THE POEM OF A LIFE

THE
POEM OF A LIFE

A biography

Louis Zukofsky

Mark Scroggins

SHOEMAKER
HOARD

Earlier versions of Chapter Two ("An Ernster Mensch at
Columbia: 1920–1924") and "Adams: Phases of History"
appeared in *Chicago Review* 50 nos. 2/3/4 (Winter 2004/5).

Cover & frontispiece photographs, Louis Zukofsky at Willow
Street, Brooklyn Heights, ca. 1958 © Jonathan Williams.
All interior photographs courtesy of Paul Zukofsky.

Every effort has been made to secure permissions. We regret
any inadvertent omission.

Library of Congress Cataloging-in-Publication Data
Scroggins, Mark, 1964–
The poem of a life : a biography of Louis Zukofsky /
by Mark Scroggins.
p. cm.
Includes bibliographical references.
ISBN-13: 978-1-59376-158-5
ISBN-10: 1-59376-158-9
1. Zukofsky, Louis, 1904–1978.
2. Poets, American—20th century—Biography. I. Title.
PS3549.U47Z835 2007
811'.52—dc22
[B]
2007011766

Book design by David Bullen
Printed in the United States of America

Shoemaker Hoard
www.shoemakerhoard.com

10 9 8 7 6 5 4 3 2 1

for
JENNIFER, PHILIPPA, and DAPHNE
my Three Graces

Contents

Preface

Louis Zukofsky could be called the "last modernist" (as one biographer named Samuel Beckett); he has been cited, just as aptly, as one of the first postmodernists. What is most important is not the name but the shape of his achievement as it unfolded over his career and as it continues to resonate into a new century. Zukofsky's was not a highly colored life; my interest in writing his biography has been to cast light on his poetry, which I am convinced is one of the highest achievements of twentieth-century writing, and grows more influential every year. The goal of this biography is not so much to tell the story of Zukofsky's life as to tell the life story of Zukofsky's writings, to trace his poetry and prose over the fifty-eight years in which he could call himself a published poet.

Most of the chapters of this book are conventional narrative, moving through the events of Zukofsky's life and career chronologically, though several chapters focus on specific bodies of work—sections of *"A"*, *Bottom: on Shakespeare*, short poem sequences. I have also written seven "interchapters," unnumbered discussions of topics in Zukofsky's writing and thought: figures who influenced him, ideas and images that obsessed him, compositional techniques to which he frequently turned. I have placed these interchapters at what seem logical points in the text, and while their arguments are integral to the biography as a whole, I expect they may be read with profit apart from the overall narrative.

. . .

In quoting from letters and notebooks, I have for the most part let misspellings and unconventional spellings stand, refraining from the intrusive "*(sic)*." This is most evident in letters by Zukofsky and by Ezra Pound, both partial to phonetic spellings and other slangy devices, but I have also preserved the typographical errors in William Carlos Williams's letters, which towards the end of his life serve as an index of Williams's declining health. In quoted letters, angled brackets (<>) indicate the letter writer's own insertions, while square brackets ([ ]) indicate my editorial clarification. Louis Zukofsky's given name was always pronounced "Louie," never "Lewis." When memoirists or transcribers of interviews have mistakenly spelled the name "Louie," I have silently corrected it to "Louis."

The titles of Zukofsky's works are apt to give copyeditors fits (the title of the short story "*It was*" is always in italics, the collection *Barely and widely* has only one capital letter, and so forth). Zukofsky himself seemed unclear as to whether the "on" in *Bottom: on Shakespeare* should be capitalized (though he leaned towards the lower case) or whether *ALL* should be spelled in all capitals. One thing is clear: Though he vacillated in his early years, Zukofsky eventually decided that the title "*A*" should without exception include quotation marks—though a number of scholars, and even a few book jacket designers, have yet to figure that out. I represent the individual movements of "*A*" without italics—"A"-1, "A"-13—but there is no consensus as to that usage, and Zukofsky himself seems to have given it little thought.

THE POEM OF A LIFE

Introduction

Louis Zukofsky liked to call his long poem "*A*" a "poem of a life," and his own was certainly a life of poetry. As a child, he would stand on the Lower East Side street and recite Longfellow's *Hiawatha*—in Yiddish—to stave off gangs of Italian bullies. Almost seventy years later, as he lay dying in a hospital on Long Island, two publishing houses—one a tiny specialty press in Vermont, the other a huge and prestigious university press—were preparing to issue his eighteenth and nineteenth volumes of poetry.

One of those books, which Zukofsky would never see, was the first one-volume edition of the complete "*A*", begun in 1928 but not finished until 1974. He had always believed, like his friend Ezra Pound, that the epic was "a poem including history," and the forty-six years of its gestation had provided plenty of history for "*A*" to include: the Great Depression, the Second World War, the cold war, Korea and Vietnam, the civil rights movement. Like Walt Whitman, whom he so admired, Zukofsky strove to be a witness to his time; unlike Whitman, who had served as a nurse during the Civil War, Zukofsky mostly recorded history unfolding from the sidelines.

When Zukofsky began writing, American poetry was in the midst of the modernist revolution. Poets like Ezra Pound, T. S. Eliot, Marianne Moore, William Carlos Williams, and Wallace Stevens were writing a poetry that strove, in Pound's words, to "make it new." They wrote about forbidden subjects—sex, the unconscious, the dark side of bourgeois existence; they questioned the place of humanity in a world without God, where history seemed driven by the forces of evolution or class struggle. The modernists changed the way poetry was written. They discarded the Victorians' artificially elevated diction, all those "e'er"s and "t'is"es, and—most crucially—they set aside the metrical forms that had served English poets since Shakespeare's day. The modernist poets sought new, irregular forms in which to cast their poems: verse of daring metrical looseness, entirely unmetered "free" verse, and even the French innovation of "prose poetry," which completely dispensed with the poetic line.

Modernist writing was not yet a part of the curriculum when Zukofsky took his education in literature. Nonetheless Zukofsky saw the future of literature in the works of James Joyce, Ezra Pound, E. E. Cummings, and T. S. Eliot, and in his twenties he made it his business to seek out and befriend Pound and Williams, two men he considered at the forefront of what was new and alive in American poetry. From the very start of his writing life, Zukofsky allied and associated himself with the modernist revolution in writing, and he would pursue the implications of that revolution as thoroughly, resourcefully, and systematically as any writer of his century.

Yet Zukofsky approached modernism—and the entire tradition of Western literature—as an outsider. He was a Jew, a first-generation American of immigrant parents, a product of the vast waves of immigration that washed upon the eastern seaboard in the decades around the turn of the century. Pound and Eliot were (like the traditionalist Robert Frost) descendents of long-established New England families, and they were assured enough in their Anglo-Americanness to feel a profound discomfort with the traditions of nineteenth-century American cultural life. For them, Western culture was an inheritance to be acknowledged or discarded. For Zukofsky, from the moment he began studying English at P.S. 7 on Manhattan's Lower East Side, that same culture was a prize to be struggled for and claimed, and only then to be weighed and assessed. From a little boy reciting Yiddish poetry on the street, Zukofsky made himself a master of the English tongue and the Western literary tradition.

Zukofsky was a poet of vast ambition, though he rarely expressed that ambition openly—in his later years, not at all. He began his career expecting to be recognized as a major figure on the literary landscape. He assiduously cultivated literary connections, wrote widely and polemically, and even spearheaded a short-lived literary movement, the "objectivists." Little in the way of fame or reputation came of this work, however, and by the late 1950s Zukofsky had suffered some two decades of public obscurity. Some of the younger poets who discovered his work in those years assumed that he was dead, so total was his eclipse from the literary scene. But Zukofsky never ceased writing. Over his writing life he produced seven collections of short poems; a novel, a novella, and a handful of short stories; two full-length books of criticism and another volume of occasional essays; a play; and two edited anthologies. With his wife, Celia, he translated the entire corpus of the Latin poet Catullus, a work that represented a major rethinking of the aims and techniques of literary translation.

Despite the range and quality of Zukofsky's other writings, his posthumous reputation will almost certainly rest upon the long poem *"A"*. The long poems produced by modernist poets reflect both their authors' continuing ambition to produce works on the scale of the major achievements of the past and the modern era's loss of faith in the traditional structures of narrative, of argumentative unity, of epic memory. These modernist long poems—among them Pound's *Cantos*, David Jones's *The Anathemata*, Williams's *Paterson*, and Charles Olson's *The Maximus Poems*—avoid straightforward storytelling: They proceed through juxtaposition, the setting side by side of disparate materials mirroring the increasingly fragmented spectacle of human history and culture in the twentieth century.

What sets *"A"* apart from the other modernist "epics" is the astonishing range of forms and shapes taken by its twenty-four movements. Zukofsky remained throughout his life a *formalist*: he considered form, consciously intended shape, inherited or invented, to be at the very heart of poetry. *"A"* incorporates a sequence of seven rhymed sonnets, a pair of canzoni (a medieval Italian form), and various passages in traditional meters and rhyme schemes. The poem also includes sections written in radical new forms: several movements based on various baroque musical forms; one based on the sections of the Roman Catholic mass; an entire play translated and adapted from Plautus's Latin; lines structured by a given word count, rather than a pattern of syllables and accents; finally, a full-scale "masque" that juxtaposes passages from all of Zukofsky's previous writings with the music of George Frideric Handel. This latter movement, "A"-24—the conclusion of the poem—was the work of Zukofsky's wife, Celia, and its place at the culmination of his long poem indicates how essential the ongoing collaboration with his wife became to him over the course of their almost forty-year marriage.

Reading "A" is like passing a season in an unfamiliar principality where the landscape is so variegated, the prospects so ample and diverse, that one is always encountering a new neighborhood, an undiscovered village, a previously unremarked vista or grotto. There are passages in "A" of mind-bending, impenetrable obscurity (some); there are passages of great beauty and lucidity (more); and there are many passages—the better part of the poem—that hover somewhere in between those two limits: that offer the reader a lyrical grace, a wry musicality, a gentle, resigned wisdom. The idiom of Zukofsky's verse is a pure and lucid English that has been twisted, torqued away from ordinary usage to make something fresh, new, and often inexhaustibly resonant. Always, however, in reading "A" one is conscious that one is reading "a poem of a life," a work in which the multifarious and oddly dovetailing particulars of contemporary history, of the events of the past, and of the whole pageant of human language, literature, and culture have been filtered and ordered through the consciousness of a single thoughtful, stubborn, sensitive, and endlessly imaginative poet.

· · ·

Zukofsky's poetic style is altogether his own. He writes a poetry of *reticence*, one in which the poet is a person who writes poems, who crafts careful structures of words; not a culture hero, a Romantic figure to be pitied, lionized, or sympathized with for the struggles he has undergone. In his mature poetry Zukofsky worked incessantly to remove the overt traces of the personal, those one-to-one connections between the work and the life so beloved of the readers of biography. In his early years, he wrote passionate love poems; in later life, he would cast his statements of love into the formal mode of valentines.

Zukofsky's work is *bare*, notably spare of metaphor, simile, and other figures of speech. He has no truck with symbols; when Zukofsky uses a word, he means precisely what the word means—though the reader may have to hunt through etymologies to figure out precisely which meaning Zukofsky has in mind.

The *sounds* of the words of Zukofsky's poems are his supreme value. But the "music" of Zukofsky's verse—and musicality is what he prized most highly in poetry—is not at all the harmonious and sometimes lulling variety of vowel, consonant, and stress to which our ears might become accustomed by Keats, Tennyson, and their followers. It is a tense, intense attention to the play of sound, a brittle and dissonant music whose analogues in actual music would be the composers of the Second Vienna School—Schoenberg, Webern, Berg.

But if Zukofsky's poetry might strike one as strange, it nonetheless offers many pleasures. There is the pleasure of sheer sound, the music of words modulating and recurring, forming into rhythmic patterns, then dissipating into others. There is the pleasure of surprise, of meeting an unexpected word or phrase, or of finding a familiar sequence of words pivoted into something new and fresh. There are jokes aplenty, for Zukofsky had a consistent, if often dry, sense of humor. There are the traditional mainstays of poetry: heartfelt but well-turned expressions of love, of mourning, of social and political indignation. Perhaps most importantly, there is the pleasure one takes in recurrences, the reappearance of words, phrases, themes, or sounds from one passage of the poem to another. Zukofsky's whole life's work, he suggested on a number of occasions, was built upon such recurrences, and it is perhaps appropriate to consider that life's work under the aspect of music: a structure built upon a finite number of themes, which are then played through for all the variety of their combinations, variations, and repetitions.

.   .   .

The complexity, gravity, and beauty of Zukofsky's writing place him among such major modernists as James Joyce, Marcel Proust, T. S. Eliot, and Ezra Pound, yet his work's critical and public reception has lagged far behind theirs. "There is no substitute," the critic Hugh Kenner has written, "for critical tradition: a continuum of understanding, early commenced."[1] Almost thirty years after Zukofsky's death, his own critical tradition is just out of its infancy. Why? First, an accident of chronology: Zukofsky, born in 1904, was about twenty years younger than the major modernist poets in whose shadow his work was first received. Though mistaken, the notion of Zukofsky as a "second generation modernist," a follower—or imitator—of the great innovators, is still the default assumption among many readers and critics. More significant, perhaps, was Zukofsky's failure to recognize that "difficult" writing is only rarely welcomed on its own terms. While Joyce produced "schemata" to explain *Ulysses* to its early readers, Eliot wrote notes to his *The Waste Land*, and Pound ceaselessly clarified his poetry in letters and essays, Zukofsky never chose to gloss his poetry for his readers (apart from answering the questions of a very few close correspondents). He wrote critical prose reluctantly, and had little patience with the genre of explication.

Zukofsky was as well plagued by singularly bad luck in publishing his books. For the first decade and a half of his career, the period during which most poets are publishing their first three or four collections and consolidating their readership, Zukofsky's poetry was not available except in transient periodicals and narrowly circulated anthologies. In fact, Zukofsky did not see a volume of his poems issued by a trade publisher until he was sixty-one years old. Zukofsky never had the attention of a patron who could underwrite the publication of his poems; nor, for the first three decades of his writing career, was he able to find a small press that could afford to print him without direct subvention.

Some have speculated that Zukofsky's obscurity in the public eye became reflected in the obscurity of his later poetry: Since Zukofsky was writing for an audience of one or two, he could afford to indulge himself in hermeticism. But Zukofsky's natural inclination was always towards the oblique and compact, the complexly interwoven; that his writing towards the end of his life developed into such breathtaking density is more readily explained as a logical evolution of the work itself than as a response to the work's reception. One of Zukofsky's inabilities, along with his inability to type, to drive a car, or to carry a tune, was his inability to tailor his language for a broad audience. On all occasions, Zukofsky hewed to his deeply idiosyncratic vision of the potentialities of language. He was fortunate to have as many readers in his own day as he did, readers willing to follow his vision: William Blake and Emily Dickinson were less fortunate.

Zukofsky had no talent for self-promotion. This failure, perhaps more than anything else, assured that Zukofsky's public obscurity would become a self-perpetuating state. An intensely private and inwardly directed man, Zukofsky could not imagine indulging in paroxysms of publicity like his younger contemporaries Allen Ginsberg and Charles Olson. Instead, he concentrated upon his art, expecting that the art alone would attract readers. Though his time in obscurity stretched from years to decades, his work is now undergoing a renaissance—and, from his point of view, perhaps, the best kind; for it has been, largely, a poets' renaissance.

Among his readers and advocates have been some of the most distinguished poets of his century: his close friend William Carlos Williams, who always deferred to Zukofsky's critical intelligence, time and again submitting his own work to Zukofsky for editing; the Northumbrian master Basil Bunting, who counted Zukofsky as one of the two contemporaries (the other being Pound) who had taught him something about the making of poems; his fellow objectivist George Oppen, and his Wisconsin friend Lorine Niedecker; Robert Creeley and Robert Duncan, each of whom repeatedly acknowledged Zukofsky's deep influence on their work. Now, at the beginning of a new century, a whole range of younger poets—most notably among them perhaps the avant-garde "Language" poets and their successors—continue to read Zukofsky as an inexhaustible source of directions for poetry.

While Hugh Kenner describes "A" as "the most hermetic poem in English,"[2] that description does little to point up the manifold pleasures Zukofsky's work offers. Guy Davenport, more happily, remarks that Zukofsky's "name may well be the best known of our time when the dust has settled around the year 2050."[3] Wherever Zukofsky

9

emerges in the centuries-long horse race of literary reputation, his life and career are remarkable in their reflection of the literary and cultural history of twentieth-century America, and his poetry stands without peer in its ingenuity of construction, its astringent musicality, and its ceaseless invention.

∞

A Lower East
Side Youth 1904–1920

LOUIS ZUKOFSKY was born in an apartment building at 97 Chrystie Street, near the Third Avenue Elevated, in the heart of Manhattan's Lower East Side, on January 23, 1904—or so the date is now recorded.[1] In a conversation seventy-four years later, Zukofsky recalled that the midwife who delivered him had filled out his birth certificate in English, which his parents—Russian Jewish immigrants, whose first language was Yiddish—could not read. They set the document aside, perhaps mislaid it. When the time came that Zukofsky needed a hard and fast date of birth, he chose an approximate day, something "close": January 29. That would prove a date of ill omen, for his mother was to die on January 29, 1927, a death that precipitated the breakup of his nuclear household.[2]

It was only when he came to apply for a passport in 1933 that Zukofsky was enlightened—a little—as to his birthday. The passport was hard enough to obtain; the midwife, of questionable literacy, had written his name as "Sallikowsky" rather than Zukofsky.[3] But that document at least contained a hard and fast birthday: January 26. Looking it over at a later date, however, Zukofsky found he had misread the midwife's handwriting, and finally discovered the "true" date of his birth, January 23. Fascinated with numbers as Zukofsky would become, he considered himself "a man with three birthdays."[4] For someone else, these confusions over names and dates might have been mere irritations or curiosities; for Zukofsky, one might hazard, they served as signs of his own multiple natures, his own *betweenness*— he was a man with three birthdays, a man with two names, a man who would leave behind the world of his fathers for a world in which he was never entirely at home. Zukofsky would live most of his life in New York, his birthplace, but at intervals he would speak of the city not as home but as "Egypt"—a land of exile.

. . .

Whatever troubles may have attended its recording, Zukofsky's birth was not a newsworthy event; hundreds of children were born each day in the crowded tenements of New York's mainly immigrant districts. By 1904, Manhattan's Lower East Side was teeming with recent immigrants and their rapidly multiplying offspring. Between 1880 and 1910, some 1.4 million eastern European Jews came to New York City, and around 1.1 million of them settled there. At the turn of the century, the Jewish Lower East Side was the most densely populated area of New York, and one of the most densely populated on earth, with more than seven hundred inhabitants per acre: one study reported that overcrowding in the Tenth Ward— Zukofsky's neighborhood—was worse than that of the slums of Bombay.[5]

To some observers, the overcrowding and poverty of the tenements were horrifying, a matter of immediate public concern. In 1890 Jacob Riis had written that the tenements

> are the hot-beds of the epidemics that carry death to rich and poor alike; the nurseries of pauperism and crime that fill our jails and police courts; that throw off a scum of forty thousand human wrecks to the island asylums and workhouses year by year; that turned out in the last eight years a round half million beggars to prey upon our charities; that maintain a standing army of ten thousand tramps . . .

In *How the Other Half Lives*, Riis presented the Lower East Side as a spectacle outshaming Dickens's London or Karl Marx's Manchester. At the same time, however, he was quick to note that these immigrants were by no means lazy. The Lower East Side was a "hive of busy industry": "Life here means the hardest kind of work almost from the cradle. The world as a debtor has no credit in Jewtown."[6]

No one would deny that the overcrowding and poverty of the Lower East Side were appalling; but the immigrants continued to come, and those who had already come continued to send for their friends and relatives from the old country. Despite hardships, to these newcomers America was indeed a land of opportunity and limitless potential. The centuries-old *shtetl* communities of eastern Europe represented a premodern, increasingly threatened way of life, and the nineteenth-century *Haskala* ("enlightenment") sought to bring eastern European Jews into the mainstream of Western thought. The *Haskala* made Jews aware of the riches of their own indigenous culture, their *Yiddishkayt*, but it as well brought into currency a whole range of ideologies—capitalism, Zionism, socialism—quite alien to the *shtetl* world, and unable to be realized within its boundaries.[7] More immediately, the assassination of Tsar Alexander II in 1881 brought an end to toleration of the Jews within the Russian Empire: new waves of pogroms washed over the Jewish communities of the Pale, and his successor, Alexander III, would revert to the consistently anti-Jewish policies of earlier tsars.[8] For many eastern European Jews in the last decades of the nineteenth century, *di alte heym* ("the old country") was becoming increasingly untenable. So, as had so many of Europe's poor for over two centuries, they looked to America.

. . .

Louis Zukofsky was a late child, the baby of the family. His father, Pinchos Zukofsky (or Zukowsky, as some members of the family would spell it), was in his midforties in 1904, and his mother, Chana Pruss Zukofsky, in her early forties.[9] Louis was the only one of his family's children to be born in the New World. Pinchos had been born sometime in the 1850s in the outskirts of Must (or Most), a small city in Lithuania (now Belarus). Chana, several years younger, was from the same town, and indeed may have been distantly related to Pinchos.

We know very little of the couple's lives before they emigrated. Pinchos and his father, Maishe Afroim Zukofsky, probably worked as farmhands, Zukofsky's wife Celia recalled in 1978. In his own elegy for his father, Louis Zukofsky would ask, "What did he not do?"

> He had kept dogs
> Before he rolled logs
> On the Niemen . . .
> What a blessing:
> He saw Rabbi
> Yizchok Elchonon
> *Walking*
> On the wharf
> In Kovno.[10]

In the old country, Pinchos and Chana Zukofsky had five children in fairly rapid succession. Two died in infancy, but three survived to grow up in the United States: Dora, born in 1888, Fanny, in 1890, and Morris Ephraim, in 1892.[11] Pinchos, like so many immigrants to America in the latter part of the nineteenth century, went to the new country alone: "His boy wept / And would not let him go. / But he kissed and kissed him and crossed / The Atlantic."[12] He arrived in New York in 1898—"with bedding in a sheet / Samovar, with tall pitcher of pink glass, / With copper mugs, with a beard, / Without shaving mug"[13]—and soon found a job in the Lower East Side garment industry.

The "sweatshop"—a small, often home-based industrial establishment in which a number of workers, each with a specific and clearly defined task, manufactured garments for a "contractor"—was not an American invention: Marx had written about the practice of "sweating" in nineteenth-century England in *Capital*. Nor was it a particularly advanced mode of capitalist production, like the assembly lines Henry Ford would later pioneer; but it was a mode that took advantage of technological innovations—the "long knife," which cut many more garments than the scissors, the sewing machine—and which enabled contractors (often German Jews) to set up profitable establishments with a minimum of start-up capital. By the turn of the century the American garment industry was in the midst of an explosive expansion, and New York City, with its ubiquitous sweat-shops manned mainly by hopeful immigrants, accounted for about two-thirds of the nation's garment production.[14]

Pinchos Zukofsky's first job in America—a "miracle," his son would call it—was at such a shop, where for six years he worked nights as a night watchman and days as a presser, one of the most unskilled and lowest-paying tasks:

> he pressed pants
> Every crease a blade
> The irons weighed
> At least twenty pounds
> But moved both of them
> Six days a week
> From six in the morning
> To nine, sometimes eleven at night,
> Or midnight . . .

There was one day on which Pinchos would not work, and his employer was one of the many who recognized the expediency of letting religious Jews take Saturday off:

> His own business
> My father told Margolis
> Is to keep Sabbath.[15]

The pay was by no means princely—the average presser at the turn of the century made twelve dollars a week[16]—but by combining this with whatever he received for his night shift ("A shop bench his bed, / He rose rested at four"[17]), Pinchos Zukofsky was able to save enough to bring his wife and children to New York in 1903.

The ill-paid drudgery of his father's working life—in 1936, well over seventy years old, Pinchos was still pressing pants, and he did not retire until he was eighty-one, on an old age pension of twenty-six dollars a month[18]—made a deep impression on his son. As memorable to Zukofsky, however, were the piety and resignation with which his father faced this endless round of backbreaking labor (the pressing irons often resulted in spinal curvature in their operators[19]) in a foreign land. Pinchos Zukofsky was an Orthodox Jew for whom faith and ritual observance were sources of sustaining strength. He opened and closed the synagogue "For over six times ten years / Until three days before he died," Zukofsky wrote after his father's death in 1950, and in numerous letters he would recall Pinchos Zukofsky's quiet resignation. Zukofsky would remember his father's kindness, how every Saturday he would take his son "To the birdstore-window to see / The blue-and-yellow Polly / The cardinal, the / Orchard oriole." That kindness was evident even to strangers:

> A beard that won over
> A jeering Italian
> Who wanted to pluck it—
> With the love
> His dark brown eyes
> Always found in others.

In a land where he was never entirely at home—Pinchos Zukofsky never learned more than a few words of English—his largeness of spirit overcame any barriers of language: "Everybody loved Reb Pinchos / Because he loved everybody."[20]

· · ·

Zukofsky never wrote a formal memoir of his childhood; what little he put down about his family background and his youth on the Lower East Side is in occasional letters and in a series of "hints & more than hints" scattered throughout his long poem "A". There was the Karchemsky family, the Zukofskys' next-door neighbors from Odessa, "where one could get tea and matzohs all year round. That was *class*." Even among the tenement Jews, there was a hierarchy, and the Crimean Karchemskys made the Zukofskys feel like "poor Litvaks."[21] There was the "one bright Sunday morning" when Zukofsky "Hit his brother's head with a shoe . . . Just like THAT, while his older brother was still sleeping. / For no reason at all."[22] There was the incident of "preventing an animal errand" which became "the family joke," when the three-year-old Zukofsky chased the family cat—presumably bent on relieving itself—down three flights of stairs and returned it to the apartment, stroking it and telling it, "you / pussy stay upstairs, // now *I'll* go / downstairs."[23] There was his confusion about Gentile physiology—"a Jewish / boy I thought / gentile boys never // peed"[24]—which may be at the source of the numerous urinary jokes throughout Zukofsky's poetry. And there were the times in his grammar school years when Zukofsky played in Bowling Green Park in knee britches, pretending to be George Washington, Wolfe, or Montcalf, brandishing "a toy sword / That cost 10¢."[25]

. . .

Given the hours that Pinchos Zukofsky worked, Louis Zukofsky could have seen little of his father during his childhood, and if his poetry is any indication, he was emotionally far closer to Chana Zukofsky, his mother. That closeness was largely registered as grief at her loss—she would die when Zukofsky was twenty-three—but Zukofsky's first major work, "Poem beginning 'The,'" composed the year before her death, deeply concerns itself with the relationship of mothers and sons. For on the Lower East Side it all came down to one's *sons*. Whatever dislocations and deprivations Pinchos and Chana Zukofsky might undergo, whatever hours Pinchos might work, were all worthwhile if they could thereby make a better life for their children—most specifically, for Morris and Louis. "The idea that they constituted a 'transitional generation' was a major cause of that stoicism which colored the whole of immigrant life," writes one chronicler of New York Jewry. "And with gratifications postponed, the culture of the East Side became a culture utterly devoted to its sons."[26] There is no way of knowing how intelligent or gifted Zukofsky's sisters Dora and Fanny were, but it is almost certain that it was Morris and Louis who received the lion's share of their parents' encouragement in educational pursuits.

Morris, twelve years older than his brother, was interested in books and literature (he would later attempt to make a living as a bookstore proprietor). He introduced the four-year-old Louis to the world of letters by taking him to the Yiddish theaters on the Bowery.[27] The drama as an art form was for the most part alien to the Jews of eastern Europe, and for the first decade of its existence (counting from 1882, when the first Yiddish theatrical production in New York took place), New York's Yiddish theater presented an unsubtle amalgam of vaudeville, light opera, melodrama, and outright farce. Only in the last years of the nineteenth century did the institution begin to move towards artistic maturity, towards the more socially and emotionally "realistic" modes that had dominated recent western European drama.[28]

One way for this theater to achieve artistic significance, its producers and actors realized, was to present Yiddish versions of important non-Yiddish drama.[29] Significantly, when he recalled his attendance at the Yiddish theater—particularly the Thalia on the Bowery—Zukofsky did not mention seeing any of the many Yiddish plays then being written. By the age of nine, however, he "had seen a good deal of Shakespeare, Ibsen, Strindberg and Tolstoy performed—all in Yiddish."[30] Not to mention Aeschylus—"at five I / heard in Yiddish / *Prometheus Desmótes* chanted"—and whatever other classics of the Western tradition the impresarios of the stage felt might draw a crowd. (The man who made the Yiddish version of *Prometheus Bound*, Zukofsky recalled, "broke one of our Vienna café chairs in wild enthusiasm over an explication de texte of Strindberg's *The Father*."[31])

Morris not only took his little brother to the theater, but he encouraged him to read poetry. By an early age Zukofsky had at his brother's prompting memorized much of Longfellow's *Hiawatha* in a Yiddish version by Solomon Bloomgarden (pen named "Yehoash"), one of the most prominent of a new generation of American Yiddish poets. The Italian boys of the neighborhood would corner Zukofsky and force him to recite, then throw him pennies.[32] Zukofsky would follow Yehoash's career closely, watching the poet move from sounding like "*very good* Heine" to "'freer' American forms" and exotic, even Oriental, subject matter that recalled the work of Ezra Pound.[33]

No doubt as important as the Yiddish theater, Zukofsky's "first exposure to letters," was his "first exposure to English," which took place at "P.S. 7 on Chrystie and Hester Streets."[34] He surely meant his first *formal* exposure to English, for the Lower East Side was by no means a monolingual enclave. Most of the immigrant Jews spoke Yiddish, but there were many other tongues heard around the neighborhood or within a few blocks, among them German, Italian, Chinese, and various Slavic languages. English itself, whether in an Irish or American accent, was becoming a lingua franca even in the most Jewish sections of the Lower East Side.[35] Zukofsky spent his earliest years in an air that resonated with the meaningful sounds of a host of different tongues. It is problematic to speak of Yiddish as Zukofsky's "first language," if one means by "language" the whole complex system of grammar, rhetoric, and notation into which one is initiated during the process of attaining literacy, of one's formal education. Yiddish, that is, was the set of sounds through which Zukofsky communicated with his family—his preschool tongue, as it were. It was a language that he never formally studied, in which he never wrote, and to whose literary productions—save for Yehoash—he paid scarcely any attention. Whatever mastery of Yiddish Zukofsky had gained before he entered P.S. 7, he would gradually lose over the many decades in which he established himself as a speaker, teacher, and writer of English.[36] Indeed, from the moment he began school, Zukofsky's main intent was to render himself a consummate master of English, the official language of the nation in which he had been born.

The New York public school system certainly encouraged such ambitions. In 1890, Riis had written that Yiddish speaking immigrants "must be taught the language of the country they have chosen as their home, as the first and most necessary step."[37] The public schools, as if in outright response to Riis's call, sought explicitly to "assimilate and amalgamate these people as a part of our American race": their foremost goal was to teach the immigrants and their children the English language, the primary vehicle of American culture and values.[38] There was no question of bilingual education; instruction was entirely in English, though school administrators were often sensitive to the needs of children immersed for the first time in an anglophone environment.[39] The parents must have viewed their children's acquiring English with some ambivalence, for English served to drive a wedge between the generations, to alienate the sons from their fathers' world, their fathers' experience, and perhaps even their fathers' faith. At the same time, however, the immigrants knew that a mastery of English was vital if their children were to escape the sweatshops.

Zukofsky thrived in the public schools. When he was about eleven, his English teacher offered prizes to every student in the class who could read through the whole of Shakespeare's plays and answer the teacher's "pretty stiff questions" about them. Zukofsky owned an illustrated Shakespeare, which he dutifully absorbed only to receive as prize a volume called *The Boy Electrician*; he envied the school's star athlete, who won Thackeray's *Pendennis*.[40] Only some five or six years after starting school, then, Zukofsky had read all of Shakespeare, whose works were to prove a constant ground to everything he would write over the next sixty-odd years.

By then Zukofsky's own poetic ambitions had awakened: "By eleven I was writing poetry in English, as yet not 'American English,' tho I found Keats rather difficult as compared with Shelley's 'Men of England' and Burns' 'Scots, wha hae.'"[41] It is perhaps prophetic of the role revolutionary politics would play in his career that of the three poets Zukofsky here recalled, the two to whom he responded most readily were staunchly leftist: the Scottish Jacobite Burns and the exile Shelley, reviled throughout England for his atheism and socialism. In "Men of England" and "Scots, wha hae," these men had written poems addressed to the common reader and calculated to inspire social movement. Keats, by contrast, would come to represent a subjectivist, impressionistic Romanticism anathema to the chiseled, precise verses that Zukofsky would value.

The English Zukofsky learned at P.S. 7 served him well, for he went on to Stuyvesant High School, a highly selective secondary school set up by the school board to prepare the children of immigrants for careers in the sciences. Zukofsky, it seems, had some vague idea of becoming an engineer. He graduated in January 1920, just short of his sixteenth birthday, with plans to attend not City College—the most proximate beacon of higher education for Lower East Side Jews—but Columbia University, the city's Ivy League institution.

. . .

When Zukofsky came to write his own brief, reticent autobiography in 1967, he struck its keynote with a specifically literary juxtaposition: "I was born in Manhattan, January 23, 1904, the year Henry James returned to the American scene to look at the Lower East Side. The contingency appeals to me as a forecast of the first-generation infusion into twentieth-century American literature."[42] When James sailed from England in August 1904, he had been away from his native land for twenty-six years. He had missed the rapid changes overtaking the United States in what Mark Twain called the "gilded age"—the rapid industrialization, the amassing of the great railroad fortunes, and most of all, the unprecedented influx of immigrants into the eastern seaboard. In the summer of 1905 James visited the Lower East Side to experience firsthand the effects of the waves of "aliens" upon the New York he had once known.[43]

Zukofsky encountered James's work early: Spurred by the notices in the papers of the novelist's 1916 death, he had read a recent reprint of James's early story "Gabrielle de Bergerac," a tale of class-violating romance in ancien régime France—"rather hard going for then for a kid of 12," he commented later.[44] In his later years Zukofsky would buy and read most of James's novels, but it was James's record of his return, *The American Scene* (which Zukofsky read in 1946), that left the most obvious traces in his poetry. Zukofsky was fascinated, to say the least, by the fact that he and James had if only for a moment shared the same streets. "H.J. intensely in / New York," Zukofsky wrote in "A"-18, "the year I was born."[45] In "A" 12, he indulged a fantasy of encountering James in his, Zukofsky's, own neighborhood:

> I have just met him on Rutgers Street, New York
> Henry James, Jr. . . .
> Practically where I was born.
> Breathing quite affectively in the mind
> Ready to chance the sea of conversation
> And unashamedly—it has been like a warm day—
> The look of a shaven Chassid . . . [46]

James's visit to the Lower East Side, as recorded in the chapter "New York and Hudson: A Spring Impression," was an experience of shock at the intensity of the "alien" "infusion" (James's terms, repeated in such running heads as "The Ubiquity of the Alien" and "The Effect of the Infusion"[47]) into the American metropolis; and following that shock, an attempt to assess what the vast waves of immigration meant, both to the immigrants themselves and to established Anglo-Saxon culture. James was appalled at the crowding of lower Manhattan, "a great swarming, a swarming that had begun to thicken, infinitely, as soon as we crossed to the East side and long before we had got to Rutgers Street. There is no swarming like that of Israel when once Israel has got a start": this was "a Jewry that had burst all bounds." "What meaning, in presence of such impressions," James asked, "can continue to attach to such a term as the 'American' character?—what type, as the result of such a prodigious amalgam, such a hotch-potch of racial ingredients, is to be conceived as shaping itself?"[48]

James's fears for the future of an Anglo-Saxon "American character" and culture were clear, but also evident was his sense that these recent immigrants were indeed making a better world for themselves. The "denizens of the New York Ghetto," he noted, "heaped as thick as the splinters on the table of a glass-blower, had each, like the fine glass particle, his or her individual share of the whole hard glitter of Israel." Even the tenement houses, in contrast to "the dark, foul, stifling Ghettos of other remembered cities," had, with their compact, efficient architecture and modern fire escapes, something of the aspect of "the New Jerusalem on earth."[49] And James knew the hopes America offered the immigrants' offspring—like Zukofsky himself: "it is the younger generation who will fully profit, rise to the occasion and enter into the privilege" of "brotherhood" with Anglo-Saxon America.[50]

James was no anti-Semite—he was a Dreyfusard, had sponsored Emma Lazarus, and was a frequent guest of the Rothschilds[51]—but his description of the Lower East Side has drawn frequent accusations of, if not outright anti-Semitism, then at best a reactionary nativism.[52] Zukofsky chose not to read *The American Scene* in that manner. "I can never, re. HJ again," he told a correspondent in 1967, "think of his visit to the East Side as anything but *benevolent*—in the decent sense of that word—willing good as against fringe benefits. His historical sense in 1904 was amazing."[53] Zukofsky had brooded long upon the final sentence of James's meditation on New York's immigrant communities, where James reflected upon "The Fate of the Language" in the hands of these new immigrants. James described the Lower East Side cafés as "torture-rooms of the living idiom," which could well presage "the surrounding accent of the future," and ended on an ambiguous note: "The accent of the very ultimate future, in the States, may be destined to become the most beautiful on the globe and the very music of humanity . . . but whatever we shall know it for, certainly, we shall not know it for English—in any sense for which there is an existing literary measure."[54]

Zukofsky would use these final phrases to castigate the painful bureaucratese of those in political power in the 1960s—particularly the terms "war on poverty" and "underprivileged"[55]—but he also knew that, out of the linguistic and cultural "hotch-potch" that was his own Lower East Side background, he had come to write a poetry that had overleapt any turn-of-the-century "literary measures," that indeed at times could scarcely be known for English, even as it aspired to be "the very music of humanity." Zukofsky himself *was* the "first-generation American infusion"—note James's word—"into twentieth-century literature," and would bring all of the energy, vitality, and linguistic multiplicity of his immigrant upbringing to bear upon the project of renovating English-language poetry.

An Ernster Mensch
at Columbia 1920–1924

Z ukofsky enrolled as a freshman at Columbia University in January 1920, just short of his sixteenth birthday. His youth was not particularly unusual; the New York public schools, under pressure from the rising population, regularly allowed bright students to skip grades and graduate early.[1] That he attended Columbia rather than a public university was a measure both of Zukofsky's talents and his ambition, but it required sacrifice on his parents' part. Even though he would live and board at home, Columbia's tuition—approximately two hundred and fifty dollars a year—was no small amount; the City College of New York, in contrast, charged no tuition at all.

To venture from the Lower East Side to Morningside Heights was also to cross a great cultural divide. By entering Columbia, Zukofsky was leaving the predominantly Jewish world of his family's neighborhood for an Ivy League that was still largely Anglo-Saxon and Protestant. About half of the student body at New York University was

Jewish, as was the overwhelming majority—over 80 percent—at City College. In contrast, Jews were distinctly in the minority at Columbia.[2] This was not merely an effect of Columbia's comparatively high tuition. There was an institutional climate of unspoken anti-Semitism in the University: There were very few Jews on the faculty—none at all in the English department—and anti-Semitic admissions policies had been established in the years after the First World War. The administration, acutely conscious of Columbia's position in the Ivy League, was worried that the college was becoming "too Jewish," too much a reflection of the city in which it was located. (As an Ivy League college song of the 1920s had it, "Oh, Harvard's run by millionaires, / And Yale is run by booze, / Cornell is run by farmers' sons, / Columbia's run by Jews.") In response, college officials instituted ostensibly "regional" quotas, whose effect was to reduce the Jewish population of Columbia from around 40 percent—New York City itself was approximately 30 percent Jewish in 1920—to around 20 percent. Nonetheless, there remained more Jews at Columbia than at Harvard, Yale, or the other Ivies, and they made their presence felt. The general Ivy League undergraduate ethos at the turn of the century was an anti-intellectual bonhomie, where college was seen as the place where one formed associations and friendships that would be useful for one's future in business, where studies were secondary to sports, fraternities, and social clubs: the ethos of the "gentleman's C." The Jews—hardworking, fanatically dedicated to their studies, often from working-class backgrounds—upset this equilibrium, forcing the scions of East Coast wealth actually to pay attention to lectures, making them lose face when class rankings were announced.[3]

Jewish students brought a respect for learning and a dedication to scholarship as part of their cultural background. "For shtetl Jews," one scholar notes, "scholarship was a moral imperative just as work was for seventeenth-century Puritans. Scholars were accorded special prestige and authority in the Jewish community. And parents encouraged and exulted in the scholastic achievements of their (male) children." There was little continuity of method between the Talmudic learning of the eastern European *kheder* and the courses of study at American universities, but the dedication to learning was clearly the same.[4] And the Jews of the Lower East Side had an even more pressing motive to do well in college: the perennial economic desire to pull themselves out of their parents' working-class milieu. However much he might respect his father's knowledge of the Torah, Zukofsky had no desire to spend his own life pressing pants.

The Jews at Columbia were for the most part a serious, hard-working lot, eager to discuss politics or philosophy, hungry to learn the traditions of Western thought and literature. They were *ernste Menschen*—earnest people—recalled one of Zukofsky's non-Jewish friends, Whittaker Chambers, using a German phrase he would pick up in his years with the Communist Party.[5] The young English instructor Mark Van Doren, newly hired in fall 1920, would acquire "the reputation of being partial to Jewish students"; he denied partiality, but admitted "that among the Jewish students in my classes there were many who fascinated me by their brilliance and by the saliency of their several characters."[6] Some of Zukofsky's classmates would go on to great distinction, as anyone who traces the careers of the students profiled in Van Doren's 1927 article, "Jewish Students I Have Known," can see.[7] There was Lionel Trilling, whose doctoral thesis on Matthew Arnold would win him appointment as the first Jew on Columbia's English faculty, and who would go on to become one of the most influential literary critics of midcentury America. There was Meyer Schapiro, who would also become a member of the Columbia faculty and a widely known art historian. Clifton ("Kip") Fadiman became an editor—at Simon and Schuster and the *New Yorker*—an indefatigable anthologist, the host of "Information Please" (a popular middlebrow radio show), and a senior judge for the Book-of-the-Month Club. Herbert Solow would become the editor of *Fortune* magazine. John Waldhorn Gassner, a diminutive Hungarian immigrant, would become a leading theater critic and Sterling Professor of Playwriting and Dramatic Literature at Yale.

And then there was Whittaker Chambers. Chambers, the first son of a more or less dysfunctional family on Long Island's South Shore, came to Columbia in the fall of 1920. Chambers entered Columbia describing himself as a Christian Scientist and political conservative; he hoped—in truly Ivy League words—to "make of myself a good man, a fine gentleman, and American patriot."[8] What his teachers and classmates remembered him for, however, were the intensity of his shifting political convictions, his practical jokes, and his remarkable literary talents. Van Doren recalled that "his poems were good," and ranked him as the "best" of the students he taught in the Twenties.[9] Chambers and Zukofsky were friends, and would discuss literature both on campus and on the Long Island beach, where Zukofsky visited him in the summer after he left college. Zukofsky also came to know Chambers's troubled brother Richard, who would commit suicide in 1926.[10]

Perhaps the most aggressively intellectual of Zukofsky's circle was the young Mortimer J. Adler, who was pursuing studies in psychology and philosophy, and of whom the 1923 Columbia yearbook commented, "they call him 'Plato.'"[11] Adler had an intense, relentlessly systematizing intelligence; he typed up his lecture notes as soon as he returned from class, and would retain those typed lectures the rest of his life. (Such a mind would serve him well in his career as an educator and as the editor of the *Encyclopaedia Britannica*.) Van Doren remembered Adler's "inimitable discourse, which was rapid and fiery, and illuminated at every turn by formal logic—itself, as he manipulated it, a shower of sparks."[12] Over half a century later, Adler would recall Zukofsky as very private, quiet, withdrawn—not at all a good conversationalist—and recall how "frail and pale" he looked.[13] But Adler may have had a great—though perhaps unintentional—effect on Zukofsky. In 1931, Zukofsky told a friend that "as a kid I wanted to be an engineer—I'd have been a swell one, but I met a fool philosopher or epistemologist, & it really was 'easier' doing nothing at Columbia."[14] Though Zukofsky would never mention his name in print (save for a submerged pun in "A"-12), that "fool philosopher" had been Adler.[15] Whether or not Mortimer J. Adler was responsible for the shift in Zukofsky's career intentions, it was philosophy and English on which he would concentrate during his four years at Columbia.[16]

.   .   .

The early 1920s were a good time to be studying literature and philosophy on Morningside Heights. Van Doren, who joined the English faculty at twenty-six, had already published books on Henry David Thoreau and John Dryden, and brought to the teaching of literature the sensibility of a practicing poet. He was an inspiring teacher, as generations of his students—among them the poets Allen Ginsberg, John Berryman, Thomas Merton, and John Hollander—would recall. Van Doren, Clifton Fadiman recalled, "calmly assumed a class composed entirely of heavy thinkers. At first this was embarrassing, for even in those days intellectuality and venereal disease enjoyed about equal prestige."[17] Louis Simpson remembered Van Doren working his way through a text so that "He seemed to be composing the book, alongside Shakespeare, or Hardy, or Yeats . . . He made us feel that we could write."[18] In "Jewish Students I Have Known," Van Doren described Zukofsky as "a pale and subtle poet who was not in fact lazy, but the memory of whose painfully inarticulate soul forbids me to use him for any purpose however respectful . . ."[19] Zukofsky was far from flattered by this description when he read it in 1927, but he retained a deep affection for Van Doren; he would keep in touch with his old teacher for the rest of Van Doren's life.

There were other luminaries in the English department, among them the heavy-set Raymond Weaver, more than anyone else responsible for the twentieth-century revival of Herman Melville's reputation, and the formidable John Erskine. Erskine was a handsome, patrician figure, given to illustrating points of his lectures by playing passages of music on the piano.[20] The great curricular innovation for which he would be remembered was the "General Honors" seminars he began in 1920, in which small groups of students read through a course of "Great Books" of Western culture. The notion of a Great Books curriculum, presenting a certain canon of works as universally essential for a higher education, was a bold one, cutting against the grain of the increasing disciplinary specialization in American universities and the popular elective system, in which students were largely free to craft their own courses of study. The success of Erskine's experiment depended much on the talent of the young instructors who ran the seminars, among them Van Doren, Weaver, and the graduate students Adler and Fadiman.[21]

Erskine was faculty advisor for the Boar's Head Society, a group of young poets and the only student club with which Zukofsky was affiliated.[22] The Boar's Head published a periodical, the *Morningside*, which like most undergraduate poetry magazines was largely an outlet for the editors' own work. Zukofsky was on the editorial board with his friends Samuel Theodore Hecht and Chambers, and all of them published poetry there regularly. Despite Erskine's support for the literary arts at Columbia, Zukofsky would remember him sourly in the fourth movement of his "Poem beginning 'The,'" written in 1926. Here Erskine was "Engprof," his lectures flung before the students like "roast flitches of red boar," and Zukofsky himself was the student struggling to stay awake in the back of the class:

173   On weary bott'm long wont to sit,
174   Thy graying hair, thy beaming eyes,
175   Thy heavy jowl would make me fit
176   For the Pater that was Greece.
177   The siesta that was Rome.

178   Lo! from my present—say not—itch
179   How statue-like I see thee stand
180   Phi Beta Key within thy hand!
181   Professor—from the backseats which
182   Are no man's land! [23]

This passage, of course, is a parody of Edgar Allan Poe's "To Helen," and an ungentle poke at the reason Erskine left Columbia: In 1925 he published a racy bestseller, *The Private Life of Helen of Troy*, which catapulted him to national fame and allowed him to ease up on his teaching and pursue a career as a concert pianist. (In 1928, he became president of the Juilliard School.) The poem's image of Erskine, pontificating upon the fact that Poe "never wrote an epic" and toying with his Phi Beta Kappa key, bespoke Zukofsky's scorn for a man whose criticism and lectures were composed of such platitudes, but whose most famous essay bore the impossibly ponderous title "The Moral Obligation To Be Intelligent."

．   ．   ．

When Zukofsky recalled his college years half a century later, it was not the English professors he named, but the philosophers. Columbia had a distinguished philosophy faculty, the most famous of whom was John Dewey, who had come to Columbia from the University of Chicago in 1904. He was a leading proponent of the pragmatist philosophy pioneered by William James and Charles Saunders Peirce, but by the 1920s he was probably more widely known as an advocate of "progressive" education. For an educational theorist, Dewey's own teaching methods left something to be desired: "He would wander around the room stopping from time to time to look out the window or examine a picture on the wall," one of Zukofsky's contemporaries recalled. "Occasionally he would say something. When he did so he appeared to be talking to himself and rarely were his remarks relevant to anything the class was supposed to be considering."[24] Adler remembered Dewey's delivering his lectures "in a low, barely audible voice, with long pauses, some stumblings, and frequent groping for words."[25]

For his part, Zukofsky had little interest in what Dewey had to say, but he was fascinated by the manner in which he said it. "It's how [Dewey] inflected his voice that mattered," he recalled in 1971, "stressing active-*ing* or a passive-*ed* that made the point of his course—sometimes as he sat on the radiator, and when it was hot of course he moved away. His educational philosophy did not interest me. The preoccupied man did."[26] Dewey's precise speech might have influenced Zukofsky's own. To the end of his life, the poet spoke English with a refined, elegant accent that showed only traces of his Lower East Side roots, and that accent—what some would recognize as a "Columbia accent" common to students of his generation—may, it has been ventured, be traced to Dewey.[27]

The philosophy professor Zukofsky remembered with affection and with intellectual respect, however, was Frederick J. E. Woodbridge. Adler recalled Woodbridge, who held the Johnsonian Professorship —a chair formerly occupied by Columbia's famous president, Nicholas Murray Butler—as "a superb lecturer, as slow in delivery as Dewey but without any hesitation; more eloquent than [fellow professor Irwin] Edman but with an eloquence that derived from the flow of his thought rather than from the flow of his words."[28] In Zukofsky's words, Woodbridge "acted his thought in his lectures."[29]

It was probably under Woodbridge that Zukofsky first made the acquaintance of two thinkers to whom he would return for the rest of his life, Baruch Spinoza and Aristotle. Woodbridge would name them as among his own greatest influences, and would teach a seminar wholly devoted to Spinoza's *Ethics* during Zukofsky's last year at Columbia.[30] In contrast to Dewey, occupied with the new gospels of pragmatism and progressive education as well as with various political causes, or to the philosophy department's other luminary, Irwin Edman (whom Adler suspected of a poverty of ideas[31]), Woodbridge worked hard to understand the philosophers of the past on their own terms, to communicate how their thought remained relevant. While Santayana was the only living philosopher to whom Woodbridge paid homage, it was clear he regarded the thought of Spinoza and Aristotle as just as vital and immediate as that of the Spanish-born Harvard professor.

Aristotle, especially, Woodbridge regarded as a thinker of major importance and relevance: "He has said everything that I have ever said or shall ever say," Woodbridge would write.[32] All too commonly, Aristotle had been dismissed as presenting a systematic philosophy that denied all of the beautiful doctrines of his teacher Plato, or had been saddled with responsibility for the entire paralyzing machinery of medieval scholasticism. In contrast, Woodbridge sought to recover the essence of Aristotle's thought unencumbered of the centuries of commentary that had obscured it. He read Aristotle as a powerful philosopher of nature, nature conceived as "a dynamic and productive system."[33] For Woodbridge, Aristotle's multifarious writings—in physics, biology, cosmology, psychology, ethics, politics, and so forth—were a systematic attempt to understand the processes of nature, a nature of which the human being is only the most self-conscious functioning element. As he concluded a 1930 series of lectures that summed up his lifetime of studying and teaching Aristotle,

> each thing is drawn to seek its good, to be what it might be, to realize its powers, to find no hindrances except in the inertia of matter and the incidents of chance, and so turn the possible into those numberless illustrations of the actual which diversify existence. Man is only the supreme illustration. The stone turned into a doorstop can illustrate it also. Man is supreme only because in him there is realized the power to say that all this is what nature is.[34]

Woodbridge's vision of Aristotle's thought deeply influenced many of his students. Adler, for one, was to become a lifelong

Aristotelian, and Richard McKeon, also Woodbridge's student, became perhaps the most eminent Aristotle scholar of the twentieth century. Woodbridge's version of Aristotle, in which the philosopher's works appeared as multiple approaches to grasping the whole of a singular system of nature, must have captured Zukofsky's imagination, for it would shape his use of Aristotle for the rest of his life.

. . .

During his four years at Columbia, beginning in the latter part of his first year, Zukofsky published almost two dozen poems in the college magazines *Varsity* and the *Morningside*. Some of them, like "Monody"—"Like crushed violets / In a faded hand, / So are / My unfulfilled dreams"—were exercises in adolescent angst, or, like "Youth," "Youth's Ballad of Singleness," and "Spare Us of Dying Beauty," hopeful assertions of boundless youthful possibility.[35] It is easy to discern what Zukofsky had been reading as he composed his own verses. "The Sea-Nymph's Prayer to Okeanos" was transparently indebted to the early H.D.; "The Faun Sees" could be the Wallace Stevens of *Harmonium*; and both "The Mystic Song" and "The Seer" were saturated with the vaguenesses of the Bengali poet Rabindranath Tagore (to whom "The Seer" is dedicated).[36]

These were poems in a late-Romantic vein, much of a piece with the late-Romantic verse Zukofsky's colleagues published in the same magazines. Indeed, when one compares Zukofsky's "Autumn Sunrise," a painfully correct sonnet commemorating an agricultural dawn, with the poem on the page facing it, Daniel T. Walden's "Spring in the City," one aspect of Zukofsky's work becomes evident: the utter absence of this city boy's actual surroundings.[37] New York itself, the Lower East Side on which he had been raised, the urban campus of Columbia, the Harlem visible from Morningside Heights, all were nowhere to be found in Zukofsky's poems, which celebrated woods and streams, the sun and the ocean, the mountains and the clouds, and (in the verse play "Earth Counts a Day") a fairy-tale-like cottage and pond.[38] The only poem with a New York setting was "Louis XIV Chamber," which meditated upon a "period" room in the Metropolitan Museum of Art (and which contained a line—"and music falling left no traces"—that would later appear in "A"-1), but even that poem's precise observations were blurred in a haze of "Lacquer, carved gold, and glass."[39]

While Zukofsky may have been writing in a weary period mode of "sensitive" observation and strenuous spiritual assertion, and while he may have found it difficult to escape his influences (one line of "Earth Counts a Day" is even lifted from Joyce Kilmer's "Trees"[40]), he was already attentive to the formal aspects of his art. Several of his poems were in free verse, but mostly Zukofsky wrote in traditional forms or in measures that evoked traditional forms. "Youth's Ballad of Singleness" is in a recognizable ballad form; "An Immortality"[41] is in a variant of Dante's terza rima; and "Earth Counts a Day," while metrically irregular, makes deft use of end rhymes. Above all else Zukofsky pursued the sonnet, the lyric form par excellence of Shakespeare, Keats, Wordsworth, and the other Romantics. More than a third of his Columbia poems were wholly credible sonnets, free of overt metrical padding, syntactic inversions, and the Elizabethan archaisms to which the neophyte poet so often resorts. As were so many poets of his generation and the generation before him, Zukofsky was striving to achieve a modern voice by exploring the meaningful potential of inherited forms.

More striking than the formal deftness of Zukofsky's Columbia poems, however, was their air of Paterian aestheticism. The English critic Walter Pater (1839–1894) was widely regarded as one of the fathers of the "art for art's sake," decadent stance in literature. In the Conclusion to his *The Renaissance: Studies in Art and Poetry*, Pater dismissed all notions that our experience of a work of art ought to be character building, world altering, or otherwise edifying. Instead, he stressed the momentary nature of human life: "A counted number of pulses is given to us of a variegated, dramatic life. . . . How shall we pass most swiftly from point to point, and be present always at the focus where the greatest number of vital forces unite in their purest energy?" One is only truly alive in the moments of greatest emotional, intellectual, and aesthetic awareness. "Success in life," according to Pater, is to "burn always with this hard, gem-like flame, to maintain this ecstacy . . ."[42]

More often than not, Zukofsky's poems dramatized precisely such moments of "purest energy." Unlike the imagist poems of Pound and

H.D., where the image became the "*adequate* symbol" for a state of mind,[43] poems of Zukofsky's like "Dark Room" and "Silver Moment" focused on the moment itself, the passing aesthetic experience that makes one truly alive: "I shall accept this moment pure, immense, / And in the useless loveliness of things / My thought shall find the world's one recompense / For all the sorrow that it brought . . ."[44] "Moments" was almost a versification of Pater's conclusion:

Our life is but a wreath of moments: these
Bring us great joys, white glory and deep pain,
Beauty's tall form, and love, and song's refrain,
And knowing these we know all verities.
Lucid like leaves in sunlight-memories,
The token of these moments to the brain,
Are the few truths that lastingly remain
To light a torch to our perplexities.

And the most perfect moment is the twilight's
When we see golden strands through mist; the sky lights
Its stars; a radiance shines through all things—
Truth, seraph with bare sword and fire-tipped wings,
We seem to see beyond our turbid strife,
Yet there is no flamed truth but that is life.[45]

Such unabashed Paterianism was by no means the rule among Zukofsky's classmates. Trilling and his circle "were very down on Walter Pater, very hostile to what we called 'aestheticism,' . . . we took him to be everything that was disembodied and precious."[46] Trilling and Adler had little patience with Paterian aestheticism, especially as reflected in the style of Professor Irwin Edman and in the work of George Santayana, one of Edman's favorites.[47] Zukofsky must have known something of Santayana's philosophy—not merely were both Edman and Woodbridge partisans of Santayana's, but Santayana wrote the introduction to the edition of Spinoza Zukofsky owned—and there are clear traces of Santayana's poetry in Zukofsky's Columbia verse, which is nothing if not "disembodied and precious."

. . .

Zukofsky spent a little over four years as a student at Columbia University. He received his master's degree in June 1924, having the month before submitted a thesis on the American historian Henry Adams.[48] While Zukofsky had been elected Phi Beta Kappa in 1923, he had never received the baccalaureate, having dropped out of the required physical education course.[49] (This, like his age at enrollment, was not particularly anomalous; Adler had similarly failed to receive his B.A. because of nonattendance at physical education, and had similarly been admitted to the graduate school anyway.[50]) Then as now, writing one's thesis on a recently dead and as yet uncanonized figure (Adams had died only six years before) was not the path to academic preferment, and Zukofsky was not offered an instructorship at Columbia. That might have been a matter of personality: quiet and withdrawn, Zukofsky perhaps seemed less than promising teaching material. And the unwritten code of anti-Semitism that reigned in the English department—and that would not be broken until Trilling was hired in 1939—almost certainly told against him. At any rate, Zukofsky's formal schooling ended in 1924 when he was twenty, and he would make no serious attempt to pursue the doctorate.

Zukofsky had made some fast friendships at Columbia: Whittaker Chambers, who was his "closest" friend there, and with whom he would remain close for several more years until Chambers disappeared into the mazes of radical politics and espionage; Irving Kaplan, an economist and statistician who would find him work in the years to come, and whose California home Zukofsky would visit on two occasions over the next decade; John Gassner, with whom he would remain in touch till Gassner's death in 1967; and Van Doren, who would rise to become one of the most prominent men of letters in America, and who would always remain on friendly and encouraging terms with his former student—if he did little actively to promote his writing.[51]

More important than personal contacts were the intellectual foundations Zukofsky had laid at Columbia. He had been introduced to and studied a number of the philosophers that would prove important to his writings: his lifelong involvement with the works of Aristotle and Spinoza, most importantly, began at Columbia. Celia Zukofsky would say many years later that her husband "read philosophy as other people eat bread,"[52] and to find a poet as seriously involved with and committed to the discourse of philosophy, we must go back to Coleridge's investment in the German transcendental tradition, or even to Lucretius's epic exposition of atomistic philosophy in *De Rerum Natura*. There were times when Zukofsky seemed to struggle against his philosophical propensity, trying to write lyrics of unadorned perception like those of his friend William Carlos Williams, but there would always be an undercurrent of philosophical questioning and systematizing in his work.

And Zukofsky gained the beginning of a lifelong literary education at Columbia. He had read widely and comprehensively over the canon of European literature, strengthening his acquaintance with the tradition of poetry.[53] While he may have scorned the superficiality of John Erskine's teaching, the basic principles of "General Honors"—that the Great Books were neither museum pieces nor the obsolete records of earlier eras, but living entities in their own right—would become an article of faith in Zukofsky's writing and criticism. Ezra Pound, one of the "new" poets Zukofsky was reading while at Columbia—no doubt outside of any formal syllabus—had written in 1910, in the preface to his *The Spirit of Romance*,

> All ages are contemporaneous. It is B.C., let us say, in Morocco. The Middle Ages are in Russia. The future stirs already in the minds of the few. This is especially true of literature, where the real time is independent of the apparent, and where many dead men are our grandchildren's contemporaries, while many of our contemporaries have been already gathered into Abraham's bosom, or some more fitting receptacle.[54]

This sense of simultaneity, the achronological *aliveness* of all great works of the imagination, was planted and confirmed in Zukofsky during his years on Morningside Heights, and would eventually flower in vast works of such complexity and global reach that it seems scarcely credible that they were produced by the same man who wrote the precious, self-centered apprentice work published in the *Varsity* and the *Morningside*.

Adams: Phases of History

Zukofsky submitted his master's thesis, "Henry Adams: Detached Mind and the Growth of a Poet," in May 1924.[1] His involvement with Adams, however, would go far beyond his Columbia years: it would prove profound and lifelong. "The man who taught me most about history," he told an audience at the American Embassy in London forty-five years later, "was Henry Adams."[2] Between 1924 and 1969, Zukofsky would refer to Adams in a number of his works, and would incorporate substantial sections of Adams's writing into his long poem "*A*".[3] But beyond the mere appropriation of the historian's words for the poet's writings, Adams's theories of history and the fundamental intellectual dilemma he represented would be immense influences on Zukofsky's entire cast of thought.

. . .

Zukofsky's Columbia thesis, sixty-three typescript pages of text, was the first full-length treatment of Adams's entire writing career, and a document that preferred to let Adams speak for himself. Zukofsky commented at lesser or greater length on most of Adams's works, but rather than directly discussing his greatest work, *The Education*, Zukofsky used quotations from Adams's autobiography as a narrative frame for the thesis as a whole: such quotations, indeed, make up more than half of the thesis.[4] In thus modestly effacing himself and letting his subject's voice be heard, Zukofsky had precedent in Adams's own work: "*The Life of Gallatin* was more than half quotation; Adams's contributions to the study of the life were the barest facts, though these were many; there was no ornament; emotion was reticent...."[5] Such "reticent" quotation was a method that Zukofsky would use throughout his career, in *The Writing of Guillaume Apollinaire*, *A Test of Poetry*, *Bottom: on Shakespeare*, and much of "*A*".

Henry Adams had been born in 1838, the great-grandson of the second president John Adams, the grandson of the sixth president John Quincy Adams, and the son of Charles Francis Adams, a lawyer, congressman, and diplomat. Scion of perhaps the first family of American politics, Henry Adams felt from an early age that success in a public career was expected of him. Such public success never came. Instead, Adams became a writer, the author of biographies, novels (the anonymous bestsellers *Democracy* and *Esther*), a nine-volume *History of the United States during the Administrations of Thomas Jefferson and James Madison*, and the two unclassifiable works upon which his contemporary reputation rests, *Mont Saint Michel and Chartres* and *The Education*. From a literary standpoint Adams's life was an extraordinary success; as Zukofsky put it, "Henry Adams lived long and wrote well."[6] In Adams's own estimation, however, he had failed miserably.

The Education of Henry Adams (first published in a "private" edition in 1907) was a withering, elegant dissection of the failure Adams conceived his life to have been. Adams blamed the failure of his "education" neither on Harvard nor on the opportunities afforded him as a secretary to the American legation in London, as a political journalist, and as the editor of the *North American Review*. Rather, he saw himself as a human fossil, a survival from an earlier era confronted with a bewildering, changing world: "What could become of such a child of the seventeenth and eighteenth centuries, when he should wake up to find himself required to play the game of the twentieth?"[7] From the Middle Ages, human society seemed to be moving with ever-accelerating speed into diverse and baffling—often self-contradictory—new directions, and late in life Adams, admitting his own abject inability to adapt to such changes, found consolation in tracing the course of the catastrophe that had wrecked his own hopes:

> Setting himself to the task, he began a volume which he mentally knew as "Mont Saint Michel and Chartres: a study of thirteenth-century unity." From that point he proposed to fix a position for himself, which he could label: "The Education of Henry Adams: a study of twentieth-century multiplicity."[8]

. . .

The subtitle of Zukofsky's thesis, "Detached Mind and the Growth of a Poet," named the dichotomy he found in Adams: "These chapters on the writing of Henry Adams illustrate two actuating forces of his nature," Zukofsky began. "Let this nature, by conceit, take on the aspect of moving waters: then, deep feeling and poetic intellect is its one continual undertow, and detached mind the strong surface current dashing in the contrary direction."[9] When he described Adams's "poetic" side, Zukofsky meant something quite congruent with the poetry he himself had been writing at Columbia: the Romantic notion of the poet as a man of deep feelings, a transmitter of powerful emotional currents. Of course, Adams was scarcely a poet, strictly speaking; he had written only two poems, "Buddha and Brahma" and "Prayer to the Virgin of Chartres" (both of which Zukofsky quoted at length). Zukofsky made an intermittent effort to argue that there were uniquely poetic qualities to Adams's prose, but here he defined poetry not as "deep feeling" but as a specific way of using words—as *technique*. One of Adams's essays, for instance, "gave the impression of precise phraseology and order of thought—two prerequisites not the least important for a poet."[10] More often, however, as when he considered the young Adams's mixture of "Detachment and the poet's receptivity for torment,"[11] Zukofsky's thesis discussed the poetic in the familiar terms of Romantic sensitivity.

He would never abandon the notion of poets as sensitive barometers of their times—what Ezra Pound would call "the antennae of the race"—but Zukofsky more and more came to define poetry in terms of technique or craft, a definition far closer to that of the modernists.

His enduring fascination with Henry Adams, I suspect, depended less on the spectacle of this New England aristocrat's emotional turmoil at the constant erosion of his life's epistemological foundations, than on the intellectual structures Adams erected to understand and chart that erosion—on the products of his "detached mind."

Brooks Adams opined that it was his brother Henry, alone of the male Adamses of his generation, who had inherited John Quincy Adams's scientific turn of mind.[12] Adams, deeply influenced by Brooks's *The Law of Civilization and Decay*, became convinced that one could make sense of the bewildering shifts Western society was undergoing by applying the laws and principles of science to the study of history.[13] He said as much in 1894 in "The Tendency of History," which argued that American historians were only following the spirit of the age in their attempt to "create a science of history," to formulate "a great generalization that would reduce all history under a law as clear as the laws which govern the material world."[14] A number of nineteenth-century historians and philosophers, among them Auguste Comte, Henry Buckle, Hippolyte Taine, and Herbert Spencer, had already argued that human society developed according to discernable laws and was conditioned by impersonal forces.[15] A truly comprehensive science of history would render irrelevant the notion of history as a chronicle of kings and administrators or a succession of heroes; most importantly for Henry Adams, it would explain why the world of the fast-approaching twentieth century would be so catastrophically alien to a child of the first half of the nineteenth.

Adams first advanced his "Dynamic Theory of History" in *The Education*. Such a theory, he argued, "defines Progress as the development and economy of Forces." Adams's theory traced "economies of force" in the development of human society, most importantly in the form of human thought itself—"the mind is itself the subtlest of all known forces." Human thought, confronted by the impersonal forces of nature, symbolized those forces under a progression of names, beginning with the "divine," and the scientific historian aimed to trace that progression and, using the tools of mathematics and the physical sciences, to determine its laws. The divine gave way around 1500, with Bacon's "new philosophy," to an era of "mechanical and chemical" forces, and "the speed of progress so rapidly surpassed man's gait as to alarm everybody, as though it was the acceleration of a falling body which the dynamic theory takes it to be." "The stupendous acceleration after 1800 ended in 1900 with the appearance of the new class of supersensual forces"—forces embodied in the Curies' discovery of radioactivity, the wireless telegraph, and the immense power of the electric dynamo, before which Adams had stood in awe at the 1900 Paris Exhibition: "to Adams the dynamo became a symbol of infinity.... Before the end, one began to pray to it; inherited instinct taught the natural expression of man before silent and infinite force."[16]

Adams intended *Mont Saint Michel and Chartres* and *The Education* to serve as contrasting studies of human thought: the former illustrating the "unity" of the mind in a "theological" age, the latter explaining how that age had given way to contemporary "multiplicity." Two years after the private publication of *The Education*, Adams sought to formalize his "dynamic theory" of history in the essay "The Rule of Phase Applied to History." He took as model the "phase" theory of the American physicist Willard Gibbs, which outlined the conditions under which matter passes from one physical state to another: solid to liquid, liquid to gas, gas to "electricity," "electricity" to "ether." Like matter, Adams hypothesized, human thought exists in various phases, and human history is the chronicle of its progression from one phase to the next. For at least ninety thousand years, according to Adams, human thought was in a Religious (or "fetishistic") Phase; the Renaissance's revolution in conceiving the universe's structure, evident in such thinkers as Bacon, Galileo, and Newton, brought human thought into a Mechanical Phase; about 1870—or perhaps as late as the turn of the century—human thought entered an Electrical Phase; and, within the next few years—or at the very latest around 2000—thought would enter a phase which marks the "limit of its possibilities," the Ethereal.[17]

Henry's brother Brooks questioned what an ethereal phase might mean: "How such an age would express itself must be to most of us problematical, since, according to Henry, only a few highly trained and gifted men will then be able to understand one another." Adams himself speculated that "Thought in terms of Ether means only Thought in terms of itself, or, in other words, pure Mathematics and Metaphysics, a stage often reached by individuals. At the utmost it could mean only the subsistence of the current into an ocean of potential thought, or mere consciousness, which is also possible, like static electricity."[18]

. . .

Adams's readers have largely passed over the "Rule of Phase" essay, seeing it as a rather embarrassing imposition of a scientific vocabulary upon the cultural insights so lovingly detailed in his earlier books.[19] Zukofsky, however, took "The Rule of Phase Applied to History" very seriously indeed. He quoted key passages from the essay in his Columbia thesis, and while he concluded that strictly considered "Truth . . . is not the standard for judging Adams' essay," he also opined that "a few may see that Henry Adams, even in disillusion, wrote poetry, and perhaps truth" as well.[20] As he grew older, Zukofsky continued to brood on Adams's work, and what had initially struck him about Adams—the conflict between conceptualizing, "detached mind" and poetic sensibility—grew less and less compelling as he pondered further the implication of the "rule of phase" and the "dynamic theory" of history.

Zukofsky published his thesis with only minor revisions as "Henry Adams: A Criticism in Autobiography" in *Hound & Horn* in 1930; he made a few more changes for its 1967 appearance in *Prepositions: The Collected Critical Essays*. As usual with Zukofsky, most of the revisions were excisions: words and sentences, overly arch or flowery phrases were pruned back to conform to Zukofsky's spare mature prose style. The only significant *additions* were to Chapter X, "Phase," where Zukofsky added a full three pages from the "Dynamic Theory of History" chapter of *The Education*. It was the largest stretch of continuous quotation in the essay, and it served to buttress by concrete historical analysis the phase theory, which, as Zukofsky had summarized it in the thesis, had seemed overly speculative and schematic.

Zukofsky could well afford to emphasize Adams's use of the "theory of phase" in 1967, for by that time Adams's thought had become an integral part of his own theory of poetic language. As Zukofsky put it in 1969, in response to an auditor who wondered that "For one who *thinks* so much in his poetry, it seems rather strange to, in fact, *hear* you speak only of its music," Henry Adams saw the attractions of events happening in the human mind—you know, the old business of action and reaction and looked at it thermodynamically. There are three states of existence: one is solid, another is liquid, and the other is gas. . . . It's the same with the materials of poetry, you make images—that's pretty solid—music, it's liquid; ultimately if something vaporizes that's the intellect.[21]

Like Dante, Zukofsky was fond of thinking in threes, and this particular trio—image, music, and intellection—had long been a constant in his critical thought. The preface to *A Test of Poetry* (1948) claimed that "The test of poetry is the range of pleasure it affords as sight, sound, and intellection."[22] In his 1950 "A Statement for Poetry," Zukofsky defined the components of poetry as "Image," "Sound," and "Interplay of Concepts."[23]

This tripartite division of the elements of poetic language clearly derived from the Poundian critical vocabulary. In his 1929 essay "How to Read," Pound distinguished three "kinds of poetry," three different aspects of language upon which a poet could choose to concentrate: *phanopœia, melopœia, and logopœia*. Phanopœia, "a casting of images upon the visual imagination," was best exemplified for Pound in image-based Chinese poetry; Provençal lyric was the purest example of melopœia, "wherein the words are charged, over and above their plain meaning, with some musical property"; and logopœia, "the dance of the intellect among words," was perhaps most clearly seen in the ironical modulations of words' connotations found in Mina Loy's early work and in Pound's own "Homage to Sextus Propertius."[24] Much of Zukofsky's 1929 essay on *The Cantos* was devoted to explicating these three terms, and he recapped them in the 1931 "'Recencies' in Poetry."[25]

By the time Zukofsky began *Bottom: on Shakespeare* (1947–1960), he had come to identify these three uses of language with the three physical states of matter—imagery was "solid," music "liquid," and intellection "gaseous"—and to value the first two states over the last. "I said solid state, liquid, gas," he told an interviewer in 1968, "as a matter of fact you can word it sense, essence, non-sense."[26] Zukofsky was part of a generation for whom Pound's imagist dictum, "Go in fear of abstractions," had become an article of faith.[27] Throughout his critical work, Zukofsky valued the evidence of the senses, presented as concrete images in the poem, and the music of the poem's words, over any abstract thinking or intellectualizing that might take place in the poem. "I don't see why Wallace Stevens ruined a great deal of his work by speaking vaguely about the imagination and reality and so on," Zukofsky said. "He can be a wonderful poet, but so much of it is a bore, bad philosophy."[28]

But *Bottom* also made evident how Zukofsky had modified Pound's critical categories, precisely by plotting them upon a historical continuum: "solid," "liquid," and "gaseous" did not merely describe different sorts of poetic language, but represented progressive stages of human language use. As he put it in *Bottom*, using the terms of "looking" (sight), "singing" (sound), and "conceiving" (intellection),

> in primitive time man *looks* around and into himself—his body and his cave to be decorated—then *looks* out and wonders how he first looked around and into himself; having reached fabling time he looks out by these means, above, underneath earth, its *heard* life that once made him speak now rarifying his picturing *sounds* of earth into *song* like those of an Odyssey; in late time he *conceives* past a vanishing point, nowhere or everywhere projecting "objects" in signs and indices which may again let him look around, into, out, up, down for an underpinning of earth . . .[29]

Or as he put it in "A"-12 (1950–1951), mapping this progression onto the semantic "fortunes of the Greek word *ruthmos*"—what we now pronounce *rhythm*—and aligning it with the Hebrew creation myth:

> So goes: first, *shape*
> The creation—
> A mist from the earth,
> The whole face of the ground;
> Then *rhythm*—
> And breathed breath of life;
> Then *style*—
> That from the eye its function takes—
> "Taste" we say—A living soul.[30]

Human language and thought, Zukofsky claimed, began in the solidity of concrete imagery, progressed to the liquid state of musical sound combination, and then evaporated into the gas of metaphysics. It was this historical progression upon which the analysis of *Bottom* was based. While Wyatt and the Elizabethan poets wrote a poetry of image and music, by Shakespeare's time we were entering an age of abstraction—a "gas age": "Shakespeare's *Works* as they conceive history regret a great loss of physical looking. They recall with the abstracted 'look' of a late time. The intellective propositions of their action anticipate the present day's vanishing point, but unlike the present's propositions still sing an earthly underpinning."[31] The progression of human language from solid to liquid to gas drives the almost five hundred pages of *Bottom*, and this historical schema undergirds most of the works of Zukofsky's maturity, from *"A"* to the short poems to the translation of Catullus. And Zukofsky—like the Shakespeare he describes in *Bottom*—saw this progression towards abstraction in a tragic light, as tragic a light as that in which Adams saw the twentieth century's increasing multiplicity. *Bottom*, *"A"*, and Zukofsky's other works were imbued with a deep nostalgia for a time of unimpeded perception, unimpeded song. "I'd like to keep it solid," Zukofsky said, "I was born in a gas age . . ."[32]

What Zukofsky had done in short was to harness Adams's scheme of history to Pound's doctrines of poetics. As so often with Zukofsky, none of the constituent elements of the composition are new—it is the combination of the "recurrences" that arrests a reader. The distinction among phanopœia, melopœia, and logopœia—sight, sound, and intellection, in Zukofsky's terms—is Pound's, but putting that distinction to work as a way of characterizing various eras' language use is Zukofsky's own complication of Pound's theory; and that complication, in turn, is fundamentally indebted to Adams's phase theory of history.

·   ·   ·

Zukofsky's involvement with Adams's work casts into sharp relief another aspect of his own thought: his respect for—even envy of—the vocabulary and methods of science, his own desire to install poetry as a discourse of scientific accuracy and verifiability rather than the vague expression of emotion. He was not alone in this. Poets, at least since Tennyson's and Arnold's attempts to come to terms with evolutionary theory, had keenly felt the cultural capital of their art being eroded by the forces of the new sciences and technologies. Some champions of poetry such as I. A. Richards, in *Science and Poetry* (1926), sought to establish it as a mode of truth-telling utterly distinct from science.[33] Many of the modernist poets, however, were inclined as well to appropriate the language of the sciences and technology to describe their own works. In *The Spirit of Romance* (1910), Pound described poetry as "a sort of inspired mathematics which gives us equations, not for abstract figures, triangles, spheres, and the like, but equations for human emotions," and his later critical works were peppered with scientific language and analogies. Zukofsky's friend William Carlos Williams described a poem as "a small (or large) machine made of words."[34]

Later in life, when Zukofsky was teaching at the Polytechnic Institute of Brooklyn, he told his students—most of them prospective engineers or scientists—that "the engineer or scientist was closer to his concept of poetry than was the liberal arts student who has less contact with and respect for design, form, and invention . . ."[35] Indeed, he saw his own poetry in architectural or engineering terms, as a structure of semantic and musical tension, rather than as the "emotion recollected in tranquility" of Wordsworth's Romantic formulation. "Whoever makes it," Zukofsky wrote, "may very well consider a poem as a design or construction."[36] In "A"-12, he described his poetics in mathematical terms:

$$\int \genfrac{}{}{0pt}{}{\text{music}}{\text{speech}}$$

An integral
Upper limit music
Lower limit speech[37]

What Zukofsky envied in the discourse of science, and what he craved for his own criticism, were precise standards of measurement and assessment—"The need for standards in poetry is no less than in science"—and to that end he never tired of repeating an aphorism from Plato: "If number, measure and weighing be taken away from any art, that which remains will not be much." His ultimate goal, one suspects, was to hit upon a critical method that would have the accuracy, reliability, and iterability of a scientific theorem:

Someone alive in the years 1951 to 2000 may attempt a scientific definition of poetry. Its value would be in a generalization based on past and present poems and always relevant to the detail of their art. All future poems would verify some aspect of this definition and reflect it as an incentive to a process intended to last at least as long as men.[38]

Zukofsky never arrived at such a "scientific definition" of poetry. By temperament and talent, he was no scientist. It was the symmetrical, crystalline conceptual structures of science and mathematics that attracted him, so much like the ruthlessly logical constructions of the philosophers he most admired—Lucretius, Spinoza, St. Thomas Aquinas, Charles Saunders Peirce. While he had a side of emotional vulnerability, even sentimentality, Zukofsky longed for the systematic order a "scientific definition" of poetry, like a phase theory of history, might provide. Ultimately, the very division he traced in Henry Adams—between "detached mind" and "poetic undertow"—was at the foundation of his own sensibility.

The Lean
Twenties 1924–1928

chapter three

W
HILE ZUKOFSKY's master's degree offered him no immediate career prospects, he spent the summer of 1924 pleasantly. Whittaker Chambers and his friend Henry Bang,
also a Columbia dropout, were camping on the Long Island
beach after their Manhattan apartment burned out. Friends would
join them there, among them Clifton Fadiman, Henry Zolinsky, and
Zukofsky. At the beach there was alcohol, steamed clams—"Whitt
ate incessantly," Zukofsky recalled—and conversation, much of
it literary. Like Zukofsky, both Chambers and Zolinsky aspired to
be poets. "Friday nights," Zukofsky remembered, were "a regular
appointment to go over stuff with Henry. Whitt thought the stuff was
genius if precipitous. Everybody thought they were difficult but out of
ordinary—which wd. make me mad . . ."[1] Already Zukofsky's poetry
was getting a frustrating reputation for obscurity: "I'd say look this
means this & this, say they're rotten, but really if you *read* carefully
you can't say they're not clear."

The beach is a major presence in the brief lyrics Zukofsky wrote that summer and the next: "air over the dune-grasses" in the early morning, the "Breaking up of a bonfire / On the beach" late at night, the sand fleas Zukofsky stirs as he walks the beach at sunset.[2] These poems were a vast step ahead of the classically orotund or feyly lyrical pieces he had published at Columbia. Some of them indeed survive into his mature collections. "Aubade, 1925," for instance, reworks the Provençal *alba* or *aubade*—a lover's morning song before departure—into a gritty portrait of the poet awakening, sweaty, cramped, and chilly, in his seaside tent:

> Kick the blanket away,
> The man of darkness has sweated enough!
> One, two, three efforts, and he stands on his feet—
> Chilled a little on the cold sands.

Wryly self-aware, the poem moves through meditations on "the state of man," a plaintive cry for communion—"Whence, if ever, then, will come sympathy?"—to a final return to the physical:

> Bah-h! so much blanket again
> Tousled hair—sleep!
>
> Swims!
> Spewing and spewn on to the land!
>   The sun is hot![3]

These poems showed that Zukofsky had been reading his older contemporaries—Wallace Stevens, H.D., Ezra Pound. He had a copy of Stevens's first collection, *Harmonium* (1923), and read it "constantly" ("I cannot imagine whose copy it was," he recalled almost fifty years later, "because I couldn't afford it"[4]), and there are traces of Stevens's vivid, elegant diction in his lyrics. The free verse of the poems—in contrast to his Columbia lyrics, few of them are in regular meters—is flexible and expressive, like that of the poems Pound and H.D. had been publishing as imagists ten years before. Most of all, they show the exuberance of a poet barely into manhood; pleased and a bit amazed at the sensation of his own body in the unfamiliar environment of sand, water, and sun; and drunk on the "freshness of discovering" the world of literature—"Joyce, Lawrence, etc, the Greeks, Latin, mediaeval, Adams, French."[5]

· · ·

49

Zukofsky had no full-time job. For a while, he worked as a tutor of English as a second language in an assembly-line operation run by Samuel Roth (who would edit *Two Worlds Quarterly* and pirate Joyce's *Ulysses* in 1927). The phone-booth-sized "classrooms" were packed closely together: "my friend who had recommended me could be heard saying no not *ket, cat*—& he could hear me[,] no not *bad, bed*." If a student failed to show up for a session, Zukofsky simply wasn't paid his fifty cents an hour.[6] He worked part-time for a while at a local post office, but was fired for refusing to work on Yom Kippur. (Not that he was planning to attend temple—something just went against the grain about having to punch the clock on the highest of High Holidays.) And he worked for a time—again, part-time—dispensing orangeade at Nedick's, a fast-food operation that sold orange drink, coffee, and doughnuts.[7]

After an early infatuation with Calvin Coolidge, Whittaker Chambers had been drifting to the political left. In February 1925, he formally joined the Communist Party.[8] Though most of Chambers's Columbia friends were sympathetic to the Party's aims, they were also suspicious of his full-fledged Party membership. Zukofsky, when Chambers told him he had joined, "squinted one eye and lifted the eyebrow of the other, so that he looked as if he were peering through a monocle. 'Do you drill in a cellar with machine guns?'" he asked.[9] (Ironically, Chambers remembered, it had been Zukofsky who first urged him to read *The Communist Manifesto*.) Both Zukofsky and John Gassner, however, were committed enough to accompany Chambers to Party meetings and have him propose them for membership. Both were rejected on the grounds that they were "bourgeois intellectuals" rather than true sons of the working class. Gassner, in the words of the presiding member, was "not the cream of the proletariat, but the scum of the bourgeoisie."[10] When Chambers took Zukofsky to a meeting of his West Side Cell, the members found the young poet altogether too nattily dressed: they suggested he join someplace on the East Side. Zukofsky was nonplussed—"What a thing to be going to! East side or west side!"—and did not renew his attempts to join the Party.[11]

Chambers and Zukofsky had remained close friends after leaving Columbia. Zukofsky had spent time with Chambers's family—his ill-matched mother and father, his charming but feckless younger brother, Richard—and he and Chambers had shared their literary discoveries, shown each other their poetry as it was written. But Zukofsky found Whittaker's new cloak-and-dagger world of espionage, infiltration, and secret names simply incredible. It seemed too far-fetched that his friend, whose entire universe five years before had consisted of literature and philosophy, should now be entering the upper echelon of the Communist Party. In the end, he thought, Whitt must be joking—he must be getting together material for a novel.[12]

Chambers was in dead earnest, eventually getting a job at the *Daily Worker*, making his way to the top of the American Communist literary hierarchy, and within a few years beginning his career as a spy for the Soviet Union. Zukofsky preferred to pursue his politics through poetry. Lenin, the much-mythologized leader of the Bolshevik Revolution, had died in January 1924. The following year, Zukofsky wrote a memorial to him, "Constellation: *In Memory of V. I. Ulianov*" (Ulianov was Lenin's birth name). The poem is in one of Zukofsky's less compelling early voices—one is tempted to call it the *large* rhetorical voice, and it owes much to Walt Whitman—but it sets up remarkable patterns of sound as it pursues a wholly classical theme: that the dead Lenin has been set in the heavens as a star to guide those struggling for justice on the earth.

> Star, of all live processes
> Continual it seems to us,
> Like elm leaves,
> Lighted in your glow;—
> We thrive in strange hegira
> Here below,
> Yet sometimes in our flight alone
> We speak to you,
> When nothing that was ours seems spent
> And life consuming us seems permanent,
> And flights of stirring beating up the night
> And down and up; we do not sink with every wave.[13]

The conceit here is not complex, but the sound of these lines, rhyming and off-rhyming at precise asymmetrical intervals, approaching, settling into, and then retreating from regular meters, is evidence of the poet's growing formal mastery.

Zukofsky was trying out other voices as well, poetic modes more closely tied to the "folk" genres of ballad and song. "During the Passaic Strike of 1926" contrasts the violence directed against New Jersey textile mill strikers with the plight of the "rich parish" of St. Mark's-in-the-Bowery, whose sexton had told Zukofsky's friend Samuel Theodore Hecht that "there was only room for two in his graveyard."

> For justice they are shrewdly killing the proletarian,
> For justice they are shrewdly shooting him dead,
> Good Heavens, when the vaults are filled in St. Mark's-
>   on-the-Bouwerie,
> How will the dead bury their dead![14]

At its height there were sixteen thousand workers involved in the Passaic Textile Strike, most of them foreign born and poorly educated. Traditional labor unions had refused to involve themselves with what began as a spontaneous walkout in protest of wage cuts, and the Communist Party's subsequent involvement made the strikers the focus of both police brutality and media red-baiting.[15] The rollicking lines of Zukofsky's poem, which comically distend the ballad form towards which they gesture, were an ironic commentary on an economic situation that itself embodied a cruder and more serious irony.

Ironical as well was Zukofsky's adaptation of Jesus's words (Matthew 8:22)—"let the dead bury their dead"—as the closing line of each stanza. As the child of Orthodox parents, Zukofsky grew up in an atmosphere of Torah. But his Columbia education, focusing as it did on the classics of English literature, gave him a taste for the language and symbolism of the Christian New Testament. New Testament images, phrases, and tropes are prominent in his early poetry. In the second half of the 1920s, Zukofsky was particularly drawn to the seventeenth-century writer John Bunyan's popular allegory, *The Pilgrim's Progress*.[16] That narrative, in which a common, working-class character finds his way out of the City of Destruction and eventually makes his way to the city of eternal life, seemed to Zukofsky an apt allegory of the worker oppressed by capital. "Bunyan, who had a conception of Deliverance by the right way, straight and narrow," Zukofsky wrote, "was, if similitudes are employed, a Revolutionary pessimist" with a "metaphysics" like that of the French socialist Georges Sorel, whose *Réflexions sur la violence* (1908) had proposed proletarian violence as the cure for the existing social order.[17] "Constellation," in its first periodical publication, begins with an epigraph from Bunyan that associates Lenin with the "ministering Spirits, sent forth to minister for those that be heirs of salvation," who guide Christian on the very last leg of his journey to the holy city.[18] And "During the Passaic Strike" is followed by a quotation from *Pilgrim's Progress*, a passage pointedly relevant to the plight of the striking workers: "*I was born indeed in your dominions, but your service was hard, and your wages such as a man could not live on.*"

Service may have been hard and wages strait, but Zukofsky was working—if not regularly. From the fall of 1924 through the end of 1926, and then from late 1928 to the end of the 1930 school year, he was a substitute teacher of high school English.[19] Substitute teaching is a sporadic, ill-paying, and stressful occupation, and even with a master's degree from Columbia—which ought to have qualified him for a college teaching position—Zukofsky could not apply for a regular high school teaching post without passing the Board of Education's examination, which he was loath to take: Surely something better than a high school classroom would present itself for a young man as bright and qualified as he was.[20] In April 1927 Zukofsky was working part-time, along with Whittaker Chambers, in his brother Morris's Greenwich Village bookstore.[21] Late in 1927 Zukofsky's Columbia friend Irving Kaplan ("Kappy") got him a job with the Industrial Relations Department of the National Industrial Conference Board, editing and writing reports on such subjects as workplace cafeterias and employee savings plans.[22] He also worked for the Educators' Association, editing a "Miscellany" section of their Volume Library.[23] He remained at the family home at 57 East 111th Street, keenly following the contemporary literary scene and writing his own poetry.

. . .

The last years of the 1920s were productive for Zukofsky in terms both of his writing and of his literary connections, but they were marred by the deaths of those close to him. The first was Whittaker Chambers's brother Richard, whose life had been sliding deeper and deeper into chaos. Richard had enrolled in college and dropped out, had made a short-lived marriage, and was more or less constantly under the influence of "poisonous Prohibition whiskey."[24] Whittaker himself frustrated two of Richard's suicide attempts. On September 9, 1926, however, Richard succeeded in killing himself, lying on two chairs and putting a pillow beneath his head in the oven of a gas range.[25] Whittaker was convulsed with grief and guilt over his inability to save his brother. Zukofsky had been close to Whittaker and his family; remembering the excitement of discovering poets, novelists, and philosophers at Columbia, and the times he and his friends had spent with Whittaker on the Long Island beach, he committed his own grief to paper. The pain of Richard Godfrey Chambers's death was to reverberate in Zukofsky's poetry for some four years, and found immediate expression in "Poem beginning 'The,'" which he drafted in the fall and winter of 1926.[26]

In the second of the six sections of that poem, Zukofsky breaks into an extended lament for "Lion-heart, frate mio":

78   Goldenrod
79   Of which he is a part,
80   Sod
81   He hurried over
82   Underfoot,
83   Make now
84   His testament of sun and sky . . .
93   Do you walk slowly in the halls of the heavens,
94   Or saying that you do, lion-hearted not ours,
95   Hours, days, months, passed from us and gone,
96   Lion-heart not looked upon, walk with the stars.[27]

Zukofsky removed Ricky's name from the final version of the poem (the draft manuscript refers repeatedly to "Ricardo" and "Richard"), but the reference to the English king Richard Coeur de Lion points inescapably to him.

The lament for Chambers's suicide, however, is merely a single moment in a long and complex poem, a work that demonstrated how entirely Zukofsky had escaped the weaknesses of his college poetry and how deeply he had immersed himself in the writings of the emerging modernist movement. "Poem beginning 'The,'" that is to say, was Zukofsky's first major work, an astonishing achievement for a poet of twenty-two. "'The'" is a long poem of 330 lines, divided into six sections. It is in a variety of voices—elegiac lyric, grandiloquent political prophecy, synthetic school song, and even a section giving voice to nocturnally wandering *cats*—but Zukofsky strikes its predominantly satirical tone in the first lines:

1 The
2 Voice of Jesus I. Rush singing
3   in the wilderness[28]

This is a *vox clamantis in deserto*, like that of Isaiah or John the Baptist, but here Jesus has become some small-time businessman with a middle initial, a pun for the harried worker of the 1920s—"Jesus, I rush!" "'The'" is an extraordinarily allusive poem, crowding in quotations from and references to over thirty items from Zukofsky's reading, but it is also strikingly catholic in its allusiveness. College cheers, the titles of Broadway musicals, pop songs, and Yiddish lullabies jostle with Dante, Sophocles, Shakespeare, and Chaucer in a scattershot and often painfully funny mix.

It is precisely in this allusiveness that "Poem beginning 'The'" most resembles its immediate model and the implicit target of its satire, T. S. Eliot's *The Waste Land*. *The Waste Land*, published in 1922, seemed for sympathetic readers to crystallize the mood of post–Great War Europe. Those first readers knew nothing of the trials of Eliot's own life, the horrors of his marriage to Vivien Haigh-Wood. Instead, in the poem's densely packed quotations from and allusions to classic literature, they saw a picture of the state in which the First World War had left Western civilization. Modernity, *The Waste Land* seemed to argue, had debased literature, had debased the life of the spirit, had debased sexuality. All that was left were "fragments" that the poem's Tiresias-narrator had vainly "shored against my ruin."[29] Traditionalist critics attacked *The Waste Land* as incoherent pastiche, but even sympathetic readers, who saw in its multivoiced form a barometer of the direction of modern poetry, were appalled by its message.

"Poem beginning 'The'" immediately announces itself as a parody of *The Waste Land*. Where Eliot's poem is divided into five sections, "'The'" is divided into six, the last given the seemingly tacked-on title "Half-dozenth Movement: *Finale, and After.*" Where Eliot appended a lengthy section of explanatory notes to his poem, numbering every tenth line to facilitate readers' flipping back and forth, Zukofsky numbers *every single line*, and then prefaces the poem as a whole with a full-page "dedication" that supplies references for particular lines. The references, however, are presented not in the order of their appearance in the poem, but in alphabetical order: "Modern advertising—163, George Moore—24, Marianne Moore—22, Mussolini—74, 75, Myself—130, 142, 167, 309, Obvious—Where the Reference is Obvious, Walter Pater's *Renaissance*—165," and so forth.[30] For a reader seeking immediate illumination, these "dedications" are practically useless. Himself an intelligent reader, Zukofsky must have suspected the relevance of many of Eliot's notes to *The Waste Land*, and he as well distrusted the whiff of pedantry emanating from them. What better way to poke fun at Eliot's punctiliousness than to push it to a scholastic extreme?

"Poem beginning 'The'" begins with a direct challenge to the modernist movement in literature, a group of writers obsessed with reclaiming the heritage of the past, "Oedipus-faced wrecks / Creating out of the dead . . ." These writers—"self-exiled men" like Pound in Italy, Eliot in London, Joyce in Paris—seem only to lament the past, rather than looking to the future. "Lord, lord," the poem implores,

. . . why are our finest always dead?
18   And why, Lord, this time, is it Mauberley's
         Luini in porcelain, why is it Chelifer,
19   Why is it Lovat who killed Kangaroo,
20   Why Stephen Dedalus with the cane of ash, . . .
26   And why if the waste land has been explored, traveled over,
         circumscribed,
27   Are there only wrathless skeletons exhumed new planted
         in its sacred wood[?][31]

(The modernist works referred to here—the "dedication" reminds us—are Pound's *Hugh Selwyn Mauberley*, Aldous Huxley's *Those Barren Leaves*, James Joyce's *Ulysses*, *The Waste Land* itself, of course, and Eliot's *The Sacred Wood*.)

The "new" writers' obsession with the past might be unhealthy; but no more healthy, Zukofsky implies, was the superficial, popularizing manner in which John Erskine had offered up the "great books" at Columbia. In the poem's fourth movement, *"More 'Renaissance',"* Zukofsky characterizes Erskine's General Honors as "Askforaclassic, Inc.":

164 Get yourself another century,
165 A little frost before sundown,
166 It's the times don'chewknow,
167 And if you're a Jewish boy, then be your Plato's Philo.[32]

That "Jewish boy," the "dedication" notes, is Zukofsky himself. As a Jew working his way through a course of Gentile classics, he must forever be Philo to the canon's Plato—the adaptor who gives a peculiarly Jewish voice to the master's thought, rather than himself the innovator.

And even among his own people, the Orthodox community, Zukofsky's desire to write poetry made him an outcast. Baruch Spinoza, excommunicated by the Amsterdam Rabbinate in 1656, wrote his philosophy in a lonely self-exile, diverting himself by grinding lenses. Now, having been initiated into the mysteries of Western culture at Columbia ("Cathedral Parkway"), Zukofsky himself finds only Spinoza for company:

55 Not by art we have lived,
56 Not by graven images forbidden to us
57 Not by letters I fancy,
58 Do we dare say
59 With Spinoza grinding lenses, Rabbaisi,
60 After living on Cathedral Parkway?[33]

On the other hand, "Assimilation is not hard," the poet says to his mother, "252 And once the Faith's askew / 253 I might as well look Shagetz just as much as Jew." (The Yiddish word *shagetz*—a non-Jewish boy, the masculine of the more familiar "shiksa"—is a particularly brutal term, deriving as it does from the Hebrew for "abomination.") This is the assimilation, however, of the double agent, as Zukofsky notes in the voice of Shakespeare's Shylock:

258   The villainy they teach me I will execute
259   And it shall go hard with them,
260   For I'll better the instruction,
261   Having learned, so to speak, in their colleges.[34]

Notwithstanding the bitterness of this adaptation of *The Merchant of Venice*, the passage strikingly presages Zukofsky's later intellectual career. Zukofsky was, in fact, "better[ing] the instruction," mastering the Western literary tradition as thoroughly as any English or American writer of his generation.

The assimilated double agent was at work in "Poem beginning 'The.'" Much as Eliot had introduced non-Western elements into *The Waste Land*—the Buddha's Fire Sermon, the Sanskrit phrases of "What the Thunder Said"—Zukofsky leavened his own poem with lively parodies of American popular culture and quotations from Jewish writers. The poem's second section, *International Episode*," is in part a dialogue about the theater between Zukofsky and his own penis, whom he addresses as "Peter Out" (more familiarly, "My Peter Out"). The titles of the Broadway shows they consider seeing are a mixture of salacious low comedy and high cultural parody, including "Dancing with H.R.H.," "The Happy Quetzalcoatl," "Tear the Codpiece Off, A Musical Comedy," "Near Ibsen," and—in an allusion to Oswald Spengler's work of cultural pessimism—"The West-Decline."[35]

"Poem beginning 'The'" is a poem of sorrows and alienations—as Zukofsky quotes Heine, another assimilated Jew writing in a Western language, "Aus meinen grossen Leiden mach ich die kleinen lieder" (Out of my great sorrows I make little songs)[36]—but it is also a poem of hope. In part that hope is political, centered in the brave new experiment of Soviet communism: "It is your Russia that is free, mother," the poet twice reminds Chana Zukofsky, in contrast to the "gastanks, ruts, cemetery-tenements" of New York.[37] And hope lies in the vigor of new poetries to which the modernists are blind. Some sixty lines of "Poem beginning 'The'"—almost a fifth of the entire poem—are translated or adapted from the Yiddish verse of "Yehoash," the poet Solomon Bloomgarden (1870–1927). Yehoash, like Pinchos Zukofsky, had come to the United States from Lithuania, and his writing was central to the flowering of Yiddish literature in the New York of the 1920s and 1930s. In addition to his own poetry and prose works, Yehoash compiled a Hebrew-Yiddish dictionary and translated the Hebrew Bible into Yiddish. The Yiddish *Hiawatha* that the child Zukofsky recited was Yehoash's translation.[38]

Yiddish writing, however, was beyond the pale of both Erskine's Great Books and the tradition extolled in T. S. Eliot's influential 1919 essay "Tradition and the Individual Talent." European writers for the most part dismissed Yiddish as a mongrelized German. Even the intelligentsia among Orthodox Judaism all too often saw the language as a mere "jargon" (*zhargon*), infinitely inferior to the *loshen kodesh* (holy tongue) of Hebrew, the appropriate vehicle for Jewish writing.[39] Like Spinoza, then, between Orthodoxy and Cartesian rationalism, and like Zukofsky himself, Yehoash is a Jew between traditions. Yehoash's poetry takes a pride of place in "Poem beginning 'The'" analogous to that which Eliot awarded to the seventeenth-century English metaphysical poets in his own work. Zukofsky adapts three of Yehoash's lyrics in "'The,'" and ends the poem with the hopeful vision of "Oif di Churvos" ("On the Ruins"):

318   By the wrack we shall sing our Sun-song
319   Under our feet will crawl
320   The shadows of dead worlds,
321   We shall open our arms wide,
322   Call out of pure might—
323   Sun, you great Sun, our Comrade,
324   From eternity to eternity we remain true to you,
325   A myriad years we have been,
326   Myriad upon myriad shall be.[40]

With these lines, the poet steps out of the "wrack" of the modernists' wasteland, out of the "shadows of dead worlds," and looks towards a new, hopeful future.

· · ·

Much of the last two movements of "Poem beginning 'The'" was directly addressed to Zukofsky's mother. In the poem she represents the old world of eastern European *Yiddishkayt* living within the new world of the American 1920s. For all the tenderness of Zukofsky's address, there was also a sense of bitter alienation. His mother, who knew only Yiddish, would never read these words: "Now I kiss you who could never sing Bach, never read Shakespeare."[41] Chana Zukofsky was ill when Zukofsky was writing "Poem beginning 'The,'" and she died on January 29, 1927, on the date that Zukofsky believed was his birthday. She had suffered for some time from a pulmonary infection, and had been home from the hospital a month when she died. Of his two parents, it was his mother to whom Zukofsky had been closest. His father Pinchos had worked crushing hours, from early in the morning until midnight; Zukofsky had barely known him during his childhood. Even physically, Zukofsky resembled his thin, sharp-boned mother more than his vigorous father.[42]

It is hard to assess Zukofsky's reaction to his mother's death, except to imagine the inevitable grief of the bereaved child. His friend Henry Zolinsky wrote a poem at the time, "On the Burial of Louis' Mother":

> She is buried away forever, Son Loya, what is left of her,
> And part of you and a part of some others are buried away,
> And she lives as sadness in the mind of you,
> Part of your permanent sorrow;
> And she will live thruout the earth,
> Part of its permanent life.

Zukofsky himself mourned his mother's death in poems far more subtle than Zolinsky's. In March he wrote two highly wrought sonnets; the latter of these questioned whether mourning his mother might be Zukofsky's response to a common mortality: "bowed with her death, we mourn / Ourselves, our own earth selves."[43] These were highly compacted, almost "metaphysical" poems, and far less immediate than the poem Zukofsky wrote in 1928 on the first anniversary of his mother's death, where he addressed a tiny potted cactus that reminded him of her:

always mortmain the oblivion of her
      in the desert of my traces—
Hannah, "grace." Grace under the moon,
      on blue velvet cloth I placed the prickly plant.[44]

The poet "tread[s] knee deep in snow" this January day, but to "Think of snow" is to "Know duration." Even as one sees the snow, knowing that it will soon enough be melted, one knows that certain things—like memory of one's mother—remain in "unseen continuance."

In his writing at least, Zukofsky would not fully come to terms with his mother's death until 1936, when he wrote the largely auto-biographical play *Arise, arise*. The more immediate effect of Chana Zukofsky's death was the gradual breakup of the family unit. Zukof-sky's brother Morris Zukowsky and sister Fanny were both married and raising families of their own. Pinchos Zukofsky was in his late sixties, no doubt worn down by almost thirty years of sweatshop labor. Eventually, Pinchos would move from East Harlem to the Bronx home where Fanny and her husband, Al Wand, were raising a family; after the spring of 1930, Zukofsky would be on his own, liv-ing with friends or in an ever-changing succession of rented rooms and apartments.[45]

. . .

"Poem beginning 'The'" was clearly something special, the most sub-stantial and successful thing Zukofsky had yet written. Of course it should be published as soon as possible, but it might also serve as a way of introducing himself to the writers he most admired. With this in mind, Zukofsky sent the poem to E. E. Cummings in May 1927: the poem was meant, Zukofsky explained, "not as the Arab merchants plead—you wan' buy?—but [as] how can I meet the only American writer I care to meet outside of a book[?]"[46] Cummings seems not to have replied. There was a far more favorable response, however, when Zukofsky, around the beginning of August 1927, submitted "Poem beginning 'The'" to Ezra Pound's new periodical, the *Exile*.

In 1927 Pound was forty-one, eighteen years older than Zukof-sky. He had been an expatriate since 1908, living in Venice, London, and Paris before finally settling down in the Italian Riviera town of Rapallo, where such literati as W. B. Yeats and Max Beerbohm maintained seasonal residences. Born in Hailey, Idaho, raised in a Philadelphia suburb, and educated in American universities, Pound had bidden farewell to his native country after losing his midwestern academic position in a scandal involving a snowstorm-stranded chorus girl.[47] Pound left with few regrets. His youthful travels had given him a taste for European living, and his training in comparative literature at the University of Pennsylvania had focused largely on the Romance languages. Most crucially, Pound had early on decided that his destiny was to be a poet, and he saw little place for belles lettres in a provincial and aggressively commercial turn-of-the-century United States.

Pound's European career is part of the mythology of "high modernism": how he became a gadfly to the London literary establishment, helping prod Yeats out of his impressionistic Celtic twilight and into a more straightforward, politically charged voice; how he "discovered" fellow expatriates Robert Frost, T. S. Eliot, and Hilda Doolittle (H.D.); how he spearheaded the literary movements of imagism and vorticism. Pound had tirelessly worked to advance the cause of "the new" in literature and the arts, promoting the careers of the sculptor Henri Gaudier-Brzeska and the composer George Antheil, writing hundreds of pages of art and music reviews, and pressing for the publication of Joyce's *Portrait of the Artist as a Young Man* and *Ulysses*. His ongoing goal, reiterated in hundreds of occasional articles and essays and in thousands of letters, was a new renaissance in the arts, a renaissance that could only be achieved by cementing connections between like-minded poets, writers, musicians, and artists, and a coalition of wealthy but discriminating patrons and intelligent readers.

By 1927, however, Pound found himself isolated. He had broken with Joyce and the Paris scene, and his friend Eliot ("the Possum"), whose *The Waste Land* he had edited into its final form in 1922, was positioning himself through his magazine, the *Criterion*, to become a mainstay of the very London literary establishment against which he and Pound had once been arrayed. And the Great War, in which Pound's friends Gaudier-Brzeska and T. E. Hulme died, had set Pound's imagination on an irrecoverably political course. No one seemed quite sure why the world war had been fought. Pound thought he had found its causes in the manipulation of public debt and national currency by powerful private interests. The only European country that seemed to be correcting these abuses was fascist Italy. In Benito Mussolini, Pound saw a larger-than-life philosopher king, an enlightened strongman not unlike the Renaissance condottiere Sigismundo Malatesta, whose exploits Pound celebrated in his Malatesta Cantos.

Pound had always kept one foot in the American camp, serving as European correspondent to various American literary periodicals. By the mid-1920s, however, his connections with the *Dial* and *Poetry* had been severely strained: While their editors still respected Pound, they would no longer print whatever he sent them, no longer took his word as to what mattered in European letters. Pound had been associated with so many periodicals in the past—not just the *Dial* and *Poetry*, but the *Egoist*, the *New Age*, the *Little Review*, and so forth—that it seems surprising that only now, with the *Exile*, had he gotten around to editing one of his own. In part, the magazine was a gesture of disgust with the periodical publishing scene in general: The *Exile* was "undertaken," Pound told Harriet Monroe in 1931, "to print what no other mag. wd. print."[48]

Indeed the *Exile* was probably the only periodical adventurous enough to publish the 330 numbered lines of "Poem beginning 'The.'" As Zukofsky wrote when he submitted the poem, "I don't suppose anybody dares print this, but if anybody does, it will be you."[49] Pound was enthusiastic in his reply: "My Dear Zukofsky: Thanks. First cheering mss. I have recd. in weeks, or months, or something or other."[50] He would print "Poem beginning 'The'" in the next issue. (The other poem Zukofsky had sent, "Critique of Antheil," Pound wasn't so sure of; along with several other Zukofsky pieces, it would eventually appear in the *Exile*'s fourth and last number of autumn 1928). Pound was delighted to have heard from Zukofsky: His letters and submissions were evidence that the life of the mind and the pursuit of poetry were not yet dead in the United States, and evidence that Pound might be able to instigate some new literary movement in his home country.

Pound immediately encouraged Zukofsky to get in touch with his nearby contemporaries. Pound was especially keen for Zukofsky to meet his old friend William Carlos Williams, just across the river in New Jersey: "Do go down an' stir up ole Bill Willyums, 9 Ridge Rd. Rutherford (W. C. Williams M.D.) and tell him I tole you. He is still the best human value on my murkn. visiting list."[51] Zukofsky dutifully contacted Williams, who, despite the tone of Pound's introduction—"By 'human value' I suppose Ezrie means that in his opinion I can't write," Williams opened his first letter to Zukofsky[52]—was eager to meet the younger poet. Williams invited Zukofsky to dinner at his home in Rutherford, but their first actual meeting took place on April 1, 1928, at the Park Central Hotel in New York, where Williams hoped Zukofsky would "rescue" him from an interviewer and a caricature artist.[53] They had dinner, and Zukofsky gave Williams one of his own poems. The next day, Williams wrote to congratulate him: "Yes, yes. You have the rare gift. . . . It is thoughtful poetry, but actual word stuff, not thoughts for thoughts."[54] From this time forward, Williams and Zukofsky were rarely out of communication long, and their friendship would prove one of the most durable influences on each of their creative careers.

William Carlos Williams, born in Rutherford in 1883, was two years older than Pound. The two had met as students at the University of Pennsylvania in 1902. Theirs was a close friendship marked by deep rivalry: Each of them was convinced of his vocation as a poet, but while Pound immersed himself in pre-Raphaelite verse and translations from medieval European literature, Williams was fumbling his way out of an overripe Keatsian idiom towards a poetry that would capture the American reality in which he lived and the peculiarly American language spoken all around him. Williams remained among Pound's closest American correspondents after Pound moved to Europe; Pound kept him updated on the literary scenes of London and Paris, the progress of his own career, and the new movements he was witnessing in literature and the arts. He also twitted Williams mercilessly about his decision to remain at home practicing medicine while Pound in Europe was at the center of the new explosion in the arts. Williams was painfully aware of his position. He read about what the "new" artists and writers—Picasso, Wyndham Lewis, Gertrude Stein—were up to, and he knew that there was precious little going on in the United States that could stand comparison with what was being done in Europe. But he was also more and more convinced that America was the proper place for American writers, the American scene and American language their proper subject matter and voice.

By the early 1920s Williams was producing works that through their dislocations of syntax, form, and argument challenged readers as aggressively as anything produced in Europe. In the prologue to his *Kora in Hell: Improvisations* (1920), Williams excoriated Pound as "the best enemy United States verse has," and called Eliot "a subtle conformist," "this archbishop of procurers to a lecherous antiquity."[55] Williams's 1923 *Spring and All*, which interwove vivid, image-centered verse with polemical prose, was in large part a hopeful response to Eliot's hopeless *The Waste Land* of the year before. *The Waste Land*, Williams would recall decades later, seemed a direct blow to the nativist American avant-garde: "It wiped out our world as if an atom bomb had been dropped upon it and our brave sallies into the unknown were turned to dust."[56] While Zukofsky's response to *The Waste Land*, in "Poem beginning 'The,'" was subversive parody, Williams's had been a frontal assault on Eliot's classicism.

Whether or not Zukofsky was closely familiar with Williams's work before he met him, he was soon to be intimately involved with it. On April 11, 1928, soon after their first meeting, Williams gave him a copy of *Spring and All*, which was to become Zukofsky's favorite of Williams's books.[57] Zukofsky spent the Fourth of July at Williams's Rutherford home, talking about writing and listening to Williams's two nieces set off fireworks. "I like Louis," Williams wrote Pound a week later.

> He has distinction. He knows and is not puffed up, offensive, perverted by what he has absorbed. He puzzles me. His mind is really silky. God knows if he'll ever do anything with it. He has no job, doesn't seem to be able to get any. They live in a tenement—under trying if not distressing circumstances—yet he is fine. And strong too. I have rarely met a person who can see as clearly, hold as firmly to his point, enjoy excellence and for a clear reason, so gracefully and find fault so convincingly—curious.[58]

Zukofsky could not but have been encouraged by the praise this poet two decades his elder gave his work, as well as the trust Williams placed in his critical abilities. Within a few weeks of their first meeting, Williams was allowing Zukofsky to read and edit his unpublished manuscripts. Zukofsky, Williams told Pound, was reading through and arranging a "pile of stuff," "work[ing] at it with remarkably clean and steady fingers."[59] That manuscript was *The Descent of Winter*, which Pound published in the fourth number of the *Exile*.[60]

Thus began one of the most important relationships of Zukofsky's and Williams's writing lives, a relationship that involved, as Zukofsky later recalled, "an unremitting exchange of letters" and "blanket orders" on Williams's part "to shorten, emend, and correct anything in your manuscript that would clean them up and save pennies—a conceptive impatience on your part sometimes that allowed the editor the poor consolation of thinking." Zukofsky visited Williams's Rutherford home often, "taking the old bus in an alley behind the Hotel Astor, or the ferry to the Erie Railroad"[61]—a route that for him resonated with Charles Francis Adams's "An Erie Raid." Zukofsky was never uncritical in his reading—even when it came to the writings of his friends—but poems and books of Williams's would occupy a central position in his imagination of what American poetry could accomplish.

· · ·

"Poem beginning 'The,'" which appeared in *Exile* 3 in the spring of 1928, brought Zukofsky another friendship. George Oppen (born Oppenheimer) was the somewhat rebellious son of a San Francisco businessman.[62] In 1926, he was enrolled in Oregon State University in Corvallis, where he spent a night in his roommate's Model T with a young woman he had met in his English class. The college administration disapproved: They expelled Mary Ruth Colby and suspended Oppen, who dropped out soon after. The couple were married the next summer, to Oppen's family's consternation. In 1928 George and Mary Oppen were living in New York. Oppen was working as a switchboard operator in a brokerage house, awaiting his twenty-first birthday, when he would come into an annuity from his late mother's and maternal grandmother's estates. On their way to a party on the other side of Manhattan, the Oppens stopped at the Gotham Book Mart, where Oppen looked through recent periodicals, including *Exile* 3. At the party were Zukofsky's friend Russel Wright, a designer, and Wright's wife, Mary. When Mary Wright learned Oppen was a poet, she suggested that he ought to meet "our friend Zukofsky." "He wrote 'Poem beginning "The,"'" Oppen said, to which Mary Wright responded, "You are the only one in the world who knows it."[63] Oppen met Zukofsky soon after; Zukofsky introduced him first to the poetry of his older friend Charles Reznikoff and then to Reznikoff himself and his wife, Marie Syrkin. Zukofsky also introduced Oppen to other of his friends: the violist and composer Tibor Serly, his Columbia friend Ted Hecht and Hecht's wife, Kate, and Williams.

The Oppens, fresh from their wanderings across the Midwest, were dazzled by the circle of writers, artists, and musicians within which Zukofsky moved. George especially formed a close bond with Zukofsky. Four years older than Oppen, Zukofsky was the first real poet he had met. Zukofsky spent many evenings at the Oppens' Brooklyn Heights apartment, discussing poetry or (in Mary Oppen's words) "any of the topics which young people discuss," talking "far into the night, night after night after night."[64] For Oppen, Zukofsky's was the closest friendship he had formed in New York, and almost certainly the most crucial friendship to him at this point in his life. Oppen looked to Zukofsky not merely as a friend but as a teacher, a poet whose own rigorous verse served as a model for contemporary poetry.[65] Oppen's early work was deeply influenced by Zukofsky's laconic sensibility.

. . .

By 1928 Zukofsky had achieved a distinctively modern poetic voice marked by its lyricism, its angularity, and its own decisive take on the modernist practices of quotation, translation, and collage. He had made that voice public by publishing a major poem, and his work was well represented in the more interesting and adventurous periodicals of the day. He had made friends among the first rank of contemporary poets, and was attracting followers and admirers among the poets of his own generation. The question of what his ultimate career might be—how, in short, he would go about earning a living—remained unsettled. That poetry was his vocation, however, was clear, and by late 1928 Zukofsky had taken the next step towards making himself a major poet. He had begun the long poem upon which his reputation would ultimately rest—"*A*".

"A Thousand fiddles playing Bach" 1928–1930

THE POEM *"A"* would be a sprawling, eight-hundred-page menagerie of forms incorporating the traces of events from forty-six years of Zukofsky's life. It would include a double can-zone, various imitations of the musical fugue, a cycle of seven sonnets, large chunks of outright collage, an entire Plautus play (in idiosyncratic translation), and as its conclusion a 350-page musi-cal score counterpointing texts from all of Zukofsky's genres to the harpsichord music of George Frideric Handel. Needless to say, when Zukofsky began his "poem of a life," he had no idea of its eventual scope.

When Zukofsky first met William Carlos Williams in April 1928 at the Park Central Hotel, he invited the older poet to hear Bach's *Passion According to St. Matthew* with him at Carnegie Hall the follow-ing Friday. Zukofsky already had a taste for Bach: "If horses could but sing Bach, mother," he had written in "Poem beginning 'The,'" and in 1926 he wrote an impressionistic poem entitled "For a Thing by Bach."[1] Williams shared his enthusiasm—"I'd give my shirt to hear the Mattaus Passion this week," he wrote Zukofsky—but was unable to make it into the city for the concert.[2] This performance, which Zukofsky attended alone, was to be the starting point for his long poem.

> A
>
> Thousand fiddles playing Bach—
>> The clear music
>>> *"Come ye daughters, share my anguish—*

it began, though readers know it better in its revised form: "A / Round of fiddles playing Bach. / *Come, ye daughters, share my anguish—*." The title, about which Zukofsky was sure from the very beginning, was a quotation of the poem's first line: *"A"*.[3]

Zukofsky had finished the first two movements of *"A"* by October 1928, and he had completed two more by July 1929.[4] He sent copies of *"A"*-1 and -2 to Williams and Pound soon after he finished them, where they met with initial enthusiasm from Williams (followed by doubtful second thoughts) and a storm of blue-penciling from Pound.[5] He submitted those movements to the *Dial*, but Marianne Moore rejected them as "inappropriate" for the magazine.[6] Zukofsky was to labor long on the poem before seeing any part of it in print. The seventh movement would appear in 1931 in *Poetry: A Magazine of Verse*, in an issue Zukofsky himself edited; the first and second movements would not appear until 1932, four years after their composition.[7]

. . .

Zukofsky's job at the National Industrial Conference Board had ended early in 1928;[8] later that year, someone suggested to him that there might be a job at the Hartford Accident and Indemnity Company. On learning Zukofsky would be visiting Connecticut, Bill Williams urged him to look up Wallace Stevens, who headed the Hartford's fidelity and surety claims department. "He is a friend," Williams wrote. "Do not fail to go to him at the earliest possible moment as he may be of assistance as a reference. Tell him you are my friend."[9] In the last week of October Zukofsky took the train to Hartford, made his way to the company's palatial headquarters ("there was this vast foyer almost a feeling of the interior of the Duomo," he recalled years later), and had his interview. Zukofsky was to be disappointed—he asked after Stevens and was told "Mr. Stevens was away."[10] While he was able to draft three short poems on the train ride there and back, Zukofsky didn't get the job at the Hartford, nor would he ever meet the poet whose work he had read "constantly" back in 1923.

By late 1928 Pound had tired of editing the *Exile*: He would leave periodicals to the enthusiasm and energy of youth. For a while, he urged Zukofsky to try establishing a book series, "The Book of the Quarter," which might include Zukofsky's poems, Robert McAlmon's short stories, Marianne Moore's collected poetry, and "some bloody work of mine." In the service of his own ideas Pound's enthusiasm was boundless: "It is rather too good a scheme to waste," he told Zukofsky.[11] Williams was more realistic about how much work and money such a small press would involve. "Let [Ezra] come across and risk his hide," he wrote Zukofsky. "That alone can put such a scheme across."[12] Williams preferred to look to newly established little magazines for publishing possibilities. Charles Henri Ford, a young poet in Mississippi, had asked Williams to serve as contributing editor to a new magazine called *Blues*. "An outlet at last," Williams wrote Zukofsky enthusiastically. "I want your poem beginning 'A' for it if the Dial isn't large enough."[13] The following April, the young writer Richard Johns invited Williams to serve as associate editor of a new magazine whose title, *Pagany: A Native Quarterly*, alluded to Williams's novel *A Voyage to Pagany*.[14] *Blues* and *Pagany*—magazines "virtually twins" in their aesthetic programs[15]—would between 1929 and 1932 publish some twenty-four of Zukofsky's poems, including "A"-1, which appeared in *Pagany*'s last issue in 1932. The first issue of *Pagany* (January 1930) included Williams's essay "The Work of Gertrude Stein," which had benefited from Zukofsky's thorough blue-penciling and additions.[16]

Zukofsky's poem "Tibor Serly," which re-creates the listener's reaction to a performance of one of Serly's compositions, was published in *Blues* in fall 1930. Serly, born in Hungary a little more than two years before Zukofsky, grew up in New York City. His was a musical family—his father had studied with Liszt—and from 1922 to 1925 he attended the Budapest Royal Academy, where he studied composition with Zoltán Kodály and became fast friends with Béla Bartók. By the time he and Zukofsky became friends in the late 1920s, he was playing viola in the Philadelphia Orchestra under the baton of Leopold Stokowski.[17] Serly already had literary interests; in 1926 he wrote settings for four of James Joyce's poems. Written in beautifully modulated two-line stanzas of two-word lines, "Tibor Serly" is reminiscent of Williams's "jazz" poems; as in so many of Zukofsky's early works, the sea is a major presence, as the sound of the orchestra becomes synesthetically identified with waves breaking on a sunset shore:

Red varnish
Warm flitch

Of cello,
They play

Scroll before
Them—Sound

Breaks the
Sunset! . . .

      Bodies
Of waves
Whose crests

Spear air,
Here rolls

The sea—[18]

Zukofsky would later pair this poem (under the title "Two Dedications") with a poem in three-line stanzas and three-word lines, written about the same time, dedicated to "Comrade D.R.," the Communist Mexican muralist Diego Rivera: "Comrade D. R.— / His murals speak: / Executives of industry, / / Rich stone heads / Conferring at tables . . ."[19] The yoking together of these two poems—the one an almost symbolist exercise in aesthesis, the other verging upon socialist realism—was an emblem of Zukofsky's divided loyalties. Rivera's murals, with their easily comprehended political message, were a "correct" subject for the socially committed artist to address.

Serly's compositions, however, and the whole realm of classical music smacked of the disengaged ivory tower, so far as Zukofsky's Party associates might be concerned.

Zukofsky enjoyed a compact but diversely talented group of friends in New York. There was Serly, the designer Russel Wright and his wife, Mary. There were his college friends Ted Hecht and Irving Kaplan. There was the poet Jesse Loewenthal, who like Hecht and Zukofsky taught high school. There was Jerry Reisman, a precocious young man who had been Zukofsky's student at Stuyvesant High; Reisman showed aptitude for mathematics and engineering, but Zukofsky was trying to encourage his interest in poetry. Perhaps most importantly, there was the poet Charles Reznikoff, one of the very few contemporary writers, Zukofsky would recall many years later, who had taught him something about making poems.[20]

Reznikoff was ten years older than Zukofsky, though the two men shared a common background; he had been born in the Jewish "ghetto" of Brownsville in Brooklyn, both of his parents Russian immigrants. After a year studying journalism at the University of Missouri, Reznikoff attended New York University Law School and was called to the Bar in 1916 (he never practiced). He spent a brief period as a salesman for his father's hat-making concern, but by the end of the 1920s Reznikoff was in his midthirties, contemplating marriage with Marie Syrkin and living on an allowance from the family business.[21] Reznikoff had aspired to be a poet from an early age, but high ambition was alien to his sweet, singularly modest nature. He published poems in Harriet Monroe's *Poetry: A Magazine of Verse* in Chicago, but when he found it difficult to interest book publishers in his work, he went ahead and published himself, eventually purchasing a printing press and setting type on his own. He issued his first book, *Rhythms*, in 1918, followed by *Rhythms II* (1919), *Poems* (1920), *Uriel Accosta* (1921), and *Five Groups of Verse* (1927). It is unclear when Zukofsky first encountered Reznikoff's poetry or first met Reznikoff, but by 1929 he was vigorously promoting his friend's work to Pound and Williams.[22] Reznikoff's poetry was deeply influenced by the imagist poetics of Pound and H.D., the vignettes of Edgar Lee Masters's *Spoon River Anthology*, Pound's adaptations of Chinese poetry, and the rhythms of the King James Bible. He wrote a clean, flexible, precise free verse that could treat his contemporary urban surroundings as readily as it could address more classical subjects. Like Zukofsky, he was keenly aware of his own position as the child of immigrant Jewish parents attempting to scale the battlements of Gentile culture; he encapsulated the dilemma in the lovely, rhythmically subtle "Hellenist":

> As I, barbarian, at last, although slowly, could read Greek,
> at "blue-eyed Athena"
> I greeted her picture that had long been on the wall:
> the head bent slightly forward under the heavy helmet,
> as if to listen; the beautiful lips slightly scornful.[23]

.   .   .

Pound, from his vantage point on the Italian Riviera, kept sending people Zukofsky's way. In 1930 the French critic René Taupin arrived in New York to take a teaching position at Columbia. Taupin was twenty-five and held a doctorate from the University of Paris; in 1929, he had published *L'influence du symbolisme français sur la poésie américaine (1910–1920)*, a landmark study of contemporary American poetry that included intelligent readings of Pound, Eliot, and Williams.[24] Taupin had corresponded with Pound while writing his book, and Pound considered the volume something of an "insider's" history of the period. Zukofsky recognized the book's importance as soon as Pound drew his attention to it. Zukofsky's review of *L'influence du symbolisme français* was published in 1931, and as soon as he had read the book he began drafting a sequel that would extend Taupin's narrative up through the end of the 1920s.[25] By the summer of 1930 he and Taupin had become fast friends.

A brief note arrived in July 1930: "Dear Mr Zukofsky— Ezra Pound says I ought to look you up. May I? I like the 'Henry Adams.' Yrs Basil Bunting."[26] Bunting was newly arrived in America, and newly married to a young woman from Wisconsin whom he had met the year before in Venice. He had no job, though his wife was a schoolteacher, and his only prospects lay in a sheaf of letters of introduction Pound had given him to various New York writers and editors.[27] Bunting had been born in 1900 in coal-mining Northumberland, where his father was a colliery doctor. The combination of an excellent education in Quaker schools and a firsthand knowledge of the brutal working conditions in the mines confirmed the young Bunting in literary aspirations and radical politics. He spent the better part of a year imprisoned as a conscientious objector at the end of the First World War, then mingled in London with the Bloomsbury circle and the Fabian Society. He studied at the London School of Economics, wrote music reviews for London periodicals, and after four years left England for Paris, where by chance he met Pound in a boulevard café. As with so many young writers, Pound's spell proved irresistible, and after working for Ford Madox Ford's *Transatlantic Review* for some months (Ernest Hemingway was his replacement), Bunting moved to Rapallo and became a member of Pound's circle of younger poets, musicians, and general hangers-on. Meeting him there, W. B. Yeats described him to Pound's mother-in-law as "one of Ezra's more savage disciples."[28]

Bunting would prove one of Zukofsky's most long-standing and valuable friends. He had a fine musical ear and a well-trained knowledge of classical forms; he was a talented linguist, fluent in French, Italian, and German, and, at Pound's suggestion, teaching himself classical Persian; and he was a gifted poet and practical critic, well aware of the most exciting directions of contemporary writing and able to follow and comment upon every turn of Zukofsky's imagination. Over the next four decades, Zukofsky and Bunting would carry on a constant, detailed correspondence, and would show themselves continually aware of their position as—in the words of Pound's *Guide to Kulchur* (1938), dedicated to the two men—"strugglers in the desert."[29]

In addition to living contacts, Pound was eager to supply Zukofsky more concrete emoluments, in the form of either paying publication or actual work. Through Pound's good offices, Zukofsky was able to publish a revised version of his Columbia thesis in the journal *Hound & Horn*, edited by Lincoln Kirstein, Allen Tate, and Yvor Winters.[30] In 1929, Zukofsky wrote a full-length essay on Pound's *Cantos*—almost certainly the first such study to be written—an essay that Pound received quite favorably. "As far as I know," he wrote

Zukofsky, "no one else has writ. a crit of me AFTER reading the work. This method has advantages. Also so far as I know you are the first writer to credit me with an occasional gleam of intelligence or to postulate the bounds or possibility of an underlying coherence."[31] T. S. Eliot would publish a chunk of this study in the *Criterion* in 1931; in the meantime, Pound secured the publication of the entire essay in the French journal *Échanges* (in René Taupin's translation), and prompted his protégé Emanuel Carnevali to translate it into Italian for the Genoan periodical *L'Indice*.[32]

Zukofsky himself, Pound thought, ought to be able to earn some money translating. When Zukofsky told him that in addition to Yiddish he knew French and German, Pound fired off a letter to Horace Liveright of the publishing house Boni & Liveright, recommending Zukofsky as a German translator.[33] In early 1930 Pound suggested to Zukofsky that he ought to translate one of Pound's own current obsessions, the German anthropologist and archaeologist Leo Frobenius's *Paideuma*.[34] Zukofsky looked over the 450-page book and concluded that "$500 would not be too much for the job—and I've a notion that one would need to spend more time on the job than the 500 bucks indicate."[35] Zukofsky did not translate Frobenius, but he found *Paideuma* interesting enough to be reading away at the book late that same year;[36] Frobenius's notion of *Kulturmorphologie* must have appealed to him, with its clear parallels to the historical theories of Henry and Brooks Adams.

In late 1929 and the first part of 1930 Zukofsky was at work translating a life of Albert Einstein for Albert and Charles Boni. *Albert Einstein: A Biographical Portrait*, by "Anton Reiser" (actually Rudolf Kayser, the husband of Einstein's stepdaughter), was less a serious biography of the scientist than a celebrity profile, and Zukofsky found the work of translating it far from congenial. He was frustrated with Reiser's rambling, directionless prose, and with his own obligation as translator to render *all* of that prose.[37] The only bit of the "job" that gave Zukofsky satisfaction was the half-page preface by Einstein himself, which reads in part:

What has been overlooked [in this biography] is the irrational, the inconsistent, the droll, even the insane, which nature, inexhaustible operative, implants in an individual, seemingly for her own amusement. But these things are singled out only in the crucible of one's own mind.

This is as it should be. For, otherwise, how could the isolation of distance be approximated?[38]

Zukofsky quoted the last two sentences to Pound: "*Maybe*," he said, "I'm learning something about language."[39] In the event, however, Zukofsky requested that his name as translator be omitted from the book.[40] Translation—or at least the drudgery of the piecework translator—was not to be his métier.

By summer 1930 Zukofsky was hurrying to finish the Einstein book, anxious to get away from New York. He had a bit of money—he felt almost a "dirty plutocrat" after receiving *Hound & Horn*'s check for the Henry Adams essay[41]—and was looking forward to spending the summer in Berkeley with his friend Kaplan, who had taken a job with Pacific Gas and Electric. "Will spend my summer in Kaigh's attic," he wrote Pound in mid-June, "and try to do my own work for a change—."[42] His "own work"—what he had found no time to pursue between teaching school and translating—was the big poem "*A*". He had managed to squeeze out two more movements of the poem, "*A*"-3 and -4, over the summer of 1929, and had finished "*A*"-5 in September, but he hoped that his vacation in the Bay Area would give him time to bring "*A*" a few stages further.

· · ·

Zukofsky marked his first cross-country trip with postcards: cornfields and babies to Williams, a portrait of Brigham Young ("An old friend?") to Pound.[43] This was the first time this New Yorker had seen the vast expanses of the American West and Midwest, and Zukofsky observed closely, judging by the cross-continental snapshots that he incorporated into "*A*"-6. Everywhere he saw the evidences of the Great Depression: closed businesses, workers idled, foreclosed farms.

Kaplan, his friend in Berkeley, may have been an economist and tax advisor, but his home proved a congenial place to try to encompass all this in poetry. Back at Columbia Kaplan had written "Paper," a literary-philosophical essay that Zukofsky admired to the point of sending copies, signed with the pseudonym "Roger Kaigh," to both Bunting and Pound. "Paper" expounded a nominalistic theory of language, and attacked the abstractions of contemporary philosophy and literary criticism as symptoms of a "paper age," ideas that must have been congenial to Zukofsky insofar as they dovetailed with Henry Adams's notion of the modern age as an era that thought in terms of "ether."[44] In Berkeley, Kaplan sought to mend Zukofsky's economic education by urging him to read Thorstein Veblen.[45] (The author of *The Theory of the Leisure Class* would turn up early the next year in Zukofsky's poetry, the source of an epigraph to "Immature Pebbles."[46])

Zukofsky's time in "Kaigh's attic" proved profitable. Over the course of four days (August 4 to August 7), he wrote the devilishly complex, virtuosic climax of the first block of movements, the sonnet sequence "A"-7. And in five more days (August 12 to August 16), he drafted the poem's longest movement to date—as long as the rest of the movements combined—"A"-6.[47] Towards the end of August, Zukofsky sent his friend Taupin a huge sheaf of poems—161 in all—and asked him to choose the best fifty and put them in some sort of order.[48] Zukofsky wanted a book manuscript. He felt "Poem beginning 'The,'" the first seven movements of "A", and his fifty best short lyrics would make a collection that could bear comparison with any poet publishing. "A good title," he thought, "would be

Poem Beginning 'The'
<hr>
'A'

In the event, Taupin proved interminably slow at winnowing the manuscripts, and Zukofsky found himself distracted by other tasks.

The year before Zukofsky had unsuccessfully applied for a Guggenheim fellowship to finance work on the poem, and was planning to apply once again.[49] In the meantime, however, rather than returning to New York, Zukofsky was off to Madison, where he had been offered a two-thirds assistantship in the Department of English at the University of Wisconsin.[50] Both Pound and Williams had written to Wisconsin on his behalf.[51] University teaching was the career for which Zukofsky had prepared in his graduate work at Columbia, and he had by now accumulated some sixteen months' experience teaching, if only at the high school level. At least, he hoped, "6 hrs or even 10 hrs a week of teaching shd. leave plenty of time" for his next project, the one he had proposed for this year's Guggenheim, a study of "How Jefferson Used Words."[52]

It was to be a characteristically idiosyncratic study—Zukofsky was less interested in the genealogies of Jefferson's political ideas (Rousseau, Blackstone, Locke) than in "how J uses the names of flowers in his garden book."[53] He would pursue the Jefferson project at Wisconsin, though it proved difficult to find a faculty member there familiar enough with Jefferson's work to advise a graduate-level project on it. In the next few months, however, "How Jefferson Used Words" would be entirely set aside, displaced by a wholly unexpected opportunity to win fame at the head of a bright, new avant-garde.

"A"-1 through "A"-7

W HY, IN 1928, did Zukofsky turn to the long poem? Aside from "'The,'" his poetry thus far had taken the form of short lyrics, sometimes strung together into thematically organized sequences.[1] Many of the major poets of Zukofsky's generation and the generation immediately before him, however, would eventually turn to the long poem. Perhaps it was implicit in the models of poetic excellence the Western tradition offered: Milton's *Paradise Lost*, Spenser's *Faerie Queene*, Dante's *Divine Comedy*, Virgil's *Aeneid*, Ovid's *Metamorphoses*. The very font of Western tradition, Homer, was remembered for his twin epics. More proximately for American poets (and more ambiguously) there was Walt Whitman's sprawling, shapeless, but undeniably energetic *Song of Myself*. When one embarked on a long poem, one had attained artistic maturity, one had declared oneself a contender for the upper ranks of a Parnassus whose highest slopes were inhabited by the great epic writers of the past. The epic-length poem, simply put, was a mark of a poet's ambition.

An epic, as the genre was defined by Homer and Virgil and extended

79

by such later writers as Tasso and Milton, was also a *public* poem. Pound liked to quote Kipling: The epic was "the tale of the tribe."[2] The long poem offered the poet a larger canvas than the lyric, a space where he could address the largest of issues. The classical epic was a "schoolbook for princes," and the Victorians had shown in poems like Tennyson's *In Memoriam* and Arnold's *Empedocles on Etna* that the long poem could speak to the most pressing intellectual issues of its society. As Pound became increasingly obsessed with the failings of the West, his *Cantos* more and more became a writing stage upon which he could analyze how Europe had declined from the cultural peaks of antiquity and the Renaissance.

Pound recognized how paradoxical his embarking upon a long poem might seem in the wake of the ultramodern imagist movement, whose poems rarely ran beyond a half page. As he wrote an old teacher in 1922, "Having the crust to attempt a poem in 100 or 120 cantos long after all mankind has been commanded never again to attempt a poem of any length, I have to stagger as I can."[3] That commandment had been handed down by Edgar Allan Poe in his essay "The Poetic Principle"—"I hold that a long poem does not exist. I maintain that the phrase, 'a long poem,' is simply a flat contradiction in terms"[4]—and passed on through Baudelaire and Mallarmé. Poe and his followers believed that poetry ought to stimulate an "elevating excitement," an excitement that was perforce transitory; a long poem, then, could be only "a series of minor poems," held together by passages of less-than-poetic intensity. That certainly seemed a fair description of such monuments of otiose storytelling as Tennyson's *Idylls of the King* or Swinburne's *Atalanta in Calydon*.

Of course, the modernist long poem could not be like the Victorian long poem; it would be neither narrative nor discursive, neither a story told nor a philosophical disquisition. Pound's foremost model for his own long poem was Dante's *Divine Comedy*—hence Pound's calling his sections "cantos," which at some point (perhaps by default) became their actual title. By the time Pound had really hit his compositional stride with the "Malatesta Cantos" (published in July 1923), the work had assumed a distinctively modernist form. The ongoing composition of the *Cantos* appears to have been greatly affected by the two landmark works of 1922, Joyce's *Ulysses* and Eliot's *The Waste*

Land.[5] *Ulysses* showed the mileage that the modern writer could get from viewing contemporary events under the aspect of timeless mythical forms. By paralleling Leopold Bloom's peripatetic day to the wanderings of Odysseus, Joyce lent resonance and significance to Bloom's mundane doings; as Eliot put it, Joyce, by "manipulating a continuous parallel between contemporaneity and antiquity," had shown modern writers a "way of controlling, of ordering, of giving a shape and significance to the immense panorama of futility and anarchy which is contemporary history."[6] *The Waste Land* had been practically a collaboration between Eliot and Pound, Pound ruthlessly editing the shapeless manuscript into something very close to its final published form. In that process, it had become clear to Pound that a long poem need not sacrifice intensity in achieving size—the poet could simply eliminate the passages of lesser intensity, cut out the connective material, and let the remaining passages generate new significance through their juxtaposition. Pound's method in *The Cantos* would be the placing side by side of disparate materials, allowing higher meanings and implications to arise from such placement, and underpinning it all with a network of references to the *Odyssey*, *The Divine Comedy*, and *The Metamorphoses*.

Zukofsky would be at some pains to emphasize that he was not familiar with *The Cantos* when he began "*A*". When he started "*A*", he told Pound in 1930, Zukofsky had only read Cantos 4, 5, and 6, and "had no inkling of the main intention of the long poem": "I had started <without knowing it,> something in 1928 which you had started in 1908 (?)—the dangers of being young and too poor to get hold of the books that matter." Zukofsky clearly recognized that his poem might be received as a mere knockoff of *The Cantos*; Lincoln Kirstein had told him, after reading a typescript of "*A*"-1 through "*A*"-5, that he saw "the same personal obscurities, but never Mr. Pound's brilliant diction."[7] But Zukofsky was resigned to such occasional misinterpretation. He tended himself to consider "influence" a matter of period styles "in the air" at a given moment; as he put it much later, speculating on possible lines of influence between his own work and that of Wallace Stevens, "with respect to vapors I prefer to settle for *this most excellent canopy, the air, look you.*"[8]

· · ·

Zukofsky wrote the first four movements of "*A*" in a sustained burst in the last months of 1928 and the first half of 1929, the fifth later that year, and the sixth and seventh in the late summer of 1930. In their earliest forms, the first six movements were published in pairs, with only nominal breaks indicated between the first and second movements of a pair. "A"-1 and -2 were subtitled "Come, ye Daughters"; "A"-3 and -4, "Out of the voices"; "A"-5 and -6, "And I:"; and "A"-7 was "There are different techniques."[9]

"A"-1 presents the dilemma of the poet's task in an unsettled time—how to navigate between the demands of an unjust, capitalistic society and the otherworldly perfection offered by art, represented here by Bach's *St. Matthew Passion*.[10] The poem begins in Carnegie Hall on April 5, 1928, where the *Passion* is being performed under the baton of Ossip Gabrilowitsch, a noted interpreter of Bach (and Mark Twain's son-in-law). Gabrilowitsch, according to the *New York Times* review of the concert the next day, had requested "plain black dress and a silent reception of the masterpiece" (in an "edited and abbreviated" score).[11] Zukofsky, in the audience, notes the "Bare arms, black dresses" of the women around him, how their ostentatious jewelry serves to "Bediamond the passion of our Lord." He cannot help contrasting this display to the "motley / Country people in Leipzig" who attended the work's premiere in 1729, when Bach was not "the Master" but merely "Johann Sebastian," "der Kappellmeister."[12]

The music is transcendent, filling Zukofsky with a vision of "perfection" through the purity of the voices of its boys' choir, but that transcendence is immediately shattered by a serpent-like usher—"No suh! / Not past that exit, Zukofsky!"—who engages Zukofsky in a dreamlike debate, invoking a picture of those boys at the seaside, their bodies defaced with sunburns. Then, as the poet steps out of Carnegie Hall, he confronts a series of contrasting New York street scenes. A tramp, "lips looking out of a beard / Hips looking out of ripped trousers"; the inane chatter of the concertgoers of the sidewalks—"Poor Thomas Hardy he had to go so soon" (Hardy had indeed died earlier that year, but at the age of eighty-seven); and "on one side street near an elevated," a group of leftist agitators urging one "Carat" to write an editorial on behalf of a group of locked-out Pennsylvania miners.[13]

These voices, competing for Zukofsky's attention, almost drown out the music he has heard, "The blood's tide as the music's, / A thousand fiddles as beyond effort / Playing." Back in his room, he sits down to write, "Not boiling to put pen to paper. / Perhaps a few things to remember . . ." Characteristically, these "few things" are *quotations*. From Pound's *Antheil and the Treatise on Harmony*: "There are different techniques, / Men write to be read, or spoken, / Or declaimed, or rhapsodized, / *And quite differently to be sung*"; from Williams's novel *A Voyage to Pagany*, spoken by a character who has himself just heard a performance of the *Passion*: "I heard him agonizing, / I saw him *inside*"; and from E. E. Cummings's play *Him*, which Zukofsky had recently admiringly reviewed: "Everything which / We really are and never quite live."[14] He falls asleep to the words of the *Passion*'s libretto: "*He came and found them— / Sleeping, indeed their eyes were full of sleep.*"[15]

The next day brings "the reverses, / As if the music were only a taunt"—like a slap in the face, the cold reality of contemporary hardship. The unemployed, "idle, shiftless, disguised on streets"; industry economists and Wobblies shouting each other down; the grotesque vision of some captain of industry, "The great Magnus," holding a sandwich, pointing at a chart, and boasting of his managerial technique: "'We ran 'em in chain gangs, down in the Argentine, / *Executive*'s not the word, use engineer, / Single-handed, ran 'em like soldiers . . .'" The only comment on this is another snatch of the *Passion*: "Open, O fierce flaming pit!"[16]

In "A"-1, then, the poet finds himself torn between his longing for imperishable art and the demands of the immediate political world around him. "A"-2 transposes this dilemma to the realm of poetics. What *ought* the poet write, and where ought he find his materials? The section begins with a grouse from "Kay" (probably Irving Kaplan), who takes the Keatsian line: "Poetry is not made of such things, / Old music . . . Society, traduction twice over." Zukofsky at first responds angrily—"What do you, Kay, know about it!"—but then begins a serious meditation on the sources of his own poetry. "The sea" is his emblem for the world of events, "nations— / Navies and armaments drilling— / Churning of old religions, epos . . . ," and as well for the cultural heritage upon which the poet draws: Agamemnon, the warrior of the *Iliad*, the music of Bach, the never-ceasing noise of industry, imperialism, and popular culture. All these things, this "sea," crowds in upon us "Wherever always we are."[17]

Despite all of this impinging upon him, and despite the noise of a very real dockside scene where sailors laugh and horse around, the poet is still able "of an afternoon" to have a vision that transcends his immediate circumstances. The moon, rising above the water, becomes an organic thing, "green, flowering, opening leaf within leaf." It has become the flower "liveforever." In "A"-2 Zukofsky steps into this flower, enters this vision, in the guise of a horse. "I have stepped with haired ankle, / As with fetlock, to the center leaf . . . Hair falling over ankle, hair falling over forehead . . ." The movement ends with the poet back in the real world, riding a train. He sees a billboard advertising Wrigley's chewing gum, its letters "blood red as intertwined Rose of the Passion," and sees (or imagines) a boy and girl lying together in a field. At the sight he is once again in the realm of the "flower," the realm of pure artistry, of music—here, as before, the music of Bach's *St. Matthew Passion*; "'*O Saviour blest*' // And the double chorus singing, / The song out of the voices."[18]

. . .

Zukofsky sent "A"-1 and -2 to Pound on December 12, 1928. Already he was planning his poem on a large scale. "So far," he told Pound, "I've planned 24 movements. I hope that will be all."[19] Pound laid into Zukofsky's script with a far from tender hand, covering the first page with circled passages and marginal comments. Of the two lines, "White matronly flounces, cloth / Over two breasts—starched, heaving," Pound circled "White," "cloth," and "Over two." Circled passages were, he noted, "unnecessary": "flounce usually is cloth." He was even more peremptory with Zukofsky's three opening lines: "A / Thousand fiddles playing Bach—/ The clear music." "[R]ubbish," Pound wrote in a large hand in the margin, connecting his comment by a line to a heavy circle around "Thousand": "probably about 30. possibly 16." As for "The clear music," that was a "Tautology—obviously if fiddles play Bach they play mus[ic]."[20]

Zukofsky took most of Pound's editorial suggestions into account when reworking the poem. The two overstuffed lines about the flounces became the more compact "Matronly flounces, /—starched, heaving."[21] Most importantly, Pound's strictures on the poem's first lines steered Zukofsky to a far stronger opening: "A / Round of fiddles playing Bach." Where the earlier opening had tried to convey the impression of vast orchestral forces—a "thousand" fiddles—the revision pivoted on a pun ("A Round" / around) that underlines the historical "repeat" that is the subject of the movement: the *St. Matthew Passion* has indeed "come around" again, almost two hundred years after its premiere. In its first lines, *"A"* evokes the circularity of history, even as it evokes the feeling of a musical "round" that has often impressed listeners of the opening chorus of the *Passion*.

"Thurr are sevrul techniques:" Pound wrote Zukofsky, "one is getting OFF the mark at the start. IF you want the pome 'A' to be read, you'll have to owront like hell on the first three pages. After that I reckon she'll go."[22] Zukofsky knew well enough that the opening passages of a poem were crucial in setting the tone and capturing the audience; and he must have been reassured by the fact that Pound agreed that this new project eclipsed all of Zukofsky's earlier writings with the exception of "Poem beginning 'The,'" still his strongest achievement. "Omitting all problems of detail," Pound wrote in response to a collection of his poems Zukofsky sent late in 1928, "'A' has more pep than the selection of short poems in yr. mss."[23]

.   .   .

"A"-3 and -4 are subtitled "Out of the voices," picking up the last line of "A"-2, but what emerges from this double chorus is far less harmonious than Bach's careful measures. The third movement begins with words from the final bass recitative of the *Passion*, sung over the dead Christ and addressed to Joseph of Arimathaea, and modulates into a lament for the suicide Richard Chambers: *"At eventide, cool hour of rest / It is your dead mouth singing, // Ricky . . . Sleep // With an open gas range / Beneath for a pillow."*[24] After a few lines of quiet grief, however, the poem breaks into a cacophony of voices from "Ricky's" past. "'Where is the Scotch?' 'Would I lie!'"; "No crossin' bridges, Rick, / No, no bridges, not after midnight!" There are almost twenty lines of bawdy double entendre about Ricky's virility ("God's-gift-to-'oman!"), and a poignant memory of childhood: "a little boy—Rain alights: / It's rai-ai-nin' . . ."[25] And then Ricky becomes (as he was in "Poem beginning 'The'") Richard Cœur-de-lyon: "'Lion-heart', a horse bridled, // Trappings rise and surround / Princelet out of history . . ." Bach's *Passion* still permeates the poet's imagination, and the poet himself takes on the role of Joseph of Arimathaea, the wealthy follower who donated his own grave so that Christ could be laid therein. "'*Go, my soul / Beg you His corpse!*' // I, Arimathaea / His mirror!"[26]

The poem's fourth movement begins with a nocturnal riverside scene: "Carousel, / Giant sparkler, boats, // (Carousel) lights of the river, / (Horses turning), // Tide turning . . ." Closely following this, however, come the voices of Zukofsky's elders, the Orthodox Jewish community. They have long since settled into their condition of exile; paradoxically, their devotion to God and the Law has left them spiritually and intellectually empty: "Wherever we put our hats is our home, / Our aged heads are our homes . . . Even the death has gone out of us—we are void."[27] Worst of all for the elders, the younger generation—"our children"—"have passed over to the ostracized." They have abandoned the study of Hebrew texts, have evolved a "jargon," a literature in the debased vernacular of Yiddish. As example of the "music" to which the elders pray God to deafen them, Zukofsky sprinkles "A"-4 with his own translations of the poetry of Yehoash, lines that evoke Pound's 1915 *Cathay* translations from the Chinese:

> Rain blows upon quiet water,
> I watch the rings spread and travel,
> Shimaunu-Sān, Samurai,
> When will you come home?—
> Shimaunu-Sān, my clear star.[28]

The elders of his community would reject this poetry as mere "jargon," but Zukofsky recognizes in Yehoash's work a specifically Jewish poetry, international in content, that bears comparison with Pound's modernist innovations.

In "A"-4, Zukofsky looks to the past, to "The courses we tide from." Most immediately, those "courses" are his heritage, the Jewish tradition and community from which he springs. However much his vocation in poetry may be rejected by the Orthodox, the Gentile world will not let him forget that he is a Jew. Zukofsky quotes, with evident irritation, Mark Van Doren's description of him in "Jewish Students I Have Known." Van Doren's condescending article had appeared in the *Menorah Journal*, among whose editors were several of Zukofsky's Columbia classmates; as Zukofsky comments, "we had a menorah, and / It is, indeed, an honor to be circumcised . . ." Even as he rejects the parochialism of the elders, Zukofsky proudly affirms his own Jewishness. His forebears may have been humble—"My father's precursors / Set masts in dingheys, chanted the Speech"—but they were no more humble than those of Johann Sebastian Bach. The first musical Bach, "A" 4 notes, was a miller who played the lute to the accompaniment of his grinding millstones: "A pretty noise the pair must have made . . . But, apparently, this is how / Music first came into our family!"[29]

. . .

The first four movements of "A" show a young poet who is sure of his material but unclear how best to deploy it. There is some delicate lyricism here, some striking juxtapositions, but much that is discursive, even clumsy. There were no models at hand for what Zukofsky wanted to do—to write a long poem that would embody the concrete particulars of his own experience and heritage, the political and social tensions of his country, and the utopian political ideals in which he believed. Eliot's *Waste Land* was too circumscribed and confined a performance. While it provided a vivid picture of the postwar West and the author's state of mind, in the end it left the poet and the reader pretty much where they had started. *The Cantos* might have offered Zukofsky an all too compelling model for the long poem, had he known them when beginning "A". Perhaps it was best that he first seriously engaged Pound's magnum opus after his own work was well under way.

Sometime in 1927 or 1928 Zukofsky drafted an outline of his twenty-four-section poem on a tiny scrap of paper, a scrap so worn he must have carried it around in his wallet for several years.[30] Beside each of twenty-four Roman numerals, Zukofsky jotted a section heading. Many of these headings have a clear relation to the themes and materials of the early movements of "A" as he would actually write them: VII is "Kay (Love-Pirate)" (see "A"-2 and -5); XVI is "Yehoash"

("A"-4); XVIII is "Coeur-de-leon" ("A"-3); and XXI is "Johann Sebastian." Other headings remain mysterious, like VI, "Helena Or among the girls" (though a "Helen Gentile" appears in "Poem beginning 'The'"), VII—"Mary-au-pres-de-ma-blonde"—or XV, "Spinet." As Barry Ahearn has noted, this would seem to be an outline, not for a sprawling life's work of a poem, but for an expanded version of "Poem beginning 'The.'"

While the details of these plans would fall by the wayside and the scope of the poem would be radically expanded, "A" remained a poem of twenty-four sections. A talismanic number: the twenty-four hours of the day; the twenty-four letters of the Greek alphabet (or the Renaissance English alphabet, in which i/j and u/v were interchangeable); the twenty-four books of Homer's epics. In his first four movements, however, Zukofsky demonstrated his aspiration to a specifically modernist poetic mode. It is a mode of parataxis, of placing widely diverse materials side by side; a collage poetics, like the cubist paintings of Picasso or the *Merzbilder* of Kurt Schwitters, where the mundane, the traditionally lyrical, the commercial, the vernacular, and even the obscene are laid one beside and upon another; a poetics of quotation, in which the words of other writers and speakers become fair game for the poet's constructivist imagination.

. . .

The various themes of the first block of "A" had been laid out in the poem's first four movements. Now, in the fifth and sixth, Zukofsky juxtaposed them in swift, piecemeal fashion. "A"-5 opens with the poet holding a brown leaf in one hand and a burning cigarette in the other, looking over the buildings of a university to where trees frame a billboard: "DUNHILL / Comfort."[31] He is once again in conversation with his friend Kay, who questions whether one can arrive at "Liveforever," the aesthetic wholeness signified by the flower, through a poetics that involves the collaging of tiny bits of memory, fragments of "origins."

Despite his friend's doubts, Zukofsky will "continue one song / Tho' its sound go two ways, / My two voices . . ." One of those two voices is the elevated diction he borrows from the libretto of the *Passion*, by which he elegizes his mother and all of Orthodox Judaism:

Purple clover,
She wore her shoes three years—
    (The soles new as the sunned black
        of her grave-turf);
Speech bewailing a Wall . . .

The other voice is slangy, humorous, as in his parody of the national anthem— "Or say, words have knees"—or his observation of an overweight Catholic woman hanging laundry, where her "laundered conception / of the B.V.D." is conflated with Pope Pius IX's dogma of "Immaculata concepcione B.V.M."—the Virgin Mary's Immaculate Conception.[32]

Zukofsky drafted "A"-6 over five days in a feverish burst of invention: he wrote René Taupin that he'd written "30 pp. of 'A' last week—I myself don't see how."[33] As long as the first five movements combined, it is a vast, vivid portrait of the United States in the Depression, a panorama in which the poet struggles to find the individual's voice within the exhausting, leveling uniformity of communal life, "Everything lowered to a mutual, common level, // Everyone the same, / Each at his best obligato of the other; / Tiredness of trying to see differences . . ." The great Romantics offer no usable model for the contemporary poet. Beethoven and Goethe offer "Words rangeless, forms only in snatches, / Melody stopped by dramatic writing . . ." Instead, Zukofsky turns to his beloved Spinoza, whose *Ethics* suggests a model of creativity as a function within an integrated system of nature, rather than the inspired afflatus of an extraordinary genius:

Natura Naturans—
Nature as creator,
Natura Naturata—
Nature as created

    He who creates
    Is a mode of these inertial systems—
    The flower—leaf around leaf wrapped around
        the center leaf[34]

Zukofsky takes Spinoza's distinction between the eternal, creative aspects of Nature—*Natura Naturans*, "nature naturing," "nature active"—and the created aspects—"*Natura Naturata*, "nature natured," "nature passive"—and applies it to the poet, who then becomes not an inspired seer or otherworldly visionary, but "a mode of these inertial systems"—a force of nature in his own right.

After advancing this figure of the poet and his task, Zukofsky sums up his poem thus far, recapping each of the previous five movements in joky, telescoped lines: "The song out of the voices, / Together! *Come ye daughters,* / Bring the music!," for instance, is half of a six-line summary of "A"-1.[35] There follows another important statement of poetics: the poem is "An objective—rays of the object brought to a focus, / An objective—naturans—desire for what is objectively perfect, / Inextricably the direction of historic and contemporary particulars." The poet's voice will, in a metaphor taken from optics, bring the "rays of the object . . . to a focus," it will make the transcendent, "objectively perfect," objectlike poem out of an array of "historic and contemporary particulars." These "particulars" include the material that has already fed the poem, Bach's *Passion* and life, Kay's cavils, Beethoven, and Goethe: "J.S.B.: his life, a particular, / His Matthew Passion, a particular, / Kay, a particular, / Ludwig Van and Go-ethe . . ."[36]

"A"-6 as a whole is a collage of such particulars. There are glimpses of Zukofsky's own life: Kay, laughing, says, "Zoo-kaw-kaw-someone opens his mouth and you copy, / When you're phosphates, they'll look you up and discover / For six years you was out of a job"; Zukofsky recalls his short stint at the "P.O." and his friend "Van"—"Dutch, flaxen, and inherited New England, / slight, / seafaring suavity . . ."[37] There are a great number of "contemporary" particulars, snapshots of the United States in the depths of Depression. They include the pugnacious political comments and inane cultural asides of Henry Ford (with sotto voce commentary by Zukofsky): "'Many people are too busy to be unemployed.' / (Especially those who have their own factories to take care of.) / 'If communism ever gets into a country and raises Ned with it, / It's because that country needs it,'" and "'I read poetry, and I enjoy it / If it says anything, / But so often it doesn't say anything,' / says Henry." "Magnus," the captain of industry from "A"-1, makes several appearances (at one point we learn that he has an entire closet devoted to his suspenders), and the degeneracy of

American capitalism is figured in "the very old stutterers, [playing] mumbltypeg in duplex Park Av. apartments, / Mumbling imperceptibly when the jack-knife stuck $25 shoe leather."[38] (One must read carefully indeed to pick up Zukofsky's patterns of recurrence—this shoe leather evokes the three-year-old shoes of Zukofsky's mother from "A"-5, and points up the distinction between the casual profligacy of the rich and the close economy of the recent immigrant.)

In contrast to these thumbnail portraits of decadent money are the pithy epigrams of Lenin ("'It is more pleasant and more useful,' / Said Vladimir Ilytch, / 'To live thru the experience / Of a revolution / Than to write about it'"), and the ongoing collectivization of the Soviet Union serves as a counterpoint to the United States as Zukofsky sees it in 1930. He sees it, for much of "A"-6, as a cross-country tourist:

> The time for hitch-hikers across country (Summertime).
> N.Y., and then desolation.
> The steel works of Gary.
> Stopped by Lake Michigan, Chicago,
> And left note he was going to Berkeley.

Towards the end of the movement he is at last in California, among "San Francisco's hills and fogs," where he can visit one of Van Doren's favorite poets, Robinson Jeffers, who lives in Carmel in "A tower, of course, theatrical stones and a tower— / In the best imitation of Sophocles—"[39]

The last pages of "A"-6 imagine a return to New York, "Three thousand miles over rails, / And adequate distribution of 'Camels' / N.Y.—Staten Island—," and once again the "DUNHILL / comfort" billboard of "A"-5.[40] The idea of "cut[ting] short the night's work" and taking his date to see "Connie's Hot Chocolates," the Fats Waller revue, reminds him that Bach as well wrote a "Kaffee Cantata," "A kind of 'Hot Chocolates' after the Passion . . ." Bach brings the poet back to the *St. Matthew Passion*, and (in a structure that will be echoed in "A"-8 and "A"-12) brings the movement, which up until this point has threatened to proliferate more or less endlessly, to a formal conclusion:

I forget—

Said:

> Can
> The design
> Of the fugue
> Be transferred
> To poetry?

At eventide, cool hour of rest [41]

. . .

The question Zukofsky asks here—"Can / The design / Of the fugue / Be transferred / To poetry?"—reveals that the formal principle undergirding "*A*" goes well beyond a haphazard collaging of various materials, but is analogous to the baroque fugue as practiced by Bach. (He says as much in a contributor's note accompanying the first publication of "A"-7, which speaks of the poem "desiring" the "potentially perfect," and "approximate[ly] attain[ing] . . . this perfection in the feeling of the contrapuntal design of the [fugue] transferred to poetry . . ."[42])

In a musical fugue, a short melody, the *subject* or *theme*, is stated in a single instrumental voice, then taken up or *imitated* by other voices. New motifs—*countersubjects*—may be introduced in counterpoint to the subject and reappear throughout the fugue much like the subject.[43] Strictly speaking, the fugue is not a *form* but a *formal principle*, a method for generating music through the contrapuntal juxtaposition of melodic motifs. Instead of melodic motifs, Zukofsky counterpoints poetic "themes" or ideas. In "A"-1 the 1928 performance of Bach's *Passion* is the subject, its 1729 premiere a restatement of that subject in another "key"; Zukofsky's quest for aesthetic perfection, and the economic hardships surrounding him, are countersubjects, motifs different from but contrapuntally related to the first theme.

How seriously ought one to take this "fugal" analogy? When Zukofsky sent "A"-1 through -7 to Pound in November, Pound recognized his fugal intentions—"recd. one development or fugue or fuagal etc. produced by Ludwig von Zuk und Sohn, on not always digested meat of his forebears."[44] But the fugue was on Pound's mind already—he had himself described the *Cantos'* structure as fugal to W. B. Yeats two years earlier.[45] Zukofsky's knowledge of music was that of an interested listener rather than an expert of any sort. He could not read music: "as far as notes are concerned," he wrote, "I can see or hear when they go up or down, & linger or proceed."[46] And while he could write beautifully *about* music, in practice he showed little ability to tell one composer or composition from another. To avoid making too much of the musical connotations of Zukofsky's "fugal" form, one should view it as a conceptual analogy—an analogy that in the first half of *"A"* gave rise to hundreds of pages of beautiful and complexly structured verse.

. . .

Zukofsky finished "A"-7 a few days before the burst of activity that produced "A"-6. The sprawling "A"-6, which had announced at the last moment that the seemingly associative progress of its collaged fragments had been governed by the principles of the fugue, provides in its last lines a bridge to "A"-7, a far more obviously structured poem: "Her soles new as the sunned black of her grave turf, / With all this material? / To what distinction, / Horses, she saw? / My—"[47] "A"-7, which indeed begins with the word "Horses," is a series of seven rhymed sonnets. The first sets the scene. The poet, sitting on a stoop, watches a street excavation which is guarded by seven wooden sawhorses:

> Horses: who will do it? out of manes? Words
> Will do it, out of manes, out of airs, but
> They have no manes, so there are no airs, birds
> Of words, from me to them no singing gut.
> For they have no eyes, for their legs are wood,
> For their stomachs are logs with print on them,
> Blood red, red lamps hang from necks or where could
> Be necks, two legs stand A, four together M.
> "Street Closed" is what print says on their stomachs . . .

The same word—"Horses"—serves to name both a noble, animate beast and these dead wooden things ("They have no manes . . . their legs are wood . . . their stomachs are logs with print on them"). The poet, however, through the power of verbal music—"airs"—can transform these lifeless barriers into mobile animals: "No horse is here, no horse is there? / Says you! Then I—fellow me, airs! we'll make / Wood horse, and recognize it with our words—"[48]

As the poem grows more high-spirited, it incorporates fragments of the *Passion* libretto and of earlier movements of *"A"*—*"See Him! Whom? The Son / Of Man*, grave-turf on taxi" ("A"-1 and "A"-5); "Then I, singing It is not the sea / But what floats over" ("A"-2); "Ricky, bro', Shimaunu-Sān" ("A"-3 and "A"-4)—and sets all of the previous themes of the poem dancing in an energetic, complex round, culminating in the sawhorses' confession that they, like everything else in the poem, are language: "words, words, we are words, horses, manes, words."[49] Words, yes, but also "manes"—with a pun on Latin *manes*, ancestral spirits[50]—and *horses*, Pegasus-steeds that can carry the poet above the constrictions of a Depression-wracked land. The movement is a remarkable, bewildering tour de force.

Back in "A"-1, Zukofsky had dismissed contemporary sonnet writers as pale imitators of Milton—"The sonneteers when I consider again and again / Limp wet blanket pentameters, / Immured holluschickies . . . persisting through polysyllables."[51] "The intention of A7," Zukofsky told Pound, "is to justify the attack on the sonneteers in A1 . . . As for *subject matter* people had written sonnet sequences—damn 'em they had—but what moved 'em was *concepts*, not a subjeck matter like two or three balls juggled in the air at once and the play got from the reflected lights in the color of them balls . . ."[52] This figure—of multiple themes and images juggled like balls, reflecting multicolored light—serves as well as any to describe the poetics of the movements of *"A"* Zukofsky would write over the next forty years.

· · ·

Bill Williams, when he got around to carefully reading the typescript of "A"-1 through -7, was impressed if somewhat puzzled. "I've read the 'A' and be God," he wrote, "it's not tawdry. Its movement calls up a world of sound in which things coccur in unused relationships—almost filed out with a file they show such marks of making on them . . . I'll not read it again until it is in print. It's like nothing else, a hard necessitous form—which is the substance."[53] Pound was less enthusiastic: "I don't think ['A'] ought to go on after your seven wollups. NOT unless you are making it a life work. Which; if I remember rightly; was not yr/ orig. intent. 'A' a work not in but showing progress."[54] Zukofsky, however, had revised his conception both of the poem's length and of the time that he would devote to it. "Yes, as far as I'm concerned *right now*," he replied, "'A' will be <a> life-work. I don't see how else, if it's going to be 2 movements a summer and 17 more to complete the 'epic' 24."[55]

Duration, "Liveforever": Time

interchapter

In April 1971 Zukofsky addressed an audience at the University of Connecticut for the Eighth Annual Wallace Stevens Memorial Program. In preparation, Zukofsky had reacquainted himself with Stevens, and that reacquaintance had blossomed into an obsession: He had spent the last three months rediscovering poems he had read fifty years before, discovering poems he had not yet encountered. Reading Stevens, he found, was participating in a conversation; that conversation had the effect of relaxing the grip of time itself: "what *dures* or endures as impersonal friendship when one poet reads another is a reading removed from yet out of time, without actual mutual influence or conscious awareness of tradition, literary handbooks or chronometers." Reading Stevens gave him, Zukofsky said, "a feeling of duration, best defined I think as Spinoza defined it, an indefinite continuance of existence."[1]

In the *Ethics*, which Zukofsky first read in 1922, Spinoza defines "duration (*duratio*)" as "indefinite continuation of existing."[2] As Harry Austryn Wolfson explains, "duration" and "time" are the same quality viewed from different perspectives: Time, that is, "is only a definite portion of duration measured by motion." In the Spinozan scheme, duration is "the attribute under which we conceive the existence of created things, in so far as they persevere in their own actuality."[3] We, as time-bound creatures, recognize the objects and persons of our world as similarly existing in time. *Duration*, their existence over time, is the aspect under which our intellects grasp them.

However, while Zukofsky might quote Spinoza in describing his reading of Stevens, what he means by *duration* is rather distinct from Spinoza's definition. Duration, as Zukofsky intends it, is synecdoche for the moment when the consciousness of the reader and that of the poet come together as one, regardless of "literary handbooks or chronometers." It is

> an instant certainty of the words of a poem bringing at least two persons and then maybe many persons, even peoples together. . . . [I]t does not matter whether the reader is the book or the book is the reader or if the grandfather is the forebear of the grandson or the grandson the forebear of his grandfather. The instant certainty of the words is all that exists for one become two.[4]

That moment of duration is a moment of oneness, a moment of "clear and distinct" knowledge—as Zukofsky puts it in "A"-22, "duration / a knowledge that verifies"[5]—and a moment literally outside of time. Poetry can take us out of our historical, chronological moment, can put us into a place that removed from what Shakespeare calls "Devouring time" (Sonnet 19) the inexorable progression that grinds us all to the same dust.

That poetry braves time is not a new idea. "Yet do thy worst, old time," reads the same sonnet, "despite thy wrong / My love shall in my verse ever live long." Here, as in Sonnet 55—"Not marble nor the gilded monuments / Of princes shall outlive this powerful rhyme"—Shakespeare adapts a theme from Horace: "This monument will outlast metal and I made it / More durable than the king's seat, higher than pyramids" (Book III, 30).[6] But Zukofsky is less interested in the poem's serving as a durable monument than in the peculiar power that poetry itself has to shift us outside of the clock's progress. His reading of Stevens, in which the affinities between the reader and the poem take the reader out of his own chronological moment, is only a particularly intense case of what is true of valid poetry in general. Wolfson notes that the word "duration" derives from the Latin *durare*, "to be hardened," from which one gets the meaning "to continue, to last, to remain"—and then it is only a step to Eluard's wonderfully punning definition of the artist's fundamental drive: "le dur désire de durer."[7]

In an early poem, "I Sent Thee Late" (1922), Zukofsky hears the waves against the shoreline as an emblem of time as empty reiteration:

Vast, tremulous;
Grave on grave of water-grave:

Past.

Futurity no more than duration
Of a wave's rise, fall, rebound
Against the shingles, in ever repeated mutation
Of emptied returning sound.[8]

Like Whitman's "Out of the Cradle Endlessly Rocking," this is a poem of the Long Island Sound, and as in Whitman, the sea speaks the same word over and over again, so that the past and the future merge into a single "repeated mutation / Of emptied returning sound."

Six years later, however, in the second movement of "*A*", Zukofsky would see the ocean again, the moon reflected as a flower on its surface:

Till of an afternoon
Launches the moon upon sea-whorl; green, flowering,
                                        opening leaf within leaf
Floats upon wave-edge; liveforever,
            pearl-clean, giant-size,
Green leathery leaf within leathery vision—[9]

The "flower" here is a succulent of the genus *Sempervivum*—"always-living," liveforever—a plant whose imbricated leaves form red, flower-like rosettes.[10] What Zukofsky has seen in this visionary moment is an order of beauty that allows him to step beyond the noise of commerce, sex, and imperialism. "The music is in the flower, / It is not the sea"—and here the sea has been explicitly associated with "nations, / Navies and armaments"—"but hyaline cushions the flower— / Live-forever, everlasting."[11]

The plant liveforever becomes in the early movements of "A" an emblem for the escape from devouring time that is afforded by the balanced structures of great art. In "A"-1, the music of Bach's *St. Matthew Passion* repeats itself in the poet's mind despite a host of distractions; it is "flower-cell in flower, live-forever before the eyes, perfecting . . ." It is an emblem for the order that the poet desires to create, as in "A"-5: "Liveforever! flower in flower heart; / Design . . ." In "A"-7, it becomes a sort of magical draught, an elixir of life, as the poet salutes "dancing bucks, / Who take liveforever! Taken a pump / And shaped a flower."[12]

By "A"-12, Zukofsky is associating liveforever with the artist's "impossible" goals, inserting his talismanic word into a passage adapted from Aristotle's *Nicomachean Ethics*:

> Happiness is not present at the start
> Like a piece of property and is only
> Accidently concerned with the good
> Of the artist—failing he must blame himself—
> He wants impossible liveforever
> While justice is to persons as well as things.
> Nothing is better for being eternal
> Or more white than white that dies of a day.[13]

The "impossible liveforever" that the artist desires is an immortality: perhaps a personal immortality, if only through the artwork, but as importantly the immortality of the work itself. In a brief meditation on the creation myth of Genesis, Zukofsky observes paradoxically that the thing created "must live forever," that in some sense it exists, removed from time, as thought in its creator's head—and even *before* it is thought:

> A source creating
> The heaven and the earth . . .
> Sweet shapes from a head

99

Whose thought must live forever—
Be the immortelle—
Before it is thought[14]

This passage strongly echoes one in "A"-8, where Zukofsky quotes a famous description of "the labor process" from Marx's *Capital*:

What distinguishes any worker from the best of the bees
Is that the worker builds a cell in his head before he constructs
    it in wax.
The labor process ends in the creation of a thing,
Which when the process began
Already lived as the worker's image.[15]

In the late 1930s Zukofsky found the human being as maker best described in Marx; by the early 1950s, with his strongest political passions cooling, he was describing the creative process as something like (in Coleridge's words) "a repetition in the finite mind of the eternal act of creation in the infinite I AM."[16]

Significantly, the longest single passage of "A"-23 (the last-composed movement of "A") extracted from a single source, a 136-line redaction of the *Epic of Gilgamesh*, revolves around its protagonist's search for immortality. The demigod Gilgamesh—"Strongest" in Zukofsky's version—dismayed by the death of his friend Enkidu ("One Kid" or "Stronger"), goes in search of Utnapishtim ("Everlasting"), the sole survivor of a world-flood analogous to Noah's and possessor of the secret of eternal youth. At the end of "A"-23's version of *Gilgamesh*, Everlasting gives Strongest the plant that will ensure his own immortality: "Take home my gift, my / secret the plant you shall / name, this journey as under / water, 'Alive-Old-Stay-Young.'"[17] Zukofsky chooses to break off his retelling of *Gilgamesh* at this point: In the original epic, Gilgamesh proceeds to lose the flower, and with it his hopes for thwarting the mortality that took his comrade Enkidu. In Zukofsky's version, however, the story ends at the moment when Strongest has attained his goal, has been given the plant *"Alive-Old-Stay-Young,"* which Everlasting now bids him name; perhaps the appropriate name would be precisely *liveforever*?

There are a few further evocations of liveforever in "A"-22 and -23, but the poet's final reference to the flower is the fourth poem of the posthumously published collection *80 Flowers*, "Liveforever":

> Wild time *liveforever* horsethyme ice
> by shard green red-purple thyrse
> shadowed stone or a flurry
> troth *orpine* kin *acre* yellow-red
> *mossy stonecrop love-entangle* your kind's
> *roof houseleek old-man-and-woman* who woo
> thatch song quicksilver cold would
> won't know All *sedum* no[18]

The plant itself is named in the poem's first line, and put in apposition (or opposition?) to both "Wild time" and "horsethyme," evoking Zukofsky's figure of the poet as horse. The poem's syntax, as in all of the *Flowers*, is dense, multivalent, and indeterminate, but on one level this seems to be a domestic scene in which the hope of aesthetic immortality has been located beneath a "*roof*" (perhaps a romantically "thatch[ed]" roof) where a "*love entangle*[d]" "*old-man-and-woman*"—Zukofsky and his wife Celia, then in their eighth and seventh decades, respectively?—celebrate their "troth" and produce "song" in spite of "quicksilver cold."

The explicit celebration of and reference to the plant liveforever as emblem of personal or artistic immortality grow rarer in Zukofsky's later poetry. One senses that Zukofsky has come to terms with the issue of immortality, has realized that to constantly strain against the bonds of time, an explicit "dur désire de durer," is to misplace one's emphasis. Just as Shakespeare's sonnets turn from their early stress on achieving immortality through art to the gritty business of negotiating the emotional and aesthetic implications of their speaker's love affairs—and thereby achieve immortality through a peerless *specificity* of language and metaphor—so also Zukofsky's poetry turns from brooding explicitly upon the mysteries of art's survival, as emblematized in the image of liveforever, to contemplating the actual workings of artistic immortality in the echoing voices of the human verbal tradition. Depicting moments that might be symbolized by liveforever, for Zukofsky, is in the long run less interesting than pursuing moments of his own special sense of *duration*.

Zukofsky read all of literature as a vast echo chamber of images, motifs, and sounds, as a simultaneous whole. His poetry is deeply rooted in the everyday and historical events through which he is living, but equally as important to Zukofsky are the moments when history and culture seem to be repeating themselves. In Zukofsky's youth, he subscribed to a Marxist teleology, looking for the advent of an end-of-history millennium in the revolution and the dictatorship of the proletariat; in his fifties, when he saw the American empire spread out across the world and threatened by nationalistic revolutions at its fringes, he found contemporary history described with striking accuracy in Gibbon's *Decline and Fall of the Roman Empire*.

As a maker of poems, Zukofsky came to believe that the modernist emphasis on "making it new," while perhaps valid in regard to poetic technique and form, was simply beside the point when applied to subject matter. In his early criticism he castigated Stevens for a "versification clambering the stiles of English influence." But in 1950 he would assert that "the *means* and *objects* of poetry (cf. Aristotle's *Poetics*) have been constant, that is, recognizably human, since ca. 3000 B.C." In his life of reading—for Zukofsky almost identical to his life of *writing*—Zukofsky came to look for and delight in the discovery of recurrences, of moments of recognition: moments when the reader found himself lifted across and out of time. Stevens's poems about reading, especially, Zukofsky told his Connecticut audience in 1971, were for him striking examples of that experience of *duration*: "It is not a temporal thing, may be felt only an instant, but that instant call it love, eternity, infinity: whatever you *want*—that's it. Stevens describes that feeling. It *dures* Stevens might be saying."[19]

It would be going too far to assert that Zukofsky entirely gave up seeking immortality in his verse, but in a move of profound intellectual generosity and openness, he came more and more to set aside that ambition in favor of an ongoing delight in the play of recurrences and resemblances across literary and cultural history, and came more and more to fashion his own poetry out of those moments of time-transcending "duration."

"Objectivists" 1930–1931

chapter six

I N OCTOBER 1930, Zukofsky received a letter from Harriet Monroe, the editor of *Poetry: A Magazine of Verse*. Zukofsky had asked her to recommend him for a Guggenheim fellowship. (His application of the year before, when Ezra Pound and T. S. Eliot had written him letters of recommendation, had been rejected; perhaps his luck would be better if he were backed by an established editor rather than a pair of somewhat suspect poets.) Of course, Monroe told Zukofsky, she would be glad to write on his behalf. More importantly, she had a proposition for him. "A recent letter from Ezra Pound spoke with admiration of your 'definite critical gift' and of the 'new group' of poet[s] in whom you are interested," she wrote. "It may be that *Poetry* has not adequately represented this group as yet, and I therefore propose that you take charge of a number—say Feb., March or May—and put in whatever poets you like up to 30½ pages of verse and 20 more of prose."[1] This invitation would set Zukofsky's career on directions he could not have anticipated, and would decades later come to regret.

From this letter can be dated Zukofsky's first emergence into the public eye, and from it can be dated the first emergence of the objectivist phenomenon. The objectivists were a group of poets who constituted the most important American poetic revolution in the middle decades of this century, with Zukofsky clearly at its head. But was his defining term—"objectivist"—a deeply considered description of the commonalities his poetry shared with that of George Oppen, Carl Rakosi, Charles Reznikoff, and William Carlos Williams, or was it an ad hoc formulation, a hastily conceived banner under which he could advance the poetry and careers of himself and his friends? In either case, through much of the 1930s Zukofsky saw the objectivist label, which seems to have hovered between a general definition of poetics and the name of a specific literary movement, as his best hope to bring his own work before a wider audience.

.   .   .

Monroe founded *Poetry* magazine in Chicago in 1912 to publish high-quality poetry and poetry reviews. Early on she enlisted Pound as the magazine's "foreign correspondent," a rather daring move, given that Monroe's own tastes ran to such writers as Vachel Lindsay, Carl Sandburg, and Edgar Lee Masters. Pound's relationship with *Poetry* was a stormy one. He fed the magazine a stream of exciting new poets—H.D., Richard Aldington, T. S. Eliot—and persuaded his established friends and acquaintances—Yeats, Rabindranath Tagore—to submit work. But he was repeatedly frustrated by Monroe's obdurately conservative sensibility, and his relationship with the magazine became tenuous after 1919, though he remained on cordial terms with Monroe.

Monroe liked Pound's suggestion that his young friend Zukofsky assemble an issue of work by a new generation of poets. "A magazine is always in danger of getting into a rut," she wrote Zukofsky, "and I should be very glad of such a definite break as your number would be."[2] Both she and her associate editor Morton Dauwen Zabel had noticed Zukofsky's work (indeed, *Poetry* had published his poems in 1924 and 1929), and they especially admired the Henry Adams essay serialized in *Hound & Horn*. Zukofsky was to have a free hand in selecting material for this issue of the magazine—aside, of course, from limitations of space.[3]

Zukofsky jumped at the opportunity to edit an issue of what was still the foremost poetry magazine in America. "Wonners will nevuHH cease," Pound wrote Zukofsky upon receiving the news from Monroe, adding (a little ruefully), "thet wummun she nevuh trusted me lak she trusts you!!!"[4] Pound was exaggerating, as he often did, but he was in large part right. Monroe was handing the controls of her magazine over to Zukofsky for an issue, no questions asked. Aside from the matter of page limits, Monroe had one condition for his editorship, spelled out and repeatedly emphasized. In her letter of invitation to Zukofsky, she had spoken of him and his younger colleagues as a "new group"—not a tendency in writing, but a movement *of writers*. Monroe stressed, in her next letter to Zukofsky, that she wanted this issue of *Poetry* to feature not just new poets, but a new *ism*. "I shall be disappointed if you haven't a 'new group,' as Ezra said," she wrote: "I think you should have an editorial showing what you and your group are aiming at and what you think of modern tendencies in general."[5] When Zukofsky began assembling materials for the issue he had no intention of promoting a movement. How could he, since no such movement or "group" existed? (As he put it to Pound, immediately after receiving Monroe's invitation, "Naturally, I haven't a 'group' or know one . . . 'Perhaps' *you* know of a new group."[6]) But Monroe expected his contributors to constitute such a group: If no such group existed, Zukofsky would have to invent one.

. . .

T. S. Eliot, a poet who assiduously steered clear of literary movements, would comment in 1944 on the phenomenon of the formal poetic group: "a small group of young writers, with certain affinities or regional sympathies between them, may produce a volume together. Such groups"—and here Eliot was thinking mostly of the imagists of 1912—"frequently bind themselves together by formulating a set of principles or rules, to which usually nobody adheres; in course of time the group disintegrates, the feebler members vanish, and the stronger ones develop more individual styles."[7] Eliot was right: whatever ideologies and aesthetics young writers may have in common are really far less important than the mere fact of solidarity, the sense of community that the group provides the young poet. Pound, who had during his London years organized at least two "movements" in contemporary poetry and the arts—imagism and vorticism—knew, no less than Eliot, the ad hoc nature of group formations. But he was also keenly aware, having overseen the publication of the first imagist anthologies and watched the ongoing popularity of Edward Marsh's five anthologies of *Georgian Verse*, that a group label could be a potent marketing device for otherwise unknown young poets.

Now, after almost six years in self-imposed exile in Rapallo, in the thick of the Fascist political experiment he so admired but far from the centers of English-language poetic innovation, Pound was trying to raise up movements that would follow in the footsteps of the imagists and vorticists. In February 1928, he had urged Zukofsky to send him manuscripts by "any of your contemporaries with whom you care to associate. Somebody OUGHT to form a group in the U.S. to make use of the damn thing [Pound's magazine the *Exile*] now that I have got it in motion."[8] There was no necessity for unanimity among the members of such a gathering ("How the hell many points of agreement do you suppose there were between Joyce, W. Lewis, Eliot and yrs. truly in 1917; or between Gaudier and Lewis in 1913; or between me and Yeats, etc.?"[9])—but he also strongly believed in the utility of groups. Zukofsky did nothing to start a New York "group" in 1928, but Pound never abandoned the notion of mobilizing a new movement of American poets, and no doubt communicated that enthusiasm to Monroe when he suggested that she allow his young friend to take over an issue of her magazine.

Zukofsky had two tasks on his hands: First, to assemble a *Poetry* issue's worth of previously unpublished work by younger poets he admired; and then, to come up with a banner, a "movement" under which he could somehow group them. Pound was certainly willing to help out on the first task. Immediately after learning that Zukofsky was to edit the issue, he bombarded Zukofsky with six letters in swift succession, totaling some twenty-odd pages of editorial advice.[10] As frenetic as those letters were, they showed a certain restraint. Again and again, Pound advised Zukofsky to follow his own instincts in selecting contributors, and cautioned Zukofsky to give himself time to make the issue as good as possible: "you are to have Feb. *OR* March *OR* May, as you like. Don't fire till you see the whites of their eyes."[11]

Pound communicated his main misgiving to Monroe herself: "My only fear is that Mr. Zukofsky will be just too Goddam prewdent."[12]

From Madison, Zukofsky set to work contacting poets and soliciting work: his Columbia friends Samuel Theodore Hecht, Henry Zolinsky, Whittaker Chambers, and Irving Kaplan;[13] his New York acquaintances Reznikoff and Oppen; poets of the left, among them John Wheelwright, Norman MacLeod, and Henry Roskolenkier; and a whole range of avant-garde poets whose work had come before Zukofsky's eyes in the little magazines and through word of mouth: Robert McAlmon, Kenneth Rexroth, Emanuel Carnevali, Parker Tyler, Charles Henri Ford, and Carl Rakosi.

. . .

Carl Rakosi was born in 1903 in Berlin, his parents Hungarian Jews. (His father had been Leopold Rozenberg; Rakosi, the name he adopted, was that of a dynasty of Hungarian national heroes.) After immigrating to America, Rakosi's father owned a jewelry shop in Kenosha, Wisconsin. Over the 1920s, Rakosi had completed a graduate degree in educational psychology, had begun and abandoned an English PhD at the University of Texas, and had worked as an industrial psychologist, a social worker, and a mess boy on a freighter. He had also written poetry—gnomic, colorful verse of an unexpected vocabulary, heavily influenced by the imagists and Wallace Stevens—and had cemented literary friendships with fellow Wisconsin writers Kenneth Fearing and Margery Latimer. Latimer had encouraged him to send poems to Jane Heap's *Little Review*, perhaps the most prominent American avant-garde organ of its day (the magazine had printed Eliot, Pound, and Yeats, and had serialized Joyce's *Ulysses*), and appearing there was enormously heartening for Rakosi.[14]

Zukofsky's letter inviting him to submit work for a special issue of *Poetry*, nonetheless, found Rakosi's personal fortunes at a low ebb. After dropping out of graduate school, he had spent a year in medical school in Galveston, until his funding ran out. In late 1930 he was in Houston teaching high school English—intractable students, a "fixed Victorian course of study from which one was not allowed to deviate"—and "in despair."[15] (Indeed, Zukofsky told Pound, Rakosi had largely abandoned writing poetry since 1925.[16]) Zukofsky's interest in Rakosi's work was a godsend: It encouraged Rakosi to continue thinking of himself as a poet, rather than as a serial failure. Zukofsky praised him highly, asked to use as many as seven pages of his work, and offered to pass poems he couldn't use on to *Hound & Horn*, *Pagany*, or the *Morada*. In letter after letter of the intense correspondence that followed, Zukofsky dissected Rakosi's poems with a careful eye, praising strong lines, questioning unclear images and over-ornate diction, and suggesting changes and improvements. (Sixty-seven years later, Rakosi would recall those blue-pencilings: Zukofsky "was a great critic, really a great critic—in his own way he was as good as Pound as a critic."[17]) Zukofsky was doing the same for his other contributors, marveling at the weakness of the work he had received from "even 'accomplished' poets," and finding the job of editing more arduous than he had anticipated.[18]

The correspondence with Rakosi was something of a consolation for the homesick and lonely Zukofsky. His closest friends—Hecht, Taupin, Reisman, Chambers, Oppen, Kaplan, and Serly[19]—were far away from the "hell-hole" of Madison. Williams was "very dear" to him, but twenty years older. And Pound, however hospitable and generous his letters might be, was a poetic and critical eminence too grand to be over-nearly approached. The tense undercurrent of the younger poet addressing the older master that runs through Zukofsky's letters to Pound, however casual the immediate tone might be, was absent in his letters to Rakosi. Rakosi was a chum, a pal—almost a surrogate brother—with whom Zukofsky could exchange smutty double entendres, lament his own career prospects, and share his somewhat fanciful aspirations: to know something about music, to learn to drive, to work with his hands.[20]

. . .

Finding the poets Zukofsky wanted to include was relatively easy, apart from the editorial labors he had to spend upon the poems they sent him, and apart from periodic cautions by Monroe that he had exceeded his page limits. But the work had to be done in haste. Despite Pound's cautions not to rush matters, Zukofsky had decided to go with a February rather than a March or May issue. Copy therefore needed to be in Monroe's hands by December 20, 1930. Since she had first written him on October 11, that left something like ten weeks to assemble almost sixty printed pages of poetry and prose. He had his opening suite: four poems of Rakosi's arranged under the title "Before You." And Bill Williams came through with just the poem Zukofsky needed to close out his selection, the sublime "The Botticellian Trees." ("By some curious trick of the imagination," Williams noted, "I have persistently kept the Alphabet of Leaves thing for just the purpose you want it for."[21]) But there still remained the matter of the "movement," the banner under which to assemble his diverse contributors.

Among the poems Zukofsky had lined up for the issue were six brief, perfect lyrics by his friend Reznikoff, under the unassuming title of "A Group of Verse." And still on his hands was "Charles Reznikoff: Sincerity and Objectification," an essay on Reznikoff's work he had finished writing back in February.[22] (Zukofsky had originally intended the essay for the *Menorah Journal*, but was put off by a rather peremptory rejection[23]) The essay was far too long for *Poetry*, and would have to be cut. In early November, responding to Pound's barrage of editorial suggestions in no fewer than *forty-three* numbered points, Zukofsky implored Pound to edit the manuscript for him.[24] Pound was already "in act of placing or trying to place" Zukofsky's essay, but agreed to recall the manuscript from whichever editor held it at the moment.[25] By the time Pound's edited version of the essay reached Zukofsky in December, however, Zukofsky had already cut the piece down to *Poetry*'s specifications.[26]

In its original form, "Charles Reznikoff: Sincerity and Objectification" was a career-spanning overview of all of Reznikoff's writings, poetry, plays, and prose works. It was a rather extraordinary demonstration of faith in a poet essentially unknown to the literary world at large. All of Reznikoff's eight volumes to date had been self-published, and public reaction to his work had been minuscule. Zukofsky's essay aimed to redress that neglect, to present Reznikoff as a poet, playwright, and fiction writer of far more than "regional" (read New York Jewish) interest, and as a writer well ahead of most of his contemporaries in matters of literary craft.

Zukofsky trimmed substantial sections devoted to Reznikoff's plays and prose works, and reduced the number of passages quoted from the poetry. The title of the resulting piece, "Sincerity and Objectification: *With Special Reference to the Work of Charles Reznikoff*," shifted emphasis from Reznikoff himself to the theoretical principles that Zukofsky adumbrated in the course of describing his work. "Sincerity and Objectification," as it was published in Zukofsky's February 1931 issue of *Poetry*, was a manifesto of poetics that would assume an importance in Zukofsky's career comparable to that of the preface to the 1802 *Lyrical Ballads* in Wordsworth's, and would become a touchstone by which generations of poetry critics sought to come to terms not with Reznikoff's work but with Zukofsky's own poetry.

"Sincerity," the first of Zukofsky's talismanic criteria, is a stance taken by the composing poet, an attitude of exceptional fidelity to both the words of the emerging poem and the facts that the poem seeks to record. In sincerity, "Writing occurs which is the detail, not mirage, of seeing, of thinking with the things as they exist, and of directing them along a line of melody."[27] Here, as so often, Zukofsky analyzes the poet's tasks into the three realms of eye, ear, and mind. When a poet is writing with sincerity, he presents the unaltered, unretouched evidence of his eyes ("the detail, not mirage, of seeing"); he seeks honestly to embody the processes of his thought about the objects seen ("the things as they exist"); and, as he writes the words of the poem, those words will form "a line of melody"—a musical, aurally pleasing sequence.

Zukofsky's rhetoric was similar to those of any number of earlier poetic revolutions, from Wordsworth's description of his own verse as "fitting to metrical arrangement a selection of the real language of men in a state of vivid sensation," to Pound's imagist strictures, a century later: "Direct treatment of the 'thing' whether subjective or objective.... [U]se absolutely no word that does not contribute to the presentation.... [C]ompose in the sequence of the musical phrase, not in sequence of a metronome."[28] What Zukofsky calls for, like Wordsworth and Pound, is a cleansing, a stripping away of rhetoric and "poeticisms." Wordsworth had sought in his lyrics to return to something like natural speech, free from the elaborate figural language and artificial rhetoric of eighteenth-century English poetry. Pound called for the poet not merely to eschew the ornamental, the abstract, and the artificial, but even to break with the structures of traditional meter. Zukofsky is more radical yet in his definition of sincerity: The poet cannot be beholden to any preconceived notion of what a poem ought to be, but must work with a constant fidelity to his perceptions, his thoughts, and the sounds of his language. Sincerity is, in short, a "preoccupation with the accuracy of detail in writing."[29] Such art is a far cry from the polished, "worked" productions of the past, just as "the perfect line of occasional drawing" or "the beginnings of sculpture not proceeded with" differ from a finished Academy painting or a polished statue.[30]

Zukofsky's prose is far from transparent. But it is clear that he intends *sincerity* as both the poet's composing stance and as a quality that can be identified in as narrow a space as a single line of verse. *Objectification* is something else altogether. It is a "rested totality" in the reader's mind, "the apprehension satisfied completely as to the appearance of the art form as an object." Zukofsky plays several variations on this definition. Objectification appears in "writing (audibility in two dimensional print) which is an object or affects the mind as such." It is "the arrangement, into one apprehended unit, of minor units of sincerity—in other words, the resolving of words and their ideation into structure."[31] If sincerity then is the poet's ideal compositional mode, and the combinations of words produced in that mode, then objectification is the larger structure into which those "minor units of sincerity" resolve. It is, simply put, *form*. Not the form of the poetic handbooks, which tell how many lines make up a sonnet or how stresses should be disposed in a line of iambic pentameter, but form as a sense of unity, an impression of "rested totality" in the reader's mind.

What Zukofsky had done was to take the strictures of Pound's imagism—a series of suggestions as to what the poet both should do and should *not* do—and add a further step: "objectification," an overall form for the poem. The "theory" of the image (in Pound's words, "An 'Image' is that which presents an intellectual and emotional complex in an instant of time"[32]) provided a rationale for short, visually striking poems, but it gave no direction as to how the poet might go about composing lengthier or more complex works. Objectification provided a higher mark for the poet to aim at, a "rested totality" created in the reader's mind by a poem that had the same self-sufficient overall form as a tangible object.

It was a high mark indeed. "At any time," Zukofsky wrote, "objectification in writing is rare. The poems or prose structures of a generation are few." Zukofsky singled out the works of the major modernists that show objectification: five poems of Williams's *Spring and All*; Marianne Moore's "An Octopus" and "Like a Bulrush"; Eliot's "Mr. Appollinax"; and, in flashes, some poems of E. E. Cummings and Robert McAlmon. And, of course, Pound: "In contemporary writing, the poems of Ezra Pound alone possess objectification to a most constant degree," Zukofsky wrote, giving his friend the most unqualified praise of the essay: "his objects are musical shapes." In contrast, "The degree of objectification in the work of Charles Reznikoff"—the poet to whom the essay was making "special reference"—"is small" (though Reznikoff's poems are "almost constant examples of sincerity").[33]

.   .   .

Zukofsky had arrived at the critical terms "sincerity" and "objectification" almost a year earlier, when he was first drafting the essay on Reznikoff. At the time, he had no idea that his article would be pressed into service as the manifesto for a new poetic movement. But with Monroe urging him to define a "new group" under which to range the poets he wanted to publish, and with the deadline for the February issue pressing down upon him, the Reznikoff essay seemed an obvious resource. What he valued most highly in poetry was something he called objectification. Why not, then, present his poets as "objectivists"? As he put it to Rakosi, he was "Cooking up a *standard* for my contributors to gather round in the *Feb. issue*—Objectivists, 1931 or something of that sort." He admitted that the notion of such a group was "Foolish—but may excite the reading booblik, hysterectomied & sterilized readers of 'Poetry'—and I owe it (maybe) to the *honor* (!) of my contributors."[34]

Zukofsky's issue of *Poetry*, in the event, appeared under the title "'Objectivists' 1931," the raised eyebrows of the scare quotes perhaps signaling the guest editor's ambivalence with the banner. Rakosi, happy to have four of his poems published at once in *Poetry*, had registered no objections to the name.[35] One imagines that most of the other poets in the issue were at the least surprised to find themselves christened "objectivists." (When he received his copy, Reznikoff wrote friends that "There is a learned article about my verse in *Poetry* for this month from which I learn that I am 'an objectivist.'"[36]) Publishing "Sincerity and Objectification" as the defining document of this collection of poems allowed Zukofsky to accede to Monroe's demands for a "new group," while simultaneously sidestepping the question of whether such a literary "movement" actually existed. In "Sincerity and Objectification: *With Special Reference to the Work of Charles Reznikoff*" and in "Program: 'Objectivists' 1931" (the brief headnote Zukofsky appended to the prose section of his *Poetry* issue) Zukofsky never claimed that he was formulating the program for a new movement, or that his principles of sincerity and objectification were somehow radical or new. In fact, one of the consistent strategies throughout both pieces was to cite the poetry of an earlier generation—Pound, Williams, Moore, Eliot, Cummings—and thereby blur the generational lines that would distinguish a new group from its precursors. "These poets," Zukofsky laconically noted, having reeled off a list of books by the above older poets, along with works by Stevens, McAlmon, and Reznikoff, "Seem to the present editor to have written in accordance with the principles heading this note. So do the contributors to this number."[37] And that, in short, was all that the poets of "'Objectivists' 1931" shared.

The "principles" Zukofsky mentions were presented at the beginning of "Program: 'Objectivists' 1931" in the form of a block of definitions:

> *An Objective: (Optics)—The lens bringing the rays from an object to a focus. (Military use)—That which is aimed at. (Use extended to poetry)—Desire for what is objectively perfect, inextricably the direction of historic and contemporary particulars.*[38]

Three definitions, each casting a different light on objectification. The optical definition emphasized the poet's focused vision, pursuing writing "which is the detail, not mirage, of seeing." A "military" definition, one might suppose, would be appropriate for the manifesto of a new avant-garde, but "That which is aimed at" seems less bellicose than simply bland. It's the "objectively perfect" poem as "inextricably the direction of historic and contemporary particulars," with its Hegelian echoes, that is most striking. While Zukofsky was quick to assure his reader that "historic and contemporary particulars" might mean *objects*—oak leaves, or the "Egyptian pulled-glass bottle in the shape of a fish" of Marianne Moore's poem—as well as *events*, his second example of the latter—"the Russian revolution and the rise of metallurgical plants in Siberia"—implied that not merely was this a poetics firmly grounded in the historical rather than the purely personal verities, but that Zukofsky remained as sympathetic to the Soviet experiment as he was when composing "Poem beginning 'The'" four years earlier. He ended "Program: 'Objectivists' 1931" with a brief parody of "a great writer"—*Lenin*: "editing this number has been too pleasant and too useful to permit further discourse about it."[39]

There were red flashes in the editorial matter of Zukofsky's "'Objectivists' 1931" issue of *Poetry*, and some of its contributors were red indeed. Zukofsky's friend Whittaker Chambers was not yet spying for the Soviet Union, but he had become closely associated with left-wing literary circles and was well on his way to becoming the "hottest literary Bolshevik" in New York.[40] Norman Macleod and Harry Roskolenkier, each of whom also had a poem in the issue, would become prominent as poets of the left. And John Wheelwright, born into a Boston Brahmin family, was assiduously trying to keep a foot in both communist and avant-garde literary camps.[41] In the contributors' notes to the *Poetry* issue, Zukofsky regretted the "limitations of page-space" that prevented him from printing work by the leftist poets Herman Spector and Sherry Mangan (as well as his friends Reisman and John Gassner).[42]

There was, however, little that could be construed as positively leftist *poetry* in the issue. Roskolenkier's "Supper in an Alms-house" most closely answers that description, and Chambers's "October 21st, 1926," with its persistent address to a "brother" and its invocation of "the motion of masses," might easily be taken as a political statement (though it originated as an elegy for his brother Richard[43]). There was a political critique implicit in the first of George Oppen's two poems, in which "Big-Business" removed itself "Above the / Plane of lunch, of wives," and Zukofsky's own "A"-7, even as it spun playful conceits into its intricate pattern of seven sonnets, had its workers cry out, "Brother, we want a meal," and openly voiced the word "revolution."[44] But on the whole, while "'Objectivists' 1931" could be said to tilt decidedly towards the left, the issue as a whole offered little that might actively contribute towards a political struggle whose literary lines were being drawn.

Perhaps the kindest that could be said for Zukofsky's issue of *Poetry* was that it was a mixed bag where some real jewels were mixed among the chaff. "Before You," the suite of four Rakosi poems that led off the issue, began on a Romantic note ("And I, my love, / skirt the cottages . . . to animate the ideal / with internal passion") but then shifted to more concrete—though colorful, and often metaphysical— imagery.[45] Zukofsky's own "A"-7, in which the themes of the first six movements of "A" were deftly crammed into seven sonnets, was on its face an astonishing tour de force, but must have been quite incomprehensible to readers not already familiar with Zukofsky's project. There were all-too-delicate, imagistic lyrics by Howard Weeks, Jesse Loewenthal, and Zukofsky's friends Ted Hecht and Henry Zolinsky. There was a dramatic monologue by Robert McAlmon, a pair of Rimbaud translations by Emanuel Carnevali, a religiously charged list-poem by Kenneth Rexroth (fittingly titled "Last Page of a Manuscript"), and a brief, impressionistic "Poem" by Zukofsky's Wisconsin student Martha Champion.

What stands out in the issue (though a reader's eye is perhaps slanted by the literary history of seventy years) is the work of the writers who would later come to be known as objectivists: Rakosi's "Before You" and Zukofsky's "A"-7—and by putting them first Zukofsky showed that he was well aware of the poems' strengths—but as well Reznikoff's six lyrics and the two poems of George Oppen's that went under the title "1930's." (They would later form sections of his 1934 volume, *Discrete Series*.) Basil Bunting contributed a sonorous poem on the process of poetic creation, "The Word," and the poetry section of the magazine closed with Williams's lovely "The Botticellian Trees," in which he records his impressions of bare tree limbs as "thin // letters that spelled / winter," now "fading" with the first spring foliage, "being modified / by pinched out // ifs of color."[46]

·   ·   ·

The "'Objectivists' 1931" issue of *Poetry* was in the hands of its contributors and subscribers by late January 1931. Zukofsky had returned
to New York for the holidays, where Basil Bunting's wife, Marion (née
Culver), an old Wisconsin acquaintance of Rakosi's, had fed him "a
swell Xmas dinner."[47] He returned to Madison on the sixth of January and soon found himself regretting the vacation. He was homesick, and missed his friends: "Write again—" he wrote Rakosi, "the
cold is better but this place ain't heaven—I should never have gone
back to N.Y.—I should never etc. . . ."[48] As the semester wore on,
Zukofsky found Wisconsin no more hospitable. He found it hard to
adjust to the faculty's midwestern mores—"They're so genial that
when a guy's quiet they think he's arrogant"—and the members of
the English department seemed to fear that he was teaching over his
students' heads: "I think you credit them wi-ith too-o much," Zukofsky's "chief" told him in a teaching evaluation.[49] And while Zukofsky
preferred to keep the news of his publications to himself, his critical
essays had come to the attention of the department, where they were
the object of general puzzlement.

Socially, Madison was sterile and stifling. Zukofsky had moved
out of his lodgings at the University Club to the Irving Apartments,
where he had a private bath and could entertain visitors without
entering "thru a gudgeous hall in which lighted bald heads pore over
newspapers"[50]—not that visitors were frequent. His few friends were
students. Martha Champion had been in one of his fall semester
courses; she was, as Zukofsky put it to Rakosi, a "swell person," and
a poet to boot.[51] Champion knew classical Greek, and she and Zukofsky amused themselves by translating passages of the *Iliad* into New
York slang.[52] With another student, Frank Heineman, he worked
through Joyce's *Ulysses*.[53] But such companions were no substitute
for the circle of friends he had left behind in New York.

Zukofsky wanted out of Madison, even though he had no clear
idea what he would do for a living if he gave up his thousand-dollar-
a-year position and returned to New York. Many of his hopes were
pinned on the Guggenheim fellowship: with the Foundation's two
thousand five hundred dollars, he could travel to Europe.[54] By March,
however, his application had once again been rejected, and his future
as a whole looked uncertain. "Do you know if I could get a job in

Urope the coming September," he wrote Pound: "in N.Y. I suppose I wd. have to march on the city hall with the others."[55] The University of Wisconsin was likely to offer him another year's work, but he was already inclined to leave, even if the department were able to upgrade his position from instructor to lecturer, with a five-hundred-dollar raise.[56] In the event, they offered Zukofsky a reappointment without a raise, which he turned down. "I don't know what I'll do in N.Y.—" he wrote Rakosi in May, "but there's no use doing this I've been doing all year."[57]

. . .

The readers of *Poetry* reacted to "'Objectivists' 1931," and Monroe printed a selection of letters received, with her own commentary, in the April 1931 issue.[58] There were some humorous notes—a Princeton student "who congratulates us upon achieving an interesting issue at last," a "Long Island editor" who returned his copy with a page of free verse demanding back "my money, my god, my money!"—but there were also more serious assessments from the poet critics Horace Gregory and Stanley Burnshaw. Gregory was guardedly generous. After expressing a touch of Wasp uneasiness at the "curious strain of Jewish nationalism" he found in the poetry, Gregory praised Zukofsky for having consolidated all "the little poetry movements of the last ten years under one banner." But he criticized Zukofsky for using Charles Reznikoff ("a man of minor abilities") as his standard of comparison and for his "tendency to speculate exhaustively about the technic of writing," a preoccupation that might eventually force the objectivists "backward into the library." Contemporary poets could not ignore, in short, "the panorama of strictly American life, including the class struggle."

Printed in full was a letter from the twenty-four-year-old Burnshaw, just beginning what was to be a very long career as a critic, poet, and editor. Burnshaw addressed a series of queries to Zukofsky whose overall import, choked by their rather bombastic language, was quite straightforward: Is objectivism (the noun was Burnshaw's— Zukofsky had been careful only to use the adjective, "Objectivist," and to set it off with quotation marks) a "programmed movement" or "a rationalization undertaken by writers of similar predilections and tendencies"? Given Zukofsky's concept of objectification (which Burnshaw confessed he could just barely puzzle out), doesn't all worthwhile poetry achieve that state? And finally, given that a number of the poems in the issue seem quite traditional in their images and sentiments, why group them under the "new" banner of objectivist?

Monroe also printed Zukofsky's detailed and rather cranky reply. Of course, Zukofsky wrote, some of the poems in the issue seemed more traditional than others, but the serious poet does not make invidious distinctions between styles of worthwhile poetry: "Poetry is 'past' or 'news' only to historians of literature and to certain lay readers; to poets (craftsmen in the art of poetry) and to competent critics, poetry." The poets Zukofsky included among his objectivists, then, may be writing in a recognizably new style or in a clearly traditional one; what counted was the degree of sincerity and objectification visible in their work. Most crucially, Zukofsky emphatically disavowed objectivism as a "programmed movement": "The editor was not a pivot, the contributors did not rationalize about him together; out of appreciation for their *sincerity* of craft and occasional *objectification* he wrote the program of the February issue of POETRY . . ."

Monroe closed her selection of responses with a postcard from Pound—"Send me four more copies—this is a number I can show to my Friends. If you can do another eleven as lively you will put this mag. on its feet"—to which she wryly commented, "Alas, we fear that would put it on its uppers!" Pound had written Zukofsky immediately upon receiving his copy of the issue, calling it a "good job."[59] Six weeks later, writing Monroe, he was more guarded: "As to Feb. *Poetry* . . . The point is that although most of the contents was average, the *mode* of the presentation was good editing. . . . Service of Feb. number perhaps not so much re what is to survive of present infants as in strong indication of what *will not* survive from former mediocrity and faintly-above-medioc. A pruning of the tree." If Monroe was dissatisfied with what Zukofsky had done, however, perhaps she should "GET some other damn group and see what it can do. What about the neo-Elinor-Wylites? . . . Or the neo-hogbutchererbigdriftites?"[60] Pound had as little patience as ever with Monroe's favorites Elinor Wylie and Carl Sandburg.

The "'Objectivists' 1931" *Poetry* issue proved a short-lived instigation to other editors. Pound speculated that he himself ought to edit an issue of contemporary French poets.[61] Basil Bunting was keen to do an issue of avant-garde British poets, but aside from Bunting himself, J. J. Adams, and the extraordinary Scottish poet Joseph Gordon Macleod, he found little of interest in the U.K.; Bunting, Pound, and Zukofsky all dismissed the works of W. H. Auden and his circle. Monroe, as well, seemed rather gun-shy about guest editors after her experience with Zukofsky; the best she would do would be to make her own selection out of poets Bunting invited, then allow him to write an introduction.[62] Zukofsky himself, now that his own issue was in print, was ready to move on to other concerns. In the spring of 1931 he had little inkling that in the objectivist movement he had raised a golem that would do his bidding only imperfectly, and would rise up to haunt him periodically for the next four decades. Through the 1930s, Zukofsky would turn to the objectivist phenomenon as a springboard to bring him the recognition he felt he deserved, and would be disappointed. In the 1960s, when he felt he had left both the "movement" and his fellow objectivists far behind, it would be resurrected by the critical establishment, and he would find himself bracketed with a group of poets with whom—in his own view—he had almost nothing in common.

At the Helm of an
Avant-Garde 1932–1933

B Y SUMMER 1931 Zukofsky was back in New York and anxious, with Pound's letters spurring him on, to keep alive whatever popular momentum the "'Objectivists' 1931" issue of *Poetry* had created. On August 19 he gave a scrappy talk, "'Recencies' in Poetry," at the Gotham Book Mart, the center of New York's avant-garde book scene. He would not offer "apologies," Zukofsky said, but provide "some explanations regarding 'Program: "Objectivists" 1931' and 'Sincerity and Objectification.'" Those essays were not meant to define a new movement in poetry, on the model of the imagists or the surrealists, but to pinpoint issues of craft perennially central to the art of poetry. "Recencies" was a paradoxical term: "only good poetry—good an unnecessary adjective—is contemporary or classical. . . . It would be just as well then dealing with 'recencies' to deal with Donne or Shakespeare, if one knew them as well as a linguistic usage not their own can know them." Whatever "objectivist" might imply, it was above all else a label for acts of poem making on a continuum with the great poems of the past. "The good poems of today are—as jobs—not far from the good poems of yesterday," Zukofsky concluded, with a nod towards the fact that Joseph Stalin, the head of the revolution, had been spending time "in his one or two rooms" reading Shakespeare.[1]

Before he left for Madison the previous year, Zukofsky had discussed with George and Mary Oppen the possibility of founding a publishing venture. The Oppens had left New York at the same time as Zukofsky, first to San Francisco and then to France, where they settled in Le Beausset, a town in the Var district not far from Cannes.[2] In October 1931, Zukofsky and the Oppens formed To, Publishers. The project's name was Zukofsky's: "*To*—as we might say, a health to—*To*" (according to Zukofsky), or "'to' in the sense of 'to whom it may concern,' as on a bill of lading or as in usage before a verb to indicate the infinitive, 'to publish'" (according to Mary Oppen). (One might also read "To" as an acronym for The Objectivists.) The project's supporting capital was Oppen's. Zukofsky, as paid editor (one hundred dollars a month), would collect material and edit the books; the Oppens, in France where typesetting and printing were inexpensive, would have the books printed and ship them to Zukofsky, who would then market and distribute them.

They had ambitious plans for the enterprise. They would begin with Williams's *A Novelette and Other Prose*, then issue Pound's collected prose in multiple volumes under the title *Prolegomena*. Also projected was Basil Bunting's translation of Federigo Tozzi's *Tre Croci* and books of poetry by Reznikoff, Robert McAlmon, and Zukofsky himself.[3] The firm ran into problems with its first publication, Williams's *Novelette*, which came out in March 1932. The Oppens received proof from their French-speaking compositors that was full of errors, and since the books were paperbound—standard practice in Europe—American customs insisted on taxing them at the higher periodical rate, which played havoc with Oppen's budget. The only way to avoid the tariff was to ship the books in bundles of twenty-five or fewer, which meant multiple trips to the post office for both Oppen and Zukofsky. In addition, it was difficult to persuade American booksellers to give shelf space to To's paperbacks.[4] When the first volume of Pound's *Prolegomena* (containing *How to Read* and the first chapters of *The Spirit of Romance*) was published in June 1932, an American publisher (Bruce Humphries of Boston) was secured to handle importation and distribution.[5]

Through much of 1931 Zukofsky had hopes that Samuel Putnam, editor of the *New Review*, would publish an issue devoted to the objectivists, and to that end he began compiling an anthology of objectivist poetry. In fall 1931 Zukofsky was expecting Putnam to issue the anthology as a book under the New Review Editions imprint, but by February 1932 the editor had backed out.[6] Oppen then agreed to publish *An "Objectivists" Anthology* as a To book. It was to be the press's third and final volume, as Oppen was finding it financially impossible to continue the venture. He gave Zukofsky the news in August 1932, along with the unwelcome information that Zukofsky's salary would be reduced to fifty dollars a month—if Oppen could afford that much—through the end of the year, when it would cease altogether.[7]

. . .

An "Objectivists" Anthology was published in the summer of 1932, and like the "'Objectivists' 1931" issue of *Poetry* presented a heterogeneous mix of poets and poetics. A number of the contributors to the *Poetry* issue had gone by the wayside—among them Whittaker Chambers, Henry Zolinsky, Jesse Loewenthal, Martha Champion, and John Wheelwright—while a few new names had been added. The smaller number of poets and more spacious format allowed Zukofsky to include larger selections of his contributors' work and substantial sections of longer poems.

The anthology was divided into three sections, the first devoted to the "epic," the second devoted to shorter lyrics, and the third and shortest to a series of "Collaborations." These were essentially Zukofsky's rewritings of his contributors' works, and while Williams was always amenable to his friend's revisions (as with the sequence "March" that ends the *Anthology*), Kenneth Rexroth attached an exasperated note to Zukofsky's revision of Part A of his "Prolegomenon to a Theodicy": "I have read this over once more. I cannot allow it to be printed with my signature. You can append a note that it has been abridged by L.Z., if you wish, or print it entire or don't print it at all. It simply makes no sense to me at all."[8] Zukofsky had cut six pages of Rexroth's rather abstract original down to three far more concrete ones; always, his impulse when it came to revision was simply to *omit*.

The *Anthology* was altogether sturdier than the *Poetry* issue, edited in much haste, had been. Basil Bunting's "Attis; Or, Something Missing" started it off with a bang: "What mournful stave, what bellow shakes the grove? / O, it is Attis grieving for his testicles!"[9] Much of the work that followed was very strong indeed: Oppen's "1930's" (later included in his *Discrete Series*); "A Journey Away," a vivid and precise nine-section poem by Rakosi; Reznikoff's brief verse play "Rashi"; a sequence of seven Williams poems, including "The pure products of America" ("For Elsie"); and T. S. Eliot's "Marina," which Zukofsky felt was the best thing Eliot had done since *The Waste Land*.[10]

Most importantly, Zukofsky included "A"-1 through "A"-7, the whole of his long poem to date. Its appearance as a single thirty-three-page stretch of printed text announced that Zukofsky, who at the age of twenty-eight had yet to publish a book of his own poetry, was a force to be reckoned with on the poetry scene. In its *"Objectivists" Anthology* appearance, with the hopeful tailpiece "To be Continued," *"A"* was setting itself up in competition with *The Cantos*, openly advertising itself as what Pound had doubted it fit to be—"a life work."[11]

The anthology as a whole was dedicated "To / Ezra Pound / who . . . is still for the poets of our time / the / most important."[12] Pound had given "over to younger poets the space offered him" in the *Poetry* issue,[13] but he contributed two rather damp squibs to *An "Objectivists" Anthology*. (Zukofsky had hoped for a Canto or two, but Pound was reserving new Cantos for paying venues.[14]) "Words for Roundel in Double Canon" was a harmless but rather unfunny attack on Bloomsbury. The other poem, beginning "Gentle Jheeezus sleek and wild" (usually referred to as "The Yiddisher Charleston"), was the lyric to Pound's idea of a popular song, a mélange of heavy-handed stage-Yiddish and black minstrelsy. The poem grew out of the obscene "Black King Bolo" doggerel Eliot and Pound had exchanged for years, and managed to be insulting to Christians, Jews, blacks, and Republicans alike. Whether or not the poem was designedly anti-Semitic (Pound worried it might be read as such—"The yittisher by itself might give deleterious impression of antisemitism which I am far from"[15]), Zukofsky was delighted with it. In an October 1931 letter to Pound (beginning "Adoinoi ECHOD-D!!!") he told Pound that he "Alwus, alwus . . . schuld sink in de voyce of de beoble—oi, alwus!"[16]

Zukofsky's mock-Yiddish here echoed Pound's own, part of a pattern of mildly anti-Semitic banter between the two. Pound's anti-Semitism was as yet nowhere near as virulent as it would become. Pound saw Zukofsky first and foremost as a poet, a disciple, a potential propagandist for modernism in the United States, rather than as a Jew. Zukofsky, himself alienated from his family's Orthodox community, viewed the Jewish cultural establishment with much the same disdain Pound felt for Bloomsbury. The editors of *Menorah Journal*, which had rejected "Sincerity and Objectification," were a retrograde "Sanhedrin," he told Pound. "Do I luf my peepul?" he wrote in 1929: "The only good Jew I know is my father: a coincidence."[17] Zukofsky and Pound would continue this affectionate—if somewhat creepy—banter well into the 1930s, when a disturbingly *serious* anti-Semitic edge would become evident in Pound's side of the correspondence.

．　．　．

An "Objectivists" Anthology received a mixed public response. Henry Bamford Parkes, an English historian teaching at New York University, concluded in the *New English Weekly* that "'Objectivism' appears to be a restatement, in pretentious and sometimes incomprehensible language, of the aims of the Imagists." Zukofsky was little more than an epigone of Pound's, and *"A"* was nowhere near as interesting as *The Cantos*.[18] In a strikingly vicious review in *Hound & Horn*, Yvor Winters dismissed the objectivists as "sensory impressionists," and commented on their lack of "rational intelligence." The anthology as a whole, he said, "is of clinical rather than literary interest."[19] (While *Hound & Horn* had published Zukofsky's Henry Adams thesis over three issues in 1930, Winters and Zukofsky had locked horns in summer 1931 over Winters's disapproving review of Taupin's *L'influence du symbolisme français*.[20])

Closer to the bone, however, was the "Open Letter to Louis Zukofsky" that Basil Bunting published in *Il Mare*, a Rapallo weekly newspaper, in early October.[21] (In 1931 Bunting and his wife had moved to Rapallo, where he saw Pound on a regular basis.) This "Open Letter" mostly addressed "'Recencies' in Poetry," the preface to *An "Objectivists" Anthology*, but it also expressed Bunting's general distrust of critical abstraction:

> If I buy a hat I am content that it should fit, be impermeable[,] of good texture, and of colour and cut not outrageously out of fashion. If I am a hatmaker I seek instruction in a series of limited practical operations ending in the production of a hat with the least possible waste of effort and expense. I NEVER want a philosophy of hats, a metaphysical idea of Hat in the abstract, nor in any case a great deal of talk about hats.

However knotty his own poetry might be, Bunting was master of a precise, Swiftian plain style in his prose; he distrusted abstraction, and felt that the prose of "'Recencies'" had moved away from anything of possible value to readers of poetry or poets themselves: "these paragraphs about poetry look to me like flights into darkness, away from ascertained or reascertainable fact to speculative mysticism, to a region I think void of anything permanently valuable."[22]

However much he might deride readers who failed to read "4 or 5 times for a meaning," Zukofsky could not deny Bunting's intelligence or goodwill, and Bunting had put his finger on a central paradox of Zukofsky's writing. Zukofsky spent a lifetime attacking abstraction, whether in critical prose or in poetry. He would write a five-hundred-page book on Shakespeare to "do away with all philosophy," and would lament that Wallace Stevens "ruined a good deal of his work by speaking vaguely about the imagination and reality and so on."[23] Nevertheless, the vast majority of Zukofsky's critical prose, from the objectivist manifestos to *Bottom: on Shakespeare* (1963), is marked not merely by tense, crabbed, and clotted syntax, but by relentless intellectual abstraction. It is as if Zukofsky's primary poetic impulse—to condense—when translated to the more expansive medium of exposition, produced prose from which not merely the connectives, but the particulars themselves, had been squeezed.

Zukofsky was in constant touch with Pound, Williams, and Bunting, and his objectivist activities brought him to the attention of another poet, as well. Lorine Niedecker was almost a year older than Zukofsky, the only child of a philandering fisherman father and a deaf mother. She lived with her parents on Black Hawk Island on Lake

Koshkonong, Wisconsin, between Milwaukee and Madison, where she had returned after a brief failed marriage.[24] Some six months after the publication of the "'Objectivists' 1931" issue of *Poetry*, which she had found revelatory, she got in touch with Zukofsky. It was the beginning of a forty-year correspondence and a lifelong friendship. While Niedecker and Zukofsky's relationship began as that of teacher and pupil, Niedecker was always a strong-minded and independent writer—she experimented extensively in surrealist modes, for instance, a style which for Zukofsky had only limited interest—and developed a mature poetics quite dissimilar to Zukofsky's. Niedecker would visit Zukofsky in New York in late 1933, and he would in turn visit Black Hawk Island in 1936. Through much of the 1930s, Zukofsky would send his manuscripts to Niedecker to be typed, and often turned to her as a sounding board for his ideas about work in progress.[25]

. . .

While the salary Zukofsky received from To, Publishers for the latter part of 1931 and most of 1932 was by no means spectacular, at least it was aboveboard, which could not be said for the scheme on which he and René Taupin collaborated from fall 1931 to spring 1932. Taupin seemed headed for a brilliant academic career; *L'influence du symbolisme français sur la poésie américaine* had won a Gold Medal from the Académie Française in 1929, and he now had a teaching post at Columbia University. He suffered, however, from an Oblomovian unwillingness to write. While at Madison, Zukofsky had been feeding Taupin ideas for his second book, *Quatre essais indifférents pour une esthétique de l'inspiration*.[26] In mid-1931, with Zukofsky back from Madison and Taupin anticipating a sabbatical leave from Columbia for spring 1932, the two came up with a "racket." As Zukofsky explained to Pound,

> I will write on [Guillaume] Apollinaire & the period & other loci when I know something about 'em. [Taupin] will appear with me as the author—or the entire author in French (without me) & then I'll 'translate' my work or book into the original English. For which I'll get $50 a month (and, probably, Taupin's other liabilities). *Not a word of this to anyone.*[27]

He did well to counsel silence—news of such an arrangement would almost certainly have cost Taupin his job. (In any event, he would leave Columbia for Haverford later in 1932.)

Zukofsky set to work teaching himself "something" about Apollinaire, and to that end "borrowed" three of the French poet's books for several months from the New York Public Library. Zukofsky's manuscript, *The Writing of Guillaume Apollinaire*, was finished in April 1932.[28] It is impossible to know whether the book's subject— Guillaume Albert Wladimir Alexandre Apollinaire de Kostrowitsky, as he was christened, "Kostro" to his friends—was hit upon by Taupin, suggested by Zukofsky, or arrived at by common agreement. There is little or no mention of Apollinaire in Zukofsky's writing or correspondence before he began the project, but he clearly devoted a great deal of time and energy to the book, reading through all of Apollinaire's principal works and consulting most of the available secondary materials.

Apollinaire, of the same generation as Pound and Williams, had been at the center of the French prewar avant garde, and was perhaps *the* preeminent French modernist poet. Zukofsky's study consisted of three chapters. The first and third discussed Apollinaire's life and works; the second (which Zukofsky called "the first Joyce in French"[29]) was a collage of passages from Apollinaire's writings. Indeed, a very large proportion of the book as a whole—well over half—was direct quotation, just as Zukofsky's Adams thesis, eight years before, had been largely made up of its subject's own words. Zukofsky's book touched upon all aspects of Apollinaire's writing career, occasionally in a leisurely, sometimes impressionistic manner. The primary theme upon which Zukofsky hung his readings of Apollinaire's work was the extent to which the Frenchman's writing was a conscious attempt to come to terms with modernity: the new century, new technologies, new social formations. Throughout his career, Zukofsky would praise poetry that embodied its own time and place. Apollinaire lived in a historical moment of bewildering flux and change, but instead of seeking "fragments" to shore against ruins, he extolled "cette joie de voir choses neuves" [the joy of seeing new things].[30]

He embodied that "joy" in a poetry not of sensibility but of intelligence and objectification, according to Zukofsky. "Connais-tu cette joie de voir des choses neuves?" asked Apollinaire, and Zukofsky replied,

> If one does, writing cannot be a matter of setting down aesthetic principle by way of filling a sketch. Writing becomes the work of making art of an intelligence, of a life, of using an era as an illustration of an emotion, of isolating the mutations and implicit historic metamorphoses of an era to record them.

This is not *quite* a matter of the poet becoming merely a "catalyst" or a "medium," as Eliot implied in "Tradition and the Individual Talent," but of the poet's subsuming his sensibility—in the Romantic sense—in intelligence: "The writing is a period of vibration off the ring of intelligence which is an object. For the intimacy revealed is not Apollinaire's, a reflection's, but that of an intelligence, the fact and a life. The writing down of this intimacy," Zukofsky argued, "has become the cast of forms of his time."[31] In Apollinaire's writing, Zukofsky wrote, echoing his own objectivist rhetoric, "Even sentimentality is objectified as in a Mozart fugue."[32]

Apollinaire could embody his time so vividly, Zukofsky argued, because he shared the spirit and the scientific equanimity of the new discipline of cultural anthropology, whose practitioners saw the differences between cultures not as an indication that one culture was more "sophisticated" or "advanced" than another, but as the result of different historical and geographical circumstance. "Working with the ardor of a good anthropologist," Zukofsky wrote, "Apollinaire recognized the effect of historical processes in every cultural phenomenon and the fundamental sameness of mental processes in all racial and cultural forms as embraced by the intelligence in the present day." Franz Boas, who had come to Columbia in 1893 and founded the country's leading department of anthropology, had argued much the same thing. Zukofsky had attended Boas's class, and clearly the tenets of Boas's "cultural relativism" had been deeply imprinted on him: "It is the quality of their experience, not a difference in mental make-up," Zukofsky paraphrased Boas, "that determines the difference between modern and primitive art production and art appreciation." Apollinaire "studied his race as tho it were 'primitive.'" Recalling his own Columbia discussion of the "poetic undertow" of Henry Adams's writings, Zukofsky wrote, "Apollinaire was a historian (or more specifically an anthropologist) in the same sense that Henry Adams was a poet . . ."[33]

Zukofsky's exposure to cultural anthropology at Columbia had an important impact on him. He would remain interested in the culture and practices of "primitive" peoples: ethnographic details appear in "'Mantis'" (1934) and thirty years later in "A"-18 (1964–1966), and the later movements of "A" are thickly seeded with allusions to non-Western cultures. In some ways, the "graph of culture" that makes up most of *Bottom: on Shakespeare* is a deeply anthropological undertaking. In part, his interest in anthropology was an outgrowth of Zukofsky's own sense of himself as an outsider within the culture he inhabited—in this much like Apollinaire, illegitimate son of a Polish mother and an Italian father, attacked by a French critic in 1911 as a *métèque*, or foreigner (the term was commonly used to single out Jews).[34] In a sense, Zukofsky was writing about himself when he addressed Apollinaire: Like the Frenchman, Zukofsky was always viewing the culture around him with the detached eye of the anthropologist.

One of the primary figures in Apollinaire's work was the *flâneur*, the stroller who wanders the urban landscape, observing. The poem "Zone," for instance, was an extended exercise in *flâneurie*. The *flâneur*, like the anthropologist, was an outsider, an observer, and in Zukofsky's poetry we can read this rhythm of undirected motion and keen, dispassionate observation. It would take Zukofsky a long time to work out fully the implications of his ambivalent relationship to the Western culture in which he was so deeply immersed, but eventually he would come to see his own marginal status as enabling, as giving him a more intimate acquaintance with "myth," the primordial word, than that of his more "scientific" contemporaries. As he scribbled to himself in 1966, thinking about early Greek drama,

> I find that my sense of myth (the word, the murmur of the oldest of my race in the body rather than my contemporaries' science of it) is deeper than their elegant thinking of it—of the blood rather than information of their superego or whatever of it. Comes probably from being a poor man's son & respectful of "knowledge" yet not so

flattered by it as to run out to always *au courant*, "like the Joneses." Of a natural shyness not dazed by advertising, what's the latest. And having only realized this by "catching up" with their information only late in my life—the expression of the primitive is more native to the primitive. . . ."[35]

.   .   .

The argumentation of *The Writing of Guillaume Apollinaire* was more considered, less aggressive than much of the prose Zukofsky had been writing. In terms of its clarity, however, the book was little improved over the tangled densities of "Sincerity and Objectification" or "'Recencies' in Poetry." When Zukofsky sent a copy of the type-script to Pound, Pound replied, "I don't know if it is YOU or René / BUT in anny kase you MUST now at once start on study of technique of FLOW. As I may have said <:> I started after Tacitus and did learn a bit about concentration/ BUT AFTER that you have <one has> to go out for the NEXT step / which is clarity/"[36] Zukofsky didn't seem to get, or want to get, the hint: "clarity, in my handy dictionary," he replied, "has two lines after it, so: ‖. Which means archaic."[37]

Clear or not, *The Writing of Guillaume Apollinaire* satisfied Taupin that his monthly fifty dollars had been well spent. The first and third chapters were printed, under both Taupin's and Zukofsky's names, in late 1933 and early 1934 in the *Westminster Magazine*, and Taupin's French translation was published as *Le Style Apollinaire* in Paris in 1934—again with both men listed as authors.[38] (Most of the French edition was destroyed in a warehouse fire soon after publication.) The second installment of the periodical publication was accompanied by a tart note: "Mr. Zukofsky has used the word *objectivist* but never *Objectivism* in connection with the work of certain poets. He disclaims leadership of any movement putatively literary or objectionist."[39]

.   .   .

For some time, Pound had been encouraging Zukofsky to come to Europe. The greatest obstacle, of course, was money: His young friend's finances remained as tenuous as ever. In August 1932 Pound had sent Zukofsky a check for $112 "on chance," to be used for "transportation (tourist class) to and *from* Europe."[40] Zukofsky was unable to travel that summer, but he was deeply touched by the gesture, and saved the check as a souvenir.[41] As a token of gratitude, he sent Pound a poem:

in that this happening
        is not unkind
it put to
        shame every kindness

mind, mouths, their words
        people, put sorrow
                on
        its body

before sorrow it came
        and before every kindness,
happening for every sorrow
        before every kindness;

Pound had it published in the next issue of *Il Mare* alongside Bunting's Latin translation, which Pound found less "incomprehensible" than the original.[42]

The following summer Pound offered a check once again, and this time announced it as a committee decision: He, Taupin, and Tibor Serly all thought Zukofsky should see Europe.[43] Even Bill Williams, the staunch nativist, felt that Zukofsky ought to go and offered his own hundred dollars: "Take Pound up. Go to Europe as soon as you can. Look around. Make notes. Learn whatever there is to learn over there . . ."[44] Zukofsky acquiesced, and sailed from New York on the *Majestic* on June 30, arriving at Cherbourg six days later.[45]

He spent nine weeks in Europe, beginning with a weeklong tour of Normandy and Brittany with Taupin.[46] Pound had especially urged him to visit Paris, sending along a list of people to get in touch with, among them Fernand Léger, Constantin Brancusi, Jules Supervielle, Hilaire Hiler, Jean Cocteau, Louis Aragon, André Breton, Salvador Dalí, and Max Ernst.[47] Zukofsky was not particularly assiduous in pursuing this visiting list, but he met Léger, saw Hiler several times, and dropped in at Brancusi's studio. The two men hit it off: "I stayed about 2 1/2 hours & he played his phonograph for me, & shook both my hands when I left (still remarking on how I resembled [Raymond] Radiguet & I again saying how much he looked like my father)."[48] Supervielle wasn't unavailable, but Zukofsky met the American poet Walter Lowenfels and the two went to hear Aragon read on the twenty-second; afterwards, the Americans argued the virtues of "proletarian poetry" behind the auditorium.[49] Zukofsky also managed to visit the cathedral at Chartres, familiar to him from Henry Adams's *Mont Saint Michel and Chartres*.

Zukofsky arrived in Budapest, Hungary, on August 7, where he met Tibor Serly, who was visiting family. Serly's relatives made Zukofsky welcome—he ate a "good goulash" at the poorhouse Serly's aunt supervised[50]—and he gave an interview to Pasztor Arpad, a reporter from the Budapest newspaper *Pesti Naplo*. When asked how he was enjoying his vacation, Zukofsky claimed not to be much interested in Europe; he was there "chiefly to meet the master of American poetry and in some sense its father, Ezra Pound." Zukofsky named Williams, Taupin, Bunting, Rakosi, Reznikoff, Rexroth, and Forrest Anderson (who had appeared in *An "Objectivists" Anthology*) as contemporary poets who "have broken with the known, customary, successful, banal forms" of conventional verse. When Arpad pressed him for specifics, Zukofsky explained that "we tend to write an expressive and musical verse rather than a magniloquent one. We seek the plasticity of words and their interrelations and musical connections rather than their denotations. We look for actual beauty (value) and not for atmosphere." As published, the interview was rather dismissive— the reporter didn't conceal his disdain for what he perceived as Zukofsky's aestheticism, his unwillingness to participate in "today's terrific struggle for life or death." Clearly Zukofsky did not fit Arpad's conception of what an American Jewish poet ought to be. Rather than "a socialist agitator, the poet of the longsuffering people who know nothing save the sweatshops of New York," Zukofsky appeared "past and above socialistic problems and class struggles. He has risen to the higher aesthetic and philosophic culture, and to their highest ranks."[51]

From Budapest Zukofsky went to Genoa and was met at the station by Basil Bunting, resplendent in a red jacket, a deep tan, and a piratical beard. The two arrived at Rapallo in time for lunch with Pound and his English wife Dorothy.[52] Zukofsky stayed in Rapallo for two and a half weeks; he was lodged in an "enormous" room in the apartment of Pound's parents (who had retired to Rapallo five years before), and while he was supposed to be eating his meals with Basil and Marian Bunting, Homer Pound's frontierlike hospitality usually persuaded Zukofsky to take breakfast with him and Isabel, Pound's mother, who "held herself like Queen Mary."[53]

Zukofsky had traveled to Rapallo to attend the "Ezuversity," as Pound had come to call it, and he spent time nearly every day with Pound and Bunting, lingering over tea and pastries on the Via Marsala or talking in Pound's study. *The Writing of Guillaume Apollinaire* had not convinced Pound of the Frenchman's significance; he felt that Joyce and Williams had covered the same ground earlier. "Perhaps there are three people who understood your Henry Adams," he told Zukofsky, "but only two will understand your Apollinaire. How do you expect to live?" At Zukofsky's request, Pound read his Canto XXX, which Zukofsky had quoted in "'Recencies'"; played "very fluidly" on the Dolmetsch clavichord in his study; and treated Zukofsky to a few "howls" of the opera he was composing based on the life of François Villon.[54]

Towards the end of August, the Ezuversity had another visitor. Eighteen-year-old James Laughlin IV, an heir to the vast Pittsburgh Jones and Laughlin steel fortune, had just finished his freshman year at Harvard. Summering in Europe, Laughlin wrote Pound on August 21 to inquire as to whether he might visit, he desired "1) advice about bombarding shits like [literary critic Henry Seidel] Canby & Co; 2) sufficient elucidation of certain basic phases of the CANTOS to be able to preach them intelligently"; and "3) to know why Zukofsky has your support." Pound replied by telegram—"VISIBILITY HIGH"—and Laughlin accordingly came.[55] To Zukofsky, the wealthy, six-foot-five-inch young man "looked like a young god . . . very handsome, strikingly handsome."[56] But the two men seem not to have hit it off in August 1933. Laughlin would return to the Ezuversity for extended stays in 1934 and 1935, and at Pound's instigation he founded a publishing house in 1936. Laughlin's New Directions would become Pound's and Williams's primary U.S. publisher. Aside from a few appearances in New Directions' annual anthology, however, Laughlin would never publish Zukofsky.

The rich young Laughlin was malleable in ways that Zukofsky, ten years older and hardened by a good deal of economic adversity, was not. Pound found Laughlin a ready convert to his own favored economic panacea, the Social Credit theory of Major Clifford H. Douglas. Zukofsky, in contrast, had seen the hardships of the Great Depression firsthand, and his reading of Marx had convinced him that the Douglasite fiscal reform Pound so favored was based on a radical oversimplification of economic reality. Pound had been urging Zukofsky to read Douglas, and it is safe to assume that their conversation in Rapallo reverted to Douglas on a number of occasions, given the frequent discussion of Social Credit in their correspondence following Zukofsky's return to the States.[57] But Zukofsky had come to Rapallo to discuss poetry, not economics, and if Pound had hoped to make a Douglasite convert of him, he was disappointed. For his part, Zukofsky had experienced in viva voce Pound's musical verse and swift critical pronouncements, but he had also received a foretaste of the obsessions into which his mentor was rapidly sliding. He left Rapallo at the beginning of September, and on the seventh he sailed back to New York.

.   .   .

The following month Faber & Faber—the publishing firm where Eliot was a director—published Pound's *Active Anthology*, which presented (in Pound's words) "an assortment of writers, mostly ill known in England, in whose verse a development appears or in some case we may say 'still appears' to be taking place . . ."[58] Among the anthology's eleven poets the objectivists were heavily represented: Along with poems by Williams, Oppen, and Bunting, Pound presented a large selection of Zukofsky's work—"Poem beginning 'The,'" "A"-5, "A"-6, and "A"-7. But Pound's comments on Zukofsky's work were far from heartening: "A whole school or shoal of young American writers seems to me to have lost contact with language as language . . . in particular Mr Zukofsky's Objectivists seem prone to this error, just as Mr Eliot's followers tend toward neo-Gongorism." How far was Zukofsky justified, Pound asked, in pursuing a "mathematical" use of language? "I think the good poem ought probably to include this dimension without destroying the feel of actual speech. In this sense Zukofsky's earlier poem ['Poem beginning "The"'] is better than his later ['A']." Pound was adopting a wait-and-see attitude about the direction of Zukofsky's ongoing long poem, neither pronouncing it wholly misguided nor assenting to it *tout court*: "you cannot expect a writer to develop all his merits simultaneously and *pari passu*," he wrote. "I know of no case where an author has developed at all without at least temporarily sacrificing one or several of his initial merits."[59]

By the end of 1933, then, Zukofsky had reached a peculiar point in his career. He was widely published and recognized (Yvor Winters groused that "Mr. Zukofsky has filled more space in the four or five leading British and American literary journals than almost any other writer of his generation"[60]). He had found himself, willy-nilly, cast as the leader of a new poetic movement whose very existence he denied. His work was read by a number of established poets—Williams, Pound, Moore, Eliot—and he had a cadre of poets of his own generation who looked to him as a critical presence—Bunting, Rakosi, Oppen, Niedecker. None of these readers, however, was willing or entirely able to follow the directions in which Zukofsky was pressing his poetry. The modest fame he had won thus far would seem only to reinforce the military connotations of the term *avant-garde*: The soldiers in the vanguard, after all, provide the enemy their handiest targets, and ultimately suffer the cruelest casualties.

Politics and
Poetry 1934–1935

TWENTY MONTHS after the publication of his *Active Anthology*, Pound wrote a "retrospect": "A dislike of Bunting's poetry and Zukofsky's is possibly due to haste.... At intervals, months apart, I remember a passage, or I re-open my volume of excerpts and find something solid. It did not incinerate any Hudson river. Neither did Marianne Moore's when it first (20 years since) came to London. You have to read such verse slowly..."[1] Pound still had little patience for Zukofsky's prose. When Zukofsky sent him a copy of the published *Le Style Apollinaire*, Pound replied, "I thought the Apol less of a g/ d/ bore in print than in typescript, but that doesn't mean I bothered to read it." Pound remained intent on converting Zukofsky to his own economic views, but he was frustrated with Zukofsky's intransigent Marxism, and made his frustrations clear in extravagantly anti-Semitic language: "Seriously, yew hebes better wake up to econ///.... If you don't want to be confused with yr/ ancestral race and pogromd

136

... it wd/ be well to modernize / cease the interuterine mode of life/ come forth by day etc."[2]

Pound did not comment on another prose work Zukofsky had shown him in 1932, "Thanks to the Dictionary."[3] Zukofsky's most experimental work yet, "Thanks" consisted of twenty-nine prose sections, many of which Zukofsky generated by throwing dice and turning to the page of one of a pair of dictionaries—a 1930 Funk and Wagnall's and a 1917 Webster's *Collegiate*—indicated by the result of the throw. That page's words and their definitions would then determine the vocabulary of a given section of Zukofsky's work.[4] The following passage, for instance, derives from page 255 of Webster's, clearly in the early *d*'s:

> Daedal: cunningly formed or working; ingenious; variegated, rich. The daimon does not clog with mire but grows over the daffodil. The bank does not wall the watercourse despite the damage. Happening as the daimon—dalliance or dawk; the dahood bearing red drupes in the southern United States; transport by relays of men or horses. Or the dahlia; and the smudge on the early daguerreotype. Dagon: half man and half fish, the god of the Philistines, trailed with the land mud and wet, his tusks thru the water, and bearing between them a flower. The dairy produces milk; Damascus once produced steel with peculiar markings as well as silks with patterns of flowers; the inhabitants of the rocks fall over the dalles.[5]

More often than not these dice throws landed Zukofsky in the early stretches of the alphabet. In keeping with "Thanks to the Dictionary"'s emphasis on *d* words, and interwoven with the more playful sections of the work (such as that above), were condensed passages from the story of King David in the book of Samuel.

Zukofsky believed the work important: While he did most of the actual writing from 1932 to 1934, he tinkered with the arrangement of the various sections through the rest of the decade.[6] This procedural approach to composition—in Mallarmé's phrase, "ceding the initiative to words themselves"[7]—was a radical alternative to the painstaking "sincerity" that Zukofsky had earlier advocated as the poet's ideal. As always, Zukofsky was fascinated by the constraints and possibilities of *form*. And what was poetic form but a set of more or less arbitrary constraints the poet imposed upon himself? Determining one's vocabulary by a throw of the dice (and surely Zukofsky had Mallarmé's *Un coup de dés* in mind at some level) was nothing more than pushing to extremes the basic principles of form itself.

"Thanks to the Dictionary" was a mark of Zukofsky's continuing interest in the activities of the more radical wing of the international avant-garde, such figures as Gertrude Stein, Marcel Duchamp, and the Dadaists. Tristan Tzara had promoted procedural composition as far back as 1920 in "To Make a Dadaist Poem," where he had encouraged readers to scissor up a newspaper article and transcribe pieces drawn at random from a bag: "The poem will resemble you . . . an infinitely original author of charming sensibility, even though unappreciated by the vulgar herd."[8] By the late 1920s, Tzara, along with Paul Eluard, Robert Desnos, and other members of the emerging surrealist movement, was being published in Eugene Jolas and Elliot Paul's *transition*. *transition* provided a forum for a range of avant-garde projects, including surrealism, collage, automatic writing, and various sorts of procedural poetics. "Thanks" was a direct response to the aesthetics Jolas was promoting; indeed, it seemed to be a deliberate flouting of one of the sentences in Jolas's "Revolution of the Word" manifesto—"THE LITERARY CREATOR HAS THE RIGHT TO DISINTEGRATE THE PRIMAL MATTER OF WORDS IMPOSED ON HIM BY TEXTBOOKS AND DICTIONARIES."[9] Instead, Zukofsky would make art, as rich and strange as anything by the surrealists, that relied precisely on the dictionary's impositions.

The centerpiece of Jolas's editorial project was the serialization of James Joyce's "Work in Progress" (*Finnegans Wake*); Zukofsky at one point referred to "Thanks to the Dictionary" as his own "work in process."[10] Joyce loomed large on Zukofsky's imaginative horizon: The Irish writer was his first great influence.[11] Zukofsky was familiar with *Ulysses* (published in 1922, but banned in the United States until 1933) as early as 1926, when he wrote "Poem beginning 'The'" ("I grew up, so to speak, with *Ulysses*," he would later recall).[12] In 1930 he had written that Joyce was "the brain and conscience . . . of his literary generation," and had traced most of what was interesting in American poetry to either Joyce or Pound. At Madison he had gone through "every word" of *Ulysses* with his student Frank Heineman, and he was aware of the ongoing "Work in Progress," which he contrasted with Stein's work in a footnote to the "Sincerity and Objectification" essay.[13] Joyce's method in *Finnegans Wake*, however, never much appealed to Zukofsky. He was interested not in what one could do with a "Jabberwocky"-like carnival of polyglot portmanteau words, but in obtaining the utmost possible poetic energy by torquing ordinary English words into new combinations.

From 1932 to 1934 Zukofsky encouraged his friend Reisman to prepare a film screenplay of *Ulysses*.[14] In 1934 they contacted Joyce through his son Giorgio, then living in New Jersey. Though not enthusiastic, Joyce seemed amenable to the idea of making a movie of *Ulysses*—"per il cinema sta bene, suppongo" [as for the film all right, I suppose].[15] Joyce received the script in June, after which there was an exchange of letters between Joyce's amanuensis, Paul Léon, and Zukofsky and Reisman. There were problems with the screenplay, Léon explained, and he suggested they take on a third collaborator. Zukofsky believed in his friend's work, and was bullish on a film treatment of *Ulysses*—he suggested Charlie Chaplin to play Bloom, or perhaps Charles Laughton[16]—but in the end nothing came of the project. The time and energy Zukofsky devoted to the screenplay, however, demonstrated that he was well aware of the aesthetic potential of the cinema. He followed Eisenstein's films, and saw cinematic montage as analogous to some of the things he was doing in his own poetry.[17]

. . .

While public interest in the objectivists as a literary movement had fizzled, Zukofsky still believed that coordinated effort among poets could be useful. Obviously, he and his friends did not present an aesthetically homogeneous front, but if they pooled their *economic* means they ought to be able to establish a vehicle to publish their own works. In spring 1933 Zukofsky projected a "writers' syndicate" under the name of "Writers Extant" (W.E.). The group's publications would be funded by the group's members—initially Zukofsky, Serly, and Taupin, though Zukofsky expected Williams and Reznikoff to join shortly—so W.E. would be beholden to no single "angel," as To, Publishers had depended on Oppen. Zukofsky had ambitious plans for this syndicate. He wanted Joyce, Wyndham Lewis, Hemingway, Yeats, and Ford Madox Ford on the advisory board, and hoped to publish volumes that would result in actual profits: a reprint of Arthur Golding's Renaissance Ovid, a Pound-edited anthology of English poetry whose footnotes would present a running critical debate between Pound and Eliot.[18]

Neither Pound nor Williams was much inspired by the idea of Writers Extant, but in October 1933 Oppen, Zukofsky, Reznikoff, and Williams, meeting in the Oppens' Brooklyn Heights apartment, formulated a stripped-down version of W.E.[19] It was called The Objectivist Press (*not* Zukofsky's idea). The pithy statement of purpose was Reznikoff's: "The Objectivist Press is an organization of writers who are publishing their own work and that of other writers whose work they think ought to be read." The press announced as its first publications Williams's *The Collected Poems 1921–1931* and two volumes of Reznikoff's, *Jerusalem the Golden* (poetry) and *Testimony* (prose).[20] Except for the Williams book, which would be underwritten by subscriptions (and ultimately turned a small profit), each author would pay for the publication of his own work. This was fine for those with jobs or annuities: Reznikoff would issue no fewer than four of his own books under imprint over the next three years, and The Objectivist Press published Oppen's *Discrete Series* in 1934. But Zukofsky, who again had no steady source of income, could not afford to bring out his own manuscript, which he was calling "55 Poems."[21]

Zukofsky worked hard to get Williams's *The Collected Poems 1921–1931* into shape, and he worked hard to promote the book. Nonetheless, the two poets' friendship was strained over the abortive project of an opera based on the life of George Washington, which Williams was trying to write with Zukofsky's friend Serly. The project stumbled through much of 1933 and all of 1934, and Williams finally threw in the towel in late 1935. An intense collaboration with Serly and Zukofsky had produced nothing, and had left Williams feeling that his friendship with Zukofsky ought to be a matter not of actual shared labor, but of each man serving as the other's "mirror." "Every year we're different men, Louis, wiser, I hope, if every year shorn somewhat closer to the hide in the matter of what genius we had," he wrote Zukofsky. "Maybe that's a good thing. I think that in our friendship there's much more to come and I for one am in a better position to appreciate it today than I was yesterday. We were too damned close for a while. That's no good."[22]

· · ·

At the beginning of 1933, American industrial production was at half the level it had been before the Crash of 1929; most banks were closed; and thirteen million people were out of work. The American electorate had eagerly responded to Franklin Delano Roosevelt's call for a "new deal" in late 1932, and ousted the Republican Herbert Hoover by a landslide. In his first term Roosevelt infused millions of dollars into the economy through public works programs. Zukofsky was among the many beneficiaries: In January 1934, he began working for Harry Hopkins's Civil Works Administration. The pay was nothing special—as he told Pound, for "6 hrs of continual insult to the intelligence" daily he received nineteen dollars a week—but at least it paid *something*, which was more than could be said of his unpaid labors for The Objectivist Press.[23]

He worked at various projects at Teacher's College of Columbia University, and it was on one of them that he met Celia Thaew. On her desk was a copy of Williams's book of visionary cultural criticism, *In the American Grain*, which she had picked up to read on the subway. Zukofsky, her supervisor, noticed the book and asked if he might borrow it overnight; the next day, he gave her some "other pages of writing" ("A"-7, in fact), and asked if she'd like to look them over. He didn't tell her they were his own work—not, that is, until she told him how she'd been struck by "what seemed a musical structure." At that, "his face lighted up. He beamed all over."[24] They struck up a friendship: Zukofsky invited Thaew to join the office group with which he regularly ate lunch; in turn, she would occasionally invite him to concerts for which she had tickets.

Celia Thaew may not have had Zukofsky's single-minded devotion to contemporary literature—she'd never heard of Williams before buying his book—but in his other area of interest, music, she had much to teach the thirty-year-old poet: She had been formally trained in music, and spent much of her time working with folk dance groups, fife and drum corps, and other school musical societies.

141

CHAPTER EIGHT: POLITICS AND POETRY : 1934–1935

She had been born on January 21, 1913, almost exactly nine years after Zukofsky, but their backgrounds were very similar. Her father, Hyman Thaew (pronounced "Tave"), was born around 1885, and came to the United States from Smilovici (or Samac Valovic) near Minsk in Belarus. His name was a Yiddish variant on the Hebrew *tov*, "good"; the Germanic spelling "Thaew"—"th" for "t," "ae" for long "a," and "w" for "v"—was arrived at with the assistance of some Ellis Island functionary. His brothers sensibly transliterated themselves "Tave."[25] Though Hyman Thaew dreamed of being a rabbi, there was no money to educate him as such. He was a tailor, but a pious tailor, blowing the shofar, chanting the service, and serving as vice president of his Brooklyn shul. Celia, the middle of three daughters, was the family's iconoclast. She wanted to be a musician, and, much against her mother's sense of economy, pursued a college degree.

Celia and Louis's was not a whirlwind love affair but a protracted courtship. They went to concerts together—Leonard Bernstein at Town Hall, for instance, playing Copland.[26] Zukofsky introduced her to his friend Serly and his brother Morris Zukowsky, and eventually they would meet each other's families. They moved imperceptibly into engagement, it seems; forty years later, Celia could remember no formal proposal. Certainly, in later years their friends would find it hard to imagine one without the other.

. . .

In the summer of 1934 Zukofsky was working on an education project whose goal was to gauge adults' learning capacities. The procedure was fairly straightforward: "I started," Zukofsky wrote,

1: with a clean tablet of conscience. This was filled suddenly with examples. I was asked to give my reaction.
2: The procedure continued with another set of examples as nearly similar as possible to the first set. I was told what to see in them, and again asked to give my reaction.
3: The procedure continued, on another day, with still another set of similar examples. I was asked again to give my reaction, and was not always told that this last reaction was a test of my being able to learn after being told how to learn.[27]

The "examples," at least in some cases, were passages of poetry, and Zukofsky was convinced that he could do better than the twenty-year-old tests his supervisors were administering. So he volunteered to work up some "examinations" himself—"For double pay—relief from being tested and time-off to do a test of my own." He was busily gathering "exhibits" when he received a copy of Pound's eccentric "textbook" *ABC of Reading*, which he greeted as a godsend. "I'm doing better than a review by your text," he told Pound. "I'm advertising it in an examination, or rather a series of 'em, I've been preparing over the last few weeks. . . . I wuz workin' like hell getting up my exhibits, when along comes your A. B. C. to verify 'em. Isn't sonny wonnerfull?!"[28]

The *ABC of Reading* was an expanded version of the long essay *How to Read* (1929), which To, Publishers had reprinted in *Prolegomena 1* in 1932. (Zukofsky extravagantly admired *How to Read*, raising some departmental eyebrows in Madison when he used it as a freshman text during his year at the University of Wisconsin.[29]) *ABC of Reading* was an iconoclastic, opinionated "gradus ad Parnassum" that distilled Pound's most important ideas about the art of poetry.[30] The first half consisted of prose apothegms, discussions of the art of poetry, and a set of rather oblique "tests" and "composition exercises" for students. The second half of the book, "Exhibits," was Pound's pocket anthology of the high points of English poetry. It was a scrappy selection: Among forty-eight passages of poetry, from Chaucer to Browning, there were no quotations from Shakespeare or Milton; the Romantics were represented by Walter Savage Landor alone; and Pound's favorite, Robert Browning, stood for the entire Victorian period.

ABC of Reading lent Zukofsky some additional "exhibits" for his own series of adult education tests, and within the next year he began shaping his collection of resonant passages into a pair of anthologies, the more important of which would become *A Test of Poetry*.[31] Zukofsky conceived of *A Test of Poetry* as a teaching anthology, an outgrowth of the work he was doing at Teacher's College. "I believe that desirable teaching," he wrote in his preface, "assumes intelligence that is free to be attracted from any consideration of every day living to always another phase of existence. Poetry, as any other object matter, is after all for interested people." *A Test of Poetry* was neither a historical nor a comprehensive anthology, but a series of comparative exhibits: "readers have rarely been presented with comparative standards to quicken their judgments. . . . To suggest standards is the purpose of this book."[32] The anthology was divided into three sections, each of which had twenty-five "units" of two to four passages of poetry, none of them very long. II.2.a., for instance, presented the same passage from *The Odyssey* in Thomas Hobbes's rather clunky pentameter and in William Morris's effusive fourteeners. II.24.a. juxtaposed the anonymous fifteenth-century "I have a gentil coke" with Williams's "The Red Wheelbarrow"—the basis for comparison, of course, being the chickens the two poems shared.

The three sections of the anthology were parallel, as the Chronological Chart at the back of the book indicated. The passages under a given number in each section were meant to be read with a specific critical consideration in mind: unit 1, for instance, exemplified "translation," unit 5 "measure," unit 6 "sound." The reader would have to consult the Chronological Chart for further information on most of the anthology's selections, however, for Zukofsky purposefully omitted titles and authors' names from the passages he presented in the first and third sections. "If the poems of Part I and III, which have been presented anonymously, interest the reader," Zukofsky wrote, "he should be moved to decide for himself their relative merits, without reference to their authorship."[33]

Zukofsky inherited this "blind" method of presenting material to students from the protocols of the Teacher's College test series.[34] The idea of presenting poetry to students anonymously, to circumvent the stock responses that authors' names elicited, was no doubt influenced by I. A. Richards's 1929 *Practical Criticism*. *Practical Criticism* was based on Richards's evaluation of Cambridge undergraduates' written responses to a set of thirteen poems—some excellent, some flawed, some banal—provided without clues to their authors' names or reputations. By analyzing these "protocols" (as he called the responses), Richards generated a taxonomy of the ways in which supposedly educated young people actually read poems; furthermore, he presented a coherent and compelling argument for the practice of "close reading," an interpretive method that over the next three decades would be institutionalized in American universities.[35]As Richards made clear, even highly trained Cambridge undergraduates often had only the foggiest notion of whether a poem was good or bad. Going one step further, Zukofsky's anthology aimed to provide its readers with standards by which to judge the poem—hence its title: "The test of poetry is the range of pleasure it affords as sight, sound, and intellection. This is its purpose as art."[36]

Such standards could best be demonstrated, Zukofsky thought, through the simple juxtaposition of successful and unsuccessful poetry—a straightforward test indeed. In the middle section of the anthology, however, he obliged his reader to the extent of including brief critical comments on each "unit." The "Comments" are to the point, and often devastating. Of Crabbe's "The Borough" and Wordsworth's "Laodamia": "Readable, honest attempts at good writing, these can hardly be said to have the emotional effectiveness of great poetry." Of Shelley's "An Indian Serenade": "The words are too often carried along in a *lull* of sound (of no intrinsic value) till they lose their connotative meanings. Or, the lines become banal."[37] More interesting are the notes that follow each Comment, and that together form a forceful and pithy anthology of Zukofsky's principles of poetics. A brief selection:

> A simple order of speech is an asset in poetry.
>
> The music of verse carries an emotional quality; when the music slackens, emotion dissipates, and the poetry is poor.
>
> Poetry convinces not by argument but by the *form* it creates to carry its content.
>
> What is foreign to poetry is the word which means little or nothing—either as sound, image, or relation of ideas.
>
> Simplicity of utterance and song go together. Song as musical, poetic form is usually defined by a continuous and complete statement of the words.
>
> Condensation is more than half of composition. The rest is proper breathing space, ease, grace.
>
> As poetry, only objectified emotion endures.[38]

When Pound first saw *A Test of Poetry* in 1950, his comment was "looks like he is following *ABC*."[39] There *are* striking continuities between the two books, not least between Zukofsky's basic test of a poem—"the range of pleasure it affords as sight, sound, and intellection"—and Pound's perennial categories of "phanopoeia," "melopoeia," and "logopoeia."[40] There is also a considerable overlap of material on exhibit: Of the forty-eight passages of poetry in Pound's *ABC*, no fewer than thirteen specific quotations were reused in *A Test of Poetry*. (Indeed, both Pound and Zukofsky concluded that the Scotsman Mark Alexander Boyd's "Fra bank to bank" may be the finest sonnet in English.[41]) Beyond that, many of Zukofsky's critical comments strike one as recast versions of Pound's obiter dicta. Clearly, Zukofsky was working within a Poundian tradition as he compiled his teaching anthology. Just as clear, however, were the conceptual differences between his work and *ABC of Reading*. The *ABC* presented a chronological sequence of exhibits with lengthy commentary, Pound's brief history of the art of poetry in English. "The ideal way to present" these exhibits, he noted, "would be to give the quotations WITHOUT any comment whatever. I am afraid that would be too revolutionary."[42] In *A Test of Poetry*, however, chronological signposts, literary-historical progressions, even great names have all fallen away, leaving the poems alone to be read and evaluated. Zukofsky took Pound's hint, which Pound himself would not follow—"I have learned that in the present imperfect state of the world, one MUST tell the reader"—and ran with it. Zukofsky was simply more inclined to let his material speak for itself, as he had done in the Henry Adams thesis and the middle section of *The Writing of Guillaume Apollinaire*.

. . .

A Test of Poetry was meant as both a statement of aesthetics and a practical teaching tool, and Zukofsky would tinker with it for half a decade before trying to find a publisher. The other anthology he compiled in 1934 and 1935 was a far different creature: *A Workers Anthology*, according to the "Editor's Preface," "illustrates the presence of revolutionary struggle and ideas in some of the *best* poetry of 2000 years."[43] The congruencies and contrasts between the two anthologies are striking. Of *A Workers Anthology*'s thirty-eight selections, over three-quarters were also included in *A Test of Poetry*; Zukofsky was drawing from the same fund of reading and research for both projects. But where *A Test of Poetry* presented its passages in anonymous snippets, juxtaposed one to another according to various critical considerations, *A Workers Anthology* presented its poems in strictly chronological order, from Ovid to André Salmon. In essence, Zukofsky was trying to recover a radical political tradition within the canon of Western literature.[44]

While Zukofsky anthologized poets regularly considered revolutionary prophets—Blake and Burns, most notably—more often he chose work out of a subcanon of poetry that had already met his own aesthetic criteria. *A Workers Anthology* gathered all the passages from *A Test of Poetry* that had any conceivable political application, from Ovid's description of the pre-economic "golden age" in *Metamorphoses* I to the religious hypocrisy of Burns's "Holy Willie's Prayer." Among them were poems of clear political relevance—Burns's "A Man's a Man," Blake's "London," Henry Clay Work's "The Year of Jubilee." But there were also pieces that had talismanic significance for Zukofsky, to which he appended remarkably strained political interpretations. Of the fourteenth-century Anglo-Irish lullaby "Lollai, lollai, litil child": "The cry of the enslaved folk is in these verses, though religion is smothering it." Of Shakespeare's dense lyric "The Phoenix and the Turtle," in which the two birds love one another with such intensity that "Property was thus appalled / That the self was not the same": "cf. Marx's emotional attack on the nationals of property.... Shakespeare, in these verses, seems to have anticipated Marx's irony with greater accuracy than just poetic instinct."[45]

The passages collected in *A Workers Anthology*, Zukofsky argued in the preface, were among the "*best* poetry of 2000 years." Their very excellence served a pedagogical function: "Lenin has said that art must unite the feelings, thoughts and wills of the masses, and awaken and develop the artist in them. The excellence of these selections should help to develop the artist in the worker, and awaken the class conscious artist to the possibilities for excellence in poetry for the masses." Despite the paraphrase of Lenin and the general party-line enthusiasm for the working "masses," Zukofsky's hope that these poems would "develop the artist in the worker" and spur "class conscious" poets to write better was remarkably out of touch with the social-realist trends of left-wing literature of the moment. In *A Workers Anthology*, Zukofsky was doing his best to serve two masters:

the political imperative that writing should serve the cause of the proletarian revolution, and the aesthetic ideals of concision, craft, intellectual density, and musicality he valued in the poetry of the past, regardless of its social intention.

. . .

Zukofsky's Marxism was heartfelt, and sprang at least in part from his own situation as the youngest child of a laborer in the garment industry. From early on, however, Zukofsky's stubborn individualism and his commitment to modernist poetics came into conflict with the regimented structures that dominated American leftist writing of the 1930s. Back in 1925, he had rejected Communist Party membership, according to Whittaker Chambers, because of his unwillingness to accept the discipline to which Party members had to submit.[46] Now he found a similar "discipline" imposed upon those who would write for periodicals on the left.

The most important of these was the journal *New Masses*. The journal had been founded in 1926 as a successor to the *Masses*, a lively leftist periodical edited by Max Eastman and Floyd Dell. Initially, *New Masses* emulated its predecessor's eclecticism, disregarding the dubious political credentials of many of its leftist contributors, even publishing pieces by nonleftists like Pound whose names lent credibility to the magazine's attempt to establish itself as a serious literary journal. By the mid-1930s, however, *New Masses* was hewing more and more closely to the aesthetics of the "Proletarian Realism" espoused by its editor, Mike Gold. Gold had been born Izhok Granich in 1893, in the same Lower East Side neighborhood as Zukofsky, and Zukofsky had met him by the end of the 1920s, though he was little impressed by this commissar of the literary Left. When Pound inquired about Gold, the installments of whose novel *Jews Without Money* had aroused his interest, Zukofsky confessed, "I don't think I've missed anything not seeing more of [Gold] in N.Y.—saw him once anyway. N. Masses a pretty bad best—I'd just as soon have H[ound] & H[orn]."[47]

Gold's idea of what sort of poetry would serve the revolution was straightforward: "Swift action, clear form, the direct line. . . . No straining or melodrama or other effects; life itself is the supreme melodrama. Feel this intensely, and everything becomes poetry—the new poetry of materials, of the so-called 'common man,' the Worker moulding his real world." The poet must eschew "verbal acrobatics": "this is only another form of bourgeois idleness. The worker lives too close to reality to care about these literary show-offs, these verbalist heroes."[48] Gold's *New Masses* promoted a simplifying aesthetic, whose ultimate goal was rhetorical: to *move* the work's reader to political action. The difference between this proletarian realist ethos and *A Workers Anthology*, which aimed to make an "artist" out of the worker or to educate the poet in the potential excellences to be found in (incidentally) class-conscious poetry, could not be more evident. And in his poetry, Zukofsky was nothing if not a "verbal acrobat."

Nonetheless, these were polarizing times, with the capitalist system seemingly on the brink of downfall and two opposed systems—communism and fascism—vying to replace it. Zukofsky felt himself obliged to declare his loyalties. In May 1935 he told Pound that he was applying for membership in the newly formed League of American Writers (an affiliate of the Soviet-sponsored International Union of Revolutionary Writers), among whose goals were to "Fight against imperialist war, defend the Soviet Union against Capitalist aggression," and to fight "against Fascism, whether open or concealed."[49] By the end of the year he was working as an unpaid poetry editor for Gold's *New Masses*.[50]

Zukofsky's only find as a *New Masses* editor was the rather charming political doggerel of Robert Allison Evans. Evans, of Pound's generation, had been a mining engineer for the Lehigh Valley Coal Company, had been sacked for making trouble about the company's business practices, and was now "on relief."[51] *New Masses* printed a double-page spread of Evans's poems in its February 4, 1936, number under the title "From the Anthracite." Zukofsky found Evans's conversation informative and diverting, and incorporated his account of 1935 Pennsylvania mining activism into "A"-8, which he had begun in August of that year.[52] Zukofsky's friendship with Evans would outlast his commitment to the Party. When Evans died in 1943 of oral cancer, Zukofsky wrote a quiet epitaph which began, "Chance broke the jaw of this man / For no will could have done so / To him / Whose life built such good will."[53]

. . .

But how was Zukofsky, in his own writing, working to advance the cause of the inevitable proletarian revolution? The review he wrote of Muriel Rukeyser's 1935 *Theory of Flight*, winner of the Yale Younger Poets competition, had clear political implications.[54] Keeping in mind that "language is a social factor, and as such its main function is to be understood," Zukofsky wrote, "communists, as poets, can do two things":

1. Write the poems everybody can understand—for example, the strike-songs which Miss Rukeyser only mentions;
2. Deal with precise fields of knowledge (science, etc.,) so as to confirm revolutionary theory in sensory values. Communists who specialize in these fields can understand this writing and explain it to the masses who under capitalism obviously find it almost impossible to pursue such fields of study by themselves.

Rukeyser, Zukofsky noted, performed the first of these well enough; she wrote ballads "nicely," if "not so well as [African American poet] Sterling Brown in BLACK WORKER AND WHITE WORKER." But when she attempted more ambitious examinations of the class struggle and its effects on the contemporary mind, her work was too often muddled, hard to follow, "submerged in an uncommonly vague mysticism." She was hampered by "the effete metaphor of Wallace Stevens, and the hazy effulgence of Hart Crane . . ." She ought to remember Marx's words, Zukofsky noted. *"There has been history*. And," he added, "there have been examples of poetic art and invention—technics": the very sort of class-conscious technical examples that Zukofsky had gathered in *A Workers Anthology*.

Zukofsky himself found it increasingly difficult to write "the poems everybody can understand." He had done so nine years before with "During the Passaic Strike of 1926"—"For Justice they are shrewdly killing the proletarian, / For Justice they are shrewdly shooting him dead"—but over the intervening decade even Zukofsky's marching songs had become more and more oblique. It is hard to imagine a workers' glee club deriving any immediate political uplift from "A madrigal for 3 voices":

Hail the tree's meadow
Where the watch
Fees no property . . .

When pigeons greet
Workers meeting –
In the valley
  of the city –
Not a chimney's
  made of putty
And the lampposts
   are high
    high
      and white—or
   red, like
no property of
   night.[55]

The poem is delicate, deft, and funny, and it includes all the correct images—workers, the death of property, the omnipresent "red"—but it is too much concerned with its own technique, its own formation of words to be set to music, to serve as the lyric for any song the average member of the proletarian masses might want to sing.

 If the typical leftist poem of the 1930s was a work that dramatized the state of things under capitalism, that crystallized revolutionary sentiment, that above all sought to *move* its reader to action, it is safe to say that Zukofsky rarely wrote such a poem. While his poems very often treated politics as subject matter, their effectiveness as political interventions was compromised precisely by the complexity of the political role Zukofsky imagined for them, "to confirm revolutionary theory in sensory values." One way of doing that was to quote Marx in the rollicking three- and four-step lines of "Song—¾ time (*pleasantly drunk*)":

   "because the
     weaver has sold
       linen;

  "the distiller
   is only able to
     sell the strong

"waters
    because the
        bible agent has already

"sold the waters
    of
    —
       life;[56]

Another, in "To my wash-stand," was to follow how the poet's morning ritual—washing his hands, observing the broken tiles of the bathroom, noting how the oval mirror reflected his profile like a coin—put him in mind of "the poor":

    so my wash-stand
in one particular breaking of the
    tile at which I have
looked and looked

    has opposed to my head
the inscription of a head
    whose coinage is the
coinage of the poor . . .

    carefully attentive
to what they have
    and to what they do not
      have[57]

The poor were always with Zukofsky—now in his thirties, he was making little more than he had as an instructor in Madison, and much of that went to support his family[58]—and in late 1934 an encounter with a stray insect in a subway station instigated yet another poetic meditation on their plight:

Mantis! praying mantis! since your wings' leaves
And your terrified eyes, pins, bright, black and poor
Beg—"Look, take it up" (thoughts' torsion)! "save it!"
I who can't bear to look, cannot touch,—You –
You can—but no one sees you steadying lost
In the cars' drafts on the lit subway stone.[59]

Nervous, thin, mantis-like himself, Zukofsky was rattled by the insect—"Don't light on my chest, mantis"—despite a newsboy telling him, "it is harmless." Unable to rescue the insect, finding no "safe leaves" in the windy stones of the subway station on which to deposit it, he could see the mantis as a parallel to the lost, vulnerable, separate "poor" around it.

The poem "'Mantis'" begins with the incident in the subway, then plays the poet's observations of the praying mantis against a half dozen other ideas, among them the entomological and biological causes for the mantis's being there; the plight of New York's Depression-era poor; the way that newspapers such as those carried by the boy earned their owners money to build edifices out of stone, like that surrounding the poet in the subway station; Provençal folklore about the mantis; various "primitive" mantis myths; and the mantis's resemblance to an aircraft.[60] The form into which Zukofsky cast all this material was a sestina, a thirty-nine-line Provençal form invented by the troubadour Arnaut Daniel and practiced most famously by his admirer Dante. Instead of using regular rhymes, the sestina repeats in shifting order the words at the ends of each line—in "'Mantis,'" *leaves, poor, it, you, lost,* and *stone*. The six line-end words are shuffled through six different permutations in six stanzas, until Zukofsky addresses the insect once more in a final three-line stanza:

Fly, mantis, on the poor, arise like leaves
The armies of the poor; strength: stone on stone
And build the new world in your eyes, Save it!

Zukofsky was proud of the poem, and immediately sent it to Williams.[61] The doctor was not convinced: "so far as I can tell after a first glance, it seems as tho the form has made you do what you never would have done otherwise: stress too heavily what should have been lightly stressed. . . . I myself dread the implications of a too regular form—our world will not stand it." Williams had put his finger on an uncertainty at the heart of Zukofsky's uses of traditional poetic forms: To what extent had the demands of the form *de*formed the expression of the poet's thoughts? Zukofsky's reply took the form of a free-verse poem, "*'Mantis,' An Interpretation*," over five times as long as "'Mantis'" itself. The poem has as subtitle a phrase of Aquinas's, "*Nomina* *sunt consequentia rerum, names are sequent to the things named*[62]—and it argues that the sestina form, as complex and seemingly arbitrary as it might appear, is ultimately the only form that can capture "The actual twisting / of many and diverse thoughts,"[63] what Zukofsky in "'Mantis'" itself called "thoughts' torsion." From the poem's inception Zukofsky had the sense "That this thoughts' torsion / Is really a sestina / Carrying subconsciously / Many intellectual and sensual properties of the forgetting and remembering Head / One human's intuitive Head."

"'*Mantis,' An Interpretation*" is a bravura performance. It incorporates the misgivings expressed in Williams's letter—"Our world will not stand it, / the implications of a too regular form"[64]—and counters them with a consideration of the history of the sestina, the circumstances of the poem's composition, the sources of "'Mantis'"'s more arcane references, and the poet's general relationship to traditional forms. The overall thrust of Zukofsky's argument is that he is free to use inherited forms, not as experiment or tour de force, but when he feels the form of his experience demands it: "as an experiment, the sestina would be wicker-work—/ As a force, one would lie to one's feelings not to use it." But the "*Interpretation*," despite its attempt to justify why Zukofsky cast a ringingly Marxist poem in a recondite form, leaves the impression that when all was said and done Zukofsky's interests lay more with the challenges of the sestina's formal intricacies than with "the situation of the poor."[65]

James Laughlin would publish both "'Mantis'" and its "interpretation" in 1936 in his first *New Directions in Poetry and Prose* annual. The poems were not published, however, by *New Masses*, or by any other journal associated with the Left. For all Zukofsky's concern with the plight of the poor, and for all his mastery of Marxist social and economic theory, his work was simply unacceptable to those like Mike Gold who demanded clarity and relative simplicity in writing. Personally speaking, Zukofsky was indeed a poet of the Left; but his poetry, while it addressed political and economic issues, was too deeply involved in the linguistic and formal experimentations of modernism to serve the Left's purposes.

.　.　.

On Christmas Day 1935, Zukofsky wrote Pound that "I guess all the 'objectivists 1931' have joined the communist party or are somewhere near it."[66] He was omitting Reznikoff, of course, who placidly continued writing and steered clear of politics. Others of that group, however, were becoming more deeply involved in the struggles of the day—to the detriment of their gifts. Rakosi had come to New York in 1935 to work for the Brooklyn Jewish Family Welfare Society. That same year he joined the Party. Over the course of the decade, he found the demands of social work and his own Marxism, which made him "lose respect for poetry itself," overcoming his desire to write. By 1941 he had ceased altogether.[67] In 1935 George and Mary Oppen also joined the Communist Party. Oppen, a stubborn individualist, had no desire to see his verbal talents put to the Party's uses. He worked for the Party as a labor organizer, not a wordsmith. He would not write another poem for twenty-four years.[68] Of the three, only Zukofsky continued to write through the rest of the decade. And while his commitment to the Left was perhaps more theoretical and less practical than Rakosi's or Oppen's, it would continue to involve him in painful contradictions.

Culture and
Design 1936–1940

T HE YEAR AFTER Zukofsky's death, Celia Zukofsky recalled that her husband had long had "a notion in the back of his head: he wanted to do just one of each particular form, one long poem, one novel, one play . . ."[1] By 1936 Zukofsky had written a considerable body of short poems, a full-length critical work (the *Apollinaire*), a piece of experimental prose ("Thanks to the Dictionary"), and the first seven movements of an epic-length poem. It seemed perfectly natural that, sooner or later, he would turn to the theater.

Much of Zukofsky's literary education had come through plays. When he was a child, his brother Morris had taken him to the Yiddish theater to see the classics of Western drama. A bit older, he had ventured out to the Provincetown Playhouse in Greenwich Village, where the plays of Eugene O'Neill, dramas by the members of New York's avant-garde, and various German expressionist works were being produced. Shakespeare, whom Zukofsky had read through by age eleven, was always a fixture of his intellectual landscape. And

Zukofsky had also been reading continental drama—Apollinaire's *Les mamelles de Tiresias*, Pirandello, and the French surrealists.[2] All of these works contributed to the idiom of *Arise, arise*, the play Zukofsky drafted in the first part of 1936.[3]

Zukofsky chose a bad time to turn to the drama. The Provincetown Players, one of the very few companies that might have considered *Arise, arise*, had been defunct since 1922. As the Depression wore on, there was little money available to produce experimental theater: What the public wanted was Broadway's musical diversions (Cole Porter's *Anything Goes* was the great hit of 1934). The left, through such companies as the Group Theater, was mounting politically aware productions like Kurt Weill's *Johnny Johnson* (1936) and Clifford Odets's rabble-rousing hit *Waiting for Lefty* (1935). But *Arise, arise*, despite its continuous effort at political relevance—"May First" is a repeated reference, the Father quotes the *Communist Manifesto* at one point, and one attendant sings the first verses of the "Internationale"[4]—could only by a great stretch be classified as a political play.

It was instead a family drama, a presentation of Zukofsky's own private anguish in the form of dream theater. The title of *Arise, arise* referred to the "Internationale"—"Debout les damnés de la terre / Debout! les forçats de la faim!" (arise, you damned of the earth, arise, you prisoners of hunger)—but it more immediately quoted John Donne's Holy Sonnet 4:

> At the round earth's imagined corners, blow
> Your trumpets, Angels, and arise, arise
> From death, you numberless infinities
> Of souls, and to your scattered bodies go.

The Son reads these lines to his mother at the play's opening, and that filial reading is the key to the play's themes. In *Arise, arise*, Zukofsky sought to commemorate the lives and lay the ghosts of two women he had loved. His mother had died in 1927, on the day Zukofsky believed was his birthday; the Son alludes to this in the first act of the play—"I never had a birthday till my mother died"—and the Attendant (as Shakespearean "Prologue") says as much two scenes later: "The day she died / Was his birthday, / He could remember it / As her day."[5] Zukofsky's sister Dora Pruss had died in 1913, when Zukofsky was only nine, shortly after the birth of her son Moe.[6] "Dead, the young remain young in the mind," the Son muses, and recalls his sister's wedding, when he was seven: "My sister's wedding took place in another hall, with probably too many relatives around to take care of, because I sat against a pillar and felt very lonely," and "My young mother wore [these earrings] at my sister's marriage, and the dancers—some of them—did not know her from the bride."[7]

Arise, arise is clearly a product of early twentieth-century experimental theater. (Zukofsky would describe the play as "an action which is at the same time a poem."[8]) Like Cummings's *Him* or Strindberg's *A Dream Play* (1902), Zukofsky's play has (in Strindberg's words) the "disconnected but apparently logical form of a dream. . . . Time and space do not exist. . . . The characters are split, double and multiply; they evaporate, crystallise, scatter and converge."[9] The Mother is both alive and dead through the scenes, which shift time frames imperceptibly, as (for instance) from her return from the hospital to the aftermath of her funeral. The Girl is both the Son's lover and his sister. The two black attendants at times speak in clumsy minstrel-show dialect, at others quote poetry and sing along with the final chorus of the *St. Matthew Passion*. The play's dialogue is a mingling of realistic conversation and found materials: Zukofsky embeds most of his translation of Apollinaire's "The Gathering" in the Son's speeches; the Son speaks as prose three lines from the Donne sonnet—"We were all there today, all whom the flood did, and fire, all whom war, death, age, agues, tyrannies, despair, law, chance had slain"; and fragments of Zukofsky's own poems appear in the dialogue.[10] Throughout the whole, music plays in the background: Byrd's "Wolsey's Wild," Mozart's G Minor Symphony, Bach's Fugue in E Minor, the *St. Matthew Passion*.

A cynical reader might take *Arise, arise* as (in the Son's phrase) "a filching poet's [words] which play on two deaths," but that offhand summary underlines how much of his own emotional circumstance Zukofsky confronted in the drama. The Mother and the absent Sister are clearly Chana Zukofsky and Dora Pruss; the Father, with his wry resignation, dovetails squarely with Zukofsky's descriptions of Pinchos Zukofsky. And even the capitalist Aunt—Zukofsky presents his characters with barely a hint of his own impoverished Jewish background—was, according to Celia Zukofsky, based on "a distant relation that had some sort of factory" where Zukofsky's brother and sisters had briefly worked.[11]

The surface political motifs of the play do not mask its real subject: the Son's grief and sense of rootlessness in the wake of his sister's and mother's deaths. "I think I regretted most," he says, "to be alive when those who had meant most to me were dead."[12] Whether or not Zukofsky meant that as a literal transcription of his own grief, the play stood as evidence of Zukofsky's conviction that a human being's happiness, his sense of at-homeness in the world, was bound up with the family relation. This was a conviction that he would not yet express in his more public poetry; it would come to the fore only after he married Celia Thaew and became a father. It is unclear whether Zukofsky made any attempt to get *Arise, arise* produced, but it would not be published for another twenty-six years, and was not performed until 1965.

. . .

As devoted as he was to New York City, Zukofsky enjoyed getting away. In the spring of 1932, he had again visited Irving Kaplan in San Francisco, taking a route that led him through the Southwest (which he commemorated in two poems, "In Arizona" and "Arizona"[13]). In September 1936, he and Reisman went to Wisconsin to visit Niedecker at Black Hawk Island, where Zukofsky was photographed awkwardly horsing around with a pellet rifle.[14] For the most part, however, Zukofsky's finances constrained him to do his traveling—as so many other Americans were doing—at the movies. The interest he had shown in the cinema since at least 1931, when he told Pound that as to "Advertising & montage, Mr. E.,—Eisenstein has nothing on us,"[15] had not at all abated. In early 1936, he attended the Museum of Modern Art's "Survey of the Film in America," where he saw an assortment of early silents by D. W. Griffith and Charlie Chaplin, *A Fool There Was* with Theda Bara, *The Fugitive* with William S. Hart, and Ben Turpin's *Clever Dummy*.[16]

These movies, along with the Soviet and surrealist cinema Zukofsky knew, paled in comparison with the fully achieved art of Chaplin's *Modern Times*, which Zukofsky saw early in 1936. He was immediately and enthusiastically recommending the film to his correspondents. "Please go see it," he told Niedecker: "[Chaplin's] problem was ours and he solved it, singing himself into modern times, making an art of his own tradition, & remaining Chaplin &"—in René Taupin's words—"notre Chaplin international." "That's *action* (*not* acting)," he told Pound, "& the local bastudly press is trying to minimize it by speaking about the ole sentimental Charlie etc."[17] By the middle of March, Zukofsky had completed an essay on Chaplin's film, a commentary on the art of the cinema and its place in the contemporary political struggle.[18]

In 1936, Charlie Chaplin was the world's most popular film actor and was increasingly recognized as an auteur of genius. His previous movie, *The Gold Rush* (1931), had been hailed as a masterpiece; *Modern Times* was, if anything, even more widely praised. The movie was both a comedy and a powerful commentary on the contemporary economic and political scene. Over the course of the film Chaplin, in his familiar persona of the Little Tramp, is subjected to an absurdly accelerating assembly line, becomes the guinea pig for a monstrous "eating machine" that would allow management to eliminate workers' lunch hours, finds himself—wholly inadvertently—carrying a red flag at the head of a crowd of marching protestors, is arrested for accidentally throwing a brick at a strikebreaking policeman, and decides that the spartan comforts of prison are preferable to the hardships of Depression-era America. The scene is always, as Zukofsky emphasized, an *American* one, so that the film becomes not just "international" humor (the Little Tramp, in previous features, could as easily have been a Cockney) but immediately relevant social commentary.[19]

The essay "Modern Times" aimed to pin down precisely what made Chaplin's art so effective in *Modern Times*, and it did so within the context of an overview of cinematic history. Zukofsky referred to the films shown at the Museum of Modern Art's "Survey," to Chaplin's own previous movies, and to a wide variety of other pictures, surrealist—Buñuel and Dali's *Un Chien Andalou*, Cocteau's *Le Sang d'un Poète*, René Clair's *À Nous la Liberté* and *Le Dernier Milliardaire*—and Soviet—Blokh's *A Shanghai Document*, Pudovkin's *Life is Beautiful*, Eisenstein's *Ten Days that Shook the World*. Zukofsky was fascinated with the developing techniques of the cinema and showed some familiarity with its technical terms; what impressed him most about Chaplin was that the director was "not taking his career as a standstill for a display of personal sensitivity, charm, or whatever," but was using his skills to keep abreast of changing cultural and technological realities: "Charlie in the past yoked himself to the world, and now lives and works in this age of gears."[20]

Chaplin's art, which was too often dismissed as mere "comedy," had entered the realm of materially aware *satire*: "Charlie's devices and 'types' live with material thoughtfulness and thus historical meaning," Zukofsky wrote, and therefore "a new idea in a Chaplin film is not merely a notion, a general sense of today, or an understanding of politics, art, life or whatever, but inventive existence interacting with other existence in all its ramifications: sight, hearing, muscular movement, coordination of all the senses acting on the surrounding world and rendering it laughable."[21] For Zukofsky, Chaplin was a major modernist artist.

. . .

Zukofsky saw a good deal of Carl Rakosi, who was now in New York. Rakosi was something of a small-town boy in the big city, and Zukofsky enjoyed showing him its cultural resources—the museums, the movies, and (when he could afford it) the restaurants.[22] In the spring of 1938 Basil Bunting arrived in New York, carrying a sextant and sporting "yeoman muscles" from a year of living alone on a six-ton sailboat, wandering around the coasts of England. Bunting's marriage had ended in 1937, and when he came to the United States the next year, he was looking for work. Zukofsky's best suggestion was that Bunting might work for Lorine Niedecker's father, who seined carp; Henry Niedecker, however, saw no place for a second man in his business, which was suffering the effects of generally fallen markets. Bunting rattled around New York until that summer, when he got a job captaining a rich man's schooner. He would hasten back to England in late 1939 after the declaration of war between Great Britain and Nazi Germany.[23]

. . .

The New Deal and its various organs would support Zukofsky—with only one short interruption—from January 1934 to April 1942. He was by no means alone: Roosevelt's initiatives, despite the derision they received in some quarters,[24] saved an extraordinary number of intellectuals, artists, and ordinary working people from starvation. Zukofsky's work with the Columbia CWA projects lasted through the first part of 1935. For the rest of that year he worked as a "feature and continuity writer and special researchist" for the municipal radio station WNYC under the auspices of the Works Progress Administration.[25] In early 1936 he was hired by the newly founded Federal Arts Project (also a WPA program) to write for the Index of American Design. An unprecedentedly ambitious project, the Index set some six thousand artists and writers to work preparing visual records of the objects produced by American crafts and scrupulously researched essays on the history and traditions of those crafts. The Index aimed to be, in Zukofsky's words, "a graphic survey of American decorative arts and crafts from the earliest colonial days to the beginnings of large-scale production."[26]

In his half decade of work on the Index, Zukofsky produced a substantial body of writing on American design: four full-length essays (some 135 typescript pages), eight complete radio broadcast scripts (eighty-seven pages in manuscript and typescript), and over forty pages of detailed notes for three more.[27] The subjects he treated—ironwork, tinware, kitchenware, carpentry, friendship quilts—were as far removed as could be imagined from the "high" art that had hitherto engaged his critical imagination. There is little indication that Zukofsky found the work at all congenial, at least initially. Indeed, he told Pound in late 1936 that he would have preferred a job with the Federal Writers' Project, which was employing the 1931 "objectivists" Kenneth Rexroth and Harry Roskolenkier.[28] (Niedecker would work for the Writers' Project from 1938 to 1942, helping compile one of the WPA's regional guides, *Wisconsin: A Guide to the Badger State*.[29])

But uncongenial jobs, in the hands of a writer of genius, have a way of turning out to be more than mere piecework. Samuel Johnson's *Lives of the English Poets*, a series of prefaces commissioned by a bookseller, was a founding document of the genre of literary biography;

Stéphane Mallarmé wrote *Les Mots anglais* (1877), a little handbook on English philology, for an educational publisher, yet the work contains some of the French poet's most fascinating observations about the properties of poetic sound and the nature of language. Zukofsky's writing for the Index of American Design showed the hand of the poet who had written the careful, concrete observation of "To my wash-stand," and the objectivist who would insist that the poet is "a craftsman who puts words together into an object."[30]

Although he had been friends for some years with Russel Wright, one of America's most prominent designers, his work for the Index was Zukofsky's first exposure to the detailed history of American handicraft traditions. The four full-length essays he completed for the project—on ironwork, chalkware, tinware, and kitchenware—include histories of the technologies and traditions of each handicraft, thumbnail biographies of the most prominent craftsmen, descriptions of the objects being illustrated by the Index's artists, lists of prominent examples of each craft available in various collections, and extensive bibliographies. Much of this, obviously, was library work, but there were also research trips around the city, like the one Zukofsky made in November 1936 to interview Thomas Hicks, General Blacksmith and Toolmaker, in the Bronx, or the trips he made to a nautical instrument shop at 69 Pearl Street, "in the heart of the shipping district," to research the "Binnacle Figure" radio script.[31] The protocols of the Index article prescribed fairly closely what information Zukofsky's essays needed to present, and left little room for imaginative digression. Nonetheless, he was able to insert bits of poetry. In "Ironwork, 1585–1856," he translated the stove inscription "Baron Stiegel ist der Mann / Der die Ofen Machen Kann," using a wry "Briticism": "Baron Stiegel is the cove / who can make an iron stove." In "American Tin Ware" he transcribed several eighteenth-century poems dealing with the tinsmith's trade.[32] None of them rose above the level of amusing doggerel, but they served, as did the anonymous ballads Zukofsky had collected in *A Test of Poetry* and *A Workers Anthology*, as "definite information on the subject dealt with."[33]

One of the "considerations" explored in *A Test of Poetry* was "anonymity," which was closely entangled with "the serious conviction and the almost unexplainable completeness of the art of simplicity out of which all folk poetry is made. Such poetry is not the property of the few 'arty,' but of everybody."[34] Like the ballads in Zukofsky's anthologies, most of the products of American design he described sprang from anonymous sources: "the majority of craftsmen who worked in tin remain anonymous. There exist only the wares they made and some few traditions connected with these . . ." Zukofsky wrote about the lives and careers of named craftsmen; most of the articles he discussed, however, were by their very nature anonymous, objects made for household use rather than aesthetic contemplation. Their nameless makers lived on through the objects themselves. As Zukofsky puts it in his first radio script, in what could serve as an epigraph to the whole of his Index writings, "In objects which men made and used, people live again. The touch of carving to the hand revivifies the hand that made it."[35] This emphasis on the made object before its maker, on the objectlike poem over the designing poet, had been a constant center of Zukofsky's thought since the objectivist days. The anonymous was Zukofsky's answer to Romanticism's heroizing of the poet, his assertion that the lasting value of humanity's makings lay in the care and craft manifested in the made object itself, rather than in the biography of its maker.

By late 1939, Zukofsky was writing radio scripts for "The Human Side of Art," a series of programs on station WNYC intended to publicize the Index's activities. The broadcast format demanded liveliness and human interest rather than the masses of information presented in the essays. In each of the scripts, Zukofsky presented himself as the Index's expert on various craft traditions or objects, interviewed, in a supposedly off-the-cuff manner, by an unnamed interlocutor. (All of this "spontaneous" material—the jokes, the interjections—was scripted in advance by Zukofsky, and comes across on the page as rather leaden.) Each interview aimed to present research on a given topic in an entertaining and easy-to-grasp manner, and Zukofsky took a number of approaches to this popularizing goal. "American Tinsmiths" presented diverting anecdotes of the lives of those craftsmen, and featured Zukofsky reading ("in character") some of the poetry he had quoted in the long essay "American Tin Ware." "The Henry Clay Figurehead" was a historical mystery story, speculating on whether a polychrome figure of the statesman Clay was an actual ship's figurehead or the "totem" of a Poughkeepsie "Henry Clay" political club.[36] And "Carpenters of New Amsterdam" was largely a series of droll tales about Dutch carpenters' drinking habits.

Even in the radio scripts, Zukofsky aimed to make larger connections. This is nowhere more evident than in "A Pair of New York Water Pitchers." In 1817 these silver pitchers were presented "by the Manumission Society of the State of New York to Joseph Curtis" as a testimonial to his work on behalf of the abolition of slavery in that state. After his first description of the pitchers, Zukofsky explains the history of slavery in the northern states. But the script takes an unexpected turn, and Zukofsky begins discussing a "brand of slavery" of which "History has minimized the evils . . . by giving it another name—indenture." The maker of the pitchers, one Joel Sayre, was likely related to Paul Sayre, a runaway indentured servant "advertised for in the *Connecticut Courant and Weekly Intelligencer* of Hartford, May 9, 1780." While indenture had the form of a contract, Zukofsky implies, it differed from outright slavery only in its limited term of service. Both forms of bondage, in Zukofsky's Marxist analysis, represent "means by which the growing mercantilism of the seventeenth and eighteenth centuries employed government sanction to transfer labor to undeveloped colonies." The passage following this, which Zukofsky deleted from the manuscript (perhaps at a supervisor's behest), was even more overtly Marxist in tone:

> Advocating the theory that wealth consists not in labor and its products, but in the quantity of hard gold and silver in a country, mercantilism encouraged mining and importation of these metals by the state and the exportation of goods as well as people who make them. It sought to increase national rather than common individual interests, and as such especially influenced the legislative policy of Great Britain. The first extensive use of indenture, as of modern slavery, occurred in the British colonies.[37]

Products of American handicraft could also testify to historical moments when labor was not yet alienated from its products. In the "collectively managed" Shaker and Amana communities of the mid-nineteenth century, a "tradition of craftsmanship" persisted while the rest of the nation became increasingly dependent on manufactured goods. Zukofsky's nostalgia for such collective labor existed in tension with his admiration for the individual artist-craftsman, like the furniture maker Duncan Phyfe. Phyfe's work, characterized by "curves so slight as to escape detection, not geometrical curves, but free hand lines based on the geometrical," represented the best of eighteenth-century aesthetics to Zukofsky: Phyfe's "art, like his time, was given over to order and freedom, simultaneously as it were." Phyfe himself, though the foremost furniture maker of his time, sought a certain anonymity: "All his life he refused to sit for a daguerreotype, so that posterity owns no portrait of him. For that," Zukofsky wrote, "we must look again at the Index plates illustrating the characteristic reeded legs, wing trimmings, stamped brass handles . . . and other distinguishing marks of his furniture."[38] The craftsman would best be known by the object made.

Zukofsky would never publish what he wrote for the Index of American Design, though at one point he would contemplate writing *A History of American Design*.[39] Nor did the Index itself quite come to fruition. None of the radio scripts he prepared was ever broadcast; the periodical and book publications of Index material would only occur decades later; and the Index itself was shut down in early 1942, shortly after the United States entered the Second World War.[40] But the Index work confirmed Zukofsky in a certain mode of cultural analysis. He had already learned from Henry Adams's *Mont Saint Michel and Chartres* how important the close examination of artifacts could be to the cultural historian. Zukofsky's Index writings fit within a tradition of cultural criticism that began with Ruskin and descended without interruption to Pound, a tradition that viewed the whole of a given human culture as a totality: The overall "health" of a culture, then, could be diagnosed from a single manifestation of that culture, a single artifact or act of making.[41] Ruskin's analysis of a wrought iron railing at the beginning of *The Crown of Wild Olive*, or his discussion of the "barbarous black lettering" of a legal document in *Fors Clavigera*, were examples of the same principle of cultural criticism that allowed Pound to assert that "finer and future critics of art will be able to tell from the quality of a painting the degree of tolerance or intolerance of usury extant in the age and milieu that produced it."[42]

As well, there is at work in Zukofsky's Index writings a political aesthetic akin to that underlying Walter Benjamin's massive

Passagen-Werk (a project precisely contemporary with Zukofsky's). Benjamin aimed to construct, out of a vast and characteristically modernist montage of texts and images, a cultural history of nineteenth-century Paris. No object or quotation was too small or insignificant to be considered, for he saw each of them as "ur-phenomena," microcosms in which the seeds of their own future were visible.[43] Zukofsky did not know Benjamin's project (which was only published in 1982), but he no doubt would have found it deeply provocative. Perhaps it would have pushed forward more decisively the Index writings' first tentative gropings at a cultural history, gropings that would finally take shape in *Bottom: on Shakespeare*'s "Graph of Culture" twenty years later.

. . .

Through the second half of the 1930s, Zukofsky carried on a running epistolary debate with Pound over issues of economic theory, a debate that sometimes resulted in verbal violence on both sides. In May 1935, Pound attacked Zukofsky ("You bloody buggaring fool," the letter begins) for holding to the Marxist doctrine that labor was a commodity: "Have you not even sense enough to USE A WORD with a meaning and let the meaning adhere to the word. A commodity is a material thing or substance / it has a certain durability. . . . I suppose it comes of being a damned foreigner and not having bothered to learn english. . . ."[44] Zukofsky responded in kind: "Yr. English language (private pauperty!)! It's like your 'call me a liberal and I'll knock yr / constipated block off,' like the line in a Fascist play we've heard about—'when I hear of culture, I cock my gun!'" Pound, "dizzy with the sweet sound of the Wop tongue," had ignored the words of his own Canto 13: "forgetting Kung's advice to the old guy on the road pretending to be receiving wisdom, You seem to think you are the Messiah."[45]

At times their exchanges were almost ludicrous, as when Pound wrote Zukofsky in June 1936, asking for Pinchos Zukofsky's opinion on the Levitical laws regarding usury.[46] The two men remained on writing terms, though Zukofsky's patience must have been sorely strained. He expressed his ambivalence in an April 1938 letter to the communist poet Walter Lowenfels: for all of Pound's "vile political mess," there was a Chinese Canto in the *Fifth Decad of Cantos* (1937) "which wd. give me a secret pang if I had to shoot him down, & no doubt he's provoked both reactions solidly enough. I'll probably say pardon me, & shoot him anyway."[47] On some level Zukofsky still viewed Pound as an artistic father—"Papa," as "sonny" addressed him in many letters.

While Zukofsky would try to reason with Pound's increasingly virulent anti-Semitism or debate it through ironical repartee, it was Bunting who saw it for what it was, and said so. Back in 1935, Pound had written Bunting that Zukofsky's work had ceased evolving, but that Zukofsky had no interest in improving it: "he wants to argue about how good his defects are, and like every other god damn KIKE (this is not for transmission) he wants to put it over, and have others admire it."[48] In late 1938, Zukofsky showed Bunting a letter he had received from Pound that began with a resounding slur, blaming German anti-Semitism on the Jews themselves: "Why curse Adolphe [Hitler] / why not git down to bed rock / NESCHEK [Hebrew: the 'bite' of usury] and the buggaring vendetta of the shitten Rothschild which has run for 150 years / and is now flopping back on jewry at large/."[49] Bunting responded in a heated letter to Pound: "Every anti-semitism, anti-niggerism, anti-moorism, that I can recall in history was base, had its foundations in the meanest kind of envy and in greed. It makes me sick to see you covering yourself with that filth. . . . To spue out anti-semite bile in a letter to Louis . . . is uncommonly close to what has got to be called the behaviour of the skunk."[50] Pound, writing Zukofsky, dismissed this as a "Lot of hot steam from Bzl."[51] Zukofsky's response was measured: "your letter," Zukofsky wrote,

> which offended Basil because he feels I'm a very Jewish Jew, which I don't feel, was written to me. It was none of his business to take it upon himself etc, but I admire him for having done it, whatever reservation I may have as to the usefulness of his actions. He thinks it may lead you to think again. Frankly, I don't. . . . As for yr. anti-semitism I believe you're no more anti- than Marx himself, tho' the cluttered mess of the rest of yr. economic & political thinking makes it appear so.

He sent Pound "the first two stanzas of a canzone"—"A"-9: "if there's poetry in <it>, you'll see it, I believe. Some insights a man never loses.—But let's not correspond about politics etc."[52]

. . .

Zukofsky's relationship with the American literary Left was no more satisfying. He was doing unpaid, part-time work for *New Masses*, and he was a member in good standing of the Soviet-sponsored League of American Writers. (He was invited to be on the editorial board of the League's abortive periodical, *American Writing*, and in July 1938, at Zukofsky's insistence, the League reversed its rejection of Robert Allison Evans's membership application.[53]) But Zukofsky was of limited use to the revolution. In part, he was tainted by his association with the fascist Pound. In a 1935 *New Masses* review of Reznikoff's *Separate Way*, the leftist poet Norman Macleod lamented "that a man of Reznikoff's caliber should be forced to descend to publication by the Objectivist Press, an outfit controlled by that consummate ass and adulator of Herr Ezra Pound (Heil Hitler and may all his descendents descend), Louis Zukofsky."[54] Back in 1933, Zukofsky could tell Pound "that as far as [the Communist Party was] concerned papa [Pound] & childt [Zukofsky] & Unk Bill Walrus [Williams] are in the same boat"[55]; but as the Depression wore on and the rise of Nazi Germany made another war seem more and more inevitable, Zukofsky felt increasingly impelled to lend his energies to the class struggle, and his closeness to Pound had irremediably tarnished his left-wing credentials.

In the latter part of the decade Zukofsky found himself caught up in a debate within the Left over the *uses* of poetry, and over whether the poet ought to tailor his or her aesthetic for a specific audience. Zukofsky was unwilling to lay aside his ideal of a complex, intellectually sophisticated poetry in favor of the simple-minded exhortation recommended by men like Mike Gold. "Proletarian realism," Gold wrote, "is never pointless. It does not believe in literature for its own sake, but in literature that is useful, has a social function. . . . Every poem, every novel and drama, must have a social theme, or it is merely confectionary."[56] Zukofsky's poetry certainly had a "social theme": "A"-8, which he labored on from 1935 to 1937, and the first half of "A"-9, which occupied the rest of the 1930s, were deeply Marxist poems. But they were dense, difficult, challenging even to readers familiar with the innovations of modernism, and incomprehensible to the rank-and-file worker.

Gold, Zukofsky told Pound, was a "confused shit-head."[57] Zukofsky argued that his own aesthetic touchstones—the critical writings of Longinus and Dante, for instance—*already* followed a logic identical to the materialist thinking of Marx and Engels.[58] The key, as he had suggested in *A Workers Anthology*, was not to write *down* to the worker, but to remain as true as possible to one's own aesthetic, in hopes that the worker would be raised to understand it. This at least was Zukofsky's argument in a "poetry discussion" at a June 1937 League of American Writers conference, where the question was debated among Zukofsky, Horace Gregory, Rolfe Humphries, Genevieve Taggard, and others. Following the conference, Zukofsky was able to read a stretch of "A"-8 for radio station WOR's League-sponsored writers' program—"& for the first time over the air the words of Marx"—which the poem liberally quoted—were "given more time than ever before."[59] This was another difference between Zukofsky and most of the literary communists of the day: With typical scholarly devotion, he preferred to get his Marxism from the source. His letters to Pound and his poems of the period are littered with quotations from Marx, Engels, and Lenin.

Such a nuanced Marxism—drawing as well on Aristotle and Duns Scotus—made little headway in the rough-and-ready, hortatory world of leftist publishing. In the latter part of the 1930s, *New Masses* published only two poems of Zukofsky's, brief excerpts from "A"-8; one, under the title "The Labor Process," was the piece he had read on the radio; the other, "March Comrades," was a wholly uncharacteristic May Day marching song.[60] These were his only periodical publications between 1935 and 1941. Harriet Monroe had died in 1936, and the new editors of *Poetry* were by no means enthusiastic about Zukofsky's work. Most of the little magazines and small presses had succumbed to the Depression. Only James Laughlin's New Directions, with an enormous steel fortune behind it, remained. Williams, a New Directions author, pressed Laughlin to publish "A".

"It can't sell," he wrote Laughlin, "but may bring the press a certain distinction.... there are moments in it of distinction unique in modern writing."[61] Laughlin heeded Williams's advice; "A"-8 appeared in *New Directions in Prose and Poetry 1938*, the third of his annual anthologies, and he announced plans to publish the whole of "A" upon its completion. (He also described the poem in the contributors' notes as an "epic of the class struggle," a description that still irritated Zukofsky fifteen years later.[62]) When the poem would be finished, however, not even Zukofsky had any idea.

. . .

"Let's not correspond about politics," Zukofsky had written Pound in January 1939; Pound replied sarcastically—"Yes. Yes. let us continue. Zucco vi prego. Will write when the days lengthen to 30 hours"[63]—and, no doubt to Zukofsky's relief, was true to his word. Zukofsky saw Pound in person (for only the second time) that spring, when Pound made a three-month visit to the United States in hopes of averting the European war he saw on the horizon. Even Pound's grand chutzpah could not obtain him an interview with Roosevelt, but he spoke to several senators and the secretary of agriculture; none of them was converted to Social Credit, however, and to that extent the visit was a failure.[64] In New York, he held court in Tibor Serly's apartment, where Zukofsky visited him. They spoke—doubtless to Zukofsky's regret—of politics. When Pound praised the radio speeches of the anti-Semitic Father Charles Coughlin, Zukofsky could only say, "Whatever you don't know, Ezra, you ought to know *voices*." "I told him," Zukofsky recalled later, "that I did not doubt his integrity had decided his political action, but I pointed to his head, indicating something had gone wrong."[65]

The two men did not resume their correspondence until early the next year, when Zukofsky asked Pound to recommend him for a Columbia-sponsored research fellowship so that he could return to his project of ten years earlier on Thomas Jefferson's style.[66] In the intervening year, Zukofsky's situation had changed radically. On August 20, 1939, he and Celia had gone down to Wilmington, Delaware, where they were married by a rabbi named Henry Tarvel. In New York City, couples hoping to be married were required to take a blood test for syphilis—the Wassermann test—which Zukofsky refused to undergo. He was also hoping to avoid New York's requirement of a religious marriage ceremony, but in Wilmington the couple discovered that they would have to find a rabbi after all; at least the phone book held a name propitiously close to the bride-to-be's Thaew.[67] Bunting sent his jesting congratulations:

> Welcome then to the great fraternity of the married. Not that I have any high opinion of conjugal bliss in recent years. However, since you are both Jewish, therefore tenacious, you will probably make a better shot of it than I did. . . . At least, it makes Celia's surname spellable. . . . When Ole Ez found me and Marian drinking German beer to celebrate two completed years of it, he bade us cheer up, the first seven years are the worst. I pass on the good news. . . . Milton wrote his tract on divorce during the honeymoon with his first wife. I await Louis' next production with interest.[68]

Pound, when he heard the news, quoted Tennyson: "Ring out wilde Bells (or ballz)[.] I trust Celia is content with you."[69] Soon after getting married, the Zukofskys moved to an apartment in the Bronx, overlooking the Bronx River and so near the zoo that they could hear the big cats roaring for their meals on weekend mornings.[70]

By 1939, Zukofsky had begun to lose his taste for left-wing politics. Marx was clearly still one of his intellectual lodestones—as evidenced by his centrality to the first half of "A"-9—but it had become increasingly hard to put up with the bloody mess that live "Marxists" had made of the master's doctrines. The Moscow show trials of 1936 through 1938, when Stalin purged his party of the very members who had brought him to power, drove countless American communists from the Party. (Zukofsky, though not a Party member, at least initially found Stalin's actions regrettable but necessary.[71]) Stalin's non-aggression pact with Hitler of August 1939, which opened the way for the Nazi invasion of Poland, proved the moral bankruptcy of Soviet communism to all but the most hardened sectarians—people like the Party members who ran *New Masses*. Zukofsky continued to associate with left-wing writers and literary groups through the end of the 1930s, but after completing the first half of "A"-9 in April 1940 he would never again attempt to explain history, or forecast its course, in Marxist terms.

. . .

Thus, circumstances directed Zukofsky's attention, as registered in the short poems he wrote in the last part of the 1930s, away from the political towards the personal, the realms of romantic and familial love. Already, he had begun thinking of these new poems—clearly separate in his mind from his still unpublished first collection, 55 *Poems*—under the title "Anew," a reference to Dante's luminous account of the history of his love for Beatrice, *La Vita Nuova*, "the new life." Seven weeks after his marriage Zukofsky drafted a poem of pure erotic abandon that far surpassed the awkward expressions of desire he had written early in the 1930s:

> Drive, fast kisses,
> no need to see
> hands or eyelashes
> a mouth at her ear
> trees or leaves
> night or the days.[72]

A little over a week later, he wrote a delicate epithalamion for the wedding of his nephew, Moe E. Pruss, the son of his dead sister Dora: "Joy / On their wedding // Love tomorrow / Loved today."[73]

Zukofsky's marriage to Celia Thaew signaled the beginning of an almost forty-year collaboration between the two, a collaboration that went far beyond Celia's typing her husband's manuscripts or answering his mail when he was ill. Perhaps most crucially, while Zukofsky had been obsessed with music and "musical form" for some years, Celia was a trained musician, one who could interpret the scores Louis could not read, and who could lend actual music to his words. Their first collaborative work was "Motet," Celia's four-part vocal setting of Zukofsky's obscene little squib on "General Martinet Gem," who, as "A"-8 told it, "mobilized and reviewed / At the Invalides / A parade of 80,000 tiny metal warriors to-day."[74] Knowing his friend's love of music and his often phallic humor, Zukofsky enclosed a copy of the setting in his January 3, 1940, letter to Pound.

After so many years of drifting from one job to another, from rented room to rented room, Zukofsky had now achieved a new stability. It was time to take stock, to assess his body of work and go about the business of getting it published. In June 1939, he collected and had typed his critical essays, under the title "Sincerity and Objectification," clearly hoping to find a publisher for them.[75] He was also circulating *A Test of Poetry* to various publishers, without success.[76] One publisher told him, "We were tempted by the idea of publishing so unusual a book but our commercial sense got the better of us, even if it is not 'sense.' We can't believe there would be enough people who would take advantage of the opportunity this book affords to give oneself an education in the understanding and enjoyment of poetry."[77]

While he was not diffident about the merits of his writing, Zukofsky viewed the business of publishing and promoting that work with some distaste. In Celia Thaew he had found a partner of unusual stubbornness and persistence, a companion who was determined that her husband's writing should be protected, published, and promoted by whatever means necessary. The first fruits of their partnership came in November 1940, when the two of them issued a privately printed edition of *First Half of "A"-9*. It was a modest publication, forty-one pages typed and mimeographed in an edition of fifty-five copies—just enough to secure copyright. But it was Zukofsky's first "book" publication since the French edition of *Le Style Apollinaire* in 1934; it was the first book to appear with his name alone as author; and it was a harbinger of more to come.

"A"-8 and *First Half of "A"-9*

ZUKOFSKY HAD WRITTEN the first seven movements of *"A"* in a few relatively brief bursts. When those movements were completed, however, he began reconsidering both the pace and the scope of his long poem. In 1930 Zukofsky had written thirty pages of "A"-6 in a single week; when he returned to the project in August 1935, with "A"-8 before him, his formal and thematic ambitions for the poem had grown. "A"-8 would be longer than any previous movement of the poem—indeed, longer than the first seven movements combined—and it would be more formally complex, as well.[1]

At the end of "A"-6, Zukofsky had asked *"Can* / The design / Of the fugue / Be transferred / To poetry?" "A"-8 would be the proving ground for that ambitious question. As Zukofsky explained to Niedecker, the movement generated a sort of "music" not primarily through the literal sounds of its words, but through a "counterpointing" of disparate thematic materials: "it must be music of the statements," Zukofsky wrote, "but not explanation ever—that's why I seem to leave out—but the reader will have to learn to read statement, juxtaposed constructs, as music." A "music," then, not of sounds but of ideas and images. As the movement grew, the complexity of Zukofsky's musical analogy grew as well, until he was arguing that the movement "shd. give sumpn like the effect of a 'mirror' fugue— i.e. each of a pair <of fugues> being the exact inversion of the other, as if it were seen in a mirror." Zukofsky knew that this musical model could only very loosely be applied to his poem:

> I'd be crazy & chust superhuman if I sat down to figger out an exact order of the materials going to make up each fugue, because fugues in words don't exist, because all the words go in one order—give one melodic line & can only suggest others between the lines going on at the same time, while in music you can & do have 2 or 3 or 4 melodies (voices) going on at the same time. So as I said—I've let the intensity with which I've felt the material determine its order & the *effect* or *suggestion* is sumpn like a mirror fugue in this section.[2]

Whether or not "A"-8's impression on a reader resembles that of a mirror fugue—one suspects Zukofsky himself would not have recognized such a musical composition—the movement, over the course of its sixty-two pages, exhibits a clear pattern of juxtapositions, transformations, and reappearances of a limited number of discrete themes. Eight, to be precise, in keeping with the movement's number. Zukofsky outlined them in a letter to Niedecker early in the poem's composition, and noted how "Each theme pumped on the organ as you say modulates or is heard against the other, then each one assumes phases of the others, appearing in different guises, but continuing to mean the same—till they'll all go together."[3]

That particular early list of eight—admittedly vague and confusing —was rethought in the course of the "A"-8's composition; Zukofsky would later summarize the eight themes of the poem for his own use in the manuscript of "A"-12. A reconstructed and mildly expanded account:[4]

1) *Labor*, both physical and intellectual: "Labor as creator, / Labor as creature," Zukofsky writes, adapting Spinoza's *natura naturans* and *natura naturata*

2) *Bach*, Bach's music, and music in general

3) *Economics*, especially as theorized by Marx and Engels, and experienced by the working classes during the Great Depression

4) *Science*, including the ideas of Einstein and Poincaré, and Thorstein Veblen's meditations on the scientific tendency of the age

5) *Nominalism* as represented in the philosophy of Duns Scotus, whom Zukofsky saw as an important precursor to dialectical materialist thinking

6) *Personal History*

7) *Literature and Art*

8) *The Adamses*, Henry, Brooks, and Charles Francis Jr., all of whom wrote keenly about the tendencies of American history; Henry, in particular, seemed to have foreseen the importance that Russia would assume in twentieth-century history

All of these themes revolve around the fundamental theme of *labor*, so that the opening lines of the movement serve as an overture to and summary of the whole:

> And of labor:
> Light lights in air,
>   on streets, on earth, in earth—
> Obvious as that horses eat oats—
>   Labor as creator,
>   Labor as creature,
> To right praise.[5]

Zukofsky's intent is clear: to cast light upon all sorts of human labor, to show how labor—in its ideal state unexploited, unalienated—is an integral element of an unfolding "nature"; and further, to dignify that labor with "right praise."

This goal makes for a poem far more rangy and heterogeneous than any of the earlier movements of "A". Zukofsky begins once again with the 1729 premiere of the *St. Matthew Passion*, advertised with unconscious wit, "THREE HOURS / AGONY / IN THIS CHURCH / GOOD FRIDAY."[6] That "agony," no doubt, was more Bach's than his audience's, since the sublime music of the *Passion* had to be produced under quite adverse economic conditions. "It is astonishing," the poem quotes Bach, "that . . musicians should be expected / to play *ex tempore* any music put before them, / . . the necessity to earn their . . bread / allowing them little leisure to perfect their technique . ."[7] This is a fundamental opposition "A"-8 explores: the thwarting of productive labor—artistic or otherwise—by the forces of capitalism. It appears in the tragically failed career of John Quincy Adams, as related by his grandson Brooks; in the vast Gilded Age money grabs of Vanderbilt and Gould, as related by Henry and Charles Francis Adams Jr. in their *Chapters of Erie*; in Robert Allison Evans's narration of strikes among Pennsylvania coal miners;[8] and in a plethora of documents, letters, and anecdotes relating to Karl Marx and Friedrich Engels, who emerge as the most clear-eyed critics of the economic system under which the poet himself lives.

Marx is not merely a theoretician in "A"-8, however; as Zukofsky was arguing in his letters to Pound, and to anyone on the American left who cared to listen, Marx had been an *artist* as well, a thinker of many sides, unwilling to send *Das Kapital* to Engels until he had brought it to a satisfactory completion:

> I am now working like a horse (Marx)
> As I must use the time in which it is possible to work . . .
> One cannot always be writing (*Das Kapital*)
> I am doing some differential calculus—
> the derivative of x with respect to y—
> I have no patience to read anything else
> Other reading always drives me back to my writing,
> Then there is still the fourth book, the historical-literary, to
>   write—
>
> . . .
>
>   I cannot bring myself to send anything
> Till I have the whole before me.[9]

In his essay on Chaplin, Zukofsky wrote, "There exists probably in the labors of any valid artist the sadness of the horse plodding with blinkers."[10] As poet, Zukofsky saw himself as such a "valid artist"—as a "horse"—and saw in Marx another such.

The movement as a whole, however, is by no means the dry political document that my summary might suggest. Instead, it is a glittering succession of contrasting and mutually illuminating fragments and anecdotes, frequently leavened with broad or subtle humor. *Chapters of Erie*'s narrative about "captains of industry" is interrupted by Doll Tearsheet of *Henry IV, Part 1*: "A captain! / God's light . . the word as odious as the word 'occupy[.]'"[11] Général Gene Gem reviews his army of tin soldiers at the Invalides, and Kokichi Mikimoto, "The Japanese Pearl King," conducts "A memorial service for the 'souls' / Of hundreds of millions of oysters / That had been 'martyred' to make Mr. Mikimoto a fortune."[12] (These latter two items seem lifted straight from the newspaper.)

There are moments when Zukofsky himself appears, moments of personal history: "the researchist in old gardens" for the WPA visiting a blacksmith in the Bronx;[13] the arrival of Pinchos Zukofsky in the new world; and Zukofsky's own childhood. In some sense, Pinchos has the crowning thought of "A"-8 as a whole, in a passage that relates the activities of human creation to the processes of nature itself:

> Plenty of eloquence,
> Words enough,
> Such hardened soldiers of fortune who became softies,
> How could they escape
> when the canals of the ear relate the head to the wood-grain of a
>   chair.
> Enough and more than enough,
> My father would not have any one curse in his home,
> Would say, we too, once were made delectable by the pipes of the
>   organ,
> Heaven of Substance, penetrant music,
> Sub-cherubim of the air—
> Above colonnade wake forms.[14]

"He who creates," Zukofsky had written in "A"-6, speaking of Spinoza's *natura naturans* and *natura naturata*, "is a mode of these inertial systems"; this conviction would remain at the heart of his long poem.

· · ·

For all of Zukofsky's talk of "mirror fugues" and eightfold themes, the *texture* of "A"-8—which moves from one block of quotation, paraphrase, or narration to another in an easy, often long-lined free verse—is not dissimilar to that of "A"-6, or several of the earlier movements of the poem. Except, that is, for two passages composed in a far tighter and more rigorously determined form, and which suggested a turn that Zukofsky's work would take in "A"-9: a *mathematical* turn.

The first passage, near the beginning of the poem, opens

> To this end, Communists assembled in London
> Sketched the Manifesto of the party itself.
> Hidden, open fight—to date that is history:
> Exploiting and exploited. When in the ice-age
> A pipe made of a lion's tooth played D and G,
> Or when glass harmonica or dining table
> Tuned their glass (plunged tones) there was history (movement
> In excavations) an economy that is,
> Which was the material clef of the music.[15]

and runs through eight more nine-line stanzas, each line of eleven or twelve syllables. The second passage is at the very end, functioning as a tailpiece to "A"-8 as a whole; it consists of three intricately rhymed ten-line stanzas, each ending with the line "Labor, light lights in air, on earth, in earth,"[16] and a six-line coda:

> Coda, see to it that the burden renew,
> Sound out thick gardens dug up in purlieu
> The shrapnel haunts; May is red blossom, berth
> Of what times' mill; blood reads the wounds, the cue—
> Luteclavicembalo—bullets pursue:
> Labor light lights in earth, in air, on earth.[17]

These are ten-syllable lines, though by no means traditional iambic pentameter. What is not immediately evident in these two passages is that they have been carefully structured in a manner that goes beyond mere rhyme or line and syllable count.

While Zukofsky was at work on "A"-8, Basil Bunting—always an indefatigable researcher into poetic form—had sent him a set of notes on Welsh prosody.[18] What arrested Zukofsky in these notes was probably a description of *cynghanedd* ("harmony"), the intricate schemes of sound correspondence out of which medieval Welsh poetry was woven. Such intricate and formalized patterings of sounds suggested to Zukofsky that there might be other means of structuring a poem than English's traditional arrangement of stressed and unstressed syllables—"accentual-syllabic" meter—and rhyme. With Reisman, who by this point was majoring in physics at City College, Zukofsky began analyzing how consonantal sounds were distributed in his own poems, and then in other poems of the English tradition. Could such distributions be described by mathematical formulae? It was Reisman—as Zukofsky described him, "a friend (or an enemy of practical prosody)"—who suggested the converse approach: Why not *compose* a poem in which the distribution of certain sounds was determined mathematically?[19]

The nine-stanza passage towards the beginning of "A"-8 and the thirty-six-line coda of the movement were composed according to Zukofsky's new notion of a mathematical *cynghanedd*.[20] Using the sounds *n* and *r* as variables, Zukofsky distributed those sounds in the lines of his poem according to precise mathematical formulae. The earlier eighty-one line passage adjusts its *n*'s and *r*'s according to certain "ratios of acceleration and deceleration," applied to three-line units of the verses. Thus, lines 31 through 33 contain three *r*'s and three *n*'s:

> Now drinks he up seas, and he eates up flocks, He's but
> A coof for a' that: he'll break his whip that guiltlesse
> Smals must die—I spec it will all be 'fiscated.

Lines 34 through 36 contain five *r*'s and three *n*'s:

> De massa run, ha! ha! De darkey stay, ho! ho!
> So distribution should undo excess—(chaseth),
> Shall brothers be, be a' that, Child, lolai, lullow.[21]

Zukofsky was simultaneously working with other constraints: Each eleven- or twelve-syllable line contains approximately four main stresses, and this particular passage is a collage of quotations from *A Workers Anthology*—Burns's "A Man's a Man," Henry Clay Work's "The Year of Jubilee," and *King Lear*, among others.

The precise equations with which Zukofsky worked have not survived. Barry Ahearn has proposed convincingly that the nine-stanza opening passage drew on "the calculus of a curve," while the thirty-six-line coda, in keeping with the poem's focus on "revolution," was based on a formula "related to a circular movement through 360 degrees."[22] Zukofsky could not have expected any reader to detect the working of these mathematical underpinnings when reading "A"-8—as a reader might immediately recognize that *Paradise Lost*, for instance, is in blank verse, or might recognize a Shakespearean sonnet about horses embedded in the fifth movement of "Poem beginning 'The.'" The effect of Zukofsky's mathematically structured work is rather more elusive; Hugh Kenner argues, perhaps overstating the case, that "Such hidden laws, presenting a different face to the poet and to us ... suspend the whole poem on some plane other than the plane of unresisted discourse, much as musical laws, though we may not know what they are, yield effects we do not confuse with random sonority."[23]

The mathematical forms of "A"-8 serve as an experiment in "practical prosody." The danger of setting aside traditional metrical forms, as both Pound and Eliot had clearly seen, was the formlessness they deplored in Whitman, Amy Lowell, and the voguish vers-librists of the 1910s and 1920s. Both Eliot and Pound believed that form was necessary to poetry—as Eliot put it, "there is no freedom in art."[24] Zukofsky, as he showed in his notion of the poem's "objectification," was wholly in agreement with them. The mathematical formulae of "A"-8 were in the purest sense an *experiment* at finding new, potentially productive structuring devices for poetry in English, just as the Italian sonnet form must have seemed revolutionary to sixteenth-century English poets. Mathematics had a powerful attraction for Zukofsky; it seemed to offer an objective, crystalline, logical description of reality—a way to make the poem, as *natura naturata*, model the actual processes of the creating world, *natura naturans*, and to do so in a manner consonant with the science Zukofsky admired.

Perhaps most importantly, the mathematical forms of "A"-8 were a self-appointed challenge to the poet himself, a formal obstacle to be overcome. Zukofsky would later speak of "my usual impulse to overcome something ... a resistance for work or working out. ... During the work it may after a while come easy, or at least must look that way to reader and when it's done it can all be scrapped."[25] In this, as in so much, Zukofsky's true forebear was James Joyce, the complex stylistic shifts and systems of parallels of whose *Ulysses* can be read as a series of self-imposed formal challenges to be surmounted, rather than as the blueprint for a work to be produced.[26] And Zukofsky's spiritual heir might be John Cage, who set forth his own version of an "impulse to overcome something" in one of the mesostic stanzas of "Composition in Retrospect":

aCt

In

accoRd

with obstaCles

Using

theM

to find or define the proceSs

you're abouT to be involved in

the questions you'll Ask

if you doN't have enough time

to aCcomplish

what you havE in mind

conSider the work finished.[27]

. . .

If the "mathematical" sections of "A"-8 had been governed by "hidden laws," Zukofsky revealed all of the machinery behind his next project when he and Celia published *First Half of "A"-9* in November 1940. "A"-9 was the most formally and conceptually complex piece of writing Zukofsky had yet undertaken; he labored on these seventy-six lines of verse for almost twenty months.[28] The poem took its metrical, stanzaic, and rhyming form from "Donna mi priegha," a canzone (song) by the Tuscan poet Guido Cavalcanti (ca. 1250–1300), whom Dante had called the first of his friends. With Dante, Cavalcanti was a master of the *dulce stil nuovo*, the "sweet new style" of poetry in the Tuscan vernacular. "Donna mi priegha" was a poem that defined love in the vocabulary of post-Aristotelian scholastic philosophy. Pound admired the poem extravagantly, but for all his praise of Cavalcanti's clarity of thought, his own translations of "Donna mi priegha" (he published three separate versions of the poem[29]) never attempted more than to *suggest* Cavalcanti's complex verse form, which consisted of five stanzas of fourteen eleven-syllable lines, followed by a six-line *commiato*, all of them bound together by a complicated system of internal and line-end rhymes. The first stanza, with its rhyming sounds highlighted, gives a taste of the whole:

> Donna mi pri**egha** perch'i volglio **dire**
> D'un acci**dente** che so**vente** é **fero**
> Ed é sí al**tero** ch'é chiamato a**more**
> Sicche chi l **negha** possa il ver sen**tire**
> Ond a'l pre**sente** chono**scente chero**
> Perch' i no **spero** ch om di basso **chore**
> Atal ragione portj chono**scenza**
> Ché **senza** natural dimostra**mento**
> Non o ta**lento** di voler pro**vare**
> Laove nascie e chì lo fá cri**are**
> E qual è sua virtu e sua po**tenza**
> L'es**senza** e poi chiaschun suo movi**mento**
> E' l piaci**mento** che'l fá dire a**mare**
> E se hom per veder lo puó mo**strare**:—

(A lady bids me, and so I would speak of an accident that is often fierce and is so haughty that is called love. Would that he who denies that were able to feel its truth! And for the present purpose I want someone who is an expert, as I do not expect that anyone base-hearted could bring knowledge to such reasoning: for without natural demonstration I have no intention of wishing to bring proof where it resides, what creates love, and what its virtue and potency may be, its essence and each of its movements, and the pleasure that makes it called love, or whether one can show it to be visible.)[30]

As Pound explains, "each strophe is articulated by 14 terminal and 12 inner rhyme sounds, which means that 52 out of every 154 syllables are bound into pattern."[31] Moreover, Cavalcanti's rhymes are disyllabic ("feminine") rhymes, far more common in Italian than in English; given the general scarcity of rhyming words in English (compared with Italian) it would seem impossible for a poet writing in English to duplicate the canzone's rhyme scheme.

Zukofsky, however, manages to do so. The first stanza of "A"-9 reads (again with rhyme sounds highlighted):

An impulse to **action** sings of a **semblance**
Of things re**lated** as **equated values**,
The measure **all use** is time congealed **labor**
In which ab**straction** things keep no re**semblance**
To goods cre**ated**; inte**grated all hues**
Hide their natur**al use** to one or one's **neighbor**.
So that were the things words they could say: **Light is**
Like **night is** like us when we meet our **mentors**
Use hardly **enters** into their ex**changes**,
Bought to be sold things, our value **arranges**;
We flee people who made us as a **right is**
Whose **sight is** quick to choose us as fre**quenters**,
But see our **centers** do not show the **changes**
Of human labor our value **estranges**.[32]

This is no disquisition on love, but an examination of labor and value. Zukofsky, using the *form* of Cavalcanti's canzone, has adapted the language of Marx's *Capital*. This stanza, for instance, draws on the "Commodities" chapter of Part I, where Marx allows commodities their own voice: "As values, commodities are nothing but particular masses of congealed labour-time. . . . If commodities could speak, they would say: 'Our use-value may interest human beings; but it is not an attribute of ours, as things. What is our attribute, as things, is our value. Our own interrelations as commodities prove it. We are related to one another only as exchange-values.'"[33]

Through its five stanzas and coda (as Zukofsky called the six-line tailpiece, or *commiato*), the poem mounts a highly abstract yet lyrical analysis of the relationships among labor, commodities, use- and exchange-value, and money. The second stanza recounts how the exchanges commodities undergo—money for productive labor, money for the products—obscure the fact that the ultimate source of capitalist profit is workers' labor. Commodities themselves would plead, the third stanza has it, that there is—or ought to be—an intimate relationship between the worker and what he makes: "Hands,

hearts, not value made us, and of any / Desired perfection the project solely, / Lives worked us slowly to delight the senses, / Of their
fire you shall find us . . ." Commodities, Zukofsky paraphrases, "are
the embodied images of perfection people have in mind, . . . they
are for the enjoyment of people, who give their lives making them,
rather than just so much work forgotten after a time."[34] The poem as
a whole is the speech of commodities themselves, carefully tracing
(in words borrowed from Marx) the stages of their production, their
alienation from the workers who made them, and their ultimate fate
as the objects of monetary transactions.

The coda turns to larger speculations, and the verse turns back
upon itself and reflects how its own production is an instance of
applied intellectual "labor":

> We are things, say, like a quantum of action
> Defined product of energy and time, now
> In these words which rhyme now how song's exaction
> Forces abstraction to turn from equated
> Values to labor we have approximated.

The poem, which was "first brought into being by this abstract
equation"—that commodities are "time congealed labor"—"has
been forced to turn from it to the labor product in the words of the
song itself, the form of which the things speaking have assumed."[35]

Pound had noted that "the canzone was to the poets of [Cavalcan-
ti's] period what the fugue was to musicians in Bach's time,"[36] and
this description must have appealed to Zukofsky. It was a tribute
to his ambition and obsessiveness that he would adapt Cavalcanti's
already difficult poem to an equally abstract subject, using equally
specialized intellectual sources. The parallels were inescapable: for
Zukofsky, Marx and Engels were scholastic authorities, as inevitable
in the twentieth century as Aristotle and Albertus Magnus were in the
thirteenth. The poem draws as well upon Herbert Stanley Allen's *Electrons and Waves: An Introduction to Atomic Physics* (1932).[37] "Donna mi
priegha" had been a state-of-the-art psychological disquisition in its
time; six hundred years later, Zukofsky revives the form as a similarly
up-to-date argument, building on what he saw as the best economic
and scientific thought of his day.

Once again, as he had in the two passages of "A"-8, Zukofsky underpinned his poem with mathematics. The first five stanzas of the poem, he explained,

> are the poetic analog of a conic section—i.e. the ratio of the accelerations of two sounds (r, n) has been made equal to the ratio of the accelerations of the coordinates (x, y) of a particle moving in a circular path with uniform angular velocity. I.e. values of
>
> $$\frac{\frac{d^2y}{dt^2}}{\frac{d^2x}{dt^2}} = \tan \theta \text{ where } \theta - \text{arc} \tan \frac{y}{x}$$
>
> are noted for five symmetrically located points. The time unit in the poetry is defined by 7 eleven-syllable lines. Each point is represented by a strophe.[38]

This meant that every seven lines, Zukofsky adjusted the relative numbers of *n*'s and *r*'s. Lines 1–7 had thirteen *n*'s and thirteen *r*'s, lines 8–14 thirteen *n*'s and fourteen *r*s. As in "A"-8, the effects of all this calculus are barely discernable—the seven-line sections toggle between thirteen and fourteen occurrences of each consonant, a modulation invisible to a reader who isn't actively counting. Indeed, despite the importance Zukofsky seemed to attach to the mathematics here—he would reprint his explanation of "The 'Form'" in a broadside twenty-six years later[39]—it is difficult to see the calculus as anything other than a final, perhaps trivial, element of complexity grafted to an already almost unbelievably complex project. Unless, that is, one takes into account Zukofsky's notion of obstacles to be overcome, and reads that calculus as another element in a complex chorus of voices and ideas held in suspension in "A"-9 as a whole. These voices—Cavalcanti and his sources, Marx, contemporary science, mathematics—are all bound together both in the ongoing "graph" of Western culture and in the poem itself, which should "fluoresce as it were in the light of seven centuries of interrelated thought."[40] *Fluoresce*—to give off light: "Light acts beyond the phase day will us into / Call a mature day" ("A"-9); "Labor light lights in earth, in air, on earth" ("A"-8).[41] Light was one of Zukofsky's obsessions in "A"-8

and -9, light as the object of the physicists' experiments and the metaphorical goal of the economists' researches. Light and seeing would
remain central to his work.

. . .

The typescript of *First Half of "A"-9* that the Zukofskys assembled and
mimeographed in November 1940 was an elaborate affair. Besides the
actual text of the first half of "A"-9, it included Cavalcanti's canzone
in Italian, twenty-five pages of excerpts from Zukofsky's sources—
Marx and H. Stanley Allen—a detailed note on "The 'Form'" of the
poem, a prose "Restatement" of Zukofsky's poem, and no fewer
than four English translations of "Donna mi priegha." Two of them
were by Pound, from his 1932 edition of Cavalcanti and from Canto
36. The other two were exercises in the vernacular of their day, just
as Dante had urged poets to set aside Latin in *De Vulgari Eloquentia*.
Reisman's "A Dame Ast Me" was a blunt Brooklynese version of the
first two stanzas of "Donna mi priegha."[42] Zukofsky's own "A foin
lass bodders" "done for relaxation" from his work on "A"-9,[43] was
a translation of the whole of Cavalcanti's canzone into a stage-Irish
brogue:

> A foin lass bodders me I gotta tell her
> Of a fact surely, so unrurly, often'
> 'r 't comes 'tcan't soften its proud neck's called love mm . . .
> Even me brudders dead drunk in dare cellar
> Feel it dough poorly 'n yrs. trurly rough 'n
> His way ain't so tough 'n he can't speak from above mm . . .[44]

This was surely a bit of high-spirited fun, but there was also clearly an
element of Oedipal rivalry at work. For Zukofsky, even as he translated Cavalcanti into the language of the streets, had still punctili-
ously preserved the meter and the feminine rhymes of the original,
a feat that Pound, his mentor and poetic "father," had deemed both
undoable and not worth attempting.

It is unclear whether Zukofsky ever gave Pound a copy of the
complete edition of *First Half of "A"-9*.[45] Pound's comment to James
Laughlin, after having read the poem alone, was that "Zuk the Zook
has just written *A-9* which appears to be compounded of donna mi

priega and Marx'z economic phallassies."[46] Williams was receptive but bewildered: "I am somewhat confused, what relation does this section of 'A' bear in relation to the whole poems as written & as projected?"[47] But he admired it enough to recommend it to George H. Dillon, an editor at *Poetry* magazine, and the poem was published there in June 1941.[48] It was Zukofsky's first appearance in *Poetry* since 1933.

Given the minuscule number of copies of *First Half of "A"-9* he and Celia had produced, Zukofsky had no reason to hope for a public response to the pamphlet. The very title of the book—"First Half"—however, spelled out the ongoing nature of his work on "*A*", and the fact that he would not begin writing "A"-9's second half until 1948—eight years after completing "A"-10—underlined the evolving nature of the project as a whole. "*A*" was no longer a long poem to be worked at seriatim, as Spenser had added books to *The Faerie Queene*. It had become a series of formal experiments to which Zukofsky would return and work at regardless of numerical ordering, a "poem of a life" in which each movement would bear the marks of the poet's lived circumstances, historical and personal, and take its place as an eccentric, impersonal record of the poet's intellectual and emotional life.

Numbers and Horses

Zukofsky's imagination was fired by the historical theories of Henry Adams and Karl Marx, the philosophical systems of Aristotle, Spinoza, and St. Thomas Aquinas, the musical structures of Johann Sebastian Bach. But a number of motifs recur throughout his writings that are far less highbrow—that seem less intellectually or artistically motivating themes than mere private obsessions. Why was this detached, unscientific aesthete, who according to family testimony could hardly balance his own checkbook, so fascinated with *numbers*? And why was this city boy, who lived most of his life with the concrete and asphalt of New York beneath his feet, who spent his single year in the Midwest in an agony of homesickness, so obsessed with *horses*?

. . .

Zukofsky's obsession with number seems at first merely superstition. Celia Zukofsky, in a brief essay on Zukofsky's relationship with Pound, gives some examples of how her husband's mind worked. He had first written Pound in 1927, and Pound had died in 1972. "1927 to 1972—the sum of the first year is equal to the sum of the last year,"

Zukofsky remarked to his wife. "It's the same thing. It's perfect. It ended as it started." Correspondences could also be more detailed: "Louis' copy of Pound's *Lustra*," Celia Zukofsky wrote, "is no. 129. Translated, to Louis it meant his own birthday, January 29."[1]

Perhaps the puzzle of his own multiple birthdays had something to do with Zukofsky's obsession with number. Clearly, the precise day on which he was born had been of little concern to his immigrant parents, but so much was keyed to numbers in twentieth-century America—one's date of birth, the hours measured out by the clock, the obscure achievement percentages that the schools translated into A's or B's—that perhaps there *had* to be a correlation between the numbers attached to a man's life and that man's fate. The numbered lines of "Poem beginning 'The'" were only an early presentiment of the role number would play in Zukofsky's poetry. His first collection was entitled *55 Poems*, a number arrived at long before Zukofsky had completed the poems that would make it up (and belied by simple arithmetic: its two sections are "29 Poems" and "29 Songs").

It was in *"A"* that Zukofsky's number obsession became most evident. Pound had begun *The Cantos* hoping to emulate the structure of Dante's *Divine Comedy*—a descent into Hell, a tour of Purgatory, and then an ascent into some Heaven—but by 1939 he admitted that without a theological geography of the sort upon which Dante had plotted his poem ("I haven't an Aquinas-map; Aquinas *not* valid now"[2]), he would find organizing his ongoing epic hard work. In contrast, whatever Zukofsky might end up writing *about* in *"A"*, from the very beginning he projected the poem within a formal armature based on *number*: twenty-four movements. The contingencies of his own life and the history through which he would live would supply the material for the poem; the number 24, with all of its various resonances, would provide the form.

If *"A"*'s movements had only numbers to distinguish them one from another, then it made sense to play upon those numbers in the movements themselves. "A"-7 was a series of *seven* sonnets. "A"-8, building on the "fugal" form first explicitly evoked in "A"-6, deployed *eight* themes. As the poem progressed, however, Zukofsky came increasingly to play upon coincidences between his movements' numbers and the numbers that figured in the events of his life. "A"-17, the

"Coronal for Floss" in memory of William Carlos Williams, corresponds to September 17, Williams's birthday. "A"-20, the "Respond for P.Z.'s tone row / At twenty," was written in 1963 for Paul Zukofsky's twentieth birthday. The three last-composed movements of the poem, "A"-21, -22, and -23, form a trinity comparable to that of Zukofsky's family circle, as summed up on the last page of "A"-23: "*Kalenderes enlumined 21-2-3 . . .*"[3] These three numbers are the birthdays of Celia (January 21), Paul (October 22), and Louis (January 23).

In the later movements of "*A*", one begins to come across references to the Pythagoreans, who based their thought upon mathematics. When in "A"-18 Zukofsky writes, "seven words heaven, eight love, nine universe," he evokes the Pythagoreans' ascription of mystical significance to specific numbers.[4] That particular numbers have specific meanings seems to have been one of the motivating forces behind Zukofsky's late word count prosodies, especially in light of the prominence of *five*-word lines in his later work ("A"-21, -22, -23, and *80 Flowers*)—five was the Pythagorean number of *marriage*.[5] Having discovered that pleasing intervals in music depended upon simple mathematical ratios, the Pythagoreans quite naturally generalized that principle and asserted that the entire universe was structured in accordance with mathematical laws, was in some sense made up of numbers. Hence the "music of the spheres," the unheard harmony generated by the movements of the heavenly bodies.[6]

I doubt Zukofsky took Pythagorean number symbolism entirely literally, but it was just the sort of philosophical system—precise, all-encompassing, with a heady tincture of moralism and mysticism—that appealed to him as a source of generative analogies. And number itself, apart from the meanings that one mystical school or another might attach to individual numerals, drew his attention on several levels. Numbers, which could be shuffled and manipulated in all manner of ways, provided a fertile source of generative *play*. Shuffling the numbers of his poems could serve to uncover new connections within the work itself and new "recurrences" from across the whole "graph of culture." As he contemplated the overall form of his last book, *80 Flowers*, Zukofsky mused that each poem would contain precisely forty words, a key quantity in the Hebrew Bible;

if one added the integers—4 + 0 = 4—one came up with four, the Pythagorean number of justice. Eight (2 x 4) lines to each poem dovetailed with the "two-by-four's" of the poem "For" in his collection "I's (pronounced *eyes*)."[7] And if Zukofsky wrote eight poems a year (*80 Flowers* was planned as a decade-long project), he would produce sixty-four lines a year: 6 + 4 = "10 (years); 8 x 10 years = 80 and again adding integers 8 + 0 = 8" (to which Zukofsky added various "eight" references from "A"-8).[8] When Zukofsky decided to add an epigraph to *80 Flowers*, making eighty-one poems total, he began a new round of "number-tumbling," in which 8 + 1 = 9, the number of the Muses and the Pythagorean universal.[9]

The more serious manipulation of numbers embodied in the mathematical arts offered Zukofsky a model of a self-sufficient, self-enclosed system of thought free from empirical contingency. Throughout the first half of "*A*", mathematics is presented as among the highest forms of mental exercise. Zukofsky himself was no mathematician, but he nonetheless attempted to incorporate the results of a differential equation into the form of "A"-9 and parts of "A"-8. In "A"-12 he would describe his own poetics in terms of calculus: "An integral / Lower limit speech / Upper limit music."[10] In "A Statement for Poetry" (1950) Zukofsky defined poetry "as an order of words that as movement and tone (rhythm and pitch) approaches in varying degrees the wordless art of music as a kind of mathematical limit." Zukofsky envied mathematics its invariable logic and crystalline structure. While the Pythagoreans had ventured into the realm of fancy by ascribing mystical virtues to particular numbers, they were right in sensing the powerful connection between number and the visible cosmos, for the whole of modern physics from Newton to Einstein would take mathematics as its primary tool for unraveling the structures and relationships of nature.

Most important for Zukofsky, however, was the vital relationship between number and his own art. It was through their experiments with music that the Pythagoreans had come to believe in the harmonic, *numerical* structure of the universe, and number, as any musician or musicologist can attest, is at the heart of Western music: the proportions between tones, the counted divisions of time. Indeed, according to a sentence of Plato's Zukofsky liked to quote, number is at the heart of all the arts: "If number, measure and weighing be taken away from any art, that which remains will not be much."[11] (This sentence is echoed in a verse from the apocryphal Wisdom of Solomon—Deus omnia facit numero, mensure, et pondere, "God created all things according to number, measure, and weighing"—which proved immensely influential on Renaissance theorists of the arts.[12]) Number was at the center of Zukofsky's imagination in large part because the processes of number—counting, measuring, weighing— were at the center of his conception of the poetic art. Poetry might be an expression of an individual's emotions; it might be an act of communication, a "letter to the world"; it might be a recording of the events of one's own time. It might be all of these things, and many more—but all of those aspects of the poetic act were incidental to its essence as the making of an aesthetic object, an object that achieved objecthood through the poet's careful application of the principles of measuring, weighing, and numbering: numbering his sounds, his syllables, his words, and his lines. The poet's was a counting that for the most part proceeded by ear, rather than by calculator (or by fingers). In "Peri Poietikes" Zukofsky cautioned the poet to "Forget terms": "Mind, don't run to mind / boys' Greeks' metres gnomes, / rummage in tee-tomes, tee-tums, tum-tees."[13] But whether the poet follows a traditional meter or seeks to forge his own new measure, the success of the poem ultimately depends on the care with which its maker has obeyed the laws of number that underlie the poetic art.

· · ·

Among the pleasures of Zukofsky's work is his frequent unwillingness to take himself too seriously. In "A"-14, a quarter century into their marriage, Celia Zukofsky makes light of one of Zukofsky's favorite motifs, the *horse*: "'your / horse complex' (C.) / 'what a preoccupation.'"[14] The figure of the horse appears so frequently in Zukofsky's poetry that one is tempted to ascribe its omnipresence to a psychological fixation, some Freudian "complex." Unlike his preoccupation with number, however, which stands as both an eccentric hobby and a perception of truths at the root of his own craft, Zukofsky's obsessive horse imagery shows him dealing in that rarest of phenomena in his writings (which are largely unmetaphorical and strangely *literal*): a *symbol*.

"Horses" are indexed in the "Dedication" to "Poem beginning 'The,'" Zukofsky's first important work, and a reader who pursues that reference will find, midway through the fifth movement ("*Autobiography*"), an ungainly but rather touching sonnet in triple meters:

224 Horses that pass through inappreciable woodland,
225 Leaves in their manes tangled, mist, autumn green,
226 Lord, why not give these bright brutes—your good land—
227 Turf for their feet always, years for their mien.
228 See how each peer lifts his head, others follow,
229 Mate paired with mate, flanks coming full they crowd,
230 Reared in your sun, Lord, escaping each hollow
231 Where life-struck we stand, utter their praise aloud.
232 Very much Chance, Lord, as when you first made us,
233 You might forget them, Lord, preferring what
234 Being less lovely where sadly we fuss?
235 Weed out these brutes as tho they were not?
236 Never alive in brute delicate trembling
237 Song to your sun, against autumn assembling.

These horses, passing through a woodland scene, stand in sharp contrast to the "old horse strewn with yellow leaves" of line 220; they are a vision of natural freedom and vitality, far away from the "gastanks, ruts, cemetery-tenements" of the Lower East Side. "238 If horses could but sing Bach, mother,—" Zukofsky writes, "239 Remember how I wished it once—/ 240 Now I kiss you who could never sing Bach, never read Shakespeare."[15]

Perhaps the child Zukofsky had some experience of horses that made him identify "these bright brutes" with a freedom and vigor in sharp contrast to the bonds of poverty, ill health, and cultural marginality within which his mother was confined. The horses he would have seen on the Lower East Side—and horses were in wide use in the city through the end of the First World War—would have been beasts of burden, drays pulling wagons or fire engines, nags pulling hansom cabs. But he could as well have seen well-fed, finely curried specimens on the popular bridle paths of Central Park. Such horses—redolent of grace, power, and vigor—might have impressed him both as emblems of sheer natural vitality and as glimpses of a longed-for freedom, both spiritual and economic. Nor could he have been unaware of the mythical figure of the flying horse, even if his most immediate vision of Pegasus was a Mobil Oil sign.

A particularly fruitful study of Zukofsky's poetry might trace all of the shifting uses he makes of horses, from the eighty-odd references to them in the index to "A" through their various appearances in the shorter poems of ALL and 80 Flowers. Guy Davenport has playfully asserted that to read "A" one must "find the horse": there is, he believes, a horse embedded in every movement. For most of the movements, finding the horse involves no more than consulting the poem's index. But "A"-9 and "A"-11 have no overt reference to horses, and it is only when we recall that these two movements are based on the "Donna mi priegha" and "Perch'io non spero" that we see the horse concealed in the name of those poems' author—Guido Cavalcanti.[16] The three lines of "A"-16—"An / inequality // wind flower"—would seem horseless, until we remember how they echo the opening of "A"-15—"An / hinny / by / stallion / out of / she-ass"—and hear the horse's whinny in "inequality." The horse in "A"-17, the self-quoting homage to William Carlos Williams, lurks in a pun, a vocal direction embedded in the Zukofskys' Catullus LI: "[voice hoarse in a throat]."[17]

In a 1961 letter to the poet Babette Deutsch, Zukofsky rounded up a number of the connotations horses held for him: "Horses—0, take it as a symbol of animal drive, or just animal delight, the kind that plays with Gulliver's hat, you remember, the human animal not as 'simple' as the horse." This horse represented for Zukofsky sheer physicality, the joy of embodiment and the joy of play. (One remembers also that Swift's Houynhyms are distinguished by a simplicity that amounts to guilelessness, a higher "rationality" that cannot comprehend the complex deceptions and self-deceptions of "sophisticated" human society.) In "A"-7, Zukofsky explained to Deutsch, the wooden sawhorses of the street excavation are "animated" by words, by the "human imagination . . . a kind of uncontrolled horse itself."[18] Here horses represent for Zukofsky a somatic, irrepressible energy that the poet channels into his creations, harnesses to transform the deadwood of his surroundings into stampeding activity.

The horse's more humble relation, the donkey, appears in Zukofsky's work as well, representing a kind of idiotic sagacity. The jackass of the college poem "Millennium of sun"—"O who will pluck geranium / With smiles before this ass's face / And tie it to his cranium / To match the ass's grace!"[19]—is a premonition of the character who will dominate Zukofsky's study of Shakespeare, the weaver Nick Bottom. In *A Midsummer Night's Dream* Bottom is "translated" by the transformation of his head into a donkey's, a substitution that allows him privileged insight into the ratios of love and reason, the eyes and the mind, that underlie all of Shakespeare's works. Bottom is the ungainly, parodic minotaur at the heart of the labyrinth that is *Bottom: on Shakespeare*.[20] As donkey, as the lowest form of "horse," he is able best to perceive the sensuous truth of the Shakespearean text, that "the good reasons of the mind's right judgment are but superfluities for saying: *Love sees*."[21]

More often, however, in Zukofsky's writing the horse is a general emblem of the poet himself. In the early movements of *"A"*, the poet becomes a centaurlike figure, full of energy and potential: "Half-human, half-equestrian, clatter of waves, / Fabulous sea-horses up blind alleys . . ."[22] At other times, the horse is simple shorthand for the poet himself: "One horse / Walked off, / The trees showing sunlight / Sunlight trees, / Words ranging forms."[23] In *"A"*-12, Zukofsky uses the figure of the horse to adumbrate his own poetics, a mixture of the romantic imagination and the seeking out of recurrences. The horse is both the wild animal and the drawer of a plow, opening up furrows that have been opened and reopened throughout recorded history:

> The horse sees he is repeating
> All known cultures . . .
> The shape of his ground seems to have been
> A constant for all dead horses . . .[24]

Zukofsky's horse, as symbol of the poet, exemplifies in turn both sorts of horses of Zukofsky's youth, the wild "bright brutes" of "Poem beginning 'The'" and the draught animals of the Lower East Side.

Zukofsky was always well aware of the sheer drudgery involved in the pursuit of art. In a 1936 essay he encapsulated that drudgery in an equine image: "There exists probably in the labors of any valid artist the sadness of the horse plodding with blinkers and his direction is for all we don't know filled with the difficulty of keeping a pace."[25] As Zukofsky grew older and more and more resigned to the abyss of public indifference into which his published works seemed to drop, images of the poet-horse as the powerful embodiment of physical and imaginative grace grew rarer and rarer. Indeed, the horses of "A"-22 and -23 seem to be ready almost for the glue factory—"the bent dray-horse," "old in / a greenhouse the stabled horse / sings sometimes."[26] But only *almost*. The final equine reference of "A"—"*sawhorses silver / all these fruit-tree tops*"—returns us to the sawhorses of "A"-7, worded into life by the poetic imagination; the latter part of the phrase is from *Romeo and Juliet*, a hopeful lover's oath from Romeo: "Lady, by yonder blessed moon I vow, / That tips with silver all these fruit-tree tops—"[27] There is life in this old nag yet, and that equine life is present abundantly—though still reined in by the "sorrow of harness"—in the epigraph to *80 Flowers*: "stem-square leaves-cordate earth race horsethyme / breath neighbors a mace nays."[28] The horse may have grown resigned to the stable, the wagon, or the plow, but he tenaciously retains his passion to gallop free on the racetrack or through "inappreciable woodlands."

The Home
Front 1940–1945

Germany invaded Poland at the beginning of September 1939. In a matter of days, Europe was plunged into a second world war. With the Soviet Union sidelined by Stalin and Hitler's nonaggression pact, the Germans hoped to dispose of their most formidable European antagonists—Great Britain and France—in fairly short order. Poland, invaded from the west by the Germans and the east by the Soviets, fell in a few weeks. In spring 1940, the Nazi Wehrmacht swept through Holland and Belgium and pressed into France. Paris fell on June 14, and a little over a week later France capitulated; the country was divided into two zones, the northern under direct German occupation, the southern—Vichy France—nominally independent, but governed by a German puppet regime.

Zukofsky, while never a fluent French speaker, was always an ardent Francophile, and his involvement with French culture went back many years. Over seven weeks of summer 1940, Zukofsky drafted "Paris," a poem lamenting the city's capture and the defeat of France.[1] "Paris," which would become "A"-10, is a striking turn from the formal and intellectual complexities of "A"-9 or the broad "fugal" structure of "A"-8. Indeed, the poem seems largely to reject even the lyrical itself: "Poor songster so weak / Stopped singing to curse"; "Let a better time say / The poet stopped singing to talk."[2] After spending most of the 1930s refusing to write the sort of immediately apprehensible, politically relevant poetry the American Left admired, with the fall of Paris Zukofsky turned to precisely that mode:

> Frenchmen resist flee to Britain
> Proclaim indissoluble union
>   of your two peoples
> Of peoples[3]

The poem is a vivid, moment-by-moment portrayal of the fall of France, interspersed with political invective—"A vicar of Christ sworn to traitors," "French and British concessioners consort / with Japanese greed / Betrayals bankers' wars from across seas / To gain the scorched earth of China"[4]—and not unmixed with irony, as in the Ionesco-like equation of Mussolini in Africa to a rhinoceros,[5] or in the more brutal

> French people, Spain's dead asked you for help
> Now you cannot ask them for help
> Do you still ask us gullible people for help
> Stop crying for France, snarls Italy
> What more could they have done
>   to merit our heel in their necks?[6]

Even in his grief and anger, however, Zukofsky had not lost his taste for structure. "Paris" is based on the form of the Roman Catholic Mass, where a Kyrie is followed by a Gloria, then a Credo, Sanctus, and Agnus Dei. Zukofsky's is an "inverted" mass, a "black" mass, in keeping with the darkness of the time and the perfidy of the Church hierarchy: "All the people of Paris / Mass, massed refugees on the roads / Go to mass with the air / and the shrapnel for a church / A Christian civilization / Where Pius blesses the black-shirts[.]" The elements of the mass appear first as isolated quotations (as the libretto of the *St. Matthew Passion* figured in "*A*"'s earlier movements), but with the Credo, they begin to become more immediate and more sinister: "*Credo* I believe // Shame // Ashamed of all people put to shame..." It is not the Lord who is holy (Sanctus), but "Sylvie / A little girl / Paul and Hélène's daughter," who sings a haunting song about the burial of her dolls. And the Agnus Dei, the Lamb of God, is not the crucified Christ but the twelve-year-old Eugene, a French boy who hangs himself when he learns that his family will be forced to eat his pet rabbit.[7] The mass, and all the most cherished symbols of the Christian world order, have been debased with the descent of that order into a new cycle of war and oppression.

Williams, always impressed with Zukofsky's uncompromising intellectuality but often puzzled at his poetry, was deeply moved by "A"-10: "Your poem is a beauty, you are fast becoming the most important and neglected poet of our time and place." Zukofsky replied diffidently, noting that "a dozen or more publishers" had rejected the poem: "The older I get, the less public notice I receive, the more skeptical I become about my own necessity. That leaves me thinking in terms of 'reputation' altogether."[8]

. . .

In the months after the fall of Paris, Zukofsky and René Taupin planned a new periodical, *La France en Liberté*, "the review of free France." From England Charles de Gaulle was proclaiming a "Free France" in exile. Similarly, Taupin and Zukofsky hoped to provide an outlet for the writing of French writers, those sympathetic to the ideals of "liberty, equality, and fraternity," and all others "still animated by the hope of better times ... who know that the intelligence can pursue its activity only when free."[9] Taupin and Zukofsky foresaw a 150-page bilingual quarterly; Taupin and the Alsatian surrealist poet Yvan Goll would be the French editors, Zukofsky the English. The Advisory Board of *La France en Liberté*, whose ultimate subtitle was "Quarterly of French refugee writers and the struggle for free France," was heavy with famous names, among them Albert Einstein, Ernest Hemingway, Princeton University dean Christian Gauss, popular historian Henrik Willem Van Loon, and William Carlos Williams. Taupin and Zukofsky had letterhead printed, and distributed a questionnaire to prospective contributors asking them to comment on the possibilities of preserving French culture "under a totalitarian regime." Zukofsky solicited an essay from Williams, "The Poet in Time of Confusion," for *La France en Liberté*, and intended to publish "Paris" (which he had decided would be "A"-10) there.[10] Zukofsky took leave from his WPA project for the first two months of 1941 and devoted himself to *La France* more or less full-time,[11] but for whatever reason—probably financial—the magazine never appeared.

. . .

In March 1941, Zukofsky was back working for the WPA, again as a writer for WNYC. Perhaps he was weary of having his poetry rejected, or perhaps, as "A"-10 suggested, it was a time to "talk" rather than to "sing," but in the early years of the war Zukofsky tried his hand for the first time at conventional prose fiction. Some time earlier, he and Reisman had revised a brief comic story by Zukofsky's brother Morris Zukowsky, "Abe Fink, Begorrah."[12] Now Zukofsky produced his own first effort at realistic fiction, "A Keystone Comedy."[13] The story of Charles Fenix and his kitchen-based, family narcotics-distribution business is meant to be funny, but wrecks itself on the shoals of Zukofsky's awkward dialogue—"Please, Ann, look at the facts!" says Charles. "My brother an elegant clown at the game sells dope pure and does not get into trouble"—and inability to keep his high-culture obsessions out of this low-culture romp: "Billy touched him on the shoulder. 'Why don't you go to sleep, Papa, instead of roosting all night like the bird in the sole Arabian tree out of Shakespeare?'"[14]

The fall of France served as stimulus for the novella Zukofsky began writing in February 1941, *Ferdinand*.[15] The work started as a short story, he told Williams in August, but "now that I look over what there is of it, it appears to me better suited for a novel."[16] He was hoping Williams would recommend him for one of the publisher Houghton Mifflin's literary fellowships on the basis of what he had already written, though his notion of where precisely the plot was headed—as outlined in the synopsis he prepared—was still rather hazy.[17]

Unlike "A Keystone Comedy," which could have taken place any-time in the first half of the century, or "Thanks to the Dictionary," which takes place in the timeless interstices between the King James Bible and the lexicon, *Ferdinand* was to be "a story of our time"—a work, like Henry Adams's *Education*, firmly situated within the unfolding history of its writer's world. The title character, Ferdinand, is the child of a French diplomat on the Italian Riviera; the family live across from a monument to Christopher Columbus—a foreshadowing of Ferdinand's removal to the United States, where he is sent to join his brother, who works in Washington. In America, he feels isolated, rootless, but consoles himself with a taste for pow-erful automobiles and directionless travel. His friends are "a varied lot": There is "a White Russian emigré passionately convinced of the good in the *workers* revolution"; an Englishman—clearly modeled on Basil Bunting—"who loved to sail with them in a catboat someone had given him" and who "diverted them with his opinion that poetry sang and spoke best in [classical Persian poet] Firdusi and his grow-ing opinion that after [Firdusi's epic] the Shah Namah it almost never sang and spoke at all"; and a young New York Jew, "the rabbin," who had "steeped himself in English and American scholarship to a degree emulating the devotion of his parents to their religion about which he never thought"—Zukofsky himself.[18]

The title character, Ferdinand, also reflects much of Zukofsky; one could argue that Ferdinand is a fictive self-portrait of the author, Zukofsky's own imagining of himself as one of the European exiles all around him during the war years. Ferdinand's fascination with cars and travel parallels Zukofsky's own (though Zukofsky, constitution-ally inept with machinery, never learned to work a typewriter, much less drive a car), and perhaps the isolation Zukofsky felt from his ancestral community finds an echo in Ferdinand's sense of rootless-ness, emblematized in the weed "Creeping Charlie" or "Wandering Jew," "with the blue, mantis-like face of its floweret," "a flower"—like the alien in America—"which thrives like a weed."[19]

Ferdinand reaches its climax in the American Southwest, where the now-orphaned Ferdinand is driving his refugee aunt and uncle on a cross-country tour. There they encounter an enigmatic Indian girl, Nina, who shares a name with both one of Columbus's caravels and a little girl Ferdinand had played with in his childhood. Ferdinand falls asleep at the wheel; in his dream his aunt and uncle have been killed in an accident, he spends the night with Nina, and with the Englishman and the rabbin he wanders into a double bill of Charlie Chaplin and Disney's *Dumbo*. He awakens to find he has merely dented a fender on a guardrail, but as they resume their trip he finds a certain peace: "He might please his aunt and uncle and speak again to his brother from whom he had become estranged. In that case, he could never get himself to tell this story or as much of it as the *rabbin*, who had lived in his time, could guess."[20]

Early on, Williams questioned the effectiveness of the "Indian scene," but Zukofsky responded, "as a matter of fact, that Indian girl was one of the images that got Ferd. going. I never slept with her, but remember the face very well—there was no other face around when we drove past her in the Arizona desert, 1932."[21] With the full manuscript before him, Williams still distrusted the ending: "I certainly do not like the phantasm, the fantasy—which seems definitely manufactured and anything but 'true' at the finish," Williams wrote. "Either you should kill everybody and follow through with the 'truth' of the story as story. Or just don't do anything. Don't have the hallucination of an accident but make them come out perfectly safely into a beautiful sunny green California valley and have a picnic lunch on the grass."[22] Stubborn as ever, Zukofsky made no change in the novella's conclusion. Indeed, he was busy planning more fictional works, partly in response to an encouraging communication from Houghton Mifflin. He had been eliminated from the fellowship competition, but an editor had expressed interest in the completed *Ferdinand*; Zukofsky knew that he couldn't expand the work beyond its novella length, but perhaps with two other short stories it might make a book?[23]

He already had "A Keystone Comedy" on hand, and the very difficulty of writing *Ferdinand*, it would seem, gave Zukofsky his single perfect short story, "*It was*."[24] This brief piece—only four pages long—is transparently autobiographical, spoken by the poet himself in the act of writing another story—clearly *Ferdinand*. He has arisen early Saturday morning, "*anxious to go on writing the story that in the dark hours did not let me rest.*" In loving detail, Zukofsky describes the surroundings of his and Celia's East 180th Street Bronx home: the river, the park across the street, the lions' roars from the zoo a quarter mile away. What makes the story so striking is Zukofsky's description of his own quandary, his own search for the next sentence of the novella:

> *Though characters must take things in their own stride—somewhere in his story the writer cannot hold back this sentence that judges them. . . . The difficulty is to judge without seeming to be there, with a finality in the words that will make them casual and part of the story itself, except perhaps to another age.*

He has barely started preparing breakfast when his wife, *"without a word,"* takes over the task; so he straightens the house in anticipation of their weekly morning walk in the park. And as he dwells—lovingly, again—on the furnishings of their shared dwelling, the sentence comes to him: *"—You were good to me."* [25]

The real interest of this curiously static little story lies in the portrait it gives us of the writer at work, worrying his night away over the next sentence of his story, convinced that the writer's life, and the life of his prose, depend on the precise joinery of every single sentence. The writer arrives at his sentence—*"You were good to me,"* a statement of gratitude, of affection—only after refreshing his senses with the surroundings of his married life. After his marriage to Celia, married love would become the primary theme of Zukofsky's poetry, and the history that so dominated the early movements of *"A"* would become no longer a protagonist in the poem, but the constantly shifting backdrop to the affectionate retreat he and Celia would create, almost out of reach of the cries and alarums of the world around them.

. . .

Although Basil Bunting had spent time in prison as a conscientious objector at the end of the First World War, he enlisted soon after September 1939; by the end of 1941 he had managed to parlay his knowledge of Persian into a posting to Iran, where the British hoped to preserve Iranian oil fields from both the Germans and nationalist Iranian interests. [26] Bunting kept in close touch with Zukofsky when he could, sending him long and vivid letters, but no doubt holding back his more cutting insights for fear of the military censors. Zukofsky was also anxious to contribute to the struggle against fascism, but his age, his always frail health, his weak eyes, and his marital status all made him a poor candidate for the military. In October 1941 he applied for a job as a translator with the FBI; he listed his height as five feet nine inches, his weight as 130 pounds, and his employer as the Index of American Design. Nothing came of the application, nor of others. In November 1942, after applying for a commission in the army, Zukofsky was contacted by an army procurement officer who "wanted a man who could speak French without the *least* hesitation, who had a vocabulary including patois, argot etc etc. <and could understand everything *anyone* speaking French might spill on him.>" Zukofsky was more straightforward than Bunting, who had probably not emphasized that his knowledge of the Iranian tongue was limited to *classical* Persian: he told Major Crawford that he "could fit the bill with a little practice."[27] The army apparently wanted someone whose language skills were more immediate.

. . .

While Zukofsky's employment prospects were tenuous throughout 1941—it looked increasingly likely that the United States would enter the war, and when that happened it was anyone's guess what would become of the WPA—Zukofsky's poetry was beginning to receive some long-deferred hearing. Thanks to the poet Norman Macleod, director of the Poetry Center at the 92nd Street YMHA, Zukofsky gave a reading at the Y on January 23, 1941, before about sixty people.[28] Zukofsky prefaced his reading—a long one, including pieces from *55 Poems*, new work from the manuscript *Anew*, a section of "A"-8, and all of "A"-10—with a talk entitled "The Objectivist Program." Whether or not there had been an objectivist "movement," Zukofsky believed that the poetic principles he had laid down ten years before still held good. After going over the history of objectivist publications, he boiled those principles down: "*Sincerity*—thinking with the things as they exist[.] *Objectification*—making another thing—a *poem*—existing so that it would seem on a par with other things." "Tonight," he said, "we want to get at the poems I'm going to read in the way I've described. And it's up to you now to judge what values of good poetry are in them. . . . And that's about all there is to the Objectivist intention."[29] Macleod at least must have been impressed, for he invited Zukofsky back the following year to take part in a symposium on poetry and the war, where Zukofsky read Walt Whitman's scathing, electrifying "Respondez!," which, he told Williams, was "a perfect poem in itself—the kind of thing that an intelligence in our time ought to be willing to live and die for."[30]

. . .

Louis and Celia Zukofsky had "published" *First Half of "A"-9* in November 1940; of the fifty-five numbered and signed copies, one went to the Register of Copyrights, and fifteen more were reserved for presentation. Zukofsky sent copies to Williams, Rakosi, Pound, and others, and hoped to sell the remaining thirty-nine for two dollars apiece. (Buyers were not beating at the door, for Zukofsky still had copies on hand as late as 1958.[31]) The couple had realized that conventional publishing outlets were simply not going to release Zukofsky's work. Laughlin, the most prominent advocate of innovative poetry and prose, had turned down *Sincerity and Objectification*, and was not enthusiastic about Zukofsky's short poems, though he was—probably to Zukofsky's chagrin—planning to do a selection of Rakosi's work.[32] It was Williams who pointed Zukofsky towards the press of James A. Decker in Prairie City, Illinois.

Decker had started publishing 1937 at the age of twenty with a secondhand press and a few cases of type. He began with a poetry journal, *Upward* (later *Compass*), publishing Moore, Williams, Stevens, and others, and rapidly expanded to printing books. Within the next five years he issued some fifty volumes of verse, among them collections by Hubert Creekmore, Charles Henri Ford, Norman Macleod, and Edouard Roditi. (He was to achieve nationwide fame in 1941 and 1942 by issuing two volumes by fellow Illinoisan Edgar Lee Masters.) By the first part of 1941, Zukofsky had come to an agreement with Decker for the long-delayed publication of *55 Poems*. Decker had not begun as an author-subsidized press, but by the early 1940s, he was accepting money from authors to print their work—usually a two-hundred-dollar investment for a print run of two hundred copies, with profits going directly to the author until the subsidy was repaid.[33] The Zukofskys probably reached a similar deal with Decker for *55 Poems*.

55 Poems was a comprehensive, carefully constructed survey of Zukofsky's poetry from 1923 to 1935. He had been tinkering with the manuscript a long time; indeed, he had prepared a typescript under the title *55 Poems* back in 1933, for possible publication by Wishard and Company in London.[34] One needed to be no more a mathematician than Zukofsky himself to see that the book's two major sections, "29 Poems" and "29 Songs," added up to *fifty-eight* poems, not even counting the collection's opener, "Poem beginning 'The'," and the two pieces at the end, "Further than" and "'Mantis'" (Zukofsky considered "'Mantis'" and "*'Mantis,' An Interpretation*" a single poem for counting purposes). A note at the book's end served somewhat to clarify Zukofsky's numerological intentions: "The six blank pages intended by Song 29, written January 29th, 1933, were filled during 1933 and the early months of 1934 with songs 11, 23, 24, 26, 27, 28. Added to the original collection their number is not included in, or for, the title of the book, namely *55 Poems*. They are dedicated rather by their subjects."[35] Song 29, "N.Y.," had been written on a talismanic birthday, Zukofsky's twenty-ninth, which fell on January 29, 1933.[36] "As planned there should be to-day / 29 songs written over two years," he wrote, but he had fallen short of that number: "I have written down twenty-three / Leaving 5 and another page blank."[37] "29 Songs," a title to which Zukofsky stuck even when it was obvious he had fallen six songs short, became less a designator of quantity than an assertion that these songs had something to do with his twenty-ninth year. The six added pieces—most of them political poems—the original version of the Note read, "are dedicated rather to the file and rank."[38]

The book begins with an epigraph from Omar Khayyám's *Rubaiyat*, reproduced in Bunting's calligraphy. "One day in Rapallo," Zukofsky told Niedecker, "B. said he always connected that stanza, never Englished by Fitzgerald, with me & wd. like to see it opening a book of mine." "We cannot speak out as many of the world's secret as are in our ledger," it reads (in Bunting's translation). "It would bring calamity upon us. Because there is not, amongst these learned people,

one with sense, not everything that is in our mind can be uttered."[39]
"Poem beginning 'The'" follows as 55 *Poems'* first poem, and the book
closes with "'Mantis,'" an impressive bracketing of the rich variety
of voices and forms between the two—as though Zukofsky were
asserting his bid for modernist mastery by opening and closing his
collection with his own updated versions of Eliot's *The Waste Land* and
Pound's "Sestina: Altaforte."

"29 Poems" is the earlier of the two main groups, dating from
1923 (the manuscript of "*tam cari capitis*" has the notation "Student
days"[40]) through 1929. "29 Songs" begins with a cluster of poems
written in Madison, including the high-spirited "It's a gay li-ife," a
light jab at Zukofsky's conceit of the poet as horse:

> There's naw-thing
>   lak po-ee try
> it's a delicacy
>   for   a horse;
>
> Dere's na-thing
>   lak pea-   nut brittle
> it's a delicacy
>   for   the molars.[41]

Poems of clear political import, like "Home for Aged Bomb Throwers
—U.S.S.R.," lie cheek by jowl with delicate, subtle love lyrics like "Do
not leave me" and airy, almost content-free constructions of tenuous
syntax and sound, like Song 12:

> Whatever makes this happening
>   Is unheard
>   To a third.
>
> Two. Where two should
>   Stand. One. One.
>   With the sun. In a wood.
>
> Tomorrow is unsought.
>   No oasis of ivy to inurn
>   Either foot or fern.[42]

The sixty-one poems of 55 Poems demonstrated that Zukofsky commanded a range, formal variety, and aural mastery surpassing that of any of his contemporaries.

Williams had given Zukofsky some phrases of endorsement for the dust jacket of 55 Poems. He reused one of those phrases, "An extraordinary sensitivity," as the title of the review he published the next year in *Poetry* magazine.[43] Williams worked hard to speak fairly of poems he admired but did not always understand. He found Zukofsky's "a dangerous sort of writing," dependent upon a reader "who is sensitive enough, trained enough and ready enough to place himself exactly in tune with it to appreciate its just observations and careful statements of fact . . ." More "explicit" writing, Williams contended, could at least be reduced to a satisfying prose "sense," but "when sense, even if ploddingly, cannot solve a sentence because of an over-absence of its parts," Williams wrote, "the fault cannot be said to lie with the reader. But to fly, we require a certain lightness—and wings. Among these poems (at their best) we have them."

.   .   .

The United States entered the war after the Japanese attack on Pearl Harbor in December 1941, and employees of the Index of American Design knew the WPA's days were numbered as the government shifted to a wartime footing. "Rumor, possibly reliable, has it our project is to end Feb. 1," Zukofsky wrote Niedecker. "We *may* be switched to make inventories of museum objects to be stored away for the 'duration'. . . . I feel like a corpse just thinking about it." By February Zukofsky was once more out of a job. He remained unemployed for about six months, but Celia's income from her teaching position was able to carry the couple through.[44] At the end of June, they moved out of their Bronx apartment to spend the summer upstate in Diamond Point, near Lake George, where they had "rented a cottage to live cheaply."[45]

For Zukofsky this time at the lake, like all vacations, was a working vacation. He had finished *Ferdinand* in mid-June. Now that "A"-8, the first half of "A"-9, and "A"-10 were written, he went back to the poem's first seven movements, completed twelve years earlier, and revised them to where they "[stood] up alongside of the later" to his satisfaction.[46] Zukofsky rarely produced multiple manuscripts of a given work. As he told Mary Barnard in 1940, "Most of my work is written before it is written down on paper, and if revised at all after that,—years later."[47] The poem, that is, had been deeply pondered before being committed to the page. If by that point it had no life or value, then it was senseless to try to improve it by fussy revision; better to discard it, as Zukofsky discarded masses of his early work. There was, however, value in returning to work after a long interval, a fresh perspective enabled by time and distance.

In the case of "A"-1 through "A"-6, this involved mostly excisions, cutting lines and phrases and making the movements more swift and compact. It also involved culling out some of the more coy self-references of the early parts of the poem. In the first published version of "A"-1, for instance, the usher had said, "Not past that exit, Zukofsky!", which became in the revised version the more plausible "Not that exit, Sir!"[48] "A"-2 had begun:

> The clear music—
> Zoo-zoo-kaw-kaw-of-the-sky,
> Not mentioning names, says Kay,
> Poetry is not made of such things,
> Old music, itch according to its wonts,
> Snapped old cat-guts from Johann Sebastian,
> Society, traduction twice over.
>
> Damn you, Kay,
> What do you, Kay, know about it!
> Wherever always we are
> Crowds the sea in upon us,
> Slivers of slugs from the seaweed,
> Tossed cuttlefish shouldering
> Ball of imperialism,
> Wave-games of its stanchions . . .

In July 1942, Zukofsky whittled that down to

> —Clear music—
> Not calling you names, says Kay,
> Poetry is not made of such things,

Music, itch according to its wonts,
Snapped old catguts of Johann Sebastian,
Society, traduction twice over.

—Kay, in the sea
There with you,
Slugs, cuttlefish,
Ball of imperialism, wave games . . .[49]

The three-part division of the first six movements—"A"-1 and -2, "A"-3 and -4, "A"-5 and -6 as single sections—was discarded so that each movement stood on its own. With these revisions, Zukofsky had put the first major block of his poem into its final form.

Zukofsky's other project that summer involved an "excellent painter" he had discovered at Diamond Point, a fifty-six-year-old Hungarian immigrant named Dometer Guczul.[50] For Zukofsky, Guczul invited "comparison with anonymous American *primitive* painters and other *primitives*"—a comparison that bracketed this Rembrandt-worshipping genre painter (whose canvases included "The Old Spinning Wheel" and "The Pickaninny") with both the anonymous craftsmen of American design and the "primitive" artists admired by Picasso and Braque. Perhaps, in writing his brief overview of the painter's solitary labors—for Guczul had never shown his work outside "of one small room in a temporary wood cottage in which he lives"—Zukofsky was recalling Pound's promotion of Gaudier-Brzeska, or Apollinaire's of the cubists; Zukofsky compared Guczul's work to that of both the *Douanier* Rousseau and Francis Picabia.[51] Williams told Zukofsky to send the essay "Dometer Guczul" to Laughlin; it was published the following year in Charles Henri Ford's surrealist magazine *View*.[52]

. . .

The Zukofskys returned to New York in early September, staying with Celia's parents in Brooklyn until they could move at the end of the month into a new apartment in Brooklyn Heights, a neighborhood they would inhabit for most of the next twenty-two years.[53] Still at a loss for work, Zukofsky renewed his substitute teaching license and began filling in for $8.50 a day in English classrooms, where he found "discipline problems" "something awful." So he settled for a job as a lab assistant at Brooklyn Technical High School; while it paid a dollar a day less, "The school is nearby, has a fine set of boys, friendly staff, and the work is pleasant."[54] He continued in the New York high schools through the end of the academic year, when he began a job editing instruction books for the Hazeltine Electronics Corporation in Little Neck, Queens.

Here finally he could contribute to the war effort: Hazeltine, like other high-tech companies, had become a defense contractor. Zukofsky edited the manuals that would allow soldiers, sailors, and airmen to operate the complex devices that Hazeltine was manufacturing for America's arsenal: radios, bombsights, the electronic systems of submarines.[55] Technical editing was a challenging business, which involved taking often linguistically challenged engineers' accounts of how their technology worked and rendering them into readable English. In late 1943 Hazeltine asked Zukofsky to prepare a report on Basic English. Basic, a "simplified, all-purpose, idiomatic" version of English, had been invented in the years after the First World War by the Cambridge linguist C. K. Ogden, and had been promoted thereafter by his student I. A. Richards. While large English dictionaries contained almost half a million words, Basic consisted of a mere "850 words, which, together with a summary of rules fill a single page."[56] Ogden intended Basic as a learning tool to afford children and non-English speakers access to English culture, but no doubt the executives at Hazeltine wondered if this simplified language might prove handy in making their technology accessible to the GIs who were its ultimate users.

Zukofsky's report on Basic took the form of a pointed "running comment" on Ogden's *Basic English: Introduction and Rules* (1938) from the point of view of both a "writer of instruction books on radio" and a poet, concerned with the most forceful and graceful uses of language. Zukofsky took a decidedly jaundiced view of Ogden's project. Of Ogden's eschewal of a number of simple verbs—"rise," "shave," and "feed" would be replaced by "to get up," "to take hair off the face," and "to take food"—Zukofsky commented, "Like Swift's Laputans, the founder of BASIC begins by building from the roof down." In the event, the user of Basic would have to use his or her limited stock of words in so many idiomatic ways that the language would become little simpler than standard English. Worst of all, Basic's rules forced its writers into graceless paraphrase and even the mortal sin (for Zukofsky) of *abstraction*:

> trying to conform to BASIC the writer of instruction books on radio by looking for a paraphrase runs the risk of losing time and conciseness. He may even end up with BASIC words which both BASIC's founder and Jeremy Bentham have called *fictions*. These make mental cowards of us all, in as much as *things* and relations of things that should be pretty close to words which stand for them become dim behind films of thought, which are so to speak fifth removed from things.[57]

By the end of the report, Zukofsky had gotten far from the implications of Basic for technical writing, and was criticizing Ogden for his underlying goal, "a common language": "the refreshing differences to be got from different ways of handling facts in the sound and peculiar expressions of different tongues," Zukofsky wrote, "is [*sic*] not to be overlooked, precisely because they have *international* worth."[58] In the end, what was worthwhile in the Basic English project, according to Zukofsky, was identical to the principles of good writing, and had nothing to do with Basic's prescriptive word list: "'To know your meaning, and to state it as simply as possible' sums up the best in BASIC. Good writing means a grasp of and a closeness to subject or object rather than an addiction to a large or small vocabulary"—or, as he put it back in 1930, "thinking with the things as they exist."[59]

. . .

Louis and Celia Zukofsky's son, Paul, was born at about 8 P.M. on October 22, 1943. The next day, in "Joe's B'klyn Restaurant," Zukofsky drafted a brief and hopeful adaptation of Guido Cavalcanti's *ballata*, "Perch'i' no spero di tornar giammai," evoking an Italy to which he hoped one day to return, and looking forward to a new family life:

To my baby Paul
(After Guido)

Since we can't go back to Tuscany, Dinty,
We'll drink to you and Celia and to Jerry

And place her there who has never seen a
                            vineyard—
Drinking Chianti with us for the days
                            when you will be growing.[60]

With a child to support, Zukofsky cast about for a job that might
pay more than Hazeltine. In October 1944, as Paul neared his first
birthday, Zukofsky moved from Hazeltine to Jordanoff Aviation
Corporation, where he again edited instruction books. During the
war it was difficult to switch jobs within the defense industry; one
had to prove that one would be more "essential" in the new position
than in the old. It made no difference to the representative of the War
Manpower Commission—one William Hauptmann—that Zukofsky
would be making more money at Jordanoff than Hazeltine, nor was
he impressed by Zukofsky's scant experience in actual engineering.
It was only when he asked, "are you L.Z. the poet?" and Zukofsky
wearily replied in the affirmative that Hauptmann said, "That settles
it," and gave him the release to change jobs. Hauptmann had read
"Poem beginning 'The'" in the *Exile* back in 1928; "As Rezy said,"
Zukofsky wrote, "if you get a book out someone'll read it."[61]

Jordanoff sent its employees to work directly with manufacturers,
so Zukofsky spent much of 1945 away from New York, in such places
as Cambridge, Massachusetts, and Towson, Maryland, where Bendix
Aviation was located.[62] Reisman was working for Bendix in Towson
as well, but Zukofsky found the work he did over 1945 isolating—he
missed Celia and Paul when he was forced to be away from them, he
was largely out of touch with his literary acquaintances, and even Taupin had been incommunicado for some two years—and intellectually
unrewarding: "Taking care of the output of eight writers turning out
3000 pages of crap for the Corps of Engineers," as he described his
postwar responsibilities in late 1945.[63]

In the fall of 1945, Laughlin told Pound that "I haven't heard
from Zuk in years. He seems to have burrowed down into his own
private little world."[64] While Laughlin was never high on the list of
Zukofsky's correspondents, he was largely right. Peripatetic work,
a new family, and the continued indifference of publishers—"I'm
certain," Zukofsky told Williams, "I'd write more if the possibility of

publication drove me to it"[65]—had pushed Zukofsky far from the public eye. *A Test of Poetry* was still making the rounds of publishers, with no taker in sight. *"A"* had been shelved for the nonce. There was one bright spot on the horizon, as the Pacific war wound to its close: The Zukofskys could anticipate the imminent publication of Zukofsky's second Decker Press collection, with the optimistic title *Anew*.

A New Life 1946–1951

THE WAR HAD TURNED against the Axis in 1943, and the great conflict spent much of 1945 winding itself down. Hitler committed suicide on April 20, and on May 8 Germany surrendered to the Allies. The Japanese would capitulate soon after the atomic bombs fell on Hiroshima and Nagasaki in early August. President Franklin Delano Roosevelt, who had shepherded the nation through twelve tumultuous years, would live to see neither victory. On April 12, 1945, three months into his unprecedented fourth term, he died of a cerebral hemorrhage. Four days after his death, Zukofsky drafted a lyric that encapsulated some of his own frustrations and griefs:

> I shall go back to my mother's grave after this war
> Because there are those who'll still speak of loyalty
> In the outskirts of Baltimore
> Or wherever Jews are not the right sort of people,
> And say to her one of the dead I speak to—
> There are less Jews left in the world,

While they were killed
I did not see you in a dream to tell you,
And that I now have a wife and son.[1]

In January 1945, Zukofsky, Celia, and Paul had moved temporarily
to Baltimore. He was working for Jordanoff Aviation in Towson, a
suburb of the city, but the three took an apartment in Baltimore itself
because they had been "refused any <and all> apartments in Towson
<because we're Jews and/or have a baby>";[2] even as the evidence of
the Nazi death camps filtered into American national consciousness,
there were still neighborhoods "restricted" to Jews. Like Whitman
in "Respondez!," Zukofsky wrote bitterly of his country, a nation of
"forced labor" where all "grace" and "gentleness" had yielded to economics and commodification:

Then I shall go and write of my country,
Have a job all my life
Seldom write with grace again, be part of the world,
See every man in forced labor,
Dawn only where suburbs are *restricted*
To people who take trains every morning,
Never the gentleness that can be,
The hope of the common man, the eyes that love leaves
Any shade, thought or thing that makes all men uncommon,

The poem's close conflates the silence of the dead with the "lovely
air" of oncoming spring:

So early and late in the fortunes that followed me from my
        mother's grave
A lovely air follows her
And the dead President who is worth it:
'Dear death, like peace, I end not speaking,
The chitchat has died
And the last smile is unwilled
I am dead, I can't talk
To blossoms or spring in the world.'

On May 3, Ezra Pound was arrested outside Rapallo by Italian partisans and placed in the hands of the U.S. Army. Early in 1941 Pound

had begun making broadcasts on Italian national radio, shortwave broadcasts aimed specifically at American listeners. After the United States entered the war, he continued the broadcasts, now under the auspices of a declared enemy. Like his Cantos, Pound's ten-minute talks were oblique and densely allusive, but they were also fiercely polemical, attacking Roosevelt and the international conspiracy of Jewish "usurers" who had led Europe into war and drawn the United States in after.[3] In July 1943, as Mussolini's government toppled under the pressure of the Allied bombing of Rome, Pound was indicted for treason. Nonetheless, in December 1943 he began broadcasting again for Mussolini's Salò government, a puppet regime sustained by the Germans in northern Italy.[4] Pound was arrested five days after Mussolini had been captured and executed by partisans. At the end of May, he was sent to a Disciplinary Training Camp near Pisa, where American soldiers who had been convicted of serious crimes were allowed to work out their sentences "by enduring one year of training 14 hours a day, one year of terrible discipline, unbroken regimentation, monotony, and constant chewing."[5] Here Pound wrote the *Pisan Cantos*.

Zukofsky was ambivalent about his old friend's plight. As he wrote Niedecker, "[Pound] believes Hitler was a saint & a martyr; Musso was weak because too human, but that the greatest political mind of our time is Stalin. Eclectic as ever. I'd hate to see him shot but that's what he deserves . . ."[6] Pound was flown to Washington to stand trial in November, and at the recommendation of the court's psychiatrist and his own legal counsel was transferred to St. Elizabeths Hospital for the Insane. In February 1946 he was declared officially "unsound," unable to stand trial—but not innocent by reason of insanity. Caught in this legal double bind, he would remain in St. Elizabeths until 1958. "It's a mad way out," Zukofsky wrote Williams, "typical of our time: glib psychiatrists, willing judges etc. As far as Ezra is concerned it doesn't make any difference, I suppose. As an old friend I hate to think of him suffering, if he is (I doubt it), but he was certainly willing to see millions suffer <while he> ranted."[7]

Zukofsky's statement on his friend, which appeared in the literary journalist Charles Norman's *The Case of Ezra Pound* in 1948, was careful, guarded, and deeply regretful. Zukofsky praised Pound's "profound and intimate knowledge and practice" of poetry, and asserted that Pound's anti-Semitism had never manifested itself to him in person: "I never felt the least trace of anti-Semitism *in his presence*. Nothing he ever *said* to me made me feel the embarrassment I always have for the 'Goy' in whom a residue of antagonism to 'Jew' remains" (emphases added). "In his presence" was disingenuous: Zukofsky had only met Pound twice in the course of their twenty-year relationship, and there had been anti-Semitism aplenty in Pound's letters to him. "He may be condemned or forgiven," Zukofsky concluded. "Biographers of the future may find his character as charming a subject as that of Aaron Burr. It will matter very little against his finest work overshadowed in his lifetime by the hell of Belsen which he overlooked."[8]

. . .

For some years Zukofsky had in mind the title *Anew* for his second collection of poems, but *Anew*'s appearance in March 1946 was indicative of both a new, postwar life and the new directions taken by Zukofsky's poetry since *55 Poems*. Once again the Zukofskys turned to James A. Decker to issue Zukofsky's poems, but where *55 Poems* had been a handsomely printed, substantial volume, *Anew* was one of the first in Decker's new series of inexpensive, small-format books, Pocket Poetry. As the dust jacket explained, "The size and format of this book is [*sic*] not intended as a novelty. We are publishing most of our new titles in this format—because we believe poetry is particularly suited to a pocket-fitting format, . . . a size that can be easily 'carried along' with the reader, especially in such a restless age as ours."[9]

Nearly all of the poems of *Anew* were written between 1937 and 1944. Some of the early poems showed Zukofsky's interest in mining his dream life for poetry. The four haunting lines of number 24, for instance, which seemed perfectly to capture the surreal atmosphere of the "Sitzkrieg" between the fall of Poland and the German invasion of western Europe—

The men in the kitchens
Their women in the foundries

The children in the wars
The old men at the boundaries[10]

—were, Zukofsky noted on the manuscript, "Dreamed, morning of Oct 28, 1939."

"*che di lor suona su nella tua vita*," the collection's first poem, also sprang from a dream, as Zukofsky explained in a note at the end of the volume: "When I awoke the exact words of the poem I dreamt were lost, but those I wrote down still seemed to follow on the events of the dream."[11] The poem presents a syntactically straightforward but puzzling personal narrative:

I walked out, before
"Break of day"
And saw
Four cabins in the hay.

Blue sealed glasses
Of preserves—four—
In the window-sash
In the yard on the bay.

Further:
The waters
At the ramp
Running away.[12]

Dream writing was very important to the surrealists, deeply influenced as they were by Freud, but what is interesting in "*che di lor suona su nella tua vita*" (its title is from *Inferno* IV.77) is how Zukofsky combines the seemingly unmediated act of dream writing with a powerful sense of intertextuality, of previous voices speaking in his own poem—of the line "Break of day," he wrote, "I was aware in the dream that I was writing a poem and also aware of verses by others"—and an awareness of the multiple connotations of each word. "The word 'bay,'" Zukofsky noted, "is what I could reconstruct later from the feeling of the action of the dream," and is meant to "convey something of all the meanings of the word 'bay': red-brown, the laurel wreath, a bay horse, a deep bark or cry, a window-bay, a large space in a barn for storage as of hay or fodder, the state of being kept at a standstill, but more specifically two meanings that seemed to include all the others, they are, an arm of the sea and a recess of low land between hills."[13] Zukofsky is offering a primer for reading his poetry: first, the reader ought to be aware of all the echoes of "verses by others" ("I walked out," for instance, recalls countless British and Irish ballads); and furthermore, the reader must be alert to all possible meanings of the poem's words.

Dream-poems are relatively rare in *Anew*. The volume's clearest internal continuity lies in its lyricism, a musical poetics at times entirely emptied of content, as in the twentieth poem:

> The lines of this new song are nothing
> But a tune making the nothing full
> Stonelike become more hard than silent
> The tune's image holding in the line.[14]

Even in poems as musically absorbed as these, however, Zukofsky could conceal great weights of background. "Glad they were there," for instance, seems an exercise in dancing meters—

> Falling away
> Flying not to
> Lose sight of it
> Not going far
> In angles out
> Of ovals of . . .[15]

—but, as Zukofsky details in a note at the end of *Anew*, has been distilled from passages of Cavalcanti, Dante's *Paradiso*, *Das Kapital*, and Henrik Anton Lorentz's *Theory of Electrons*.[16]

Several poems stand out for the specificity of their references. "1892–1941" details a visit to Rock Creek Cemetery in Washington, D.C., where Henry and Clover Adams lie buried beneath an enigmatic bronze figure by Adams's friend August St. Gaudens: "Characterless lips, straight nose, sight, form no clue / (are none too great sculpture) to portrait or you." (The year 1892 was when Adams first saw St. Gaudens's memorial to his wife; 1941 was the year of the Zukofskys' visit to the cemetery.)[17] There are two epithalamia, or marriage songs, for Zukofsky's nephew Moe E. Pruss and for his brother Morris's daughter Florence. There are the first of the many Valentine poems that would appear in Zukofsky's collections. And there are several poems addressed explicitly to Celia, the deftest of them an adaptation of the seventeenth-century poet Sir Charles Sedley's "A Song to Celia" in which Zukofsky reproduces Sedley's meter and rhyme words. Sedley's poem ends:

> Why then should I seek farther Store,
>   And still make Love anew;
> When Change it self can give no more,
>   'Tis easie to be true.[18]

Zukofsky alters Sedley's lyric from a conventional declaration of love to a meditation on how *Anew* itself would memorialize the love Louis and Celia shared:

> And if your ear hear me I store
>   It in our book *Anew*
> Where we last who make Sedley—more
>   Than he was perhaps—true.[19]

One notes how Zukofsky has made play with the senses of "true": Sedley's remaining faithful to a single lover has become his telling the *truth* in his verse. This making anew of the old—the appropriation, adaptation, or allusion to previous authors' words—was to become more and more prevalent in Zukofsky's work, until he would build an entire branch of his poetics upon the use of such preexisting literary templates.

.   .   .

There were a number of brief reviews of *Anew*, but the most substantial assessment came from Bill Williams. Williams had responded enthusiastically to the book when he first received it—"Wonderful! Metrically I can see at once that it is the only adult verse being written today"[20]—and he elaborated his praise in his review "A New Line Is a New Measure," published in the *New Quarterly of Poetry*. "This poetry," Williams wrote, "is lyric in a way that we have hardly sensed at all for a century." "In Zukofsky's work," he specified, "there are many excellences clustered about the main one of a new understanding of the line structure, which is the great novelty bearing the others." Reading Zukofsky, Williams could "hear a new music of verse stretching out into the future." Most strikingly, Zukofsky's love poems were not *about* love, as love poetry in the past had been: "They don't try to SAY anything where nothing can be said. They seek to *embody* love in the words. To make love."[21]

In early 1943 Williams had entrusted Zukofsky with a manuscript of poems tentatively entitled "THE (lang) WEDGE" or "The Language." Zukofsky had edited the book sensitively but thoroughly, cutting Williams's typescript from 115 to 82 pages. Williams adopted almost all of Zukofsky's suggestions, and was so grateful that he dedicated the book—finally published as *The Wedge* in September 1944—to Zukofsky.[22] His next project, however, the long poem *Paterson*, he did not show to Zukofsky in manuscript, preferring to let him see the first installment when New Directions published it in early 1946. Williams, one suspects, was more comfortable letting Zukofsky work with his collections than with a single large project; he trusted Zukofsky's skills at sequencing, arranging, and weeding out individual poems, but perhaps felt vulnerable about embarking upon a long poem in his late fifties, while Zukofsky had already been at work on his own for almost twenty years.

Celia Zukofsky had been composing musical settings for Zukofsky's poems since soon after their marriage, and by 1948 had set some fourteen of his lyrics. In 1946 she did a setting of Williams's poem "The Pink Church," and between 1943 and 1949 she completed a setting for piano and voice of Shakespeare's *Pericles, Prince of Tyre*.[23] No doubt the Zukofskys hoped eventually to get *Pericles* performed by professional musicians, but in the meantime they had to settle for informal after-dinner performances, such as the one the couple gave Zukofsky's old Columbia professor Mark Van Doren, who inscribed his latest book "to C & LZ, composer and best singer of 'Pericles.'" "I guess he liked it & really meant he didn't mind my singing," Zukofsky commented wryly. "That's the only way we can get people to hear it unfortunately."[24]

. . .

In March 1946 Zukofsky left Jordanoff Aviation to join Techlit Consultants, a technical writing firm his friend Reisman had started the year before.[25] It was an uneasy time to be in the technical writing business, particularly since in late 1945 Louis and Celia had bought their first home, a handsome four-story row house at 30 Willow Street, Brooklyn. They moved there at the beginning of May 1946. It had been overly optimistic of Reisman to start a technical writing firm at the end of the war, and Techlit Consultants was feeling the crunch by the end of 1946. If business did not pick up in the new year, Reisman told Zukofsky, he would have to cut his staff to a bare minimum in order to stay afloat.[26] Zukofsky left Techlit in January 1947, and around the same time ended his seventeen-year friendship with Reisman.

In February, Zukofsky started as an instructor of English at the Polytechnic Institute of Brooklyn, which would be his institutional home for the rest of his career. While Brooklyn Polytechnic (or "Poly," as the students knew it) had little investment in the humanities—its students pursued degrees in engineering and the hard sciences—its reputation was strong and growing; research done by its faculty had been instrumental to the Allied development of radar during the war. Brooklyn Polytechnic was experiencing a postwar boom, as thousands of returning veterans entered college under the GI Bill. Such enrollment pressures were no doubt responsible for Zukofsky's mid-academic-year hiring. His department chair was a Professor Saidla, "a nice old Danish American" who had taught with Pound at Wabash College in Indiana in 1907–8. Zukofsky thought he would do all right at Poly: "I'll be there a good long time while there are students (i.e. till next war)."[27]

. . .

The war's last year had been a time of economic uncertainty and "drudgery" for Zukofsky, and he had written very few poems in 1945. In May of that year, however, seeing his son learning to speak set Zukofsky once again to thinking about poetry in the broadest terms. "When you were 19 months old," he addressed Paul, "your ability to say 'Go billy go billy go billy go ba,' much faster than I could ever say it, made me take some almost illegible notes on poetry out of my wallet. The time had come for me to fill the vacuum I abhorred in my life as much as you had filled it in yours."[28] The essay Zukofsky worked up from those "notes" over the next year and a half, "Poetry / *For My Son When He Can Read*," was his most comprehensive meditation on his art, a thoughtful, tender consideration of the place of poetry in the human world.[29] The essays of the objectivist years—"Sincerity and Objectification" and "'Recencies' in Poetry"—had been tied up in the business of commentary and literary polemic. Now, feeling very much beyond the jostle of the poetry marketplace, addressing a projected reader—his infant son—with no investment in any literary quarrels, Zukofsky set out to formulate his deepest sense of what poetry was, and what it was *for*.

Poetry is an art that enables one to live in one's own moment, and simultaneously an art of memory: "without poetry," Zukofsky writes, "life would have little present. To write poems is not enough if they do not keep the life that has gone. To write poems may never seem enough when they speak of a life that has gone." The poet is not merely a lone, self-absorbed singer, but a craftsman whose makings are part of an overall *paideia*, an educative program to train human beings to live humanely in society. Even when silent, the poet is not idle, "but secretly measures himself against each word of poetry ever written. Furthermore, if he is of constant depth, he thinks of others who have lived, live, and will live to say the things he cannot say for the time being. People who do this are always working."[30] Every poem it is possible to write has been preceded by a myriad of poems and will be followed by another myriad, will take its place among those poems and be judged in comparison with them. "Originality," then, is an empty goal, just as chronology and geographic distance are categories of interest only to literary historians, biographers, and other pedants.

The poet "measures" himself, Zukofsky writes, with Plato's words never far from his mind: "If number, measure and weighing be taken away from any art, that which remains will not be much." "Someone alive in the years 1951 to 2000," Zukofsky muses, "may attempt a scientific definition of poetry." He himself will not do so: for all his citations of Einstein, Poincaré, and Lorentz, and for all the calculus in "A"-8 and -9, Zukofsky was no scientist. But he can consider how poetry, like science, is one of humanity's fundamental ways of encountering the world, and how poetry—again like science— depends on "standards," measures. Those who would reject an objective "standard of song," Zukofsky argues, must realize that the words of a poem stand in the same relation to the poet's experience and environment as the language and symbols of science do to the physical world: "The choice for science and poetry when symbols or words stop measuring is to stop speaking." Ultimately, poetry's "aims and those of science are not opposed or mutually exclusive," Zukofsky writes; it is "only the more complicated, if not finer, tolerances of number, measure and weight that define poetry [which] make it seem imprecise as compared to science, to quick readers of instruments."[31]

Poems, like the equations and theories of science, are "but phases of utterance," human beings' seeking to organize and "speak" the world around them. "The action that precedes and moves towards utterance moves towards poetry"—not just the action of the poet and the scientist, but that of the architect, the dancer, the economist and historian, the painter and musician, and even the weaver—"all who achieve constructions apart from themselves, move in effect toward poetry."[32] As for the poet, his "specialized concern" must be first "to avoid clutter no matter how many details outside and in the head are ordered," "For his second and major aim is not to show himself but that order that of itself can speak to all men"—an order that Zukofsky associates with music.

But what of poetry in the postwar world? "The poet wonders why so many today have raised up the word 'myth,' finding the lack of so-called 'myths' in our time a crisis the poet must overcome or die from, as it were, having become too radioactive." Why pursue myths, "when instead a case can be made out for the poet giving some of his life to the words *the* and *a*"—as Zukofsky had himself done in "Poem beginning 'The,'" and was still doing in "*A*"—"both of which are weighted with as much epos and historical destiny as one man can perhaps resolve. Those who do not believe this are too sure that the little words mean nothing among so many other words."[33] Zukofsky's challenge was to go largely unheeded: While postwar American poetry would turn not to myth, but to the plainspoken or plaintively personal—even the "confessional"—Zukofsky would remain almost alone in his determination to unravel the "epos and historical destiny" of the "little words."

The final page of "Poetry / *For My Son When He Can Read*" presents a handful of lines from Zukofsky's own poetry and brief quotations from five "friends"—Bunting, Pound, Williams, Niedecker, and Reznikoff. "My intention should appear even more complete to you," Zukofsky tells Paul, "if I say that I shall be most the poet when Celia finishes her music to the words of 'Pericles.' For the work she has put into them has often made us hear 'Shakespeare' speak." Paradoxically, perhaps, the poet is "most the poet" not when he is composing, but when he is most open to the words of others.

Almost as an afterthought, Zukofsky appends the entire text of "Respondez!" ("Whitman's greatest poem"), which "could more easily have served the definition of poetry we anticipate[.]"[34] Whitman's bitterly satirical poem, revised in the wake of the Civil War, takes on new life as a savage indictment of post–World War II American complacency and materialism. Like Whitman, Zukofsky believed passionately in the democratic ideals upon which America had been founded, and like Whitman he grieved at the betrayal of those ideals. Throughout the 1950s and 1960s, he would survey the course of American democracy with outrage and sorrow, but that outrage and sorrow would appear in his writings—as here, when he speaks through Whitman—not in his own voice, but in the voices of others.

．　．　．

Zukofsky took to university teaching, at least at first. He didn't formally lecture, "tho I seem to find it no difficulty to fill any 50-minute period with a 'lecture' prompted by whatever it is, on the spur of the moment. The kids seem to like it, but my own ears ache a little—& sometimes more than a little—from my own talk. Not that it ain't good talk, but it ain't the grief of poetry."[35] After his first spring at Brooklyn Polytechnic, Zukofsky spent the summer at Colgate University teaching Shakespeare and English Renaissance literature as a visiting assistant professor.[36] Zukofsky was no happier in upstate Hamilton, New York, than he had been at Madison seventeen years

before. Before he left Colgate, he drafted two wry quatrains drama-
tizing his own exhaustion and playing upon the toothpaste family
whose fortune had endowed the institution:

Lese-Wiat, from Colgate

Colgate, Farewell, that hath me bound
And with an ointment laved my teethe
Until mine own voice tired, the sound
A quiet wasting summer's breath

Babylon his flood is stilled
Babel her tower doeth tie my tongue
In the willow path there it hath swilled
My spirit, His case, and young.

Editor's note—Last line: slow, penitentially[37]

(When Zukofsky came to publish the poem, he substituted "Caul
Gate" for "Colgate.") Zukofsky had impressed his students—"One
in fact wrote a whole essay—very good—to say that before he took
my Renaissance course he had learned nothing"—but it was just such
praise, Zukofsky speculated, that had deterred the "staid & quarrel-
some faculty" from asking him to stay on.[38]

That summer Zukofsky met Omar Pound, who was attending
Ezra's old alma mater, Hamilton College, some twenty-five miles
from Colgate, while his mother Dorothy lived in a Washington apartment and spent her days with Ezra at St. Elizabeths. Omar barely
knew Ezra and Dorothy, since he had been raised in England. He
had served two years in the U.S. Army during the war. Zukofsky liked
Omar, seeing in him a reflection of himself decades earlier: "Nice kid
... likes Cummings, worships him, doesn't approve of his pa's politics
but feels he's a benevolent uncle—like me—& somehow tied 1933 &
1947 together. Glad I looked him up."[39]

Teaching Shakespeare that summer spurred Zukofsky to begin
another project, in part a response to Celia's musical setting of
Pericles, Prince of Tyre. Bottom: on Shakespeare would occupy him for
the next thirteen years. It seems to have germinated in the conflu-
ence of Zukofsky's reading of Shakespeare for his Colgate classes,

the comprehensive syllabus of the literature survey he was teaching at Poly ("We begin with prehistoric times & go to Dante—Hell by Jan[uary]"), and a notion he was developing, dating back to his work on Henry Adams, about the progression of human consciousness. "I evolved a theory of how 'man' in everything proceeds from concrete to abstract," he wrote; "might show it off in 'A' sometime."[40] Zukofsky would take his time with *Bottom*; he had no deadlines pressing him, and could pursue the only sort of critical prose he had once considered "permissible": "The direction of this prose, tho it will be definition, will also be poetry, arising from the same source or what to a third reader might seem the same source as the poetry—a poetically charged mentality."[41] As *Bottom* accreted over the years, the evolving direction of the work—commentary, philosophy, anthology, collage—would increasingly render problematic the conventional distinctions between poetry and prose, text and commentary.

. . .

A Test of Poetry had been finished since 1940, but no publisher had shown interest. In 1948 the Zukofskys finally decided to do it themselves, as an Objectivist Press book. The last volume the press had published had been Reznikoff's 1936 *Separate Way*; no one associated with the venture objected to Zukofsky's reviving the imprint. He ran into problems with reprint permissions, however: Williams was glad to let Zukofsky quote his poetry in *Test*, and even offered to help with the printing costs, but Emily Dickinson's estate wanted permissions fees that Zukofsky was unwilling or unable to pay.[42] Worst of all, Zukofsky's manuscript included over three hundred lines of Pound's work, and Pound did not respond from St. Elizabeths to Zukofsky's request to quote them.[43] In the end, Zukofsky made his own versions of *Odyssey* 11 to replace passages from Pound's first Canto, and would later reuse them in "A"-12.[44]

A *Test of Poetry* was published in September 1948; the Zukofskys were out of pocket some eight hundred dollars for the five hundred sets of printed sheets.[45] Its front jacket carried blurbs by Williams, Mark Van Doren, and Zukofsky's college classmate Clifton Fadiman, now editor of the Book-of-the-Month Club. Zukofsky sent a copy to Wallace Stevens, one of whose poems he had included in the anthology, and received a polite but ambiguous reply: "Let me thank you for your book. This is so arranged that the contents pick up a particular interest. It just so happens that one of the things I have been thinking about recently is the absence of the element of interest in so much poetry."[46] The book received respectful reviews in the *New York Times Sunday Book Review* and the *Nation*, but sparked no great interest among readers.

If it did not make Zukofsky famous, *A Test of Poetry* could at least help his teaching career. At the end of the 1947–48 academic year, Zukofsky had presented Professor Saidla with the published version of "Poetry / *For My Son When He Can Read*," along with the poems he had published that year, and the old man had promised to argue for his promotion. A year later, with *Test* in print, Zukofsky received a letter from the president of Poly informing him that "effective September 1, 1949," he had been promoted to assistant professor, with the annual salary of $4,200.[47]

It was becoming clear to Zukofsky that Brooklyn Polytechnic Institute was a job, rather than an intellectual or artistic home. His teaching load was heavy, and few of his students cared about poetry. Nor did his colleagues have much time to discuss literature, with the exception of Edward Dahlberg, who taught at Poly for a few years, beginning shortly after Zukofsky arrived.[48] Dahlberg, four years older than Zukofsky, had made a name in the 1930s with such brutal but well-written examples of social realism as *Bottom Dogs* (1929) and *From Flushing to Calvary* (1932). In his 1941 *Do These Bones Live?*, Dahlberg had recast himself as a scornful Old Testament prophet, excoriating the sterility of American culture in an ornate prose sprinkled with learned allusions. Dahlberg—mercurial, waspish, and monstrously egotistical—was not easy to deal with, but Zukofsky sympathized with Dahlberg's feeling of having been passed over by the literary world. For his part, Dahlberg saw in Zukofsky an intellectual rigor and a set of aesthetic standards akin to his own. At Dahlberg's suggestion, the English poet and art critic Herbert Read, editor at Routledge and Kegan Paul, would arrange for Routledge to issue an English edition of *A Test of Poetry* in 1952, using sheets of the Objectivist Press edition.

·   ·   ·

In the summer of 1948, in order to keep Paul clear of a polio epidemic in New York City, the Zukofskys rented a place in Lyme, Connecticut, a resort town several hours to the northeast. The following summer, they purchased a fifteen-by-twenty-foot, two-room clapboard cottage in neighboring Old Lyme, and would spend that summer and the next struggling to make the place livable, continually fighting its antiquated plumbing and tendency to flood with every heavy rain: While the cottage sat on the edge of a marsh, the Zukofskys had been assured that it had not flooded since the hurricane of 1938.[49] Finally, after their third vacation in Connecticut, they gave up and sold the property.

They did make some friends in Old Lyme. The poet-artist Kenneth Patchen and his wife, Dorothy, were there, whom the Zukofskys saw a good deal of, and there was a "lovely lady" (in Paul Zukofsky's words), Helen Taggart, who became "a close family friend" for a number of years to come.[50] Everyone was taken with Paul, who at the age of five already showed a remarkable talent on the violin. Old Lyme, however, was a rather Waspish enclave, and Zukofsky was made uncomfortably aware of his own Jewishness, judging from what he wrote there. Part I of "Chloride of Lime and Charcoal" is Zukofsky's Old Lyme poem. Its first section recalls making their water potable by introducing "a bag / With a mixture of lime and charcoal" into the well. The second commemorates a housewarming gift of zinnias from Mrs. Appleby, who with her husband held the mortgage on the cottage:

> Zinnias you look so much like Gentiles
> Born among butcher furniture
> Who lived Easter and Christmas . . .
> To whose salt marsh—it happens I like
> cattails—Jewish I am mortgaged.

The poem acknowledges the kindness, even "sweetness," of these Gentiles who had allowed the Zukofskys into their community, but in its last stanzas Zukofsky reflects, not without bitterness, that the position of the Jew in mid-twentieth-century America is little different from his place in the Egypt of Exodus:

> As your rose, pink, yellow, and orange
> Are mixed in the melting pot

That the kindness of our mortgagers
Created with you at leaving you at our door
And tho your givers begin to shake hands with my kind . . .
So: these are your lancent leaves, tubular stems
Stopped in the lotus or artichoke of your sepals
Of Egypt.[51]

Zukofsky liked the Applebys' son John ("Jackie"), who served as
the handyman on the place—"you ask what I can do— / My name
is Jackie / I am Jack-of-all trades," he says in "Chloride of Lime and
Charcoal"—and who was surprised, when he first met Zukofsky, that
the "Professor" would address him as "Mister."[52] Jackie was particularly fond of Paul, and he sent the family a series of fond but gram-
matically shaky letters after he joined the army and was sent to Korea
in early 1951; Zukofsky would incorporate them into "A"-12.[53]

Paul was a precocious child. In 1948 Louis and Celia enrolled him
in the Mannes School of Music, where he studied violin. In 1951, dissatisfied with the public schools, they applied to the Board of Education for permission to teach Paul at home themselves. They had an
ambitious curriculum planned: music, of course, came first. Celia
would teach him arithmetic and handwriting; Louis would teach him
writing and reading. For the summer of 1951, Zukofsky planned for
the two of them to read the *Iliad*, the Bible, "Breasted's Ancient History; maybe some Shakespeare." Eventually, perhaps, astronomy,
"birds, beasts & flowers," and Greek and Latin;[54] one suspects
Zukofsky wanted to work through these languages as much for his
own benefit as his son's.

Zukofsky was delighted in his son's musical talent; he liked to
imagine himself—despite his frequent inability to distinguish one
composition from another—as Leopold Mozart to Paul's Wolfgang
Amadeus. In 1950 Zukofsky began a whimsical fiction, "Little Baron
Snorck," largely a roman à clef about his son's progress. "Little," of
course, was Paul Zukofsky. Celia was "Verchadet [from the Yiddish
'cloudy'] von Chulnt," Louis himself "Dala Baballo von Chulnt."
(Zukofsky had originally assumed the name "Leon," in keeping with
his fascination with his own name's cognates—German *löwe*, "lion,"
for instance.[55]) The puns generating other names were somewhat
more labored. Zukofsky's brother-in-law Al Wand was the Count

"Murda-Wonda": back in the 1920s, Al had worked for the infamous New York gangster "Dutch" Schultz.[56] "Little Baron Snorck" showed a wit and deftness of handling notably absent in Zukofsky's previous fiction, but there was only so much he could write about his son's career when the boy was barely seven years old. After eight chapters, Zukofsky laid the manuscript aside.

. . .

The past returned to haunt Zukofsky in early 1949. The August before, Whittaker Chambers, now a senior editor at *Time* magazine, was subpoenaed by the House Un-American Activities Committee (HUAC). Chambers had defected from the Communist Party in 1938, and had become something of an anti-communist crusader within the Time-Life organization. Since his defection, Chambers had been debriefed by the FBI several times,[57] but the true bombshell came in the public HUAC hearings of August 1948: Chambers accused Alger Hiss, president of the Carnegie Endowment for International Peace and a former State Department aide, of having been a Soviet spy. Hiss in turn denied any involvement with espionage or with the Communist Party. On December 15, a grand jury indicted him for perjury.[58] The charge was technical: Everyone knew that Hiss was on trial for spying, and all eyes were on the trial.

The FBI showed up at 30 Willow Street on March 18, 1949. The Bureau had a slim file on Zukofsky, including notes from an October 1941 interview when Zukofsky applied for a job as translator for the FBI; they knew of his publications in *New Masses* in 1937 and 1938; they had received an anonymous letter in 1935, describing Zukofsky as a "Communist writer"; and they had a fall 1941 membership roll of the League of American Writers, on which Zukofsky appeared as a member.[59] This was far less than the bureau had on William Carlos Williams. But in the first months of 1949, in preparation for the Hiss perjury trial, the Bureau had extensively interviewed Chambers,[60] and he had named the two Columbia friends he had recruited for the Party back in 1925: John Waldhorn Gassner and Louis Zukofsky.

The FBI agents who interviewed Louis and Celia were looking for information on Chambers, anything that could bolster the testimony offered by this overweight, rumpled, self-confessed ex-spy against the counterstory that would be presented on behalf of the handsome, impeccably credentialed Hiss. Zukofsky knew this—the two agents told him that they were looking for "character references" for Chambers[61]—but he also knew that elements of his own past might not bear public exposure. After all, he had applied for membership in the Party back in 1925; he had written for the *New Masses*, had socialized with many of the most prominent literary communists of the 1930s, and had belonged to the League of American Writers. Since then, he had worked as a technical writer on projects directly related to the American war effort, and he now taught at a polytechnic institute, teaching the future engineers who would defend America against the Soviet threat. He had been at Brooklyn Polytech for barely two years; if nothing else, public revelation of his political past might put his job in jeopardy.

The FBI report of the March 18 interview describes both Louis and Celia as "extremely guarded," though "not uncooperative." As Celia Zukofsky described it some years later, they were closer to being scared stiff.[62] The whole business quickly turned farcical. "Louis had never been a member," Celia recalled, "and he couldn't even remember when he had been in Wisconsin and of course Louis was so mixed up that the FBI was correcting him and saying 'Oh no, excuse me, you were in Wisconsin in 1930, you're getting your dates mixed up.' And finally they said, 'We're sorry but we really couldn't use you as a character reference because you haven't seen him in so many years.'"[63] According to the FBI's notes, Zukofsky said he had known of Chambers's Party membership—as had his entire circle of Columbia friends—but had no idea of how serious Chambers's involvement was. Zukofsky made no mention of his own attempt to join the Party.

Hiss was convicted of perjury in January 1950. The FBI interviewed Chambers concerning Zukofsky again in October 1951, but he could furnish them no information more recent than 1933, when he had run into Zukofsky in Penn Station and exchanged greetings.[64] While some memos flew back and forth between Bureau offices and agents made phone calls to verify Zukofsky's current address and occupation, the FBI did not return to Willow Street. His file was not closed until May 11, 1953, when an agent concluded that since Zukofsky's ties to the Left were two decades old and "this investigation has not disclosed any recent Communist activity by the subject," the Bureau could go off to hunt fresher scents.[65] The Chambers business, and the whole leftist moment of Zukofsky's youth, were now behind him.

. . .

In the summer of 1950, Zukofsky drafted much of the second half of "A"-9 and sketched a tentative rhyme scheme for "A"-11, which he wrote the following spring.[66] In the summer and early fall of 1951, after having accumulated material for who knows how long, he drafted "A"-12, a movement as long as the first eleven combined, in a single fourteen-week burst of composing.[67] He had brought his great poem to its midway point, and—as he had back in 1940 after completing "A"-10—he would allow it to lie fallow again for the better part of a decade.

The great shadow over "A"-12 was the death of Zukofsky's father. After a brief illness, Pinchos had died of a heart attack on April 11, 1950. He had been Zukofsky's only parent for twenty-three years, a steadfast example of gentleness and Spinozistic fortitude. One of his last concerns before leaving for the hospital was the money he had put aside for the synagogue; his children found "About three dollars and less than a dollar in pennies I guess."[68] They were unsure whether to "Put 91 or 95 / On his tombstone."[69] The Zukofskys had named Paul for him, a clear violation of the Jewish tradition of naming children for the dead rather than the living, but "I knew Pinchos would not mind / Their 'English' names being the same . . . 'our Hebrew names are not the same. / Bless him, may he live / 120 years.'"[70] Pinchos's last words to Zukofsky, visiting the hospital the day before he died, were "Isn't visiting over? / Go home, / Celia must be anxious, / Kiss Paul."[71]

Zukofsky was grieved for his sister Fanny—Pinchos had lived with her and Al for all of their married life—but he was as well grieved to lose his last living link to the world of European *Yiddishkayt*. Of his father's possessions, he took seven Hebrew books: the Bible in five volumes, the Psalms, and a collection of commentaries by the Jewish fathers. "I told [Fanny] I teach the Bible in school among other things. We live in such different worlds, only the simple fact of sister and brother brings us together."[72] Despite his pedagogical excuse—the assimilated professor of English to his unassimilated sister, whose principal language was still Yiddish—Zukofsky took these books not so much for his teaching as for a remembrance of his father, a tangible link to the long tradition of Jewish piety that had been broken when Zukofsky himself turned his back on the elders and devoted his life to the monuments of Gentile culture. Over the next decades, Zukofsky would incorporate more and more of the Jewish tradition into the "graphs of culture" laid out in *Bottom: on Shakespeare* and the second half of *"A"*.

"A"-9 (second half) through "A"-12

W HEN ZUKOFSKY began "A" in 1928, he was twenty-four and single, a poet with boundless ambitions, solid beginnings, and unclear potential. Everything had changed in the twenty-two years between the "round of fiddles playing Bach" that opened the poem and the second half of "A"-9, which Zukofsky finished in 1950. Zukofsky was well into middle age, a homeowner twice over, and a husband and father; he had published two collections of poetry, yet his work still seemed fated to obscurity. The future, which he had once measured in terms of his own lasting literary fame, he now saw embodied in his son. It was not surprising, then, that the movements of "A" composed after 1940's "A"-10 showed Zukofsky's attentions turning from the world of class struggle and revolutionary change to the more private realm of the family.

The two halves of "A"-9 are the most striking index of that shift. The first half (1938–1940) had adapted the words of Karl Marx to the form of Cavalcanti's "Donna mi priegha," and was an extended poetic restatement of the labor theory of value. When he returned to the poem ten years later, Zukofsky rewrote his earlier canzone—preserving the mathematically determined distribution of n's and r's, the complex rhyme scheme, often the same rhyming words—using the terminology of Baruch Spinoza's *Ethics*.[1] Where the first half of "A"-9 was a Marxist definition of *value*, the second half was a Spinozan definition of *love*. Its first stanza (which may be compared to the first half's beginning, on page 185) reads as follows:

> An eye to action sees love bear the semblance
> Of things, related is equated,—values
> The measure all use who conceive love, labor
> Men see, abstraction they feel, the resemblance
> (Part, self-created, integrated) all hues
> Show to natural use, like Benedict's neighbor
> Crying his hall's flown into the bird: Light is
> The night isolated by stars (poled mentors)
> Blossom eyelet enters pealing with such changes
> As sweet alyssum, that not-madness, (ranges
> In itself, there tho acting without right) is—
> Whose sight is rays, "I shall go; the frequenters
> That search our centers, love; Elysium exchanges
> No desires; its thought loves what hope estranges."[2]

The syntax is more dense, inverted, and abbreviated than in the earlier work, and demands more careful unraveling. In addition, the poem is saturated with references to outside texts: "Benedict's neighbor / Crying his hall's flown into the bird" paraphrases a passage from the *Ethics*, where Spinoza refers to a man "who I heard the other day shouting that his hall had flown into his neighbour's chicken . . ."[3] In addition to Spinoza, there are references to herbal lore and classical mythology. Aside from the overt reference to "Benedict," however, and a trio of Greek proper names—"Elysium," "Apollo," "Hyacinthus"—these references are nowhere "keyed" for the reader; Zukofsky never went to the trouble of preparing a bundle of aids for this canzone, as he had with *First Half of "A"-9*. In *First Half* he had given the world (as he put it in number 42 of *Anew*) "all my hushed sources,"[4] but the world had paid no attention. Henceforward, Zukofsky would pepper his poetry with uncited quotations and veiled references, and he would let the poetry stand without gloss or key.

"Sweet alyssum" in that first stanza provides a foretaste of another aspect of Zukofsky's mature poetics. (The plant was once thought to cure insanity, thus "sweet alyssum, no-madness."[5]) There is at least one flower embedded in every stanza of the second half of "A"-9: "rose" in the second, "dandelion" in the third, "Balm or jewelweed" in the fourth, "hyacinth" (in the myth of Apollo and Hyacinthus) in the fifth, and "sweet alyssum" again in the coda. These *flowers*, I suspect, are intended as a submerged pun on a couple of passages from the *Ethics*: "The more any image has reference to many things, the more frequent it is, the more often it *flourishes*, and the more it occupies the mind"; and "The more an image is associated with many other things, the more often it *flourishes*."[6] In *Bottom: on Shakespeare* Zukofsky speaks repeatedly of his desire to show how the definition of love he finds in Shakespeare "flourishes" in the light of a vast array of other texts.[7] The fact that Zukofsky has tucked a flower into each stanza of the second half of "A"-9 suggests the increasingly arcane procedures of his later poetry, where the structural and thematic underpinnings of the verse become less and less evident to the reader of the poetry's surface, more and more submerged or "hushed."

The second half of "A"-9 also plays variations on a theme that had become central to Zukofsky's thought: the idea, in short, of the reliability and perfection of the physical sense of vision, as against the abstractions of the intellect. *Bottom*, as it expanded, was becoming an endless descant on the themes of sight, mind, and love in Shakespeare. Zukofsky words it most succinctly as a proportion: "*love : reason :: eyes : mind* . . . Love needs no tongue of reason if love and the eyes are *1*—an identity. The good reasons of the mind's right judgment are but superfluities for saying: *Love sees* . . ."[8] For all his emphasis on the *music* of poetry, Zukofsky continually ranked vision as a higher good—better than hearing, and far better than the immaterial rationalizations of the intellect. It is no accident that the second half of "A"-9 begins, not as the first had, with an "impulse to action"—"impulse" suggesting the abstractions of contemporary physics, or perhaps even the "passions" Spinoza so deprecated—but with "An *eye* to action." There are images of eyes and seeing in every stanza of the second half of "A"-9, as Zukofsky couples his ethics of seeing with the love he finds defined in Spinoza, and with the state of "salvation, blessedness, or liberty" Spinoza proposed as the thinker's goal.[9] Indeed, all of the movements of *A* that Zukofsky wrote during 1950–51—the second canzone of "A"-9, "A"-11, and "A"-12—can be read, like *Bottom*, under the conjoined signs of Spinoza's *Ethics* and Zukofsky's own philosophy of love and the eyes.

. . .

After the formidable intellectual and formal density of "A"-9 and the thunderous historical rhetoric of "A"-10, "A"-11 comes as a quiet display of lyric virtuosity, an almost entirely private utterance.[10] The movement is dedicated to Celia and Paul, and is the poet's address to his own song, figured in the first line as a "river." At the age of forty six, Zukofsky is imagining his own death, and the grief of those who would be left behind:

> River that must turn full after I stop dying
> Song, my song, raise grief to music
> Light as my loves' thought, the few sick
> So sick of wrangling: thus keeping,
> Sounds of light, stay in her keeping
> And my son's face—this much for honor.[11]

There follow four ten-line stanzas, each of them with the same complex pattern of terminal feminine rhymes, each of them ending with the word "honor." The unexpected word "turn" in that first line—for in the English poetic tradition, one more often expects a river to "flow" or to "run"—gives the key to Zukofsky's formal model: Cavalcanti's Ballata XI, which begins "Perch'io non spero di *tornar* gia' mai" (Because I do not hope ever to return).[12] Like Zukofsky's, Cavalcanti's poem is addressed to the song, urging it to go—in the absence of the poet himself—to the poet's beloved and present itself as token of his devotion. "A"-11 takes its metrical and rhyme scheme from "Perch'io non spero," with the exception of the repeated "honor": Cavalcanti's first stanza ends "onore," but its remaining stanzas use that as a *rhyme* sound, ending "dolore," "core," "Amore," and "valore."

"A"-11 is a masterpiece of delicate music and thorny syntax, drawn from verse to verse in tenuous webs; the ear delights in the music, while the meaning seems just out of reach. It ends with a single sentence in which the poem itself speaks to the poet's son, a fine example of the movement's delicate music:

Honor

His voice in me, the river's turn that finds the
Grace in you, four notes first too full for talk, leaf
Lighting stem, stems bound to the same branch that binds the
Tree, and then as from the same root we talk, leaf
After leaf of your mind's music, page, walk leaf
Over leaf of his thought, sounding
His happiness: song sounding
The grace that come from knowing
Things, her love our own showing
Her love in all her honor.[13]

It is difficult to overstate the richness of the syntax here. In the last four lines, for instance: "knowing / Things" could be read as "knowing about things" or as "things which know"; "her love our own showing / Her love in all her honor" is a delightful tangle—is "showing" a noun or a gerund? if the latter, does it follow "her love" (with "our own" in apposition to "her love," or as the object?) or "our own"?—all resolving into heartfelt praise of Celia's love and "honor."

Some of these lines echo earlier movements of "A": "The flower—leaf after leaf wrapped around the central leaf" of "A"-6, "The roots we strike" of "A"-4, for instance.[14] Of "the river's turn," Hugh Kenner notes that in musical terminology, a "turn" is "An ornament consisting of four tones, the first a degree above and the third a degree below the principal tone which comes in the second and fourth positions"[15]—thus "four notes" in the following line. These four notes are four voices sounding in the poem (just as the first half of

"A"-9 had sounded the voices of Cavalcanti, Marx, and contemporary physics). First of course is Cavalcanti, from whose ballata the poem takes its form. The others are less obvious. The second voice is the American poet Joseph Rodman Drake (1795–1820), whose river poem "Bronx" Zukofsky had copied on a note card and included with the materials for "A"-11. It begins

I sat me down upon a green bank-side
   Skirting the smooth edge of a gentle river,
Whose waters seemed unwillingly to glide,
   Like parting friends who linger while they sever;
Enforced to go, yet seeming still unready,
   Backward they wind their way in many a wistful eddy.[16]

Zukofsky had quoted "Bronx" in poem 15 of *Anew*, and Drake's poem occupied a special place in his heart: It evoked the apartment overlooking the Bronx River in which he and Celia had lived when they were first married.[17]

The third "note" is the sixteenth-century physician and alchemist Paracelsus. In 1951 the Bollingen Foundation published a selection of his vast and heterogeneous writings, and Edward and R'lene Dahlberg had given a copy of the book to Zukofsky.[18] Paracelsus's writings present a fascinating portrait of Western thought on the verge of modernity. Paracelsus stressed the empirical practice of medicine, yet believed fervently in alchemy for its promise of the wealth-spinning "philosopher's stone." Paracelsus saw the world in terms of systems of correspondences, exemplified in astrology, where one could distinguish clear connections between human destiny and the movement of the heavenly bodies. The human being was a microcosm, a "little world" reflecting the structure of the "great world," the universe as a whole.

Zukofsky incorporated a striking number of references to Paracelsus in "A"-11 and "A"-12. When Zukofsky addresses his poem, "Take care, song, that what stars' imprints you mirror / Graze their tears," he plays on Paracelsus's assertion that "The starry vault imprints itself on the inner heaven of man." When he refers to his son's violin, "thread gold stringing / The fingerboard pressed in my honor," he alludes to an alchemical symbol: "*aurum musicum*, wire or thread gold, used for the stringing of musical instruments." And when he speaks of "His second paradise," he refers to Paracelsus's *De vita longa*: "The striving for wisdom is the second paradise of the world."[19]

More important than Paracelsus to "A"-11, however, is Spinoza's *Ethics*, words that had been running through Zukofsky's mind for almost thirty years. Spinoza is the fourth "note" of the movement, his definition of "honor" its presiding spirit. "Honor, song, sang the blest is delight knowing / We overcome ills by love" is tied to three propositions in the *Ethics*. In Proposition LII, Part IV, Spinoza defines a proper "self-complacency," "pleasure deriving from the fact that man regards himself and his power of acting," as a very high good, and "inasmuch as this self-complacency is more and more cherished and encouraged by praises . . . we are led in life principally by the desire of honour . . ."[20] Such honor, Proposition LVIII explains, "is not opposed to reason, but can arise from it."[21] In Proposition XLIV, Part III, we learn that "hatred which is entirely conquered by love passes into love, and love on that account is greater than if it had not been preceded by hatred."[22] Honor, as Spinoza defines it, is others' acknowledgment of one's ethical, spiritual uprightness—the "grace" that one manifests in composing a beautiful poem, or playing well upon an instrument. It is for Zukofsky the acknowledgment of bonds of family and of love, bonds cemented in a shared artistic endeavor that includes his own writing, his wife's composing, and his son's violin playing.

What is extraordinary about "A"-11—aside from its delicate lyrical virtuosity—is that Zukofsky composed this intensely personal statement to his wife and son largely using the words of others. This is not a matter of half-remembered echoes of read texts cropping up in his own verses; as the manuscript of the poem makes clear, Zukofsky knew precisely which passages of Spinoza, Drake, and Paracelsus he was alluding to. Aside from the reference to "the blest" in the third stanza (Baruch/Benedictus = "blest"), these references and borrowings are entirely silent, entirely unsignaled. Like the second half of "A"-9, "A"-11 is a foretaste of the poetry Zukofsky would write for the last two decades of his life: overtly or obliquely lyrical, formally cunning, often intensely personal verses worked out of a vast array of fragments of preexisting texts.

. . .

Zukofsky drafted all of "A"-12, which would come out to over 130 printed pages, in a little less than four months. He was himself somewhat bemused by the inequity of scale between the forty-six-line "A"-11 and this leviathan movement, as he notes towards the end:

> A kind of childlike
> Play this division
> Into 24,
> Enough perhaps for
> 12 books in this one
> All done in a summer
> After a gathering of 12 summers.[23]

After the tense, obsessively tight formal constraints of "A"-9 and "A"-11, "A"-12 seems a sprawling, almost leisurely assemblage of materials.[24] While three or four outside texts might appear in a single stanza of "A"-11, while the syntax of a passage of "A"-9 might require multiple readings to extract even a provisional "sense," "A"-12 presents its quotations for the most part in large, recognizable blocks of up to two pages, sometimes prominently citing their sources, in a syntax that is—if somewhat foreshortened—generally comprehensible.

This does not mean, however, that no formal principles underlie the movement. For one thing, there is still the notion of the fugue, and of baroque music in general. The movement's first line— *"Out of deep need"*—alludes to "When we are in deepest need," the melody upon which Bach based his last chorale prelude.[25] According to one account, Bach interrupted the composition of his monumental *Art of Fugue* in order to dictate that chorale prelude: "the fourfold 19th fugue" of the series, Zukofsky writes, "Stopped here / With the last Choral-Prelude / Told his son-in-law Altnikol."[26] The intended fugue, musicologists have surmised, was to have been something never before attempted, a *quadruple* fugue, deploying four separate themes in counterpoint. One can read "A"-12 as the verbal analogue of such a quadruple fugue. In his own fugue, Bach based the third theme on the letters of his name, BACH (in German musical terminology, B = B-flat, H = B-natural). Similarly, Zukofsky structures the enormous edifice of "A"-12 around the letters B A C H, which appear in acrostic form on the poem's second page:

Blest
Ardent   good
Celia   speak simply, rarely   scarce, seldom—
Happy, immeasurable love
    heart or head's greater part unhurt and happy
    things that bear harmony
    certain in concord with reason.[27]

"B" is Spinoza—Baruch, of course, means "blest." "A" is Aristotle, to whose works, like Spinoza's, Zukofsky had been returning for decades. "C" is Celia. And "H" is Paracelsus, whose surname was Hohenheim. These four thematic centers Zukofsky presents, juxtaposes one to another, and "counterpoints" as if he were writing a fourfold fugue.

It is less cumbersome, however, to see the movement as structured around various groups of four. "Four horses," writes Zukofsky, evoking both Revelation and his own favorite figure for the poet, "like four notes" (tying the movement back to the "four notes" of "A"-11).[28] There are four elements in the BACH acrostic; there were four elements in ancient physics—earth, air, fire, and water—which, as Barry Ahearn notes, appear "in some form on every page of the movement." As Burton Hatlen points out, the movement revolves as well around four members of the Zukofsky family: Louis himself, Celia, Paul, and Paul's grandfather, Pinchos.[29]

Yet neither the fugal analogy nor the principle of fours fully accounts for the form of "A"-12. Zukofsky may have conceived of "A"-8 as a "mirror fugue" of sorts, but the texture and movement of "A"-12—its succession of themes and subjects, its sometimes rambling progression—are far less tightly woven than even the most otiose baroque fugue. And while sets of four are prominent in the movement, an enormous amount of material escapes whatever four-termed taxonomy one applies to it. "A"-12 is not quite the "ragbag" that Pound had once called his *Cantos*, but its broad weave is capacious enough to encompass whatever caught Zukofsky's attention. "*A*" is a poem taking shape in parallel to the lived life of its poet, opening itself to the contingencies that that life encountered.

The movement begins with a condensed statement of its theme—"Timed the theme Bach's name"[30]—and recounts, through several abbreviated and conflated creation myths, Zukofsky's evolving theory of the development of human consciousness from "solid" to "liquid" to "gaseous" states, a theory he was simultaneously pursuing in *Bottom: on Shakespeare*. Then the poem runs through a dazzling, heterogeneous array of materials: a valentine from Paul to Louis, enclosed within a drawn heart;[31] dozens of passages from Shakespeare, many of them from *A Midsummer Night's Dream*; an aphorism of Schoenberg's—"A Chinese sage speaks Chinese, / But the important thing is / What does he say?"—quoted from a *New York Times* article by the composer Roger Sessions;[32] bits of Paracelsus; longer passages of Spinoza and Aristotle; and much else. Many of these quotations, like this lovely unrhymed couplet adapted from Spinoza—"Voice without scurf or gray matter, / For the eyes of the mind are proofs"[33]—explore themes that Zukofsky was working through in *Bottom*. Indeed, "*A*"-12 and *Bottom* were conjoined works, and the prose work serves as the best possible commentary on "*A*"-12.

About ten pages into the movement, Zukofsky defines his "poetics" in mathematical terms, as "An integral / Lower limit speech / Upper limit music." However much his verse might move between these two "limits," the crucial element of "constancy" must be present. Such constancy leads Zukofsky into a long and moving remembrance of his father: "Poetics. With constancy. // My father died in the spring." Zukofsky's memories of his father are warm, straightforward, and touching, but always aware of the modern world, as when Albert Einstein's words comment on Pinchos Zukofsky's Spinozan "simplicity":

> Had he asked me to say Kadish
> I believe I would have said it for him.
> How fathom his will
> Who had taught himself to be simple.

247

Everything should be as simple as it *can* be,
Says Einstein,
But not simpler.

Although Pinchos—"Paul" to his American neighbors—was dead, in some sense he lived on in his grandson Paul, and Zukofsky intersperses memories of his father with accounts of his own son. (Not coincidentally, the Aristotle text drawn upon most frequently in "A"-12, the *Nicomachean Ethics*, was written by Aristotle, son of the physician Nicomachus, for his own son Nicomachus.) Paul's amusing but poetic malapropisms—"My eyes are bloodshy"—are juxtaposed with Pinchos's life story and with fragments of Jewish culture: Jacob's struggle with the angel, Moses's rules for the Sabbath, a selection of Hasidic proverbs from Martin Buber's *Ten Rungs: Hasidic Sayings*.[34]

Most important in this poem are *recurrences*, moments of repetition or near-repetition of material either that had already appeared in Zukofsky's poems or that he had encountered in his reading or experience. Stein, Zukofsky notes, began *The Making of Americans* with an anecdote from Aristotle; and much of modernism, in fact, had been an attempt to breathe new life into ancient culture, from Leopold Bloom's odyssey in *Ulysses* to the fertility rituals of Eliot's *The Waste Land*. Zukofsky goes a step further: For him, all human culture is a seamless continuity, an ongoing tapestry of writers, artists, and thinkers happening upon ideas, motifs, and expressions that have had analogues in earlier works and will have other analogues in later works. "Much Shakespeare in Aristotle,"[35] Zukofsky wryly notes, brushing aside all notions of temporal priority, dismissing intellectual history as the chronicle of *progress* in human thought or expression. "The horse," Zukofsky writes, clearly referring to himself as poet,

> sees he is repeating
> All known cultures
> And suspects repeating
> Others unknown to him,
> Maybe he had better not
> Think of himself

Hunting so to speak
Sowing so to speak
Composing always.[36]

Why should he be surprised or worried to recognize that original-ity is an illusion? After all, haven't all artists worked from the same materials? What delights Zukofsky—and provides the fundamental poetics of both "A"-12 and *Bottom*—are moments of cross-textual, cross-cultural recognition, when

> instances from "different" cultures, surprisingly inwreathed,
> Seem to look back at one another,
> Aristotle at Shakespeare (both so fond of blind heroes)
> And blest Spinoza at Shakespeare—
> How?
> . . . none has to read the other yet it happens.[37]

This would prove his most long-standing delight, the teasing out of "recurrences" in the works of widely differing authors, as well as within his own oeuvre. As he wrote Niedecker in a letter of consola-tion after her mother's death (quoted in "A"-12),

> Each writer writes
> one long work whose beat he cannot
> entirely be aware of. Recurrences
> follow him, crib and drink from a
> well that's his cadence . . .[38]

Or as he puts it somewhat later in the poem, referring to an "Ameri-can blue block-print . . . Of ships and Seminoles" that he and Celia were using as curtains at the Old Lyme house, fabric "Recut / So often for the windows / Of different places we have lived in": "We begin early / And go on with a theme / Hanging and draping / The same texture."[39] Recurrence was for Zukofsky the most basic prin-ciple of all art. Without the meaningful recurrence of tones, music was but noise; without the recurrence of sounds and motifs, poetry was chaos. He would build the rest of his career on the exploration of various forms of recurrence.

. . .

If one could read all of human culture in terms of such recurrences, one could also read the events of one's own life as repetitions of events that had been played out many times before. The story which governs "A"-12, as it had Joyce's *Ulysses*, is the *Odyssey*, Homer's epic of the wanderings and homecoming of the Greek warrior Odysseus. Near the beginning of the poem, Zukofsky writes, "Have your Odyssey / How many voiced it be."[40] Pinchos Zukofsky's journey—to the new world from Russia, and then "for over six times ten years," to devoutly "open and close the synagogue"—was "A longer journey than Odysseus'."[41] Later, Zukofsky transcribes letters the family received from John Appleby of Old Lyme, now a private in the army on his way to the war in Korea. Jackie's letters have none of the culturally illuminating power of the contents of Sigismundo Malatesta's mailbag in Pound's Canto IX, or the accusatory immediacy of Marcia Nardi's letters in *Paterson*. But in Jackie's travels Zukofsky saw repeated the ancient patterns of the *Odyssey*, in particular the descent into hell (*Nekuia*) that occupies the center of Book 11. Zukofsky introduces Jackie's letters with a passage from his own version of *Odyssey* 11 (the same one used in *A Test of Poetry*), and punctuates the letters with further lines from the *Nekuia*. Jackie's account of his arrival at Camp McNair in Japan—"When we got there, there was a sign at the gate in Japanses. (This is hell) You can believe that. You couldn't walk anywhere with out getting all mad"—is followed by the laconic quotation, "followed / The shore to wet hell."[42]

Whenever one sets out on a long journey, Zukofsky implies, one reenacts the *Odyssey*. The child Paul inadvertently perceives the contemporaneity of all ages, showing a clearer "grasp of the present" than the politicians Zukofsky has been quoting: "Does Lars come from Troy / Where all those men fell? / (He had misheard: / *Troy* for *Detroit*.)"[43] Joyce would have understood and approved.

The wanderings of an Odysseus inevitably culminate in a *nostos*, or homecoming. "A"-12 ends in such a homecoming, though Zukofsky's own wandering has been but a 130-page odyssey through his memories, his present experience, and his own library. The poem ends at the beginning of the *Odyssey* itself, Homer's invocation to the muse:

Tell me of that man who got around
After sacred Troy fell,
He knew men and cities
His heart riled in the sea
As he strove for himself and his friends:
He did not save them.
Tell us about it, my Light,
Start where you please.[44]

Zukofsky's muse is of course Celia; her name, cognate with the Latin *coelis*, sky, gives the poet his illumination: thus, "my Light." (Thus also, throughout the movement, his references to Celia as an "eye of sky," which as well incorporates the last two syllables of his own name.) If Zukofsky has been Odysseus, then Telemachus is obviously Paul; and Penelope is Celia herself, around whom the other three elements of the BACH acrostic cluster in its last appearance, which closes the movement:

Blest
Ardent
Celia
         unhurt and
Happy.[45]

Zukofsky recognized that this quiet homecoming, this *nostos*, would be the close of the first half of "A". He sensed as well, I believe, that the movements of the poem's second half would show new directions in his work—they would be, in many ways, the work of a different poet than the man who had written "A"'s first twelve movements. The time had come for Zukofsky to empty his files, to divest himself of his earlier self's projects. "I clear my desk of clippings," he writes some fifteen pages from the end of "A"-12, and proceeds to do just that: in the pages that follow, he lays out a rich menagerie of quotations, superseded drafts, notes and titles for discarded works, and stray "clippings"—"Anybody's welcome to it. / Take: a raft of stuff."[46] Zukofsky's notes are apt to set the reader daydreaming about what his discarded projects might have amounted to. There are "Notes for different plays / I'd have done in my twenties / At the slightest encouragement," among them "*The Windows*: the drama of a textile plant," a musical; two operas, one of them "Ovid's *Metamorphoses* / That would sing Golding"; several short stories; two novels; and a stack of nonfiction works.[47]

The only record of many of these works is their mention here in "A"-12 (notes for others have been preserved among Zukofsky's papers); almost none of them were ever written. The two exceptions are the story "*It was*" and the final item, *Graph: Of Culture*. Zukofsky would include "*It was*" as a preface to *Ferdinand* when he published the novella a decade later. The notion of a "graph of culture," a plotting of thematic recurrences across the entire spectrum of human culture, would prove one of the central structuring principles of *Bottom: on Shakespeare*.

· · ·

After he finished "A"-12, Zukofsky would lay aside his long poem for another nine years, not returning to it until 1960. This was not at all surprising, for while Zukofsky liked to stress slow and painful composition—"Emphasize detail 130 times over—or there will be no poetic object," or "Six nights on one page, / No complaint. / Only in the end to write it / Exactly as sketched / in the first draft"—when he was in the midst of a piece, he actually tended to write rather rapidly. Much of the first half of "*A*" had been produced in relatively short periods of activity, rather than the day-in, day-out writing advocated by so many creative writing gurus. When he finished "A"-12, Zukofsky knew that another twelve movements awaited. But he had no desire to hurry them; they could wait until the contingencies of his own life summoned him back to "*A*". In the meantime, he counseled his long-suffering typist to "Give some thoughts to a performance / Of your *Pericles*, Celia," and turned his own attention to *Bottom: on Shakespeare*.[48]

Spinoza: Geometry and Freedom

In early 1951, at the suggestion of Zukofsky's friend Edward Dahlberg, the editor of *Tomorrow* invited Zukofsky to review George Santayana's latest book, *Dominations and Powers*, a discursive and remarkably *long* meditation on political theory.[1] Zukofsky's review, "The Effacement of Philosophy," is largely a reflection on Santayana's intellectual debt to Spinoza—both of them materialist philosophers concerned with political theory: Santayana comes off far the weaker of the two. These two philosophers had loomed large in the philosophy curriculum at Columbia, but while Santayana was not an important figure in the mature Zukofsky's mental landscape, Spinoza supplied the philosophical underpinnings for much of Zukofsky's work. The way of life Spinoza outlined in his *Ethics* suggested to Zukofsky a mode of being in the world that he found deeply compelling, if hard of attainment. And Spinoza's "geometrical" method of presenting his philosophy in the *Ethics* harmonized entirely with Zukofsky's own aesthetics of "mathematical" form; indeed, the system of thought of the *Ethics*, and the manner in which Spinoza presented that system, were largely identical to the structure that Zukofsky found underlying the world, and that he sought to imitate in his poetry and prose. When he came to sort through his books at the end of his career, Zukofsky would date his first reading of Spinoza to 1922. The "blessed" philosopher had been with him all his adult life.

. . .

Baruch Spinoza—his given name would be latinized to "Benedict"—was born in Amsterdam in 1632 to a family of Sephardic Jewish merchants. His Portuguese ancestors were *marranos*, Jews forcibly converted to Catholicism who continued to practice their religion in secret; by the beginning of the seventeenth century there was a sizable community of such former *conversos* living in the Dutch republic, where they were allowed to resume the open practice of their faith. By the age of twenty-four Spinoza had rejected the fundamental creeds of Orthodox Judaism, and in 1656 he was formally excommunicated from the Jewish community.[2] For the rest of his short life Spinoza lived in quiet, ascetic obscurity in the Low Countries, where he carried on a correspondence, combatively philosophical and largely devoid of personal news, with a wide range of fellow seekers of knowledge. He had made a name for himself in 1663 by publishing a "geometrically ordered" exposition of the philosophy of René Descartes. Ultimately, however, Spinoza rejected Descartes' division of the world between the realms of "extension" and "thought": Much of Spinoza's greatest work, the *Ethics*, can be read as a rethinking and rejection of Cartesian dualism.[3] Spinoza's anonymous *Theological-Political Treatise* was officially banned in 1670, and the *Ethics* would be published only after his death.

Spinoza's works met with incomprehension or derision for the better part of 150 years. The most common charge was that he was an "atheist," on account of his rejection of traditional conceptions of the deity. Spinoza held that the totality of existent being was itself God—hence his phrase *"Deus sive Natura"* (God, or Nature). As Spinoza argues in the first part of the *Ethics*, there is, and by definition can only be, a single, infinite substance ("God, or Nature"), which manifests itself in "Infinite things in infinite modes." "Whatever is, is in God [or Nature], and nothing can exist or be conceived without God." God, and the various modes by which he is expressed, can be viewed under the attributes of both thought and extension.[4]

This does not imply, as in Descartes, that thought and extension are separate realms, only that they are different attributes by which the same single substance can be grasped. We, as human beings (finite modes of God), can conceive of God, or Nature "as an active and creative principle, intelligible in and through itself," for which Spinoza borrows a scholastic phrase, *natura naturans* ("nature naturing"). Or we can conceive of God, or Nature as passive, "the product of creation, as the working out of a creative endeavour through the infinite and finite modes of the one true substance"—as *natura naturata* ("nature natured").[5]

Spinoza's *Ethics* is also concerned with the origin and nature of human emotions; the strength of those emotions, and how they hold us in "servitude"; and how, through "the power of the intellect," we can obtain freedom from them. Spinoza's universe is absolutely determined. All of the modes of the world, human beings included, arise from the necessity of God's own nature. As human beings, we experience emotions as *actions* to the extent that we are aware of the necessary causes of those emotions, as *passions*—things that hold us in servitude—to the extent that we are ignorant, or have only a confused idea of their necessary causes.[6] Human freedom—peace of mind, emancipation from the lacerating effects of passions—comes through one's understanding as fully as possible the entire system of modes, attributes, and interlinked necessary causes that make up the whole of nature, or God. "The more we understand individual things," Spinoza claims, "the more we understand God," and our understanding, or intellectual love of God (*amor intellectualis Dei*), "is the greatest good that we can desire according to the dictate of reason." This *amor intellectualis Dei* constitutes "salvation, blessedness, or liberty"; it "is not the reward of virtue, but virtue itself." The truly wise man, Spinoza concludes, occupies himself with learning and knowing, for only by such knowledge can he achieve peace: "the wise man, in so far as he is conceived as such, is scarcely moved in spirit: he is conscious of himself, of God, and things by a certain eternal necessity, he never ceases to be, and always enjoys satisfaction of mind." Such equanimity in the face of an often hostile world is no doubt hard to achieve—"But," Spinoza writes in the *Ethics*' last sentence, "all excellent things are as difficult as they are rare."[7]

· · ·

The words of Spinoza's *Ethics* echoed in Zukofsky's mind much of his life. As his mother lay ill in 1927, he turned them over in a poem written three days before her death:

(**Spinoza in a Winter Season**)

Now sings the January wind
A winter lullaby
For all deep thoughts concerning God—

God's thought with other things dinned
Earthward by the wind, then towards the sky
Straight on the air with shout and prod.

And there is sun, much
Sun, even for the sickest in the other room—
'Infinite things in infinite modes

Must follow from the divine nature being such'—
And the sun dances on our yellow broom,
And where I nurse, or merely stare, corrodes.[8]

"Infinite things in infinite modes (that is, all things which can fall under the heading of infinite intellect) must necessarily follow from the necessity of divine nature," reads the sixteenth Proposition of the *Ethics'* first part.[9] This Spinoza, a source of comfort or cosmic perspective, contrasts sharply with the Spinoza of "Poem beginning 'The,'" written the fall before: "54 Let me be / 55 Not by art have we lived, / 56 Not by graven images forbidden to us / 57 Not by letters I fancy, / 58 Do we dare say / 59 With Spinoza grinding lens, Rabbaisi, / 60 After living on Cathedral Parkway?"[10] The young Zukofsky, alienated both from the tradition of Western literature and philosophy he had been taught at Columbia and from the Orthodox faith of his fathers, could take only bitter comfort in the similar situation of the philosopher, expelled from his own community and regarded as a dangerous atheist by the Christian world.

The *Ethics*, among other things, was something of an early modern self-help book, a guide to leading a satisfied life. If there exists a "popular" reading of Spinozistic philosophy, it involves the calm resignation that Zukofsky saw exemplified in his own father;

Pinchos, he wrote in 1931, was "the only pious example of Spinoz-istic philosophy I've ever met—who has nothing but is resigned."[11] Such resignation—a key element in the "blessedness" invoked in the *Ethics*—was especially difficult for a poet as ambitious as Zukofsky. Towards the end of his life, when decades of readerly indifference and petty literary politics had hardened Zukofsky's public face into a thin-lipped bitterness, he would assume that resignation as a mask of passive-aggressive defense against the world. But Spinozistic resigna-tion appealed to him early and late, in large part because it represented the ethical triumph of the intellect over the passions, the overcoming of the unruly emotions by the power of the analytical mind.

It was not merely Spinoza's ethical "teachings" that remained with Zukofsky. Zukofsky read him as a living thinker whose ideas had lost none of their immediacy over three centuries. The first half of "*A*" is thickly dotted with references to Spinoza, references that cast light on how Zukofsky conceived of his own poetics. As early as "*A*"-6, Zukofsky situated the poet within the system of *natura natur-ans* and *natura naturata*, as "a mode of these inertial systems."[12] The dialectical materialism that so dominated the first nine movements of "*A*" could be read as an intellectual descendent of Spinoza's refusal to separate the realms of thought and extension. In the mid-1930s, Zukofsky cited Engels's *Historical Materialism*—"It is impossible to separate thought from matter that thinks"—and quoted the medi-eval philosopher Duns Scotus's question whether it was "impossible for matter to think?" as support; he was almost certainly aware that Marxist thinkers had interpreted Spinoza's work as an important forerunner of Marx and Engels's dialectical materialism.[13]

If the Spinoza of the first nine movements of "*A*" was bound up with Marxism, the Spinoza Zukofsky built upon in "*A*"-11, "*A*"-12, and *Bottom: on Shakespeare* was a philosopher of perception, an ana-lyst of the relationship between the senses and the mind, and above all else, a theorist of *love*. Early in *Bottom*'s long exposition of love, reason, the eyes, and the mind, Zukofsky introduces a series of quo-tations from Spinoza central to the problems his volume as a whole addresses. Among them is a proposition upon which he had based a poem fifteen years before, "Desire which arises from reason can have no excess."[14] The note to Proposition XX, Part V of the *Ethics*—

unhealthy states of mind owe their origin for the most part to exces-
sive love for a thing that is liable to many variations, and of which we
may never seize the mastery. . . . From this we conceive what a clear
and distinct knowledge . . . can do with the emotions, namely, that
if it does not remove them entirely as they are passions . . . at least
brings about that they constitute the least possible part of the mind.
. . . Moreover, it gives rise to a love towards a thing immutable and
eternal . . . and of which we are in truth masters[15]

—implies, for Zukofsky, that only when the rationalizations of the
mind cede preeminence to the evidence of the senses are our desires
rightly invested. The passage, of course, means something entirely
different in the context of the *Ethics*, but Zukofsky's aim in writing
Bottom was not so much to bolster his own argument with authorita-
tive citations as to concatenate disparate texts that played variations
upon the "love : reason :: eyes : mind" theme. Indeed, Zukofsky
implies, Spinoza's work is most useful for his own project in *Bottom*
when read obliquely, for the short space between Shakespeare and
Spinoza represents the leap between "sense (the *universal* term for
singular feeling)" and "essence (the *universal* for singular *being*)." We
recognize here a recasting of Zukofsky's solid/liquid/gas scheme:
"When Shakespeare argues his interest is largely sense, tho essence
always encroaches," Zukofsky writes; in contrast, "When Spinoza
argues his interest is largely essence, tho (as in Aristotle) sense is
hardly ever forgotten . . ." Or, as Zukofsky put it more informally in
1969, "I love Spinoza, but he is the gas stage and it really started for
our time about then."[16]

Spinoza was also, of course, one of the four pillars of "A"-12, his
name the B of the B-A-C-H acrostic, "blessed" echoing both the
Hebrew Baruch and the state of blessedness described in the final
part of the *Ethics*. Out of the great stretches of the *Ethics* worked into
that movement, the central quotation is from Part V, where Spinoza
argues for a kind of immortality: "The human mind cannot be absolutely destroyed with the human body, but something of it remains,
which is eternal." Spinoza is not asserting a personal afterlife, but
rather speculating that some part of the human being, viewed "under
a certain species of eternity" (sub specie aeternitatis), has no part in
time. We have no conscious experience of eternity, "But nevertheless

we feel and know that we are eternal. For the mind no less feels these things which it conceives in understanding than those which it has in memory. For the eyes of the mind by which it sees things and observes them are proofs."[17] Zukofsky's version sets "the eyes of the mind" in sharp contrast to the obfuscations of the rationalizing intellect: "Voice without scurf or gray matter, / For the eyes of the mind are proofs."[18] The "eyes of the mind" here are the concrete physical senses, working in harmony with the reason to see things as they actually *are*, to see the beloved ones around whom the poet's work revolves.

The poet's eye in "A"-12 and *Bottom* does not merely look towards his immediate surroundings, but seeks to see all moments of culture "under the aspect of eternity." "Can love rouse a thing of the past," Zukofsky asks, "And not see it as present?"[19] If all ages are contemporaneous under the aspect of eternity—and Zukofsky had been arguing that since at least 1930[20]—then any speaker's voice can contribute to the conversation about love: Aristotle, Paracelsus, Shakespeare, Jackie Appleby, or Paul and Celia themselves. All are woven together to compose the complex tissue of "A"-12, a "weave" that is as well a "music": "For all inwreathed / This imagined music / Traces the particular line / Of lines meeting / by chance or design."[21] As in *Bottom*, the various voices, images, and "lines" work together to make the definition of love "flourish." As Spinoza puts it, "The more any image has reference to many things, the more frequent it is, the more often it flourishes, and the more it occupies the mind."[22] Insofar as he seeks to make a single definition or image "flourish," and insofar as he seeks to read all culture sub specie aeternitatis, Zukofsky works from profoundly Spinozan premises.

.   .   .

Like other seventeenth-century "rationalists," Spinoza believed that the order of nature was reflected in the order of human ideas—to the extent, that is, that those ideas were "clear and distinct."[23] For Spinoza, the most obvious self-evidently true ideas were those of mathematics and geometry. He presented his *Ethics*, therefore, in a "geometrical method" modeled after Euclid's *Elements*. Each section begins with a list of self-evidently true "definitions" and "axioms" from which the "propositions" that follow are derived, all buttressed by an elaborate structure of "proofs," "corollaries," and "notes." This geometrical method has been responsible for unnumbered readers laying the *Ethics* aside in frustration. Zukofsky, however, was delighted by that method. "The wonderful thing about Spinoza's philosophy to me," he said in 1969, "is that out of 8 definitions and 7 axioms he builds the whole system."[24] This is not to say that Zukofsky believed that the quasi-mathematical structure of Spinoza's philosophy somehow underwrote its accuracy or truth. Rather, he found a powerful *aesthetic* attraction in the geometrical method, a method by which the thinker erected a complex intellectual structure out of a strictly limited number of principles and materials, all the while keeping those principles and materials in the forefront of his readers' attentions. (Zukofsky showed a similar enthusiasm for Ludwig Wittgenstein's *Tractatus Logico-Philosophicus*, organized numerically around "seven main propositions and not many subordinate ones."[25])

"The parts of a fugue," Zukofsky quotes Bach in "A"-12, "should behave like reasonable men / in an orderly discussion," and for Zukofsky the fugue, where subject and countersubject were introduced, counterpointed, and built upon to create "harmony / certain in concord with reason," was a compositional principle akin to Spinoza's method of definitions, axioms, and proofs.[26] Zukofsky's affection for such formalized systems of thought was surely related to his affection for the languages of mathematics and science. But his attraction to sciences and mathematics was ultimately an *aesthetic* one: They were beautiful, and the beauty of their equations and theorems reflected the beauty of the natural world. "Like mathematical formulae," he told the same audience in 1969, "that's pure abstract state, but who's not to say that that is as beautiful as some botanical convolvulae or something like that."[27]

Paracelsus appealed to Zukofsky through his recognition of the isomorphism and interrelatedness of the various spheres of existence: the stars and human destiny, the micro- and macrocosms. Bach had a similar vision of an ordered universe: "The order that rules music, the same / controls the placing of the stars and the feathers / in a bird's wing."[28] Spinoza, more than any other thinker, had made a philosophical system out of that sense of order, and an ethics that could bear him through the fluctuations of a painful and disappointing life. "Few philosophers have had the sense of order as supremely as Spinoza had it," wrote Zukofsky's professor Frederick J. E. Woodbridge. "The beauty of it in him for a modern reader lies in his freedom from *epistemology* and the confusions of *subjectivism*."[29] *Epistemology*—the theory of knowledge, of how and whether we truly know the objects of our senses—was for Zukofsky a waste of time better devoted to "thinking with the things as they exist." "It is assumed that epistemological problems do not affect existence," he wrote in 1930.[30] Zukofsky dealt with *subjectivism*—the enshrining of the poet's individual consciousness—in "Poetry/*For My Son When He Can Read*." The poet's first aim, he writes there, is "to avoid clutter" so that "the order of his syllables will define his awareness of order. For his second and major aim is not to show himself but that order that of itself can speak to all men."[31]

Spinoza was central to Zukofsky's imagination, not merely as a theorist of love or as a proponent of a rational ethics of self-respect and benign complacency, but as an *artist*, one who perceived the interlinked orders of the mind and the world and sought to embody them in a work of equal structure and proportion. That, after all, was the goal of Zukofsky's own poetic endeavor, which, like all excellent things, was as difficult as it was rare.

The Great
World 1952–1957

AMERICAN POETRY in the 1950s was far less experimental and rambunctious than it had been two decades before. The modernists born in the last decades of the nineteenth century were now distant elders, their most shocking rebellions tamed or forgotten. Pound was a traitor shut up in a madhouse. Williams, at work on some of what were to be his most famous poems, remained in Rutherford in comparative obscurity. Wallace Stevens, strolling each morning to his job at the Hartford, continued to refine his meditations on reality and the imagination, paying little attention to younger poets. Marianne Moore, whose acerbic formal experiments had given way to slacker and more discursive parables in verse, had been embraced by the reading public as a lovable eccentric, known more for her tricorn hat and her support of the Brooklyn Dodgers than for her poetry. The greatest living American poet, public consensus would have it, was Robert Frost, a staunch old-style formalist who had spent years crafting his image as a plainspoken New England farmer.

The experiments of modernism seemed far behind, and this was nowhere more evident than in the cultural eminence of T. S. Eliot, who by the 1950s had come to embody the literary establishment that he and Pound had attacked back in the 1910s and 1920s. He had been awarded the Nobel Prize in 1948, the capstone of his institutionalization, and spent his energies analyzing the troubles of modern society in such prose works as *Notes Towards the Definition of Culture* and middlebrow plays like *The Family Reunion* and *The Cocktail Party*—all of them, ultimately, in the service of his "Anglo-Catholic" Christianity.

It is difficult to overestimate Eliot's literary influence in the 1950s: his authority as a critic and a poetic model (especially in the *Four Quartets* of 1943) was well-nigh papal for American writers. Eliot's early critical writings, along with the works of I. A. Richards and others, had given rise to the "New Criticism," a movement that would come to dominate the reading of poetry in the American academy. New Critical methods worked best with the seventeenth-century metaphysical poets or such moderns as Eliot and W. H. Auden. The poets who came to public prominence in the postwar years—among them Robert Lowell, Randall Jarrell, Karl Shapiro, and Elizabeth Bishop—were much under the sway of the New Criticism (poetry, as never before, was becoming an *academic* pursuit) and worked in the shadow of Auden, Eliot, and Yeats. They wrote finely crafted, formally traditional poems fitting comfortably into the English lyric tradition, and seemed to want to forget the upheavals that had characterized American verse culture in the 1930s. As Delmore Schwartz, a prominent member of this generation, put it towards the end of the 1950s, "what was once a battlefield has become a peaceful public park on a pleasant Sunday afternoon."[1]

These poets were not reading Zukofsky. If they recognized him at all, it was as a relic of the 1930s, a minor soldier of Pound's failed revolution. On the threshold of his sixth decade, Zukofsky had not seen a single volume of his poetry published by a major commercial press. *Poetry* would occasionally print his poems, and there were always "little" magazines—run by individuals, or out of college English departments—that would welcome his work; but to the tastemakers of American poetry, Zukofsky's writing could have been from another planet.

Yet not all of American literary life in the 1950s was a reflection of postwar society's gray flannel conformity. Across the country, isolated pockets of poets sought to effect another "revolution of the word" comparable to that of modernism. Many of these poets looked to Pound and Williams as still-living heroes of the modernist revolution, and some of them were discovering Zukofsky's work as well. Charles Olson was among the most influential of these "postmodernists" (he was the first to use that term in a literary context).[2] Six years younger than Zukofsky, Olson had long considered Pound the most important living American poet, and soon after Pound was incarcerated in St. Elizabeths Olson began visiting him. He found Pound tired, often incoherent, but brilliantly stimulating. Pound mentioned Zukofsky to Olson as one of his "old friends."[3]

Olson was in the process of finding his way to a poetics based upon the collaging of fragments characteristic of Pound's and Williams's writings, but Olson's work was to have an energy and dynamism that outstripped that of his masters. He laid out his poetics in the 1950 essay "Projective Verse," where he argued against traditional form and metrics in favor of what he called "composition by field." The poem must be "a high-energy construct and, at all points, an energy-discharge." In order to attain such energy, the poet must realize that "FORM IS NEVER MORE THAN AN EXTENSION OF CONTENT."[4]

Much in "Projective Verse" struck Zukofsky as repeating positions he himself had staked out two decades before in his objectivist essays. Olson's insistence that "form is never more than an extension of content" echoed Zukofsky's emphasis on the poet's necessary "sincerity" to achieve "objectification," goals having little to do with traditional formal schemes. Zukofsky had anticipated Olson's exploration of the typewriter as scoring device for the voice in "'Recencies' in Poetry," where he included "Typography" among the "components of the poetic object": "certainly—if print and the arrangement of it will help tell how the voice should sound."[5] Perhaps most frustrating for Zukofsky was Olson's proposing a new poetic stance, "objectism," which was "the getting rid of the lyrical interference of the individual as ego, of the 'subject' and his soul . . ."[6] This seemed no more than a restating of what Zukofsky had asserted back in 1931: "A poem. A poem as object. . . . Perfect rest—or nature as creator, existing perfect, experience perfecting activity of existence, making—theologically, perhaps—like the Ineffable—"[7] Worst of all, Olson posited his "objectism" in explicit contrast to a defunct movement of Pound's and Williams's "which got called 'objectivism.' But that word," Olson continued (clearly overlooking Zukofsky's repeated disavowals of any "ism" and his dissociation of his term "objectivist" from any "philosophical etiquette"), "was then used in some sort of a necessary quarrel, I take it, with 'subjectivism.'"[8] "So much criticism," Zukofsky told Thomas Merton some years later in reference to "Projective Verse," is "current restatement of what's been said more simply previously." Olson, in dismissing "objectivism," clearly "hadn't read me at all or misread me—or he'd have left well enough alone as it was."[9] Celia Zukofsky was more blunt: "Louis always felt that Olson's essay on Projective Verse was really a take off on his own critical writings . . . a restatement of what Louis had said re the Objectivists."[10]

Olson was to become a major force in alternative American poetry. In 1948, he took a temporary teaching post at Black Mountain College, an innovative liberal arts institution in North Carolina (replacing his friend Edward Dahlberg), and in 1951 he returned as rector. In the five years of Olson's rectorship Black Mountain was one of the most lively centers of the arts in the country: its faculty would include the musicians and composers John Cage, David Tudor, and Stefan Wolpe, the painter Franz Kline, and the choreographer Merce Cunningham. Olson invited Zukofsky himself to teach at Black Mountain—his phone call to New York was the two poets' only conversation—but the salary was less than that of Brooklyn Polytech, and the idea of moving to rural North Carolina was even less attractive than moving to Madison had been in 1930.[11] Zukofsky would follow Olson's career in magazines and books, but while he admired the "lyrical spareness" of some of Olson's poetry, he was put off by Olson's army of disciples and promoters and impatient with Olson's didacticism.[12]

.   .   .

While Olson was the confirmed leader of what literary history would come to label the "Black Mountain Poets," Zukofsky's work had a presence at the college, thanks in large part to a pair of young poets in Olson's orbit, Robert Duncan and Robert Creeley. Born in 1919, Duncan had recognized poetry as his vocation after reading H.D. in high school, and in 1937 he set himself to learning what modernism in poetry consisted of besides *The Waste Land*. That year he read (in the files of Pound's the *Exile*) Zukofsky's "Poem beginning 'The'" and (in *New Directions 1936*) "'Mantis'" and "'*Mantis,' an Interpretation*." He found these poems revelatory in how they showed "a kind of self-consciousness in which not the poet but the act of writing was this 'self'—an active conscience in making . . ." Much later, Duncan would summarize the shift he keenly intuited in 1937: "If a neo-Platonism presides over the poetics of Pound, and it does, then we have broken with Plato in Zukofsky and a neo-Aristotelianism takes its place."[13]

After absorbing Williams's *The Wedge* (1944) and *Paterson I* (1946), Duncan found that he could begin to fit Zukofsky within a lineage of poets that ran from Williams to himself. Duncan's was a notoriously eclectic aesthetic, and Zukofsky would join a varied company: Duncan described his own poetics in 1954 as "brew[ing] another cup / in that Marianne Moore—/ E.P.—Williams—H.D.—Stein—/ Zukofsky—Stevens—Perse—/ surrealist—dada—staind / pot . . ."[14] Duncan wrote Zukofsky in the summer of 1947, and a warm exchange of letters ensued. Zukofsky sent him a copy of *Anew*, which Duncan took with him when he and his partner, the artist Jess Collins, went to Mallorca in 1955.[15] There he lent it to the young poet, fiction writer, and editor Robert Creeley.

Creeley, born in Massachusetts in 1926, had dropped out of Harvard during his senior year, having realized that he wanted above all else to be a writer.[16] By the mid-1950s, he was several years into an intense, voluminous correspondence with Olson. In late 1953 Olson asked Creeley to become the editor of Black Mountain College's new literary magazine, the *Black Mountain Review*. The first issues of the journal focused heavily on Olson's own work. It was Edward Dahlberg, also living on Mallorca at the time, who suggested that Creeley ought to approach Zukofsky about contributing to the magazine.

Creeley knew Zukofsky only as one of the dedicatees of Pound's 1938 *Guide to Kulchur*, but Dahlberg informed him that Zukofsky was still alive and writing, if in obscurity—still a "struggler in the desert." Soon after, Duncan brought *Anew* and his typed collection of Zukofsky poems.[17] For Duncan, Zukofsky represented a "particularly Jewish urbanism" and a link to the esoteric traditions of the Kabbalah (Duncan's own inclinations ran towards the mystical); more importantly, Zukofsky was a "master craftsman."[18] Creeley concurred. In the next two years, he published Zukofsky in each of the last three issues of *Black Mountain Review*: a chunk of "A"-12, two excerpts from *Bottom: on Shakespeare*, and the sequence "Songs of Degrees."

Creeley had taught at Black Mountain College in 1954, and he returned there from Mallorca in the summer of 1955, where he communicated his enthusiasm for Zukofsky's work to various students, among them the poet Joel Oppenheimer and the writer Fielding Dawson. Creeley came out to the Zukofskys' 30 Willow Street, Brooklyn, home later that year. He overshot his subway stop, spent his last coin making good his mistake, and arrived "tentative, confused, and literally penniless." Creeley was deeply moved by Louis and Celia's kindness to a young, bedraggled, impecunious stranger: They gave him not merely subway fare, but a five-dollar bill, an overcoat of Louis's, and a packed lunch for his return to North Carolina the next day.[19] There grew up between Creeley and Zukofsky a warm and intense friendship. Though Creeley's actual visits were not numerous and their correspondence was not voluminous, the two men shared a "metaphysical rapport" (in Celia Zukofsky's words), a common sense of what the poem consisted of and what the poet strove for. For Creeley, Zukofsky was a living example of how one could dedicate oneself to one's art and the extraordinary writing that could result from such dedication. "Each of us needed someone," he later recalled, "not to listen to our whining, but to serve as model to the possibilities of our own concentration and art. . . . Louis Zukofsky served us as this extraordinary sense of what, after all, one was committing oneself to, if poetry was the art that was possible."[20]

Creeley's early work had been heavily influenced by Hart Crane's and D. H. Lawrence's poetry; he had come a bit later to Williams and then Olson. After he began reading Zukofsky and sending him his poems in manuscript, Creeley's poetry began to turn to the "unobtrusive, intensive wordplay" that was so characteristic of Zukofsky's. As he had been with Rakosi, Niedecker, and Williams, Zukofsky was a keen editor, quoting passages he liked from the poems and recommending excisions. He saw great accomplishment and promise in Creeley's poems, and admired *The Gold Diggers*, the volume of short stories Creeley had published in 1954.[21] Zukofsky would review Creeley's chapbook *The Whip* for *Poetry* in 1957[22]—a gesture indicating the depth of friendship he felt for the younger poet, since by that point Zukofsky had entirely abandoned "occasional" criticism—and would write several letters of recommendation on Creeley's behalf for various grants and teaching posts.

· · ·

After he finished "A"-12 in October 1951, Zukofsky had laid the long poem aside and devoted his energies to *Bottom: on Shakespeare*. *Bottom*, which had expanded from an essay on certain motifs of sight and mind in Shakespeare to a comprehensive examination of Shakespeare's epistemology, and then to a tracing of the problems exemplified in Shakespeare's work through the whole of Western culture, had become an all-consuming project, an obsession that left Zukofsky time only for brief forays in verse. The poems he wrote during the rest of the 1950s were mostly brief and almost without exception occasional—prompted, that is, by the events of his life. Almost every year from 1951 to 1957 he wrote a Valentine's Day poem. In 1952, in "On Valentine's Day to Friends," he remembered those closest to him: Celia, Paul, Edward and R'lene Dahlberg, Niedecker, Helen Taggart, and Taupin.[23] Three valentines for Celia from 1953 and 1954 became sections 1, 2, and 4 of "Songs of Degrees."[24] "The Record" was a valentine to his wife and son, a remembrance of the recording *Eine Kleine Nachtmusik* Celia had given him before they were married and a commemoration of Paul's performance of the music in a concert that fell on her forty-third birthday.[25]

Other occasions were less happy. In 1953, the day before Christmas, Celia's father, Hyman Thaew, died of a coronary thrombosis; his funeral was held on December 27, the following Sunday. Riding in the funeral procession, melancholy—on the way to bury "one of the few good men I knew"—Zukofsky idly noted how even the shop signs seemed to reflect a world in which poetry and music had become debased. As he put it in a poem drafted that same day,

Being driven after the hearse thru suburbs—
 the dead man who had been good
 and by a coincidence my father-in-law,
I sped by shop signs:
 Handel, Butcher, Shelley, Plumber
a beautiful day, blue wintry sky
such is this world.[26]

One of the minor intricacies of this quiet poem is the pun—"the dead man who had been *good* "—on his father-in-law's name, Thaew, from Hebrew *tov,* "good."

. . .

While the Zukofskys liked to spend their summers outside of the city, Paul's education occupied more and more of their attention. In early 1952 he began taking lessons under the supervision of the legendary Juilliard violin pedagogue Ivan Galamian, and that summer and the following the entire family went to upstate New York so Paul could attend Meadowmount, the music camp Galamian had established in 1944.[27] The first summer there Zukofsky wrote "Spook's Sabbath, Five Bowings," a playful poem whose five sections mimed five different methods of bowing the violin: *spiccato, martelé, grand détaché, collé,* and *staccato.*[28]

In the summer of 1954 the Zukofskys made a cross-country trek that included the South, the Canadian Rockies, and the West Coast. The vacation began with a rather touching reunion: though there had been no communications between Zukofsky and Pound since 1948, Zukofsky wrote Pound to inquire if they might visit him in Washington at St. Elizabeths. Pound replied: "Sure, bring deh fambly. I didn't know you had one."[29] And if Paul was as fine a violinist as Zukofsky claimed, perhaps he could play Canto LXXV, an arrangement of sixteenth-century composer Clément Jannequin's "Chant des Oiseaux"? The Zukofskys arrived at St. Elizabeths on the afternoon of July 11, where they found Pound stationed on the lawn in a folding chair. The two poets had not seen each other in fifteen years, and their meeting was warm. They spoke of Pound's current writing, of plans to get him out of the asylum, and—less welcome for Zukofsky—his same old economic and political obsessions, as strong as ever. Then Paul played for the old poet: Jannequin's song of the birds, followed by the preludio of Bach's Third Partita. Pound was pleased and impressed, and Zukofsky left him with a copy of *Anew*.[30] Pound wrote him later that day: "imp. at p/ 15. I now divide poetry into what I CAN read and what I cannot. I hv/ read thus far and expect to read to the end. I note that you have got OUT of influence of E.P. and Possum [Eliot] / NO longer the trace of linguistic parasitism that I noted with surprise on rereading some early Zuk. about 1942."[31]

It was a long-overdue recognition on Pound's part that could only have been gratifying to Zukofsky. The summer before, in reaction to Pound's *Pisan Cantos*, Zukofsky had drafted a meditation on King David, the prophet Ezra, the destruction of the Jerusalem Temple, and the experience of exile. This poem, "'Nor did the prophet,'" began "I know why David moves me, / Ezra, he did not pound / 'The worst bastard of them all' / Never chartered nor coddled his ground."[32] In Canto LXXIV, the first of the *Pisan Cantos*, Pound had written, "to redeem Zion with justice / sd/ Isaiah. Not out on interest said David Rex / the prime s.o.b."[33] Pound sounds here one of the *Pisan Cantos'* leitmotifs, the notion of rebuilding, of holding fast to a spiritual ideal in the midst of the war's destruction. In the Detention Training Camp, he had been reading the Old Testament and finding much to admire: the prophet Isaiah's admonition that "Zion shall be redeemed with judgment" (Isaiah 1.27), the Psalmist David's assurance that "He that putteth not out his money to usury" shall be blessed (Psalm 15.1, 5). In the *Pisan Cantos*, Pound aligned the task of rebuilding Western culture with that of rebuilding the Temple after the Babylonian Captivity.

Zukofsky's "'Nor did the prophet'" is suffused with the language of the Hebrew Bible; as references, Zukofsky appends a list of passages from Ezra, I Chronicles, II Samuel, and Genesis. But where the book of Ezra described the rebuilding of the Temple by the returned exiles, Zukofsky presents a picture of Jewry in a condition of permanent exile—or non-exile, since a people without a Temple cannot be exiled therefrom:

The sound in the temple built after exile
Is never worth the sound
At the earth where no temple stood
And on which no law of exile can fall.

Zukofsky condenses into a very few lines the prophet Ezra's description of the Temple's rebuilding, and how Ezra, dismayed by his backsliding people's intermarriages with the Gentiles, "Rends coat, plucks hair of his head and his beard / Sits down astonished . . ."

In "'Nor did the prophet'" *Ezra* is both the Hebrew prophet and the poet *Ezra* Pound, whose agonies in the DTC (movingly described in the *Pisan Cantos*) are contrasted with the ways in which Pound had been most un-Davidic. King David, for instance, refused to drink the water of the well of Bethlehem, which his men had risked their lives to bring him: "*is not this* the blood of the men that went in jeopardy of their lives?" (2 Samuel 23.17). Pound, in contrast, by overlooking the evil of the Nazi and fascist regimes he supported, "does not stop from drinking water / As blood is shed." His moral obtuseness has become aesthetic failure, so that he "Does not see morning without a cloud / Upon tender grass without rain" (see 2 Samuel 23.3–4, a description of the "just ruler"). Zukofsky ends the poem—in its 1953 first draft—both tenderly and bitterly. "On this earth / We will not—nor did the prophet much—mention / David." There has been enough criticism for now; no need once again to mention David, "the prime s.o.b.," "The worst bastard of them all."

Zukofsky speculated that he might use the lines of "'Nor did the prophet'" in "A"-13, but he would not publish them in a magazine, "apart from a volume of verse"—no doubt because he was shy of making too public a statement about his old friend.[34] In January 1955, with the visit to St. Elizabeths still very much on his mind, Zukofsky returned to the poem and added the first and last stanzas. In the first, Paul speaks, and his father replies: *The man is our friend? / Our friend.* In the last, the birds themselves have taken up that refrain:

The birds sing:
The man is our friend,
Our friend.[35]

Where before "'Nor did the prophet'" had been a response to the *Pisan Cantos* and an oblique reflection on the themes of exile and return, these two framing stanzas recast the whole poem as a meditation on that afternoon in Washington where ideological differences had been subsumed under a common love of music.[36]

From Washington the Zukofskys traveled to North Carolina and then turned westward. They stopped at Black Hawk Island to visit Niedecker, whose father had recently died. The trip included the Canadian Rockies, Los Angeles, the Bay Area (where he gave a reading at Berkeley radio station KPFW), and British Columbia.[37] Zukofsky's lasting memories of this trip, as he would recount them several years later in "A"-13, were of vivid details of scenery, landscape, and flora: Jefferson's "natural air-conditioned cellar at Monticello"; "the South's crepe myrtle"; "Tall trees and waterfalls / But falls and falls of trees / Douglas firs redwood"; "Oregon: Crater Lake saw / No order except its intense blue that / Clouds over it do not change"; "the misnamed temples / Of Grand Canyon's absurd sunsets"; "The tourist emerald of Lake Louise [in Banff National Park, Alberta] / Set in the glacier"; "the soft mountains of Canmore . . ."[38] It would be a mistake to dismiss the Zukofskys as homebodies; they were, it is true, most comfortable in New York, but they shared the postwar American passion for tourism, even that brand of tourism promoted as "seeing America first."

·   ·   ·

It had been almost a decade since Zukofsky had published a book of poems. He had been collecting and arranging poems for some time—"Some Time" was the title he envisaged for his next collection. Its title poem had been on hand since 1949: "Some time has gone / Since these were written: / The cause runs off—/ A child's mitten."[39] As usual, however, finding a publisher presented a problem. Concurrent with the emergent "underground" poetry scene was the rise of an alternative publishing industry, exemplified in such tiny outfits as Creeley's Divers Press, Lawrence Ferlinghetti's City Lights Pocket Poets series, and Jonathan Williams's Jargon Society. These presses took as models earlier small presses like Leonard and Virginia Woolf's Hogarth Press, but most of all they looked to James Laughlin's New Directions, which had made a range of new writers and some of the most important of the modernists widely available in inexpensive paperback editions. That ethos of getting the poems into print and available, no matter how cheaply they might be printed, was foreign to Jonathan Williams. Williams—who, despite his press's collective title, *was* the Jargon Society—was an aesthete, a lover of fine printing and elaborate bindings. Born in 1929 and brought up in Highlands, North Carolina, Williams had in 1951 published a broadside poem of his own as Jargon 1.[40] He continued issuing books and pamphlets under the Jargon Society imprint after he came to Black Mountain College later that year to study photography. At the college he fell under Olson's influence, and in the years to come the Jargon Society would publish two volumes of Olson's *Maximus Poems*, as well as books by fellow Black Mountain poets Creeley, Duncan, and Joel Oppenheimer.

It was Duncan who told Williams that he ought to publish Zukofsky.[41] In May 1955 Williams sent Zukofsky a bundle of Jargon books—new poetry by Olson, Creeley, Kenneth Patchen, and himself—and inquired whether he might be interested in doing a book with the press.[42] Zukofsky replied by subscribing to Jargon's forthcoming titles by Kenneth Rexroth and Patchen and indicated that he did indeed have a manuscript on hand, and would be interested in working with Jargon.[43]

Williams was delighted with the poems of *Some Time*, and determined that they should be presented in a format that did justice to their beauties. While serving in the army in Stuttgart, Germany, Williams had discovered the fine print shop of Dr. Walter Cantz. Williams wanted *Some Time* to be printed by Cantz in an especially sumptuous edition, in the format of "a Japanese book . . . with uncut pages and a string binding."[44] Zukofsky was pleased with Williams's concern for his book's tangible aesthetics, but he was intimidated by the prospective costs: two dollars apiece for three hundred copies, or a dollar fifty apiece for five hundred. Neither man would have to foot the bill, however: Williams would solicit subscriptions for the edition, which would consist of three hundred regular copies (three dollars) and fifty copies of a boxed and signed "author's edition" (five dollars); for ten dollars, one could be a "patron" to the edition and have one's name included in a list in the book.[45]

By 1955, Zukofsky was fifty-one—in Williams's words "already a

worn and bemused man, but an infinitely kind, patient, and respon-
sive one as well";[46] he had developed a deep distaste for the "business" of literary publishing, the various pits in which the artist soiled
himself to get his work out to an audience. The Jargon Society's subscription policy had the advantage of freeing the poet and publisher
from immediate financial involvement, but Zukofsky found this process of hat-in-hand solicitation just plain embarrassing. He nonetheless supplied Williams with a list of the names and addresses of over
sixty prospective "patrons" and subscribers—including members of
his own family and in-laws, old college friends, acquaintances from
Old Lyme and Elizabethtown, and practically every poet, writer, and
artist Zukofsky knew who might have disposable income.[47]

Zukofsky's advance copy of *Some Time* finally arrived on March 1,
1957 (its official publication date was September 1956), and despite
his impatience on behalf of his subscribers, Zukofsky found himself
pleased. Propitiously, his German-American postman recognized the
return address on the package, and remembered that the Cantz'sche
Druckerei had published the first edition of Heine. The book itself,
Zukofsky noted, was "vurry purty": "Had no idea that you intended
uncut blank pages inside," he told Williams. "Ain't seen that since my
brother's green morocco copy of Omar Khayyam at the age of seven,
which sticks in memory, tho it must have gone with his bookstore
almost 30 years ago, too."[48] Williams himself was delighted with how
the book had turned out: He still considers it the most beautiful piece
of bookmaking the Jargon Society ever had a hand in.

Some Time brought together work Zukofsky had written over the
past sixteen years (a number of the poems, in fact, had been originally
intended for *Anew*). Much of *Some Time* consisted of short—sometimes slight—poems strung together into longer sequences, so that
they gained weight and resonance from their position among other
poems. *Some Time* also emphasized voices that had been less evident
in Zukofsky's first two collections. Here, for instance, one could find
Zukofsky the author of humorous or "light" verse, such as the three
poems of "Michtam": "Lese-Wiat, from Caul Gate," Zukofsky's farewell to Colgate University; "Romantic Portrait," a jesting description
of Zukofsky's friend Stephen Seley; and "With a capital P," inspired by
a 1948 letter from Basil Bunting in Persia: "I have just distinguished

myself by smashing my car twice in one month, after having never had an accident of any sort before," Bunting wrote: "I have left the embassy and now represent the Press, capital P":[49]

> To the Gentlemen of the Press
> With a capital P
> A plea that in what sodden state he be
> He will not veer nor keep his head on he
>
> Attend him Star!
> Especially in his motorcar.[50]

Zukofsky's poetic ear had become acutely sensitive to the gradations of verbal tones, so that even when he is deploying the most outrageous rhymes and extravagant bilingual puns, as in the first stanza of "Spook's Sabbath"'s second movement—

> No sins or
> Faux pas
> Disturb a *repas*
> À l'hôtel
> The
> Hotel Windsor[51]

—the poem's sonic deliberation belies the slightness of its texture.

In other poems of *Some Time*, Zukofsky distilled everyday observation and close examination of the outside world into miniature "machines"—to use William Carlos Williams's famous metaphor—in which there was no superfluous word or syllable, where even the smallest particle of language contributed its note to the poem's fragile music. It was appropriate to set the words of the first part of "So That Even a Lover" on the cover of *Some Time*, for that poem exemplifies much of what makes the book so extraordinary:

> Little wrists,
> Is your content
> My sight or hold,
> Or your small air
> That lights and trysts?

Red alder berry
Will singly break;
But you—how slight—do:
So that even
A lover exists.[52]

Zukofsky had become a twentieth-century poet by attending to the
work of poets with fine ears—H.D. and Pound among them—and
he had trained his own lyric sense by decades of attention to the wiry
cadences of Elizabethan and Cavalier lyric. He had purged his poetry
of rhetoric and grandiloquence, leaving structures of sound through
which the evidence of the eyes and the affections of the heart could
clearly shine: the poem, in the metaphor he had invoked in "A"-6 and
in the objectivist essays, was a focusing device, a *lens*.

In the *New York Times Book Review*, Kenneth Rexroth—Zukofsky's
former fellow objectivist, now an éminence grise on the San Francisco poetry scene—wrote that "Louis Zukofsky is one of the most
important poets of my generation." The poems of *Some Time* were
"exercises in absolute clarification, crystal cabinets full of air and
angels." Twenty-five years after *An "Objectivists" Anthology*, Rexroth
had forgotten his irritation at Zukofsky's rearrangement of his poems
and hailed *Some Time* as a collection "more important and moving (or
more exemplary and instructive to the young)" than any "likely to be
published for some time." He was right, especially about the influence
Zukofsky's work would shortly begin to exert upon younger poets.

.   .   .

The publication of *Some Time* came at a busy time for the Zukofskys.
Zukofsky had been promoted to associate professor at Poly in May
1955; later that year they put the Willow Street house on the market,
with no success. By February 1956 they were making arrangements
for Paul's Carnegie Hall debut, scheduled for the end of November.
Reserving the hall was a fairly straightforward matter; far more
challenging was *filling* the auditorium, so the thirteen-year-old violinist would perform to a full and receptive audience. Louis and
Celia gave away scores of tickets to relatives, friends, and acquaintances, to Zukofsky's colleagues and superiors at the Institute, and to

newspaper critics. Even Pound, still in St. Elizabeths, pitched in. The Zukofskys had taken to sending him parcels of candy and cookies, and after Paul's performance on the madhouse lawn, he had taken a keen interest in the young violinist's progress. He sent Zukofsky a long list of people who might want to come; Zukofsky was deeply touched: "Breaks my heart thinking of you typing out all those addresses."[53] E. E. Cummings and his wife promised to come, and invited the Zukofskys over for tea (the first time the two men had seen each other since 1948). James Laughlin, "believing such things should be supported," refused Zukofsky's offer of free tickets and phoned the box office for five seats. Laughlin had paid his ten dollars to be a patron for *Some Time*, and Zukofsky had some faint hopes—though he was too proud to approach Laughlin directly on the subject—that New Directions might reprint *A Test of Poetry*.[54]

The recital went off well. Bill and Floss Williams were there (they had bought five tickets), as were the president of Brooklyn Polytech and many others, including the poet Babette Deutsch and Zukofsky's old professor Mark Van Doren, who were delighted to renew a twenty-year lapsed acquaintance when they chanced to find themselves seated next to each other.[55] Zukofsky himself had "the grippe" and "a running fever," but he wrote the next day to thank the Williamses for coming into the city. Four weeks later he was writing Williams to congratulate him on winning a five-thousand-dollar prize from the Academy of American Poets.[56] His old friend, after many years laboring on the fringes of the literary world, was finally beginning to receive public acknowledgment. Zukofsky must have wondered when—or if—his own turn would come.

. . .

The following summer, with *Some Time* finally in print and Paul's debut behind them, the Zukofskys took their long-delayed European tour. First, however, they finally sold the 30 Willow Street house. They were tired of the place's size and upkeep—the extra space seemed to invite a constant stream of family and visitors—and were happy to move into a much smaller apartment at 135 Willow, only a ten-minute walk from Poly. Amid the busyness of moving house and packing for the journey, Zukofsky tried to make some business arrangements:

He wrote to D. G. Bridson, an old associate of Pound's now working for the BBC, to inquire whether he might be able to read his poetry on the radio, or Paul might be able to play.[57] Bridson was unable to arrange anything for either of them, but he promised to meet Zukofsky when he was in London—as did T. S. Eliot and Dahlberg's friend Sir Herbert Read, both of whom held influential positions in British publishing.

The family sailed on June 18 and arrived at Plymouth a week later. They saw Stonehenge on Salisbury Plain, and the eighteenth-century resort towns of Bristol and Wells. On the last weekend of the month they went to Worcester, where they stayed with Gael Turnbull and his family.[58] Turnbull, a twenty-nine-year-old Scottish physician and poet, was almost alone among British poets in having some sense of the emergent currents in American poetry, and what those currents owed to Williams Carlos Williams and Zukofsky. While practicing medicine in northern Ontario, he had discovered the work of Creeley and Olson and had begun publishing in their company. Turnbull had been in touch with Zukofsky for some months, having sent him a copy of one of his early chapbooks, *A Libation*. He was in the process of establishing a press, Migrant Books, in order to distribute Creeley's *The Whip*. He showed the family the sights of Worcester, and took them to the nearby Malvern Hills, famous from Langland's *Piers Ploughman*.[59]

By far the greatest service Turnbull did for Zukofsky was to put him back in touch with Basil Bunting. After spending much of the war in Persia, Bunting had worked in Tehran for the British embassy (and for British Intelligence); in 1948 he had married a fourteen-year-old Iranian girl. The marriage, legal in Iran but highly irregular in English eyes, had ended his diplomatic career, and he had been jobless from 1950 to 1951, though hard at work on a magnificent long poem on Middle Eastern themes, *The Spoils*, drafts of which he sent Zukofsky on a regular basis. Bunting and his wife, Sima, returned to Iran late in 1951, where he was correspondent for the *Times* (and probably again employed by British Intelligence). He was expelled from Iran in March 1952 by the nationalist Prime Minister Mossadeq. Bunting returned to Northumberland, where he and his family lived in near poverty. He worked the night shift at a Newcastle newspaper, suffered from deteriorating eyesight, and had let almost all of his literary friendships lapse. When the young Gael Turnbull turned up on his doorstep one day, having seen his name and address on a list of subscribers to an American poetry magazine, Bunting had his first taste of being sought out by a younger generation of poets.[60]

Bunting was pleased, in a melancholy way, to hear from Zukofsky: "Most welcome. How often I've wished to see you again. And how little profit you can now extract from what's left of me."[61] But he would be glad to see the Zukofskys in the "great hideous home" that he had recently been able to buy, thanks to a legacy left him by an aunt, and which he had grandiloquently named "Shadingfield." So from Worcester the Zukofskys traveled north, stopping at Stratford-on-Avon and Edinburgh, and made their way to Bunting's home outside of Newcastle. They stayed there with Bunting's substantial household—Sima and their two children, Bunting's aged mother, and Sima's fifteen-year-old nephew—and Bunting, taking some time off from the paper, showed them the sights of the northeast, including Durham Cathedral. "We cheered him," Zukofsky commented, "they feasted us . . ."[62]

From Northumberland they went to London, where they visited museums and tried to advance Zukofsky's career. Sir Herbert Read, who had arranged Routledge's 1952 publication of *A Test of Poetry*, was "vegetarian pheasant-eyed Yorkshire" and sympathetic; unfortunately, Routledge only published two volumes of poetry a year, and had no room for Zukofsky on their list.[63] T. S. Eliot had been a director at Faber & Faber for some years now; back in 1951 he had sent Zukofsky two letters on behalf of the firm rejecting, respectively, *Ferdinand* (which Bunting had sent his way) and a collection of Zukofsky's poems.[64] When the Zukofskys came to see Eliot in his London office, he was very friendly, "almost bounding with cordiality," but could offer no hope of Zukofsky's being published in England by Faber, either.[65]

They left Dover for Calais on July 17, and the next eight weeks were a time of almost continuous movement, a frenetic cramming-in of places and sights. For four days they were in Paris, where Zukofsky admired Ossip Zadkine's "Orpheus" in the Petit Palais; unfortunately, the sculptor about whom Zukofsky had written the poem "for

Zadkine" (1944) was on vacation, and could not be visited.[66] They toured Mont St. Michel and Chartres, which Henry Adams had discussed so eloquently. Then they made a pilgrimage through the country of Pound's troubadours, visiting Poitiers and Périgueux, which Zukofsky found "perhaps the most wonderful place of all that's left of the middle ages, [a] magnificent ruin allowed to rot amid shit." Celia balked at entering some of the enclosed spaces at Lascaux, so when he emerged with Paul, Louis described the cave paintings "so well she felt she'd seen them." [67]

The family then worked its way across the French Riviera to Italy and Rapallo. There was no Pound there now, and the place was "worse than Coney Island when it's 100 degrees." In Siena, however, they visited Pound's mistress, Olga Rudge. If Zukofsky's first trip to Europe in 1933 had been prompted by his desire to meet Pound, in some sense this second, far longer tour was an attempt to take in the Europe that had made Pound—the Europe he had memorialized in his poetry and prose, from *The Spirit of Romance* through the *Cantos*. Time and again, Zukofsky would drag his long-suffering family to see another town, painting, or building mentioned in Pound's writings.

After Florence and Rome, they headed to Pound's old stomping grounds on the Adriatic, Ravenna and Venice. In Ravenna, Zukofsky found Dante's monumental tomb "like all shrines or most monstrous," but was awed by the mosaics in the darkened mausoleum of Galla Placidia, of which Pound had written, "in the gloom the gold / gathers the light against it." [68] They visited the places associated with the Roman poet Catullus—Verona, Sirmio, and Lake Garda—and went to Milan, where Zukofsky found himself unexpectedly impressed by the Leonardos: "I never dreamt he was so great an artist," he confessed, having always judged the works by reproductions.

Zukofsky's most significant encounter in Italy, as far as the "business" of poetry went, was in Florence, where he met Cid Corman. Corman was thirty-three in 1957, and already an influential figure in experimental American poetry.[69] In 1949 he had founded a weekly poetry radio program in Boston (a program on which Robert Creeley had given his first public reading). Creeley had asked Corman to gather poems for a magazine Creeley planned, the *Lititz Review*.

When Creeley's funding fell through, Corman decided to make use of the material he'd collected in a little magazine of his own, *Origin*. The first series of *Origin* ran from 1951 to early 1957, and presented a dazzling range of new poets in the Pound-Williams tradition: Olson, Creeley, Duncan, Turnbull, Paul Blackburn, Denise Levertov, and Theodore Enslin. Throughout, Olson bombarded Corman with streams of editorial advice, much as Pound had taken Zukofsky in hand back in 1930 for the "Objectivists" issue of *Poetry*.[70]

By the summer of 1957, Corman had folded the magazine and was teaching in Florence. Both Jonathan Williams and Gael Turnbull had told Zukofsky that he ought to look up this young man, and Turnbull wrote Corman to tell him that the Zukofskys were on their way. Corman had been reading *Black Mountain Review*, in which parts of "A"-12 appeared, and he was eager to meet the poet whose lines had such a "delicate strong music." Their day together was cordial; they saw the Fra Angelico in San Marco and rode a bus up to the little church of San Miniato in Fiesole—the day was hot, the crowds were thick, and the family decided to stay in the bus and enjoy the view of Florence from the hill. They parted, promising to keep in touch. Over the next decade, Corman would become one of Zukofsky's closest correspondents, and his most loyal publisher.[71]

After the churches and museums (and motor scooters) of Italy, Switzerland was a welcome relief—a country of clean streets and quiet natural spectacles—though perhaps a bit dull. From Geneva the Zukofskys returned to Paris, and on September 10 the family sailed from Le Havre, arriving back in New York eight days later, weary but at least no longer seasick.

Going
Westward 1958–1960

ZUKOFSKY WROTE little during the four summer months the family spent in Europe in 1957. Though he had lugged his collected Shakespeare across much of western Europe, he had managed to eke out only a "few pages" of *Bottom*.[1] While on trains between Stratford, Windermere, and Edinburgh, and in hotels in Rapallo and Berne, he had drafted the poem "Stratford-on-Avon," which remembers the family's visit to Shakespeare's birthplace; the poem contrasts the bard-loving American tourist—who knows his Shakespeare very well indeed, as clusters of quotations indicate—with the bard's rather provincial contemporary townsfellows: "The one blotch / On the Shakespeare arms / In Stratford," comments a Stratfordian, "Is the Memorial Theatre / A Woman planned." Knowing the complexity of Shakespeare's female characters, the "family of three" replies quietly, "That may not be so bad / If it turns out well."[2]

Far more important, however, was the long poem "4 Other Countries." Zukofsky began taking notes for and drafting "4 Other Countries" in Europe: he worked on it for a full year, finishing in September 1958.[3] Almost nine hundred lines in compact quatrains, "4 Other Countries" was Zukofsky's longest poem outside of *"A"* itself, and represented a culmination of the poetics of observation and condensation that he had been pursuing for so long. It also represented a straining against the boundaries of the short poem and short poem sequence, forms to which he had confined himself since *"A"*-12. In the 219 quatrains of "4 Other Countries," Zukofsky sought to *compress* the experience of the family over three months in Europe. In the first stanza—

> Merry, La Belle
>   *antichi*, tilling—
> of pastime and
>   good company:[4]

—"Merry" is England, as in "Merry Old England"; France is "La Belle," according to the sentimental French formulation, La Belle France; Italy, full of the relics of the Roman Empire and the Renaissance, is "antiquities" or "antiques," *antichi*; and Switzerland, agricultural and ordered, is "tilling." The Zukofskys' three months abroad had indeed been a way of passing time—a "pastime"—but the poem is also an evocation or reconstruction of time past. There was plenty of "good company" on the tour: the company of those met on the way, like Basil Bunting and the various inhabitants of the countries who speak in the poem; the company of those absent, in particular Pound in Rapallo; and the company, especially in France and Italy, of figures from the past: Bertran de Born and Girault de Borneil in Provence; Henry Adams, along with a host of painters and sculptors, in Italy; the nameless early Christians in Rome; Shakespeare in Verona (by way of Juliet's Tomb); and the poet Catullus in Verona's environs.[5]

The 1950s were a great decade for American travel in Europe—fares were inexpensive, the dollar was strong, and European countries, still recovering from the world war, welcomed infusions of tourist currency. Poems about European travel became almost a set genre during the 1950s as American poets, armed with Fulbright grants and guidebooks, came over by the score. "4 Other Countries" bore little resemblance to the poems appearing in American books and periodicals, which uneasily pondered the relationship of American culture to the monuments of ancient Europe, the social relationships spawned by the experience of tourism, and the implications of America's emergence as an imperial power, the new Rome.[6] There is little anxiety in "4 Other Countries," rather a continuous wonder at the sounds and sights of the places traversed, a rapidly moving mosaic of colorful bits and pieces of England, France, Italy, and Switzerland. Though the poem begins in England (with the stereotypical teatime) and ends with the three travelers back in the United States, it records only the high points, the "luminous details" that had arrested Zukofsky's attention. He makes no attempt to convey the larger experience of travel—the spaces of transit, the cuisine, the hotels, all the paraphernalia of the conventional travelogue. Europe, in "4 Other Countries," is a constellation of fascinating moments, scenes, and artifacts, rather than a vast alien experience.

The lines of "4 Other Countries"'s quatrains are flexible in length, and the syntax—always grammatical, though often attenuated—leads the reader's eye from quatrain to quatrain, so that images and places scroll forward in a delicate but inexorable procession. A few stanzas describing the buildings of Ravenna are exemplary:

> So the unribbed
>> vault at
> San Vitale
>> hints at the rib
>
> But remains
>> where
> the eye can take in
>> gold, green and blue:
>
> The gold that shines
>> in the dark
> Of Galla Placidia,
>> the gold in the

The center building
is 97 Chrystie Street,
New York City, where
Louis Zukofsky was
born in 1904

Pinchos Zukofsky,
Louis Zukofsky's
father, in a formal
portrait, circa 1900

Zukofsky in May 1929

Louis Zukofsky
at twenty-two, 1926

Mary Wright, Russel Wright, and Zukofsky
(riding the motorcycle) at Coney Island in 1929

William Carlos Williams,
a portrait given to Zukofsky in 1930

Ezra Pound (left) and G. Saviotti, a postcard sent to Zukofsky from Rapallo in 1931

Becky and
Hyman Thaew,
Celia Thaew
Zukofsky's
parents,
circa 1909

Zukofsky's passport,
issued in 1933

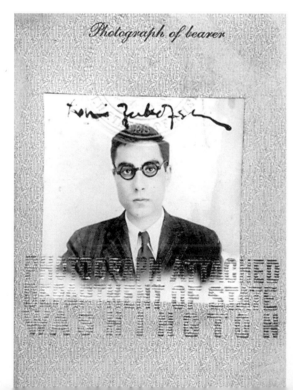

Celia Thaew in 1933

Celia Thaew Zukofsky,
February 1943

Zukofsky, a formal portrait from November 1941

Celia and Louis Zukofsky in
Old Lyme, August 1949

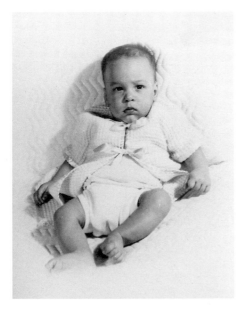

Paul Zukofsky,
February 26, 1944

William Carlos Williams,
Louis and Celia Zukofsky,
and Floss Williams in the
Williamses' Rutherford
garden, August 1959

A page of the draft
notes to *80 Flowers*

Round vault rug of stone
    that shows its
pattern as well as the stars
    my love might want on her floor [7]

The poem ends with an evocation of Colorado's "Red Rocks" amphi-
theater, whose "natural acoustics" are conditioned by the flanking
"Sandstone shapes / they call / *Creation* / and *Shipwreck*." So too the
poet, with his eyes "near wreck"—nearly crossed—can "create," from
staring at the x-shaped words of a Railroad Crossing sign, the following summary of his trip:

RAIL   CROS (S)
SING   ROAD
of pastime
    and good company.

One might certainly write travel poetry "on the fly," as it were, as
Zukofsky had done with "Stratford-on-Avon," but for the more ambitious and grandly successful "4 Other Countries," Zukofsky needed
practically a year to find a form and a metric suitable for his aims, and
found himself taking the advice of his own poem: "Go home. / There
you may / think of it." [8]

Perhaps the most enthusiastic and touching response to "4 Other
Countries" came from Bill Williams. The two men's friendship
remained strong. Williams had published his *Autobiography* in 1951,
written from unreliable memory and under the stress of ill health,
and though the book largely passed over Williams's friendship with
Zukofsky and presented an inaccurate account of the objectivists,
Zukofsky did not chide his old friend, but complimented him by quoting a passage of "A"-12: "The mind is not free to remember or forget
/ Any thing the opened hand feels." [9] Williams had a stroke in March
1951, and another in August 1952. His illness and its accompanying
depression had been exacerbated by the controversy over his appointment as Poetry Consultant to the Library of Congress in 1952. Red-
baiters in the government and the press had raised so many questions
about Williams's 1930s leftist associations that the appointment had
been held up, pending an FBI investigation, until his term of service

was practically over. Still, the consultantship, however vexed, was an official recognition of Williams's lifetime of writing, like the various prizes and awards he would win through the early 1950s.[10]

In October 1958, as Williams lay recovering from yet another stroke, Floss read "4 Other Countries" to him. "I don't care if I never write another line and hope not to do it after Floss has just read me the 4 Other Countries," he wrote Zukofsky; "I am warmed at this poem to the roots of my being." After all of the years when Williams had conceded to Zukofsky his intelligence, his determination, his stubborn adherence to his own aesthetic, but expressed doubts about his friend's work, it was this poem that finally convinced him of Zukofsky's gift: "the address to the task, your reticenses what you have elided from the text and what, at the same time you have chosen to includ—I hate to say—marks you for the genius you are, in this poem—but that's enough. You have come through this once. I will hold you to this for the rest of my life."[11]

. . .

Williams was not the only one of the first modernist generation who was paying attention to Zukofsky's work. As editor of the *Dial*, Marianne Moore had rejected pieces of Zukofsky's in 1926, but in recent years there had grown up between the Brooklyn neighbors a cordial, if not close, friendship. She had enjoyed *A Test of Poetry* ("I am getting pleasure from your book . . . the miscellaneous is in some instances not a deadness but treasure") and even from a "preliminary glance" at *Anew*, she told him, "I see that our views in many respects indeed coincide."[12] In September 1957, Zukofsky received word from Jonathan Williams that the National Book Award committee was interested in seeing copies of *Some Time*; the mystery of how this had come about was cleared up by a letter from Moore, a member of the committee, who offhandedly noted that she had asked the entire committee to read the book before beginning their deliberations. Despite a few moments of high hopes on Zukofsky's part, nothing came of this: Since it had been published in Germany, *Some Time* was ineligible for the prize.[13]

Even more tempting than the National Book Award, however, was the possibility of seeing the first half of "*A*" in print. Emanuel

Navaretta, a building contractor, had developed a keen interest in Zukofsky's poetry. He had signed on as a "patron" for *Some Time*, and in the spring of 1957 he set about convincing Zukofsky to allow him to publish *"A"* as a book.[14] To Navaretta, Zukofsky was reluctant, pointing out "all the hazards" of his committing himself to such a major project; to Jonathan Williams he was rather more enthusiastic, since Navaretta proposed to work through Jargon.[15] Zukofsky went so far as to specify the cover design he'd like Williams to use—a large aleph, the Hebrew letter corresponding to "A." Williams spent some time hunting for just the right aleph in the Manuscript Division of the Library of Congress: not merely should it look "rather like a saw-horse" (as in the saw-horses of *"A"*-7), but it should also be somehow "Cabbalistic."[16]

Zukofsky was uncomfortable working with a patron, and he was even more uncomfortable when Navaretta solicited Bill Williams to write a preface for the volume.[17] As chance would have it, Williams had already been tinkering with a piece—not so much on *"A"* as on his friend's poetry in general—and he gladly consented to overhaul it for Zukofsky's book. But Zukofsky knew how ill Williams was, and worried that writing a preface for a poem so involved with Marxist thought might well plunge Williams into the same political controversy that had marred his appointment to the Library of Congress.[18] When Williams finally sent along his script, rambling, diffuse, and studded with typos, Zukofsky went through it as carefully as he had the work Williams had sent him almost thirty years before, correcting and sharpening the phraseology, trying to push the piece a bit closer towards what he considered an accurate evaluation of his work.[19] Zukofsky defended the value of the essay to Jonathan Williams: "it's sweet of him to have done anything at all.... The value of the piece is in what it says—and it is an intelligent statement: and besides it's late Bill."[20] For the moment at least, Williams's labor was in vain. Navaretta, who had been so enthusiastic about underwriting *"A"* *1–12* when he first contacted Zukofsky, had gotten cold feet: in September 1958 he confessed that he was not at all sure that he could commit himself to financing the book's publication. Zukofsky had reached the end of his patience. "When I see Jonathan or if he phones me," he wrote Navaretta, "I shall tell him to count me out on 'A' ..."[21]

. . .

While *Some Time* was being published Zukofsky had drawn Lorine Niedecker's attention to Williams's Jargon Society. Zukofsky and Niedecker's friendship had undergone vicissitudes over the years, inevitable in a relationship sustained almost solely by correspondence. As Paul was growing up, Zukofsky had sent Niedecker frequent letters describing his progress. Niedecker felt very much a member of the familial circle, and from 1949 to 1953 wrote a long series of poems revolving around the boy's violin training, his bons mots, and the general air of child-prodigy expectation with which his parents regarded him. She sent these "For Paul" poems to Zukofsky regularly, accepting, modifying, or rejecting the revisions that he, the inveterate editor, suggested. Zukofsky at first encouraged Niedecker's project, but ultimately the Wisconsin poet's desire to be a part of the Zukofsky family came to feel all too presumptuous, and Zukofsky would no longer encourage Niedecker's recycling of his correspondence into poetry. The "For Paul" poems trailed off.[22]

The two poets remained enthusiastic readers of each other's work. Niedecker wrote a brief review of *A Test of Poetry* in 1948, and in 1955, for the *Quarterly Review of Literature*, she wrote a lengthy critical article on his poetry as a whole.[23] In late 1956 she proposed a collection of her own to Jonathan Williams, "For Paul and Other Poems." Niedecker wanted Zukofsky to write a foreword to the book, but Zukofsky balked. As he told Jonathan Williams, "while I've said in the past that she's the Emily [Dickinson] of our time, and still think so," he would not write on her behalf. There was no reason to think that his endorsement would "do her *any* good among the young let alone the old." More importantly, since she had recently published an article on his own work, for Zukofsky to in turn promote her collection "would make it evident log-rolling. Besides I don't want to do blurbs for anybody—feel too old & crabbed—& it just keeps me from finishing that damned *Bottom* book."[24] Niedecker decided that in the absence of a Zukofsky "testimonial" she ought to shelve the idea of immediate publication.[25]

. . .

In the spring of 1957 Zukofsky received an invitation from Ruth Witt-Diamant, the founding director of the Poetry Center at San Francisco State College, to deliver a six-week course at the center that summer. Witt-Diamant, who had taught at San Francisco State since 1930, was a woman of force and insight, and the center was able to bring a string of distinguished poets to San Francisco, among them Muriel Rukeyser, Allen Tate, Stephen Spender, Louise Bogan, Robert Lowell, and Charles Olson.[26] The idea of inviting Zukofsky came from Robert Duncan, who had become Witt-Diamant's assistant in 1956, after returning to the Bay Area on the closing of Black Mountain College.

The Bay Area in the late 1950s was alive with poetic activity, so much so that later writers would speak of a "San Francisco Renaissance." That "renaissance" was closely associated with the rise of the so-called Beat generation of poets and prose writers: a crucial moment for both the Bay Area poetry scene and the Beat movement had been the October 13, 1955, reading at the "6" gallery in San Francisco by Michael McClure, Gary Snyder, Philip Whalen, Philip Lamantia, and Allen Ginsberg, who gave the first public performance of his long poem *Howl*. The Beat controversy only added intensity to a poetic scene that was already vibrant. Kenneth Rexroth, who had served as master of ceremonies at the "6" reading, was a longtime San Francisco resident, a respected elder to the poets there; Kenneth Patchen had also settled in the Bay Area, and was reading his poetry to jazz accompaniment; Lawrence Ferlinghetti's City Lights bookstore provided a place for poets to meet and sell their small press books. At the Poetry Center, a close coterie of poets—Robert Duncan, Robin Blaser, and Jack Spicer—was engaged in an intense exploration of the implications of the modernist revolution, spiked with psychoanalysis, tarot cards, and other varieties of mysticism.

Although Duncan was an enthusiastic partisan of Zukofsky's work, Zukofsky was not Witt-Diamant's first choice for the summer of 1957; but since ill health and depression made it impossible for Theodore Roethke to attend, she put in a last-minute invitation to Zukofsky, who wired his acceptance.[27] He was not anxious to take on extra teaching, but the engagement would give the family an excuse—and money—to do some traveling over the summer. They would travel at a leisurely pace, seeing Denver, Salt Lake City, and Yellowstone National Park along the way to San Francisco; perhaps they might visit Mexico on the way back.[28]

The teaching itself would not be onerous: There were no papers to grade (Zukofsky's perennial complaint about Poly), and as for lectures, Zukofsky planned simply to work his way—"with interpolations"—through his most important five essays. "I do not like lectures," he told Witt-Diamant. "I intend speaking to the students, better speaking with them as I read these."[29] He would arrange to collect the essays, which could be mimeographed for students at the center. The rest of the course would be illustration, "from the Book of the Dead until now"—*A Test of Poetry* would suffice as text. Over the next few weeks, the Zukofskys set to work preparing his "course packet": Louis rereading and marking revisions in the published copies of his essays, Celia typing a clean copy of the whole. The result, ready for duplication when Zukofsky's class started in late June, was the sixty-page pamphlet *5 Statements for Poetry*.

5 Statements for Poetry was a carefully considered selection out of what had become a substantial critical oeuvre.[30] Placed together as a teaching tool, these five texts summed up Zukofsky's sense of what the poem and the act of poetry were. Three of them were over a quarter century old, the pieces he had written on behalf of the objectivists: "Program: 'Objectivists' 1931," "Sincerity and Objectification: *With Special Reference to the Work of Charles Reznikoff*," and "'Recencies' in Poetry." Added were the more recent pieces "Poetry/*For My Son When He Can Read*" (1946) and "A Statement for Poetry" (1950). In his brief foreword, Zukofsky stressed the continuity of all five essays: "These five essays may be viewed as stops in the excursion of a poet who wished to imbue criticism with something of the worth and method of his craft—poetry. In this sense, four of the pieces are restatements of the constant theme first expressed as 'Sincerity and Objectification' in 1930."[31]

Zukofsky's revisions to his essays for *5 Statements for Poetry* were few: He cut out a couple of topical references—Roosevelt disappeared from "Poetry/*For My Son When He Can Read*," as did Lenin and Stalin from "Program: 'Objectivists' 1931" and "'Recencies' in

Poetry"; he updated bibliographical references and deleted lists of books and periodicals that would make little sense in 1958.[32] No doubt the haste with which he had to prepare 5 Statements goes some way towards explaining why Zukofsky chose not to tamper with his old essays; that he decided to leave those statements practically untouched, however, stands as evidence of the *constancy* of Zukofsky's poetics. His technique had gained in grace and deftness over the years, his poetry had grown in density and complexity, but his fundamental convictions regarding the nature and craft of poetry had not changed. Whatever he had written since 1930 about poetry, in the end, was but a "restatement" of "Sincerity and Objectification."

The Zukofskys came to San Francisco in June, where they sublet an eighth-floor apartment on the edge of the city. They visited Duncan and his companion Jess in Stimson Beach,[33] thirty miles outside of town, spent a pleasant evening with Rexroth and his wife, and saw the Patchens, whom they had known at Old Lyme. Uncharacteristically, Zukofsky found himself being courted and lionized, besieged by so many invitations that he had to postpone spending time with the ever-loyal Duncan.[34] The family "had fun" seeing some of poet James Broughton's plays performed one evening, and another evening met Muriel Rukeyser at a cocktail party. Zukofsky gave two public readings: On July 2, he read at the college, and the following week he read at the San Francisco Museum of Art, where "all the factions of the S.F. scene talked to each other," as he told Corman. "So I guess I must be the prince of peace."[35]

Duncan was a regular attendee of Zukofsky's class at San Francisco State, as were Joanne Kyger, Ebbe Borregaard, and George Stanley, poets closely associated with Jack Spicer. Duncan's repeated attempts to get Spicer to meet the Zukofskys were unsuccessful; Spicer commemorated them in an ambiguous poem, "Conspiracy": "A violin which is following me . . . It follows me like someone that hates me." Spicer, who spent much of his short life deeply frustrated by his poetry's lack of public recognition, would later show a deep familiarity with Zukofsky's work. Stanley was so influenced that he would expend considerable effort over the next year trying to rid his poetry of echoes of Zukofsky.[36] Another student, an older woman named

Jehanne Biely-Salinger Carlson, was so taken with Zukofsky that she would propose editing an anthology including "the more neglected old and 'exciting' new": Zukofsky, Bunting, Reznikoff, Niedecker, and others Zukofsky might suggest. Carlson would eventually back out of the project, leaving Zukofsky frustrated over the trouble to which he had gone and the expectations he had raised in his friends.[37] The greatest effect of his visit to San Francisco was the strengthening of his relationship with Duncan. Zukofsky had become an indispensable element of Duncan's personal "map" of twentieth-century verse, and through Duncan, Zukofsky would exert an influence on Bay Area poetry for another twenty years.[38]

The Zukofskys left San Francisco in early August, and were back in Brooklyn by the middle of the month. They'd cancelled the trip to Mexico: The Mexican railways were on strike. After spending a muggy night in New Orleans, they returned to New York, where Zukofsky hoped to get some writing done before the beginning of the semester at Poly.[39] Paul was looking towards his second Carnegie Hall recital, which was scheduled for February 6 of the next year.

. . .

While Zukofsky was rather glum about the protracted delays of *Some Time* and the increasingly evident undependability of Navaretta's *"A"* project, he had assembled enough new short poems over the past two years to make a new collection. As he put it to Celia, "it would make a nice book," which was something of a private code: It would make a nice book, that is, whenever Celia had a chance to type up the manuscript. She asked for "a clean copy first—because if I start dictating I often lag to revise—which drives her crazy." When Zukofsky had produced the "clean copy"—sixty-five pages in his best, still crabbed but legible handwriting—Celia took the manuscript to a printer and arranged for three hundred facsimile copies to be printed and bound.[40] This lovely little book—numbered and signed—sold for five dollars a copy.[41]

The book's title, at Celia's suggestion, was *Barely and widely*, phrases taken from reviews of Paul's playing and Zukofsky's poetry, as Zukofsky specifies in the title poem:

> *Barely*
>   **and**
>   *widely*
>
> love
>
> they say—
>   in these words—
>
> of Paul
>   "barely
>   twelve"
>
> and of me
>   "widely
>   published
>
> throughout
>   a long
>   career"[42]

Its cover design featured a tangle of Zukofsky's handwriting, "part of the original draft of the poem '4 Other Countries.'"[43] *Barely and widely* was largely an occasional collection. Its twelve poems included "Stratford-on-Avon," two valentines for 1957 and 1958 ("A Valentine" and "This year / that valentine is late"[44]), "Head lines" from their San Francisco trip, and a pair of poems describing—of all things—ashtrays. These two show Zukofsky at his most minimalist, condensing minute examination into a series of spare quatrains where sounds resonate among themselves like a set of subtle wind chimes:

Ashtray

The baited
bear
on
the ashtray

shows more
flare
than the
tramp

in his whip
tho
perhaps
enough's

there
to
give them
heart.[45]

More expansive—almost orchestral, in comparison with "Ashtray"—
are such poems as "You who were made for this music" and "The
Heights," which presents the view from the family's Brooklyn Heights
apartment as an exercise in monochrome cinematography.[46] The
centerpiece of *Barely and widely* was "4 Other Countries," which demonstrated not merely that was Zukofsky a master of close observation
and small structures of verse, but that he could string those observations into a long and masterful whole—an *epyllion* ("little epic") in
mosaic, as it were: "mosaic // Tesserae / animal and / abstract, each
/ is animate."[47]

Barely and widely was the Zukofskys' most radical end run around
the complications of the poetry industry: In one gesture, Celia had
taken upon herself the roles of publisher, book designer, and patron.
She acted as well as the book's promoter, sending out almost two
hundred typed postcards announcing the publication—and receiving back far fewer orders than she had hoped. Two months after
Barely and widely's publication, they had sold only twenty-six copies.[48]
Zukofsky was particularly disgusted that after giving a reading at Poly
he failed to sell a single copy of the book.[49] The Zukofskys had tried
to take the process of publishing Zukofsky's poetry out of the unreliable hands of those in the publishing "business," and found that they
themselves were no better at that business than the publishers they
had so come to distrust.

After serving in the army in the Second World War, George Oppen had moved with his wife and daughter to Redondo Beach, California. In the highly anti-communist atmosphere of the postwar moment, the Oppens found themselves the targets of increasing FBI attention because of their work for the Party before the war. In 1950 they went into exile, moving to Mexico City.[50] In 1958, after a quarter-century hiatus, Oppen began writing poems again.[51] The Oppens came north in November to visit their daughter Linda, attending Sarah Lawrence College. George had been in touch with Zukofsky in August, when he responded to a letter of Zukofsky's. (Oppen's half sister, June Oppen Degnan, who had seen the Zukofskys in San Francisco, had given Zukofsky her brother's address.) "I found pieces of Rezi's poems and yours," Oppen told Zukofsky, "going through my head during the whole war."[52] There was nostalgia in Oppen's letter, along with a recognition that his and Zukofsky's was no longer a friendship of young men at the start of their careers, but of two men nearing old age, their moment of shared endeavor far behind them.

The Oppens returned to New York in May 1959, and this time they invited the Zukofskys to ride back with them to Mexico City. Louis and Celia had no vacation planned for the summer, and it would give the family the chance to see Mexico that they had missed the summer before. They would fly back "family rate," and the whole trip would be brief, "just a short jaunt."[53] The drive itself, with five people in a single car, was long and tiring—"I have (not making vows)," Zukofsky wrote, "no intention of riding in anyone else's car again."[54] The monotony was broken when Oppen (behind the wheel) hit a stray heifer, who in fright smeared the car with dung. Zukofsky commemorated the incident in the second section of "Jaunt," a series of brief poems about the journey:

The cow scraped by
the hood of the car
leaped its frightened
dung its avatar
that gentle
(not the hood)

the ungentle
driver
escaped.

What struck Zukofsky about the Mexico trip, and what made its way
into "Jaunt," were the sights around Verona, Ohio, which put him in
mind of *Romeo and Juliet* and *Two Gentlemen of Verona*; the cavalier attitude of the Mexicans towards their own antiquities ("Rune // ruinin'
/ runs // Mexico"); and the stunning view from the airplane—it was
Zukofsky's first flight—on the way back to New York:

Physical
geography
a sea of cotton or
a fluff of icebergs or
waterfalls, trees, gigantic
mushroomed ivories
Chinese of whatever animal . . .[55]

While the family had seen the pre-Aztec pyramids at Teotihuacán,
the convent of San Augustín, and the eighteenth-century town of San
Miguel Allende, Zukofsky found Mexico City "overrated—a mush-
room culture imitative of U.S."—and Mexico as a whole "the least
interesting of foreign countries we've been in, except Canada."[56]

The Oppens would end their Mexican exile next year and move to
New York, and for a while Oppen and Zukofsky would maintain their
friendship. But for George and Mary, the Mexico trip—two weeks
in close quarters with the intensely directed and almost hermetically
sealed Zukofsky family unit—had shown them that their relationship
with Zukofsky would never be as close as it had been almost thirty
years before.[57]

. . .

After their 1957 meeting in Florence, Zukofsky and Cid Corman had
become frequent correspondents. They answered each other letter
for letter, and Zukofsky kept Corman closely apprised of the progress of his own work. In early 1958 Corman moved to Japan, where
through contacts with Gary Snyder and others he had secured a teaching post at a women's college. Though he as yet had no idea of reviving

Origin as a magazine, he was publishing books of poetry—mostly his own, but also collections by Snyder, William Bronk, and Gael Turnbull—under the Origin Press imprint. Corman was deeply devoted to Zukofsky's work, and when Zukofsky told him at the end of 1958 that Navaretta's scheme for publishing *"A"* had fallen through, he immediately offered the services of Origin Press.[58]

Money remained the perennial obstacle, but the Zukofskys managed to come up with funding for an edition of two hundred clothbound copies of *"A"* 1–12.[59] This time around, in sharp contrast to their experience with *Some Time*, there were no delays: Zukofsky mailed the typescript in late July, and by October Corman was reading proof.[60] By Christmas 1959 Zukofsky had a copy of *"A"* 1–12 in hand.[61] *"A"* 1–12 was a handsome book, just short of three hundred pages, bound in red cloth with a facsimile of Zukofsky's signature stamped on the front boards. There were a number of typographical errors, of course—like *Ulysses*, the book had been printed by craftsmen whose first language was not English, and Corman, its only proofreader, had the unenviable task of spotting errors in a very long, complex poem not his own.[62] One typographical matter Zukofsky had settled definitively in November: The poem's title was *"A"*, *with* quotation marks—it was a quotation, after all, of the poem's first line, and (more playfully) "if A's traced back to the aleph, the ox head, the quotes are the horns."[63] The volume concluded with a reprint of Zukofsky's "Poetry / *For My Son When He Can Read*" and the note William Carlos Williams had written for the book back in 1957.

Looking over his twenty-five years' labor, finally bound in a single volume, led Zukofsky to reflect on his own place in twentieth-century poetry: "Having just 'finished' Whitman with my classes," he wrote Corman, "this historical judgment follows reading 'A' 1–12 as book: Ez underrated Whitman; I feel—I have never felt that before—that I follow out of Walt more than I realized; especially in the sense that I am more of my time, as he was of his, than are my immediate elders born ca 1875–1894."[64]

. . .

Zukofsky had something of a banner year in 1960; not merely was there the arrival, at the beginning of February, of the remaining

149 author's copies of *"A" 1–12*, but on May 8—Mother's Day, as it happened—Zukofsky finally finished *Bottom: on Shakespeare*. He had labored on the book for almost thirteen years, and had accumulated a fair copy of over a thousand manuscript pages. He had as yet no idea who might want to publish this elephantine work, but he knew he wanted it published. It had become clear to him that there was emerging a young and interested audience for that work: aside from Corman, Creeley, Duncan, Turnbull, Snyder, Jonathan Williams, and the students at San Francisco State, Zukofsky was receiving letters of interest and praise—and often manuscripts—from a host of younger poets, among them Larry Eigner, Theodore Enslin, and Frank Samperi. With *Bottom* finished, there were other projects to be tackled. He and Celia had begun translating their way through Catullus in 1958, at first in odd moments, later more intensively. Above all else, the time seemed right to begin the second half of *"A"*.

Shakespeare:
The Evidence of the Eyes

The works of William Shakespeare, which Zukofsky had first seen performed in Yiddish at the Thalia, were an integral part of his entry into the English language, and those works always remained at the center of Zukofsky's imagination. But for many modernist poets, Shakespeare's works were not an inspiration but an insuperable *block*, a monolith of universally admired "genius" that had to be surmounted or bypassed; and for *American* modernists, their sense of belatedness in the face of Shakespeare's achievement was exacerbated by his Englishness, the fact that the single greatest poet in their language was a foreigner. Some of them reacted almost savagely. In "The Descent of Winter," William Carlos Williams asserted that "the only human value" of writing "is intense vision of the facts"; in contrast, Shakespeare "By writing . . . escaped from the world into the natural world of his mind. . . . Such a man," Williams concluded, "is a prime borrower and standardizer—No inventor. He . . . does not go forward, sinks back into the mass."[1]

299

The more internationally inclined American modernists constructed their own traditions, artistic genealogies in which Shakespeare became something less than central. T. S. Eliot always acknowledged Shakespeare's preeminence in the drama, but he looked towards Dante and the seventeenth-century metaphysical poets for models of a new verse. Pound, more radically, declared himself the heir of a pan-European tradition that centered on the troubadours, Dante and Cavalcanti, a few nineteenth-century French poets, and Robert Browning. Shakespeare was entirely omitted from *ABC of Reading*; Pound justified himself in *Guide to Kulchur* by noting that "the bard is both read and ably discussed by others almost sufficiently."[2]

Perhaps because as a first-generation American Zukofsky was in some sense coming to the received tradition of Anglo-American letters from the *outside*, he never tried to set aside, discount, or otherwise circumvent Shakespeare. Not that he took Shakespeare's plays or the characteristic metaphorical richness of Shakespeare's blank verse as a model for his own poetry: Like other modernists, he was to find more immediate stimulus to his own practice in the *songs* scattered throughout the plays than in their dialogue or soliloquies. But he never ignored Shakespeare or sought to dethrone him. *Bottom: on Shakespeare* was the fruit of more than fifty years' engagement with Shakespeare's works, and this enormous book, which combines literary criticism, intellectual history, philosophy, and practical prosody, is one of the central works of Zukofsky's oeuvre.

. . .

In 1961 Zukofsky drafted a brief statement, "Bottom, A Weaver," that laid out his retrospective sense of the book:

> To me *Bottom: on Shakespeare* is:
> 1. A long poem built on a theme for the variety of its recurrences. The theme is simply that Shakespeare's text throughout favors the clear physical eye against the erring brain, and that this theme has historical implications.
> 2. A valid skepticism that as 'philosophy of history' (taking in the arts and sciences) my book takes exception to all philosophies from Shakespeare's point of view ('Shakespeare's,' as expressed above and as excused by my preface to the book.)

3. A continuation of my work on prosody in my other writings. In this sense my wife's music saves me a lot of words.
4. A poet's autobiography, as involvement of twenty years in a work shows him up, or as in the case of Shakespeare his words show it, are his life.[3]

One could do worse than to approach *Bottom* on the basis of those four items.[4]

I: "A long poem built on a theme for the variety of its recurrences"

Bottom: on Shakespeare is a book with a thesis, the claim that "Shakespeare's text throughout favors the clear physical eye against the erring brain." This claim had appeared in "A"-12, and it continues the emphasis on the physical senses in the objectivist essays of the early 1930s. It can be stated as a "definition of love as the tragic hero."

> He is Amor, identified with the passion of the lover falling short of perfection—discernment, fitness, proportion at those times when his imagination insufficient to itself is an aberration of the eyes; but when reason and love are an identity of sight its clear and distinct knowledge can approach the sufficient realizations of the intellect.

More compactly, the theme can be reduced to a "proportion": *"love : reason : : eyes : mind* [.] Love needs no tongue of reason if love and the eyes are *I*—an identity. The good reasons of the mind's right judgment are but superfluities for saying: *Love sees*—if it needs saying at all in a text which is always hovering towards *The rest is silence*."[5] Much of *Bottom* demonstrates how this proportion is played out through the entire canon of Shakespeare's works: with a happy outcome in the comedies (and "romances"), an unhappy in the tragedies.

Zukofsky saw little value in an arbitrary distinction between "prose" and "poetry." "Sometimes you do a thing in verse, and sometimes you do it in prose," he said in 1969. "To me they're both poetry."[6] What made *Bottom: on Shakespeare* a "long poem" was not the musicality of its sentences or any more vaguely defined "poeticisms," but the fact that he had built the book "on a theme for the variety of its recurrences."

When he said that *Bottom*'s governing theme "has historical implications," Zukofsky referred to the theory of the evolution of human thought and expression that had been gestating in his mind since he had read Henry Adams back in college. In its earliest stage, human thought and expression worked in terms of "solids," of the tangible and trustworthy images and data supplied by the physical senses; as human culture grew more complex, it moved away from these images to a more "liquid" state of music and song; and finally, by a further step of abstraction, humanity entered a "gas age" of discourse, where thought and language existed in a "gaseous" state, neither making use of the direct evidence of the senses nor exploring their own inherent music, but simply rearranging the empty counters of metaphysics and abstract philosophy. Shakespeare stood on the cusp between the two latter ages: while his work is saturated throughout with "liquid" musicality, he nostalgically harks back to a "solid" age of reliance upon the physical senses, and regrets his own place in an emergent "gas" age.[7]

2: "A valid skepticism"

Zukofsky took epistemology, the theory of knowledge—and its evil sibling, skepticism—as the epitome of what was wrong with philosophy. Like Pound and Pound's friend T. E. Hulme, and like Adams and Shakespeare (in his own reading of them), Zukofsky had little patience with abstraction; the most pernicious abstraction of all was the theory of knowledge, the philosophers' stubborn and ultimately irrational doubting of the evidence of their own senses. Or perhaps it would be better to say their all too *rational* doubting of their senses, for epistemological questioning is the clearest possible instance of the physical eye's betrayal by the reasoning intellect. The poet's task, Zukofsky explained back in 1930, was "thinking with the things as they exist," and it could be "assumed that epistemological problems do not affect existence"; in 1968, he would repeat precisely those values: "Any artist lives with the things as they exist. I won't go into the theory of knowledge. I don't care how you think about things, whether you think they are there outside of you, even if you disappear, or if they exist only because you think of them. In either case you live with things as they exist."[8]

Bottom: on Shakespeare incorporated much philosophy: There were

large stretches of Plato, Aristotle, Aquinas, Spinoza, and Wittgenstein, along with shorter or longer references to a number of other philosophers. But Zukofsky's project manifested a "valid skepticism" towards all these thinkers (as opposed to the "invalid" skepticism that would deny the clear knowledge offered us by the physical senses), and judged them—"took exception" to them—by the yardstick of the "*love : reason : : eyes : mind*" proportion. Zukofsky would later claim that he had "done away with epistemology" in *Bottom*. He summed up the book even more bluntly in 1969: "I wrote 500 pages about Shakespeare just to say one thing, the natural human eye is OK, but it's that erring brain that's no good, and he says it all the time."[9]

3: "A continuation of my work on prosody"

All of Zukofsky's writings had been in some sense "work on prosody," insofar as his poems had ceaselessly sought to explore how words could be knit together into poetic structures. While Zukofsky had little patience with the codifications of prosodists, he had nothing but respect for the achievements of past poets who wrote in "conventional" forms. The danger, as he saw it, was to take a given form as an end in itself, to forget that it had arisen under the pressure of a poet's need to express a certain experience or fulfill a certain "tune." *Bottom: on Shakespeare* presents itself as a "work on prosody" most clearly in Zukofsky's attempt to rescue Shakespeare from critics and prosodists who would have him adhere to a rigid, regular blank verse throughout his plays. If a few lines show metrical irregularities, then Shakespeare is praised for his flexibility; if many lines are irregular, then the text is deemed corrupt or the work of another hand. For Zukofsky, the "prosodical and musical rule" of Shakespeare's verse is best expressed in Hamlet's sentence: "the lady shall say her mind freely, or the blank verse shall halt for't."[10] Zukofsky had said something similar in his own poem "Peri Poietikes" (literally "On Poetics," the title of Aristotle's treatise), when he parodied the last line of Sir Philip Sidney's first *Astrophil and Stella* sonnet, "'Foole,' said my Muse to me, 'looke in thy heart and write'": in Zukofsky's version, "What about measure, I learnt: / *Look in your own ear and read.*"[11]

Shakespeare's prosody, *Bottom* argues, "is but the consent of rule of thumb—however more accomplished it is than most accomplished prosody—to the germ of the writing, the recurrent insistence of the theme that defines and unfolds it": the theme of love and the eyes. The prize exhibit here is *Pericles, Prince of Tyre*—Zukofsky's favorite of the plays—which had been problematic for Shakespeare's critics ever since Ben Jonson: It was either a deeply flawed piece of work, an inexcusably corrupt text, or the product of Shakespeare's collaboration with an inferior poet.[12] While critics might deny Shakespeare's authorship of parts of *Pericles* because they do not recognize his prosodic "fingerprint" on those passages, it is in precisely those passages that Zukofsky recognizes "Shakespeare," Shakespeare as a body of texts that expand upon a single proposition: "The play of *Pericles* moves me most by its devotion to the tragic insight of the poet's measure as it invokes the *definition of love* which is thematic to the entire canon." And *Pericles* is entwined with music, literal and thematic, to a degree rare even among Shakespeare's plays. "In *Pericles* especially," Zukofsky wrote, "the rarefying as against the lovable constant eye of the definition of love of all the plays acts thru the art of song . . ."[13]

Aside from the play's investment in song, Zukofsky believed that his "wife's music"—her setting of *Pericles, Prince of Tyre*—had saved him "a lot of words," had done much of the prosodic analysis that he might have attempted in prose. Celia Zukofsky had begun composing music for *Pericles* as early as 1943, several years before her husband began writing *Bottom*, and completed the piano version of her setting in 1949.[14] That setting had languished in the desk drawer aside from occasional "performances" Celia and Louis would give friends such as William Carlos Williams and Mark Van Doren. In her own preface, Celia Zukofsky dissociated what she had written from conventional "opera," and stressed that her setting was meant solely to bring out the music inherent in the play's text: "Shakespeare's words for me do not need 'opera' in the traditional sense—arias, duets, choruses, ballets, etc. The music I have set down . . . is a form of heightened speech, faintly trying to keep pace with Shakespeare's words, which in their rhythmic, tonal order are music in themselves."[15]

If poetry was, in the words from Dante's *De Vulgari Eloquentia* that Zukofsky was fond of quoting, "nothing else but the completed action of writing words to be set to music,"[16] then there could be no more thorough prosodic examination of Shakespeare than a musical setting that sought to follow the music already inherent in Shakespeare's lines. Zukofsky, therefore, at the beginning of *Bottom*'s long, theoretically dense Part Two, would call his wife's setting of *Pericles* "the one excuse for all that follows" after the section's first four pages.[17]

4: "A poet's autobiography"

Zukofsky wore his rather thorough knowledge of Shakespearean commentary lightly. What interested him *least* was the tradition of reading Shakespeare biographically: "Guessing at the chronology of the forty-four items of the canon," Zukofsky wrote, "the critics have been insistent on seeing his ideas grow, his feelings mature, his heart go through more exploits than a heart can, except as may be vaguely intimated from the beat and duration of any of the lines or works." To read the *Works*, that is, as Shakespeare's emotional autobiography. It would be simpler and more fruitful "to consider the forty-four items of the canon as one work, sometimes poor, sometimes good, sometimes great, always regardless of the time in which it was composed, and so, despite defects of quality, durable as one thing from 'itself never turning.'"[18]

But even as he seeks to read a "Shakespeare" defined as a set of writings, rather than as a historical individual, Zukofsky knows that "any poet" inevitably writes her- or himself into the work: The poet "knows, unfortunately, that his writing with fleshly pencils will be loosely considered the issue of himself."[19] In the 1960s and 1970s Zukofsky would freely admit that his works, whether in verse or prose, stood as records of a particular poet's life—an autobiography despite himself. "In a sense the poem is an autobiography," Zukofsky wrote in a statement on the jacket of the 1967 reprint of *"A" 1–12*: "the words are my life." In the foreword to that volume, he would call *"A"* "a poem of a life—and a time."[20]

. . .

The structure of *Bottom: on Shakespeare* makes no concessions to what readers might expect from a work on Shakespeare. The book begins with a twenty-page prefatory piece, Part One, explaining that

"Shakespeare" will be treated as a set of texts and themes, rather than a living individual. Part Two is subtitled "*Music's master*: notes for Her music to *Pericles* and for a graph of culture." It is a theoretical statement, commenting upon Celia's *Pericles* setting and laying the conceptual groundwork for the rest of the book. "*Music's master*" is almost sixty pages long, an exposition of the "love/eyes" theme that ranges from straightforward prose to maddeningly condensed, almost entirely opaque exposition. Citations from Shakespeare, especially *Pericles*, provide the basis for the argumentation, but there are also ventures into Aristotle's *Posterior Analytics*, *Metaphysics*, and *De Anima*, a brief discussion of Boole's *Laws of Thought*, and a more expansive tour through Wittgenstein's *Tractatus Logico-Philosophicus*. Zukofsky does not present these difficult texts in anything like a reader-friendly manner. On the contrary, his usual practice is to quote a passage of the author at hand—often quite abstruse—and then comment upon it in a highly oblique manner, tying it to Shakespeare and the other texts around it through fragmented quotations and offhanded puns. Zukofsky's prose makes no concessions to simplicity or clarity of exposition; it recalls Zukofsky's comment on the prose of Thorstein Veblen: "Veblen was the kind of man who'd give you a bag of bees and walk off."[21] "*Music's master*" juxtaposes texts much as "*A*" does: It is a conversation where Shakespeare, Zukofsky, Spinoza, Aristotle, Wittgenstein, and the rest speak together as equals.

This principle of juxtaposing voices from various places and eras takes on even broader scope in *Bottom*'s Part Three, "An Alphabet of Subjects," which occupies over three-quarters of the book—346 pages. This "Alphabet," which incorporates the "graph of culture" referred to in "*Music's master*," consists of twenty-six chapters, one for each letter of the alphabet. The "Alphabet"'s centerpieces, which take up over two-thirds of Part Three, are "Continents" and "Definition." In "Definition," Zukofsky himself (the "I") engages in a dialogue with his son (the "Son"), justifying, expanding upon, and providing illustration from each one of Shakespeare's works for his "*love : reason : : eyes : mind*" proportion. It is a bravura seventy-six pages, and possibly the most readable section of *Bottom* as a whole. In the vast (160 pages) chapter "Continents," Zukofsky arranges a compendium of chronologically ordered quotations from ancient and medieval Jewish, Near Eastern, and scholastic writings, and English, French, and American literature, all casting light upon the "definition" of love and the eyes he had derived from Shakespeare. "Greeks" and "Latine" are similar in structure to "Continents," tracing parallels to Shakespeare's imagery and thought in classical Greek and Latin authors.

The remaining chapters, while all addressing Shakespeare to one degree or another, vary widely in scope and purpose. "Forgotten," which opens with a typically self-pitying quotation from Edward Dahlberg—"I am the forgotten man"—is a consideration of Shakespeare's late collaboration *The Two Noble Kinsmen*. "Ember Eves" hovers around various images of candles and burning, moving from the Zohar, to René Descartes' *Meditations*, to Michael Faraday's "The Chemical History of a Candle," all as illustration of human culture's movement into a world of (in Henry Adams's words) "physics stark mad in metaphysics." "Julia's Wild" spins a lovely twenty-one-line poem from a single line of *Two Gentlemen of Verona*, "Come, shadow, come, and take this shadow up," rearranging and repunctuating the words through twenty variations. "Qu'ai-je?" is a joke, quoting *Merry Wives of Windsor*: "Od's me! Qu'ai-j'oublie?" (what have I forgotten). "She who typed this," writes Zukofsky, mindful of Celia's monumental labors, "assured me: *Nothing!*"[22]

The book closes with "Z (*signature*)," which nods towards Zukofsky's long poem—"'A'—pronounced how? With a care for the letters and out of them their sound"—and ends with an invitation to his wife's music for *Pericles*:

> For there is the happiness—
> > of *i*'s that delay notes in Haydn's setting for *smiling at grief*, which makes the singer's lips smile—
>
> > of the 'blessed' apart from 'shape' we 'know' in the Adagio of Handel's Violin Sonata, opus 1, number 3—
>
> > of an exercise by Bach for Anna Magdalena—
> as the music of Part 4 of this work takes over with no excuse for using a modern text of *Pericles*—the love:
> > τουτο δὲ πρὸς ἕνα.[23]

The Greek phrase means "and (all) this towards one"—the "one," presumably, being Zukofsky himself, acknowledging his wife's love as manifested in her own work on Shakespeare.

While "Z (*signature*)" is the last chapter of the book, the last-written section was—appropriately—the "P" chapter, "Pericles." Zukofsky datelines "Pericles" with dates that bracket the whole of *Bottom*'s composition, "(thought, 1947–1960)," and ends the chapter with a line of King Simonides's, addressed to his daughter Thaisa; she is curious as to why the most poorly dressed of her suitors (Pericles in disguise) has taken as his motto "In hac spe vivo" (in this hope I live). "He hopes by you," the King replies, "his fortunes yet may flourish."[24] It is a typically Zukofskyan way to end and knit together his work, for at once he acknowledges how his own labors had flowered in the atmosphere of Celia's love and refers once again to his beloved Spinoza: "The more an image is associated with many other things, the more often it flourishes."

. . .

A fortuitous set of circumstances enabled Zukofsky to get *Bottom: on Shakespeare* into print with far less delay than the eight years that had elapsed between the completion of "A"-12 and the publication of "A" *1–12*. Around 1959 Charles Norman, who in 1948 had solicited Zukofsky's "Work/Sundown" for his collection *The Case of Ezra Pound*, approached Zukofsky about a biography of Pound he was writing. Zukofsky allowed him to read Pound's letters to him, and recalled in some detail his own 1933 trip to Rapallo to meet Pound.[25] In July 1960 Norman asked Zukofsky to "look over" the completed biography; he asked what Zukofsky planned to do with *Bottom*—Zukofsky had no clear idea—and then made arrangements for the manuscript to be considered by Macmillan, his own publishers.[26] Macmillan, a large commercial house, was not interested.

In a letter to Williams, Zukofsky compared *Bottom: on Shakespeare* to Samuel Taylor Coleridge's *Biographia Literaria*;[27] the comparison suggests that Zukofsky had for some time been taking the long view of his own career and achievements. Zukofsky had preserved the correspondence of the poets who had meant the most to him—Pound, Williams, Bunting, Niedecker—and since 1953 he had been considering another sort of "autobiography," this one a compilation of letters received. It would be a chronicle of his writing life as reflected in what others had written to him, and would thereby preserve his customary taciturnity while showing how deeply he had been a part of his time.[28] Zukofsky had shelved the letters when he grew too deeply immersed in *Bottom*, but he returned to them in 1959, and sent the preface for this collection to Williams in October 1960:

> Hamlet's *Let be* might speak for omissions from the originals of these letters, and also for what is here in the order it was received over nearly forty years. *A man's life's no more than to say "One"* while the various perception—of a time perhaps—remains.[29]

Part of his reason for contacting Williams—at this point Bill was too ill for casual correspondence—was to secure reprint permissions: Zukofsky had reason to believe that the University of Texas would be publishing the letters as a book.

In 1960 Zukofsky was approached by Lew David Feldman, a dealer in rare books and manuscripts. Feldman, who affected a flamboyant appearance—large floppy hats, a silver-handled cane, fine fur coats—was the head of the House of El Dieff (L-D F) and the most important buying representative of the Humanities Research Center (HRC) at the University of Texas.[30] Harry Huntt Ransom, the University's provost, had founded the HRC in 1958 with the ambition of establishing "a center of cultural compass, a research center to be the Bibliothèque Nationale of the only state that had started out as an independent nation."[31] His dream was enabled by the extraordinary funds he was able to coax from the oil-rich coffers of the Texas legislature: Texas in essence wrote Feldman a blank check to acquire rare books and manuscripts, and through the 1960s he spent unheard-of sums to make the HRC's one of the world's greatest collections of twentieth-century literary materials.

Feldman had read Norman's life of Pound, and realized that Zukofsky, featured prominently in the biography, almost certainly had letters from Pound that the HRC would want to acquire.[32] The HRC, Feldman told Zukofsky, wanted his letters from Pound and Williams; they were also willing to acquire the manuscripts of Zukofsky's own writings. The HRC had no way of knowing whether Zukofsky's manuscripts would eventually prove valuable, but the Pound and Williams material, with scattered items from Cummings, Moore, T. S. Eliot, and others, was clearly worth a good deal of money.[33] Zukofsky was not interested in cash; he wanted his collection of letters received published. In late 1960, through Feldman's offices, Zukofsky reached an agreement with the HRC: He would give them the letters, along with about three thousand pages of his own manuscripts; in return, they would pay him a thousand dollars, would establish a special collection to house the materials—the "Louis Zukofsky Manuscript Collection"—and would publish his selection of his friends' correspondence.[34]

The problem with publishing others' letters, of course, was obtaining their permission. Most of Zukofsky's correspondents were amenable, but Pound and Bunting were another matter. Pound, officially "incapable" of standing trial, had been released from St. Elizabeths in May 1958. He returned to Italy soon after, where he lived in turn with his wife, Dorothy, in Rapallo and his daughter, Mary, and her family in the Tyrol. His health was failing, and by the time Zukofsky contacted him about the letter collection he was beginning to recede into silence and depression. Bunting had firm principles about correspondence: He habitually destroyed letters received, and had no desire to see his own in print. With permissions not available from two of his central correspondents, Zukofsky reluctantly abandoned the letters project.[35]

Towards the end of 1960, Zukofsky arrived at a solution: Instead of the correspondence received, the HRC would print *Bottom: on Shakespeare*—in two volumes, with Celia's setting of *Pericles* constituting the second. For most of the time he was working on *Bottom*, Zukofsky had not considered his wife's music an integral part of the work, or even a companion volume, but by early 1960 he had decided the two works ought to be printed together, "even if it's only 50 copies at $25 the copy," he told Corman.[36] Zukofsky, Feldman, and the HRC arrived at a complex arrangement. Upon receipt of the letters and manuscripts from the House of El Dieff, the HRC would pay Feldman ten thousand dollars. One thousand dollars of that would go to Zukofsky; another thousand would be retained by Feldman (Zukofsky was not apprised of this latter stipulation). Feldman in turn would "donate" eight thousand dollars to the HRC to underwrite the publication of 1,040 copies of *Bottom*. The Zukofskys would receive one hundred copies of the book, as would Feldman, and in addition Louis and Celia would be paid a 25 percent royalty on copies sold.[37] There was no consideration of reprints; F. W. Roberts, the director of the HRC, believed that 1,040 copies would be more than enough to keep the book in print for the rest of his, Feldman's, and the Zukofskys' lives.[38] The oddest provision of Zukofsky's contract, however, was that Feldman wanted the book to be dedicated to him. Zukofsky was happy enough to comply, though the language settled upon for the dedication—"*To* / LEW DAVID FELDMAN / *who made it possible*"— evidenced no emotional attachment on Zukofsky's part.[39]

When it became clear that Texas would publish a two-volume *Bottom: on Shakespeare*, Celia Zukofsky revisited her piano score of *Pericles*, orchestrating it for a spare ensemble of strings, woodwinds, and brass—no more than three instruments playing at any one time, and the "Gower songs" accompanied only by lute. She completed her orchestration by June 24, 1961, a month after Zukofsky had sent the final typescript of *Bottom* off to Austin.[40]

The HRC hired Kim Taylor, an English book designer living in Austin, to design the book and publish it under his own Ark imprint—though the volume would be printed in Texas and distributed by the University of Texas Press. Taylor was a sensitive and inspired designer, but this was a huge project. The original publication date—April 1962—was repeatedly pushed back, and at the eleventh hour, as finished books were being received from the printer in August 1963, Taylor discovered that the second volume was missing a section of Celia Zukofsky's autograph score.[41] A new signature had to be tipped into the existing bindings, necessitating a further delay. Review copies had already gone out, and the book's official publication date remained 1963, but Zukofsky was wearily willing to put off actual publication for "what now seems to me the most auspicious moment—Shakespeare's baptismal date (nearest we know to his birthday) April 26"—April 26, 1964, the four-hundredth anniversary of the playwright's baptism.[42]

. . .

By the time *Bottom: on Shakespeare* was finally released—in two handsome volumes, boxed—Zukofsky was looking forward to the publication of his collected short poems by a major trade publisher. He was about to move into something like the public eye, and to achieve a measure of very long delayed fame. One might view the HRC arrangement as a devil's bargain: Had Zukofsky held on to his papers for a few more years, he might have gotten far more for them. But Zukofsky was satisfied with what he had obtained, and saw his relationship with the HRC as part of a campaign directed towards literary history in the long term. *Bottom* was now in print, which was no small thing; more importantly, Zukofsky had established an archive to hold his work and the record of that work. Over the rest of the Zukofskys' lives, they would sell at least six more batches of papers to the HRC. The money was welcome, but more comforting no doubt was the sense that by his presence in the archive, Zukofsky would be taking his place with the other authors so collected—among them Williams, Pound, and Joyce.

The Darker
World 1961–1963

chapter sixteen

IN THE FIRST MONTHS of his marriage, Zukofsky translated a little
poem by the Latin poet Catullus:

Miserable Catullus, stop being foolish
And admit it's over,
The sun shone on you those days
When your girl had you
When you gave it to her
       like nobody else ever will.
     . . .
So long, girl. Catullus
             can take it
He won't bother you, he won't
             be bothered:
But you'll be, nights.
What do you want to live for?

Whom will you see?
Who'll say you're pretty?
Who'll give it to you now?
Whose name will you have?
Kiss what guy? bite whose
               lips?
Come on Catullus, you can
             take it.[1]

"Catullus viii" recasts Catullus in a punchy New York vernacular, but it retains a traditional notion of the translator's task—to bring the verse of another time into the idiom of today.

In early 1958, Zukofsky returned to Catullus, this time beginning with the poem in which Catullus dedicates his finished and bound collection of poetry to his friend Cornelius: "Whom do I give my neat little volume / slicked dry and made fashionable with pumice? / Cornelius, to you . . ."[2] Over the next eight years, Zukofsky would translate his way through Catullus's complete works: 108 short lyrics, eight longer poems (including an *epyllion*, a short epic), and a handful of fragments.[3] This translation was a collaborative effort: Each of its periodical installments, and the book in which the poems were collected, were published under the names "Louis and Celia Zukofsky." Zukofsky's Latin was sketchy at best.[4] For knowledge of the meaning, the pronunciation, and the rhythms of the Catullan text, he relied on Celia. The couple quickly evolved a working method for their joint translation. On the left leaf of each two-page spread of their working notebooks, Celia would copy out the Latin text in red ink, mark each line's scansion, and insert, on alternate lines, an English "pony" that followed the word order of the original and indicated its more thorny grammatical turns. Louis would scribble notes, parallels, and rough drafts into all available spaces, and then, on the facing page, would draft his finished English version.[5] "I did the spade work," Celia later explained, "Louis then used my material to write poetry—*good poetry*."[6]

The results were radically different from "Catullus viii." Here, for instance, is the 1958 version of the same Carmen 8 that Zukofsky translated in 1939 (with the Latin interwoven):

Miss her, Catullus? don't be so inept to rail
Miser Catulle, desinas ineptire,
at what you see perish when perished is the case.
Et quod vides perisse perditum ducas.
Full, sure once, candid the sunny days glowed, solace,
fulsere quondam candidi tibi soles,
when you went about it as your girl would have it,
cum ventitabas quo puella ducebat
you loved her as no one else shall ever be loved.
amata nobis quantum amabitur nulla.

      . . .

Vale! puling girl. I'm Catullus, *obdurate,*
vale, puella. iam Catullus obdurat,
I don't require it and don't beg uninvited:
nec te requiret nec rogabit invitam:
won't you be doleful when no one, no one! begs you,
at tu dolebis, cum rogaberis nulla.
scalded, every night. Why do you want to live now?
scelesta, vae te. quae tibi manet vita?
Now who will be with you? Who'll see that you're lovely?
quis nunc te adibit? cui videberis bella?
Whom will you love now and who will say that you're his?
quem nunc amabis? cuius esse diceris?
Whom will you kiss? Whose morsel of lips will you bite?
quem basiabis? cui labella mordebis?
But you, Catullus, your destiny's *obdurate.*
at tu, Catulle, destinatus obdura.[7]

This is still recognizably the Catullus of "Catullus viii"—asserting the incomparability of his own love, scolding his unfaithful mistress, and asserting (desperately, and unbelievably) his own self-sufficiency—but the language has become far stranger, far more fresh. It has been pulled into the gravitational field of Catullus's Latin *sounds.* "Miser Catulle, desinas ineptire, / Et quod vides perisse perditum ducas" (literally "Poor Catullus, it's time to quit your folly and see what's gone as gone") has become "Miss her, Catullus? don't be so inept to rail / at what you see perish when perished is the case." Zukofsky has conveyed the gist of Catullus's lexical "meaning" while imitating not merely the rhythms of the Latin lines, but their vowel and consonant sounds: Line 1's "ineptire" ("to talk foolishly") is echoed in "inept to rail," while "vale, puella. iam Catullus obdurat" ("farewell, girl, henceforth Catullus is resolved") crosses to English as "Vale! puling girl, I'm Catullus, *obdurate*," darting an added sting by rendering "puella" as "*puling* girl."

Catullus 8 was fairly early in the project. As the Zukofskys got further and further into Catullus's poems, Zukofsky would try harder and harder to hew to the sound of the Latin, producing less familiar sorts of English "sense." The logic of all this was clear to Zukofsky, if not to many of his bewildered readers. A poem was a pattern of sound traced by the voice on the air; the delight in patterned sound was at the base of the poetic impulse. The art of poetic translation, however, had for much of its history confined itself to another aspect of the poem, its "meaning." Why ought not the poet devote himself to trying to reproduce what had been most immediate to Catullus himself, and to his first readers and listeners—the sounds and rhythms of the Latin words?

"This translation of Catullus," wrote the Zukofskys in a 1961 "Translators' Preface," "follows the sound, rhythm, and syntax of his Latin—tries, as it is said, to breathe the 'literal' meaning with him." The "literal" meaning: not the "plain sense," but the *litterae*, the letters scoring the sounds Catullus uttered. A "Poet's Preface"—which Louis alone signed—makes this even plainer: "This version of Catullus aims at the rendition of his sound. By reading his lips, that is while pronouncing the Latin words, the translation—as his lips shape—tries to breathe with him."[8] Zukofsky knew that such a translation would find little favor among professional classicists, but he was determined to follow his own obsessions wherever they might lead; reputation was no longer an issue, or at least he would no longer admit it to be such.

. . .

But reputation was coming to him, whether he pursued it or not. In November 1960 he taped a reading for the Library of Congress, and later that month he flew to Toronto to read at the Poetry Center at the

invitation of the Canadian poet Raymond Souster. That was a satisfying experience: He was able to sell all of the books he had brought,
and "everybody felt my work was *not* difficult."[9] He read at the café
Les Deux Mégots in August 1961, where the audience included his
old friend Reznikoff and a number of younger poets—Robert Kelly,
Paul Blackburn, Gilbert Sorrentino—and then gave a reading before
the Literature Club at Bard College, Annandale-on-Hudson (this at
the invitation of Kelly, who had recently joined Bard's faculty): "who
would have thought Saul Bellow, whose work I've never read, has
been interested in mine for a long time and came to hear me . . ."[10]
In February 1961, Zukofsky was invited to spend two summer months
at the Yaddo writers' colony in Saratoga Springs; he turned down the
offer, since writers' families were barred from accompanying them.[11]
Around the same time Zukofsky learned that he had been awarded
a three-hundred-dollar prize from the Longview Foundation in
recognition of a series of passages from *Bottom* appearing in *Poetry*
magazine the year before. The award notification came with a personal note from the critic Harold Rosenberg, whom Zukofsky had
met during his time with the WPA back in the 1930s: "Happy about
this, Louis."[12]

Zukofsky's relationship with *Poetry* had markedly improved over
the late 1950s. The magazine had gone through a number of editors
since 1936, none of whom entirely shared Harriet Monroe's vision
of the journal as a vessel featuring the best of both traditional and
modernist poetries. The poet Karl Shapiro edited the magazine from
1950 to 1955; he commissioned Zukofsky to review a book about
Williams in 1950, and published one of Zukofsky's short poems in
1954, but that was all the exposure Zukofsky would receive for a half
decade in the magazine that had invited him aboard as guest editor
back in 1930.

Things changed in 1955, when Shapiro was replaced by the poet
and theologian Henry Rago. Rago was a talented manager and an
editor of rare vision: He recognized that *Poetry*'s task was to be, as
T. S. Eliot had put it, not a magazine but an institution, and he
believed that the journal should aim to provide a venue for the best
poetry being written, of whatever school or style.[13] Over the next
decade, Zukofsky would develop a warm working relationship with

Poetry; Rago solicited Zukofsky's work regularly, and *Poetry* printed a substantial number of Zukofsky's shorter poems, a selection from *Bottom*, and a number of the "Cats" (as Louis and Celia came to call the Catullus translations). From 1963 on, *Poetry* would practically serialize the ongoing movements of *"A"*.

Poetry was a prestigious place for his work, but perhaps as important to Zukofsky was the fact that the magazine *paid*. He and Celia were by no means well off, and the checks that came in from such magazines as *Poetry*, the *Nation*, and the *Paris Review* were welcome; they stood in sharp, professional contrast to the growing number of "little" magazines that wanted to print a Zukofsky poem, but had no funds to pay for it. Lew David Feldman, who continued to negotiate the sale of Zukofsky material to the HRC, counseled Zukofsky that "I shouldn't give things away as in the past"; and whatever financial motives he might have, Zukofsky felt that on some level Feldman had his best interests at heart.[14]

In November 1960 *Poetry* published a review of *"A"* 1–12 by Denise Levertov, one of the poets associated with Creeley's *Black Mountain Review* and Cid Corman's *Origin*. She brought to their discussions a passionate commitment to new poetry, a deep knowledge of the traditions of English verse, and—courtesy of her British education—a clear, lively, and uncluttered prose style. By 1958 collections of her poetry had been published both by Ferlinghetti's City Lights and Jonathan Williams's Jargon Society.[15] Levertov's review, "A Necessary Poetry," was largely a polite confession of her inability to figure out what was going on in the poem. Zukofsky's was "the voice of a man of refined, meditative intelligence speaking with intense seriousness," and the music of his poetry—"austere in melody, beautifully reticulated in counterpoint"—seldom fell flat.[16] "We must try to awaken our own intelligence to follow the intricacy of his thought," Levertov wrote, "and when that fails (as with me, certainly, it often does) we must let the subtle music of his sounds enter us, that is, we must stop trying so hard and see if form itself won't begin, after a while, to present content to us."[17] This was an observation much in line with Zukofsky's own discussions of his poetry. But Levertov found "A"-6 and "A"-8 reminiscent of Pound at his worst ("a patchwork that is excruciatingly hard to see as a whole") and could make nothing of

"A"-7 or "A"-9. She closed with a complaint about the small print run and high price of the book; a more widely available "A" 1–12 would serve as a counterbalance to "the diet of public confession, made without care for craft" being fed the young—they "might learn from Zukofsky of 'That order that of itself can speak to all men.'"[18]

Zukofsky was frustrated that Levertov—whom he had met, and with whom he was on friendly terms—waited until after her review had been accepted to ask Zukofsky about the parts of "A" she hadn't understood. She had waited, she explained, because she didn't want to have an "unfair advantage" over readers who approached "A" 1–12 without being able to ask the poet for elucidation. Zukofsky was enraged. To live by such notions of English "sportsmanship" was "just like bloody British hypocrisy, arrogance, and double-dealing in politics," he fulminated to Corman. Wasn't the reviewer's task to mitigate the "myopia" of the reading public, rather than to display such myopia herself? Zukofsky phoned Levertov to tell her so, and the conversation left him with a poor opinion of Levertov's critical skills and literary ethics: "by such ethics all of us are buried."[19] (Zukofsky's anger had abated by the time the review was published, and he would drop Levertov a brief note of apology and best wishes.[20])

"A" 1–12 received only one other review, a brief note (in an omnibus review of books by Pound, W. H. Auden, and Jonathan Williams) by Hugh Kenner, an English professor at the University of California, Santa Barbara. It was published in the National Review, run by Kenner's friend William F. Buckley Jr.; Kenner served as that magazine's poetry editor.[21] Zukofsky found Kenner's review "to the point," doubtlessly enjoying the way it put recent Auden in its place in comparison with "A", though he was still doubtful about the Creeley-Olson-Zukofsky "nexus" Kenner had mentioned in a recent issue of Poetry.[22]

. . .

Zukofsky was pleased with the job Corman and his collaborator, the designer Will Petersen, had done on "A" 1–12. In the spring of 1961 he entered into discussions with them about doing another book: 5 Statements for Poetry. This time Zukofsky foresaw a book of wider commercial appeal, perhaps even a textbook: He mentioned a print run of around a thousand copies. Zukofsky pulled back from the scheme after consulting a copyright lawyer: Since the 1958 edition of *5 Statements* had been copyrighted in the United States, a new edition could not be printed overseas and imported for sale—by the letter of the law that would be piracy. Corman responded that the government was unlikely to prosecute a case of copyright piracy when the original edition had consisted of 110 stapled pamphlets, but Zukofsky was obdurate. "That I should bother with copyrights at all," he wrote, "—well, you know I have some sentiments about my 'afterlife'. . . ."[23] Instead, he suggested, Origin Press might do a collection of his fiction: "*It was*," "A Keystone Comedy," *Ferdinand*, and "Thanks to the Dictionary," under the title *It was*. Later in 1961, Origin Press published a 250-copy edition, uniform with "*A*" *1–12*, of *It was*.

Since late 1959 Corman had been plotting to revive *Origin* magazine. This time around, Corman decided to dispense with formal subscriptions: The magazine would be sent free to individuals or libraries who wrote Corman and requested it, and who demonstrated continuing interest by "responding" to it by letter at least once a year. Corman would finance this series of the magazine by selling his letters from the poets involved to various research libraries. The first series of *Origin* had begun under the tutelage of Charles Olson and had revolved around his work; this second series, Corman decided, would center upon Zukofsky.[24] Zukofsky was published in each of the fourteen issues of the second series of *Origin* (1961–1964). *Origin* published excerpts from *Bottom: on Shakespeare* and a large number of the Catullus translations; most notably, over its first four issues *Origin* serialized "*A*"-13, Zukofsky's return to his central project. Zukofsky had not added to "*A*" since he had completed "*A*"-12 in 1951. He had told Corman in September 1959 that he hoped to live up to Corman's high hopes for the poem's second half, but "I'm just holding back as long as I can, probably another year or two (tho I've rafts of notes & most of the 'plan' in my head) . . ."[25]

No doubt seeing the first half of "*A*" in print, along with the prospect of nearing the end of *Bottom*, prompted Zukofsky to return to the poem in the summer of 1960, several months ahead of his stated schedule.[26] Though long, "*A*"-13 had little in common formally with the vast, vaguely "fugal" "*A*"-12. Instead it was a "partita"—a composition in five parts modeled upon Bach's Second Violin Partita in D Minor, a composition that Paul, not coincidentally, was practicing in preparation for his third Carnegie Hall recital, scheduled for February 1961.[27] Zukofsky completed "A"-13 in September 1960, and once again laid the long poem aside to concentrate on the Catullus translations.[28]

. . .

Corman's *Origin* was not merely an outlet for Zukofsky's own poetry, but a venue to which he could encourage his friends to submit their work. Corman had boundless energies: He wrote enormous amounts of poetry and carried on numerous correspondences, commenting in detail on poems offered to the magazine and leaving no hopeful contributor awaiting a response. One suspects that Zukofsky came to see Corman as a trustworthy and convenient party to whom he might "hand off" the literary correspondences he himself had come to find burdensome. This was certainly the case with the young poet Frank Samperi, who had first gotten in touch with Zukofsky in the summer of 1957. An orphan, Samperi lived with aunts in Brooklyn, and a debilitating mental illness—Samperi himself simply called it "fear"—made it difficult for him to hold down a job.[29] He was a voracious reader and an indefatigable autodidact. More often than not, his lengthy letters to Zukofsky were accompanied by multiple poems, poems whose lineation was deeply influenced by the modernists but whose reliance on the more abstruse elements of Dante and Aquinas often took them into realms of abstraction that Zukofsky found uncongenial. Zukofsky encouraged Corman to print Samperi in *Origin*, and encouraged the young man in his epistolary relationship with Corman. After a while, Samperi's letters—long, weighted with lengthy quotations, religiously earnest, and emotionally needy—must have become a burden that Zukofsky was eager to share, if not rid himself of entirely. Finally, Samperi pulled himself together enough to marry, and in spring 1964 he and his wife moved to Kyoto, Japan, where Corman lived, and where Samperi—like Corman—would teach English.[30]

Another problematic correspondence was Zukofsky's longstanding exchange with Lorine Niedecker. He admired her poetry as much as ever; he told his students at Brooklyn Polytechnic that she was "the best American woman poet after Marianne Moore," and wrote Corman that he considered her "the best poetess of our time, the Emily [Dickinson], but without the metaphysical Host etc."[31] She was also a very isolated and needy poet; after her father's death in 1954, Niedecker had supported herself on the rent of some cabins she had inherited, but by 1957, with failing eyesight, she was making ends meet by scrubbing floors at the Fort Atkinson Memorial Hospital. In 1960, Zukofsky encouraged her to send poems for *Origin*, and he was glad to see a close correspondence spring up between Corman and Niedecker.[32]

Zukofsky, however, was still troubled by the extent to which Niedecker's poems recycled events of his own family circle. He wrote irritably to Corman in June 1961 concerning Niedecker's poem "Now go to the party," which had appeared in *Origin* 2. Readers might well wonder why the same incident—Paul Zukofsky's appearance at a 1952 costume party at Meadowmount, dressed as Confucius—had been described both in Niedecker's poem and in "A"-13, part iii (scheduled to appear in *Origin* 3).[33] Niedecker got the incident, Zukofsky explained, from a letter he had written her "at the time": "but you can't *make up* poems that'll hold up *whole* about such incidents even if friendship moves you," Zukofsky wrote. "It becomes sentiment of the affections etc."[34]

In late 1960, Zukofsky asked Gael Turnbull, now living in Ventura, California, and running Migrant Press, to send Niedecker a copy of *The Dancers Inherit the Party*, the first collection by the Scottish poet Ian Hamilton Finlay.[35] The short poems of *The Dancers* combined a fine ear for the spoken language, a playful but constant formal restraint, and a high-spirited sense of occasionally surreal humor. Zukofsky was right to expect that this Scot, so in love with the vernacular, the odd, the "wee," would find a kindred spirit in Niedecker.[36] Finlay and his companion Jessie McGuffie were in the process of founding a small press, and in the summer of 1961 they asked Niedecker if the Wild Hawthorn Press could publish a selection of her poems. Once again, as she had with "For Paul and Other Poems" back in 1956, Niedecker asked Zukofsky to write an introduction for the book, which was to be titled *My Friend Tree*. (The introduction was Finlay's idea.) Once again Zukofsky refused: "It's a promise—an oath?—I swore to myself after finishing Bottom that I would not do another line of criticism in my life. I've just refused to do one for Rezy. . . . Besides your book can and should stand on its own."[37]

Finlay and McGuffie followed *My Friend Tree* (1961) with a brief pamphlet of Zukofsky's poems, *16 Once Published*. They wanted a short "factual" introduction, either by Zukofsky himself or by Corman, for this volume as well: an understandable request, considering they were proposing to introduce Zukofsky's work to an unfamiliar audience. But Zukofsky was adamant: "If my poems are worth anything they are my biography," he told McGuffie; "if I am to have my readers they need only the text to go by, to 'catch up' in an arbitrary world, so to speak."[38] *16 Once Published* was Celia's selection of poems from Zukofsky's four previous collections, *55 Poems*, *Anew*, *Some Time*, and *Barely and widely*. Each of the poems in *16 Once Published* was dated, and bibliographical information was provided on the table of contents. One could read the poems, arranged in roughly chronological order, as a chronicle of Zukofsky's entire adult life, from the 1925 Long Island beach of "Pass on, you still dead to the sound of a name," through the wartime capacitors of 1944's "It's hard to see but think of a sea," to the minute domestic scenes of "An Incident" (1955) and "Ashtray" (1958). This method of life-writing—telling the story of a life through judicious selection from the subject's writings—was of a piece with the blocks of quotations that made up much of the Henry Adams thesis, and would find its purest form in Zukofsky's 1970 *Autobiography*.

In 1962 Finlay started a journal, *Poor. Old. Tired. Horse.* (he borrowed the title from a line of Creeley's) which showcased Finlay's wide-ranging interests in new poetries in English and other languages, and established him as one of the most prominent figures in an emergent British poetic avant-garde. Zukofsky would appear in only one issue of *Poor. Old. Tired. Horse.*, for while Finlay greatly admired his work, Zukofsky's intensely musical, fundamentally *verbal* work had little in common with the visual and "concrete" poetries that Finlay was pioneering and promoting. Zukofsky may have written intelligently on Apollinaire's "calligrammes" back in the 1930s, but his own poetry's greatest appeal was always to the ear, rather than the eye.

. . .

Zukofsky had also begun to find followers among his students at Brooklyn Polytechnic. In January 1959, a group of students, most of them associated with Poly's literary magazine *Counterweight*, formed a "poetry club" and asked Zukofsky to serve as advisor.[39] Among those students were Ernie Raia, Dick Sheeler, and Hugh Seidman, who had transferred from M.I.T. the year before and who was to become the editor of *Counterweight* in fall 1959. That same fall Zukofsky finally mustered enough students to offer his elective course "Essentials of Poetry," using his *A Test of Poetry* as textbook, and just before Christmas he read to them from his advance copy of *"A"* 1–12.[40] In the poetry club, the students would read and discuss their own poems, or Zukofsky would read from *"A"* or *Bottom: on Shakespeare*. When Seidman interviewed him for the Poly newspaper, Zukofsky made the most of his position at a polytechnic institute: Zukofsky "feels the engineer is closer to his concept of poetry than the liberal arts student," Seidman wrote. "He considers the engineer or scientist to have more contact with and respect for design, form, and invention than the liberal arts student who would perhaps tend to imitate other poets and convention."[41]

Under Zukofsky's advisement, the poetry club invited visiting readers, including Williams, Corman (temporarily back in the United States), and George Oppen.[42] The poetically inclined students at Poly were a tiny minority, but they were deeply impressed by and fiercely loyal to Zukofsky. Seidman, in particular, found in Zukofsky almost a surrogate father, an authority figure whose example constituted tacit permission for Seidman to pursue his own poetic ambitions.[43] After graduate school in theoretical physics, he worked as a computer programmer and continued to write; his first book, *Collecting Evidence*, would be published in 1970 as part of the Yale Younger Poets series.

Zukofsky's influence persisted with other students for some years after they left Poly. Raia went on to work as a technical writer, and at a party he met another member of that trade, Michael Heller, a

Rensselaer Polytechnic graduate. Raia showed him Zukofsky's work, which was to prove decisive for Heller's own, and introduced him to Zukofsky himself.[44] Sheeler joined the navy after Poly, and remained in touch with his old teacher; learning that Sheeler would be visiting Scotland, Zukofsky encouraged him to look up Ian Hamilton Finlay. To Finlay's grief and anger (and to Zukofsky's embarrassment), Sheeler's visit to Edinburgh proved all too successful: He and Jessie McGuffie fell in love, and announced their engagement. Finlay's admiration and friendship for Zukofsky would outlast his momentary rage—after all, Zukofsky had no control over what his ex-student might do—but Zukofsky's responses to Finlay's heated letters and Sheeler's note of rather defiant apology were characteristic: To apologize would be simply "to open wounds," he told Finlay, but he had cut off all communication with Sheeler.[45]

. . .

Age was beginning to tell on Zukofsky, and along with the physical complaints that increasingly punctuated his letters—arthritis, neuralgia, dental problems—he was beginning to see the members of his generation dying off. On June 3, 1962, Zukofsky's brother-in-law Al Wand died. He and Fanny had been married thirty-five years before at her dying mother's bedside.[46] Al's death touched Zukofsky deeply; as he told Corman, Al's "wit and profound profanities made us happy."[47] Zukofsky would mourn his brother-in-law in "Atque in Perpetuum A.W.," which begins with an outrageous pun on Al's name, quotes some of his bons mots, and ends by suggesting that the ex-gangster's verbal humor has passed to his eighteen-year-old nephew, the violinist Paul:

> Alias to a wand the height lowered
> sleep well who woke every half hour
> on the hour with last breath joked
> two legs were mine walk 'Glad to
> hear your voice' 'Glad to hear my
> own voice.'
>
> . . .
>
> The scholarly string player has a theory

of his tone the old hour listens
'I don't understand a thing you're saying
but it's terribly'—sleepily—'out of tune.'
Counting sevens an ornament unto my wound.[48]

The poem's title is an allusion to Catullus CI, the poet's farewell to his dead brother: "atque in perpetuum, frater, ave atque vale" (and for ever, brother, hail and farewell).

In "Atque in Perpetuum" Zukofsky was indeed "counting sevens": each line of the poem contains seven words. Once again, as when he composed parts of "A"-8 and "A"-9 according to mathematical principles, Zukofsky was rethinking the formal bases of English verse. The most widely adhered to method of measuring the poetic line in English, from the Renaissance on, had been some form of accentual-syllabic meter, counting both accents and syllables: The iambic pentameter line, for instance, in its purest form contains ten syllables and five alternating stresses: "My **mis**tress' **eyes** are **no**thing **like** the **sun**." Pound, Auden, and others, working from the model of Old English verse, had experimented with accentual lines, which counted stresses but placed no strictures on the number of syllables. Marianne Moore, most radically, had pioneered a purely syllabic verse that prescribed the number of syllables to a line but made no rules as to the pattern of their accents. To count *words*, as Zukofsky was increasingly to do in his later poetry, is something else altogether.

A prosody in which line length is based on number of words means that rhythmic patterns like the iambic pentameter are no longer binding upon the poet, and that the actual sounded lengths of the lines might vary widely: The thirteen-syllable "helicopter and turbojets. It used to shower," then, is by number of words "equivalent" to the seven-syllable "I am a son of the soil." The word count line allowed Zukofsky the same flexibility of rhythm and sound values that he had found in metrically "free" verse, and allowed him to exploit free verse's most characteristic ways of generating formal movement: The unconscious stress the reader places on the first and last words of a line, the various energies produced when the syntax flows from one line to the next without punctuation ("enjambment") or pauses at the end of a line ("end-stopping"). At the same time, however, the word count imposes a constraint upon the poet, a frame within which he has to work—as the painter is constrained by the size and shape of the canvas, or the composer by the range and tonal characteristics of the instrument for which he composes. The word count was perhaps a minimal constraint, compared with the traditional accentual-syllabic line or even with Moore's lines of counted syllables, but it signaled that Zukofsky in his later work, as much as in the sonnets of "A"-7 or the canzoni of "A"-9, regarded form as a fundamental element of the poetic art.

The Pythagoreans had assigned particular qualities to each integer: four was "justice," five was "marriage," and, as Zukofsky notes in "A"-18, "seven words heaven, eight love, nine universe."[49] It was appropriate, then, in writing of his deceased brother-in-law, and attempting to assuage the "wound" that death had dealt him, that Zukofsky would resort to a seven-word line, an emblem of "heaven."

．　．　．

The travails of age and the griefs of mortality were little mitigated by the increased attentions of the young. The counterestablishment movements in American poetry, which aside from the Beat writers had remained largely underground through much of the 1950s, had exploded into public view with Donald M. Allen's groundbreaking 1960 anthology, *The New American Poetry*.[50] *The New American Poetry* classified into groups (San Francisco Renaissance, Black Mountain, etc.) a wide range of writings that had been appearing in small press pamphlets, obscure little magazines, and mimeographed journals, and anthologized many of the younger poets who had been in touch with Zukofsky: Duncan, Creeley, Jonathan Williams, Allen Ginsberg, Joel Oppenheimer, and others. Zukofsky was coming to be seen as a key elder statesman to a generation of poets who had ranged themselves against the institutional forces of the "glossy" magazines, the large trade publishers, the emergent networks of creative writing programs, grants, and prizes, and the academy in general.

This is not to imply, however, that these poets did not take teaching positions when they could get them. Jerome Rothenberg, born in the Bronx in 1931 and raised with Yiddish as his first language, was by 1962 teaching at the Mannes School; he was "the school's *entire* humanities dept.," Zukofsky noted, and in that capacity hosted a reading series that included Zukofsky, Levertov, Duncan, Paul Blackburn—another young poet who had gravitated to Zukofsky— and Robert Kelly. Rothenberg was in the early 1960s adumbrating the "deep image," a visionary poetics derived from Blake, García Lorca, and others. Kelly, his younger coexplorer of the deep image, was a multilingual, polymathic talent—"a mountainous Brooklyn Dr. Johnson, but gentle Irish voice and blue eyes," Zukofsky described him.[51] With his friend George Economou, Kelly and his wife, Joan, visited the Zukofskys in Brooklyn Heights, where they listened to the older poet scrutinize "the minute particulars of some poem, studying it aloud as if Zukofsky were trying to see its breath."[52] In 1960, the Kellys and Economou founded a journal, *Trobar*, largely an outlet for "deep image" poetry. Zukofsky was skeptical of the whole deep image business; he praised certain lines of Kelly's from *Trobar* 3, remarking that he anticipated good things from the young poet, "without or with 'deep image' or even having to remark how deep can it be without being swamped."[53]

Despite his reservations about the editors' poetics, Zukofsky gave *Trobar* a poem to print in 1963, and he was similarly generous to a whole raft of fledgling little magazines: *Neon* (edited by Gilbert Sorrentino), *Burning Deck* (Keith Waldrop), *Folio* (Clayton Eshleman), *Blue Grass* (Hank Chapin), and others even more obscure. Zukofsky preferred seeing his poetry published in such paying venues as *National Review* or *Poetry*, and he continued to send work to Corman for *Origin*, but he was heartened by the interest young editors were showing and conscious of the value of having his writing appear in these "progressive" venues. He had been irritated by his exclusion from *The New American Poetry*, presumably on the basis of his age (though Donald Allen had solicited work from him, and Charles Olson, only six years Zukofsky's junior, had been included), but he felt far closer to this new generation of poets than to most of his own contemporaries.[54]

One magazine with which Zukofsky formed a lasting relationship was the lively and eclectic *Kulchur*, bankrolled and partly edited by Lita Hornick. *Kulchur* (founded in 1960) took its name from Pound's *Guide to Kulchur*, and aimed to be more than a "literary" magazine, including commentary on all the arts and on a wide range of cultural and political issues.[55] Gilbert Sorrentino, who was guest editor for the fourth issue, asked Zukofsky ("whom I badly wanted to see the magazine for an outlet," Sorrentino recalled[56]) for a contribution, and in 1961 Zukofsky gave him "Modern Times," the essay on Charlie Chaplin he had written back in 1936.[57] The following year, *Kulchur* would print for the first time Zukofsky's play *Arise, arise*, another product of the 1930s.[58] Over 1962 and 1963 *Kulchur* would reprint much of Zukofsky's criticism, including all of *5 Statements for Poetry*.[59]

While Zukofsky had abandoned the idea of an Origin Press edition of *5 Statements*, he still wanted to see the essays between covers. He suggested to James Laughlin in early 1961 that New Directions might do a reprint of *A Test of Poetry*, and when Laughlin showed interest, Zukofsky offered a combined volume: *A Test of Poetry* and *5 Statements for Poetry*.[60] Laughlin felt *5 Statements* was too difficult for undergraduates (the presumed market for the book), so he returned it immediately. *Test*, Laughlin said, was a fascinating selection of material, but the commentary was "too sophisticated for the average student," and to be a *really* useful textbook, the anthology ought to have "suggestions for the teacher, questions for the student, theme topics and so forth." Laughlin was interested, however, in the Catullus, and thought he could see a place for the Zukofskys' version in New Directions' series of bilingual "classics."[61] Zukofsky, with a long history of Laughlin's rejections in mind, was skeptical: "Well, we're still cordial," he told Corman. "If he ever turns out *Cat*—I'll be stunned. But my work is still 'fascinating.'"[62]

So it was back to the small presses, and Zukofsky welcomed Kelly and Economou's suggestion that Trobar Press (*Trobar*'s book publishing arm) issue his newest collection of short poems.[63] *I's (pronounced eyes)* was a tiny pamphlet collecting ten poems Zukofsky had written in 1959 and 1960, along with the 1937 "Motet" in Celia's four-voice setting. As cover image, Zukofsky chose a reproduction of a poem in the calligraphy of the Japanese monk Ryokan (1775–1831); the scroll was Cid Corman's, who was so delighted with its grace that he had lent it for successive yearlong intervals to a number of his friends.[64] *I's (pronounced eyes)* begins with "(Ryokan's Scroll)," a lovely, minimal lyric that incorporates a translation of Ryokan's poem:

dripping
words

off

a
long
while

the
first
snow

out
off
where
blue

    eyes

    the
    cherry
    tree's
    petals [65]

Zukofsky was enchanted by the scroll; he fancied he could make out an "LZ" in the calligraphy, as he recalled in "A"-14: "at / the scroll's / first hanging // found my / own initials." [66] When Corman received a copy of *I's (pronounced eyes)*, he immediately told Zukofsky that the scroll on the book's cover had been printed upside down. Zukofsky acknowledged the error—not his, for he had marked how the calligraphy should be oriented—but he would not complain to Kelly or Economou. [67] As he put it in "A"-14, it was "not // the worst / erratum / for 'the // blossoms to / fall up.'" [68] Perhaps, in a world of mounting mortality, it was even a hopeful emblem.

·   ·   ·

Early in 1963, Zukofsky and William Carlos Williams's thirty-five year friendship was ended by Williams's death. Bill's last years had been darkened by increasingly debilitating illness—a bout of colon cancer, depression, and strokes, which left him unable to read and barely able to type with one hand. He had thought *Paterson* complete when its fourth book was done, but returned to it over the mid-1950s and wrote a fifth; in early 1961 he got no further than a few pages into a sixth volume.[69] His last series of poems—*Pictures from Brueghel*—was completed by 1960. Zukofsky was in close touch with Williams through 1960, and Bill's deterioration saddened him. He made sure that Williams received a copy of *"A" 1–12*, which Williams took with him to Florida in the winter of 1960; he was unable to follow Floss's reading of it, however—"I find my mental processes much retarded lately," he told Zukofsky—and lent the book to his friend, the critic Kenneth Burke, who was staying in the next bungalow.[70] (Burke wrote Williams a three-page letter about *"A"*, which delighted Zukofsky with its generous praise and careful analysis.[71]) Later that year Cid Corman visited Williams and read two hours' worth of the book to him. Corman's "persistence won the day," Williams told Zukofsky; "it was a pleasure for me to hear it—far simpler than I had ever envisioned it and more lyrical than I was ever able to envision it."[72]

On March 4, 1963, Williams's wife, Floss, went to wake him, only to find that he had quietly passed away the night before. Paul Blackburn, who had gotten the news from television, phoned the Zukofskys with word of Williams's death. They went out to Rutherford for the funeral, where the graveside was thronged with Williams's townsfolk, among them many whom he had helped deliver into the world.[73] It was a day of the sort of weather Williams had celebrated in many poems: "we went in pouring rain and came back in cold wind," Zukofsky told Corman. Afterwards, Floss had coffee in the house for family and a few close friends—the Zukofskys, Paul Goodman and his wife, the critic M. L. Rosenthal, and Williams's publisher Laughlin. Laughlin, moved by Zukofsky's grief, tried to comfort him by alluding to *Spring and All*: "don't despair, Zuk, it'll be spring soon."

Zukofsky had remembered his friend Williams on a number of occasions in his own poetry. Among them were the fourth section of "Chloride of Lime and Charcoal," which quotes Homer to describe the Rutherford poet-physician—"A soothsayer, a doctor, a singer / and a craftsman is sure of welcome / where he goes"—and the fifth section of "Songs of Degrees," which equates the precision of Williams's poetic speech with the deadly marksmanship of a Wild West desperado:

> **William**
> **Carlos**
> **Williams**
>
> **alive!**
>
> thinking of
> Billy
>
> The kid
> shoots
> to
> kill[74]

Now Zukofsky turned back to his papers to memorialize his old friend. During the twelfth and thirteenth of March, just over a week after Williams's death, Zukofsky went through his files and compiled a twelve-page collage of quotations from his own work that pertained to Williams or that he associated with Williams, along with a few short communications that Williams had sent him. It was a comprehensive, if brief, history of their friendship and artistic partnership, from Zukofsky's quoting *A Voyage to Pagany* in "A"-1, through his anthologizing of Williams in *An "Objectivists" Anthology*, his incorporation of Williams's comments on "'Mantis'" into "'*Mantis,' an Interpretation*," his work on the manuscript of Williams's *The Wedge*, and Celia's settings of some of Williams's poems. This "Coronal"—dedicated to Floss—included as well ample evidence of Zukofsky's admiration for Williams's work. It concluded with a facsimile reproduction of Williams's scrawled signature—his illness evident in the misspelled "Carolos"—in Zukofsky's copy of *Pictures from Brueghel and Other Poems*.[75]

By the time Zukofsky received a request from Henry Rago to contribute a specimen of "work in progress" for *Poetry*'s October issue, he had decided that the "Coronal" was "A"-17. 17 because Williams had been born on Constitution Day, September 17; he would have turned eighty in September 1963. As Zukofsky put it to Rago, offering him the typescript of "A"-17,

> The intervening movements of "A" (following 13 which has been printed) are still notes—largely in my head, and may take some years to write down. I try not to hurry "A" but let its form happen. But when I felt the need to gather the enclosure after Bill's death, I skipped a few movements in my long poem to make the number of this movement correspond with the day of his birth. Other movements of "A" were not written in chronological order, trusting the sequence would work out.[76]

"A" was proceeding by a mixture of plan and contingency: As had been his practice from the beginning, Zukofsky had the next movements, and perhaps the shape of the whole, blocked out in his mind; and as from the beginning, the poem took its final form in response to the events of Zukofsky's life.

, , .

John F. Kennedy was assassinated on November 22, 1963. Kennedy's death united a nation, linked together more than ever through television news, in shock and grief. It must have been much on Zukofsky's mind when he went up to Cambridge, Massachusetts, on December 14 to read at Harvard University's Adams House. He had been invited by a young poet and student of French literature, George Michael Palmer (he would later shed the "George" and publish simply as Michael Palmer). The previous summer, at a poetry conference in Vancouver, Palmer had met Olson, Levertov, and Ginsberg, and had heard Zukofsky lavishly praised by Robert Creeley. He seized the opportunity of a reading series the following semester to invite Zukofsky to Harvard, where he gave a "stunning, beautiful, beautiful reading." Despite Zukofsky's "pared down" thinness, the impression he gave of "radical asceticism" ("he took up only a small part of the chair," Palmer recalled), his audience was deeply impressed by the "precise, anti-rhetorical manner" in which he read passages from "A"-12, the first half of "A"-9, a smidgen of *Bottom*, and some shorter poems.[77] It was Zukofsky's first venture into the Ivy League since leaving Columbia almost forty years before.

The next day Zukofsky drafted a brief poem on the train back to New York:

After Reading

After reading, a song

a light snow
a had been fallen

the brown most showed
knoll trunk knot treelings' U's

The Sound marsh water

ice clump
sparkling root etc

and so far out.[78]

The poem, in Zukofsky's most delicate, imagistic manner, and hearkening back to the imagery of Williams's *Spring and All*, concentrates hard upon the immediacies of perception, shutting out the worlds of politics and public mourning. Zukofsky's own grief over Kennedy's death would find expression the next year in "A"-15, when he returned to his long poem in a final, decadelong sustained haul of composition.

Short Poems:
Contingencies
and Sequences

THE COLD COMFORT James Laughlin had offered Zukofsky in March 1963, as they drank coffee with Floss after Bill Williams's funeral—"don't despair, Zuk, it'll be spring soon"—came in the wake of a conversation about the prospects of New Directions' publishing the Catullus translations. Zukofsky had not raised the subject, nor did he trust Laughlin's professed desire to see the Catullus in print from New Directions. While Laughlin had devoted enormous energy to making available the works of Zukofsky's friends Williams and Pound, he had never offered to do a book of Zukofsky's. What definitively set Zukofsky against Laughlin was New Directions' 1962 publication of collections by two other objectivists, George Oppen and Charles Reznikoff. These books were copublished (and presumably in large part underwritten) by the *San Francisco Review*, a magazine edited by Oppen's half sister June Oppen Degnan, a well-to-do

San Francisco socialite and Democratic activist. The *Review*'s starting a publishing imprint in collaboration with New Directions had been Degnan's idea, though clearly she relied on her poet brother's advice in choosing a selected volume by Reznikoff—whom Oppen admired intensely—as the new imprint's first publication.

Oppen had consulted Zukofsky on the selection of poems for Reznikoff's book, *By the Waters of Manhattan*. Zukofsky would scarcely deny his old friend his belated success, but it must have rankled Zukofsky when New Directions/*San Francisco Review* announced in early 1962 that they would be publishing, simultaneously with *By the Waters of Manhattan*, a collection of new Oppen poems, *The Materials*. Why, if New Directions/*San Francisco Review* seemed bent upon reviving the objectivists from the pit in which that group had slumbered for the last three decades, would they not publish Zukofsky—who, after all, had theorized, engineered, and named the whole "movement"?

Oppen protested that he himself had favored doing a Zukofsky volume from the beginning of the venture, and that so far as he knew, so had Laughlin. It was June Degnan, her brother said, who opposed publishing a *collected* volume of Zukofsky's short poems.[1] It is easy to imagine how Zukofsky felt betrayed in this business, and how it soured his recently renewed friendship with Oppen. In the early days of the two poets' relationship, Zukofsky had been the teacher, the mentor. It was he who launched the objectivists and had argued on their behalf in the pages of the literary magazines. While Zukofsky's poverty had prevented him from having more than an editorial role in the Objectivist Press, Oppen had been able to underwrite his own *Discrete Series*, after which he had abandoned poetry altogether for a quarter century—a quarter century during which Zukofsky had never stopped writing in the face of almost universal public indifference, and a quarter century during which Zukofsky had disseminated his own work through self-publication, subscription, and self-subsidized printing.

Now, barely four years after Oppen had returned to writing, he was seeing his book of poems published by James Laughlin, the same publisher who had been putting Zukofsky off for decades, and with the connivance of a wealthy magazine editor who happened to be his half sister. To add insult to injury, in September 1962 Zukofsky received an invitation to a party at the Gotham Book Mart celebrating the publication of *The Materials* and *By the Waters of Manhattan*; the invitation spoke about both Oppen's and Reznikoff's participation in the objectivist movement, but made no mention of that movement's creator, Zukofsky himself.[2]

The English poet Charles Tomlinson, visiting the Zukofskys in August 1963, could see clearly that their friendship with George and Mary Oppen had suffered a shock unlikely to be mended.[3] Oppen himself told Tomlinson that New Directions/*San Francisco Review* might—just *might*, for he could not answer for Laughlin or for his sister—be willing to do a selected Zukofsky, but matters were "too awkward" for him directly to propose that possibility to Zukofsky.[4] Oppen suggested that Tomlinson drop Zukofsky a hint about trying the Degnan-Laughlin team with a selected manuscript, but as Tomlinson spent time with Zukofsky, it became evident to him that Zukofsky had no interest in issuing a selected poems at this point in his career. Zukofsky made it clear to Corman in early 1964: There would be no further selected volumes of his work before the publication of *ALL*—the title under which he had conceived his collected short poems for some years now.[5]

Zukofsky had been published in selections twice now, first in *16 Once Published*, and again in *Found Objects*, a slim volume of twelve poems. Hank Chapin, a young instructor at the University of Kentucky and editor of *Blue Grass*, had proposed doing a Zukofsky issue of his magazine, and that proposal was eventually superseded by the idea of a collection. Like *16 Once Published*, *Found Objects* was a career overview of Zukofsky's short poems, its contents running in reverse chronological order from the as-yet-uncollected "The Ways" (1962) to 1926's "Poem beginning 'The.'" What interested Zukofsky as he made the selection was how time and distance had removed the poems from their original biographical and emotional contexts, had made them appear not his own work but as "found objects." As Zukofsky put it in the pamphlet's preface,

> With the years the personal prescriptions for one's work recede, thankfully, before an interest that *nature as creator* had more of a hand in it than one was aware. The work then owns perhaps something of the look of *found objects* in late exhibits—which arrange themselves

as it were, one object near another—roots that have become sculpture, wood that appears talisman, and so on: charms, amulets maybe, but never really such things since the struggles so to speak that made them do not seem to have been human trials and evils—they appear entirely *natural*.[6]

Zukofsky had the end of his short poem-writing in sight, the completion of the string of "little" books that would together make up *ALL*. *ALL*'s final installment was a very short collection with the coda-like title *After I's*. This twenty-six-page chapbook was published in 1964 by Ron Caplan, editor of the Pittsburgh-based magazine *Mother*, under the imprints "Mother Press/Boxwood Press." With *ALL* completed, Zukofsky looked for a publisher. Jonathan Williams had been making noises for some years about the Jargon Society doing the book, but Zukofsky had reached the end of his patience with small presses. This time around, Zukofsky had determined, his work was to be brought out by a professional publisher, and at that publisher's own expense. Oppen's advice—that Zukofsky's collected poems "should be published as you've been publishing, without overhead to speak of, on volunteer labor, etc."[7]—was worse than insulting, for it showed how profoundly Oppen had misunderstood the constancy and continuity of Zukofsky's dedication to his art, and the intensity of his struggle over the past two decades to see his poetry published and properly distributed.

· · ·

Looking over the six volumes of short poems that make up *ALL*, one is struck by their *occasionality*: not that each poem is explicitly addressed to a named occasion (though many are), but that so many of them spring directly out of specific moments of Zukofsky's life and, however obliquely, address those moments. In 1823 Goethe talked to his young acquaintance Eckermann about the relationship between the poem and its occasion:

> The world is so great and rich, and life so full of variety, that you can never want occasions for poems. But they must all be *occasioned*; that is to say, reality must give both impulse and material. . . . All my poems are occasioned poems, suggested by real life, and having therein a firm foundation. I attach no value to poems snatched out of the air.[8]

Strip this statement of Romantic bombast, and Zukofsky would agree; his poetics is concerned first and last with "thinking with the things as they exist," with following the course of "historic and contemporary particulars." The poem, he wrote, "necessarily deal[s] with a world outside it"; "The revolutionary word if it must revolve cannot escape having a reference."[9] At the same time, the poem is not merely the record of the occasion, but itself a new creation. Zukofsky's poems, though they spring out of lived experience, are not merely representations of that experience, "imitations" in the sense of a mirror held to nature; the act of making poems is an imitation of the processes of nature, of Spinoza's *natura naturans*, "nature as creator."

The short poems collected in *I's (pronounced* eyes) and *After I's* approach a limit of pure occasionality, court dismissal as shirt-cuff notations of passing experience redeemed by flashes of wit or turn of phrase. Goethe's criterion of the "universal and poetic" appears rather outsized when applied to such squibs as the third section of "I's (pronounced *eyes*)," Zukofsky's response to an old photo of Paul—"Fiddler Age Nine / (with brief-and violin-case) // Sir Attaché Détaché"[10]—or the eleventh section of "The Old Poet Moves to a New Apartment 14 Times":

When the walls
are dismantled
realize
the horror
of dust

but also
where a curtain
kept the dust from
the walls,
a white

that with most
things packed shows how
little one needs
waiting for the movers

to come.[11]

Zukofsky never shies away from the microscopic, and Zukofsky never has much truck with the "universal"—at least directly. The only path to the "big" issues is by way of the minute particulars out of which the poem is woven. In the later books of *ALL*, Zukofsky concentrates more and more on the contemporary, on the immediate events of his life. That the poems resulting are more openly occasional, however, does not mean that they strive any less intensely for the "rested totality" of objectification, "the apprehension satisfied completely as to the appearance of the art form as an object."[12]

Even at their shortest, Zukofsky's short poems usually show strong if sometimes playful internal cohesion, as in the briefcase/violin-case pun of "Attaché Détaché," or in the cross-laced sound patterns of "For": "Four tubas / or / two-by-fours."[13] As important, however, is Zukofsky's technique of stringing various, often formally and thematically dissimilar, short poems into longer sequences, thereby coaxing more complex meanings out of them by their position within a larger structure. Zukofsky had always been careful about the ordering of his poetry collections: The orders of the poems in *55 Poems* and *Anew* were repeatedly revised. Early in his career, Zukofsky had gathered his poems into at least two named groups, "18 Poems to the Future" (1926) and "Answering Calamus" (ca. 1928), but it was only in the poems of *Some Time* that the sequence becomes a central structuring mode for his short poems. One could do worse, in assessing Zukofsky's shorter poetry, than to consider a few of the sequences that make up almost half of the last four collections of *ALL*.

"Light" (*Some Time*, composed 1940–1948)

At least thirteen of the fifteen sections of "Light" had been composed between 1940 and 1943 and intended for *Anew*, but for one reason or another Zukofsky omitted them from the 1946 collection. In the spring of 1948, he added two further poems and arranged the resulting fifteen poems under the title "Light."[14] The sequence begins with a fearsomely scientific little poem that probably draws upon Zukofsky's wartime technical writing work:

An instruction booklet on a certain effect in which
Mass becomes o
Inertia approaches ∞

Light is critical
Time, immaterial
Distance, inside out.[15]

The poems that follow, however, have nothing to do with Einsteinian relativity or the physics of light. Poem 2 is an observation of a mansion with lawn jockey; its rhymes—"jigger," "outrigger," "figure," "trigger"—pointedly avoid the word the house's owners, one imagines, use quite unthinkingly: "nigger."[16] Poem 3 watches the wartime film *Tarzan Triumphs*, which pits the ape-man against the forces of the Third Reich, and while winking at the homoerotic overtones of Tarzan's relationship with the "boy," reflects on how easily geopolitical troubles are overcome in the movies: "'Nazi,' Tarzan says / And lures some celluloid to the lion's maw: / And all the earth's problems are solved."[17] In Poem 4, God ("LL.D.") writes his letter of resignation; in 15, in almost Dr. Seussian abandon, a mosquito and a fish dance to the refrain of "Happy / is / music! // The flute / The flute / The flute!."[18] These poems, along with smiling celebrations of Valentine's Day, Christmas, and the onset of Daylight Saving Time, make clear one implication of the title "Light": this is *light* verse, not to be taken too seriously.

The sequence's fifteen poems also contain a couple of more somber notes. "R.A.E." is Zukofsky's epitaph for Robert Allison Evans, whose death has taken him precisely *out* of the light: "Let him dead find such repose / That will not dull the days / He is not in the sun—/ Our ills and our plaints."[19] In Poem 9, Zukofsky is walking in Central Park and meets a trio of "DP's"—displaced persons, refugees—from Germany, a man and his two small children. The man asks Zukofsky to take the trio's picture with his "small box camera," and gives the poet—always spectacularly clumsy with mechanical objects—directions:

It was easier to
Handle his contraption
Than a song.
"The man took our picture, papa?"
"Yes, because we looked nice." . . .
I have one print here.[20]

Here light has become the element that fixes memory—"The sun caught them in sky and clouds"—and Zukofsky, in taking the photograph (literally "light-print"), has impressed "one print" on his own memory, and on his own page.

The poems of "Light" explore various implications of their title: light as a physical phenomenon; light as the medium of photography; light as an emblem of life; the cinema as an animated projection of light; the shifting light of the various seasons and holidays; "light" verse as a particular, perhaps underrated literary genre. But the poems refuse to be subsumed under any single thematic heading; they bear what Wittgenstein called a "family resemblance" to one another, a "network of similarities overlapping and crisscrossing," of affinities shared among some members and not others.[21] This notion of "family resemblance" can help us discern the odd unities of Zukofsky's short poem sequences.

"Songs of Degrees" (*Some Time*, composed 1953–1955)

In the King James Bible, fifteen of the Psalms (120–134) carry the superscription "A Song of Degrees." The Hebrew is *Shîr hamma ʿlôth*, which the Revised Standard Version translates as "Songs of Ascents"; scholarly opinion is divided about the term's meaning, but it is generally agreed that these Psalms have something to do with the Jerusalem Temple, and they have been traditionally associated with the return of the Jews from the Babylonian captivity.[22] Pound had been struck by the phrase; in 1913 he published three brief, vivid groups of lines as "A Song of the Degrees"; "degrees" suggested to him differing degrees of light and shade, of the perception of color and shape.[23] When Zukofsky gathers seven poems under the title "Songs of Degrees," however, his concern is with the measuring of degrees of *sound*. The first two poems of the sequence, in fact, seem almost laboratory experiments on the effects of lineation and breath. Each of them is entitled "With a Valentine"; the first reads:

Hear, her
Clear
Mirror,

Care
His error.
In her
Care
Is clear.[24]

Twelve words, eight of them rhymes or slant rhymes to the first "Hear"; "His" and "is" full rhymes; and only "in" remaining unrhymed. Although the stanza has precedents in Zukofsky's earlier poetry (compare "A"-11's "Take care, song, that what star's imprint you mirror / Grazes their tears; draw speech from their nature"[25]), in these lines Zukofsky has condensed the complex rhyming of "A"-9 or "A"-11 into a pure, hard musicality.

Two days after writing the first "With a Valentine," on Valentine's Day 1953 Zukofsky returned and wrote the second: five variations on the original stanza, each of which manipulates the punctuation and lineation of the same twelve words to bring out new aspects of their aural and semantic interrelations:

Hear her
(Clear mirror)
Care.
His error.
In her care—
Is clear.
. . .
Hear
Her
Clear,
Mirror,
Care
His
Error in
Her—
Care
Is
Clear.[26]

343

This is indeed an intensive exploration of the "degrees" of language, of how "number, measure, and weighing" obtain in the poet's art.

It is rather a shock to move on to the third section of "Songs of Degrees," "'Nor did the prophet,'" with its heavy weight of biblical reference and the burden of guilt it imputes to Zukofsky's friend Pound. It is as though the chiming *r*'s of "With a Valentine" have melted into Jannequin's birdsong, which is broken by the dense, scriptural discourse of the body of the poem. The fourth poem, "Happiest February," is Zukofsky's valentine for 1954, a compact lyric in his best, but still oblique, greeting-card style.[27] The fifth is "William Carlos Williams alive!," a poem which reminds one of the tentative, exploratory syntax of Williams's early lyrics; the poem is a tribute to Williams in his own voice, though with a peculiarly Zukofskyan twist: As the narrow lines descend the page, they trace the quick movements of Williams's mind by examining the shapes and sounds of his initials:

> reach
> C
> a cove—
> call it
> Carlos:
>
> smell W
> double U
> two W's,
> ravine and
> runnel:
>
> these
> sink
> high
>
> in
> high
> fog
>
> which
> as

it
lifts,

the other
world
is
there:[28]

The sixth poem, "A wish," finds Zukofsky on his way to work, meditating on the Latin lesson of *The Merry Wives of Windsor* 4.1, remembering that Bach was said to have taught his choirboys Latin, and making a "mirror fugue" out of one of Mistress Page's sentences:

Look, where his master comes;
'tis a playing-day,
I see.

See I, day-playing
a 'tis;
comes master his
where,
Look.[29]

The sequence ends with a look towards spring in "March first," where a chorus of children "are making a hell of a noise," defying their parents, and "Rehearsing"—for a school play?—"We are the generations of leaves."[30]

As collective title for these seven poems, "Songs of Degrees" is less descriptive than suggestive. "Degrees" implies the degrees of measure and weighing of sound and syllable so important to poetry, as in the "With a Valentine" poems; "degrees" evokes the Jerusalem Temple, so central to "'Nor did the prophet.'" "Happiest February" and "March first" invoke "degrees" as a measurement of the changing weather, while "A wish" just barely suggests "degrees" as a measurement of educational attainment. As readers, we concede that all of these meanings are (or might be) implied by the title, but that the title impresses no unity upon the seven poems arranged under it. We read them and note their intelligence, charm, and wit, and observe how they are embedded in the circumstances of Zukofsky's life: If they have an ultimate unity, it lies in that common place from which they have all sprung.

"I's (pronounced *eyes*)"

(*I's* (*pronounced* eyes), composed 1959–1960)

Zukofsky composed the eleven wee poems that make up "I's (pronounced *eyes*)" over the course of 1959 and the first part of 1960; most of them appear in letters to Cid Corman, copied thriftily in the margins of Zukofsky's blue aerograms. It was not until the summer of 1961, however, that Zukofsky combined them under a single title.[31] "I's (pronounced *eyes*)," Zukofsky told L. S. Dembo in 1968, was "the short way" of doing away with epistemology, which is what the 450 pages of *Bottom: on Shakespeare* had sought to do.[32] These are eleven tiny poems about perception, written from an epistemological perspective in which the "eye"—the organ of perception—is conflated with the "I," the perceiving subject.[33] The opening poem presents the process in a nutshell:

Hi, Kuh,

those
gold'n bees
are I's,

eyes,

skyscrapers.[34]

Zukofsky looks at a billboard of Elsie, the Borden cow; he greets her, "Hi, Kuh" (*Kuh* is "cow" in German, with a pun on "haiku"), then reflects on the "Christmas crystallography" he sees through astigmatic and myopic eyes without his glasses, when the lights of skyscrapers are "gold'n bees / . . . I's, // eyes . . ." "*I* see this? Yes," Zukofsky told Dembo. "The eyes see it? But there's also an object out there. All right, whichever way you want."[35]

It is possible to read all eleven poems of "I's (pronounced *eyes*)" as oblique or direct reflections on the question of how the seeing eye knows the objects seen. More fun, however, to read them as a series of gnomic and witty reports from an "I" who is also an "eye"—and as importantly, an *ear*: These poems play delightful games with sound, from the puns of "Fiddler Age Nine" and "For," to the precisely rendered speech of "Angelo // the Superintendent's / Porto Rican Helper," to the "poetically" blue final poem, "Azure": "Azure / as ever / adz aver."[36]

"The Old Poet Moves to a New Apartment 14 Times"
(*After I's*, composed 1962 from notes dating to 1960)

In February 1962 the Zukofskys moved to their last Brooklyn home, a two-story apartment at 160 Columbia Heights. The place was wonderfully quiet, the "tiniest duplex," with a living room and kitchen on the tenth floor and, on the eleventh, a work room for Louis and Celia ("the Library!") and a room for Paul. Best of all were the view to the southwest—"we're right over the promenade & look towards Staten Island & the narrows, towards the sea!"—and the sunlight that flooded the rooms all day long.[37] To commemorate the occasion, Zukofsky assembled a fourteen-part sequence, "The Old Poet Moves to a New Apartment 14 Times." (He had just turned fifty-eight, but Zukofsky had been thinking of himself as an old man for some years now.)

The sequence begins with two sections of ironical self-description:

1

"The old radical"
or surd—

2

I's (pronounced eyes)
the title of his last

followed by *After I's.*
"After"—*later* or
chasing?[38]

Yes, Zukofsky had been a political "radical" in his younger days, but couldn't that term be taken in a mathematical sense, making him an irrational number, a "surd"—$\sqrt{2}$, for instance? And how is one to take the "after" of *After I's*: Is it a simple matter of temporal progression, or a confession that for all of his ocular rhetoric Zukofsky is still "chasing" a definition of the eye or the "I," the self?

The time of moving house, when one is confronted with all of the *objects* one has accumulated, is inevitably a time of self-reflection, of contemplating the manner in which one has spent one's life. In "The Old Poet"'s fourth section, *"Aleatorical indeterminate,"* with the chance-based music of John Cage very much on his mind, Zukofsky ponders the relationship of chance, the poet's compositional choices, and the temptation of preexisting meters—

> to be lucky and free and original
> we might well be afraid to think
> we know beforehand exactly
> what we're doing
>
> rather let it happen[39]

—the announced goal of so many of the free-verse poets Zukofsky saw emerging around him, a poetic epitomized in Allen Ginsberg's "first thought, best thought" mantra. But even as the poet works without "beforehand" knowledge of precisely where he's going,

> the 'illogical' anticipation,
>
> music, has always been explicit
> as silence and sound have
>
> in the question
> how long is a rest to rest.

Music is always the poet's concern; the relationship of "silence and sound" is as important to Bach as to Cage, and is encapsulated in the question of "how long is a rest to rest."[40]

Even in "the 'old' metered poetry" of the Augustans who wrote in predetermined forms, "freedom also happens / tho a tradition precounts." When "the Augustan" writes a line of pentameter, "someone before him / is counting for him / unless it happens"—and this is a point deeply relevant to Zukofsky's imitations of earlier poets' forms, and to the translations in which he sought to capture the "literal" voice of the poets translated—"that the instant has him / completely absorbed in that someone: / a voice not a meter."[41] In its last line, the poet playfully turns this upside down: "but sometimes a meter's a voice." "Sometimes," Zukofsky explained, "you discover what you think is a measure and it's the same as that objectivist voice . . ."[42] This has nothing to do with "the *new* in the sense of *novelty*," but can be found as far back in English as Chaucer and Wyatt. The poet must write with as full as possible a knowledge of the traditions of verse form and meter, and can neither dismiss out of hand work that falls into a traditional meter nor allow a predecessor to do his "counting for him." The key, as always, lies in his awareness of music, of "silence and sound," of "how long is a rest to rest."

Other sections of "The Old Poet" are more immediately topical, from a description of a "tray," a "great copper boiler cover end" the couple had from the furnace of Celia's mother's house, which is compared to the shield of Achilles; to a contrast between the singing of Patrick, the old garbage man at Willow Street, and that of the fourteen-year-old on the floor beneath them who "wailed to her / banjo / and danced the twist" as the Zukofskys moved their cartons of books; to the touching wonder of "Tiny sarah golden" (Paul Blackburn's girlfriend), who "so taken in // by the beauties / of the suites / wondrously // assumed / her friends' new / apartment // had fabulously / called in / an interior decorator."[43]

This new apartment, as welcoming as it seemed, did not insulate Zukofsky from the world's events. In section 10, the view from the roof is contrasted with newspaper accounts of the Auschwitz doctor Josef Mengele and a scene of urban unrest in La Paz, Bolivia. In the twelfth section, Zukofsky's meditation on his own writing and his place within the poetic scene—increasingly withdrawn—is juxtaposed with the nation's current obsession, the "space race" set off by the Soviet Union's Sputnik launches. The sequence ends with a peaceful panoramic view of the new apartment, with special attention to Celia, "the caryatid of the 10th floor":

She brings me all things
the caryatid of the 10th floor . . .

the water bringing all of the continents,
the oceans
otherwhere towards the windows[44]

In his new lodgings the poet has found the space and quiet he needs
to produce his work. His windows, however, look out upon water that
brings "all of the continents" into his view. In *Bottom: on Shakespeare*
"Continents" was a metaphor for the entire tradition of the written
word, the vast archive of human thought upon which Zukofsky could
draw. The same is true here, with the addition of the immediately
particular—the correspondence of his friends ("the valentine of / the
sweet fat friend"—Robert Kelly—"so heavy he cannot carry his draw-
ers"[45]), the constant information rushing in through the newspaper,
the radio, the television. Zukofsky's aerie on Columbia Heights may
have been a refuge from the noise of the streets, but it was no ivory
tower: Rather, it was a receiving station for the vast flow of data that
would be transmuted into the ongoing movements of *"A"*.

· · ·

Zukofsky had pressed his short poems almost to a limit of occasionality in the later volumes of *ALL*, but it was not that occasionality that
persuaded him to abandon the short poem form at the end of *After I's*.
(He would, after all, continue to embody the events of the moment, in
even greater detail, in the sections of *"A"*.) More than anything else,
it was a matter of husbanding his resources, of wisely spending his
remaining time. Zukofsky was acutely aware that he was now an *old*
poet, and he had before him a daunting range of projects to complete:
the remainder of the Catullus translations, ten more movements of
"A", and, when time permitted, the "funny book" he had begun in
1950, "Little Baron Snorck."[46]

 The penultimate poem of *ALL*, "The Translation," was the last
to be composed (in 1964), and constitutes both a meditation on
Zukofsky's own phonetic translating process and an homage to Celia,
his partner in the Catullus. "Wonder / once / whence / *mulier* //
woman—"[47] it begins, and wanders through a maze of etymologies,

parallel English sounds, and Greek cognates, arriving finally at a
phrase from a biographical note on Zukofsky in a 1963 Italian anthology: The note describes *16 Once Published* as "A cura della moglie del
poeta, che ha tratto poesie"—*edited by the poet's wife* [moglie], *who has
selected the poems*.[48] And "*moglie*," Zukofsky closes the poem,

that
   would

be
   mulier
that
   would

be
   wife
that
   would

be
   soft—
a
   sleeping

breath
   sof-
t-
   t [49]

Zukofsky's short poetry would end, neither with a bang nor a whim-
per, but with a quiet acknowledgment of the central role Celia had
played in his work over the last quarter century.

Becoming a
Classic ^{1964–1966}

ROUD OF THE Jargon Society's printing of *Some Time*, Jonathan Williams was keen to publish more of Zukofsky's books,
and by 1963 was planning an inexpensive paperback reprint
of *A Test of Poetry*. He also hoped to do Zukofsky's collected short
poems. For his part, Zukofsky would have no more "small press"
eccentricities: The collection must be printed in the United States
so that he could secure lasting copyright; it must be funded by some
method other than subscription; it must be available in bookstores;
and Zukofsky *must* receive royalties on copies sold.[1] Financial matters
had begun to weigh on Zukofsky's mind. He and Celia lived for the
most part simply and thriftily, but Zukofsky felt that his own poetry
ought no longer to be a financial liability: It was time that his vocation began to *bring in* some money, rather than drawing it off. From
now on, Zukofsky would insist on being paid for his public readings;
he would resent requests for poetry from magazines that could offer
no money (though he would more often than not acquiesce to such

requests); and he would no longer be involved, either as patron or as the implicit source of "begging" letters, in the funding of his own books.

In late 1964, *Test* was reprinted by the Jargon Society in cooperation with Corinth Books, an imprint run by Ted and Eli Wilentz, owners of the Eighth Street Book Shop in New York. Corinth specialized largely in the Beat poets, but had collaborated with Williams on books by Creeley, Olson, and Zukofsky's contemporary, the visual poet Bob Brown.[2] The paperback Jargon/Corinth *Test of Poetry* was a far more striking artifact than the 1948 Objectivist Press edition had been. Its cover was "a palimpsest giving Zukofsky's sense of the poetic tradition across time and geography": there was a stanza of Sappho's Greek, Catullus's translation of the same passage "blown up from the Latin incunabula," a facsimile of the Zukofskys' working notes for the translation of the passage, a cursive rendering of Sir Philip Sidney's translation, and finally, in a modern typeface, William Carlos Williams's version of the passage.[3] Whether the cover was Jonathan Williams's or Zukofsky's idea, it did a splendid job of visually representing Zukofsky's sense of the poetic tradition as a "constant ground."

In May 1964 Denise Levertov, who had just become poetry advisor to the publisher W. W. Norton and Company, contacted Zukofsky. Norton wanted to start a poetry series, and Levertov wondered if Zukofsky was interested in their doing his "Selected, Collected, or New, poems?" The opening remarks of her letter must have struck Zukofsky with bitter irony: "I assume that your publication by noncommercial publishers has been, for many years, a matter of choice, so I won't be surprised if you say no to what I am about to propose; but I'm going to ask you anyway, because it doesn't seem right to me that the work of such a peculiar and influential poet should not be more readily available."[4]

Zukofsky was more than interested in the prospect of Norton publishing him: It was not at all by his own choice that his work had been issued by "non-commercial publishers" for so long. Within two weeks of contacting Zukofsky, Levertov had Celia's two-hundred-page typescript of the collected poems in hand, and negotiations had begun.[5] Norton initially wanted a book of no more than 160 pages, but agreed in their first draft contract to 204 pages—the length of the typescript. Celia, however, had single-spaced the poems, and the line counters at Norton protested that the printed length of *ALL* would amount to something over four hundred pages, far more than the publisher had committed to.[6]

Levertov was unremittingly enthusiastic about the project. (Her enthusiasm, she insisted to Zukofsky, had nothing to do with the fact that Creeley and Robert Duncan had been pressing her about Zukofsky for some time now.[7]) Eventually Norton and Zukofsky reached a compromise: In early 1965, Norton would publish *ALL: The Collected Short Poems 1923–1958*, which would include *55 Poems*, *Anew*, and *Barely and widely*, and six months after that—"depending on sales etc"—they could exercise an option to do *ALL: The Collected Short Poems 1956–1964*, including *Some Time*, *I's (pronounced eyes)*, and *After I's* (as yet unpublished, but under contract to be printed by Mother Press later in 1964).[8] Zukofsky broke the news to Williams gently—"By all human and humane rights this ALL shd. be your book," he told him—but he was clearly pleased with the deal, sweetened as it was by a two-hundred-fifty-dollar advance, which would buy the Zukofskys a new sofa.[9]

At almost the same time, Zukofsky achieved publication on the other side of the Atlantic. In June 1964, the English poet Nathaniel Tarn, an editor at the London firm Jonathan Cape Ltd., wrote Zukofsky to inquire about the possibility of Cape publishing his work. By mid-1965 Cape had committed to doing an English edition of *ALL*, and was very interested in also reprinting *"A" 1–12*.[10] Zukofsky gave *ALL* and *"A" 1–12* to Cape for British publication, and intimated that they had an option as well on his further work—the second volume of *ALL*, the *Catullus* when it was finished, and further installments of *"A"*; but he had also reached an agreement with Donald Rapp of another London firm, Rapp & Carroll, for the publication of his collected critical essays under the title *Prepositions*.

Prepositions was a far more compendious collection of Zukofsky's criticism than either the unpublished 1939 grouping "Sincerity and Objectification" or the 1958 *5 Statements for Poetry*. For one thing, Zukofsky had written a number of critical pieces since 1939: In addition to the major essays "Poetry / *For My Son When He Can Read*" and

"A Statement for Poetry," there were among others his reviews of Santayana's *Dominations and Powers* ("The Effacement of Philosophy") and Vivienne Koch's *William Carlos Williams* (part II of "William Carlos Williams"), his piece on the painter Dometer Guczul, and an amusing review of new books of Blake criticism ("*Golgonooza?*," in dialogue form) written for *Poetry* at the behest of Henry Rago in 1965.

Nor was this collection merely a reprinting of previously published material, as *5 Statements* had been. In his "Prefatory Note" to *Prepositions*, Zukofsky observed that "the changes from the original drafts are few—mostly omissions."[11] Those omissions, however, at least in the case of the three objectivist essays of the early 1930s—"Program: 'Objectivists' 1931," "Sincerity and Objectification: *With Special Reference to the Work of Charles Reznikoff*," and "'Recencies' in Poetry"—constituted radical alterations of the original texts. In *5 Statements*, the three objectivist essays had taken up thirty-five typescript pages; for *Prepositions*, Zukofsky ruthlessly recast them into the seven-and-a-half-page essay "An Objective." What he cut, for the most part, were topical and contextual references: Where before the objectivist essays had been documents deeply rooted in their historical moment—a moment in which Zukofsky had been striving to establish a critical program for himself and his friends, in effect to promote a "movement"—their new incarnation as "An Objective" served to generalize Zukofsky's statements of poetics, cutting them free from specific texts and the local struggles of literary politics. Once freed from such contingencies, the statements of "An Objective" could be read, not as descriptions of objectivist poetry—a term which for Zukofsky had become tainted by the recent promotions on behalf of Oppen and Reznikoff—but as descriptions of poetry in general, of a piece with "Poetry / *For My Son When He Can Read*" and "A Statement for Poetry."[12]

Other essays underwent more restrained nipping and tucking. The Henry Adams thesis, in particular, was divested of all traces of its academic origins: footnotes, bibliography, its review of previous scholarship. Zukofsky believed that "Henry Adams"'s first publication in book form was historically propitious: When he received the contract for *Prepositions*, he told Cid Corman that "Since it includes

the H. Adams"—which lingered significantly on Adams's speculations about Russia—"maybe a good omen that we'll have gotten
together with the Russians, for what it's worth, to allay some of the
madness."[13] The madness, that is, of the cold war. Zukofsky's fascination with the space race was merely one aspect of his deep-seated
worry about the ongoing struggle between the free world and the
Soviet bloc.

In keeping with the more heterogeneous nature of its contents,
the title of *Prepositions* was less specific than either "Sincerity or
Objectification" or *5 Statements for Poetry*. The "Prefatory Note"
summarized Zukofsky's sense of his criticism as a fundamentally
prepositional activity, addressed towards specific objects: "The essays
in this volume may be viewed as steps in the excursion of a poet
who wished to imbue criticism with some of the worth of his own
craft. . . . As the title *Prepositions* of this book may propose—the critic's
constant intentions to the things he discussed directed, after all, such
ways of speaking as: *for*, *with*, and *about*."[14] *Prepositions* is divided into
three sections, "For," "With," and "About," each of them characterized by the prepositional stance of its overall heading. The essays of
"With" comment upon individual figures—Pound, Williams, Cummings, Chaplin, and so forth—in the manner of a critic attempting
to think and feel along *with* each figure. The essays of "About" are
more detached assessments of ideas and bodies of work, including
Zukofsky's own: "Influence" and "Poetic Values," two paragraphs
extracted from Zukofsky's 1930 review of René Taupin's *L'influence
du symbolisme français sur la poésie américaine (1910–1920)*; the essay
on Basic English he had written for Hazeltine in 1943; "Bottom, *a
weaver*," an introduction to a public reading from *Bottom*; and the
preface to *Found Objects*. The first section, "For," condenses *5 Statements for Poetry* into three essays, and simultaneously condenses that
volume's title into a single word.

Rapp & Carroll published *Prepositions* in England in June 1967,
and soon afterwards informed Zukofsky that they had arranged
with Horizon Press of New York to release an American edition the
following year, using copies of the book printed in England.[15] Rapp
& Whiting (for Donald Carroll had left the company in fall 1967)
wanted to publish Zukofsky's poetry, but he had already committed

it to Jonathan Cape.[16] In the U.K. Zukofsky's work had acquired a clear attraction for established publishers.

The cultural upheavals of the 1960s, where Allen Ginsberg was mentioned in the same breath as Bob Dylan and the Beatles, made for an atmosphere far more welcoming to "advanced" poetry than the conformist 1950s. But Zukofsky must surely share some of the blame for the belatedness of his emergence on the trade publishing scene. Robert Creeley, for instance, had seen a collected volume of his poems issued by Scribner's as early as 1962. Years of rejections had fixed Zukofsky's attention too closely upon Laughlin's New Directions, which through the 1940s and much of the 1950s had seemed his only natural option for publishing. Though Zukofsky might complain to his closest correspondents about the policies of the large houses, there is little evidence that he ever tried to place his poetry with them. When major publication happened for Zukofsky, it came by way of publishers' solicitations: Denise Levertov, Nathaniel Tarn, and Donald Carroll approached Zukofsky, not the other way around. He might wait and he might complain, but he would do nothing to attract the attention he so desired. Perhaps there was a masochistic pleasure in the very waiting and complaining.

．　．　．

By the mid-1960s Zukofsky had established a substantial audience among American poets and readers of poetry. In January 1964 he gave a reading with Paul Blackburn at the Five Spot Café ("where Thelonious etc held out of old—I had not heard of the spot"); Ginsberg showed up with his companion Peter Orlovsky, their appearance a sure sign of Zukofsky's acceptance by the hip younger generation. ("Allen with a rose for me," Zukofsky told Corman, "which I gave to C.")[17] A week and a half later, Zukofsky read with Reznikoff at the Guggenheim Museum. Zukofsky had first seen the famous structure—one of Frank Lloyd Wright's most celebrated commissions—back in 1960, half a year after its opening: "the exterior sand color, clean sand of the unending curve of the concrete, is very lovely and where it meets the straight walls they hold together, as tho he were hiding all he knew of San Vitale," he wrote Corman; "I had no idea it would be so good, or that I'd even like it, from photographs. The light inside is gentle white. It is down on the sidewalk, crowded by other buildings, apartments, when it should be perhaps in a close clearing of woods. And the concrete—I don't know why—is already cracking. Our 'abstract' art is here quite 'ancient.'"[18]

The organizers of the event—the Academy of American Poets—had scheduled Zukofsky to read in this temple of modernity along with Reznikoff and George Oppen, but Zukofsky refused to share the stage with Oppen. Robert Kelly introduced Zukofsky in words that were both lyrical and appropriate: "If I say 'Zukofsky's music', I mean that precise handling of word sounds & word silences, the weights & durations of words, constitutes the organizing principle of the work. . . . Zukofsky's work is a miracle of precision to me. Precise apprehension is the vigor of his music. It carries to us that 'news' Dr. Williams spoke of, that news found in poems, & for lack of which men perish miserably every day."[19] The reading went well, though Zukofsky found the event almost fantastic, "so much of a dream (a word I don't like to use often) of 40 years, I must have met Rezy just about that many years ago, and now for the first time reading with him . . . and of all the fantastic phantasms a lawyer showed up with whom I had played as a kid of 4 & seen only for about 5 minutes at Columbia in my undergraduate days to ask if I'd read Fitzgerald's This Side of Paradise or something."[20]

. . .

After a little over two years in the Columbia Heights apartment Zukofsky had celebrated in "The Old Poet Moves to a New Apartment 14 Times," the Zukofskys moved house again at the end of June 1964, this time to Manhattan; it was the first time Zukofsky had lived in the borough of his birth since 1939. It looked as though Paul would leave New York for Buffalo in the fall, so the four rooms of the Brooklyn apartment would be too spacious for Louis and Celia alone; in addition, the rent was proving a burden: Zukofsky was finding "income taxes and rent more than half the salary," and there was no sign that the Poly administration would promote him to full professor.[21] Their new apartment was at 77 Seventh Avenue (Zukofsky found the string of sevens propitious), on the border of Greenwich

Village, and the vestibule of the building was decorated with "the biggest Vermeer you've ever seen"—a vast enlargement of a Vermeer painting.[22] They were happy with the L-shaped studio, and Zukofsky enjoyed the pleasurable shock of being back in Manhattan: "almost the feeling of staying at a hotel in a foreign city & when we walk (tho we tire fast) all the old streets are so new."[23]

By the summer Zukofsky had begun planning new movements of "A". He had completed "A"-13 back in 1960, and since then he had drafted several brief, occasional movements. In March 1963, he had assembled "A"-17, the "Coronal" in memory of William Carlos Williams. In October of that year, he wrote "A"-20, a "Respond for P.Z.'s tone row / at twenty."[24] Paul had turned twenty earlier that month, and had been composing music for some years. "A"-20 lists the titles of twelve pieces Paul had written, in four different orders, followed by an eight-line poem that Paul had written at nine in response to one of the poems in *A Test of Poetry*, Henry VIII's "As the holly groweth green."[25]

In May 1963, Zukofsky had written the shortest of "A"'s movements, "A"-16:

An

inequality

wind flower[26]

This little poem is something of an enigma. Its probable inspiration was a houseplant on the terrace, fighting an unequal battle against the harbor wind. But I suspect it was as well associated in Zukofsky's mind with the civil rights struggle in the South: In the notebook materials from which Zukofsky worked on "A" in 1963, the first draft of "A"-16 appears amid a series of references to the atrocities of state troopers and white supremacists in Alabama.[27]

Zukofsky gave "A"-16 to Corman for *Origin* 14, to be published in July 1964. Corman was discontinuing the magazine after that number, several issues earlier than he had expected, because of a break with his collaborator Will Petersen. *Origin*'s second series had served Zukofsky well, putting a great deal of his work into print, but when Corman started a third series of the magazine in 1966, he found Zukofsky no longer eager to send him poems. Zukofsky was diplomatic—"it'll give me more pleasure to see Origin's pages taken up by those who haven't had their chance yet," he wrote[28]—but his attention was by now wholly focused on "*A*", which Henry Rago of *Poetry* was practically serializing. *Origin* had been a pathbreaking journal in its day, but *Poetry* offered Zukofsky both payment and a far larger audience.

By mid-August of 1964, Zukofsky was back at work on "A"-14, and was hoping to finish "A"-14, -15, and -18 before the semester began.[29] Though he had been assembling material for these movements for some time, in the event he was able to complete "A"-14, "A"-15, and the first thirty-eight lines of "A"-18 only by the year's end, when he turned back to the Catullus translation.[30] The speed with which Zukofsky drafted "A"-14 and -15 (four weeks for the former, eight weeks for the latter) belied the two movements' density of reference, complexity, and grace of formal organization. At sixty Zukofsky was nearing the height of his powers as a poet—an astonishing apogee that he would sustain over the next fourteen years.

.   .   .

By Christmas 1964, Zukofsky and Celia decided that the coming semester would be his last at Brooklyn Polytechnic.[31] He had been in harness at Poly for eighteen years now, shouldering a heavy teaching load, worn out from the drudgery of talking about literature to legions of uninterested "plumbers"[32] and marking stacks of student themes. He had been continually snubbed by his administrators, passed over for promotion, denied raises, and—perhaps the last straw—denied a half-pay sabbatical for 1965–66.[33] Now, with the income from Zukofsky's pension and social security (though that would not begin until he turned sixty-two in January 1966),[34] supplemented by whatever could be brought in from his selling poems and giving readings, they felt they might just be able to get along without the Poly salary.

Zukofsky had every right to feel himself a man of letters over 1964 and 1965. In 1964 no fewer than three of his books were published:

the selection *Found Objects* in April; *After I's* in September; and the Jargon/Corinth reprint of *A Test of Poetry* in December. And he was beginning to receive reviews in venues that had never before noticed his work. The (London) *Times Literary Supplement*, which still clung to its old policy of reviewers' anonymity, published a "very careful and painstaking" review of *Bottom* in August; Reznikoff telephoned Zukofsky to read it out to him.[35] The author was the English poet Charles Tomlinson, who had for some time been in contact with Zukofsky. In late 1964 Tomlinson edited a special issue of William Cookson's journal *Agenda* devoted to Zukofsky—the first such number of any periodical.[36]

In early 1965 the *Nation* ran David Hayman's review of *Bottom*, a respectful but somewhat perplexed assessment that compared *Bottom* to Mallarmé's *Un coup de dés*, Joyce's *Finnegans Wake*, and Pound's *Cantos*, and described Zukofsky as "one of the knights of the word triumphant who have in this century discovered new uses for the path cut during the last century for art's sake."[37] More unequivocal was Gilbert Sorrentino's notice of *After I's* in the *New York Sunday Herald Tribune*: Zukofsky's "work is utterly, absolutely necessary to any serious American poet working today. He is a *major* poet. . . . To ignore him is akin to a French publisher of the time ignoring Mallarmé—yet he is ignored."[38] Zukofsky received a congratulatory phone call about the review from W. W. Norton, who seemed to take it as "a great find for advance publicity for *ALL*. . . . Now they *know*, as old Bill looking out of his deer-like eyes would have nasalized—they picked a WINNAH!"[39]

Sorrentino was himself a poet very much under Zukofsky's influence, and there was no shortage of younger poets and writers who looked to Zukofsky as a great exemplar: Creeley, Duncan, Jonathan Williams, Levertov, Corman, and Samperi, of course, but also Michael Palmer, Clark Coolidge, Theodore Enslin, Joel Oppenheimer, Kenneth Irby, Larry Eigner, and Ronald Johnson—among many others. And Zukofsky had begun to establish a presence in the academy, largely as a side effect of his relationship with Ezra Pound, whose critical "industry" was flourishing alongside that of Joyce. Since 1960 Zukofsky had been in correspondence with Hugh Kenner, a Canadian scholar who had written *The Poetry of Ezra Pound*, the first full-length study of Pound's writing, and a work that may be said to have opened the floodgates of subsequent academic criticism of Pound.[40] By 1960, Kenner was chair of the department of English at the University of California, Santa Barbara, and the author of a half dozen books, among them studies of Joyce, Wyndham Lewis, and T. S. Eliot; he had established himself as perhaps the foremost critic of modernist writing. Kenner also reviewed for *Poetry* magazine and served as poetry editor for the *National Review*, where he published Zukofsky on several occasions. Kenner was intrigued by Zukofsky's work, and just as intrigued by his connections with the great old men of the first modernist revolution, Pound and Williams. Kenner was perhaps the first scholar to visit Austin (in 1963) to examine the materials in the "Louis Zukofsky Manuscript Collection"; he was making plans for his magnum opus, *The Pound Era*, a comprehensive examination of English-language modernism in which Zukofsky's work would surely play a role—how large, it was too early to tell.[41]

Like his friend Kenner, Guy Davenport had an encyclopedic mind, wrote critical prose of rare insight and vigor, and was a dedicated student of the modernists. Like Kenner, he had paid court to Pound at St. Elizabeths—where Pound tried to set him to translating Leo Frobenius's *Paideuma*—and had visited the old poet in Italy after his release in 1958. In 1964 Davenport had taken a position at the University of Kentucky in Lexington, leaving a job at Haverford, where the year before he had met Jonathan Williams on one of Williams's periodic "barnstorming for poetry" sweeps of American campuses. That year Davenport initiated a correspondence with Zukofsky, and in July 1965 he invited Zukofsky to Lexington to take part in the University's yearlong centennial celebrations.[42] Those celebrations were well funded and multidisciplinary, and Davenport was in charge of inviting speakers in the arts and humanities, among them Kenner, the novelist Eudora Welty, the polymathic scientist and inventor Buckminster Fuller, and the filmmaker Stan Brakhage. The University offered Zukofsky a princely sum for appearing—a thousand dollars plus expenses—and Zukofsky accepted, scheduling his visit for the last week of September.

The Zukofskys' sojourn in the bluegrass state was in part a comedy of incongruities. When they arrived in their Pullman car on a warm Kentucky fall morning, Zukofsky was wearing gloves, a beret, and an overcoat with the collar turned up against possible drafts. The waitress at their hotel delighted him with her question, "Are you folks from the U.S.A.?," and served Zukofsky toast with gravy, assuming that "toast" was what a New Yorker must mean when he ordered "biscuits." A reading of *Barely and widely* at a local community college went badly, Zukofsky continually wandering away from the microphone, Davenport shepherding him back: Few in the audience heard him, and most of those who did were mystified.

Davenport, however, had prepared the students in his seminar for Zukofsky's visit, telling them they were in for a visit from a "master poet of the highest order, unrecognized by the critics or any public." Zukofsky read to them from his own poems, and he and Davenport read from the *Catullus*, Davenport reading the Latin and Zukofsky his English translations. Zukofsky spoke of Shelley, who had wasted his genius through facile and sentimental writing, and of Blake, who had preserved his by never writing down to any audience. All of the students had copies of *Bottom*. The Zukofskys left Lexington knowing that Louis's critical reputation was secure in at least one American institution of higher learning.

. . .

If he had a range of new admirers, Zukofsky had not entirely left behind the objectivist associates of his youth. With Oppen he was no longer on speaking terms. But he remained friendly with Reznikoff, now in his seventies, though the two men saw each other only rarely. In 1965 Zukofsky heard once again from Carl Rakosi. Rakosi had abandoned poetry in 1941, around the time New Directions published a selection of his verse. He did not take up writing again until April 1965, when he received a letter from the English poet Andrew Crozier praising his early poems.[43] Later that year Rakosi wrote Zukofsky, giving him news of his grandchildren and his new poems, and wondering if Zukofsky might be able to suggest a publisher, since James Laughlin would not be able to get a volume out until 1967. Zukofsky's reply was friendly but unhelpful: "I'm glad you're writing poems again—and I hope I will read them in a published volume soon. . . . I wish I could suggest whom to write to, but since my publishers never ask for suggestions I won't affront them."[44]

In spring 1963 Lorine Niedecker had married Albert Millen, moved to his Milwaukee apartment, and retired from her job cleaning hospital floors. She had discovered a new financial and emotional stability, and her correspondence with Zukofsky reflected a newfound productivity in her poetry. In 1965, inspired almost certainly by Zukofsky's abortive plans for a "letters received" collection, she began sorting through and editing the over thirty years' correspondence she had received from Zukofsky. Niedecker wanted to produce a book that would distill "just the essence, tincture of Z!, a drop to a page, that constant, deep-in spot in his being."[45] She worked several months scissoring apart and numbering autograph letters, taping the scraps to cardboard backing, and finally typing the fragments into a 370-page typescript, which she mailed to Zukofsky on September 18.[46] Zukofsky had not encouraged Niedecker in this project, and he had no inclination to tackle this massive manuscript. "As I told Lorine," he wrote Corman, "I haven't the heart nor the time for two years at least to look into that mountain of letters that I'm sure ought to be cut down to a hill—but I'm the one to do it if I allow any of 'em to appear at all. So much of it is already in my work—& the Cats and more 'A' come first."[47] Zukofsky did not want any of his letters included in the special Niedecker issue of *Origin*'s third series Corman was planning for the following summer, and he insisted that Niedecker send him the carbon copy she had retained of the letters typescript.[48]

· · ·

In August 1965, almost thirty years after he had written the work, Zukofsky's play *Arise, arise* had its first production. When Zukofsky wrote the play in 1936, he seemed to have missed the cultural moment in which it might have been produced—the moment of the first American theatrical avant-garde, when the Provincetown Players had mounted their production of Cummings's *Him*. Now, in the mid-1960s, the cultural wheel had turned full circle, and there was an efflorescence of little companies springing up at off Broadway and off-off-Broadway venues, anxious to produce the experimental dramas of such playwrights as Sam Shepard, James Schuyler, Frank O'Hara, and LeRoi Jones—all of whom were also poets. Jerry Benjamin, who directed *Arise, arise* at the Cinematheque Theatre in the Village, had the year before directed Jones's *The Baptism*, which savagely attacked American bourgeois religion and sexual mores. In these years of growing discontent over Vietnam, assaulting middle-class values was a given in the alternative theater; but *Arise, arise*, with its odd mix of emotional formalism and left-wing politics, was something else altogether. Listening to a rehearsal, Zukofsky found the words he had written three decades before "affecting," but "nothing to elate me."[49]

The opening night went well: "The actors on the whole showed great seriousness," Zukofsky wrote, "sometimes a little too palpable as to the political notes (& I never want those, as I think it would be obvious to anyone with insight, to *lecture*)—but they did prove that the insights I had then remain fresh—& what I saw then is politically being 'acted' out now."[50] Acted out, that is, in the increasing protests on American campuses against the Vietnam War. While Zukofsky had regarded the 1964 Republican Party candidate, Barry Goldwater, with undisguised fear and repugnance, he had little respect for President Lyndon Johnson, whom he called "the high school principal in the White House."[51] Zukofsky considered America's involvement in Vietnam a colossal blunder, and by October 1965 Zukofsky felt that "The only cheer in the world [is] the protests against the draft: maybe there's some point in working after all."[52] But while Zukofsky was deeply troubled by the war in Vietnam, and while he would express that disquiet in various passages of "*A*", he mostly kept his disquiet to himself, unlike such poets as Levertov and Ginsberg, for whom the war became a repeated leitmotif that threatened to drown out every other melody or voice in their poetry. Zukofsky had done his share of activism back in the 1930s; now, on the verge of old age, he preferred to devote his energies to artifacts that he trusted would have scope far beyond the present crisis.

ALL: The collected short poems 1923–1958 was released by Norton at the end of April 1965, and received a respectable number of reviews in newspapers and journals across the country. *Poetry* magazine ran two reviews of the book, as part of a special issue devoted to Zukofsky's work that also included the whole of "A"-14.[53] Charles Tomlinson's former tutor, Donald Davie, published an acute and respectful review in the *Nation*, demonstrating that Zukofsky's work could appeal even to readers of a conservative, formalist disposition.[54]

Zukofsky was beginning to experiment with luxurious, small-print-run editions of single poems, among them "Finally a Valentine" from the Piccolo Press in Gloucestershire; "An Unearthing" (the first thirty-eight lines of "A"-18) from a set of printers at Harvard; and, also from Harvard, "I Sent Thee Late," a fragment of his juvenilia that Celia felt worth saving.[55] *Iyyob*, the opening passage of "A"-15, was printed in a sumptuous chapbook by Turret Books, the press run by English poet and art critic Edward Lucie-Smith (one of its designers and printers was the poet Tom Raworth).[56] The most anomalous of these micropublications was the *"A" Libretto*, which—in a throwback to their procedure with *First Half of "A"-9* and *5 Statements for Poetry*—the Zukofskys typed and mimeographed themselves.[57] The *"A" Libretto* was a twenty-one-page anthology of excerpts from all of the movements of the poem to date. Louis and Celia had sent the typescript to Paul in October 1964, hoping that he might use it as a libretto for a composition of some sort: "probably not for uproar (opera)—all roars up to you—more oratorio?"[58]

. . .

At the end of 1965 the Zukofskys accepted an invitation to the Yaddo writers' colony at Saratoga Springs, where they hoped to complete "in silence" the last bit of the Catullus—the long and recalcitrant Carmen 64, a four-hundred-line miniature epic on the marriage of Peleus and Thetis.[59] The rural estate that made up Yaddo had been offering a retreat for writers since 1926; William Carlos Williams had stayed there, as had Zukofsky's Columbia acquaintances Clifton Fadiman and Lionel Trilling. Families were explicitly forbidden, and the Zukofskys had turned down an opportunity to visit four years earlier because of that;[60] this time, however, the administrators recognized Celia as a full collaborator on the Catullus. The translation moved along at a steady clip, with Zukofsky taking increasing pleasure at rendering Catullus's ornate verse into his own "Shixespearean grandeurs."[61] The couple had come to Yaddo on December 14 planning to return to New York on February 6, but Zukofsky's productivity kept them on until the twenty-sixth.[62] He completed the "Peliaco" (Carmen 64) on February 1, and began work on "A"-19 on February 11.[63] It was the beginning of a furious round of composition. Zukofsky would work on "A"-19 for the next three months, and even as he wrote "A"-19, he returned to "A"-18, which he had begun back in December 1964; he started the main part of the movement on March 8, and completed it a little short of seven weeks later, April 28.

By the end of May 1966, then, Zukofsky had completed twenty movements of his "poem of a life," and he and his wife had finished the Catullus translation that had occupied them for the better part of eight years. His short poems, the first half of "A", and his criticism were in print or under contract to be published. The fame that had eluded Zukofsky for so many decades now seemed within his grasp.

Translation: The "Literal" Meaning

interchapter

The translation that Louis and Celia Zukofsky finally published under the title *Catullus: Gai Valeri Catulli Veronensis Liber* was to the casual eye an extremely odd production. For James Laughlin, the effect of their versions was "somewhat monstrous, certainly not Catullus and not typical Zukofsky."[1] Both points were debatable: the Zukofskys' Catullus probably *sounded* more like the Latin poet than any previous English version; and careful readers of Zukofsky could recognize its thorny cadences, impacted syntax, and shifts of verbal register as eminently Zukofskyan. The "Peliaco," for instance, in the Zukofskys' version begins:

> Pelion could one time prong its top worthy keel in pines
> ancestor lugged clear to Neptune in his sea purr on thus
> to Phasis what flood tides on the fees of Aeetes,
> came elect young ones ace, Argive eye robe awry pubes,
> aureate time hoped on there's Colchis afar to raid pelt home,
> asea soon what deep salt sough hit at the careerer poop in
> cerulean currents abeyant knees a fir oar palm ease;[2]

—a rendering of the Latin sounds of

> Peliaco quondam prognatae vertice pinus
> dicuntur liquidas Neptuni nasse per undas
> Phasidos ad fluctus et fines Aeeteos,
> cum lecti iuvenes, Argivae robora pubis,
> auratam optantes Colchis avertere pellem
> ausi sunt vada salsa cita decurrere puppi,
> caerula verrentes abiegnis aequora palmis;

A "literal" translation, from the Loeb Classical Library edition Zukofsky used, runs thus:

> Pine-trees of old, born on the top of Pelion, are said to have swum
> through the clear waters of Neptune to waves of Phasis and the realms
> of Aeetes, when the chosen youths, the flower of Argive strength,
> desiring to bear away from the Colchians the golden fleece, dared to
> course over the salt seas with swift ship, sweeping the blue expanse
> with fir-wood blades . . .[3]

A reader with a certain amount of patience and goodwill (and a slightly ribald sense of humor) can see how much of Catullus's dictionary meaning Zukofsky has managed to reproduce in his own version, even though that version might not provide the immediate lexical aid the high school Latin student wants to smuggle under his or her desk.

The Zukofskys did not expect their Catullus to be greeted with warm approval by professional classicists, but neither did Zukofsky anticipate the anger that the translation would elicit in some quarters. In the *New Statesman*, a reviewer pronounced the translation the product of "complete lunacy" and "unbelievable crankiness." Burton Raffel wondered for whom this version of Catullus would be of *use*: "The Latinist can read Catullus in Latin: he does not need, nor presumably is he interested to read, that 'a ventum horribilium atque pestilentem' can be aped (but not translated, no) as 'o vent them horrible, I'm not quite, pestilent mm.' The non-Latinist wants to know, as well as he can, what Catullus said and how he said it. Can he get anything—*anything*—from this?" *Encounter*'s reviewer found the translation evidence of the decline of Western civilization: "The Hun is at play—worse still, *at work*—among the ruins."[4]

In their anger and almost palpable sense of personal affront, these reviewers echoed the University of Chicago Latinist William Gardner Hale, who had in 1919 attacked Ezra Pound's "Homage to Sextus Propertius": "If Mr. Pound were a professor of Latin, there could be nothing left for him but suicide . . ."[5] Like Hale half a century before, Zukofsky's reviewers had fundamentally misunderstood the method and intentions of the translation before them; and like Hale—but with far less excuse—they had willfully ignored the modernists' revolution in poetic translation.

Early on Pound had asserted the importance of poetic translation: "A great age of literature," he wrote around 1916, "is perhaps always a great age of translations." He was discussing Renaissance translations of the classics—Gavin Douglas's *Aeneid*, Christopher Marlowe's *Amores*, Arthur Golding's *Metamorphoses*, George Chapman's Homer—within the explicit context of his own nascent drive to "break with tradition," to "desert the more obvious imbecilities of one's immediate elders."[6] Poetic translation was, early and late, an integral part of Pound's renovation of English verse: from his early Provençal lyrics, through the Anglo-Saxon "Seafarer" (1911), the Japanese Noh plays (1914–15), the Chinese poems of *Cathay* (1915), the "Homage to Sextus Propertius" (1919), to his later versions of Confucius's *Classic Anthology* and the plays of Sophocles.[7]

For Pound, the goal of poetic translation was not to provide an English-speaking reader the "meaning" or lexical sense of the original poem; rather, the translator's task lay in the creation of a new poem that somehow brought the power, the *virtù*, of the original over into English—a *virtù* far more important than the dictionary meaning of the original. In order to bring the power of a poem into English, to create an impact on the reader commensurate with that which the poem might have had on its original auditors, Pound used a variety of archaisms in his own English; he sought to reproduce complex and unfamiliar foreign verse forms; and most importantly, he refused to be bound by contemporary rules or norms of English verse. Pound layered languages and contexts. "Homage to Sextus Propertius," in large part a translation of the Latin poet, was also a commentary on post–Great War London, and was sprinkled with playful "translatorese" and outright anachronisms. Canto I was a translation of the *nekuia* (the descent into Hell) of *Odyssey* 11, rendered in an alliterative, accentual verse Pound adapted from the Old English; not a translation from Homer's Greek, either, but from a sixteenth-century Latin crib, which Pound saw as emblematic of the Renaissance revival of classical learning.

Like Joyce, Pound was a gifted linguist: He had studied some eight foreign languages, and was quite at home in at least five of them.[8] Zukofsky had nowhere near Pound's facility with tongues; more importantly, however, he evolved a conception of the aims and bases of poetic translation that was fundamentally different from Pound's. Pound's translational practice, however much it went against the grain of contemporary superstition, could be traced back to an older tradition, what Ben Jonson called poetic "imitation," the poet's ability "to convert the substance or riches of another *Poet*, to his owne use. . . . Not, to imitate servilely, as Horace saith, and catch at vices, for vertue: but, to draw forth out of the best, and choicest flowers, with the Bee, and turne all into Honey . . ,"[9] Pound's translations took their place, then, not with the prose "ponies" of the Loeb Classical Library, but with Fitzgerald's *Rubaiyat of Omar Khayyam* and Samuel Johnson's "The Vanity of Human Wishes" and "London" (both based on Juvenal). Imitation, however, was not Zukofsky's aim in his translations, which represent a radical rethinking of the act of poetic translation and a further development of Zukofsky's own poetics of cultural "recurrence."

· · ·

The notion of translation at which Zukofsky ultimately arrived no doubt reflected his own relationship, if not to language itself, then to the phenomenon of *languages*. Zukofsky was born, as it were, in the interstices between tongues. His parents and immediate family spoke Yiddish; in the streets where he grew up, he would have heard Yiddish, English, and a rich variety of other languages. The neighborhood bullies for whom he recited the Yiddish *Hiavatha* themselves probably spoke Italian at home. The first language Zukofsky *studied* was the English he learned in the public schools, and such a late exposure to what would be his primary tongue must have given him a deep-seated sense of the ambiguity of language itself, of the inherent *translatability* of words. More important was the sense he had that language, before it was a vocabulary, a grammar, a system of words represented by various marks on paper, was a system of physical *sounds*, a set of articulated grunts and cries that varied from one community to another, but that always found its source in the speaker's *body*.

Over the course of his career, Zukofsky translated from a wide variety of languages. In some of them, such as Yiddish and German, he might have been near fluent; in others—French, Italian—he had a competent reading knowledge. In Greek, Latin, and Hebrew, his grasp was shakier, always propped up with various "ponies." In yet others, like Welsh, he probably would have been able to make nothing of a street sign or a menu. Despite this wide disparity of "commands," the act of translating was central to Zukofsky's poetic art, and this centrality was one mark of his participation in a modernist move-ment in which one of the poet's goals was to revivify contemporary verse by drawing new strengths from alien sources.

Such is clearly the case with Zukofsky's earliest poetic translations, versions of the Yiddish poems of "Yehoash," Solomon Bloomgarden. In their context—"Poem beginning 'The'" and "A"-4—it is clear that these translations are in part meant as publicity for Yehoash, utterly unknown outside of Yiddish-speaking literary circles. In "A"-4, Zukofsky Englishes a passage of Yehoash's in which the Yid-dish poet takes on a Japanese voice:

> Der regen blezelt sich in shtillen vasser.
>> Kuk ich vee dee ringen shpreyten sich fanander:
> Shimauneh-Sān, du Sumurai blasser,
>> Ven vestu kum'n fun din vaiter vander?
>> Shimauneh-Sān, mein heller shtern . . .[10]

In Zukofsky's English:

> Rain blows, light, on quiet water
>> I watch the rings spread and travel
> Shimaunu-Sān, Samurai
>> When will you come home?—
>> Shimaunu-Sān, my clear star.[11]

This is competent translation, and poetry of a quiet beauty, but Zukofsky has not yet moved beyond a "period style"—the orientalism of Pound's *Cathay*.

In the early 1930s Zukofsky was involved in translation on a purely practical basis. He translated several essays from René Taupin's French for publication in American periodicals, and for one of them he translated some passages of André Salmon's verse. Zukofsky's work on *The Writing of Guillaume Apollinaire* resulted in a few translations from that poet. Zukofsky's translation of a German biography of Albert Einstein was pure drudgery, work so indifferent to him that he asked that his name as translator be omitted from the published book. In the early 1940s, when Zukofsky was involved with *La France en Liberté* and the exiled French literary community, he translated a few poems by Alain Bosquet and rendered a *ballade* by the fourteenth-century Guillaume de Machault.[12] All of these were occasional performances, and reflected nothing of the commitment to translation as a central poetic act that characterized Pound's ceaseless renderings of foreign texts.

Zukofsky's deepest involvement in translation did not begin until 1958, when he and Celia embarked upon their complete Catullus.[13] Catullus was in many ways a natural choice for Zukofsky, a comfortable "persona" to take on—since, as Pound had shown, the translator-poet was always to some degree putting on the mask of the poet translated. Gaius Valerius Catullus (84–54 BCE) was a quintessentially urban poet. "Contemporary New York," Guy Davenport has remarked, "is probably as close an historical rhyme to Catullus' Rome as we are likely to find";[14] for Zukofsky, Catullus was a fellow city-dweller, a "guy," as he called him in numerous letters—*Gai*. Catullus's poems include both passionate, much-anthologized love poems and spectacularly obscene flytings: the sort of poems Zukofsky, who had called himself the "Manhattan Mauler," who had written a poem beginning "Send regards to Ida the bitch," and who embedded the names of personal enemies and despised public figures into the dense texture of the later movements of *"A"*, would have been happy to have written.[15]

Catullus was not just a lover and a literary brawler, however, but a learned, exquisitely sophisticated poet, whose work showed great affinities with the work of such Hellenistic poets as Callimachus in its dense, ornate diction and complex web of references to earlier texts: a poetics, one might venture, quite akin to Zukofsky's. And Catullus, however much his poetry might reflect the realities of Julius Caesar's Rome, was not himself a Roman; he was a native of Verona, an outlander who had come to Rome at the age of eighteen, and a poet who would always carry himself with a sense of unease among Roman natives—just as the Jewish Zukofsky would always labor at a disadvantage in a literary culture of poets bearing the venerable New England names of Eliot and Lowell.

The Zukofskys' version of Catullus, as they announce in the "Translators' Preface," follows "the sound, rhythm, and syntax of his Latin—tries, as it is said, to breathe the 'literal' meaning with him." Or as the "Poet's Preface" has it, "This version of Catullus aims at the rendition of his sound."[16] There is some precedent for this in Pound's translations—"The Seafarer" had attempted to reproduce the rhythms and alliterative patterns of the Anglo-Saxon original, resorting occasionally to homophonic puns that uncharitable critics called "howlers"—but for the most part the Zukofskys' procedure is entirely new, and indicates a radical shift from earlier conceptions of the goal of a poetic translation.

For Pound, the goal of translation was a transference of affect: The poem should strike the present reader in some way similar to how it struck its original audience. Zukofsky clearly is interested in such an effect, but he seeks to achieve it by working back to the most basic properties of words—their sounds, their weights and measures as human utterances. Zukofsky well knew that the composing poet as often as not attends first and foremost to the music of the verse, and worries about the "meaning" later. Before poems are marks on paper, before they are lines and stanzas, and even before they are expressions of meaning, they are sequences of human breath modulated into patterns of sound.

"So much of the word," Zukofsky said in 1968, "is a physiological thing," an affair of the body: "I like to keep the noises as close to the body as possible, so that (I don't know how you'd express it mathematically) the eye is a function of the ear and the ear of the eye . . ."[17] Poetry is for Zukofsky largely a somatic affair, a matter of the poet's making sounds through his physical organs. As a sort of mental experiment, Zukofsky argues in "A Statement for Poetry," one can imagine language divorced from meaning, a purely aural "movement of sounds":

> It is this musical horizon of poetry (which incidentally poems perhaps never reach) that permits anybody who does not know Greek to listen and get something out of the poetry of Homer: to 'tune in' to the human tradition, to its voice which has developed among the sounds of natural things, and thus escape the confines of time and space, as one hardly ever escapes them in studying Homer's grammar.[18]

In other words, by reproducing the sounds of Catullus's Latin in his translation, Zukofsky allows the English-speaking reader to "tune in" to the Roman poet's voice, to experience an essential aspect of Catullus's poetry that a more conventional translation would ignore altogether. The translation attempts to "breathe with" Catullus; as we read it, we breathe with Catullus as well, and find our own lungs, lips, and vocal cords reproducing the movements of those of a poet two thousand years dead.

.   .   .

Zukofsky was to put the technique of homophonic translation he had pioneered in his and Celia's *Catullus* to increasing use in the years to come: translation by sound, that is, became one of the foundations of Zukofsky's later poetic technique. In "A"-21, largely a translation of Plautus's play *Rudens* (*The Rope*), Zukofsky applied a modified version of his Catullus technique, cramming each hexameter line of Latin verse into a single five-word English line, at the same time attempting to preserve as much of the Latin sound as possible. Modifying this formal goal, however, were the pressures of the dramatic form: Zukofsky wanted to achieve an English *Rudens* that was, if not playable, at least readable as a dramatic script. To an even greater degree than *Catullus*, which was salted with English vernacular from the fifteenth century onward, "A"-21 makes use of English and American slang; it is the hippest, most identifiably "Sixties-ish" of Zukofsky's poems. The last movements of "*A*", "A"-22 and -23, are vast collages, much of which consists of material homophonically translated—"transliterated," as the critics have taken to saying—from foreign texts: Latin, Greek,

Hebrew, French, Provençal, Spanish, and who knows what else. The eighty-one short poems of Zukofsky's last collection, *80 Flowers*, are similar concatenations on an even more compressed scale.

When one acknowledges that Zukofsky's primary aim in translation is to carry over the sound of the original text, the question of preserving the original's lexical *meaning* does not vanish, but rather reappears in a new light—as one of the manifold challenges such a procedure presents. Homophonic translation, that is, can be seen as one of the progressively more complex formal systems Zukofsky imposed upon himself over the course of his career, "rules all but impossible to keep" (in Guy Davenport's phrase): writing seven sonnets for "A"-7; composing an eightfold "mirror fugue" for "A"-8; preserving the meter and rhyme scheme of Cavalcanti's "Donna mi priegha" while using phrases from *Das Kapital* and *The Ethics* ("A"-9); shoehorning Plautus's hexameters into still-comprehensible five-word lines ("A"-21); writing thousand-line geological and literary histories of the world ("A"-22 and -23). To write over a foreign text is to use that text as a formal template for a new English poem; the difference between this and traditional literary translation is that Zukofsky's primary adherence to the original is on the level of sound, rather than dictionary meaning, rhetoric, or movement of thought.

When Zukofsky translates a text in a language closely related to English, a language with a high proportion of English cognates—Latin, as in *Catullus* or "A"-21, or French, as in the Mallarmé passages of "A"-19—he is able to hew more or less closely to the dictionary meaning of the original. The *Catullus* translations can be mapped onto the conventional translators' meaning of Catullus: They make "sense" in ways that are directly related to the Latin original. When Zukofsky works with a language further removed from English the results become stranger, further both from the original text's dictionary meaning and from the norms of conventional English.

The magnificent "Iyyob" passage at the beginning of "A"-15 is from the book of Job (Iyyob). The transliteration of sounds is remarkably close to the original, as several Hebrew readers have attested, but the "meaning" goes far astray: "Brine I hear choir and weigh by care—/ Why your ear would call by now Elohim" translates phrases of Job 28.7, in the King James Version, "When the morning stars sang together, and all the sons of God shouted for joy . . ."[19] All that remains of the dictionary meaning is the "choir" of morning stars or sons of God and (for the reader who recognizes one of the Hebrew divine names) "Elohim." When Zukofsky begins "Bearded Iris" (from *80 Flowers*) "Gay ore geek con candlelows," the first four words transliterate the title of Virgil's *Georgics*—in the Greek, *Georgicon*.[20] But the dictionary meaning of Virgil's title—"poems having to do with farming"—has been entirely lost in this strange series of English words.

Early in "A"-23 is an eleven-line passage of baffling transliteration, beginning

Ye nó we see hay
io we hay we see
hay io we sée no
we see knee (windsong bis)[21]

In his manuscript, Zukofsky noted beside these lines, "Arapaho Song (tuned sounds not words— peyote cult?)." At this point, Zukofsky's homophonic translation has reached a zero degree of formal constraint but unlimited semantic potential: By transliterating words that even in their home language have no intrinsic meaning—that are merely "tuned sounds"—Zukofsky can generate an English text whose sound is wholly based on a preexisting template, but whose meaning is entirely indeterminate. It is at this "musical horizon of poetry" (as he had earlier called it) that Zukofsky turns aside, refusing to impart an English semantic complexity to an original that is only "tuned sounds." The Arapaho song of "A"-23, while it might make use of common English words ("we," "see") and gesture towards the "iô" of Greek ecstatic song, is for the most part like its original, a series of enthusiastic but meaningless sounds. But as we read it—and this was Zukofsky's intention—we breathe and chant along with its original performers (whether or not we choose to enhance our performance with peyote).

Even when he was working with a text whose meaning he only tenuously grasped, Zukofsky took the task of translation as an act of homage, a tribute paid to a previous voice. In his roman à clef *Little / for careenagers*, the character Dala (who represents Zukofsky) is continually puttering away at a series of phonetic translations from

the Welsh. Zukofsky himself began these translations at the suggestion of Jon Price, whom he had met at a reading at Yale University in
March 1967; Price had sent him a copy of some classic Welsh poems
from Gwyn Williams's *Introduction to Welsh Poetry*, along with a note:
"I thought you might like to try your hand at these."[22] The bits of
Welsh poetry that appear throughout *Little* were clearly a self-mock-
ing version of the Catullus translations, a series of English versions
even more crabbed and distant from conventional English than
the Catullus. Dala's version of a passage from the *Black Book of Car-
marthen*, for instance:

> O T'd aerie too hid *his* Strad
> dear is 'nt rue cade weary cad
> m' need awe ah gnaw nim (bl') gad[23]

The "Strad" perhaps refers to the character Little's violin playing,
but any other connection between these lines and their immediate
context within the novel, and any clear English sense within the
lines themselves, are hard to come by. The character Dala himself
calls these translations "welshings," perhaps in the sense of "cheats"
or "fakes":[24] They represent playful, off-the-cuff versions of what
Zukofsky and Celia, with infinite pains, had spent almost eight years
doing with Catullus.[25]

But while the flashes of Welsh in *Little* might seem mere whimsy,
jokes at the expense of a character who is the epitome of the preoccupied, craft-obsessed poet, Dala himself—Zukofsky's stand-in—sees
them in a more sober light. They are expressions of affection for his
aged friend Gwyn Yare, "whose memory of youth was one extended
eisteddfod": "Dala moved to compassion by the wide back span
of the old man's uplifted head longed to master more than a little
Welsh—thinking: if only he could render its sounds in English that
made sense, and repay and delight his friend with loyalty in kind."[26]
This passage points to something fundamental to all of Zukofsky's
acts of translation: No matter how idiosyncratic or willful the products of those translations might seem, Zukofsky always approaches
a previous text with an attitude of *loyalty*.

"A"-22, "A"-23, and *80 Flowers*, the culminating achievements of
Zukofsky's writing career, are largely composed of passages either

quoted from English-language sources or translated—both conventionally and homophonically—from foreign texts; they represent deeply condensed versions of the same sort of cultural collage Zukofsky had essayed in *Bottom: on Shakespeare*'s "Graph of Culture." They are the stringing together not so much of cultural touchstones in the manner of Pound as of bright and resonant instances of language Zukofsky has come across in his reading. Translation, whether conventional or transliterative, is in this context always an instance of the other practice central to Zukofsky's poetics: *quotation*. To quote is to acknowledge that another has already said what one wants to say, and to bring that saying and that speaker to life in one's own verse. To translate is similarly an acknowledgment of the other's voice, an attempt to "escape the confines of a time and place" and bring that voice to life for (or *through*) a contemporary reader.

Translation was central to Zukofsky's poetics because it allowed him to embody in the movements of words and sounds the patterns of recurrence that constituted the history of human culture. "The horse," he wrote in "A"-12, "sees he is repeating / All known cultures / And suspects repeating / Others unknown to him . . ." Poetry itself, Zukofsky believed, was made up of repeated motifs: "All art," Zukofsky would tell an interviewer, "is made, I think, out of recurrence."[27] Only through quotation, and through its more specialized subsidiary, translation, could the poet hope to hint at the magnificent echo chamber that was his conception of the human cultural order.

"A"-13 through "A"-20

WHILE ZUKOFSKY had come to think of "*A*" as a "poem of a life," he did not feel compelled to work on the poem at any regular pace; the movements came when they needed to come, called up by circumstance or inner need, on no set schedule. "A"-16, -17, and -20, which Zukofsky wrote relatively quickly in 1963, were each called forth by a specific occasion: "A"-17, the "Coronal," by the death of William Carlos Williams in 1963; "A"-20 by Paul Zukofsky's twentieth birthday; and "A"-16—as I have speculated—by the news of the civil rights struggle in Alabama in spring 1963. He began a final push in late 1965, when the Catullus translations were almost complete.

It is appropriate to consider the eight movements of "*A*" Zukofsky drafted between 1960 and 1966—"A"-13 through "A"-20—as a single block, for in them Zukofsky arrives at a poetic idiom related to but distinct from that of the earlier movements: what one might call "mature Zukofsky" (in contradistinction to the "late Zukofsky" of "A"-22 and -23 and *80 Flowers*).[1] Mature Zukofsky telescopes or condenses the poetics that characterized "A"-8 or "A"-12: It is a continuously flowing texture of often oblique syntax, the immediate personal observation shifting to the historical or literary reference, quotations from friends and family members cheek by jowl with quotations from the newspapers and the classics, moods shifting from the somber to the whimsical, all unified by a single controlling consciousness, an "arranger" (to borrow a term from Joyce criticism) who occasionally speaks in his own voice, but who is just as comfortable expressing himself through a collage of previous texts. Like Joyce, Zukofsky arrived at an ideal of the literary work as a pattern of cunningly worked repetitions, a maze of varied and repeated motifs. In reading *"A"*, one attends to the most minute repetitions and continuities, trusting—and then discovering—that they provide the keys to deeper and more comprehensive patterns.

"A"-14, "A"-18, and "A"-19 are all composed of word-counted lines, the prosody Zukofsky had first essayed in the 1962 elegy "Atque in Perpetuum A.W." As Zukofsky told Creeley in 1964, "I'm counting words—just realizing that's been the life's intention in this game (& now that I'm conscious of it to make it sound as if that thought never occurred to me)."[2] To measure his lines by counting words, Zukofsky realized, was the prosody he had always been working towards: a metric of minimal constraints but enormous flexibility, upon which he could erect whole armatures of additional method—the transliteration of foreign texts, the mosaic-like collaging of quotations, the numerologically significant choices of how many stanzas, how many lines per stanza, how many words per line—a metric that allowed him all of the rhythmic and accentual freedoms of "free" verse, yet still bound his lines in the formal structure that he believed was of the essence to poetry.

In 1973, the English magazine *Agenda* printed the responses of ten American poets to its questionnaire "on rhythm." In response to the last question, *"Do you pay any attention in your metrical work to length as opposed to stress of syllable or to syllable count?,"* Zukofsky had written, "All 3 as (or since) I count words: cf. H.J.'s preface to *The Golden Bowl* (N.Y. edition) . . ."[3] In James's words, "the painter of the picture or the chanter of the ballad (whatever we may call him) can never be responsible *enough*, and for every inch of his surface and note of his song . . ."[4] For Zukofsky, himself a "chanter of the ballad" who believed he could "never be responsible *enough*" for every "note of his song," the word count prosody gave him "the most instead of least to answer for," the responsibility to pay attention not merely to number of words, but to length of syllable (what the prosodists call "quantity"), syllable stress, and number of syllables. While Zukofsky had carried out his share of formal experiments over the years—the sonnets of "A"-7, the sestina "'Mantis,'" the canzoni of "A"-9, and even the calculus of sounds in "A"-8 and -9—in the word count line he had arrived at his truest and final form, and he would continue counting words for the rest of his writing life.

. . .

"A"-13's first page announces that this long movement is a partita, a composition in various formally disparate parts; Zukofsky had told Corman early in the movement's composition that his formal model was Bach's Second Partita for Solo Violin, in D Minor.[5] Zukofsky had been hearing that composition, one of the great pieces in the violin repertoire, a good deal lately—Paul was practicing it that summer in preparation for another Carnegie Hall recital early in 1961. Bach's partita consisted of five dance-form movements—*allemande*, *courante*, *sarabande*, *gigue*, and *chaconne*—and Zukofsky conceived of his own five movements as somehow related to Bach's, though he had no strict parallels in mind.[6]

The first section comes in spare, three-line stanzas, and takes on the voice of the sententious father giving advice to his son, as though the poet at fifty-six had become Polonius: "A daughter has her mother's virtues / Everybody has enemies / The sick want company // Inheritances are not worth the hope." The poem lingers on the contents of the Zukofskys' home—a whole range of tchotchkes, "glass earrings / In the black snuff box // that was your father's mother's / Heirloom"—and quotes a letter from Pound—"*Thanks / for passover delicacies / specially the black bambino*."[7] Throughout the section, Zukofsky moves among the realms of the domestic, the larger world, and the discourses of moral philosophy.

The second section begins with a parody of Psalm 68, "Why hop ye, ye high hills?":

Why hop ye so, ye little, little hills?
And wherefore do ye hop?
It is because to us today, there
Comes the lord bis*hop*.[8]

(It continues with increasingly silly rhymes on "skip" / "bis*hip*"
and "up" / "bis*hup*.") The section's musical parallel is the *courante*
movement of Bach's partita, which means "flowing," appropriately
enough, given that the section's setting is the Brooklyn Esplanade,
where Zukofsky and his son sit and watch the harbor. They have visited 12th Street in Manhattan and walked all the way home, crossing the Brooklyn Bridge: "My lean old shanks hurt," Zukofsky
complains.[9] Much of section ii is a dialogue between Louis and Paul—
commenting on what they see from the Esplanade, rambling through
the semirandom associations of two clever, sometimes cynical inter-
locutors who well know each other's eccentricities.

The section as a whole is a tribute to Zukofsky's New York, an
affectionate tour through his own memories of the city and the literary and historical associations those memories evoke. Zukofsky,
at this peaceful moment, hopes for peace in the world at large, and
perhaps sees a presentiment of it in Khrushchev's September 1959
visit to the U.S. Zukofsky quotes a number of Khrushchev's pungent
sayings, especially "Even an animal / If you feed him becomes kind";
the Russian's "peasant parables," he hoped to Corman, would have
an "effect on diplomatic gibberish: everybody, even the stupidest will
stutter but talk peace."[10]

The competition between superpowers that threatened domestic peace was emblematized, for Zukofsky, in the space race, whose
immediate target was the moon. As section ii ends, Zukofsky and his
son stand before their apartment door, reading the mail and reflecting
on the Soviet moon probe "Lunik Three / (the third) / Which is now
nearer / The moon certainly / Than either to Moscow or New York."
The section ends with Zukofsky's intentionally awkward translation
of a thirteenth-century English poem on the Man in the Moon:

Man in the moon stand and stride
On his forked goad the burden he bears
It is a wonder that he does not slide,
For doubt lest he fall he shudders and sheers.[11]

It would not be Zukofsky's final comment on the space race, which fascinated and terrified him.

"A"-13's third section is a nocturne of sorts, the poet's meditations after his son has gone to bed. The section moves comfortably among the immediate events of the poet's life and the furniture of his mind: his memories, anecdotes collected who knows where, books read and passages remembered—all coming back to his happiness and satisfaction in the domestic:

> If I collect these things to live
> It is that I think my eyes, ears and mind are still good.
> If I quote it is myself I have seen
> Coming back to learn conveniently from one book:
> *It is not night when I do see your face.*[12]

There is a pervasive air of the Orient in section iii; perhaps instigated by Pound's interest in Confucianism, Zukofsky had grown more and more to identify with Asian thinkers and Asian aesthetics.

Section iv corresponds to the *gigue*, or jig, in Bach's Partita, and perhaps Zukofsky meant his spare quatrains to evoke the rhythm of that dance. It is an inventory of the contents of Zukofsky's wallet, and also an inventory of his life: "five / owned / snapshots"; a label from Paul's violin; a blank check and various addresses and phone numbers, "all written / mi- / nus- / cule on odd // scrap paper." All of this matter, "carefully / hy- / phen- / ated,"

> pours
> in
> the measure
>
> maze I planned
> song
> long
> since and that
>
> would not be
> hur-
> ried[13]

—a reference, one assumes, to the tiny scrap of paper on which Zukofsky wrote the earliest plan for "*A*" back in 1927, and which he carried in his wallet for decades after.[14]

The fifth and final section of "A"-13 begins with the view from the "five contiguous windows" of the Zukofskys' tenth-floor Willow Street apartment, and slowly moves, like a camera eye, over the roofs of the neighborhood, to the "water hidden and open below" of the harbor, to Manhattan, "the fantastic island / To the North / That but for a little green / Is entirely buildings / And pavement . . ."[15] The poet's consciousness has become almost wholly *eye*, an observer that makes the familiar sights of the cityscape strange by dwelling upon their visible details. The Empire State Building "watch[es] over" the city "As tho it were / A bestiary / Whose crowned fable / Of animal / That goes up / Is its bullet head," and Zukofsky imagines the skyscraper's searchlight shooting miles away into the countryside, where it lights "the nights / Of the young in the woods."[16] The poem, however, draws back from this outreaching "Radius," withdraws into the immediate domestic scene, Louis and Celia together at night:

Or two, three
Numerous
Only the image of a voice:
Love you.[17]

Like "*A*"'s previous two movements, "A"-13 starts from and returns to the scene of the family, the unit that had become the basis of all of Zukofsky's creative endeavors.

. . .

Literary critics have made much of Zukofsky's turn to—or even "retreat" to—the domestic in the second half of "*A*". For some, this emphasis on the family unit served to push the poetry into the realm of the hermetic, of private utterances intended for an audience of two, rather than for a more general readership. Other critics have regretted Zukofsky's "abandonment" of the explicit political argumentation of much of the first half of "*A*". But Zukofsky's long poem, from its very inception, was concerned with the family, with the sources of the self: "the courses we tide from" ("*A*"-4).[18] However much the first half of the poem had involved itself in the world of left-wing politics, it had more importantly been a portrait of the poet himself, in which his mother, his father, his friends, and his personal relationships had all played important roles. Zukofsky had sought to define his poetics within a Marxist conception of labor, but he had from the beginning also located his writing within the framework of Spinoza's ethics, whose linchpin was *love*. When Zukofsky eventually found himself rooted in a household of musicians, it was only natural that he would turn his attention from the frustrating world of class politics to the richer, more imaginatively satisfying realms of his small apartment: his books, his wife's and son's scores, Paul's violin, Celia's piano.

The three-person circle of his family was not a cell to which Zukofsky confined himself, but a base from which his imagination could range across the centuries and the continents. The newspaper and television brought him the news of the day, and far more enduring accounts of the actions of humanity were at hand in Gibbon, Plutarch, Henry Adams, and in books of poetry, in Pound's phrase the "news that stays news." For Zukofsky, the domestic was never only domestic, but always opened out upon its broader historical moment, and from there upon the universal. When he wrote, his immediate audience was of course his family, but his ultimate audience was a community of readers across the years. Perhaps he can be forgiven for failing to take into account the "literary" readers of his own day, who had already repaid his labors with several decades of quiet indifference.

. . .

Zukofsky wrote the thirteen-hundred-odd lines of "A"-14 in just a little over a month, but the notes upon which he drew for the movement dated back as early as August 1961. If his notes looked disorderly— quotations from his reading, things he had heard on television or seen in the paper, sayings of Paul's or Celia's—Zukofsky's method was systematic. He made his notes on tiny sheets of looseleaf paper in a ring binder, and then would sift those notes into the working draft of the movement at hand, which he wrote on the verso pages of a spiral notebook (the recto were reserved for a clean copy, suitable for Celia's typing). When he had finished a given movement, he removed the looseleaf sheets from the ring binder for filing, replacing them with clean pages. For "A"-13, he would jot next to a passage the number of the section of the movement into which it would go; when that bit of verse had been drafted, he crossed out the notebook passage. (In the case of "A"-18 and -19, which he worked at simultaneously from the same set of source notes, he would write an "18" or "19" beside each passage used before striking it through.)

The bulk of "A"-14 consists of three-line stanzas, most of them of either two- or three-word lines. There are exceptions, of course, lines of one or four words, and irregular stanzas: like any sensitive poet, Zukofsky did not enslave himself to his chosen form, and did not hesitate to violate it when he saw fit. The movement is subtitled "beginning *An*" (a nod backwards to "Poem beginning 'The'")—and its first word is indeed "An"; a few stanzas further on, "A"-14 announces itself as "*First of / eleven songs / beginning An*."[19] The poem itself had begun with "A", and "an" is but a variant of "a," the indefinite article placed before a word beginning with a vowel. Each of the remaining movements would begin with the word (or syllable) "an," another one of the formal constraints Zukofsky used to underline the coherence of his work.

"A"-14 begins with yet another meditation on the space program, then shifts through a dizzying array of Zukofskyan source texts, all somehow transmuted to fit the music of his lean, short stanzas. There are transliterated passages from the Psalms' Hebrew, bits of a biography of Bach, some smatterings of Montaigne, and—most strikingly—a run of fifty-seven continuous stanzas distilled from Milton's *Paradise Lost*.[20] Pound had dismissed Milton as a baleful influence on English poetry, and Eliot had also deplored the Puritan poet's rolling periods and Latinate syntax. Zukofsky himself had had few good words for Milton (*Samson Agonistes* made it into *A Test of Poetry* largely as an example of good verse overcome by rhetoric[21]), but he had little control over what texts he was to teach at Poly. One of the few things he managed to accomplish when teaching Milton in spring 1963 was "to get the *meat* out of *Paradise Lost*, about 2 solid pages of the 12 books for future 'A' perhaps."[22] Those "2 solid pages" are spread out, in six-word stanzas, over six pages of "A"-14, and provide a fascinating insight into Zukofsky's working methods, his sense that the "meat" of Milton was not the stormy rhetoric that so delighted the Romantics, but lay buried deep beneath layers of windy verbiage.

Also incorporated into "A"-14 are several passages from Joseph Conrad's *Heart of Darkness*. Conrad's 1899 novel was a stark parable of race relations, showing the savagery implicit within ostensibly "civilized" Western culture, and for Zukofsky it appeared an appropriate commentary on the violence directed at southern civil rights protestors.[23] In close proximity to a set of Conrad quotations, "A"-14 alludes to the May 1963 Birmingham marches where protestors were swept "down / by pressure / hoses, the // cutting streams / strip[ping] the / bark off // trees," and the September bombing of the 16th Street Baptist Church, where "four / little girls" died.[24]

The events of the history through which he was living fascinated, repelled, and sometimes amused Zukofsky, from "The voice of / episcopal goldwasser Polyuria" (Barry Goldwater) to the gallows humor with which the Russians regarded nuclear war: "In fallout / shroud yourselves calmly / walk, avoid panic."[25] History cast him back upon the old texts that had sustained him so long—Shakespeare in particular—and prompted him to recollect his own American experience ("A"-14 is peppered with Zukofsky's childhood memories) as a first-generation American approaching the literature and culture of a nation that, it was now clear, had in 1904 barely begun to confront its own deepest divisions.

. . .

History made its mark perhaps most clearly and coldly in "A"-15, which Zukofsky began a couple of weeks after he finished "A"-14, and completed two months later.[26] This, after the muted tributes of "Finally a Valentine" and "After reading, a song," is Zukofsky's poem of mourning for John F. Kennedy. It is also a poem of mourning for Bill Williams, who had died the spring before Kennedy: "he would / miss," Zukofsky comments laconically, ambiguously, "living thru / the assassination."[27] The movement opens with "An / hinny / by / stallion / out of / she-ass," forty lines of transliterated Hebrew from the book of Job: "He neigh ha lie low h'who y'he gall mood / So roar cruel hire . . ."[28] For the most part, this "Iyyob" passage adapts the words of the Lord, speaking to Job out of the whirlwind. But while the

388

deity's words in the Bible can be read as providing cold comfort to Job, who has lost his possessions, his children, and his health, Zukofsky's transliteration of them gives the impression less of divine providence than of sheer, inarticulate lament.

The two objects of Zukofsky's lamentation weave around one another in "A"-15: Williams, the great poet of the American vernacular, "aged in a suburb," who would never—unlike the other poet who had died that year, Robert Frost—be an "international / emissary / at least not / for his President"; and Kennedy, whose death "the nation / a world / mourned / three days in / dark and in / daylight / glued to / TV."[29] Much of "A"-15's treatment of Kennedy's death addresses its public aspects—the grim pomp of the funeral, the nation's collective shock and grief, the expressions of sympathy from around the world—but Zukofsky permits himself a moment of uncharacteristic straightforwardness to recall his own poetic relations with the president:

> *Finally a valentine*
> before his death
> had he asked for it
> I should have inscribed to him,
> *After reading, a song*
> for his death
> after I had read at Adams House[30]

At the heart of "A"-15 is an extended quotation from Gibbon's *Decline and Fall of the Roman Empire*, a passage in which Gibbon seeks to draw lessons for contemporary Europe from the fall of Rome: "This awful revolution may be / usefully applied to the instruction of the present age," Zukofsky quotes, and by quoting implicitly argues the passage's twentieth-century applicability. The capitalist West, America in particular, is in Zukofsky's eyes a tottering empire like fifth-century Rome, weakened by internal divisions and self-seeking ideologies. "The savage nations of the globe are the / common enemies of civilised society," Gibbon continues, "and / we may inquire . . . whether Europe is still / threatened with a repetition / of those calamities which formerly oppressed the arms and institutions of Rome."[31]

Two hundred years after Gibbon, Zukofsky applies the historian's words to Africa, where European colonies were rebelling and asserting their independence throughout the 1950s and early 1960s. In 1781, Gibbon had concluded that "Europe is secure from any future irruption / of barbarians; since before they can conquer, / they must cease to be barbarians . . ."[32] The liberty sought by African revolutionaries, Zukofsky noted cynically in 1960, was "to be only as 'free' as Firestone etc. *The Tempest* handled all the complications a long time ago. Comes of having 'taught them language'—the wrong kind 'European Free Market.'"[33] If the "civilization" the revolutionaries of the third world hope to attain is merely some version of Western capitalism, to what extent have they gained by that civilizing process?

Zukofsky seems to have read Gibbon for the first time in 1954, and later he would ascribe his final rejection of Marx to that reading.[34] Zukofsky's reading of Gibbon could not have persuaded him that Marx's analysis of the capitalist system—for which Zukofsky never showed any affection—was mistaken. Rather, Gibbon, by showing him how the conditions of the postwar world replicated those of the decaying Roman Empire, confirmed Zukofsky in his sense that Marx's Hegelian optimism, his hope for an imminent dictatorship of the proletariat to be followed by a classless society, was as much a fable as the golden age in Ovid's *Metamorphoses*. Humanity would indeed progress—in science, in technology, in material power—but each new discovery would lead to further opportunities for folly and destruction.

"A"-15 ends with a concatenation of scenes: the Zukofskys in Williams's home, waiting for the other mourners to return from Bill's interment; two passages from the *Iliad* (Nestor praising Odysseus's horses, and the grief of Hecuba and Thetis after Hector's death, with a catalogue of Thetis's fellow nymphs bewailing the fallen hero); and finally, a brief floral scene:

> *negritude* no nearer or further
> than the African violet
> not deferred to
> or if white, Job
> white pods of *honesty*
> *satinflower*[35]

These six lines wind together a number of thematic threads. The herb honesty is also known as "moonwort, satinwort, or satinflower," according to Taylor's *Encyclopedia of Gardening, Horticulture, and Landscape Design*, a reference book Zukofsky would use in the years to come.[36] Its Linnean binomial is *Lunaria annua*, as "A"-14 tells us: "*Lunaria annua honesty* // this side the / moon."[37] The final lines of "A"-15, then, bring into conjunction the revolutionary ideology of *négritude*, the patience through suffering of Job, and the continuing race to the moon, an emblem of the superpower struggle in the midst of which the nascent African nations find themselves caught. The African violet was originally brought from Africa, as were the ancestors of present-day African Americans.[38] America ought to be a place, Zukofsky's lines imply, where such diverse blooms as the African violet and the white flower honesty can live alongside one another, as they do in Celia's houseplant collection.

. . .

Given the spareness of "A"-16, the transition from "A"-15 to "A"-17 is likely to detain the casual reader only a moment; but the elegance of Zukofsky's joinery here, how the poet has engineered the movements to fit one into the next, is masterful. "An / inequality / wind flower," "A"-16 reads. "An / inequality" precisely repeats the first sounds of "A"-15, "An hinny" (the "an" forces one to elide the aspirate—"an 'inny"). "Inequality" brings to mind the inequalities that Zukofsky has pondered in "A"-14 and "A"-15: between first world and third world, between black and white within the United States, where all are supposedly created equal; "wind flower," suspended delicately towards the bottom of the page, picks up on the short *i* of "*i*nequality," and ends the movement on a dying fall. But it also picks up on the floral scene at the very end of "A"-15, and leads into the "Coronal"—a crown or garland of flowers—of "A"-17. Windflower is the Greek *anemone*: the "an"-word beginning "A"-17 is "Anemones." Such patterns of phonetic, thematic, and literal recurrence give *"A"* its unity: The harder one stares at the poem, the more one discerns such patterns.

. . .

Zukofsky took up "A"-18 and -19 as he and Celia were completing the *Catullus*. He worked on them more or less simultaneously, and completed the movements in the spring of 1966. After the mourning of "A"-15, -16, and -17, they show a renewal of energy in the poem, and are the culmination of Zukofsky's work in what I have described as his "mature" style. "A"-18 begins with a lovely but melancholy lyric in which Zukofsky imagines his own death, as he had in "A"-11, and mourns not for himself but for the bereaved Celia:

> An unearthing
> my valentine
> If I say it now will
> it always be said.
> I always know
> it is I who have died
> yet in that state
>
> sorrow for you
> by yourself.[39]

But the poem rapidly shifts into a more lively eight-word line: "I am here," Zukofsky proclaims, "let the days live their / lines," and shortly thereafter tells us the old joke of the sailor with the tattooed penis (in this version, it revolves around "SWAN" and "SASKATCH-EWAN").[40] The thought of Zukofsky's death runs like an undertow beneath the verse, however: "When I am dead in the empty ear / you might ask what was he like away / from home," Zukofsky writes, and follows with a not unflattering self-portrait: "on his job more patient with / others than himself . . . not an efficient man only an observant . . ."[41]

The movement is a mixture of the elegiac and the newsworthy, a brooding upon the still-firm realities of art and familial love—"eight words a line for love," Zukofsky writes, explaining the Pythagorean significance of his meter—even as the events of the world trudge on around them.[42] Zukofsky is sick at heart about the Vietnam War. He puns bitterly on the periodic official "body counts" of dead enemies, "How many killings per Diem Phu on Nhu," and sums up the whole Indochina venture in an anecdote lifted from the papers, where a force of South Vietnamese and American soldiers deploy automatic weapons, mines, and hand grenades in a fruitless attempt to rid a Vietnamese pond of a giant carp local villagers take to be a reincarnation of the Buddha.[43] Can the poet and his wife, Zukofsky wonders, in their retreat from the world's affairs, their attempt to emulate the white herb honesty, escape the moral darkness into which their nation has fallen?

> only in my love's
> room did her plants not burn: in world's
> hanger great room *honesty* a shade gray
> the unminded plant burned with all others where
> white is at least as false as true
> that fittest survives.[44]

"A"-19 is quicker and sparer by far than the previous movement, in large part due to its stanzaic form: thirteen-line stanzas, two words per line, ending with a three-word line. Thirteen, Zukofsky believed, was his lucky number; he says as much in the thirty-first stanza ("my / luck is / 13"[45]), and of course the digits of 31 reversed are themselves 13. The entire movement circles around the notion of luck. "No ill-luck," the first stanza of the main section begins, and "A"-13 contains numerous allusions to luck, chance, and "hazard," a term Zukofsky has picked up from the French (*hasard*) of the poet Stéphane Mallarmé. Mallarmé was much interested in chance, from his early poem "Le Guignon" (The run of bad luck) to the late *Un coup de dés jamais n'abolira le hasard* (A throw of the dice will never abolish chance). The spirit of Mallarmé hovers over "A"-19; most of the words of the first seven thirteen-word stanzas are drawn from various of Mallarmé's short poems, either through translation or transliteration, and his poems and prose works are quoted throughout the movement.[46]

Zukofsky had previously shown little interest in Mallarmé, high priest of a *Symbolisme* that regarded poetry as a sacred act, an investigation into the grounds of spiritual existence. Paul Zukofsky, however, had in the early 1960s become interested in Mallarmé, largely by way of the French composer Pierre Boulez's settings of "Le Vierge, le vivace et le bel aujourd'hui" and "Une dentelle s'abolit." In November 1963, Paul bought a copy of Jacques Scherer's *Le "Livre" de Mallarmé*, a detailed study and scrupulous transcription of the manuscript notes for Mallarmé's unwritten magnum opus: "A book," as Mallarmé described it to Paul Verlaine, "quite simply, in many volumes, a book which is truly a book, structured and premeditated, and not a mere collection of random acts of inspiration. . . . The Orphic explanation of the Earth which is the sole task of the poet and the supreme literary game."[47]

Zukofsky found his interest in Mallarmé stirred by Scherer's presentation of the notes toward this grand work; as he describes it in "A"-19,

> What book?
> what book?
> entire enough
> to take
> the place
> of all
> the books
> and of
> the world itself[48]

Zukofsky praises "How generously / Mallarmé's late / thought minds / 'the book,'" and he also alludes repeatedly to Mallarmé's profession, like Zukofsky's that of a reluctant teacher of English: "drudging / professing to / make pure / the speech / of a / scrawling race."[49] Zukofsky's interest in Mallarmé comported uneasily with his own investment in concrete reality. Mallarmé seems bent on "making all / of the / universe purely / of speech," Zukofsky writes, but "I'd rather not // preempt my / horse from / actual pavement / or green." Early in his life, Zukofsky had dismissed Mallarmé, he told Guy Davenport; reading him now, he found a *solidity* to the language he had earlier missed: "What I didn't see then is how *literal* [Mallarmé] is read from word to word and that the 'eloquence' and 'symbolisme' are really very minor components to be shook off early." In one of its aspects, then, "A"-19 is an homage, "this / maybe not / too late / tribute to / once Stéphane Mallarmé."[50]

The poem is an homage to Mallarmé, but it is of course much more. Zukofsky celebrates his son's achievements: much of "A"-19 is taken up with the events of the 1963 Paganini Prize competition in Genoa, in which Paul had performed. Scattered throughout are updates on the race to the moon and various bits of current events, as though the poem were a radio receiver with its dial being turned, pausing over one station after another. All is held together by continual reference to the theme of luck or chance, and by the parallel formal structure of number: "why / you should / have patience," Zukofsky addresses his reader,

> ranging random
> numbers (my
> luck is
> 13) and
> if I
> voice thru
> Demetrius 'Egypt
> . . singing harmonies
> of seven vowels
>
> hymning gods'[51]

The latter quotation is from the treatise *On Style* by the fourth-century BCE Greek orator Demetrius of Phaleron,[52] and serves to point up, through its emphasis on "seven vowels," Zukofsky's own sense of the interdependence of the poetic and the numerological. Number and chance, as in a Mallarméan roll of the dice, are always intertwined; but the Pythagorean lore that studs the stanzas of "A"-19 suggests that for Zukofsky one's luck is less a matter of sheer chance, of "le hasard," than the manifestation of obscure forces and structures underlying the everyday, and manifesting themselves in number.

The poem ends with a nod to Mallarmé, a talismanic quotation from *Pericles, Prince of Tyre* (I.i.16–17), and a burst of numbers:

> Mallarmé (not
> the hat)
> the face
> a covert
> look might
> make one

shy of
song *From*
thence sorrow
be *ever*
raz'd nine
so soon twenty[53]

Nine is in medieval numerology the angelic number, after the nine orders of angels; it is also the number of the translunary world, which is divided into the nine spheres of the empyrium, the stars, and the seven planets. More concretely, there are seventy-two stanzas in the main part of "A"-19, and $7 + 2 = 9$. Twenty was Paul Zukofsky's age in 1963, when he went to Paris and bought *Le "Livre" de Mallarmé*, and it is the number of the poem's next movement, at which Zukofsky has arrived "so soon."

"A"-20 is relatively simple and straightforward after the complications of "A"-18 and -19; it would serve the reader as something of a breather before the long, complex stretch of the poem's final four movements. When he finished "A"-19 at the end of May 1966, Zukofsky already knew what would constitute "A"-21, and he had a more or less clear idea of what "A"-22 and -23 would involve. (He also knew that their planning and composition were likely to take some years.) He had as yet no firm notion of how he would end his "poem of a life," but he trusted that time would provide the answer to that problem.

Retiring 1966–1969

IGURES LIKE KEATS, Shelley, and Rimbaud have fixed the notion of poetry as a young person's art; but Wallace Stevens, continuing to build his temples of the imagination into his seventies, or William Carlos Williams, struggling at seventy-nine to type new poems with a single, palsied finger, are more useful models of poetry as sustained life's work. In 1958, Jonathan Williams published *Lunar Baedeker and Time-Tables*, a new collection of the seventy-one-year-old Mina Loy's poems. The blurb Zukofsky wrote for the book's dust jacket summed up the admiration he felt for her constancy in poetry: "Miss Loy last heard of in the 1920s remains a poet more than thirty years later—which is the test of a poet."[1] Zukofsky knew that he himself had passed this test: he too had "remained a poet."

When he retired from Brooklyn Polytechnic in 1965, Zukofsky was sixty-one, and in the thirteen years that remained to him would produce some of his most accomplished and influential work. He would write his only full-length novel, and he would accomplish something William Carlos Williams, Ezra Pound, and Charles Olson had been unable to do: He would complete his long poem, leaving *"A"* behind him as the only American modernist epic whose author had been able to achieve a satisfactory closure. In the last movements of "A" and in *80 Flowers*, the suite of short poems that followed "A", Zukofsky would press the poetics of his mature period to new levels of density, compression, and musicality, in effect reinventing modernist poetry itself. In the process, he would leave behind many of the readers who had come to admire the short poems of *ALL* and the moving personal statements of "A"-12. For the most part, readers of poetry have yet to catch up with "late" Zukofsky.

The years of Zukofsky's retirement were punctuated by all the marks of worldly success: publication of over two dozen books, pamphlets, and broadsides; a series of prizes, well-paid invited readings, an honorary doctorate; *festschrifts*, critical articles, and university dissertations devoted to his work. This success, however, had come too late. "I have stopped living for the literary life—and C was never in it," he told Corman in 1966; as for "the writing, the drudgery"—that was "itself habit, horse habit."[2]

Zukofsky's old friend Basil Bunting had also been through hard years, but his fortunes were changing by the mid-1960s. After the 1965 publication of his 1950–51 long poem, *The Spoils*—a publication brought about by the younger poets Tom Pickard, Michael Shayer, and Gael Turnbull—Bunting found himself the object of renewed attention, and was inspired enough to commence a new long poem, *Briggflatts: An Autobiography*, which was published in 1966 to immediate critical acclaim.[3] At Hugh Kenner's invitation, Bunting came to the United States to spend the 1966–67 academic year at Santa Barbara and to give a series of readings. Bunting hoped for a happy reunion with Zukofsky in the spring, when he would read at the Guggenheim, but Zukofsky, fearing "drafts," refused to attend the reading. They spent (in Bunting's words) "A painful hour" together; Basil found his old friend "very bitter and, strangely, very jealous."[4]

.   .   .

After making preliminary notes for some months, Zukofsky began drafting "A"-21 in mid-August 1966.[5] Like *Catullus*, this movement was to be a translation from the Latin, and like *Arise, arise*, it was to be a drama: a version of Plautus's comedy *Rudens* (*The Rope*). Plautus (ca. 254–184 BCE) was like Catullus an outlander, a native of Umbria rather than metropolitan Rome. By adapting the Greek "New Comedy" to the Latin vernacular, he provided the foundations for a truly Roman drama. Zukofsky knew Plautus's influence on Shakespeare: *The Comedy of Errors* was based on Plautus's *Menaechmi*, and Plautus's *Miles Gloriosus* (Braggart Soldier) was one model for Falstaff. In *Rudens*—a comedy of familial separation, shipwreck, identification through childhood talismans, and the ultimate reunion of a father and lost daughter—Zukofsky saw an analogue to, even a source for, Shakespeare's last romances, in particular *Pericles, Prince of Tyre*.[6] Most scholars trace the plot of *Pericles* to a tale recounted in John Gower's *Confessio Amantis*; Zukofsky's conviction that the play derives from Plautus's *Rudens* was a minority, if not a lone, opinion. But the parallels are striking: both the overall similarities of the two plays' plots, which revolve around separation, shipwreck, and recognition, and the more specific congruences of comic action—both *Rudens* and *Pericles* get comedic mileage out of the byplay of unrefined fishermen and the attempt by pimps to debauch a virginal heroine.

Plautus's Latin, based on second-century Romans' everyday speech, was far from the lyrical, densely allusive language of Catullus, and Plautus's medium, the public entertainment, could not have been further from Catullus's personal lyrics and literary set pieces. So Zukofsky forged yet another idiom to render *Rudens* into English. As with *Catullus*, he sought to preserve as much of the *sound* of the Latin as possible; but he did so within the compass of his now-standard word count line: one five-word English line for each line of Plautus's Latin hexameter. This formal decision forced condensation, evident in the very names of the characters: "Daemones," the father in *Rudens*, became "Dads" in "A"-21, the heroine "Palaestra" became "Polly"; "Sceparnio," the rascally servant, became "Scape."[7] "A"-21 was *Rudens* recast in a slangy, jazzy language reminiscent of Beat-era coffeehouses or countercultural Haight-Ashbury. It was "crabbed"—a word Zukofsky increasingly used to describe his own language (and one which fit his handwriting even more closely)—but it was also racy, funny, capturing beautifully the zany movement of Plautus's original—which, like Shakespeare's early comedies, made no pretensions to be serious "art."

A little over a week after Zukofsky began "A"-21, his brother Morris Ephraim died. Like Zukofsky's sisters Dora and Fanny, Morris had been born in Russia; though twelve years older, of the siblings he was closest in age to Zukofsky. Morris was the black sheep of the family.[8] He had run a bookstore near Union Square in the 1920s, but after the failure of the business in 1927, his life became a chronicle of rootlessness.[9] Morris had married in 1919, but he and his wife separated around 1930. He stayed in touch with his two children, but did not support them. He tried restarting the book business at least twice, with no success.[10] For a while he worked for a cousin as a cutter in the garment district. Mostly he sponged off his family.[11] By 1966, he was living in a small apartment near his son Daniel in Mount Vernon. Fanny had phoned him there on August 22; receiving no answer, she asked his son to go by and check on him. Daniel Zukowsky found his father dead, alone in his book-filled apartment. Zukofsky often regretted his brother's lifestyle, but he felt a special bond to Morris. Alone among the members of Zukofsky's family, Morris had been interested in books and literature, and he had communicated that interest to his little brother from an early age. It was Morris who had persuaded Zukofsky to memorize Yehoash's *Hiavatha*, and it was Morris who had taken him to the theater, where he had first seen Shakespeare performed.[12]

"A"-21, then, would be at least in part a tribute to Zukofsky's brother, who had introduced him to poetry and the theater. Morris is alluded to early in the movement in one of the (non-Plautine) "(*Voice off*)" passages, which quotes *Midsummer Night's Dream* II.i.98—"*nine / men's / morris*"—and at the very end of *Rudens*, Zukofsky inserts a passage that recalls the pleasure that he, the child of an impecunious immigrant family, took from those trips to the playhouse with his older brother:

> poorest we had all
> droll roll and gambol risk
> of a playful sea Saturday
> matinee and night and Sunday
> matinee and night child in
> the morris harp[13]

With "A"-11 ("*for Celia and Paul*") and "A"-17 ("A CORONAL for Floss"), "A"-21 is one of the three movements of the long poem with an explicit dedication: "dedicated to / the memory of John Gassner / and my brother Morris Ephraim."[14] John Waldhorn Gassner had been a close friend of Zukofsky's at Columbia, one of the few Zukofsky had kept in touch with. He had become a well-known theater critic and drama scholar, writing and editing over three dozen books. Since 1956, he had been Sterling Professor of Playwriting and Dramatic Literature at Yale, and it was in New Haven, where Zukofsky read in March 1967, that Zukofsky had last seen him. Shortly after their meeting—a warm affair, and their first time together in almost fifteen years—Gassner suffered a heart attack. He died on April 2.

On April 6, Zukofsky sent Gassner's widow Mollie a copy of five pages of "A"-21. Zukofsky had told no one he was translating *Rudens*, but he knew that John would have been delighted; he had finished the enclosed lines "last Sunday after several days with John on my mind all the time, not knowing what was happening and hoping, looking forward to when we all could meet again and he could read the whole play."[15] He had sent a "choral passage" from Act IV of *Rudens*, a long, lyrical series of three-word lines commenting obliquely on the profession of Greaves, the fisherman. They included the poignant lines

> friends hard to
> hold, leaves' sway
> on fall's branch
> all colors remembered
> delight the ground
> tho 't blows.[16]

Gassner had been just a bit under a year older than Zukofsky. His death, and Morris's, must have reminded Zukofsky of how short a time he might have to fulfill his ambitions for his work. In his letter of consolation to Mollie Gassner, and in other letters in the years to come, he would cite the traditional Jewish measure of long life, which Pinchos Zukofsky had pronounced upon the infant Paul back in 1943: "Bless him, may he live / 120 years."[17]

In contrast to the nine years the Zukofskys had devoted to Catullus, translating *Rudens*—nine-tenths the length of Catullus's entire oeuvre, by word count[18]—occupied Zukofsky barely six months. His Latin was surer for the time he had spent with Catullus, and perhaps the very comic velocity of Plautus's text spurred him to a greater speed in Englishing it. But despite the Marx Brothers–like humor of *Rudens'* dialogue and the play's inevitable comic resolution, there is an undercurrent of melancholy to "A"-21, audible mostly in the series of quiet "*(Voice off)*" passages. They are voices from a world outside the play: snatches of Spinoza, of Shakespeare, of Izaak Walton's *Compleat Angler*, of the poet-inventor Buckminster Fuller, and of the earlier movements of *"A"*. Sometimes they comment upon or accompany the action: The words of the *St. Matthew Passion* from "A"-1, "*ye lightnings, ye thunders*," precede a description of a storm.[19] At others they seem the voice of the poet himself, commenting on contemporary culture: "Op-and-Pop art, bare engineers bare / 'what the traffic will bear.'"[20] One "*(Voice off)*" passage Zukofsky titled "Song" and sent to the *New York Times*, which published it on the editorial page:

> Old friends
> when I was young
> you laughed with my tongue
> but when I sang
> for forty years
> you hid in your ears
> hardly a greeting
>
> I was
> being poor
> termed difficult
> tho I attracted a cult
> of leeches
> and they signed *love*
> and drank its cordials
> always for giving
> when they were receiving
> they presumed
> an infinite forgiveness

With my weak eyes
I did not see
assumed a bit
of infinite myself
arrogating hypocrisy
to *no* heart
but stupidity [21]

The poet Harvey Shapiro was so appalled by the "aloneness" of "Song"
that he paid a special visit to Zukofsky, "to see him, to make him know
how he is read and honored." Paradoxically, Shapiro discovered the
Zukofskys "triumphantly happy." [22] Shapiro had had no way of seeing
the next two stanzas of this passage, which Zukofsky had not sent the
Times, and in which the poet acknowledges the "young friends" who
are *not* "leeches," and cuts them free of his influence:

if I'm not dead
a dead mask smiles
to all young friends
still young where else
it says *take care*
prosper
without my tongue
only your own [23]

. . .

One cause of Zukofsky's "happiness"—if happiness is the right
word—was seeing his work in print. At Nathaniel Tarn's recommendation, Jonathan Cape issued a photo-offset reprint of Norton's
ALL: The collected short poems 1923–1958 in England in May 1966. Tarn
was enthusiastic about Zukofsky's work, and he had the ear of Tom
Maschler, Cape's editorial director. [24] In October Cape reprinted the
Origin Press *"A" 1–12*, "errata miraculously corrected in the photo-
offset enlarged type." [25] The book was still out of print in America,
but Maschler had plans there, as well. George Plimpton, the editor
of the *Paris Review*, had in collaboration with Doubleday & Company
established a book imprint, Paris Review Editions. (The motto of the

series, Plimpton proclaimed on the books' dust jackets, was "'making no compromise with the public taste,' in the phrase sanctified by the *Little Review*.") Maschler contracted with Paris Review Editions for them to bring out an American edition of *"A"* *1–12*. Plimpton and company in turn contacted Robert Creeley, whose work was enjoying extraordinary popular success, to write an introduction for the volume.[26] Zukofsky also contributed a brief foreword of his own, which began "a poem of a life—and a time. The poem will continue thru 24 movements, its last words still to be lived."[27] That talismanic phrase—"a poem of a life"—also appeared on the book's cover when it was published in September 1967 (though the handsome cover collage by Alex Gotfryd failed to include the quotation marks enclosing the "A"—not the last time those "horns" of the ox-aleph would be overlooked).

In late 1966, Norton exercised its option and published the second volume of Zukofsky's short poems, *ALL: The collected short poems 1956–1964*, and Cape issued an English edition in October of the following year. That summer the London-based Turret Books (who had published a chapbook of *IYYOB*, the Job-song from the beginning of *"A"*-15) printed a limited edition of *"A"*-14, and Rapp & Carroll issued *Prepositions: The Collected Critical Essays* in June 1967.

· · ·

In the fall of 1967 Zukofsky turned once again to a project he had laid aside some years before: the novel *Little*. Zukofsky had drafted the first eight chapters of *Little* back in 1950. In 1959 he had drawn up a prose outline for the entire book, and he continued making occasional notes through 1967.[28] John Martin of Black Sparrow Press in San Francisco had written Zukofsky that July asking to do a book; Zukofsky had replied immediately, offering the first eight chapters of *Little*, now almost seventeen years old.[29] Black Sparrow was a young press with a deep investment in the tradition of poetry Zukofsky represented: Martin had just published a book of Robert Kelly's, and was planning to do one of Creeley's the next year. By the time the 250-copy edition of *Little*, *a fragment for careenagers* was published in December 1967, Zukofsky was hard at work on the rest of the novel.

The outline Zukofsky had drafted in 1959 specified "A comic novel of 60,000 to 75,000 words, 35 chapters, whose running theme is an allegory of 'our universal society only about six thousand years old' . . ." *Little* was to be a roman à clef, a chronicle of the early life and career of Paul Zukofsky—Little Baron von Snorck—in the company of his parents, Madame Verchadet von Chulnt (Celia) and Dala Baballo von Chulnt (Louis). The characters of the novel are versions of real people known by or to the Zukofskys, their identities disguised with more or less wit: Helen Taggart becomes "James Madison," Ezra Pound "R. Z. Draykup" ("from his habit of 'draying' on one's kopf"), Ivan Galamian "Imam Betur" ("because better was [quite properly] the highest word of praise that he knew").[30]

Little is a nostalgic chronicle of the Zukofskys' life from Paul's birth in 1943 to his second Carnegie Hall recital in February 1959, a portrait of the Zukofskys at home, with every detail highlighted for comic effect: Verchadet is just a bit *too* sardonic and self-effacing, Little a bit too clever and keen, and Dala himself more than a little too long-suffering, impractical, and involved with his largely incomprehensible "welshing." The prose of *Little*, however, shows a grace and mastery absent from Zukofsky's earlier fictions (save for "*It was*"). Like Joyce or Proust, he found his surest fictive voice when writing veiled autobiography, and the gentle humor that pervades even the most disappointing turns of *Little*'s plot—the mixed reviews of Little's Great Hall performance, for instance[31]—makes it clear that Zukofsky regarded the early years of his son's musical career as something of a golden time in the family's life. Or, in the awkward musical metaphor that ends the 1959 outline, Little's "immediate family becomes a redeeming triad braving the hazardous chromatics of Little Baron's career as virtuoso on which his mind is always set."

. . .

In February 1967, the *Critic* published Thomas Merton's glowing review of *ALL: The Collected Short Poems, 1956–1964*. Merton, ten years younger than Zukofsky, was a Columbia graduate (like Zukofsky, a student of Mark Van Doren's), a bestselling author, and a Trappist monk. He was deeply invested in contemporary literature, and found in Zukofsky a scrupulous care for language that made his poetry "a kind of recovery of paradise . . . the living line and the generative

405

association, the new sound, the music, the structure, are somehow grounded in a renewal of vision and hearing so that he who reads and understands recognizes that here is a new start, a new creation. Here the world gets another chance."[32]

W. W. Norton forwarded the review to Zukofsky, and—obviously moved—he wrote to Merton to thank him.[33] The two men began a brief but intense correspondence, sending each other copies of their books. Merton praised *Bottom: on Shakespeare*—"it's like getting the Anatomy of Melancholy from Burton himself: a book into which everything has gone"—and noted perceptively that "A"-7 was "a most marvelous Easter fugue."[34] Zukofsky was amused by the coincidence that Merton's abbey name was "Brother Louis"; as he put it to Guy Davenport (also a correspondent of Merton's), "the honesty of the man moves me."[35] Merton, deeply involved in the literary world (he had published some twenty-six books), "presumed" to mention Zukofsky's work to a Doubleday editor; Zukofsky in turn revealed that Doubleday would be publishing *"A" 1–12* in their Paris Review Editions series that fall.[36]

There was also literary conversation of a less businesslike cast. Merton was reading Charles Olson's *Selected Writings*, which Robert Creeley had edited for New Directions in 1966; what did Zukofsky make of Olson? Zukofsky replied that he liked the "lyrical bits" of *The Maximus Poems* and Olson's earlier work, and "the loneliness of the man has my sympathy and respect." But he had serious reservations about the "didactic wisdom and oratorical tone" of Olson's critical pronouncements, and the way he seemed to attract disciples who were more interested in advancing a cause than in the craft of poetry writing. In June 1967 Merton warmly recommended Ronald Johnson's new book of poetry, *The Book of the Green Man*. For Merton, it was "one of the finest things I have seen anywhere . . ."[37] Zukofsky didn't mention that Johnson (formerly Jonathan Williams's companion) had visited him on several occasions in the late 1950s, and his response to the book was decidedly tepid: "Yes, I've read *Green Man*, readable as you say. More power to Dr. Johnson—i.e. Young Dr. J.—hard to keep up these days."[38]

Late in 1967, Merton solicited work of Zukofsky's for his new magazine, *Monks Pond*. All of his poetry was either in print, under contract, or in process, Zukofsky replied—"I expect to be working quietly with nothing new until 1970 at the earliest"—but Merton was welcome to reprint "Thanks to the Dictionary," which had appeared in the 1961 Origin Press *It was*: "I doubt if more than a dozen of the out-of-print collectors of this book ever read it . . ."[39] In December 1968 Merton was accidentally electrocuted in his Bangkok hotel room shortly after addressing a meeting of Asian Benedictines and Cistercians. Cid Corman's father died about the same time, and Zukofsky bracketed his death with Merton's in a note of consolation to Corman: "To say anything seems too much—your father, Tom Merton dying alone—the sorrows remain human."[40] But he wrote no elegy for the occasion; it was time to husband his energies for the final two movements of "*A*".

. . .

In January 1968 Zukofsky gave another reading at the Guggenheim Museum, like his 1964 reading sponsored by the Academy of American Poets. This time, the stage was his alone. Allen Ginsberg introduced him, and afterwards there was a reception at the Park Avenue home of *Kulchur*'s Lita Hornick.[41] "I read at the Gugg. Mus. last night, just four years to the day I read there last," Zukofsky wrote Davenport the next day. "To great 'acclaim' etc and fame has me now so wrung out I can barely hold the BIC with which I'm writing this."[42] Earlier that month, Zukofsky had been contacted by L. S. Dembo, a Pound scholar at the University of Wisconsin. Dembo was interested in the objectivists: He wanted to mount a conference on the movement at Madison later that year and bring all four of the original players— Zukofsky, Oppen, Rakosi, and Reznikoff—together again.[43] Zukofsky had had enough of objectivists: He would not participate in such a meeting, though he would be happy to come to Madison to give a reading, if the University could supply his travel expenses and his now-standard five-hundred-dollar fee. Without Zukofsky, there was little point in an objectivists' "conference," so instead Dembo arranged for all four of the poets to visit Madison that spring *seriatim*.

Zukofsky was there on May 16, where he allowed himself to be interviewed by Dembo for the journal *Contemporary Literature*, which had been running a series of interviews with contemporary writers.

Zukofsky discussed his poetics in general and offered detailed interpretations of "The Old Poet Moves to a New Apartment 14 Times"
and the first poem of "I's (pronounced *eyes*)." When Dembo raised the
issue of the objectivist movement, however, Zukofsky was anxious to
set the record straight:

> In the first place, objectivism . . . I never used that word; I used the
> term 'objectivist,' and the only reason was Harriet Monroe's insistence
> when I edited the 'Objectivist' number of *Poetry* . . . she told me, 'You
> must have a movement.' I said, 'No, some of us are writing to say
> things simply so that they will affect us as new again.' 'Well, give it a
> name.' . . . Anyway, I told Harriet, 'All right, let's call it "Objectivists,"'
> and I wrote the essay on sincerity and objectification. I wouldn't do
> it again today.[44]

"The objectivist, then," Zukofsky concluded, "is one person, not a
group, and as I define him he is interested in living with the things
as they exist, and as a 'wordsman,' he is a craftsman who puts words
together into an object."[45] That was Zukofsky's final word.

Before Zukofsky arrived, Dembo had already interviewed Rakosi,
Oppen, and Reznikoff, and with each of them he had spent some
time trying to pin down their sense of what "objectivist" meant.
Ironically, it was Oppen, whom Zukofsky now regarded with such
bitterness, who had best understood the objectivist manifestos: "I
learned from Louis, as against the romanticism or even the quaint-
ness of the imagist position, the necessity for forming a poem properly, for achieving form. That's what 'objectivist' really means . . . the
objectification of the poem, the making of an object of the poem."[46]
No doubt to Zukofsky's chagrin, Dembo published all four interviews
as a single section—"The 'Objectivist' Poet"—in *Contemporary Literature* in spring 1969, thereby giving rise to a still-thriving critical
industry devoted to objectivist poetry: a category defined not as a
timeless description of poetic craft (as Zukofsky would have it), but
as the work of Zukofsky, Oppen, Reznikoff, and Rakosi (with the
occasional addition of Basil Bunting and Lorine Niedecker).

The day after the interview with Dembo in Madison, the Zukofskys had a final meeting with Lorine Niedecker. They had not seen
her since their 1954 visit to Black Hawk Island. Niedecker's own literary fortunes had improved: Michael Shayer's Fulcrum Press would

be issuing her new work *North Central*, and Jonathan Williams was preparing a career-wide collection of her writing, *T&G: The Collected Poems 1936–1966*. Niedecker enjoyed the meeting: "I find letters don't do it (over a period of 14 years, no!)—talking clears the air and brings out half a laugh here and there. A glance and a certain tone makes all the difference."[47]

. . .

Nathaniel Tarn had worked for Jonathan Cape as an "advisor" since 1964, but in 1967 he was hired as the general editor of a new imprint, Cape Editions. Jonathan Cape had also spun off another new imprint, absorbing Barry Hall and Tom Raworth's little Goliard Press to form Cape Goliard, whose goal was "to publish avant-garde poets, mainly American but with quite a few British and foreign, in the spirit of the little press" but with the marketing power of Jonathan Cape.[48] For Zukofsky, these developments meant that his work could in effect be issued under three different English imprints. In early 1969 Jonathan Cape issued the second volume of *"A"*, *"A" 13–21*, and Cape Goliard published the complete *Catullus*.

In early 1968 Maschler had agreed to do *Ferdinand* and *"It was"* as a small volume in the Tarn-edited Cape Editions series.[49] "My suggestion to you," Maschler told Zukofsky, "is that you consider yourself committed to us on both sides of the Atlantic and that you simply pass any offers from either side through to us."[50] Maschler was as good as his word, arranging the American publication of *"A" 1–12*, and working out a somewhat less advantageous deal with Paris Review Editions for *"A" 13–21*.[51] Maschler's other American intervention on Zukofsky's behalf proved more long-lasting. Richard L. Grossman of Grossman Publishers, which had gained spectacular publicity in 1965 with Ralph Nader's automotive industry exposé *Unsafe at Any Speed*, was looking to beef up the literary side of his publishing, and reached an agreement with Jonathan Cape—who had an impressive line of avant-garde American poets, among them Olson and Zukofsky—to publish and distribute Cape books (including Cape Editions and Cape Goliard titles) in the United States. Grossman would release an American edition of *Ferdinand* in February 1969, and an American *Catullus* in October, four months after its English release. Even after

Jonathan Cape pulled the plug on Cape Editions and Cape Goliard in late 1969 and ceased publishing Zukofsky, Grossman continued to issue his books.

. . .

Celia Zukofsky had been her husband's full collaborator on the Catullus translations, but she was his partner in other aspects of his creative life as well. Celia was largely responsible for Louis's archival legacy: She kept a running bibliography of his publications, a list of his readings and public appearances, and, most astonishingly, a list of every known mention in print of his name and works—by 1969, over seven hundred items. In fall 1968, John Martin's Black Sparrow Press agreed to publish part of Celia Zukofsky's record of her husband's work as *A Bibliography of Louis Zukofsky*.[52] Martin clearly knew his market (primarily scholarly libraries), for two hundred fifty copies of the three-hundred-copy signed and numbered print run had been sold before the actual publication date.[53]

More important than her role as her husband's bibliographer, however, was the fact that with her musical training Celia Zukofsky could realize her husband's poetry in a way that he—who never learned to read music or play an instrument—could not. Celia had been setting Louis's short poems to music since 1940, when she had composed "Motet," and by 1952 she had accumulated some twenty-two settings to eighteen poems. These settings had been neither performed nor printed (except for "Motet," published in *I's (pronounced eyes)*), but Zukofsky had at least since 1962 intended for his wife's versions of his poems to appear in print together.[54]

In 1967 Zukofsky was notified that he was to be included in a survey of midcentury authors, and asked to write a brief biographical statement for the volume. That biographical statement—less than a single typed page—became the text of Zukofsky's *Autobiography*, one of the most unusual books ever to bear that title.[55] The *Autobiography* consists of five very short paragraphs of autobiographical prose, interspersed among Celia's twenty-two settings of the short poems. What Zukofsky wanted to be remembered for, aside from the few details he provided in the *Autobiography*'s prose—his immigrant background, his friendships with Pound and Williams, his deep commitment to his family—was the *music* of his poems, and that music was best displayed in Celia's settings. If poetry was, in Dante's words, "the completed action of one writing words to be set to music," then his poetry had been further completed—realized—by his wife's settings. "The composer set the words to the 'forms' I asked for," Zukofsky wrote, "to which I had perhaps no right, unable to compose them myself; but in following my wish or whim she also did something else—showing me that apart from my impositions on my words and her, the words had potentially their own tunes which she followed even more carefully to complete for me."[56] Zukofsky arranged the *Autobiography* in the latter part of 1969, and it was published by Grossman in April 1970. While the music was clearly credited to Celia Zukofsky, the cover and title page bore Louis's name alone; not for the last time, it was as if the couple's combined labors had been subsumed under a single collective name.

Celia Zukofsky would sometimes express diffidence about her own knowledge of her husband's work, but it is difficult to overestimate her knowledge of and involvement in that work. That knowledge and involvement was most clearly displayed in the "L. Z. Masque" that she began just before Christmas 1966. Unlike the masques performed at the courts of James I and Charles I, Celia's "L. Z. Masque" was not a visual spectacle, but it aimed to combine the verbal and musical arts in ways reminiscent of the early modern stage. It was to be a five-voiced score. One of those voices would be musical, to which the other four would be counterpointed: not *set*, however, since the words were to be spoken; in Celia's words, "The words are NEVER SUNG to the music." The music determined the overall pace of the vocal parts, and provided another, "voiceless" voice. The other four voices spoke selections from Zukofsky's published writings: "Thought" from the essays of *Prepositions*; "Drama" from *Arise, arise*; "Story" from the 1961 *It was*, Zukofsky's collected fiction; and "Poem" from *"A"*.[57] "The masque," Celia explained, "is centrally motivated by the drama," *Arise, arise*; the passages of *Arise, arise* spoken by the "D" voice were Celia's starting point, the emotional and thematic framework upon which the other disparate passages were plotted.

Celia Zukofsky had completed a first version of the "L. Z. Masque" within six months, using music by Chopin, Couperin, Frescobaldi,

Haydn, and William Byrd.[58] At Paul's suggestion, she reworked the entire score using Handel's *Pièces pour le Clavecin* ("Harpsichord Pieces") as the musical base. She had finished this final version by March 1968, and presented it to her husband as a gift. Zukofsky was delighted. The "L. Z. Masque" showed that at least one reader—the reader who meant most to him—had been able to see all of his work, verse and prose, fiction and criticism, as a unit, a single system of recurrences. As Zukofsky put it in the preface he drafted for the masque, "the gift—/ she hears / the work / in its recurrence."[59]

Just as Celia's music to *Pericles* had saved Zukofsky "a lot of words" concerning prosody in *Bottom: on Shakespeare*,[60] the gift of the "L. Z. Masque" did him the immeasurable service of providing a fitting conclusion for *"A"* as a whole. The "L. Z. Masque," Zukofsky decided, would be *"A"*-24, the summing up of his "poem of a life." The great unfinished long poem was an uncomfortable tradition: Spenser had completed only six books of *The Faerie Queene*; Williams had kept adding to *Paterson*; and it looked as though Pound would never complete *The Cantos*. The problem of closure was especially acute for such a work as *"A"*, which did not rely upon a traditional narrative, which incorporated such a wide variety of forms, and which took its materials not merely from Zukofsky's reading but from the ongoing events of his life and the history through which he was living. The darkest possibility was that the poem would be closed by the poet's death, leaving it an unfinished fragment like Shelley's "The Triumph of Life" or Dickens's *Edwin Drood*. Some of these apprehensions were allayed by designating the "L. Z. Masque" *"A"*-24. Zukofsky still had *"A"*-22 and *"A"*-23 to write, but he could at least rest assured that his long poem had a fitting ending: a conclusion, crafted by his closest reader, that combined music and drama to manifest the recurrences and continuities that had underlain his entire writing life.

. . .

The second half of the 1960s saw Zukofsky's work honored with prizes and official recognition. In 1966, Zukofsky won the two-hundred-dollar Oscar Blumenthal–Charles Leviton Prize from *Poetry* for *"A"*-14 and *"A"*-15, and Jonathan Cape's edition of *"A" 1–12* was selected as the Poetry Book Society's December recommendation.

The Doubleday/Paris Review "A" 1–12 was nominated for the National Book Award in 1968. And in 1967 and 1968, Zukofsky won awards from the National Endowment for the Arts, for "A"-15 and "A"-18 respectively. In 1969, Marcella Spann at the University of Texas submitted the first doctoral dissertation devoted to Zukofsky, *An Analytical and Descriptive Catalogue of the Manuscripts and Letters in the Louis Zukofsky Collection at the University of Texas*.

Younger poets were paying Zukofsky attention and homage, though he was more inclined to be irritated than grateful these days. He had lost his taste for seeing his work appear in tiny, small-circulation magazines started by the young, and since Corman had wound up the second series of *Origin*, he had reserved most of his new work for *Poetry*, occasionally throwing a previously published short poem or a brief Catullus translation to some soliciting little magazine. But he no longer had much faith in those venues. The case of Clayton Eshleman had been instructive. Eshleman, while a student at Indiana University, had edited *Folio*, the university's literary magazine; he had visited Zukofsky in New York in 1959 and solicited a chunk of *Bottom*, only to return much of it at the insistence of one of Indiana's Shakespeare scholars.[61] In 1967, Eshleman started the quarterly *Caterpillar*; among the magazine's features was a regular "Test of Translation," modeled after *A Test of Poetry*. Eshleman solicited and received a brief "Cat" from Zukofsky for the spring 1968 issue, which also included Niedecker's "Wintergreen Ridge" sequence. But Eshleman did not send Zukofsky a contributor's copy—for good reason: By far the longest piece in the issue was a vast, incoherent, violently erotic poem by Eshleman himself, "The Moistinsplendour," datelined "A Night Before Xmas ev. NYC. 8 p.m.—3 a.m. 1967."[62] Zukofsky no doubt would have been offended (if not simply bored) by the poem's spasmodic, ranting structure, but he was disgusted and enraged by a series of passages in which Eshleman, in the course of exorcising himself of poetic influences, imagined Louis and Celia having sex. "If you must review *our* Catullus," Zukofsky wrote Corman the next summer, "do not have it printed in Eshleman's *Worm* or any of his projects. Celia and I feel intensely that we want nothing to do with him."[63] Zukofsky had made a rule of treating the older poets from whom he had learned with respect and deference, with—a word he never used lightly—

loyalty. If what the new generation of poets counted as loyalty amounted to the uncovering of their forebears' nakedness—in print—then the less he had to do with the young, the better.

In May 1969 the Zukofskys were in London, where he read at the Camden Festival of the London Poetry Secretariat. Zukofsky's return to London was an experience of unfamiliar lionization. He and Celia were driven along the Vauxhall Bridge Road, plastered with posters announcing ZUKOFSKY IS COMING, and rode under a banner, stretched from lamppost to lamppost, that read WELCOME TO CAMBERWELL LOUIS ZUKOFSKY.[64] He read at the festival with fellow New Yorker Kenneth Koch, and was "guest of honor" at the Diamond Jubilee Dinner of the Poetry Society of Great Britain, where he was pleased to see Gael Turnbull win a prize.[65] He taped a reading at the offices of Jonathan Cape. In London Zukofsky met Bunting's friend Tom Pickard; best of all, Zukofsky was able to meet the Welsh poet David Jones, author of the complex, labyrinthine poems *In Parenthesis* and *The Anathemata*.[66]

The newspapers interviewed Zukofsky in his London hotel. Edward Lucie-Smith, writing for the *Sunday Times*, described him as "so very thin, so precise, that it seems as if a statue by Giacometti had bred with a puff of thistledown."[67] Raymond Gardner of the *Guardian* saw Zukofsky as a "tall, grey haired, gaunt figure (he calls himself a skeletal apparition) whose thick jet eye brows bursting over the spectacles belie his stooped frailty." Zukofsky seemed apprehensive about his upcoming reading, recalling his performance at Les Deux Mégots in 1961: "I was in a coffee bar," Zukofsky said, "and I am afraid that I am rather staid. My pants are pressed, and I really don't like coffee bars. For one thing they are usually draughty."[68] ("Drafts" had been Zukofsky's bête noire for some years now.)

To round off this exhausting week, Zukofsky read on May 21 at the U.S. Embassy at Grosvenor Square. The English critic Kenneth Cox was there, and described the event in detail in a letter to Niedecker. Cox had long been fascinated by the clean, hard lines of such American poets as Zukofsky, Creeley, and Niedecker, and had become a penetrating commentator on their work.[69] In the question-and-answer session after the reading, there was but a single question: "Michael Shayer lobbed a pebble, perfect in time and aim, right in the middle of the pond, and the ripples widened out, wider and wider, till Zukofsky was stopped by some underling, the cultural attache I presume."[70] Cox was right: Shayer's remark—"For one who *thinks* so much in his poetry, it seems rather strange to, in fact, *hear* you speak only of its music"—was just the prompt to get Zukofsky talking.[71] And talk he did, outlining his theory of the stages of human culture and poetry (solid, liquid, gaseous), summing up the "500 pages" of *Bottom: on Shakespeare* in a single sentence ("the natural human eye is OK, but it's that erring brain that's no good, and [Shakespeare] says it all the time"[72]), reminiscing about the objectivist movement, and concluding with two parallel passages from "A"-13 and *Bottom*.

On October 16, Zukofsky read at the University of Texas; to celebrate his visit, the HRC arranged an exhibition of some of the manuscripts and letters in the Louis Zukofsky Manuscript Collection. In November Zukofsky returned to Austin for an "International Festival of Poetry" whose participants included Creeley, Robert Duncan, Czeslaw Milosz, Octavio Paz, and Jorge Luis Borges. Clearly, in some quarters Zukofsky was beginning to be recognized as among the very first rank of poets of his century.

Recognition, however, Zukofsky felt, ought to find its proper channels, and the enthusiasm of the young often outran their sense of propriety and property. Michael Shayer was so enchanted by Zukofsky's response to his question at the embassy that he made a transcript of Zukofsky's speech, which Tom Pickard printed in Newcastle later in 1969. The Zukofskys learned of the publication of *The Gas Age: Louis Zukofsky at the American Embassy, London, May 21, 1969* through a book dealer's catalogue; Shayer and Pickard had not sent them a copy of this unconventional act of homage—or, as Zukofsky preferred, this act of "piracy" with its "unauthorized mangled transcription" of his own words.[73] Shayer, learning of Zukofsky's anger, wrote him the next year, identifying himself as the questioner from the reading, apologizing for *The Gas Age*, and expressing his deep admiration for Zukofsky's work.[74] Still resentful at the liberties Shayer and Pickard had taken, Zukofsky did not reply. Ever thrifty, however, he had obtained a copy of *The Gas Age* and was correcting it for possible inclusion in an expanded edition of *Prepositions*.

Quotation

In his early poetry, whether lighthearted or painfully earnest, Zukofsky never indulged in quotation. He only began to quote with 1926's "Poem beginning 'The,'" an explicit response to Eliot's 1922 *The Waste Land*. In that poem Eliot quoted pervasively, and his notes citing the sources of his quotations failed (in his words) to "spike the guns" of the critics who accused him either of outright plagiarism or of constructing a patchwork monstrosity out of other poets' lines.[1] Zukofsky attacked *The Waste Land* in "'The,'" but "Poem beginning 'The'" took Eliot's use of quotations as an important resource for the contemporary poet. Once he began making use of borrowed language in his works, Zukofsky would never cease doing so, and indeed his late work consists almost entirely of material that is in some way or another quoted.

Along with translation—itself a form of quotation—quoting or referring to earlier texts is one of the hallmarks of modernist poetry. In the eighteenth century, poetry was a vehicle for conveying shared social truths; as Pope put it, "True wit is nature to advantage dress'd, / What oft was thought but ne'er so well express'd." The repetition of timeless verities was a central element of this art, and paraphrasing

416

and translating earlier works were honored practices. With the Romantics, however, a new conception of the poet as inspired, *individual* singer became dominant, and with this conception came a devaluing of the poem's explicit relationship to earlier works. Quotation, in short, fell out of favor in Anglo-American poetry in the nineteenth century, precisely to the extent to which readers sought to uncover the "originality" of the poet.

In his 1919 essay "Tradition and the Individual Talent" Eliot tried to defuse this emphasis on originality and on the poet as personality (or celebrity); he argued that all worthwhile art builds upon a tradition, an order of "monuments" to which the new poet can hope to add but never supersede.[2] For Eliot and Pound, quotation was an explicit recognition of the fact that the poem would take its place within an order of compositions whose beginning is coterminous with the beginnings of recorded literature.

Eliot's and Pound's practice of incorporating earlier writers' words into their own work was to become general among one wing of early twentieth-century writing, and with some distortions one can even construct a brief taxonomy of "high" modernist quotation: Eliot tended to quote previous authors in order to lend "atmosphere" to his own poetry, and to draw attention to parallels between what he described and what had been described before. Pound did the same, but more often he quoted what he called "luminous details," textual moments that briefly and memorably fix important cultural and historical facts. Marianne Moore, in poems that she first collected under the title *Observations*, used other writers' language—often that of guidebooks and other ephemera—when she saw that something had been said more memorably than she herself might say it: Quotation in her work was the acknowledgment of careful and specific language use. E. E. Cummings quoted the language he heard around him, the conversations of the barroom and the street, and often constructed his poem entirely out of punchy and spicy bits of the vernacular.[3] Zukofsky made use of all of these types of quotation.

· · ·

The early movements of "*A*" refer to a very few outside texts, notably the *St. Matthew Passion* libretto, and while these movements ("A"-1 through "A"-7) evoke *Passion*-related themes—death, resurrection, judgment—they quote the *Passion* not in any systematic or structural manner, but as evocation of the *Passion*'s power and symmetry: its symbolic force as a beautiful, realized musical structure rising above history. At the same time, however, Zukofsky quotes material from a biography of Bach that emphasized the *Passion*'s embeddedness in eighteenth-century economics. Most of the other quoted material in the first seven movements of the poem, aside from touchstone quotations from Pound, Cummings, Yehoash, and Spinoza, consists of subliterary discourse, voices from the newspapers, the picket lines, the street. Zukofsky praised poets, Whitman in particular, for having embodied the times in which they lived, and these early movements of *"A"* aim to embody the United States in the years around the beginning of the Great Depression. To capture the economic and political moment, Zukofsky quotes Lenin, John D. Rockefeller, Henry Ford, and an array of voices from the newspapers.

In "A"-8, Zukofsky was still concerned with contemporary politics and economics, but he had begun to treat the contemporary within a broader context—in what one might call a more "Poundian" manner. Quotation of contemporary voices and documents, while still important, is contextualized by masses of quotations from earlier texts. Bach is of course still present, but overshadowed by passages from John Quincy, Henry, and Charles Francis Adams, Marx and Engels, Shakespeare, and a condensed anthology of passages from the *Workers Anthology* on which Zukofsky was working. By this point in his poem, it seems, Zukofsky had begun to believe that contemporary history did not speak for itself, but must be illuminated by the texts of the past.

The definition of quotation, however, might in Zukofsky's case be expanded to include the evocation not merely of other writers' words, but of their *forms*. In this sense, "A"-7, while it quotes verbatim few literary texts other than the *Passion* libretto, alludes to the English Renaissance sonnet sequence (Sidney, Spenser, Shakespeare) and to the whole tradition of the English sonnet from Wyatt to Cummings. While the first half of "A"-9 only literally quotes Marx's *Capital*, the poem's form—the canzone—is a sort of quotation of Cavalcanti's "Donna mi priegha." Similarly, "A"-11 bases itself on Cavalcanti's ballata "Perch' io non spero." "A"-11 also embeds quotations from or allusions to Spinoza, Paracelsus, and the nineteenth-century American poet Joseph Rodman Drake. This sort of quotation, where the reader is at no point informed (by speech tags or quotation marks) that the words he is reading have been quoted, will become the basis of Zukofsky's later work.

. . .

In "A"-12 there is a quantum leap in the number of works Zukofsky quotes, and there is also a shift in the overall view of poetic creativity that those quotations imply. The range of materials quoted is broader than in any earlier part of the poem, ranging from the *Rig Veda* and the *Odyssey* to Gertrude Stein and Martin Buber. There are large swatches of Aristotle, Plato, and Spinoza, and Shakespeare is represented by quotations from at least half a dozen separate works. The Bible—Ecclesiastes and 1 Samuel—appears, as do letters from the foot soldier "Jackie" and to Lorine Niedecker. There is a new stress on the immediate context of Zukofsky's own family. In "A"-12 quotation is an index not of the originality of the poet's vision, but of its continuity with past vision. In "A"-12 Zukofsky announces his renunciation of the Romantic ideal of "originality." The poet's task, he implies, is to play variations, more or less graceful, upon the themes that earlier poets have sung. It is a gesture of profound humility. Where Pound ransacked history in order to announce his own discovery of a cure for the ills of the capitalist West, Zukofsky concedes, out of his own encyclopedic exploration of culture, that—in the words of the Preacher—there is nothing new under the sun. When the poet believes himself most original, he is almost certainly repeating the achievements of some earlier writer.

One need not quote previous writers verbatim, however, in order to acknowledge one's place in a tradition. In his use of preexisiting materials, Zukofsky both nods towards previous writers and participates in the general twentieth-century artistic movement towards collage, towards the construction of the new artwork out of the fragments of the old: Picasso and Braque's cubist collages, Max Ernst's surrealist narratives constructed out of magazine illustrations, Kurt Schwitters's *Merz* construction, Charles Ives's and Alfred Schnittke's quoting compositions.

. . .

"A"-22, "A"-23, and *80 Flowers* are the culmination of Zukofsky's late poetics of quotation. In these poems, the five-word line is composed almost entirely of words either quoted directly from English sources or translated/transliterated from foreign texts. There are no signposts to the sources of the quotations (nor are there consistent indications —italics, quotation marks—that something is being quoted), and often a single word stems from several widely disparate sources. For instance, three words of "A"-23—"*úp-on a rouncy*"—both refer to Don Quixote's horse Rocinante *and* quote the "Prologue" to the *Canterbury Tales*, "He rood upon a rouncy" (l. 390).[4]

What is a reader (not a scholar) to do with such dense, uncited quotation? It is theoretically possible to trace the sources for all of the words used in "A"-22, -23, and *80 Flowers*, but it's entirely unclear that such sourcing will in any way "unlock" the poems' meanings. Scholars have done breathtaking work in figuring out where Zukofsky's quotations come from, but while they can point to general principles behind his selection of works to quote, they are unable to demonstrate any compelling, systematic connection among the quotations' sources. Zukofsky's late quotations, in short, have no precedent in modernist poetic practice. In Pound's later Cantos, every quoted phrase can be traced to a given source and serves as a pointer *to* that source. A phrase from Justinian's *Institutes*, for instance, relates to a particular aspect of his legal code that Pound finds salutary. The quotation embedded in the poem fits the poem into a web of significances in large part borrowed from the quotation's original context. But it is difficult to apply this principle of Zukofsky. What for instance does one make of the last words of "A"-13—"*love you*"? In his manuscript materials, Zukofsky notes that he borrows the words from *The Winter's Tale* (II.i.6). But Shakespeare was not the first English speaker to put them together, and far from the last—indeed, these very words were probably uttered (with no thought of quotation) within Zukofsky's own family circle. As readers of "A"-13, do we seek to incorporate their meaning with that of the words that have preceded them in the poem—

Or two, three
Numerous
Only the image of a voice:
love you [5]

—or do we take their source in *Winter's Tale*, where the child Mamillius chooses between babysitters—

MAMILLIUS No, I'll none of you.
FIRST LADY Why, my sweet lord?
MAMILLIUS You'll kiss me hard, and speak to me as if
I were a baby still. (*To Second Lady*) I love you better.

—as somehow pinning them down, determining their meaning?

Unlike Eliot and Pound, Zukofsky refused to provide glosses for his readers, and indeed suggested on a number of occasions that knowledge of his words' sources was not necessary for a reading of his poetry. He told the editor Henry Rago, who had commented on the provenance of the threads of which Zukofsky had woven his poem, "I'd rather the public not be bothered by my 'notes'. . . . The biographers would do better to read the poetry—or the 'woven' as you say." [6] "'A''s references," he wrote Cid Corman, "the context must 'explain' em or reveal them." [7] We must learn to read the *surface* of Zukofsky's text as closely as possible, for the original sources of the words that he has used will never explain the finished tapestry into which they have been woven.

. . .

Ferreting out sources, however, can sometimes lead to revelations, personal resonances that Zukofsky has buried in the poem. For instance: "A"-23 concludes with a twenty-six-line "ABC" in which the letters of the alphabet appear sequentially in emphasized positions— "Bach's," "Cue," "Don't," "Eden," and so forth. It ends with the z of Zukofsky's signature: "Z-sited path are but us" (and a pun, the commentators tell us, on Arbutus Road, where Paul Zukofsky lived at the time). [8] The six words that immediately precede this "ABC," however, are puzzling:

421

no protest .. wise .. provident .. reach.

Zukofsky's notebooks and drafts for "A"-23 reveal that these last five
words come from Patricia Hutchins's 1965 *Ezra Pound's Kensington*,
which itself quotes an article Ezra Pound published in January 1913 in
the *New Age*. I quote Hutchins at length, since Zukofsky transcribed it
at length in the working notebook for "A"-22 and -23 (I have emphasized the words Zukofsky quotes in "A"-23):

> Pound had seen two things in London that could compare to nothing
> but Kipling's sea monster.
>
> 'Once in Regent Street, going towards Oxford Circus. It had lost
> a leg, from the knees. It must have been fresh from the hospital, for
> the cicatrice was still red. It must have had on the clothing worn at
> the time of the accident, for the breeches were torn and showed the
> surgeon's job. The other in Oxford Street, near Hyde Park. It was
> compact and beer fed and sore-eyed and nearly blind with hunger.'
>
> 'These hulks were no worse to look at than many others, but they
> were striking in this, that they were not inert . . . not Verhaeren's
> *Pauvres Gens aux Gestes la et indulgents*. The first moved swiftly, with
> great swings between its clumsy crutches, the second apparently
> slowly yet with a recklessness that marked its movement from that of
> anything else in the crowd about the bus-stop. The legs moved stiff
> from the hips, with no bend at knee or ankle. Each of these things
> moved in rhythm regular as a metronome, moved by a force unreason-
> ing as that of a tree or a flood. The first was young, the second over
> forty. Neither looked to the right nor left. They neither asked nor gave
> one time to offer them alms. They made **no protest**. . . .'
>
> Pound then formulates some ideas on practical education and
> mentions American attempts to clear the slums and how the Jews, 'this
> **wise** and **provident** people' put their children to trades. Over there he
> had watched the slum children using trams to **reach** the parks.[9]

The word "race," I suspect, is taken from Hutchins's description of
the Russian Jew John Cournos, which directly precedes this passage:
"he found [Pound] 'the kindest man that ever lived', and without a
trace of malice."

These phrases, then—"no protest .. wise .. provident .. reach"—

must have had powerful resonance for Zukofsky. Here, at the very end of "*A*", the long poem he had begun almost half a century before so much in Pound's shadow, is Zukofsky's final acknowledgment of his mentor, his final act of loyalty. Despite the controversy that had dogged Pound's name since the war, despite the poisonous anti-Semitism that marred his greatest work, despite the hurtful things he had written to Zukofsky himself—despite all this, there had been a time when Pound had dealt honorably with the Jews, that "wise and provident people."

These resonances, however, are entirely inaudible to Zukofsky's reader. The source of many of Zukofsky's lines can be traced by a careful examination of the draft materials at the HRC, but these working materials are not a road map for interpretation; they are a set of working notes for the poet himself.[10] We can rest assured that various systems, in Hugh Kenner's words "hidden laws, presenting a different face to the poet and to us"[11]—historical timelines, selective translation and transliteration, uncited quotation—underlie the vast majority of Zukofsky's later poetry; and it is no surprise that Zukofsky planned them out for himself in his working notes. But to look immediately *beneath* the poetry, before one has grappled with the text and texture of the poetry itself, is to traduce the poem.

Zukofsky's poetry does indeed present two "faces" to the poet and to the reader, much as any poem will have radically different resonances for its writer and its reader. The writer will have memories of the poem's circumstances of composition, his own state of mind, the relationships in which he was (or wished to be) involved, the landscape outside his window. And every reader knows that these resonances are largely irrecoverable. The precise sources of Zukofsky's quotations are like such resonances: They were important to the poet, they have a decisive impact on the poem as it stands in its finished form, but they are not—cannot be—the master key to the poems' interpretation. It has been claimed that the completeness of the archival material for the later movements of "*A*" and *80 Flowers* suggests that Zukofsky intended this material to stand as an interpretive key for the poems. I would argue that it indicates merely the obsessiveness of his later working methods. How else could he have kept track of the material he was manipulating? The notes are monuments of scribbled, overwritten, often illegible micrography. The only person who could possibly make out what Zukofsky was up to much of the time was Zukofsky himself.

. . .

Zukofsky came to a realization—I believe sometime while he was working through the "graph of culture" that makes up most of *Bottom: on Shakespeare*—that human culture as a whole was an echo chamber, a series of repetitions and variations on a limited number of inexhaustible themes. Much of the joy he took in quoting previous writers lay in the discovery of what he valued in his own work, the "recurrences" of ideas, emotions, and manners of expression. *Bottom* found its Shakespearean theme of eyes and mind throughout human thought, and Zukofsky consistently took delight in discovering a phrase or an idea repeated at a vast distance in time and space: "instances from 'different' cultures, surprisingly inwreathed, / Seem to look back at one another, / Aristotle at Shakespeare (both so fond of blind heroes) / And blest Spinoza at Shakespeare . . . none has to read the other yet it happens."[12] The poet-horse does not create in the Romantic sense (as in Coleridge's imagination, a repetition of divine creation): he "sows," "composes," and above all "hunts," hoping to find the recurrences in culture out of which to "compose" his own poem.

Zukofsky was interested in the aesthetics of the "found object," the piece of language that in itself had poetic power, that itself constituted a poem when "framed" as poetry on the page. Many of his later short poems consist of bits of speech quoted verbatim. The latter movements of "A" consist almost entirely of such "found objects," bits of language that Zukofsky had come upon in his reading or listening, put together in a way that suggests to me not so much collage as *mosaic*. The art of the mosaic, largely dismissed in the Victorian era—Ruskin saw it as a branch of ornament, rather than a true medium—saw a revival in the eyes of modernists such as Yeats and Pound, who sang the praises of such Byzantine mosaic work as the church mosaics of Ravenna and Rimini. (In "A"-12, Zukofsky writes of "A sound akin to mosaic."[13])

What distinguishes fine mosaic work from mediocre—San Marco from the New York subway—is both the quality of the materials and the excellence of the overall design. Byzantine mosaic work represents the culmination of a centuries-old art form: The Byzantine artists were masters in designing figures and space, and their painstaking technologies produced an unsurpassed array of different colors and textures of mosaic glass. In ransacking the history of Western literature, Zukofsky clearly felt that he was taking the shiniest, most colorful materials for his own "mosaic-work." As well, "A"-22, "A"-23, and *80 Flowers* dispose those bits of language on carefully considered, bold, and striking "designs"—most obviously, the six-thousand-year timelines of the two movements of "A".

While Zukofsky was obviously a product of his century, and a product of literary modernism—the last of the great modernist poets—there is something wonderfully archaic about his art. Its syntax, its prosody, its grasp of the contemporary world—all mark it as quintessentially modern, but in its larger structures, and in its essence as a collage of quoted material, it hearkens back to the wall mosaics of first-millennium Byzantium, and beyond that to a Homer who composed his works as a collage of found phrases and well-worn metrical units, disposed upon the "foreseen curve" of a traditional tale every one of his auditors would have already known. To quote in poetry might be the hallmark of the moderns, but quotation—in the larger sense—is as old as poetry itself.

At Port 1970–1978

T HE LAST EIGHT YEARS of Zukofsky's life were quiet. His letters, once expansive and voluble, became briefer and briefer: short notes of thanks, holiday greetings, acknowledgments of books received. Often he let Celia answer his mail for him. Zukofsky now had readers and publishers, but the worldly rewards his works might procure seemed paltry in comparison with some undefined immortality, a "liveforever" to be attained only through his writing. So he concentrated harder and harder upon that writing, until his world dwindled down to the three members of his family and the series of self-imposed tasks before him on his tiny, neatly organized desk.

Even before the 1970s began, Zukofsky had lost a powerful and influential sponsor of his work, one whom he had come to regard as a friend. Henry Rago had become the editor of *Poetry* magazine in 1955, and over the next fourteen years had restored it to its position as the most prestigious American poetry journal. "Rago's intelligence," Zukofsky told Mary Ellen Solt, "is generous and open and that's the function of an editor to let the light thru the verbal pages."[1] Rago had shown a rare catholicity of taste: He had published the poets of Zukofsky's generation—Rexroth, Oppen, Rakosi, Niedecker—the poets of the "New American Poetry" and others who looked to Zukofsky as influence—Creeley, Duncan, Olson, Levertov, Ed Dorn, Gil Sorrentino, Larry Eigner, Frank Samperi, Ronald Johnson—even as he published poets from a more "mainstream," antimodernist tradition: Anne Sexton, Mona Van Duyn, Karl Shapiro, Mark Van Doren, John Hollander.

Rago had taken a special interest in Zukofsky's work. During Rago's editorship, Zukofsky had appeared in the magazine seventeen times; *Poetry* had essentially serialized "A"-14 through "A"-21 (with the exception of "A"-16 and "A"-20), and had devoted its October 1965 issue to Zukofsky's work. Zukofsky was grateful to Rago for his loyalty, so much so that he embedded the editor's name in the final passage of "A"-18: "The grapevine heard: / 'Have fun Henry R.'"[2] As Zukofsky told Rago in a letter, the lines were "Remembering your writing to me about the discretion of keeping the Oct. 1965 issue of *Poetry* a secret—imparted to a mutual friend before you had imparted it to me. . . . I'd have used your full second name, except that I prefer not to be bumptious—all remembrances in 'A' are personal to me . . ."[3]

Rago announced that he was taking a year's sabbatical from *Poetry*, and a few days after stepping down in May 1969 he died of a heart attack. Zukofsky was grieved by Rago's untimely death (the editor was only fifty-three); he was convinced that it had been hastened by the petty feuds, obstinacies, and eccentricities of the poets among whom he had made his career.[4] Rago had named as his substitute—now by default his successor—the Canadian poet and classicist Daryl Hine. Hine's own poetry was devoted to traditional forms and meters, and he set much stock in the "wit" and "irony" admired in American academic circles. Under his editorship, *Poetry* took a sharp turn to the aesthetic right.[5] In July 1969, Hine wrote Zukofsky asking if he would contribute to the November issue of *Poetry*, which was to be a memorial to Rago. Zukofsky replied with a few brief but deeply considered sentences about the late editor: "We met only once for perhaps five minutes and wrote to each other rarely. But if as I have always hoped poetry is beyond a day's occasions, I can only say now that my dedication to him at the end of 'A'-18 informed all of it, that otherwise it might have turned out differently. And I feel certain that his insight and quiet kindness knew this."[6] Hine did not print Zukofsky's letter, nor did he acknowledge receiving it.

To his credit, Hine (perhaps out of loyalty to Rago's memory) continued publishing "A", even when Zukofsky launched upon the dense and obscure waters of his last phase. *Poetry* magazine ran "A"-22 over two issues in 1973 and 1974. Hine, receiving a "nasty, stupid letter" (in Celia Zukofsky's words) from a reader protesting the poem's obscurity, sent a copy to Zukofsky, wondering if he wanted to respond. "That settled it for Louis," Celia recalled: "He never answered the letter and he never sent anything to Daryl Hine after that."[7] Perhaps, indeed, that was the response for which Hine had hoped. But the business severed Zukofsky's connections to the magazine that had given him his first real start back in 1931.[8]

. . .

In April 1970 Grossman released the *Autobiography* in a handsome edition, the music printed in brown and the text in black. The arresting, out-of-focus photograph of Zukofsky on the dust jacket was the work of Guy Davenport's friend Ralph Eugene Meatyard, a Lexington photographer who had met the Zukofskys at Davenport's house in 1965 and had visited them in New York to take their pictures. In September Grossman published *Little*. The novel's curious subtitle, "for careenagers," Zukofsky explained in his introduction to a reading on WNYC that November, "implies ships leaning on their sides, sometimes in drydock for repairs."[9] He had drafted a verse epigraph to the book: Its first version played upon the legalisms sheltering the roman à clef: "All resemblance in this book / to living persons is surely not / coincidence. But who is he to / sue the first stone in celebrating?"[10] The final version was more compact:

> Where coincidence
> intends no harm
> who will sue the
> first stone in
> celebrating?[11]

In contrast to the silence with which Zukofsky's first books had been received, *Little* was reviewed in at least twenty literary magazines and major newspapers. The poet Hayden Carruth, who had written warmly of *"A"* *13–21* in the *Hudson Review* earlier that year, reviewed the novel as the "book of the week" for the *Chicago Daily News'* weekly magazine.[12]

Zukofsky's work was penetrating beyond the English-speaking world, as well. The French poet Anne-Marie Albiach's translation of the first half of "A"-9 appeared in the spring 1970 issue of the Paris journal *Siècle à Mains*.[13] (Zukofsky had urged Albiach, "Any syllable you can omit is one saved in my poetics. And if the French can literally *sound* near the English the better . . ."[14]) Later that year *Les Lettres Nouvelles* published Serge Fauchereau's translation of "A"-20.[15] Facilitated by the English poet (and jazz violin enthusiast) Anthony Barnett, Zukofsky's poetry had established a beachhead among the French, attracting the attention of such young avant-garde poets as Albiach, Fauchereau, Claude Royet-Journoud, Jacques Roubaud, Jean Daive, and Emmanuel Hocquard.

In July 1970 the Italian press Guanda Editore published *Da A*, a translation of movements from the first half of *"A"* and of short poems from *55 Poems* and *Anew*, along with William Carlos Williams's note from the Origin Press *"A"* *1–12*.[16] That same year a Spanish translation of *Ferdinand* was published in Barcelona.[17] The Prague magazine *Svetova Literatura* printed "A Statement for Poetry," "A"-2, "A"-10, and selections from "A"-12 and -15, all in Czech.[18] With his own delight in the materiality of language, Zukofsky must have been fascinated to see his work coming back to him in these foreign guises, shapes, and sounds.

. . .

On November 30, 1970, Lorine Niedecker suffered a stroke; she fell into a coma from which she never emerged, and died on New Year's Eve.[19] Her last years had been relatively happy ones, and certainly productive. Niedecker had continued to correspond with the Zukofskys and follow Zukofsky's career, but with a certain detachment. She read *Little* and recognized many of its incidents from Zukofsky's letters, but also found its account somewhat distancing: The book was "enchanting in the way some of those TV Munsters was . . ."[20] The poet with whom she carried on the most intense correspondence now was Cid Corman, and Corman was her literary executor. When Niedecker died, her husband followed her instructions and destroyed her letters received. There was a large mass of Zukofsky material, however—manuscripts and typescripts of various poems and prose pieces he had sent her over the years—which Millen sent to the HRC. He and Niedecker had already, at Zukofsky's suggestion, sold Texas Zukofsky's letters to her.

. . .

In early 1971, Zukofsky was invited to read and speak at the Eighth Annual Wallace Stevens Memorial Program at the University of Connecticut at Storrs. (The agent of this invitation was the English professor Marcella Spann, who had been one of Ezra Pound's regular visitors at St. Elizabeths; her doctoral dissertation had been a catalogue of manuscripts and letters in the HRC's Zukofsky collection.) If Zukofsky followed the lead of the poets who had held the lectern in previous years, he would say a few words about Stevens, read his own poetry, and then present a series of awards to younger poets. But preparing for the event, Zukofsky found himself unexpectedly immersed in Stevens. He read his way through all of Stevens's poems and essays: "I did not intend an essay. I felt myself speaking to Stevens for three months. It's really as simple as that."[21]

By 1971 Wallace Stevens, more than any of the modernist poets except Eliot, had become a part of the literary canon: His collected works were all in print, his poems in all the anthologies; his poetry was being taught in schools and universities across the country; and scholars and critics were publishing a steady stream of commentary on his work. In many ways, the elevation of Stevens to "classic" represented a defeat for the poetic tradition of Pound, Williams, Moore— and Zukofsky. Back in 1930, Zukofsky had compared Stevens unfavorably with Williams and Pound, chastising him for an "attenuated 'accessibility to experience'" and for "a versification clambering the stiles of English influence."[22] But by 1971 Zukofsky was no longer so interested in literary politics. Now that Stevens had reached his secure place at the forefront of twentieth-century poetry, and

Zukofsky himself had attained a degree of recognition, Zukofsky was interested in tracing the moments of correspondence between Stevens's work and his own.[23]

Zukofsky's Stevens Memorial Lecture, then, was largely an auto-biographical talk, Zukofsky's wandering back over his poetic education and career, using his reading of Stevens as a series of signposts. There were a number of communications between and almost-meetings of the two poets: Zukofsky's attempting to meet Stevens when he interviewed for a job at the Hartford in 1928, Stevens's writing a preface for the Objectivist Press edition of Williams's *Collected Poems*, Stevens's letter of thanks for a copy of *A Test of Poetry*, which included one of his poems.[24] More important, however, were the moments of unconscious conjunction between the two men's work, which Zukofsky detailed with some humor ("There is our use of horses and donkeys thruout our poetry," for instance[25]). Zukofsky admitted that he had given up reading Stevens back in the 1930s, "impatient with his and anybody's use of the words *reality* and *imagination*," the latter a touchstone of Romantic poetics, the former for Zukofsky a manifestation of the "gas age" in language. Zukofsky now recognized that "tho they seem to be philosophizing," Stevens's poems had as their ultimate end not philosophy, but *music*. "Coming to his work late, I am moved by the fact—as I would wish it in my own work—that his music thruout has not been impaired by having philosophized."[26]

In the end, Zukofsky confessed, reading Stevens "for the last three months I felt that my own writing, without my being aware of it, was closer to his than to that of any of my contemporaries in the last half century of life we shared together."[27] Once again, as he did so often, Zukofsky had returned to his sense of unconscious "recurrence," of the poet's repeating or paralleling the achievements of the poets that had gone before him, and of literature itself as a series of such recurrences. To underline what he and Stevens shared, at the end of the lecture Zukofsky read an "antiphonal sequence" of six Stevens poems, followed by six passages from his own work, ending with the sentence from *Little*, "I too have been charged with obscurity, tho it's a case of listeners wanting to know too much about me, more than the words say."[28]

Zukofsky felt that the Stevens talk was important; he arranged to have a tape of the lecture sent him that summer, and revised Celia's transcription into the piece "For Wallace Stevens," which he intended for an expanded edition of *Prepositions*.[29] The lecture was evidently a great success (one auditor would refer to Zukofsky's reading as a "stirring performance"[30]), and shortly thereafter the head of the Connecticut English department—no doubt at Spann's suggestion— invited Zukofsky to return to Storrs in the fall as a guest professor.[31] Zukofsky accepted the invitation and proposed a six-session seminar entitled "Poetics as Autobiography": "meaning by that not confession, but the use of the printed text of my own writing of about 50 years for whatever awareness it shows of 6,000 years of 'culture' (not limited to 'English') that offers interdepartmental interest for discussion." The syllabus that Zukofsky prepared that October was more succinct: "Subject: Poetry as autobiography, considering Zukofsky's whole work as *one* work, as the *Year by Year* chronology (available first meeting) suggests."[32] This was to be a seminar that demonstrated the unity and continuity of the whole of Zukofsky's writing life. Conveniently, Norton would be issuing a single-volume edition of *ALL: The collected shorter poems* in the middle of October, in time for his students to purchase it as one of their course "texts."

George F. Butterick, who had studied with Charles Olson at Buffalo, was present at the "Poetry as autobiography" seminar, and decided to preserve his memories of this "live occasion" with Zukofsky for posterity. Of the first day, Butterick wrote: "Louis comes early with Celia, saying he wanted to be the first there. His hair is cut short; white shirt, stiff short collar; greenish suit jacket and greenish tie with regular all-over pattern; charcoal pants. Trim. . . . The first thing he does is close windows: 'I suffer literally from drafts, not metaphorical winds.'" Perhaps Butterick, fired with Olson's sweeping pedagogical style, was not the ideal recorder of Zukofsky's seminar, for his memoir registers continual impatience with Zukofsky's attention to minute particulars: "The impression: benchwork. A watchmaker; a care for the 'littles'; a sedentary persistence." Butterick's colleagues had even less patience with Zukofsky, for attendance at the seminar dwindled over the course of the six sessions from eighteen participants to around ten.[33]

The Connecticut seminar was not a particularly happy experience for Zukofsky—he had been snubbed by the University's poet in residence, only twenty people had shown up for his public reading on November 8, and the Internal Revenue Service's share of his pay, he complained to Corman, made the trip barely worth the effort[34]—but one suspects that on some level Zukofsky took the guest professorship as a vindication; indeed, the new single-volume Norton *ALL* announced him as "presently . . . guest professor at the University of Connecticut."[35]

Though Zukofsky was glad to be shut of academia, and though he had himself foresworn the writing of literary criticism, he was not displeased to see his work being discussed in academic circles. In addition to Hugh Kenner and Guy Davenport, Zukofsky had been contacted by professors interested in his work from all over the continent: L. S. Dembo at Madison, Spann at Storrs, and Peter Quartermain at the University of British Columbia, Vancouver. At Syracuse University, the young poet John Taggart had begun a doctoral dissertation on objectivist poetics that would be largely a commentary on Zukofsky's work.[36] Zukofsky had little patience, however, for readers who wanted direct help with his poetry. Zukofsky was happy with Kenner's work, he told Davenport, but even happier with Kenner's self-sufficiency: "Ah yeah he sure did his homework on 'A' 1–12—and never asked a question (which is bliss to me who don't want to eddicate nobody)."[37]

. . .

The New York City winters had grown increasingly hard on Zukofsky as he neared his eighth decade: the cold, the snow, the polluted air, and the general inconvenience of the bustling city were proving too much for a frame bent by arthritis and lungs worn down from a lifetime of heavy smoking. He and Celia traveled to Bermuda in January 1972, where Zukofsky enjoyed the milder climate and made notes on the events of the journey and the unfamiliar plants of the island—all intended, of course, to be worked into "A"-22 or -23. While they were in Bermuda, Zukofsky's sister Fanny Wand, his last surviving sibling, died.[38] The following summer the Zukofskys moved again, this time to a third-floor apartment at 240 Central Park South. The 77 Seventh Street place had "gone co-op, beyond my means or interest,"

Zukofsky told Corman. "Besides the neighborhood depressed me more and more. We moved in a week ago & think we'll like it—an older building, a lower floor (better for power shortages) and we do see green . . ."[39] The plant liveforever had always figured largely in Zukofsky's imagination, but now, after a lifetime spent among the asphalt and concrete of New York, peering at words on printed pages, Zukofsky was becoming increasingly obsessed with the varieties and the lore of plant life. In 1969 he had bought Celia Norman Taylor's *Encyclopedia of Gardening* and Asa Gray's *Manual of Botany*; ostensibly, the books were aids for his wife in her cultivation of houseplants, but in the years to come Zukofsky would consult them as assiduously as he did the ten-volume *Century Dictionary* he had bought "for Paul" around 1950 (and which remained with Louis and Celia long after Paul had left the household).[40]

Zukofsky had been taking copious notes towards the last movements of "*A*" for some years now, and on Valentine's Day 1970 he jotted down a three-line, six-word poem that would become the opening of "A"-22:

AN   ERA
ANY TIME
OF   YEAR

Zukofsky was much taken with this resonant fragment, and arranged to have it printed as a color "poetry postcard" (blue type on a yellow field) later that spring.[41] Zukofsky then proceeded to expand upon these six words, until he had written twenty five-line stanzas of five-word lines: with "AN ERA," a 103-line "overture" to "A"-22 that was published as a limited edition chapbook in December of that year, under the title *Initial*.[42] Then, in accordance with his original five-year plan, Zukofsky laid aside this momentary burst of "inspiration" and went back to taking notes; he would resume work on "A"-22 in March 1972.[43]

The main section of "A"-22 was well under way by August, when Grossman published "A"-24, Celia's "L. Z. Masque." Zukofsky gave a couple of readings that fall, one of them at Temple University in Philadelphia. In late 1972 the Zukofskys accepted an invitation from the Rockefeller Foundation to spend five weeks at the Foundation's

"Study and Conference Center" at Bellagio, Italy. The Foundation's Villa Serbelloni was a beautiful complex on the Bellagio Promentory, with spectacular views of Lake Como, a spot redolent with literary associations. As interesting to Zukofsky, however, were the Villa's extensive formal gardens, where he talked with the gardeners and took notes on the flowers. In the couple's five weeks at Bellagio Zukofsky was able to draft another hundred lines of "A"-22, bringing the movement past its midpoint, for "A"-22 and -23 were each to consist of a thousand lines.[44] Zukofsky picked up "A"-22 again on his sixty-ninth birthday, January 23, 1973, and wrote straight through to the end, finishing on April 14. The day before, April 13—thirteen being his lucky number—he had begun "A"-23. The completion of his "poem of a life" was in sight.

. . .

Zukofsky's work was receiving increasing attention from the outside world in the 1970s, but Zukofsky sometimes took that attention with an ill grace. Grossman published *Arise, arise* as a book in April 1973, and that summer The Cubiculo mounted seven performances of the "L. Z. Masque" in New York City.[45] (Kenner was able to attend on June 21, and the discussion afterwards, according to Davenport, "amounted to a public conversation between the poet and Hugh Kenner."[46]) Serge Fauchereau directed a performance on RTF (Radiodiffusion-Télévision Française), Paris, in February 1974. John Taggart, who had taken a teaching job at Shippensburg State College in Pennsylvania, devoted the fifth issue of his little magazine *MAPS* to Zukofsky, publishing pieces of criticism and appreciation by Kenneth Cox, Kenner, Michael Heller, Corman, Davenport, and others. Zukofsky was not pleased, however: He disliked the portfolio of Meatyard photographs that Taggart had published, and he was disgusted that Taggart had printed a long essay by the English poet Eric Mottram on the politics of "*A*".[47]

The isolation of Zukofsky's last years was summed up in a touching memoir by his friend Fielding Dawson. "He didn't know how well his work was known, nor did Celia," Dawson wrote, "but as Louis was so often feeling ill, he had a curious double reputation. He was almost as well known for his ill isolation as he was for his work, and in that sense, it is sad to say, he was taken for granted, and in an even sadder sense, he took himself for granted." The writers and poets of Dawson's circle recognized Zukofsky as a "genius without peers," the preeminent poet of his generation and, after the deaths of Charles Olson in 1970 and Ezra Pound in 1972, the most important living American poet.[48] But Zukofsky's own ill health and hypochondria, his embeddedness in the family circle of Celia and Paul, and the diffidence and reticence he had developed over decades of public rejection—all these projected a Greta Garbo–like aura of self-imposed and self-desired isolation that repelled approach. Fame and respect had come to Zukofsky in his old age: Much of that respect, however, was never communicated to him, but "taken for granted"; and much of the rest he viewed with distrust and suspicion.

. . .

In October 1973, the Zukofskys moved to Port Jefferson, a town on the Long Island Sound. Paul was living there, and the couple's move to Port Jefferson was probably as much to be near him as to give Zukofsky's lungs and nerves respite from the urban environment. In many ways, the move to Long Island served to compound Zukofsky's isolation. He and Celia had lived their entire lives in the city, and they found the shift to a suburban setting disconcerting. Neither one could drive, so they depended on neighbors or taxicabs to run the smallest errands. Their friends in New York rarely made the trip out to visit them; the Zukofskys in turn found the combined taxi and train ride into the city more trouble than it was worth. As of March 1975, they had not returned to New York for a single visit.[49]

But there were advantages to having their own cottage. For once, there was no concern about space. Not that the Zukofskys took up space—on the contrary, the small house at 306 Broadway seemed larger and airier because of the acute orderliness with which they had arranged their sparse furnishings, and there were no stacks of papers or books: they took no newspaper, Zukofsky had been disposing of his collected manuscripts to the HRC, and for some years now he had been whittling down his book collection.[50] What was new was the space the house afforded for plants, both inside and in the yard. Celia had long grown houseplants, and now her horticultural interests were contributing as well to her husband's poetic pursuits. As early as the late 1960s, Zukofsky had been contemplating the work he would take up when "*A*" was finished; by 1974, he had settled upon the title *80 Flowers*, a coronal of short poems about flowers and plants that were intended to occupy him until his eightieth birthday.[51]

Zukofsky had begun the first hundred-line section of "A"-23 (its "An-song") in April 1973; by September 17, 1974, he had worked his way to the last twenty-six lines of the movement's total one thousand, a block of lines that would form "A living calendar, names inwreath'd"—an alphabetically structured summary of his influences, obsessions, and loves.[52] Four days later he had reached the thousandth line, and was able to write beneath the last line of the manuscript, "'A'-23 completed 12.30 pm Sat Sept 21/74."[53] The "poem of a life" was finished.

"*A*" had occupied Zukofsky for a little less than forty-six years, all told—the better part of half a century. For some writers the completion of such a massive, life-filling project would leave a sense of emptiness, directionlessness. (Joyce, for instance, seemed to have no idea what he would do after he finished *Finnegans Wake*.) But Zukofsky was already beginning work on his next project, which he had forecast fifty-two lines from the end of "A"-23: "10 years—80 flowers."[54] On the same day he began the twenty-six-line "living calendar" that concludes "A"-23, Zukofsky began transferring notes from his "A"-23 notebook to a new set of looseleaf pages that would become the basis for *80 Flowers*.[55]

By the beginning of 1974 Zukofsky had a contract from Grossman to publish "A"-22 and -23, and he assumed that they would be eager to do all of "*A*" in a single volume at some future date, as well.[56] "*A*" 22 & 23 was published in September 1975 in an edition uniform with *Ferdinand* and *Arise, arise*. Since the demise of the English Cape Editions and Cape Goliard, Zukofsky no longer had a British publisher, but Asa Benveniste of Trigram Press obtained rights from Grossman to do an English "*A*" 22 & 23 in late 1977.

These two thousand-line movements, daunting in their verbal complexity and suggestion and rich in a sort of thorny music, received few public performances: two of them, at Franconia College in May 1974 and Johns Hopkins University almost exactly a year later, were Zukofsky's last full-length readings. The young poet Robert Grenier, editor with Barrett Watten of the little magazine *This* and faculty member at Franconia College, had invited Zukofsky to visit New Hampshire; he was scheduled to read there in December 1973, when he would meet with Grenier's class devoted to "The Work of Louis Zukofsky"—the first such class ever offered at a college or university.[57] An ice storm forced postponement till the following May. Zukofsky gave a bravura performance of sections of "A"-22 and the opening "An-song" of "A"-23, among other poems. In the discussion period afterwards, Grenier asked a long, convoluted question about the relationship of poetry and nature; "Bob, I take my hat off to your intensity," Zukofsky replied, "but I don't understand what you're saying."[58] Later, the Zukofskys were driven back to the Boston airport by a young friend of Grenier's living in Cambridge, the poet Bob Perelman. They chatted in the car, and when Zukofsky learned that Perelman had a master's degree in classics, he began explaining to him how sections of "A"-23 imitated the sounds of various Greek texts.

This reading at Franconia, and Zukofsky's meetings with Grenier and Perelman, were an emblematic moment in the transfer of Zukofsky's legacy to a new generation of poets—what William Carlos Williams had called, so many years ago, "another wave of it."[59] In the first issue of *This* (1971), Grenier had proclaimed "I HATE SPEECH," a clear rejection of the talk-based poetics of much of the postwar New American poetry. Instead, he and his young contemporaries sought models of poetry that would complicate the relationship of the spoken word and the printed poem, that would reemphasize language as material reality and social medium. In that same manifesto, "On Speech," Grenier had reprinted as exemplary a passage from Gertrude Stein's *Tender Buttons* and "Azure," the last poem of "I's (pronounced *eyes*)."[60] Within the next decade, Grenier, Perelman, and other poets who were assiduously reading Zukofsky—Barrett Watten, Ron Silliman, Lyn Hejinian, Bruce Andrews, Charles Bernstein, Rae Armantrout, and Erica Hunt, among many others—would emerge as the first real avant-garde in American poetry since Black Mountain and the San Francisco Renaissance: the loose, bicoastal tendency known as "L=A=N=G=U=A=G=E," "Language-centered writing," or, most simply, "Language Poetry." Like the objectivists and the modernists before them, the language poets, while profligate of manifestos, would have few overarching commonalities. But they would acknowledge and promote the legacy of Zukofsky's work into the last decades of the century.

. . .

In May 1975 the Zukofskys traveled to Baltimore, where Louis was to read at Johns Hopkins University at Hugh Kenner's invitation. Zukofsky welcomed the attention of this Canadian professor who was becoming the dean of modernist critics; he believed that Kenner was his truest advocate in the academy. He was happy when Kenner moved from Santa Barbara to Hopkins in 1973, which he hoped would permit more frequent visits to the Zukofskys in New York.[61] Kenner had touched upon Zukofsky's work in his monumental history of modernism, *The Pound Era*, and he treated it more fully in *A Home-made World*, his study of the American modernists.[62] Kenner's was a lively, polymathic mind; in many ways, he had shaped the academic study of both Pound and Joyce, and he thought he might attempt a Zukofsky book one day. Kenner played host to the Zukofskys when Zukofsky read at Hopkins in 1975, and again in September 1976, when they came to Baltimore for a program to celebrate the University library's acquisition of Celia's collection of her husband's publications. Kenner had brokered that acquisition—fifty-four books, 125 copies of magazines and anthologies in which Zukofsky's work had appeared—yet another instance of the Zukofskys' paring their household down to the barest essentials.[63]

Kenner's influence proved helpful in other ways. By the end of 1975, it was clear that Grossman was not interested in publishing a one-volume *"A"*. Although he no longer taught in the University of California system, Kenner was still on very good terms with August Frugé, director of the University of California Press, which had published *The Pound Era*. By early 1976, Frugé had firmly committed to California's doing a single-volume *"A"*, and had also expressed interest in an expanded *Prepositions*. The Zukofskys were more than pleased: As Zukofsky put it to Kenner, "we were overwhelmed by a miracle, and owe it all to your and Mary Anne [Kenner]'s valor."[64]

Zukofsky prepared an "Index to Definitions" for *Prepositions*, and he and Celia in collaboration—but mostly Celia—prepared an index for the whole of "*A*".

While Kenner had yet to find the time to write on Zukofsky at length, his own long experience in the academy had shown him the value of a "critical industry" for an author's reputation: After all, his *Poetry of Ezra Pound* had been the starting point for two decades of criticism on that poet, and his own doctoral dissertation, published as *Dublin's Joyce* in 1956, remained a book with which Joyce scholars had to reckon. Kenner encouraged his graduate student Barry Ahearn to write a dissertation that would result in the first book-length study of Zukofsky's work.[65] Ahearn would visit the Zukofskys in Port Jefferson in late 1977.

No doubt the fact that Kenner would be in attendance in part attracted Zukofsky to Orono, Maine, in June 1975, when the University of Maine hosted a "Symposium on Ezra Pound's 90th Birth Year." Carroll F. Terrell, a professor there, edited the Pound journal *Paideuma* and was interested in Zukofsky—perhaps more for his connection with Pound than on his own merits. At the conference, Hugh Kenner chaired the panel on which Zukofsky sat, along with Pound biographer Michael Reck and two associates of Pound's from St. Elizabeths days. Zukofsky read and ad-libbed his way through Pound's 1913 piece, "Through Alien Eyes"—the same essay he had quoted towards the end of "*A*"-23.[66] When the discussion turned to Pound's anti-Semitism, Zukofsky held his tongue for a quarter of an hour, then rose and pronounced his own, firsthand opinion: "Now I've heard about as much of this as I want to hear. And I want to say that I have never once in Pound's presence felt the kind of embarrassment I always feel in the presence of a 'Goy' who is anti-Semitic. Not once."[67] Zukofsky had said this back in 1948, and it was his final word on the unlucky, misguided friend to whom his loyalty had never faltered.

. . .

Belated recognition continued to trickle in. In May 1976 the American Academy and Institute of Arts and Letters announced that Zukofsky was one of the recipients of an "award for creative work in literature." At the 1977 commencement ceremonies at Bard College at Annandale-on-Hudson, where his old friend Robert Kelly had become one of the most prominent members of the faculty, Zukofsky was awarded an honorary Doctor of Letters degree. Back in the 1960s, Zukofsky had repeatedly told young questioners that it was useless to try to enter the academy without a doctorate—one would end up at a place like Brooklyn Polytechnic. One can only speculate with what emotions he finally received the doctorate at seventy-three.

Zukofsky was by no means idle in his suburban retirement. On December 27, 1974, he began drafting the eighty-one poems of *80 Flowers.*[68] He had planned for the project to occupy the better part of ten years, until his eightieth birthday—1984—but as so often he grew consumed with the labor and its difficult pleasures: He finished twenty-three "flowers" over the course of 1975, and another twenty-six in 1976. By the end of 1977 he had completed the seventy-sixth, "Weeds," and on January 21, 1978—Celia's sixty-fifth birthday—he finished the collection with another Z-signature, "Zinnia." With *"A"* and *80 Flowers,* two works of daunting complexity, depth, and musicality, now at the printers, Zukofsky set to work on his next project: "Gamut: 90 Trees."

"A"-21 through
"A"-24

IT IS DIFFICULT to overestimate Celia Zukofsky's contribution to her husband's work. Her most significant gift to him was the "L. Z. Masque," which became "A"-24 and which can be read as the catalyst that enabled Zukofsky to bring his long poem to a successful end. This is speculation, of course; but there is no evidence that in 1968, when Celia gave him the "L. Z. Masque," Zukofsky had any idea as to how to finish "A". "A"-24 relieved him of that responsibility. The "L. Z. Masque" is a crystalline and strikingly realized overview of Zukofsky's life's work. By juxtaposing the four voices of her husband's work (Thought, Drama, Story, Poem—*Prepositions*, *Arise, arise*, *It was*, and "A") against one another, and by plotting them all on the framework of Handel's harpsichord pieces, Celia is able to demonstrate, musically and dramatically, the unity of her husband's writing, what he had referred to back in "A"-12: "Each writer writes / one long work whose beat he cannot / entirely be aware of."[1]

The movement as it exists between the covers of "A", one must emphasize, is only a *score*, a piece that must be realized in performance rather than simply read. Silently reading "A"-24 all too easily gives one the impression of (in one reviewer's words) "five non-profit educational stations going at one time."[2] Even in performance the movement at times descends into an impenetrable babel of voices, though Celia Zukofsky specified that "Each voice should come through clearly";[3] but more frequent than moments of muddle are the moments of *space*, when Handel's music alone, or the music and one or two voices alone, are heard—and when one can clearly discern words, ideas, or motifs in juxtaposition. On the whole, "A"-24 is strikingly successful in presenting the "recurrences" in Louis Zukofsky's writings.

Although "A"-24 is the only movement of the poem that Zukofsky himself did not compose, it is perhaps paradoxically the most "personal" of the later movements of *A*. Knowing her husband and his work intimately, Celia Zukofsky chose to relate all of Zukofsky's poetry and prose to perhaps the most emotionally close to the bone of all his writings, the 1936 play *Arise, arise*. "The masque," she specifies at the beginning, "is centrally motivated by the drama."[4] At the heart of *Arise, arise*, and therefore at the heart of "A"-24, is the family. In *Arise, arise*, Zukofsky had dramatized his mother's death, his own position as the bereaved son. Chana Zukofsky's death in 1927 was the signal event of Zukofsky's early life, a loss that reverberated through much of his work, as Celia was well aware. That loss, however, would be compensated by the happiness that Zukofsky would find in his own family, his wife and musical son, as Celia indicates at the close of the last section, "Son." Over the last notes of Handel's "Fugues"—evoking the "fugal" forms earlier in *A*—the Son of *Arise, arise* addresses his mother: "New gloves, mother?" Simultaneously, the poem voice speaks the last line of "A"-20, from a poem Paul Zukofsky wrote at age nine: "What is it, I wonder that makes thee so loved . . ."[5] "Gloves" and "loved" sound simultaneously, producing a choral "love," and "mother" sounds alone, the final word of the poem. Like Zukofsky's first major work, "Poem beginning 'The,'" "A"-24 can be read as a poem addressed to his mother. But the ending as well incorporates the voices of the family trio: Paul, the son whose line is quoted, Louis, both son and father, and Celia herself, both the arranger of "A"-24 and the mother within this new household.

If "A"-21 was a movement backwards—back to the roots of Shake-spearean drama, back to the sounds of Latin verse, back to the earli-est years of Zukofsky's life—and "A"-24 a distillation of the central themes of his writing, demonstrating its fundamental themes and recurrences, then "A"-22 and -23, like *Bottom: on Shakespeare*'s "graph of culture," would move outward over the whole recorded range of human culture—and beyond that, to the geological and natural histories within which that culture had grown and developed. In "A"-22 and -23, Zukofsky settled decisively into what one might call his *late* poetics, a mode of writing radically different from the mod-ernist obliquities and juxtapositions of the first movements of *"A"*. A reader encountering "A"-1 through "A"-7 in the 1932 *An "Objectiv-ists" Anthology*, for instance, might be able to point out the places in which Zukofsky is writing "like" Pound, or Williams, or Cummings, or whomever. But the verse of Zukofsky's last decade is like nothing before it in English.

Each of the two last-composed movements of *"A"* consists of one thousand five-word (with rare exceptions) lines. Most of these lines are made up of words, phrases, and passages quoted, paraphrased, translated, or transliterated. The effect is of dense, rich, but alien lyricism; a sense of something happening at every moment, but with its "meaning" more often than not just beyond our grasp, rendered tenuous by a consistently ambiguous syntax and a baffling obliquity of reference:

> Claque-law—bard hard, fire yet:
> miracle porker-lane, apple, birch, greetings:
> calf-eyed, pie betide thee . . gore
> *off* head a great delight
> beguile war in the nightingale—
> *lullaby to your bounty*, lulla
> tree, snow-lee—eyry air goad.[6]

Here we have several faces of Zukofsky's compositional practice: transliteration, in that the most obdurately strange-sounding lines are imitations of the sounds of bits from various medieval Welsh poems; translation and paraphrase, for *"lullaby to your bounty"* ren-ders the gist of two lines of Gwelchmai's *Gorhoffed* (whose title gives us "gore / *off* head"); and quotation, for that same *"lullaby to your bounty"* is spoken by the clown Feste in Shakespeare's *Twelfth Night*.[7]

The verse is not always this baffling. There are passages of delicate (though never *lulling*) lyricism, and stretches of narrative, though we can rarely entirely follow the story being told. These last movements of *"A"*, unlike most other verse passages of similar length in English poetry before them, are never formulaic. Our attention might flag because of the severe demands Zukofsky places upon it—we are always called upon to actively construe an ambiguous, recalcitrant syntax—but the jagged, irregular music of the words never allows the reader's attention to lapse into the half-asleep, half-aware state so often provoked by Shelley, Tennyson, Swinburne.

The two thousand lines of "A"-22 and -23 are the culmination of Zukofsky's twinned poetics of quotation and translation—really aspects of a single practice. Formed out of a radical concatenation of various materials, they sound a strange and fragmentary music. "A / child learns on blank paper," Zukofsky comments in "A"-22, "An old man rewrites palimpsest."[8] For decades Zukofsky's writing had moved towards the condition of the palimpsest—the overwritten parchment, in which an original text is still visible in the interstices of the new. In "A"-22 and -23, he achieves that condition: a wholly original poetic text, in each of whose details the voices of others can be heard.

Zukofsky viewed these two movements as "histories." In the spiral notebook in which he gathered his materials for "A"-22 and -23, the various elements for the two movements are sorted into two-page spreads, one for each century from pre-3000 BCE to the present. These elements—lines, phrases, longer passages—were then sifted, in roughly chronological order of their origins, to the drafts of either "A"-22 or "A"-23 (each of which was drafted in a separate spiral notebook).[9] But while the two movements proceed historically, they are "histories" largely devoid of that genre's proper names. Towards the beginning of "A"-22, Zukofsky writes, "History's best emptied of names' / impertinence met on the ways."[10]

After the 103-line "Initial," which serves as something of an overture to both movements, "A"-22 begins with an account of a volcanic island rising from the sea floor. It closes with the Zukofskys in Bermuda, wondering at the unfamiliar flora and taking shelter from a sudden storm. The movement concerns itself with natural history, with the geological processes and life cycles of growing things within which human culture arose. Human language, and thereby human thought, take form within the context of these vast geological processes. In its middle passages, Zukofsky concatenates vast stretches of proverbial and philosophical wisdom from the pre-Socratics, other Greek philosophers, and such "alien" traditions as Buddhism. (The effect is reminiscent at times of the early sections of "A"-13.) There is no overall "gist" to these *obiter dicta*, only a clear sense of human philosophy—or "wisdom"—as at its best a response to the growth and cycles of the natural world: "How to write history, policy / an unteachable gift of nature: / farmer prophesies better than poet."[11] "A"-22 ends with the poet in the "*still-vext Bermoothes*" of Shakespeare's *Tempest*, an "old . . . stabled horse" who "sings sometimes," and whose song takes the form of a "cento reading"—a patchwork, a medley of quotations.[12]

. . .

If "A"-22 is a "history" in which human speech, philosophy, and wisdom literature take place within a prior and more fundamental context of natural processes, then in "A"-23 Zukofsky turns his attention more specifically towards the *human*. In the records of language, of poetry in particular, Zukofsky traces a "saving history" by which the voices of human beings separated by the widest cultural and temporal gulfs can still be heard:

> the saving history
> not to deny the gifts
> of time where those who
> never met together may hear
> this other time sound *one*.[13]

Like the bulk of *Bottom: on Shakespeare*, and like *A Test of Poetry*, "A"-23 is a "graph of culture," a writing of the entire history of human word making, from the "tuned sound not words" of the Arapaho song that begins the main section all the way down to the present, the "music, thought, drama, story, poem" of the "L. Z. Masque."[14]

The range of material Zukofsky incorporates into "A"-23 is as vast as in "A"-22. At the very beginnings of human poetry making are the wordless Arapaho chant and an "Australian Aranda song" that sounds "Akin jabber,"[15] but these "primitive" modulations of sound—and Zukofsky himself, student of Franz Boas, knew how sophisticated the so-called "primitive" actually was—give way to the extended narrative of *Gilgamesh*, the earliest of Western epics.[16] There follows a mosaic of passages from the archaic Greek (Hesiod, Sappho, Anakreon, the Homeric Hymns) and the Hebrew Bible (Joel, Micah, Jeremiah, Habakkuk, Ezekiel, Isaiah, Malachi, the Psalms—by no means an exhaustive list). Though Zukofsky had confessed to "a dream of named history" at the end of "A"-22, and though the first passage of "A"-23 had announced that "older / desire chances naming," the sources of these passages remain obdurately buried, the identifications of their original speakers subsumed in the music of their words.[17] Towards the halfway point of the movement, we begin to move into more familiar (for English-speaking readers) territory: the Greek and Roman classics, often as reinterpreted and translated by Renaissance writers. Passages in early modern spelling—"*So to / ourselues we bride an air / clear, a ligh and brethe*"—begin to creep in.[18] The last few pages of the central section of "A"-23 comprise a pocket anthology of British verse, from *Beowulf* and the *Mabinogion*, through Chaucer and the medieval Welsh bards, to Elizabeth I's translation of Boethius and Shakespeare.

Like "A"-22, "A"-23 consists of an eight-hundred-line central section, bracketed by two hundred-line "framing" passages.[19] The opening hundred lines, in five-line stanzas, constitute something of a meditation upon "*A*" as a whole. It begins:

An unforeseen delight a round
beginning ardent; to end blest
presence less than nothing thrives:
a world worn in whose
happiest reins preempt their histories

which cannot help or hurt
a foreseen curve where many
loci would dispose and *and's*
compound creature and creature together.[20]

Here we have three elements of "A"-12's B-A-C-H acronym: "blest," "ardent," "happy"; all that is missing is "Celia," though her presence suffuses this first section, and her name appears some fifteen stanzas on—"what / submerged name in coldénia"—encapsulated in one of the plants she tends.[21] The poem itself is "a round," as in the first words of "A"-1, "beginning ardent; to end blest." It is "a foreseen curve"—for Zukofsky, though he had little idea in 1928 what would go into "A", knew from the beginning that it would be a "curve" of twenty-four movements—upon which Zukofsky has plotted, or "disposed," the contingencies of his life and his times, often with no more grammatical linkage than a simple conjunction: "and's / compound creature and creature together."

"A"-23's last one hundred lines are among the richest and densest of the poem, often setting materials from two or three different sources together in a single line. It is as though the poem, nearing its end, has speeded its pace into a final burst of activity, a final frenetic gathering-in of the gleaming bits of culture to which Zukofsky would pay homage. Names begin to appear, if lightly cloaked in punning guise: "cold-ridge" for Samuel Taylor Coleridge, "Jubilant agony" rewording Christopher Smart's *Jubilate Agno*.[22] The poem's last twenty-six lines are "A living calendar, names inwreath'd," in which a multitude of talismanic names appear, both outright—Bach, Handel, Eden (Richard Eden, author of the 1577 *History of Travaile*)—and as puns: "For / series distributes harmonies, attraction Governs / destinies" distills a dictum of the French utopian Charles-Marie Fourier; "Land or" is Walter Savage Landor, "Most art" is Mozart.[23] The movement ends with an acknowledgment of the poet's wife, who had composed the five voices of the "L. Z. Masque," and the poet's son, at the time living on Arbutus Road: "music, thought, drama, story, poem / parks' sunburst—animals, grace notes—/ z-sited path are but us."

· · ·

Zukofsky was seventy years old when he completed "A", and with some optimism was projecting his next work, *80 Flowers*, to occupy his next decade. Celia Zukofsky, ever mindful of her husband's future reputation, suggested that he ought to produce an index for "A", "as a help, a guide for anyone wishing to give a course, a lecture, anything on L.Z." Zukofsky demurred: "the reader will have to find his own way," he told his wife; but he responded more favorably to Celia's well-calculated suggestion that he produce an index of only three words—his perennial "a," "an," and "the." For some days Zukofsky laid aside work on *80 Flowers* to index the passages of *"A"* in which the articles were of primary importance: seventy-three references to "a," forty to "an," and seventy-three to "the." California, however, was scarcely swifter than Jonathan Williams's Jargon Society in its publication schedule, and while the Zukofskys were cooling their heels Celia Zukofsky "amused herself" by compiling an "Index of Names & Objects" for the poem as a whole. Her index ran to several *thousand* library cards, which amused Louis—"you feel in italics and think in capitals," he told her. But he consented to wade through the mass and "eliminate what he thought unnecessary," eventually pruning it down to thirty-six typescript pages, "thoroly reduced to the marrow."[24]

For some time Zukofsky had been fascinated with the index as form. The dedication to "Poem beginning 'The'" was actually an index of references within that work; "*'Mantis': An Interpretation*" incorporated a miniature index of the subjects touched upon in "'Mantis'"; and the index to *Bottom: on Shakespeare* was a substantial work in its own right. An index offered, as it were, a poetics of its own, a way of further condensing and focusing on the concerns of a given book, which would then be organized on the purely abstract basis of the alphabet—a fortuitous ordering for a poet whose major poem began with the alphabet's first letter and whose surname began with its last.

The principles that governed the index to *"A"* were fairly rigorous. Proper names were only indexed if they had explicitly appeared in the poem: "Pith or gore has" in "A"-22 clearly refers to Pythagoras, and "A"-21's "one lean buck / take heart grow fuller" is Buckminster Fuller, but neither of those passages was indexed under those names.[25] The index offered Zukofsky, the laureate of excision, a perfect laboratory to perform such operations on his own work. To single out seventy-three occurrences of "a"—a word that almost certainly appears several thousand times in *"A"*—was itself a commentary on the poem, and by some logic a poem-by-excision in its own right. Concurrently with the "Index of Names & Objects" to *"A"*, Zukofsky drew up an "Index to Definitions" for the expanded *Prepositions*.[26] It was a brief document (only two pages), utterly devoid of proper names—though *Prepositions* itself was rife with them—and with a large number of its terms receiving only a single reference. Like the index to "*A*", it served as implicit commentary on the thought of the poet who had written the essays of *Prepositions*: The four most-cited terms were "music," "philosophy," "poetry," and "history."

California was in no hurry to issue *Prepositions*. (Zukofsky would never see the book, for it was not published until 1981.) They were little more expeditious with "*A*", and by May 1978, with *80 Flowers* completed, the Zukofskys had only seen the first set of page proofs. They were pleased by the "'typographic' unity" of the book, despite the lengths to which California had been driven in economizing on this vast venture: "*A*" *1–12* had been entirely reset from the Double-day/Paris Review edition, but "*A*" *13–21*, "*A*" *22 & 23*, and "*A*"-*24* were photo reprints of their earlier appearances. Many old errors were corrected, but new errata had crept in. Nonetheless, when Celia Zukofsky finally received the printed copies of the book in January 1979, she was pleased. "It is BEAUTIFUL," she wrote Hugh Kenner. "I know Louis would have felt as I do about it."[27]

80 *Flowers* and "Gamut: 90 Trees"

FTER THEY LEFT the city in October 1973, there were few things that could persuade Louis and Celia Zukofsky to venture out of their Long Island retreat. Apart from a very few sorties, Zukofsky spent his last four and a half years in Port Jefferson, hard at work. The traditional labor of the retiree, of course, is to tend one's garden, and in a sense that is precisely what Zukofsky did: He wrote *80 Flowers*, a work that joins a long line of horticultural poems from Vergil's *Georgics* to Erasmus Darwin's *The Botanical Garden*.[1]

For Zukofsky a flower poem would not be simple or straightforward as Emerson's address to the "The Rhodora" or Tennyson's "Flower in the Crannied Wall." Zukofsky wanted firsthand knowledge of each of the plants of which he wrote—a desire that would press Celia into a constant round of container gardening over the next three years (Louis was a gardener only on paper): "*Substance*,"

he wrote in his *"Plan"* for *80 Flowers.* "Only those flowers I have actually seen and whatever botany I can learn in 10 years."[2] The latter
phrase was crucial, for the experience of nature in Zukofsky's poetry
was never direct, never unmediated. In *80 Flowers* he would treat each
plant not merely from the standpoint of its phenomenal appearance, but through the lens of its scientific description and of all of
the botanical and literary lore that had accumulated about it over the
centuries. For *80 Flowers* Zukofsky "spent, oh, hours, weeks, months
just on research," Celia Zukofsky recalled. "And when Louis started
on research there was no stopping him. Then he just went to the
bitter end, every definition, every connotation, every annotation, it
just went on and on."[3]

It was not merely that Zukofsky was painstakingly combing
through his favored botanical sources (*Gray's Manual of Botany*
and *Taylor's Encyclopedia of Gardening*), tracking down every cross-
reference and seeking out every source text cited. These eighty poems,
in their brief compass, were to be as well a summation and condensation of Zukofsky's own life's work: "*Form.* 8-line songs of 5-word
lines: 40 words to each poem, growing out of and *condensing* my previous books, 'A', *All, Arise, arise, Bottom: On Shakespeare, Catullus, Little*
etc." To incorporate in 640 lines not merely the botany and botanical
lore of the eighty flowers, but the range of projects represented in the
personal drama of *Little* and *Arise, arise,* the lyricism of *ALL,* the vast
concatenation of quotations of *"A"* and *Bottom,* the phonetic translations of *Catullus*—a stupendous ambition. And like *Bottom* and *"A",*
the poems of *80 Flowers* would reach back throughout the entire history of Western literature, winding in the Shakespeare always at his
fingertips, the Greek and Latin classics so important to him, and the
novels he was making his way through (Thomas Hardy and Henry
James in particular).

The sequence begins with an epigraph:

Heart us invisibly thyme time
round rose bud fire downland
bird tread quagmire dry gill-over-the-ground
stem-square leaves-cordate earth race horsethyme
breath neighbors a mace nays

sorrow of harness pulses pent
thus fruit pod split four
one-fourth *ripens* unwithering gaping[4]

This is the poet's invocation in epic fashion to a muse, to "Heart us" in the labors to come. The poet's "race" is against "time," increasing age, a homophone for the fragrant herb thyme, which the Greeks would burn on the altar to their gods. Time, and the pun time/thyme, would be central to the poems of *80 Flowers*, which had been plotted on a strict schedule, and which represented yet another attempt on Zukofsky's part to achieve a durable immortality, "liveforever." The poem's galloping rhythms, as well as its reference to "horsethyme" and to the "sorrow of harness" (as well as the pun "nays"/neighs), suggest that once again, as he has done so often, Zukofsky is figuring the poem as horse, as the emblem of speed and freedom bound for the nonce into the harness of labored form. But in this epigraph the horse-poet is champing at the bit to begin the course ahead, and the prospect—despite the "sorrow of harness" and "pulses pent"—is one of ripeness, of fruition, of open, ageless success: "one fourth *ripens* unwithering gaping."

The surface texture of this verse is even more daunting than that of "A"-22 and -23. The words are for the most part familiar demotic English, but the syntax is almost impossible to nail down. Is "time" a noun or a verb? What parts of speech are "rose," "bud," "fire," and "tread," all of which hesitate between the nominal and the verbal? Where, in these entirely unpunctuated lines, are we to place the pauses upon which syntactic sense so crucially depends? All eighty-one of the poems of *80 Flowers* are of a piece in this syntactic ambiguity; they seem to be composed of shards of sentences, broken from their original contexts and mosaicked into place within the five-word, eight-line grid of the poems, where to the casual eye they form opaque ranks of nouns, adjectives, and gerunds. The verbs that act as the "muscle" of ordinary English prose syntax must be extricated from forms that look like nouns or even adjectives. And there are no final answers as to how a given line ought to be read: Before our eyes, the words shift from pattern to pattern as we try out various possibilities.

All this takes place, of course, within a formal frame as binding as any traditional sonnet. The five-word line, uniform throughout the last stretch of "*A*"—"*A*"-21, -22, and -23, had become his "default" meter, an oblique homage to the ubiquitous English pentameter line. Eight, the number of lines to each poem, had grand numerological resonance. It was the Pythagorean number of love: "And love be an 8 in a precise walk," Zukofsky had written in "A"-8; "A"-18's word count lines had contained "eight words to a line for love."[5] Each poem would then consist of forty words, another talismanic number: the Flood of Genesis lasted forty days and nights; the Children of Israel had wandered in the wilderness for forty years; in the Hebrew Bible forty years was generally considered the length of a generation.[6] Each two-page spread would display eighty words—the same number as flowers in the collection as a whole.

Numerology aside, the eight-line poem, five words to the line—with *very* occasional exceptions (as in the last line of the epigraph), and with sometimes elephantine hyphenations ("gill-over-the-ground") counting as single words—provided Zukofsky a flexible but delimited form within which to work: a defined parterre, as it were, within which he could plumb the implications of each flower he approached. And those implications (etymologically, what is "folded in") go well beyond what is visible on the poems' surface. To return to the epigraph for a moment: Zukofsky's working notes for the poem show that "Heart us" is Zukofsky's transliteration (with an added aspirate) of the Greek *artos*, "bread"; "thyme" recalls both *thýmos*, "thyme," and *thymós*, "soul, spirit, passion, heart." "[R]ose bud fire" recalls Isaac D'Israeli's essay "Introduction of Tea, Coffee, Chocolate," where the prime minister's father related how the "Norwegians on the first sight of roses, dared not touch what they conceived were trees budding with fire." "[B]ird tread quagmire dry gill-over-the-ground" condenses materials concerning the Elizabethan herbalist John Gerard, while "unwithering" invokes both Shakespeare's Cleopatra and a passage from Herman Melville's *Pierre; or, the Ambiguities*. The "sorrow of harness" can be traced to a review of a 1972 biography of Albert Einstein, who described himself as "*a horse for single harness, not cut out for tandem* or team work."[7] Almost every word of each of the *Flowers* can be traced to a source in Zukofsky's reading: it is either a quotation, an allusion, a transliteration, or a translation—and often several at once.

Zukofsky's goal in *80 Flowers*, then, was of a piece with the other works of his late poetics: to forge a new poetic object, within the confines of a strict form, out of the whole range of readable culture and the constant infringements of present existence and contingency. That present existence was the course of Zukofsky's quotidian existence in Port Jefferson with Celia, surrounded by the real plants that were, after all, the primary subjects of the writing. Contingencies could be events: "scald scold honor the bard," which closes "Oxalis," may be linked to Zukofsky's 1977 honorary degree from Bard College, as well as to Shakespeare, the "bard" of Avon.[8] Contingencies could as well be events related in communications from others: "poor tom's a / cold . . . one bluegreen eye" of "Thyme" both quotes *King Lear* and refers back to a 1969 letter in which Guy Davenport told the story of his duplicitous Persian cat Max, who had entered his household "one bitterly cold day" to become "our cat," and who later turned out to have been simultaneously enjoying the board of two other sets of masters.[9] Or such contingencies could be more humble, as in the "young's churning old rambler's flown / to sky" of "Starglow," which under one of its aspects refers to a Port Jefferson neighbor's defunct automobile—an AMC Rambler.[10]

. . .

80 Flowers was Zukofsky's most private project: None of the poems were offered to magazines, nor did Zukofsky read any of them in public. (At Johns Hopkins in December 1975, Zukofsky read the twenty-three flowers completed thus far to a *very* private audience—Hugh Kenner and his tape recorder—and discussed "Bayberry" in some detail.[11]) Zukofsky's conception for the book's actual publication was little more public. On December 21, 1977, Zukofsky wrote the Stinehour Press in Lunenberg, Vermont, inquiring as to what the press would charge to produce a strictly limited edition of his new poems. (The Stinehour Press was Paul Zukofsky's suggestion; he had been impressed with the work they had done for the composer and poet John Cage.) The Zukofskys found suitable Stinehour's terms for producing a hardcover, slipcased edition, "using good materials and workmanship but not fancy or ostentatious in any way."[12] The book was announced to appear in June 1978; it would be published in a signed and dated edition of only eighty copies, and would be available—for one hundred fifty dollars a copy—only from Celia Zukofsky.[13]

Why, at this point in his career, did Zukofsky opt for such a limited and expensive edition of poems that represented the culmination of his life's work? Why, now that his poetry was in print or forthcoming from such major publishers as Norton and the University of California Press, did Zukofsky return to the artisanal production methods he had pursued with *First Half of "A"-9* and *Barely and widely*? One plausible explanation is financial: If the book sold out at one hundred fifty dollars a copy, the Zukofskys would realize a net profit of over ten thousand dollars on the edition. As well, publishing Zukofsky's work with the Stinehour Press allowed the Zukofskys a control that they had been forced to relinquish when dealing with larger publishers. Norton's *ALL*, while welcome indeed, had proved disappointing in its cramped typography, and California's *"A"* was proceeding at a snail's pace. Working with Stinehour and their own capital, the Zukofskys could be assured that *80 Flowers* would appear in a handsome, suitably readable edition, and in a timely fashion. And there was nothing to prevent Zukofsky from incorporating the Flowers into a larger collection at some future date.

And perhaps the terms of the Stinehour *80 Flowers* represented Zukofsky's final ambivalent judgment on his work and his audience. Maybe, after all, Zukofsky had no more than eighty readers in the world (certainly, as he often complained, no one was taking the trouble to visit him and Celia in Port Jefferson): but those eighty readers would have to *pay* this time around, and finally, for once in his life, Zukofsky would receive fair wages for his poetic efforts.

· · ·

When the Zukofskys concluded their arrangements with the Stinehour Press in early January 1978, Zukofsky was three poems away from completing the collection. On January 21, 1978, Celia's sixty-fifth birthday, Zukofsky finished the last of the Flowers, "Zinnia":

With prayer-plant eyes annually winter-leggy
zinnia miracles itself perennial return
blest interim strength lengthening coreopsis'-summers
actual some time whereso near
zebra-fragrant sharpened wave currents tide
new moon to full sunrise
sunset enable ships seaworth slow-rounds
rosette lancers speared-yucca's white night [14]

It is another signature, like the "Z (*signature*)" of *Bottom* or the "z-sited path" of "A"-23, and a seasonal poem, like so many of the Flowers—in this case a poem written in the depths of winter, but anticipating the "perennial return" of the warm season, "blest interim strength lengthening coreoposis'-summers." The cycles of the seasons—and by this point in composing *80 Flowers* Zukofsky had watched his wife's plants grow and bloom through three full turnings of the year—are mirrored in miniature in the cycles of the months and the tides ("sharpened wave currents tide / new moon . . . slow-rounds") and of the individual days ("sunrise / sunset") As Celia's birthday poem, "Zinnia" (the vowels of whose title significantly overlap those of Celia's name) is a celebration of almost forty years of married life, another marking, like the title of the 1956 collection *Some Time* (which it quotes), of shared existence and shared observation of the "recurrences" of life and art. *ALL* had been dedicated to Paul Zukofsky, offered up to the younger generation. *80 Flowers*, from its very inception, was intended as a collection revolving around the dual axis of Louis and Celia; its dedication reads simply "*to C.*"

. . .

Soon after Zukofsky finished "Zinnia" he and Celia sent a completed typescript of *80 Flowers* to the Stinehour Press.[15] Zukofsky took no holidays from his labors, however. At least since 1975 he had been contemplating the work which would follow *80 Flowers*: "a book entitled *Gamut: Trees ninety 5's*[*] <[*]final title decided Apr 20/75>—that is, (for the year 2000) 90 poems of 5 five-word lines each."[16] There was a clear overlap between the projects of *80 Flowers* and "Gamut."[17] Various notes gathered in the course of the *80 Flowers* research were

eventually transferred into the "90 Trees" notes, and a passage originally drafted in January 1977 for a "90 Trees" epigraph was incorporated into "Windflower."[18]

Between February 5 and 11, 1978, Zukofsky drafted the only surviving poem of "Gamut: 90 Trees," "Much ado about trees":

> Much ado about trees lichen
> hugs alga and fungus lives
> off each other hoe does
> dear owe dear earth terrace
> money sunday coffee poorjoe snow[19]

These are a quirky, minimal twenty-five words, perhaps forecast-
ing a new stripped-down demotic language for "90 Trees." They
tell us something about the interrelations of alga and fungus (which
together are lichen); they transliterate the binomial for the button-
weed, *Diodio teres*, as "dear owe dear earth terrace"; they allude to the
plant poor joe, of the coffee family. The poem ends with "snow"—as
well it might, written in February—and thereby alludes to the "Snow-
flake," "Snowdrop," and "Snow-Wreath" of *80 Flowers*. As with any
early-February poem of Zukofsky's, it is safe to speculate that "Much
ado" is a valentine, perhaps evoking the warmth of "sunday coffee"
shared by the poet and his wife on a snowy day.

The Stinehour Press sent proofs of *80 Flowers* as promised; they
were returned (mostly) without mishap—only one error slipped past
the Zukofskys' proofreading eyes—and the book went into production.[20] Soon afterwards, the University of California Press sent page
proofs for the massive single-volume *"A"*, a far more complex and
problematic text, in which Louis and Celia had to look out for the
accumulated errors of six different sets of typesetters,[21] and to which
they had to key the page references for the index upon which they
had collaborated.

Zukofsky had been a master of hypochondria for some decades
now; his intolerance of "drafts" had become almost legendary, and
heavy smoking had seriously damaged his lungs. (He had with great
difficulty reduced his intake to four or five cigarettes a day.[22]) Nonetheless, despite a constant round of various "aches," he had suffered
no major illnesses, had never undergone surgery. On the morning of

May 11, 1978, after suffering a couple of days of the abdominal pains he had always associated with simple indigestion, Zukofsky got out of bed, only to collapse to the floor. An ambulance took him to Port Jefferson's Mather Hospital. On the doctor's advice, Paul cancelled a Washington, D.C., concert engagement.

The pains, it turned out, were symptoms of a perforated duodenal ulcer—an ulcer, almost certainly, that had gone untreated for some time. Peritonitis set in, and Zukofsky slipped into a coma. He went into cardiac arrest and died the next day, May 12, 1978.[23] Zukofsky's cause of death, John Cage later remarked to Paul Zukofsky, was precisely the same as that which had carried off James Joyce thirty-seven years earlier. Joyce and Zukofsky, alike in their desire to rethink the fundamentals of their art even as they clung to its traditional pleasures, alike in the grand, culture-spanning ambitions of their great works, and alike in their stubborn determination to pursue their own aesthetics undeterred by public scorn or indifference, were—by the sort of coincidence in which each of them would have delighted—alike in their manner of passing.

Afterword 1978–1980

THE *New York Times* ran a rather perfunctory obituary for Zukofsky, but Zukofsky's friend Harvey Shapiro, editor of the paper's Sunday book review supplement, commissioned a memorial essay from Hugh Kenner. In "Louis Zukofsky: All the Words," published a month after Zukofsky's death, Kenner forecast one afterlife for Zukofsky—as the subject of scholarly research. "They will still be elucidating" Zukofsky's works, Kenner wrote, "in the twenty-second century, and perceiving what Zukofsky saw in words such as a, the, from, to, about."[1] The scholars were already hard at work. Kenner's student Barry Ahearn was revising his dissertation on "*A*" for book publication, and in May 1979, Kenner himself signed a contract with the University of California Press for a brief book to be entitled "Zukofsky's Eye." Aside from a never-published essay on "The Translation," nothing came of that project; nor did Kenner make any progress on the edition of Zukofsky's correspondence with William Carlos Williams that he considered pursuing in the years after Zukofsky's death.[2]

Celia Zukofsky maintained a warm correspondence with Kenner

and his wife Mary Anne in the months after her husband died. Kenner had a large hand in assembling the special Zukofsky issue of *Paideuma*, the Pound journal, that Carroll F. Terrell edited late in 1978. An impressive array of friends and admirers recalled and paid homage to Zukofsky there, among them Ronald Johnson, Gael Turnbull, Robert Creeley, Robert Kelly, Harvey Shapiro, Hayden Carruth, Robert Duncan, and Charles Tomlinson. Despite his never-mended, two decades–old break with Zukofsky, George Oppen—already showing the early symptoms of the Alzheimer's that would take his life in 1984—sent a brief and touching note: "Zukofsky's brilliance—his example and his brilliant comment—were revelatory to me—my first step beyond adolescent poetry."[3] Basil Bunting, thinking back over his own almost-half-century friendship with Zukofsky, summed up his colleague's temper as an "admirable" stubbornness:

> It took more than two thousand years of violent opposition to make the Jews as stubborn as the best of them are. Sometimes I don't like it; but everyone admires and even loves that stubbornness in Spinoza, Zukofsky's favourite amongst philosophers; and the stubbornness L.Z. used in his verse and in his detailed criticism is just as admirable.[4]

In September 1978 Celia Zukofsky spent a week with the Kenners in Orono, Maine, where Kenner taped her in conversation with Terrell on the subject of her husband's life and work. Terrell and Kenner both recognized the importance of such firsthand accounts of a poet, and Terrell published excerpts from the interview in the memorial *Paideuma*.[5] Determined to do whatever he could in the service of Zukofsky scholarship, Terrell edited *Louis Zukofsky: Man and Poet* in 1979, a large volume that reprinted most of the *Paideuma* memorial issue and added about two hundred pages of critical commentary, a selection of Zukofsky's own "Discarded Poems," an annotated bibliography of secondary literature on Zukofsky, and a rambling biographical profile of Zukofsky by Terrell himself (which incorporated most of the text of his conversations with Celia).[6] The book was dedicated "To Celia." Celia was pleased by the *Man and Poet* volume, as she had been pleased by the University of California Press *"A"*, which finally turned up in January 1979.

In the months after his death, there were other homages to

Zukofsky. In summer 1978, six young Bay Area poets—Kit Robinson, Steve Benson, Carla Harryman, Lyn Hejinian, Barrett Watten,
and Bob Perelman (who had driven Zukofsky back to Boston after his
reading at Franconia in 1974)—mounted a performance of "A"-24
at a San Francisco coffee shop, a performance that was repeated in
November at the Poetry Center of San Francisco State University and
at the University of California, Davis.[7] In early 1979, the poet Hugh
Seidman arranged a "Commemorative Evening for Louis Zukofsky"
at the P.E.N. American Center, an evening at which he, Allen Ginsberg, Creeley, and Celia Zukofsky herself spoke. Seidman had been a
student of Zukofsky's at Poly almost twenty years before, but he had
long since fallen out of touch with his old teacher.

The commemorative evening at the P.E.N. Center was a rather
moving affair. Ginsberg, who had known Zukofsky only distantly and
who had never quite digested his poetry, spoke in rather general terms
of Zukofsky as "a model of manners, humor, a kind of rectitude, and
a courage in pursuing near scientific studies of the musical qualities
of language and the measurements of sound and its placement on
the page."[8] Seidman remembered his own years at Poly with great
affection: "I was eighteen years old," he recalled, and Zukofsky "was
awesome to me in those days . . . the way the father is awesome to the
son." Seidman and his friends had "loved" Zukofsky, and remembered "the almost rabbinical kind of wisdom" he had shown in his
poetry and criticism.[9] For his part Creeley recalled Zukofsky's "particular friendship with me"—not that he claimed to have been a special intimate of Zukofsky's, but he remained in awe of the "generous
and particular regard" Zukofsky had shown him.[10] Creeley himself
seemed taken aback when Celia Zukofsky said, "If Louis had to pick
the friends that were dearest and closest to him, it would be Ezra
Pound, Robert Creeley, and William Carlos Williams for a while."
"But I never knew that," Creeley replied.[11]

·   ·   ·

If the April 1979 event at the P.E.N. Center in New York was something of a lovefest, the homage to Zukofsky that took place at the
San Francisco Art Institute four months before had been something
else altogether: a clash of personal egos, of poetic ideologies, and of

poetic groups, and a clash that demonstrated that there was already under way a struggle over Zukofsky's poetic inheritance. The event, held under the auspices of the Poetry Center at San Francisco State University and organized by its new director, Tom Mandel, had featured a screening of the "outtakes"—constituting a substantial film in themselves—from Richard Moore's 1965 National Educational Television documentary on Zukofsky, followed by commentary and discussion from two Bay Area poets, Robert Duncan and Barrett Watten.[12]

Duncan had been reading Zukofsky for some forty years now, and Zukofsky had counted him as a friend and a staunch supporter; Duncan had been the first to show Zukofsky's work to Creeley in Mallorca back in 1955, and had introduced Zukofsky's poetry to other poets of the Black Mountain circle. For Duncan, by the mid-1950s Zukofsky was "one of the two contemporary poets"—the other being Olson—"whose work I knew to be clearly directive of my own attentions."[13] Through his job at the Poetry Center, Duncan had brought Zukofsky to San Francisco State in 1958 for the summer session that prompted 5 *Statements for Poetry*. By the late 1970s, Duncan was a towering figure on the Bay Area poetry scene: uncompromisingly experimental in his open-form, visionary, eclectic poetry, which drew upon both the techniques of the modernists and the emotional resources of English Romanticism, and intimidatingly erudite in a wide range of literary, philosophical, and mystical fields.

Watten was a rising figure on that same poetry scene. Almost thirty years younger than Duncan, he was one of the younger writers who were coming to be known as Language poets. Watten and the other five poets who had performed "A"-24 earlier that year— Harryman, Hejinian, Perelman, Robinson, and Benson—were all associated with this movement. The Language writers were for the most part Marxists, deeply politicized by the experience of Vietnam; they were well studied in the poststructuralist thought making its way across the Atlantic from France; and they were closely acquainted with Zukofsky's poetry, both through individual reading and through discussion and reading groups centered on his work. For his part, Watten had been reading Zukofsky for ten years, since he was twenty years old.[14]

The actual screening of the NET film proved far less gripping than the fireworks surrounding it.[15] Introducing the film, Duncan spoke at length about Zukofsky's life and career, mentioning the names of numerous San Francisco poets whom he had known and influenced, and recalling his own friendship with Zukofsky. Watten's presentation after the movie was far more formal and analytic. He pondered the paradoxes inherent in Zukofsky's statement, "The words are my life"; he considered the contradictions of *"A"* as a whole, in which the familial celebration of "A"-12 coexisted with the explicit Marxism of "A"-8; and he analyzed—using an overhead projector and various marked-up passages of Zukofsky's work—a range of Zukofsky's structuring devices, including the mathematics that figures in "A"-8 and -9. In many ways, the talk was typical of the Language poets' approach to the writers who had most influenced them, from Stein and Khlebnikov to Olson and Zukofsky: a dispassionate technical analysis, a dogged uncovering and examining of internal contradictions that largely bypassed or downplayed notions of the "great work" and its master builder.

Clearly agitated—indeed, almost apoplectic with exasperation—Duncan returned to the stage. (He had already tried to retake the podium *during* Watten's presentation.) It was as though Watten, by analyzing, dissecting, and graphically mapping the structures of Zukofsky's writing, had somehow violated the poet to whom they were paying homage. Duncan's response, in the words of his student David Levi Strauss, was to launch "into a fiercely impassioned defence of Zukofsky's work." Duncan read "Zinnia," the last poem of *80 Flowers* (the existence of which the majority of his audience was learning of for the first time), and proceeded to lovingly unpack the poem, from its title (which begins with Z and ends with A) to "the incredibly rampant riming between the lines and 'the world' outside the lines."[16] What set *this* sort of analysis apart from what Watten had done—aside from the fact that Watten was delivering a carefully prepared analysis while Duncan was furiously improvising as he strode back and forth across the stage—lay in Duncan's attitude towards language and the figure of the author: "I in no way believe," Duncan said, "that there is such a thing as 'just language,' any more than there is 'just footprints.' I mean, it is human life that prints itself

everywhere in it and that's what we read when we're really reading."
In Duncan's eyes, the Language writers, by viewing language as a
structure that preceded, and even superseded, the individual subject,
had gotten it precisely backwards: language, and especially the language of a poet as powerful as Zukofsky, was preeminently the trace
of a human consciousness, the makings of a sensitive and masterful
individual artist.[17]

Duncan had the last word that evening, but his abrupt and unfair
dismissal of Watten in December 1978 was merely the first skirmish
in a series of "poetry wars" that would roil the Bay Area poetry community for the better part of the next decade, pitting the writers who
saw themselves as the spiritual heirs of the San Francisco Renaissance, the Black Mountain poets, the Beats, and other midcentury
experimental traditions against the Language poets, caricatured over
and over as soulless technocrats, antilyrical theorists, and humorless,
politically rigid commissars of a new poststructuralist Stalinism in
verse.[18] Somewhere beneath the rhetoric, of course, was a struggle for
control over the reading series, little magazines, reviews, and book
series that flourished in the Bay Area. But it is notable that the immediate locus of this struggle was the artistic legacy of Louis Zukofsky:
To whom did he "belong"—to the poets who had known him and
loved his work for so many years, seeing it as (in Milton's words) "the
precious life-blood of a master spirit"? Or to this new generation of
upstarts, who read Zukofsky with both a technical and a critical eye,
and who took his works not as a sort of limit-text of modernism, but
as a fertile source of suggestions for new permutations and depar-
tures?[19] Within seven months of his death, Zukofsky had emerged
as the single most valuable literary property for both the "old" and
"new" avant-gardes in American verse culture. While the mainstream
poetry establishment would continue to ignore his achievements for
another two decades, by the close of the 1970s Zukofsky was firmly
entrenched at the very center of an "alternative canon" of American
poetry.

. . .

Celia Zukofsky, one hopes, remained ignorant of these internecine
struggles over her husband's name—Hamlet and Laertes, as it were,

465

scuffling in Ophelia's grave over who had loved her more. Alone in their Port Jefferson house, Celia worked as she had always worked: to produce order and ensure the survival of her husband's legacy. Less than a month after Louis's death, she told the Kenners that she was occupying herself with yard work and with compiling "a card file of Louis' books—his library I mean—those with notes and marginalia, those without etc."[20] She had other projects on her hands as well. Later that summer she received the final proofs of the University of California Press's *"A"*—all eight hundred pages of them—and set to work reading them for errors and retyping the index she and Zukofsky had prepared, so that its page numbers would match those of the new edition. She had further publication plans in mind. In mid-1978, she established C.Z. Publications, in order to facilitate the reprinting of Zukofsky's texts and the publication of Zukofsky-related materials that she might gather. In October 1978, she prepared a brief type-script of "L.Z.'s notes to *80 Flowers*," with "selection and comments by Celia Zukofsky." She intended for it to be printed, like *80 Flowers* itself, by the Stinehour Press.[21]

The "notes to *80 Flowers*" were never published, but in 1979 C.Z. Publications issued Stinehour's printing of Celia Zukofsky's *American Friends*, a slim volume that juxtaposed brief quotations from seventy-five American writers, arranged chronologically from Nathaniel Ward (b. 1578) to Ernest Hemingway (b. 1898), with brief quotations from Zukofsky's works. The book was dedicated *"to Louis on his seventy-fifth birthday,"* which would have fallen on January 23, 1979. "He was never old, never ceased easily to be young," Celia wrote on the dedicatory page; "his faculties, passions, illusions, detachments of thought and flights of mind made it impossible to be younger in spite of inevitable submissions to health and age." The selections in *American Friends* were an outgrowth of Celia's work with her husband's library and manuscripts, "a result of sorting books, faded pages and old notes. It is as Americans that Louis read most meaning into the works of these 'friends.' The L.Z. extracts are *my* impression of how one human being *may* have operated with such love and perfection."[22] The jux-taposition of materials in *American Friends*—sometimes the Zukof-sky "extracts" directly comment on the quoted material, sometimes the two passages have a thematic relationship, sometimes a crucial word or cadence is carried from a non-Zukofskyan text to a Zukofskyan—is by turns amusing, illuminating, and provoking, and shows how closely Celia and Louis Zukofsky's reading habits had come to parallel one another's over the almost forty years of their marriage.

While Zukofsky's poetry was now in print, much of his other work remained hard to come by. The 1964 Jargon/Corinth *A Test of Poetry*, for instance, was unavailable, so Celia Zukofsky came to an agreement with Norton: They could manufacture and distribute a new edition of *Test*, which would be published under the C.Z. Publications imprint. This third edition of *Test*, which came out in 1980 and was available in both hardcover and paperback, had a far wider circulation than either of its earlier incarnations.

In the last months of 1979 Celia Zukofsky was preparing yet another text for C.Z. Publications, an edition of some of Zukofsky's marginalia. The typescript of "Marginalia by Louis Zukofsky" that Celia prepared in November and December of 1979 transcribed Zukofsky's markings in three books he had been reading at the very end of his life: Thomas Hardy's epic verse drama *The Dynasts* (bound with *The Queen of Cornwall*), John Dryden's *Don Sebastian*, and Samuel Butler's *The Way of All Flesh*. As with every task she set her hand to, Celia Zukofsky's transcriptions were scrupulous. She copied out words and passages Zukofsky had marked, and transcribed much of what he had written in the margins. For the most part, Zukofsky's markings consisted of philological notes on words in the text, brief comments on passages, and cross-references to passages in Shakespeare, Spinoza, and his own writings. But Celia Zukofsky knew that the joviality of the sentence of Paul Zukofsky's quoted in "A"-12—"Wait till they find out / Where you took most of 'your' poetry"[23]—was in the service of a deeper truth: that her husband's writing, under one aspect a theoretically endless system of "recurrences," drew much of its sustenance and substance from what he had read. Future readers, if they cared to ferret out the sources of Zukofsky's borrowings or sort out the uses he had made of his reading, might be glad to have a careful distillation of the marks he had made in some of the books he was reading as *80 Flowers* drew to a close.

. . .

But Celia Zukofsky's concentration on these projects relented over the course of 1980, in large part due to illness: She was suffering from cancer of the colon. Among her last meditations upon her husband's work, however, was one collaborative project that was wholly private. "1939–1978" is a gathering of twenty-two leaves of the tiny loose-leaf notebook paper Zukofsky himself preferred, bound between two plain pieces of cardboard by bits of elastic string. The dates, of course, mark the years of the Zukofskys' marriage. Each page was headed with a year, and on each page, in a steady and legible hand, Celia copied one or two brief passages her husband had written during that year. This selection was no more or less than a continuation of the couple's shared creative life, which had been marked by a series of collaborations: *Bottom: on Shakespeare*; the Catullus translation; the *Autobiography*; and "A"-24, Celia's "L.Z. Masque." The passages that make up "1939–1978" focus on Zukofsky's expressions of love, of contentment in the familial sphere; it is Celia Zukofsky's love poem to her husband's memory, expressed—in best Zukofskyan fashion—in his own words.[24]

The last survivor among the couple's parents, Celia's mother, Becky Thaew, died in June 1980. Her daughter Sophie had never had the heart to tell her that her son-in-law Louis had died two years before, or that her daughter Celia was ill.[25] Celia Thaew Zukofsky died in Port Jefferson on November 18, 1980.

Acknowledgments

Specific debts are acknowledged in the notes, but I am obliged in one way or another to all of the following: Barry Ahearn, Roger Ariew, Charles Bernstein, Joel Bettridge, Sarah H. Brown, Oliver S. Buckton, the late Ric Caddel, Mary Cameron, Ron Caplan, Stephen Collis, the late Cid Corman, William A. Covino, Jean Daive, Michael Davidson, Thom Donovan, Mary Faraci, Norman Finkelstein, Stephen Fredman, Benjamin Friedlander, Andrew Furman, Serge Gavronsky, the late Rita Gelb, Roger Gilbert, Alan Golding, Michael Golston, Robert Hass, Burton Hatlen, Molly Hite, Martha Hollander and Jonathan Bumis, the late Ronald Johnson, Kevin Killian, Richard Kostelanetz, Joel Kuszai, Hank Lazer, Michele J. Leggott, Herb Leibowitz, Chris Long and Gia Houk, David LoSchiavo, Alec Marsh, Mark McMorris, Marcella Munson and Ben Kolstad, Kristen Murtaugh, Ira B. Nadel, Cary Nelson, Peter O'Leary, Mark Osherow, Johnny Payne, Marjorie Perloff, Peter and Meredith Quartermain, Henry Rubin, Nicholas Salvato, the late Lillian Milgram Schapiro, Thomas W. Sheehan, Kenneth Sherwood, Richard Sieburth, Alfred Siegel, Ron Silliman, David Stein, Eirik Steinhoff, Paul Stephens, Susan Stewart, John Taggart, Anthony Julius Tamburri, Sam Tanenhaus, Nathaniel Tarn, Alan Thomas, Keith Tuma, Jeffrey Twitchell-Waas, Robert Von Hallberg, Barrett Watten, Jonathan Williams, David Wray, and Robert Zamsky. The final stages of drafting the book were eased by the efficient labors of Denise M. Gravatt and Manuel Jaramillo, graduate research assistants to the Department of English at Florida Atlantic University.

I have benefited from conversations and formal interviews with the late Robert Creeley, the late Guy Davenport, Theodore Enslin, Michael Heller, Tom Mandel, Michael Palmer, Bob Perelman, the late Carl Rakosi, Hugh

ACKNOWLEDGMENTS

Seidman, Harvey Shapiro, and the late Gael Turnbull. Members of Louis and Celia Thaew Zukofsky's families were generous in sharing information in letters and interviews, and I thank Florence Feigenblum, Sophie and Julius Rubin, Arnold Wand, and Daniel Zukowsky. Paul Zukofsky proved an invaluable resource and sounding board at every stage of this project.

My thanks go to the following librarians and curators: Robert Bertholf and Michael Basinski of the University of Buffalo's Poetry/Rare Books Collection; Jonathan Montaldo of The Thomas Merton Studies Center, Bellarmine College; Tony Power of The Rare Books/Contemporary Literature Collection, W.A.C. Bennett Library, Simon Fraser University; William L. Cook of Western Illinois University Libraries Archives and Special Collections; Robert Maggio of the Port Jefferson Free Library; Bill Armstrong of Florida Atlantic University's Wimberley Library; and most of all the staff of the Harry Ransom Humanities Research Center, University of Texas, among them Pat Fox, Debbie Armstrong, Tara Wenger, Director Thomas Staley, and the indispensable Cathy Henderson. I am grateful to the HRC for a fellowship that enabled me to spend substantial chunks of three summers working through their Zukofsky collections.

Sections of the work were presented at the University of Louisville's Twentieth Century Literature Conference in 1999, 2001, 2003, and 2006, at the Modern Language Association Convention in 2001 and 2003, at the Cornell University conference "Some Futures for the 20th Century" in 2002, at the "Re-reading Louis Zukofsky's *Bottom: on Shakespeare*" symposium at the University of Buffalo in 2003, and at the University of Maine's "Poetry of the 1940s" conference in June 2004. I thank my students at Florida Atlantic University, both undergraduate and graduate, and the members of the FAU Lifelong Learning Society for allowing me to share this work with them. Earlier versions of Chapter 2 and "Adams: Phases and History" were published in *Chicago Review*.

One of the great pleasures of this process was renewing an old friendship with Sam Stoloff, who was instrumental in seeing this book into print. Eric Murphy Selinger, another old friend, lifted me out of the Slough of Despond along the way more times than I care to remember. For indispensable recreation, I thank the boys in "Fluke" (Johnny Payne and Olly Buckton), Mike Grillo and the "Acetythane" axis, and the highly rhythmical Richard Potter.

Guy Davenport's essays first attracted my attention to Zukofsky some twenty-odd years ago, and his letters and conversation sustained my work in a myriad of ways over the past two decades: His death in January 2005 deprives this book of one of its keenest readers.

I am grateful to my loving but rarely intrusive family: my mother, Nelle Scroggins, and my in-laws Richard Low, Barbara Bonn, and Stephanie Low. I am pleased that Jennifer A. Low refused to set aside her own scholarly work while I burrowed my way through the Zukofskyan mountain, but conversations with her have left their mark throughout this book—and few paragraphs of its text have escaped her ruthless blue-penciling. Our daughters Pippa and Daphne have spent their entire lives in a household with a Zukofsky biography in progress, but they seem to have escaped relatively unscathed.

Appendix

Zukofsky, Reisman, Niedecker

In the two years after Louis Zukofsky's death, Celia Zukofsky was interviewed several times about her husband's life and career: by Carroll F. Terrell in September 1978 and August 1979, and by Barry Ahearn on September 17, 1978, and May 16, 1980. Excerpts from the first interviews were woven by Terrell into the biographical overview, "Louis Zukofsky: An Eccentric Profile," published in his edited collection *Louis Zukofsky: Man and Poet* in 1979.[1] The Ahearn interviews were published in 1983 in the journal *Sagetrieb*.[2]

Some years later—at least a decade after the Zukofskys' deaths—Jerry Reisman contacted Burton Hatlen, editor of *Sagetrieb*, and offered the magazine his response to those interviews, "On Some Conversations with Celia Zukofsky," which was published in *Sagetrieb* in its Winter 1991 issue.[3] Reisman had been a friend of Zukofsky's from 1929, when Zukofsky was his high school teacher, to 1947, when there was a decisive break in their friendship. There is ample evidence, both in Zukofsky's letters and in the letters of his correspondents, of the close relationship he and Reisman shared. Zukofsky was a mentor to Reisman in the young man's attempts at writing, and Reisman contributed his own mathematical and scientific expertise to Zukofsky's work.

Reisman's response to the interviews with Celia Zukofsky consisted of a number of minor quibbles about details and a lengthy account of his relationship with both Zukofskys. This account painted Louis and Celia Zukofsky in a most unfavorable—even scandalous—light, and was marked by a rather bitter animus against both Celia and, to a lesser degree, Louis Zukofsky.

Since both Zukofskys had been dead more than ten years, and since Paul Zukofsky had been only three years old at the time their friendship with Reisman ended, there was no one to contradict him.

In spring 1986 Reisman had been contacted by Glenna Breslin, a scholar working on a biography of Lorine Niedecker.[4] She hoped to substantiate a story Mary Oppen had told her about Zukofsky and Niedecker's relationship; Reisman agreed with and filled out Oppen's account, though both of them asked that they be cited anonymously in Breslin's published work.[5] Later, at the request of Jenny Penberthy, he wrote a brief memoir, "Lorine: Some Memories of a Friend," which was published in Penberthy's edited volume *Lorine Niedecker: Woman and Poet*.[6] Reisman asserted that Niedecker and Zukofsky had been lovers during Niedecker's 1933 New York visit, that Niedecker had become pregnant, and that Zukofsky had insisted that she have an abortion.

While Glenna Breslin first heard of Niedecker's New York visit from Mary Oppen—she might well have read about it in Oppen's 1978 auto-biography—all of the details of the Niedecker/Zukofsky "affair" derive from Reisman. George and Mary Oppen met Niedecker in New York in the early 1930s, but there is no evidence that they knew much of anything about her friendship with Zukofsky at that time, or for many decades after. Their few mentions of the 1930s-era Niedecker are marked by vagueness and inaccuracy. In a 1963 letter to his sister June Oppen Degnan, George Oppen writes of Niedecker as having visited New York "for a few days in 1930 or so"—which directly contradicts Reisman.[7] And in the half-page account of Niedecker's visit to New York in *Meaning a Life*, Mary Oppen asserts incorrectly that Niedecker had been a student of Zukofsky's at the University of Wisconsin.[8]

As attractive as the genre of literary gossip may be, I am unwilling to accept Reisman's two documents at face value. Reisman's quibbles about Celia Zukofsky's memory for details in "On Some Conversations"—whether Zukofsky's sister Fanny Wand lived in Brooklyn or the South Bronx, whether Reisman's sister lived in the South Bronx or Riverdale—seem remarkably trivial, even petty, directed as they are at a woman in her midsixties, attempting to remember events of over four decades before. And his assertions about other matters, such as the authorship of the Taupin-Zukofsky Apollinaire book and the *Ulysses* screenplay, seem uniformly directed towards minimizing Zukofsky's participation in those projects and making him seem mean-spirited. It is impossible to verify or refute Reisman's account of the reasons for his break with the Zukofskys; a note from Zukofsky that Reisman cites as implicitly proving Reisman's financial interest in the Zukofskys' 30

Willow Street house does no such thing, though it does provide an example of Zukofsky's occasional waspishness.[9]

Whatever the cause of that break, it left bad blood on both sides, and the greatest animus seems to have been between Reisman and Celia Zukofsky. Reisman's dislike of her is palpable throughout "On Some Conversations," and reaches almost embarrassing pitches in his letters to Cid Corman from 1988 to 1998.[10] Clearly in "On Some Conversations" Reisman is writing with an axe to grind, and the ultimate target of his resentment is Celia Zukofsky. It is impossible to determine whether such resentment is warranted or not, but its final result is to cast doubt upon the reliability of such a resentful narrator.

Reisman's account of his and Zukofsky's relationship with Niedecker, "Lorine: Some Memories of a Friend," is a brief document and shows few internal inconsistencies (though such inconsistencies and improbabilities occur between Reisman's published pieces and his letters to Cid Corman explaining and expanding upon them); but it must be read with the memoirist's own bias in mind. It is simply impossible to reconstruct the precise nature of Zukofsky and Niedecker's relationship in the 1930s. The Zukofsky–Niedecker correspondence has been so thoroughly culled and edited by the poets themselves that the emotional core of their relationship has been largely obscured. Neither poet, it is clear, wanted the details of their private lives to be resurrected by biographers.

Reisman's accounts have been taken up with some enthusiasm by those who would cast Louis Zukofsky as the villain in a psychobiography of Lorine Niedecker (a psychobiography that perforce portrays Niedecker as *victim*). More troublingly, serious scholars of Niedecker's and Zukofsky's poetry have begun to take their early "love affair" as a biographical given, on no better evidentiary grounds than Reisman's accounts. But those accounts do not constitute proof of anything. In regard to Zukofsky's relationship with Niedecker and Reisman's relationship with the Zukofskys, the events in which Reisman shows himself most deeply emotionally invested, Reisman's reliability is undercut by his evident animosity towards Louis and Celia Zukofsky. At best, these two accounts are long-after the fact memories of a profoundly biased participant; at worst, they are reconstructions of history driven by resentment. I have thought it best, therefore, to pass over Reisman's comments in the body of this biography.

Notes

The most important resource for Louis Zukofsky's biographer is the Louis Zukofsky Manuscript Collection in the Harry Ransom Humanities Research Center at the University of Texas at Austin. That collection contains an almost complete manuscript record of Zukofsky's writings, as well as major collections of his correspondence received, including most notably letters from Ezra Pound, William Carlos Williams, and Basil Bunting. The Manuscript Collection also holds collections of Zukofsky's letters to Carl Rakosi, Lorine Niedecker, and Cid Corman. (Zukofsky's letters to other correspondents, however, are dispersed in other collections or are held in private hands.) At every point in this biography, I have had recourse to the Harry Ransom Center's holdings. Central as well to this project has been an enormous manuscript and typescript record assembled by Celia Zukofsky, to which I refer in the notes as "CZ Dossier." The Dossier includes drafts of Celia Zukofsky's unpublished "L.Z.'s Notes to 80 Flowers," typed collections of reviews and notices of Zukofsky's books, a complete bibliography of Zukofsky's publications, and an exhaustive listing of every book, essay, and article that mentions Zukofsky's name. The "CZ Dossier" includes much else: an annotated list of Zukofsky's public readings, a chronological account of his addresses, a list of Celia Zukofsky's musical compositions and publications. The Dossier has proved a resource second in importance only to the Louis Zukofsky Manuscript Collection.

I have dated Zukofsky's poems using the dates he appended to their manuscripts, though it is not entirely clear whether such dates represent the date of composition or the date when Zukofsky arrived at a "fair copy" of a given poem. In some instances, I have referred to the catalogue of his library (which Zukofsky began in his last years and which Celia Zukofsky completed after his death) to figure out when Zukofsky first read a given book. I am grateful to Robert Zamsky, who transcribed Celia Zukofsky's index cards into a tabular file, for furnishing me with a copy of this list. The list itself, along with a host of other useful materials—bibliographies, chronologies, scrupulously prepared annotations, and much more—can now be found on Jeff Twitchell-Waas's invaluable website "Z-site: A Companion to the Works of Louis Zukofsky" (http://www.ofscollege.edu.sg/z-site/). The "Z-site" is a marvelously rich and lovingly prepared scholarly resource, and promises to open a new era in the reading and interpretation of Zukofsky's works.

References and Abbreviations Used in Notes

WORKS BY LOUIS ZUKOFSKY

"A" = "A" (1978; Baltimore: Johns Hopkins University Press, 1993)

AOA = An "Objectivists" Anthology, ed. Louis Zukofsky (Le Beausset, Var, France: To, Publishers, 1932)

Apollinaire = The Writing of Guillaume Apollinaire, ed. Serge Gavronsky (Middletown, CT: Wesleyan University Press, 2004)

Arise = Arise, arise (New York: Grossman, 1973)

Autobiography = Autobiography (New York: Grossman, 1970)

Bottom = Bottom: on Shakespeare, 2 vols. (1963; Middletown, CT: Wesleyan University Press, 2002)

CF = Collected Fiction (Normal, IL: Dalkey Archive Press, 1990) [I quote from the paperback edition, whose pagination differs from that of the original hardcover.]

CSP = Complete Short Poetry (Baltimore: Johns Hopkins University Press, 1991)

Prepositions+ = Prepositions+: The Collected Critical Essays of Louis Zukofsky (Middletown, CT: Wesleyan University Press, 2000)

Test = A Test of Poetry (1948; Middletown, CT: Wesleyan University Press, 2000)

Useful Art = A Useful Art: Essays and Radio Scripts on American Design, ed. Kenneth Sherwood (Middletown, CT: Wesleyan University Press, 2003)

COLLECTIONS OF LETTERS

Pound/Zukofsky = *Pound/Zukofsky: Selected Letters of Ezra Pound and Louis Zukofsky*, ed. Barry Ahearn (New York: New Directions, 1987)

Williams/Zukofsky = *The Correspondence of William Carlos Williams and Louis Zukofsky*, ed. Barry Ahearn (Middletown, CT: Wesleyan University Press, 2003)

NAMES OF PERSONS

BB = Basil Bunting
CC = Cid Corman
CZ = Celia Thaew Zukofsky
EP = Ezra Pound
JL = James Laughlin
JW = Jonathan Williams
LN = Lorine Niedecker
LZ = Louis Zukofsky
PZ = Paul Zukofsky
RC = Robert Creeley
RD = Robert Duncan
RT = René Taupin
WCW = William Carlos Williams

LIBRARIES AND ARCHIVES

Beinecke = Beinecke Rare Book and Manuscript Library, Yale University, New Haven, Connecticut

Buffalo = The Poetry/Rare Books Collection, University of Buffalo, Buffalo, New York

HRC = The Harry Ransom Humanities Research Center, University of Texas, Austin, Texas

Lilly = The Lilly Library, Indiana University, Bloomington, Indiana

SFU = The Rare Books/Contemporary Literature Collection, W. A. C. Bennett Library, Simon Fraser University, Burnaby, British Columbia

TMSC = Thomas Merton Studies Center, Bellarmine College, Louisville, Kentucky

OTHER

CZ Dossier = Celia Thaew Zukofsky's collection of Zukofsky materials
MS = manuscript
TS = typescript

Notes to Chapters

Introduction

1. Hugh Kenner, *The Pound Era* (Berkeley: University of California Press, 1971), 415.
2. "*A*", dust jacket blurb.
3. Guy Davenport, *Every Force Evolves a Form: Twenty Essays* (San Francisco: North Point Press, 1987), 91.

Chapter One *A Lower East Side Youth: 1904–1920*

1. On the Third Avenue "L," see "*A*" 183.
2. See LZ to Carl Rakosi, 6 January 1931 (HRC). In his Columbia University transcripts LZ's birthday is given as February 1, 1904.
3. LZ to RT, 11 June 1933 (KSU); see also Mary Oppen, *Meaning a Life: An Autobiography* (Santa Barbara: Black Sparrow Press, 1978), 145.
4. Barry Ahearn, *Zukofsky's "A": An Introduction* (Berkeley: University of California Press, 1984), 10; LZ explained his multiple birthdays to Ahearn in conversation, and he also mentions them in a letter to CC of 23 January 1960 (HRC). LZ would "celebrate" January 29 as his birthday at least as late as 1959, perhaps to avoid overlap with his wife's birthday, January 21; see LZ to LN, 3 February 1959 (HRC).
5. Irving Howe, *World of Our Fathers: The Journey of the East European Jews to America and the Life They Found and Made* (New York: Harcourt Brace Jovanovich, 1976), 69.
6. Jacob Riis, *How the Other Half Lives: Studies Among the Tenements of New York* (1890; New York: Dover, 1971), 2, 85, 86.
7. Howe, *World of Our Fathers*, 15–20.
8. Howe, *World of Our Fathers*, 5–7.
9. After Pinchos Zukofsky died in 1950, his children were unsure whether to "Put 91 or 95 / On his tombstone" ("*A*" 155).
10. "*A*" 151–22.
11. CZ as interviewed in Carroll F. Terrell, "Louis Zukofsky: An Eccentric Profile," in *Louis Zukofsky: Man and Poet* (Orono, ME: National Poetry Foundation, 1979), 35–36.
12. "*A*" 151.
13. "*A*" 83.
14. Riis, *How the Other Half Lives*, 97–104; Howe, *World of Our Fathers*, 154–59.
15. "*A*" 152; see Howe, *World of Our Fathers*, 82.
16. Howe, *World of Our Fathers*, 158.
17. "*A*" 152–53.

18. LZ to EP, 11 July 1936 (*Pound/Zukofsky* 183); *"A"* 154.
19. Howe, *World of Our Fathers*, 156.
20. *"A"* 155, 153, 154; Morris Zukowsky's daughter Florence Feigenblum recalls the affection evident between her grandfather and an African American policeman in the neighborhood, even though neither man could understand the other (author interview, 15 February 2001).
21. LZ to CC, 7 October 1959 (HRC).
22. *"A"* 83.
23. *"A"* 355; see LZ to CC, 16 October 1959 (HRC).
24. *"A"* 350.
25. *"A"* 211.
26. Howe, *World of Our Fathers*, 251, and 249–55 *passim*.
27. *Autobiography* 33.
28. On the Yiddish theater, see Howe, *World of Our Fathers*, 460–96.
29. On Yiddish adaptations of Shakespeare, see Joel Berkowitz, *Shakespeare on the American Yiddish Stage* (Iowa City: University of Iowa Press, 2002).
30. *Autobiography* 33.
31. LZ to CC, 28 June 1960 (HRC).
32. LZ to CC, 28 June 1960 (HRC); see *"A"* 340. LZ recalled knowing *Hiawatha* in Yiddish by age five, but Yehoash's *Hiawatha* was not published in book form until 1910. Perhaps the Italian boys' pennies were the source of LZ's sadly enduring misconception that one might actually earn money from poetry.
33. LZ to Hugh Kenner, 30 January 1974 (HRC).
34. *Autobiography* 33.
35. Howe, *World of Our Fathers*, 128.
36. According to PZ, CZ regarded LZ's Yiddish as very poor; while he spoke it to some extent with the members of his birth family, LZ and his wife (herself a fluent Yiddish speaker) almost never used it with one another.
37. Riis, *How the Other Half Lives*, 106–7.
38. Stephan F. Brumberg, "The One-Way Window: Public Schools on the Lower East Side in the Early Twentieth Century," in *Remembering the Lower East Side: American Jewish Reflections*, ed. Hasia R. Diner, Jeffrey Shandler, and Beth S. Wenger (Bloomington: Indiana University Press, 2000), 138; Brumberg quotes educational historian Ellwood P. Cubberly.
39. Howe, *World of Our Fathers*, 275–76, and, on education in general, 271–80.
40. *Prepositions+* 28.

41. *Autobiography* 33.

42. *Autobiography* 13.

43. Ahearn, *Zukofsky's "A"* 1–4; see Steve Shoemaker, "Between Contact and Exile: Louis Zukofsky's Poetry of Survival," in *Upper Limit Music: The Writing of Louis Zukofsky*, ed. Mark Scroggins (Tuscaloosa: University of Alabama Press, 1997), 23–30.

44. LZ to Hugh Kenner, 29 July 1967 (HRC).

45. *"A"* 397.

46. *"A"* 148–49.

47. Henry James, *The American Scene*, in *Collected Travel Writings: Great Britain and America*, ed. Richard Howard (New York: Library of America, 1993), 455, 457.

48. James, *The American Scene*, 464, 456.

49. James, *The American Scene*, 465, 466–68.

50. James, *The American Scene*, 455.

51. Alex Zwerdling, *Improvised Europeans: American Literary Expatriates and the Siege of London* (New York: Basic Books, 1998), 198.

52. For instance Peter Conn, *The Divided Mind: Ideology and Imagination in America, 1898–1917* (Cambridge: Cambridge University Press, 1983), 42–44.

53. LZ to Hugh Kenner, 7 August 1967 (HRC).

54. James, *The American Scene*, 471.

55. LZ to Hugh Kenner, 7 August 1967 (HRC).

Chapter Two *An Ernster Mensch at Columbia: 1920–1924*

1. See Mortimer J. Adler, *Philosopher at Large: An Intellectual Autobiography, 1902–1976* (New York: Macmillan, 1977), 2. LZ recalls his years at Columbia in his lecture "For Wallace Stevens" (*Prepositions+* 24–38), and CZ addresses them in conversation with Carroll F. Terrell, published as "Louis Zukofsky: An Eccentric Profile," in Terrell, ed., *Louis Zukofsky: Man and Poet* (Orono, ME: National Poetry Foundation, 1979), 31–74, and in Barry Ahearn, "Two Conversations with Celia Zukofsky," *Sagetrieb* 2, no. 1 (Spring 1983): 113–31. See also Ahearn, *Zukofsky's "A": An Introduction* (Berkeley: University of California Press, 1983), 11–37.

2. Sam Tanenhaus, *Whittaker Chambers: A Biography* (New York: Random House, 1997), 22.

3. Stephen Steinberg, *The Academic Melting Pot: Catholics and Jews in American Higher Education* (New York: McGraw-Hill, 1974), 11, 13–16.

4. Steinberg, *The Academic Melting Pot*, 60–62.

5. Tanenhaus, *Whittaker Chambers*, 22.

6. Mark Van Doren, *The Autobiography of Mark Van Doren* (New York: Harcourt, Brace and Company, 1958), 130.

7. Mark Van Doren, "Jewish Students I Have Known," *The Menorah Journal* 13 (June 1927).

8. Tanenhaus, *Whittaker Chambers*, 3–20, 21.

9. Van Doren, *Autobiography*, 128; Tanenhaus, *Whittaker Chambers*, 24.

10. Tanenhaus, *Whittaker Chambers*, 38, 54.

11. Ahearn, *Zukofsky's "A"*, 11.

12. Van Doren, *Autobiography*, 133;

13. Barry Ahearn, 6 December 1977 interview with Adler; see Ahearn, *Zukofsky's "A"*, 11.

14. LZ to Carl Rakosi, 6 January 1931 (HRC).

15. LZ intimated as much in an 11 March 1977 letter to Barry Ahearn; the pun—"A sum (you say) / Post-mortemer"—is in "A"-12 (*A* 145). See also Ahearn, *Zukofsky's "A"*, 115.

16. LZ's Columbia transcripts—admittedly incomplete—imply that he had concentrated on English and philosophy from the outset. Nonetheless, the shift from engineering to the humanities, whether true or not, was part of LZ's self-mythology, both in his 1931 letter to Rakosi and his 1977 communications with Barry Ahearn.

17. Clifton Fadiman, "Some Recollections of Great Teachers," in *University on the Heights*, ed. Wesley First (Garden City, NY: Doubleday, 1969), 64.

18. Louis Simpson, "Ideas and Poetry," *University on the Heights*, 28.

19. Van Doren, "Jewish Students," 267.

20. Paul R. Hays, "Forty-three Years of Columbia," *University on the Heights*, 157.

21. See Justus Buchler, "Reconstruction in the Liberal Arts," in *A History of Columbia College on Morningside* (New York: Columbia University Press, 1954), 113–16, Adler, *Philosopher at Large*, 30–31, and Van Doren, *Autobiography*, 131–33.

22. Fon W. Boardman Jr., "After Class," *A History of Columbia College*, 173, 176; Ahearn, *Zukofsky's "A"*, 12.

23. *CSP* 15.

24. Hays, "Forty-three Years of Columbia," 158.

25. Adler, *Philosopher at Large*, 28.

26. *Prepositions+* 30.

27. Mary Oppen, *Meaning a Life: An Autobiography* (Santa Barbara: Black Sparrow Press, 1978), 93–94.

28. Adler, *Philosopher at Large*, 29.

29. *Prepositions+* 29–30.

30. Frederick J. E. Woodbridge, *Nature and Mind: Selected Essays* (New York: Columbia University Press, 1937), 3; Adler, *Philosopher at Large*, 47.

31. Adler, *Philosopher at Large*, 26–27.

32. Woodbridge, *Nature and Mind*, 21.

33. *Aristotle's Vision of Nature*, ed. John Herman Randall Jr. (New York: Columbia University Press, 1965), 70; this book collects a series of lectures from 1930.

34. *Aristotle's Vision of Nature*, 98–99.

35. "Monody," *The Morningside* 9, no. 2 (November 1920): 38; "Youth," *The Morningside* 9, no. 3 (December 1920): 99; "Youth's Ballad of Singleness," *The Morningside* 12, nos. 3–4 (March–April 1923): 47–48; "Spare Us of Dying Beauty," *The Morningside* 10, nos. 5–6 (April–May 1922): 158.

36. "The Sea-Nymph's Prayer," *Varsity* (February 1921): 8; "The Faun Sees," *The Morningside* 9, no. 7 (April 1921): 239; "The Mystic Song," *The Morningside* 10, no. 2 (December 1921): 42; "The Seer," *The Morningside* 9, no. 5 (January 1921): 153.

37. "Autumn Sunrise," *The Morningside* 10, no. 3 (February 1922): 157.

38. *The Morningside* 10, no. 1 (November 1921): 1–8.

39. *The Morningside* 10, no. 5 (December 1921): 42.

40. "From the rain whose mouth to the earth is pressed" (4). The HRC holds a printed copy of the poem with LZ's autograph revisions, including the alteration of "mouth" to "feet."

41. *The Morningside* 11, no. 1 (November 1922): 10.

42. Walter Pater, *The Renaissance: Studies in Art and Poetry* (1893 text), ed. Donald L. Hill (Berkeley: University of California Press, 1980), 180–81.

43. Ezra Pound, "A Retrospect," in *Literary Essays*, ed. T. S. Eliot (New York: New Directions, 1968), 5.

44. "Silver Moment," *Varsity* (March 1921): 19; "Dark Room" appears on the same page.

45. *The Morningside* 10, nos. 5–6 (April–May 1922): 157.

46. Lionel Trilling, *The Moral Obligation to Be Intelligent: Selected Essays*, ed. Leon Wieseltier (New York: Farrar, Straus & Giroux, 2002), 342–43.

47. Adler, *Philosopher at Large*, 26–27.

48. It is unclear whether LZ's degree was awarded in English or philosophy. In Ahearn, "Two Conversations," CZ could not recall that LZ had written the thesis for any specific advisor, such as Mark Van Doren: "I think that he was pretty much on his own" (121–22).

49. This according to CZ, in Ahearn, "Two Conversations," 121.

50. Adler, *Philosopher at Large*, 20–21.

51. CZ in Terrell, *Louis Zukofsky: Man and Poet*, 50–52, 65.

52. Hugh Seidman, Allen Ginsberg, Robert Creeley, and Celia Zukofsky, "A Commemorative Evening for Louis Zukofsky," *American Poetry Review* 9, no. 1 (January/February 1980): 26.

53. In the card catalogue of books he prepared during the last years of his life, LZ recorded purchasing or reading the works of Dante, Chaucer, Webster, Tourneur, Wyatt, Marlowe, Jonson, Cranshaw, Bunyan, and others during his time at Columbia; this list, which represents only those actual volumes he retained into the late 1970s, suggests broader actual reading from 1920 to 1924.

54. Ezra Pound, *The Spirit of Romance* (New York: New Directions, 1968), 6.

Interchapter *Adams: Phases of History*

1. The thesis, dated May 7, 1924, is in Columbia University's Butler Library. I cite it as "Henry Adams: Detached Mind," to distinguish it from the successive revised versions LZ published in *Hound & Horn* in 1930 and *Prepositions* in 1967.

2. *Prepositions+* 169.

3. For Adams in "A"-8, see Barry Ahearn, *Zukofsky's "A": An Introduction* (Berkeley: University of California Press, 1983), 79–83, 85–90. Sandra Kumamoto Stanley's *Louis Zukofsky and the Transformation of a Modern American Poetics* (Berkeley: University of California Press, 1994), 26–45, discusses LZ and Adams.

4. LZ comments on this in a note to the first installment of "Henry Adams: A Criticism in Autobiography" in *Hound & Horn* 3, no. 3 (April–June 1930): 339–40.

5. *Prepositions+* 98.

6. *Prepositions+* 87.

7. Henry Adams, *The Education of Henry Adams*, in *Novels, Mont Saint Michel, The Education* (New York: Library of America, 1983), 730, 723.

8. Adams, *The Education*, 1117.

9. "Henry Adams: Detached Mind," 1.

10. *Prepositions+* 106. "Henry Adams: Detached Mind" reads "Beauty" for "Poetry" in this passage, but LZ changed his wording for the publication of the essay's second installment in *Hound & Horn* 3, no. 4 (July–September 1930): 527.

11. *Prepositions+* 87.

12. Henry Adams, *The Degradation of the Democratic Dogma*, ed. and intro. by Brooks Adams (New York: Macmillan, 1919), 35.

13. The circumstances in which Adams formulated his ideas are summarized in David R. Contosta, *Henry Adams and the American Experiment* (Boston: Little, Brown, 1980), 91–94.

14. Adams, *Degradation of the Democratic Dogma*, 126, 127.

15. Contosta, *Henry Adams*, 33, 64–65.

16. Adams, *The Education*, 1153, 1155, 1162, 1164, 1067.

17. Adams, *Degradation of the Democratic Dogma*, 305–8.

18. Adams, *Degradation of the Democratic Dogma*, 115, 308–9.

19. See for instance R. P. Blackmur, *Henry Adams*, ed. Veronica A. Makowsky (New York: Harcourt Brace Jovanovich, 1980), 273–74.

20. "Henry Adams: Detached Mind," 54; LZ changed "truth" to "fact" in the magazine publication of the third installment of "Henry Adams: A Criticism in Autobiography," *Hound & Horn* 4, no. 1 (October–December 1930): 63.

21. *Prepositions+* 169.

22. *Test* vii.

23. *Prepositions+* 21.

24. Ezra Pound, *Literary Essays*, ed. T. S. Eliot (New York: New Directions, 1968), 25.

25. *Prepositions+* 78–83, 209.

26. *Prepositions+* 242.

27. Pound, *Literary Essays*, 5.

28. *Prepositions+* 242. On Zukofsky's anti-abstractionism and his championing of the concrete senses, see Mark Scroggins, *Louis Zukofsky and the Poetry of Knowledge* (Tuscaloosa: University of Alabama Press, 1998), 45–117.

29. *Bottom* 1.87, emphases added.

30. *"A"* 126. Compare *Prepositions+* 55.

31. *Bottom* 1.88.

32. *Prepositions+* 170.

33. I. A. Richards, *Science and Poetry* (London: Kegan Paul, Trench, Trubner and Company, 1926).

34. Ezra Pound, *The Spirit of Romance* (1910; New York: New Directions, 1968), 5; William Carlos Williams, *Selected Essays* (1954; New York: New Directions, 1969), 256. On the modernists and the discourse of science and technology, see Ian F. A. Bell, *Critic as Scientist: The Modernist Poetics of Ezra Pound* (London: Methuen, 1981), and Lisa M. Steinman, *Made in America: Science, Technology, and American Modernist Poets* (New Haven, CT: Yale University Press, 1987).

35. Hugh Seidman, "Louis Zukofsky at the Polytechnic Institute of Brook-

lyn (1958–1961)," in *Louis Zukofsky: Man and Poet*, ed. Carroll F. Terrell (Orono, ME: National Poetry Foundation, 1979), 99.

36. *Prepositions+* 19.

37. *"A"* 138.

38. *Prepositions+* 6.

Chapter Three *The Lean Twenties: 1924–1928*

1. See Sam Tanenhaus, *Whittaker Chambers: A Biography* (New York: Knopf, 1997), 38–39. LZ's reminiscences about the beach are contained in a fragmentary letter to LN dated (in LZ's hand) "ca. 1941" (HRC).

2. These quotations are from a TS of his unpublished juvenilia LZ had prepared in 1941 (HRC). The TS, *The First Seasons*, bears the *nom de plume* "Dunn Wyth." As LZ explains on the title page, "*The First Seasons* (including *The First Book*) was written by me ca. 1920–1924 and is not to be published, as the pseudonym intended then; (pronounce 'done with.')" The TS is dated 23 January 1941, LZ's thirty-seventh birthday. Of the fifty-nine poems in this collection, only XXIV of *The First Seasons* was salvaged for his later collections; it appears as "I Sent Thee Late" in "A"-18 (*"A"* 391).

3. *CSP*, 30–31, MS dated 24 September 1925 (HRC).

4. *Prepositions+* 30.

5. LZ to LN, fragment dated "ca. 1941" (HRC).

6. LZ to CC, 13 June 1960 (HRC).

7. CZ recounts these jobs to Carroll F. Terrell in Terrell, "Louis Zukofsky: An Eccentric Profile," in Terrell, ed., *Louis Zukofsky: Man and Poet* (Orono, ME: National Poetry Foundation, 1979), 52. LZ mentions the Nedick's job in a 6 January 1931 letter to Carl Rakosi (HRC); the post office appears in "A"-6 (*"A"* 29).

8. Tanenhaus, *Whittaker Chambers*, 45.

9. Whittaker Chambers, *Witness* (New York: Random House, 1952), 207. Tanenhaus claims this unnamed friend was Clifton Fadiman (*Whittaker Chambers*, 50), but CZ identifies him as LZ (Terrell, ed., *Louis Zukofsky: Man and Poet*, 51).

10. Tanenhaus, *Whittaker Chambers*, 532n.47.

11. CZ, in Terrell, ed., *Louis Zukofsky: Man and Poet*, 51. LZ would recount this version of the affair to both Hugh Kenner and Guy Davenport. Whittaker Chambers, however, told the FBI in October 1951 that LZ had indeed been accepted by the Party, but had only remained a member for "approximately a month." According to Chambers, LZ left the Party because he "was such an intense individualist and was not likely to be

subjected to the discipline of the Party." At any rate, Chambers recalled that LZ "did not take an active part in the meetings of the English Speaking Branch of the Party, but merely sat in as a 'listener'" (FBI dossier on LZ, report dated 1 November 1951).

12. CZ, in Terrell, ed., *Louis Zukofsky: Man and Poet*, 51–52.

13. *CSP* 21; MS dated 3 August 1925.

14. *CSP* 26; MS dated 18 April 1926.

15. See Paul L. Murphy (with David Klaassen and Kermit Hall), *The Passaic Textile Strike of 1926* (Belmont, CA: Wadsworth, 1974). While there were plenty of instances of police violence against the strikers, there hadn't been any actual "shooting," despite what LZ's poem implies.

16. LZ dated his first reading of *Pilgrim's Progress* to 1922.

17. "A Preface," *The Exile* 4 (Autumn 1928): 86. This brief prose piece, dated 17 October 1926, is the preface to LZ's "18 Songs to the Future," a group of lyrics he sent EP in February 1928 (see *Pound/Zukofsky* 9). Each of the eighteen poems of this group was prefaced with a Bunyan epigraph, but only "During the Passaic Strike of 1926" retains the epigraph into its book publication; the manuscript version of number 11 of *55 Poems* (*CSP* 28, manuscript in HRC) has a Bunyan epigraph as well. Sorel's *Réflexions sur la violence* was translated by EP's friend T. E. Hulme in 1914 as *Reflections on Violence*.

18. The poem was first published in *The Exile* 4 (Autumn 1928): 84–86; LZ removed the Bunyan epigraph when he reprinted the poem in *55 Poems* (Prairie City, IL: Decker, 1941).

19. In 1941 LZ applied for a job as a translator at the FBI; as part of the October 31 job interview, he supplied these as the dates of his employment with the New York City schools (FBI dossier on LZ, report dated 22 October 1951, summarizing 31 October 1941 interview). CZ does not record this substitute teaching in her table of LZ's jobs (Terrell, ed., *Louis Zukofsky: Man and Poet*, 62–63), but LZ mentions it in a 6 January 1931 letter to Carl Rakosi (HRC).

20. LZ would finally take—and fail—the examination in March 1930; see LZ to EP, 19 March 1930 (Beinecke), and Charles Reznikoff to Marie Syrkin, 10 March 1930 and 17 March 1930, *Selected Letters of Charles Reznikoff, 1917–1976*, ed. Milton Hindus (Santa Rosa: Black Sparrow, 1997), 107, 113.

21. Tanenhaus, *Whittaker Chambers*, 56–57.

22. Celia Zukofsky dates this work from October 1927 to March 1928 (Terrell, ed., *Louis Zukofsky: Man and Poet*, 62); in his job application

interview with the FBI in October 1941, LZ dates his work for the National Industrial Conference Board from January 1927 to January 1928 (FBI File on LZ, report dated 22 October 1951). LZ discusses the work in a 16 January 1931 letter to Carl Rakosi (HRC).

23. LZ to Carl Rakosi, 16 January 1931 (HRC).

24. Chambers, *Witness*, 178.

25. Chambers, *Witness*, 181–82; Tanenhaus, *Whittaker Chambers*, 54.

26. The draft dates for "Poem beginning 'The'" are on the holograph manuscript of the poem in the HRC. "Ricky," LZ's nickname for Richard Chambers (he appears to have been "Dickie" to his brother), appears in several of the early movements of "*A*", the latest being "*A*"-6, whose earliest TS (HRC) is dated "Aug 12–16 / 1930."

27. *CSP* 12.

28. *CSP* 9.

29. T. S. Eliot, *Complete Poetry and Plays, 1909–1950* (New York: Harcourt Brace Jovanovich, 1971), 50.

30. *CSP* 8.

31. *CSP* 9, 10.

32. *CSP* 14–15.

33. *CSP* 11.

34. *CSP* 17.

35. *CSP* 13–14.

36. *CSP* 20.

37. *CSP* 16.

38. On LZ's use of Yehoash, see Harold Schimmel, "Zuk. Yehoash David Rex," in Terrell, ed., *Louis Zukofsky: Man and Poet*, 235–45.

39. Norman Finkelstein, "Jewish-American Modernism and the Problem of Identity: *With Special Reference to the Work of Louis Zukofsky*," in *Upper Limit Music: The Writing of Louis Zukofsky*, ed. Mark Scroggins (Tuscaloosa: University of Alabama Press, 1997), 73.

40. *CSP* 20.

41. *CSP* 17.

42. CZ, in Terrell, ed., *Louis Zukofsky: Man and Poet*, 38–39, 36.

43. These two sonnets, "The silence in the good that you were wrought of" and "Someone said, 'earth, bowed with her death, we mourn" are dated 10 March 1927 and 15 March 1927 (HRC). They were published in *The Dial* 85, no. 6 (December 1928): 459.

44. *CSP* 33.

45. In a 6 January 1931 letter to Carl Rakosi (HRC), LZ speaks of the "break up of it all" four years earlier.

46. LZ to E. E. Cummings, 20 March 1928 (HRC), in which LZ specifies that he sent the poem in May 1927.

47. See J. J. Wilhelm, *The American Roots of Ezra Pound* (New York: Garland, 1985).

48. EP to Harriet Monroe, January 1931, *Selected Letters of Ezra Pound, 1907–1941*, ed. D. D. Paige (1950; New York: New Directions, 1971), 230.

49. Quoted in Charles Norman, *Ezra Pound* (New York: Macmillan, 1960), 292.

50. EP to LZ, 18 August 1927 (*Pound/Zukofsky* 3).

51. EP to LZ, 5 March 1928 (*Pound/Zukofsky* 7).

52. WCW to LZ, 23 March 1928 (*Williams/Zukofsky* 3).

53. WCW to LZ, 28 March 1928 (*Williams/Zukofsky* 3–4); Paul Mariani, *William Carlos Williams: A New World Naked* (New York: Norton, 1981), 272.

54. WCW to LZ, 2 April 1928 (*Williams/Zukofsky* 4–5).

55. *Imaginations*, ed. Webster Schott (New York: New Directions, 1970), 26, 24.

56. *The Autobiography of William Carlos Williams* (New York: Random House, 1951), 174.

57. *Prepositions+* 47; LZ's inscribed and dated copy of *Spring and All* is in the HRC.

58. WCW to EP, 12 July 1928; *Pound/Williams: Selected Letters of Ezra Pound and William Carlos Williams*, ed. Hugh Witemeyer (New York: New Directions, 1996), 87.

59. WCW to EP, 17 May 1928; *Pound/Williams* 82.

60. *The Descent of Winter*, *The Exile* 4 (Autumn 1928): 30–69.

61. *Prepositions+* 47.

62. See the introduction to Oppen's *Selected Letters*, ed. Rachel Blau DuPlessis (Durham: Duke University Press, 1990), x–xx, and Mary Oppen, *Meaning a Life: An Autobiography* (Santa Barbara: Black Sparrow Press, 1978).

63. Oppen, *Meaning a Life*, 84–85.

64. Oppen, *Meaning a Life*, 91; Burton Hatlen and Tom Mandel, "Poetry and Politics: A Conversation with George and Mary Oppen," in *George Oppen: Man and Poet*, ed. Burton Hatlen (Orono, ME: National Poetry Foundation, 1981), 42.

65. Oppen, *Meaning a Life*, 94.

Chapter Four *"A Thousand fiddles playing Bach": 1928–1930*

1. *CSP* 17; "For a Thing by Bach," *Pagany* 1, no. 4 (Fall 1930): 23.

2. WCW to LZ, 2 April 1928 (*Williams/Zukofsky* 5).

3. LZ to CC, 17 August 1959 (HRC).

4. The TS of the first seven movements of *"A"* (HRC) dates movements 1 and 2 "October 10 / 1928 / New York" and 3 and 4 "July 11, 1929. / New York."

5. WCW to LZ, 17 October 1928 (*Williams / Zukofsky* 17); but see also WCW to LZ, 20 December 1928 (*Williams / Zukofsky* 25), which is much less enthusiastic; LZ to EP, 12 December 1928, EP to LZ, 24 December 1928 (*Pound / Zukofsky* 24–25).

6. LZ to EP, 12 December 1928 (*Pound / Zukofsky* 24).

7. *"A"* (Second Movement) appeared in *Poetry* 40, no. 2 (April 1932), and *"A"* (First Movement) appeared in *Pagany* 3, no. 3 (Summer 1932). The first seven movements of the poem appeared as a whole in *AOA* in 1932.

8. LZ told the FBI in 1941 that the job at the NICB had lasted from January 1927 to January 1928 (FBI Dossier on LZ, memo dated 22 October 1951); CZ's list of her husband's jobs dates the work from October 1927 to March 1928, *Louis Zukofsky: Man and Poet*, ed. Carroll F. Terrell (Orono, ME: National Poetry Foundation, 1979), 62.

9. WCW to LZ, 26 October 1928 (*Williams / Zukofsky* 20).

10. *Prepositions+* 31, where LZ misremembers the date as 1927.

11. EP to LZ, 2 November 1928 (*Pound / Zukofsky* 18–19).

12. WCW to LZ, 28 October 1928 (*Williams / Zukofsky* 21).

13. WCW to LZ, December 1928 (*Williams / Zukofsky* 24).

14. The history of *Pagany* is traced in *A Return to Pagany: The History, Correspondence, and Selections from a Little Magazine, 1929–1932*, ed. Stephen Halpert with Richard Johns (Boston: Beacon Press, 1969).

15. Jacqueline Vaught Brogan, *Part of the Climate: American Cubist Poetry* (Berkeley: University of California Press, 1991), 120.

16. See, among others, WCW to LZ, 3 November 1929 (*Williams / Zukofsky* 47). "The Work of Gertrude Stein" is collected in Williams's *Imaginations*, ed. Webster Schott (New York: New Directions, 1970), 346–53.

17. Jeanne Behrend and Michael Meckna, "Serly, Tibor," in *Grove Music Online*, ed. L. Macy, accessed 25 January 2007 at <http://www.grovemusic.com>.

18. *CSP* 37; MS dated 4 February 1929.

19. *CSP* 38; MS dated 25 February 1929.

20. Hugh Seidman, "Louis Zukofsky at the Polytechnic Institute of Brooklyn (1958–61)," in Terrell, ed., *Louis Zukofsky: Man and Poet*, 100.

21. Milton Hindus, "Introduction" to *Charles Reznikoff: Man and Poet* (Orono, ME: National Poetry Foundation, 1984), 16–23; Marie Syrkin, "Charles: A Memoir," *Charles Reznikoff: Man and Poet*, 37–38.

22. LZ sent EP a selection of Reznikoff's writings in November 1929; see

Pound/Zukofsky 27. In May 1929, WCW wrote LZ that he had read the Reznikoff work LZ had sent him, and "I've got to have a talk with Charles Reznikoff." Reznikoff's work gave WCW "a feeling of great honesty . . . and a sturdy resistance to a cheap art . . ."; WCW to LZ, 7 May 1929 (*Williams/Zukofsky* 31).

23. Charles Reznikoff, *Poems 1918–1936: Complete Poems Volume I*, ed. Seamus Cooney (Santa Barbara: Black Sparrow, 1976), 107.

24. Paris: Les Presses Modernes, 1929.

25. The review was entitled "Imagisme," *The New Review* 2 (May–June–July 1931). The critical "sequel" was "American Poetry 1920–1930," *The Symposium* 2, no. 1 (January 1931), reprinted in *Prepositions+* 137–151.

26. BB to LZ, 11 July 1930 (HRC).

27. Keith Alldritt, *The Poet as Spy: The Life and Wild Times of Basil Bunting* (London: Aurum, 1998), 68. Details of Bunting's life are taken from this volume.

28. Alldritt, *The Poet as Spy*, 63.

29. Ezra Pound, *Guide to Kulchur* (1938; New York: New Directions, 1970), 5. BB's letters to LZ—long, lively, and consistently fascinating—are in the HRC. Unfortunately, BB habitually destroyed received correspondence, so LZ's letters to him have not survived.

30. The three sections of the essay were published in *Hound & Horn* in May, July, and October 1930.

31. EP to LZ, 31 October 1929 (HRC).

32. "The Cantos of Ezra Pound (one section of a long essay)," *The Criterion* 10, no. 40 (April 1931); "Ezra Pound: Ses Cantos," *Échanges* 1, no. 3 (1930) (the French translator is identified as RT in EP to LZ, 6 May 1930 [HRC]); "Cantos di Ezra Pound," *L'Indice* (April 10, April 25, May 10, 1931).

33. LZ to EP, 7 March 1928 (Beinecke). EP's letter to Liveright is described in *Pound/Zukofsky* 229.

34. EP to LZ, 14 February 1930 (HRC); Leo Frobenius, *Paideuma: Umrisse einer Kultur- und Seelenlehre* (Munich: Beck, 1921). On EP and Frobenius, see Guy Davenport, "Pound and Frobenius," in *Motive and Method in The Cantos of Ezra Pound*, ed. Lewis Leary (New York: Columbia University Press, 1954), 33–59.

35. LZ to EP, 6 March 1930 (Beinecke).

36. LZ to EP, 5 November 1930 (*Pound/Zukofsky* 62).

37. LZ to EP, 18 June 1930 (*Pound/Zukofsky* 35).

38. Anton Reiser, *Albert Einstein: A Biographical Portrait* (New York: Albert & Charles Boni, 1930), v.

39. LZ to EP, 27 May 1930 (Beinecke).
40. On the flyleaf of his copy of the book (now in the HRC), LZ wrote, "I did not wish to have my name as translator appear in this book—a 'job' except for Albert Einstein's preface—on which I worked in the winter of 1929 and the spring of 1930."
41. LZ to EP, 21 April 1930 (Beinecke).
42. LZ to EP, 18 June 1930 (*Pound/Zukofsky* 35).
43. LZ to WCW, 23 July and 25 July 1930 (*Williams/Zukofsky* 69); LZ to EP, 25 July 1930.
44. There is a TS of "Paper" in the HRC that is dated 1922–1923. Another TS, like the HRC TS bearing only the pseudonym "Roger Kaigh," turned up in BB's papers and was mistakenly published as BB's in a posthumous collection, *Three Essays*, ed. Richard Caddel (Durham, UK: Basil Bunting Poetry Centre, 1994). Andrew Crozier, in his essay "Paper Bunting," *Sagetrieb* 14, no. 3 (Winter 1995): 45–74, sorts out the misattribution, discovers some interesting facts about Kaplan, and makes some crucial connections between the ideas of "Paper" and the thought of both BB and LZ.
45. LZ to EP, 8 September 1930 (*Pound/Zukofsky* 41).
46. *CSP* 41–42; the poem's MS title is "Sunday, April 12, 1931: Madison, Wis."
47. The dates are taken from the TS of "A"-1 through -7 in the HRC. The table of contents of later collections of "A" dates "A"-7 "1928–1930," but it is clear that this is a mistake deriving from the inclusive dates LZ wrote on the final page of the TS of "A"-1 through "A"-7.
48. LZ to RT, 29 August 1930 (Lilly). LZ was almost certainly exaggerating when he told RT he had a thousand poems in manuscript, but ruthless deletion seems to have been his modus operandi. Between 1930 and the publication of 55 *Poems* LZ must have destroyed at least a hundred poems.
49. LZ quotes the Foundation's letter of rejection in a letter to EP, 10 March 1930 (Beinecke); on his renewed application, see LZ to EP, 12 December 1930 (*Pound/Zukofsky* 78).
50. LZ to EP, 18 June 1930 (*Pound/Zukofsky* 35).
51. WCW to LZ, 27 May 1930 (*Williams/Zukofsky* 65); EP to LZ, 10 June 1930 (HRC).
52. LZ to EP, 18 June 1930 (*Pound/Zukofsky* 35).
53. LZ to EP, 5 November 1930 (*Pound/Zukofsky* 60). In 1951, LZ would include "How Jefferson Used Words" in a list of abandoned works in "A"-12 ("A" 257).

Chapter Five *"A"-1 through "A"-7*

1. In February 1928 LZ sent EP a sequence entitled "18 Poems to the Future" (see *Pound/Zukofsky* 9), and in November of that year he submitted a group of poems entitled "Answering Calamus" to the *American Caravan*. "Answering Calamus" is mentioned in LZ to EP, 19 November 1928 (Beinecke); the poems were not published, and have not survived.

2. Kipling used the phrase in 1906, and EP quotes it to describe his own Cantos in *Guide to Kulchur* (1937; New York: New Directions, 1970), 194, among other places.

3. EP to Felix E. Schelling, 8 July 1922, *Selected Letters of Ezra Pound, 1907–1941*, ed. D. D. Paige (1950; New York: New Directions, 1971), 180.

4. *Essays and Reviews*, ed. G. R. Thompson (New York: Library of America, 1984), 71.

5. Ronald Bush, in *The Genesis of Ezra Pound's Cantos* (Princeton: Princeton University Press, 1976), analyzes the influence of these two works on Pound's evolving poem.

6. *"Ulysses*, Order, and Myth," *Selected Prose of T. S. Eliot*, ed. Frank Kermode (London: Faber & Faber, 1975), 177.

7. LZ to EP, 12 December 1930 (*Pound/Zukofsky* 79). LZ emphasized that he didn't know the early Cantos when he began *"A"* in 15 January 1959 and 1 September 1959 letters to CC, as well as an undated fragmentary letter to LN (1953?) (all HRC).

8. For "in the air," see "Influence," a fragment of his 1930 review of RT's *L'influence* . . . (*Prepositions+* 135); the Stevens remark, which quotes *Hamlet*, II.ii.299–300, is from LZ's 1971 talk "For Wallace Stevens" (*Prepositions+* 34).

9. These subtitles were removed and the paired movements were decisively separated when LZ revised the first seven movements of *"A"* in summer 1942. While most of LZ's revisions consist of excisions, there are a number of alterations in phrasing (sometimes significant) in the early movements of *"A"*; in the following discussion of *"A"*-1 through -7, I will quote from the earlier published versions as collected in *AOA* 112–55.

10. My comments on these sections of *"A"* are much indebted to Barry Ahearn, *Zukofsky's "A": An Introduction* (Berkeley: University of California Press, 1983).

11. Olin Downes, "Music," *New York Times* (6 April 1928).

12. *AOA* 112–13.

13. *AOA* 113–14. In a 25 May 1960 letter to CC (HRC), LZ identifies "Carat" as Mike Gold, an indefatigable communist agitator and a vociferous promoter of socialist realism in writing.

14. LZ names these three sources obliquely: EP as "Atheling," the pseud-
    onym under which he wrote music reviews in London during the 1910s,
    WCW as "Carlos," and Cummings as "Estlang," his middle name.

15. *AOA* 114–15.

16. *AOA* 116–17.

17. *AOA* 118.

18. *AOA* 119–20.

19. LZ to EP, 12 December 1928 (*Pound/Zukofsky* 24).

20. EP's annotated TS of "'A' / First and Second Movements: 'Come, ye
    Daughters'" is in the Berg Collection of the New York Public Library;
    its first page is reproduced in *The Hand of the Poet: Poems and Papers in
    Manuscript*, ed. Rodney Phillips et al. (New York: Rizzoli, 1997), 185.

21. *AOA* 112.

22. EP to LZ, 24 December 1928 (*Pound/Zukofsky* 25).

23. EP to LZ, 3 February 1929 (HRC); LZ mentions sending the collection
    in a 19 December 1928 letter to EP (Beinecke).

24. While the typographical error "Rickey" in *AOA* has not been noted in
    that collection's errata sheet, the name appears as "Ricky" in "A"-3 and
    -4's earlier appearance in *The New Review* 2 (May–June–July 1931): 83.

25. Whittaker Chambers recalls the incident in *Witness*: "The other memory
    is of my brother. He is standing on our front porch, dressed in one of
    those shapeless wraps children used to be disfigured with. It is raining
    softly. I am in the house. He wants me to come out to him. I do not want
    to go. In a voice whose only reproach is a plaintiveness so gentle that it
    has sounded in the cells of my mind through all the years, he calls: 'Bro
    (for brother), it's mainin (raining), Bro.' He calls it over and over without
    ever raising his voice" (*Witness*, 95).

26. *AOA* 121–23.

27. In their first appearance in *The New Review*, these first two lines read
    "Wherever we put our hats is our home, Hebrews, / Our aged heads . . ."

28. *AOA* 124–25.

29. *AOA* 126–28. For details of Bach's life, LZ draws on Charles Sanford
    Terry, *Bach: A Biography* (London: Oxford University Press, 1928).

30. This document is in the HRC. Ahearn describes it eloquently in *Zukof-
    sky's "A"* (38).

31. In the earliest typescript of "A" 1–7 (HRC), "A"-5 is dated "Sept 9/29." The
    date assigned it on the contents page of the complete "A"—1930—would
    appear to be in error. I discuss "A"-5 at this juncture because LZ chose to
    publish it along with "A"-6 as a single unit: "Fifth and Sixth Movements:
    'And I:'"

32. *AOA* 130–31.

33. LZ to RT, 18 August 1930 (Buffalo). The HRC TS is dated "Aug 12–16/1930."

34. *AOA* 133–34.

35. *AOA* 134. Interestingly, "Ricky" (Richard Chambers) is a central figure in this two-page summing-up, playing a larger role than he does in the movements themselves; in 1942 LZ deleted most of the references to "Ricky."

36. *AOA* 136. LZ's spelling of Goethe probably pokes fun at nineteenth-century American mispronunciations of the name, by which a poet might lay an honorific "wreath" on the tomb of "great Go-ethe." The insight is Guy Davenport's.

37. *AOA* 139, 141–42.

38. *AOA* 137, 141, 142.

39. *AOA* 143, 145, 147–48. According to Ahearn, LZ did indeed visit Jeffers during this trip to California (*Zukofsky's "A"* 60).

40. *AOA* 148. I say "imagine" a return to New York because it appears from the evidence of the TS dating of "A"-6 and of LZ's letters that LZ composed all of "A"-6 in Berkeley. There is no evidence that he returned to New York before moving to Madison in September 1930.

41. *AOA* 150–52.

42. "Contributors' Notes," *Poetry* 37, no. 5 (February 1931): 294. The text prints "figure" where I have inserted "fugue," but this is clearly a misreading of LZ's hand.

43. See Willi Apel, *The Harvard Dictionary of Music*, 2nd ed. (Cambridge, MA: Belknap Press of Harvard University Press, 1969), 335. I discuss LZ's use of "fugal form" in much greater detail in *Louis Zukofsky and the Poetry of Knowledge* (Tuscaloosa: University of Alabama Press, 1998), 185–225.

44. EP to LZ, 27 November 1930 (*Pound/Zukofsky* 75).

45. In "A Packet for Ezra Pound" (1928), Yeats says that EP told him that *The Cantos*, when complete, would "display a structure like a Bach fugue" (J. P. Sullivan, ed., *Ezra Pound: A Critical Anthology* [Harmondsworth: Penguin, 1970], 100).

46. LZ to EP, 12 July 1931 (*Pound/Zukofsky* 111).

47. *AOA* 152.

48. *AOA* 152–53.

49. *AOA* 153, 154, 155.

50. See Hugh Kenner, *A Homemade World: The American Modernist Writers* (New York: Knopf, 1975), 172.

51. *AOA* 115.
52. LZ to EP, 12 December 1930 (*Pound/Zukofsky* 80).
53. WCW to LZ, 18 January 1931 (*Williams/Zukofsky* 78–79).
54. EP to LZ, 27 November 1930 (*Pound/Zukofsky* 76).
55. LZ to EP, 12 December 1930 (*Pound/Zukofsky* 78).

Interchapter *Duration, "Liveforever": Time*

1. *Prepositions+* 25, 24–25.
2. Baruch Spinoza, *The Ethics and On the Correction of the Understanding*, trans. Andrew Boyle (New York: Dutton, 1967), 38; the text and pagination of this edition are identical to those of the 1916 edition LZ owned.
3. Harry Austryn Wolfson, *The Philosophy of Spinoza* (1934; New York: Meridian, 1958), 1.353, 1.347, quoting *Cogitata Metaphysica* I, 4.
4. *Prepositions+* 27.
5. *"A"* 522.
6. Ezra Pound, *Translations* (New York: New Directions, 1963), 407.
7. Wolfson, *The Philosophy of Spinoza*, 1.341.
8. *CSP* 3.
9. *AOA* 119.
10. See Michele J. Leggott, *Reading Zukofsky's 80 Flowers* (Baltimore: Johns Hopkins University Press, 1989), 148; my whole discussion of "liveforever" is indebted to Leggott, 141–64.
11. *"A"* 7.
12. *AOA* 117, 129, *"A"* 41.
13. *"A"* 237; compare *The Basic Works of Aristotle*, ed. Richard McKeon (New York: Random House, 1941), 939–40 (*Nicomachean Ethics* 1096a–b).
14. *"A"* 142.
15. *"A"* 61; compare Marx, *Capital*, trans. Eden and Cedar Paul (New York: Dutton, 1930), 1.170.
16. Samuel Taylor Coleridge, *Biographia Literaria; Or Biographical Sketches of My Literary Life and Opinions*, ed. George Watson (New York: Dutton, 1965), 167.
17. *"A"*-23, *"A"* 540–43; LZ adapts N. K. Sandar's translation of *The Epic of Gilgamesh* (Harmondsworth: Penguin, 1960).
18. *CSP* 326. But not *quite* LZ's final word on the flower: in 1975, while gathering materials for *80 Flowers*, LZ discovered that the flower "liveforever" was not *Sempervivium tectorum*—the plant described in *"A"*-2, and whose vernacular names are alluded to in "Liveforever" ("*roof houseleek* [and] *old-man-and-woman*")—but was instead one of the *Sedum*

genus, perhaps *telephium*. (Another of that family, *Sedum acre*, is *"mossy stonecrop."*) At any rate, in the sixty-eighth poem of *80 Flowers*, "Telephus Sedum," LZ went on to implicitly acknowledge the discovery of his botanical misidentification. Both poems incorporate various names of and allusions to all three species, *Sempervivum tectorum*, *Sedum telephium*, and *Sedum acre*. See Leggott, *Reading Zukofsky's 80 Flowers*, 159–61.

19. *Prepositions+* 138, 20, 24–25.

Chapter Six *"Objectivists": 1930–1931*

1. Harriet Monroe to LZ, 11 October 1930 (HRC).
2. Harriet Monroe to LZ, 11 October 1930 (HRC).
3. The upper limit for an issue of *Poetry*, Monroe explained, would be thirty-one pages of poetry and twenty-seven of prose. Harriet Monroe to LZ, 17 December 1930, 18 October 1930 (HRC).
4. EP to LZ, 24 October 1930 (*Pound/Zukofsky* 45, 47).
5. Harriet Monroe to LZ, 13 October 1930 (HRC).
6. LZ to EP, 13 October 1930 (Beinecke).
7. T. S. Eliot, "What Is Minor Poetry?," *On Poetry and Poets* (New York: Noonday, 1961), 36.
8. EP to LZ, February 1928 (*Pound/Zukofsky* 6).
9. EP to James Vogel, 23 January 1929 (*Selected Letters* 222).
10. EP to LZ, 24 October 1930, 25 October 1930 (two letters), 28 October 1930 (*Pound/Zukofsky* 45–58); also EP to LZ, 27 October 1930 (HRC) and 28 October 1930 (HRC/Beinecke).
11. EP to LZ, 28 October 1930 (*Pound/Zukofsky* 54).
12. EP to Harriet Monroe, 24 October 1930 (*Selected Letters*, 228).
13. Strictly speaking, Kaplan did not contribute to the *Poetry* issue, but LZ cannibalized some phrases from one of his letters to make the poem "University: Old Time." See *Pound/Zukofsky* 120–21.
14. See Elizabeth Losh, "Carl Rakosi," in *Dictionary of Literary Biography, Volume 193: American Poets Since World War II, Sixth Series*, ed. Joseph M. Conte (Detroit: Gale Research, 1998), 294–304, and Rakosi's autobiography in *Contemporary Authors Autobiography Series*, Volume 5, ed. Adele Sarkissian (Detroit: Gale Research, 1987), 193–210.
15. August Kleinzahler and George Evans, "An Interview with Carl Rakosi," *Conjunctions* 11 (Fall 1988): 220.
16. LZ to EP, 17 November 1930 (Beinecke).
17. Author interview with Carl Rakosi, 29 December 1998.
18. LZ to Carl Rakosi, 3 December 1930 (HRC).
19. LZ to Carl Rakosi, 6 January 1930 (HRC).

20. LZ to Carl Rakosi, 6 January 1930 (HRC).
21. WCW to LZ, 15 October 1930 (*Williams/Zukofsky* 74).
22. The MS of the essay in the HRC is dated 4 February 1930.
23. LZ to EP, 19 December 1929 (*Pound/Zukofsky* 27), LZ to EP, 12 January 1930 (*Pound/Zukofsky* 32).
24. LZ to EP, 6 November 1930 (*Pound/Zukofsky* 65–66).
25. EP to LZ, 18 November 1930 (*Pound/Zukofsky* 74).
26. EP sent off the revised manuscript on 21 November; LZ acknowledged its receipt on 9 December. EP to LZ, 21 November 1930 (HRC); LZ to EP, 9 December 1930 (Beinecke).
27. "Sincerity and Objectification: *With Special Reference to the Work of Charles Reznikoff,*" *Poetry* 37, no. 5 (February 1931): 272–85; *Prepositions+* 194.
28. *William Wordsworth,* Oxford Authors series, ed. Stephen Gill (Oxford: Oxford University Press, 1984), 595; Ezra Pound, *Literary Essays,* ed. T. S. Eliot (New York: New Directions, 1968), 3.
29. *Prepositions+* 199.
30. *Prepositions+* 194.
31. *Prepositions+* 194.
32. Pound, *Literary Essays,* 4.
33. *Prepositions+* 196–97.
34. LZ to Carl Rakosi, 7 December 1930 (HRC).
35. Kleinzahler and Evans, "Interview with Carl Rakosi," 222.
36. Charles Reznikoff to Albert and Mildred Lewin, 4 February 1931, *Selected Letters of Charles Reznikoff, 1917–1976,* ed. Milton Hindus (Santa Rosa, CA: Black Sparrow Press, 1997), 156.
37. "Program: 'Objectivists' 1931," *Poetry: A Magazine of Verse* 37, no. 5 (February 1931): 268–72; *Prepositions+* 190.
38. *Prepositions+* 189.
39. *Prepositions+* 192; the sentence adapts the last line of Lenin's *The State and Revolution,* "It is more pleasant and more useful to live through the experience of a revolution than to write about it."
40. The phrase is Joseph Freeman's, quoted in Sam Tanenhaus, *Whittaker Chambers: A Biography* (New York: Random House, 1997), 70.
41. See Alan Wald, *The Revolutionary Imagination: The Poetry and Politics of John Wheelwright and Sherry Mangan* (Chapel Hill: University of North Carolina Press, 1983).
42. "Notes," *Poetry: A Magazine of Verse* 37, no. 5 (February 1931): 295.
43. The poem's original title was "September 8, 1926," the date of Richard Chambers's suicide; Whittaker Chambers notes that the poem was "read in court by the Hiss defence to prove something about me that

I never quite understood," yet Chambers's biographer argues that the poem is not merely an elegy but that its language also accurately reflects Chambers's late-1920s political views (Chambers, *Witness*, 183; Tanenhaus, *Whittaker Chambers*, 55).

44. *Poetry: A Magazine of Verse* 37, no. 5 (February 1931): 256, 245, 244.

45. Carl Rakosi, "Orphean Lost," *Poetry: A Magazine of Verse* 37, no. 5 (February 1931): 237.

46. *Poetry: A Magazine of Verse* 37, no. 5 (February 1931): 266.

47. LZ to Carl Rakosi, 31 December 1930 (HRC).

48. LZ to Carl Rakosi, 16 January 1931 (HRC).

49. LZ to Carl Rakosi, 24 January 1931 (HRC), LZ to Carl Rakosi, 20 March 1931 (HRC).

50. LZ to EP, 5 November 1930 (*Pound/Zukofsky* 59). In a 14 February 1931 letter to Carl Rakosi (HRC), LZ reminded him of the Irving's reputation as a "house of iniquity."

51. LZ to Carl Rakosi, 6 February 1931 (HRC).

52. LZ to EP, 5 February 1931 (*Pound/Zukofsky* 90).

53. LZ to CC, 9 November 1958 (HRC).

54. LZ to Carl Rakosi, 24 January 1931 (HRC).

55. LZ to EP, 16 March 1931 (Beinecke).

56. LZ to Carl Rakosi, 20 March 1931 (HRC).

57. LZ to Carl Rakosi, 21 May 1931 (HRC).

58. "The February Number," *Poetry: A Magazine of Verse* 38, no. 1 (April 1931): 51–58.

59. EP to LZ, 12 February 1931 (*Pound/Zukofsky* 93).

60. EP to Harriet Monroe, 27 March 1931 (*Selected Letters*, 231–32).

61. EP to LZ, 22 January 1931 (*Pound/Zukofsky* 92–93).

62. EP to LZ, 3 April 1931 (HRC).

Chapter Seven *At the Helm of an Avant-Garde: 1932–1933*

1. *Prepositions+* 203, 208, 215; the MS of the lecture is on sixty-five 3-by-5-inch note cards (HRC).

2. Mary Oppen, *Meaning a Life: An Autobiography* (Santa Barbara: Black Sparrow, 1978), 90, 126. See George Oppen, *Selected Letters*, ed. Rachel Blau DuPlessis (Durham, NC: Duke University Press, 1990), 1. The chronology of the Oppens' movements and the publishing scheme is unclear.

3. LZ to EP, 10 December 1931 (*Pound/Zukofsky* 117).

4. LZ to WCW, 16 March 1932; Mary Oppen, *Meaning a Life*, 131; Tom

Sharp, "The 'Objectivists' Publications," *Sagetrieb* 3, no. 3 (Winter 1984): 45.

5. Donald Gallup, *Ezra Pound: A Bibliography* (Charlottesville: University of Virginia Press, 1983), 49.

6. The HRC holds a typed card soliciting poems for the projected New Review Editions anthology, listing 15 October 1931 as a deadline for contributions. On Putnam's withdrawal from the project, see LZ to WCW, 17 February 1932 (*Williams/Zukofsky* 124).

7. LZ to EP, 8 August 1932 (*Pound/Zukofsky* 132).

8. *AOA* 192.

9. *AOA* 33.

10. LZ to EP, 9 November 1930 (*Pound/Zukofsky* 71).

11. EP to LZ, 27 November 1930 (*Pound/Zukofsky* 76).

12. *AOA* 27.

13. Contributors' Notes, *Poetry* 37, no. 1 (February 1931): 295.

14. In an 8 September 1931 letter (HRC), EP told LZ the price of a new Canto was two hundred dollars.

15. EP to LZ, 4 October 1931 (HRC). Opinions about the anti-Semitism of "The Yiddisher Charleston" have varied. Stephen Fredman claims the poem "features anti-semitism as the umbrella under which a collection of anti-Christian, racist, and misogynist views are gathered," *A Menorah for Athena: Charles Reznikoff and the Jewish Dilemmas of Objectivist Poetry* (Chicago: University of Chicago Press, 2001), 130, while Rachel Blau DuPlessis reads the poem as "A real vaudeville routine, showing, as with Eliot's 'Sweeney Agonistes,' that Pound identified with the verve of the groups he also berated and sometimes despised," *Gender, Race and Religious Cultures in Modern American Poetry, 1908–1934* (Cambridge: Cambridge University Press, 2001), 174.

16. LZ to EP, 15 October 1931 (Beinecke).

17. LZ to EP, 12 January 1930, 19 December 1929 (*Pound/Zukofsky* 32, 27).

18. "Two Pounds of Poetry," in *Ezra Pound: The Critical Heritage*, ed. Eric Homberger (London: Routledge & Kegan Paul, 1972), 239, 241.

19. Yvor Winters, "The Objectivists," *Hound & Horn* (October 1932): 158–60.

20. The HRC holds a galleyed exchange of vitriolic letters between LZ and Winters that were set in proof by *Hound & Horn* but never published.

21. "Lettera aperta a Louis Zukofsky," *Il Mare*, 1 October 1931.

22. "Basil Bunting Obiter Dicta," ed. Dale Reagan, in *Basil Bunting: Man and*

Poet, ed. Carroll F. Terrell (Orono, ME: National Poetry Foundation, 1981), 240–41, 242.

23. *Prepositions+* 229, 242.

24. Jenny Penberthy, *Niedecker and the Correspondence with Zukofsky* (Cambridge: Cambridge University Press, 1993), 3–100.

25. LN saved carbon copies of the LZ texts she typed, and often typed up Zukofsky's comments on his work for her own reference. These materials are in the HRC.

26. Paris: Presses Universitaires de France, 1932. LZ's copy of the book in the HRC contains LZ's notation, "(collaboration) / i.e. outlined / plan of book for R. T." LZ sent RT outlines and ideas for the "inspiration" book in letters of 17 January 1931 and 27 March 31 (Lilly), and mentioned to EP on 7 December 1931 that he was working on the "bibliography and ideaology" [*sic*] of Taupin's book (*Pound/Zukofsky* 109).

27. LZ to EP, 30 June 1931 (*Pound/Zukofsky* 106–7).

28. The MS and TS of *Apollinaire* are in the HRC. While it is unclear how closely LZ consulted with RT while writing the book, the text seems to be wholly LZ's. The MS, signed and dated "Louis Zukofsky / for / R.T. / April 19, 1932," is complete in LZ's hand except for some penciled interlinear translations in RT's hand. The TS has corrections—French accents and clarifications of French words—in RT's hand, but no substantive changes.

29. LZ to EP, 15 December 1932 (*Pound/Zukofsky* 139).

30. "La Victoire," from *Calligrammes*, quoted in *Apollinaire* 14.

31. *Apollinaire* 16; for Eliot's analogy, see *The Sacred Wood* (1920; London: Methuen, 1960), 53–54.

32. *Apollinaire* 10.

33. *Apollinaire* 32, 176, 192, 168. In addition to the ideas of Boas implied in LZ's description of Apollinaire's method, LZ explicitly cites the work of Leo Frobenius (34, 190).

34. Serge Gavronsky, Introduction to *Apollinaire* 25.

35. Notebook entry dated 19 December 1966, among the notes for "A"-21 (HRC).

36. EP to LZ, 6 December 1932 (*Pound/Zukofsky* 137).

37. LZ to EP, 15 December 1932 (*Pound/Zukofsky* 138).

38. "*The Writing of Guillaume Apollinaire*: Le Flâneur, I—Il y a," *Westminster Magazine* 22, no. 4 (Winter 1933): 9–50; "*The Writing of Guillaume Apollinaire*: III - & Cie," *Westminster Magazine* 23, no. 1 (Spring 1934): 7–46; *Le Style Apollinaire* (Paris: Les Presses Modernes, 1934).

39. *Westminster Magazine* 23, no. 1 (Spring 1934): 6.

40. EP to LZ, 16 August 1932 (*Pound/Zukofsky* 135).

41. LZ to EP, 2 September 1932 (Beinecke); EP to LZ, 21 September 1932 (HRC).

42. *CSP* 46–47; since the poem's MS is dated 22 June 1932, this cannot have been written in direct response to Pound's gift. BB's translation, a model of compact and elegant Latin composition, can be found as "Verse and Version" in his *Complete Poems*, ed. Richard Caddel (Oxford: Oxford University Press, 1994), 134.

43. Undated (May 1933?) copy in LZ's hand of a postcard from EP (HRC).

44. WCW to LZ, 6 May 1933 (HRC).

45. LZ to EP, 15 June 1933 (*Pound/Zukofsky* 150).

46. *Pound/Zukofsky* 236.

47. EP to LZ, 10 July 1933 (HRC).

48. LZ to RT, 7 August 1933 (Lilly).

49. LZ to EP, 20 July 1933 (Beinecke); Walter Lowenfels remembered the meeting in a letter to LZ of 15 December 1964 (HRC).

50. LZ to CC, 28 November 1959 (HRC).

51. "Louis Zukofsky: American Vanguard Poet," *Pesti Naplo* (13 August 1933). I quote from an English TS in the HRC that EP typed directly from Tibor Serly's impromptu translation (typos silently corrected).

52. My account of LZ's visit to Rapallo follows Charles Norman, *Ezra Pound* (New York: Macmillan, 1960), 316–19, which is based on interviews Norman conducted with LZ.

53. Norman, *Ezra Pound*, 317.

54. Norman, *Ezra Pound*, 316, 317–18; LZ to Hugh Kenner, 9 October 1962 (HRC).

55. *Ezra Pound and James Laughlin: Selected Letters*, ed. David M. Gordon (New York: New Directions, 1994), 3; see Humphry Carpenter, *A Serious Character: The Life of Ezra Pound* (Boston: Houghton Mifflin, 1988), 527–28. Laughlin's own numerous memoirs of EP tend to gloss over his first visit to Rapallo, and to my knowledge he never mentions meeting LZ there.

56. CZ, quoted in Carroll F. Terrell, "Louis Zukofsky: An Eccentric Profile," in *Louis Zukofsky: Man and Poet*, ed. Terrell (Orono, ME: National Poetry Foundation, 1979), 49.

57. EP to LZ, 8 January 1933 (*Pound/Zukofsky* 141).

58. Ezra Pound, ed., *Active Anthology* (London: Faber & Faber, 1933), 5.

59. Pound, *Active Anthology*, 253–54.

60. "The Objectivists," 160.

Chapter Eight *Politics and Poetry: 1934–1935*

1. Ezra Pound, *Selected Prose, 1909–1965*, ed. William Cookson (New York: New Directions, 1970), 399–400.

2. EP to LZ, 6[–7] May 1934 (*Pound/Zukofsky* 158), ellipses original.

3. LZ to EP, 15 December 1932 (*Pound/Zukofsky* 139).

4. See Peter Quartermain, "Writing and Authority in Zukofsky's *Thanks to the Dictionary*," in Mark Scroggins, ed., *Upper Limit Music: The Writing of Louis Zukofsky* (Tuscaloosa: University of Alabama, 1997), 154–74.

5. *CF* 272–73.

6. Quartermain, "Writing and Authority," 158.

7. "L'œuvre pure implique la disparition élocutoire du poëte, qui cède l'initiative aux mots . . . "; "Crise de vers," *Œuvres complètes*, ed. Henri Mondor and G. Jean-Aubry (Paris: Gallimard, 1945), 366.

8. Tristan Tzara, *Seven Dada Manifestos and Lampisteries*, trans. Barbara Wright (London: John Calder, 1977), 39.

9. *In Transition: A Paris Anthology—Writing and Art from Transition Magazine 1927–1930*, ed. Noel Riley Fitch (New York: Doubleday, 1990), 19.

10. Jenny Penberthy, *Niedecker and the Correspondence with Zukofsky, 1931–1970* (Cambridge: Cambridge University Press, 1993), 25.

11. In the outtakes to a 16 March 1966 interview for the National Educational Television program *USA: Poetry*, LZ said that "Joyce . . . affected me, before I knew anybody."

12. LZ to CC, 11 September 1960 (HRC). "'The'"'s reference to *Ulysses*— "Out-journeyed only by our Stephen, bibbing of a day" (*CSP* 10)—is proof positive only of a general awareness of the book, not an actual reading.

13. LZ to CC, 9 November 1958 (HRC); *Prepositions+* 197n.2.

14. Joseph Evans Slate, "The Reisman-Zukofsky Screenplay of 'Ulysses': Its Background and Significance," *The Library Chronicle of the University of Texas at Austin* 10, no. 21 (1982): 115–20.

15. *Letters of James Joyce, Vol. III*, ed. Richard Ellmann (New York: Viking, 1966), 326–27.

16. Slate, "The Reisman-Zukofsky Screenplay," 120.

17. See LZ to EP, 14 December 1931 (*Pound/Zukofsky* 121) and 17 February 1935 (*Pound/Zukofsky* 161).

18. LZ to EP, 17 April 1933 (Beinecke).

19. George Oppen to Charles Tomlinson, 5 May 1963, *Selected Letters*, ed. Rachel Blau DuPlessis (Durham: Duke University Press, 1990), 82–83. The account of this meeting in William Carlos Williams's *Autobiography* (New York: Random House, 1951, 264) is inaccurate.

20. LZ to EP, 23 October 1933 (Beinecke).

21. LZ to EP, 23 October 1933 (Beinecke).

22. WCW to LZ, 22 October 1935 (*Williams/Zukofsky* 221). On the opera, see Paul Mariani, *William Carlos Williams: A New World Naked* (New York: Norton, 1981), 336, 341–42, 355–58, 373–75. Mariani overstates when he claims that "Williams would be so upset that he would even stay away from Zukofsky for several years" (341); on 19 December 1935, less than two months after he gave up the opera, WCW invited LZ to join him for dinner in the city (*Williams/Zukofsky* 224).

23. LZ to EP, 12 April 1934 (*Pound/Zukofsky* 156).

24. CZ quoted in Carroll F. Terrell, "Louis Zukofsky: An Eccentric Profile," in *Louis Zukofsky: Man and Poet*, ed., Terrell, (Orono, ME: National Poetry Foundation, 1979), 54–55; much of the narrative of LZ and CZ's early relationship is drawn from this interview. CZ misdates their first meeting to fall 1933; LZ did not begin work for the CWA until 1934.

25. Author interview with Sophie (Thaew) Rubin, 9 November 2000. The Ellis Island source of the name Thaew is according to CZ; Sophie Rubin believes Hyman Thaew learned to spell his name thus from a Russian teacher in the old country before emigrating.

26. CZ in Terrell, "Louis Zukofsky: An Eccentric Profile," 56.

27. This description of the Columbia project is from the foreword to an early (22 August 1937) manuscript of *Test* (HRC).

28. LZ to EP, 27 June 1934 (Beinecke).

29. LZ to RT, 22 September 1930 (Lilly).

30. *ABC of Reading* (1934; New York: New Directions, 1960), 9.

31. The earliest manuscript of *Test* is dated 22 August 1937, but its colophon reads, "This collection was compiled in 1934 in New York City." According to CZ's "Year by Year Bibliography," LZ continued to work on the anthology into 1940.

32. *Test* vii.

33. *Test* vii.

34. In an undated set of "Directions" related to *Test* and its origins (HRC), LZ wrote, "If you have seen any of them [the poems] before, please read them as if you were seeing them for the first time. Their merit, or lack of it, does not depend upon the reputation of their authorship." The first section, he commented, was prescribed by the "WPA" (i.e., the CWA), though he probably "reworded" it; the second was his own.

35. I. A. Richards, *Practical Criticism* (London: Kegan Paul, Trench, Trubner, 1929).

36. *Test* vii.

37. *Test* 86, 91.

38. *Test* 48, 50, 52, 58, 65, 81, 87.

39. David M. Gordon, "Three Notes on Zukofsky's *Catullus*," in Terrell, *Louis Zukofsky: Man and Poet*, 375.

40. *ABC of Reading*, 37.

41. *ABC of Reading*, 134; *Test* 66–67.

42. *ABC of Reading*, 95.

43. *A Workers Anthology* exists in a fifty-four-page carbon copy TS in the Basil Bunting Poetry Archive, Durham University (UK), dated 8 March 1935.

44. He was not alone in doing so; Marcus Graham's 1929 *Anthology of Revolutionary Poetry*, for instance, had included poems by Blake, Shelley, Whitman, and William Morris among a section of "Forerunners." Cary Nelson, *Repression and Recovery: Modern American Poetry and the Politics of Cultural Memory, 1910–1945* (Madison: University of Wisconsin Press, 1989), 149.

45. *A Workers Anthology*, 3, 16.

46. FBI file on LZ, report dated 1 November 1951 (paraphrasing an FBI interview with Chambers).

47. LZ to EP, 5 November 1930 (*Pound/Zukofsky* 62).

48. *Mike Gold: A Literary Anthology*, ed. Michael Folsom (New York: International, 1972), 207–8.

49. LZ to EP, 11 May 1935 (Beinecke); Daniel Aaron, *Writers on the Left: Episodes in American Literary Communism* (1961; New York: Columbia University Press, 1992), 485–86n.8.

50. LZ to EP, 25 December 1935 (Beinecke).

51. LZ to EP, 25 December 1935, 18 January 1936 (Beinecke); see Barry Ahearn, "Zukofsky, Marxism, and American Handicraft," in *Upper Limit Music: The Writing of Louis Zukofsky*, ed. Mark Scroggins (Tuscaloosa: University of Alabama Press, 1997), 90.

52. *"A"* 83–86; note the address to "Bob" on 86.

53. I quote from the manuscript of "Robert Allison Evans" (HRC), dated 1 April 1943. LZ later shortened the title to "R.A.E." and omitted the fourth line (*CSP* 120).

54. The review, "Muriel Rukeyser's Poems," survives as a single undated carbon copy typescript in the HRC; I suspect the review was drafted for *New Masses*.

55. *CSP* 92; the poem, originally titled "Worker's Burden: A madrigal for 3 voices unaccompanied," is dated 27–28 February 1935 (HRC).

56. *CSP* 61, MS dated 8 December 1933.

57. *CSP* 53, MS dated 13 December 1932.

58. In an 11 May 1935 letter to EP (Beinecke), LZ mentions "my weekly stint of $21 which leaves me 75¢ a day when I've done what I can for the starving family." Given that LZ had noted that he was paying seven dollars a week for his previous room (LZ to EP, 20 October 1934 [Beinecke]), he seems to have been contributing almost half his salary towards his family's support.

59. *CSP* 65–66.

60. LZ borrowed much of the folkloric and ethnographic material about the mantis from Roger Caillois's "La Mante religieuse," *Minotaure* 5 (1934): 23–26; see "The Praying Mantis," in *The Edge of Surrealism: A Roger Caillois Reader*, ed. Claudine Frank, trans. Claudine Frank and Camille Naish (Durham: Duke University Press, 2004), 66–81. See Michael Golston, "Petalbent Devils: Louis Zukofsky, Lorine Niedecker, and the Surrealist Praying Mantis," *Modernism/Modernity* 13, no. 2 (2006): 325–47.

61. MS dated 27 October 1934; WCW comments on the poem to LZ on 30 October 1934 (*Williams/Zukofsky* 202).

62. *CSP* 67; the phrase appears in Dante's *La Vita Nuova*.

63. *CSP* 68; LZ translates a phrase from Dante's *La Vita Nuova*.

64. *CSP* 67, 70.

65. *CSP* 69. See John Taggart, "Zukofsky's 'Mantis,'" in *Songs of Degrees: Essays on Contemporary Poetry and Poetics* (Tuscaloosa: University of Alabama Press, 1994), 51–66; Michael Davidson, "Dismantling 'Mantis': Reification and Objectivist Poetics," *American Literary History* 3, no. 3 (Fall 1991): 521–41; and Mark Scroggins, *Louis Zukofsky and the Poetry of Knowledge* (Tuscaloosa: University of Alabama Press, 1998), 311–21.

66. LZ to EP, 25 December 1935 (Beinecke).

67. "Carl Rakosi," *Contemporary Authors Autobiography Series*, Volume 5, ed. Adele Sarkissian (Detroit: Gale Research, 1987), 207–8.

68. Oppen, *Selected Letters*, xiii–xiv.

Chapter Nine *Culture and Design: 1936–1940*

1. Carroll F. Terrell, "Louis Zukofsky: An Eccentric Profile," in *Louis Zukofsky: Man and Poet*, ed. Carroll F. Terrell (Orono, ME: National Poetry Foundation, 1979), 66.

2. On the Yiddish theater, see *Autobiography* 33; on the Provincetown Playhouse, see *Prepositions+* 29. LZ mentions Pirandello in his 1928 review of Cummings's *Him* (*Prepositions+* 84); that he had read surrealist drama is Terrell's suggestion (*Louis Zukofsky: Man and Poet*, 41–42). In a 1936

letter to LN, LZ speculates on how Cocteau would read the play; see Jenny Penberthy, *Niedecker and the Correspondence with Zukofsky, 1931–1970* (Cambridge: Cambridge University Press, 1993), 113n.34.

3. The MS (HRC) specifies that the play was finished 27 June 1936.

4. *Arise* 33.

5. *Arise* 1, 10, 25.

6. According to Florence Feigenblum, LZ, and Dora Pruss's niece, Dora Pruss died in childbirth (author interview, 15 February 2001).

7. *Arise* 51, 39.

8. Note dated 18 May 1950, accompanying a TS sent to Isaku Hirai of the magazine *Shigaku* (HRC).

9. "Author's Note" to *A Dream Play*, *Six Plays of Strindberg*, trans. Elizabeth Sprigge (New York: Anchor, 1955), 193.

10. Apollinaire in *Arise* 14, 18: the translation as a whole is reprinted in Terrell, ed., *Louis Zukofsky: Man and Poet*, 158; Donne in *Arise* 23; the Mother's speech, "We mourn only ourselves, our own earth selves" (*Arise* 17), adapts "earth, bowed with her death, we mourn," *The Dial* 85, no. 6 (December 1928): 459. The Son's "Graced, graced, the eyes grow black with dancing" (*Arise* 50) quotes an unpublished poem of LZ's from 1923(?), *Louis Zukofsky: Man and Poet*, 149.

11. Terrell, ed., *Louis Zukofsky: Man and Poet*, 58. Morris Zukowsky's daughter Florence Feigenblum recalls that Dora Pruss's husband owned a dress factory where Morris had once worked (author interview, 15 February 2001).

12. *Arise* 43.

13. *CSP* 45. "In Arizona" (datelined "Route No. 180, on the way to Globe, Arizona") was written 28 April 1932, and "Arizona," (dated the next day) was originally titled "towards Phoenix, Arizona."

14. LZ EP, 9 September 1936 (HRC); the photograph is reproduced in Jenny Penberthy, ed., *Lorine Niedecker: Woman and Poet* (Orono, ME: National Poetry Foundation, 1996), 40.

15. LZ to EP, 14 December 1931 (Ahearn, *Pound/Zukofsky* 121).

16. See Joseph Evans Slate, "The Reisman-Zukofsky Screenplay of 'Ulysses': Its Background and Significance," *The Library Chronicle of the University of Texas at Austin* 10, no. 21 (1982): 124, for these titles; LZ mentions going to the "Survey" in an undated fragmentary letter to LN (HRC). On LZ, WCW, and film, see David Kadlec, "Early Soviet Cinema and American Poetry," *Modernism/Modernity* 11, no. 2 (2004): 299–331.

17. LZ to LN, 10 February 1936 (HRC); LZ to EP, 14 February 1936 (Beinecke).

18. MS of "Modern Times" (HRC) dated 18 March 1936.

19. *Prepositions+* 62.

20. *Prepositions+* 58, 62, 63.

21. *Prepositions+* 60.

22. Author interview with Carl Rakosi, 29 December 1999.

23. Keith Alldritt, *The Poet as Spy: The Life and Wild Times of Basil Bunting* (London: Aurum, 1998), 90–97.

24. My mother, who grew up in Depression-era rural Kentucky where the WPA was building roads, recalled that the popular explanation for the acronym "WPA" was "we piddle around."

25. LZ to EP, 8 April 1935 (*Pound/Zukofsky* 166–67).

26. *Useful Art* 192.

27. On Zukofsky's Index writings, see Barry Ahearn, "Zukofsky, Marxism, and American Handicraft," *Upper Limit Music: The Writing of Louis Zukofsky*, ed. Mark Scroggins (Tuscaloosa: University of Alabama Press, 1997), 80–93; Ira B. Nadel, "'A Precision of Appeal': Louis Zukofsky and the *Index of American Design*," *Upper Limit Music*, 112–26; and Kenneth Sherwood's Introduction to *Useful Art* 1–13. A good overview of the Index is Holger Cahill's "Introduction" to *Treasury of American Design: A Pictorial Survey of Popular Folk Arts Based upon Watercolor Renderings in the Index of American Design, at the National Gallery of Art,* 2 volumes (New York: Abrams, n.d.), xix–xxvii.

28. LZ to EP, 8 December 1936 (Beinecke).

29. Penberthy, *Niedecker and the Correspondence with Zukofsky,* 107n.14.

30. *Prepositions+* 232.

31. On Hicks, see Ahearn, "Zukofsky, Marxism," 82; that trip is recalled in "A"-8 (*"A"* 97). On the "Binnacle Figure," see *Useful Art* 169.

32. *Useful Art* 52, 69–71, 77.

33. *Test* 89.

34. *Test* 103.

35. *Useful Art* 77, 119.

36. *Useful Art* 157, 159, 151–54.

37. *Useful Art* 165, 167.

38. *Useful Art* 106–7, 184.

39. LZ mentions this title among a list of unwritten but contemplated works in "A"-12 (*"A"* 257).

40. There is no mention of these radio programs in the files and logbooks of WNYC (Nadel, "'Precision of Appeal,'" 119); on the closing down of the Index, see Cahill, xxiv.

41. See Michael Coyle, *Ezra Pound, Popular Genres, and the Discourse of Culture* (University Park: Pennsylvania State University Press, 1995).

42. John Ruskin, *The Crown of Wild Olive* (London: Dent, 1908), 4–8; *Fors*

Clavigera: Letters to the Workmen and Labourers of Great Britain, 4 volumes (Boston: Aldine, n.d.), I.215; Ezra Pound, *Guide to Kulchur* (1938; New York: New Directions, 1970), 27.

43. See Susan Buck-Morss, *The Dialectics of Seeing: Walter Benjamin and the Arcades Project* (Cambridge: MIT Press, 1989), 73–77.

44. EP to LZ, 28 May 1935 (*Pound/Zukofsky* 168–9).

45. LZ to EP, 7 June 1935 (*Pound/Zukofsky* 172).

46. EP to LZ, 25 June 1936; LZ replied on 11 and 16 July 1936 (*Pound/Zukofsky* 181–6).

47. LZ to Walter Lowenfels, 7 April 1938 (SFU).

48. EP to BB, May 1935, quoted in Peter Makin, *Bunting: The Shaping of His Verse* (Oxford: Clarendon Press, 1992), 78.

49. EP to LZ, 2 December 1938 (HRC).

50. BB to EP, 16 December 1938, quoted in Makin, *Bunting*, 79.

51. EP to LZ, 7 January 1939 (HRC).

52. LZ to EP, 18 January 1939 (*Pound/Zukofsky* 198–99).

53. LZ to EP, 18 January 1936 (Beinecke); LZ to Franklin Folsom (Executive Secretary of the League), 8 July 1938 (HRC); Franklin Folsom to LZ, 13 July 1938 (HRC).

54. Norman Macleod, "Pain Without Finish" (review of *In Memoriam: 1933*), *New Masses* 16 no. 10 (5 March 1935: 23–4.

55. LZ to EP, 15 April 1933 (*Pound/Zukofsky* 148).

56. *Mike Gold: A Literary Anthology*, ed. Michael Folsom (New York: International, 1972), 207.

57. LZ to EP, 18 January 1936 (Beinecke).

58. LZ elaborated this position at length in an undated typescript letter addressed to [Kenneth] Burke, [Isidor] Schneider, and [Edwin Berry] Burgum (HRC).

59. LZ to LN, 7 June 1937 (HRC).

60. "The Labor Process," *New Masses* 24 no. 5 (27 July 1937); "March Comrades," *New Masses* 27 no. 6 (3 May 1938). For a detailed discussion of "March Comrades," see Mark Scroggins, *Louis Zukofsky and the Poetry of Knowledge* (Tuscaloosa: University of Alabama Press, 1998), 155–61.

61. WCW to James Laughlin, 4 December 1937, *William Carlos Williams and James Laughlin: Selected Letters*, ed. Hugh Witemeyer (New York: New Directions, 1989), 17–18.

62. James Laughlin, "Notes on Contributors," *New Directions in Prose and Poetry, 1938* (Norfolk, CT: New Directions, 1938), n.p. For LZ's complaints, see an undated (probably 1953) letter to LN (HRC).

63. EP to LZ, 10 February 1939 (HRC).

64. Humphrey Carpenter, *A Serious Character: The Life of Ezra Pound* (Boston: Little, Brown, 1988), 558–61.

65. *Prepositions+* 165; see Carpenter, *A Serious Character,* 561.

66. LZ to EP, 3 January 1940 (Beinecke); see *Pound/Zukofsky* 202. The HRC holds a TS by LZ, dated 4 January 1940, entitled "Outline of Project for a Study of the Writings of Thomas Jefferson."

67. Terrell, ed., *Louis Zukofsky: Man and Poet,* 57.

68. BB to LZ, 31 August 1939 (HRC).

69. EP to LZ, 6 February 1940 (HRC).

70. LZ to EP, 23 February 1940 (HRC); on the cats, see *"It was," CF* 181. The couple moved to 1088 East 180th Street on 15 September 1939 (CZ Dossier).

71. LZ provided a detailed rationale for Stalin's purges in a 9 September 1936 letter to EP (Beinecke).

72. *CSP* 209; MS dated 12–13 October 1939.

73. *CSP* 94–95; MS dated 21 October 1939.

74. *CSP* 209; *"A"* 94.

75. Marcella Booth, *A Catalogue of the Louis Zukofsky Manuscript Collection* (Austin: Humanities Research Center, University of Texas, 1975), 187. The TS, dated 22 June 1939, includes "Henry Adams: A Criticism in Autobiography," "Ezra Pound: His Cantos," "Sincerity and Objectification," "American Poetry 1920–1930," "Two Related Notes," and "Modern Times." Sometime later, LZ would add "Thanks to the Dictionary."

76. In 1943, WCW told James Laughlin that LZ had been trying to sell the book "for five years"; WCW to James Laughlin, 21 February 1943 (Witemeyer, ed., *Williams and Laughlin: Selected Letters,* 86).

77. Quoted in LZ to EP, 23 February 1940 (Beinecke).

Chapter Ten *"A"-8 and First Half of "A"-9*

1. Drafts for *"A"* 8 are dated from 5 August 1935 to 14 July 1937—three weeks short of two years' work. On "A"-8, see Barry Ahearn, *Zukofsky's "A": An Introduction* (Berkeley: University of California Press, 1983), 72–100; Luke Carson, *Consumption and Depression in Gertrude Stein, Louis Zukofsky and Ezra Pound* (New York: St. Martin's Press, 1999), 150–68; and Tim Woods, *The Poetics of the Limit: Ethics and Politics in Modern and Contemporary American Poetry* (New York: Palgrave Macmillan, 2002), 75–82.

2. LZ to LN, 9 November 1935, 28 January 1937 (HRC).

3. LZ to LN, 9 November 1937 (HRC); see Ahearn, *Zukofsky's "A",* 75–76.

4. Here I adapt Ahearn's convincing "compromise tally," *Zukofsky's "A",* 77.

5. *"A"* 43.

6. *"A"* 43.

7. *"A"* 45, ellipses in original.

8. *"A"* 72–73, 96–98, 86.

9. *"A"* 57.

10. *Prepositions+* 63.

11. *"A"* 76; see *Henry IV, Part 1*, II.iv.133–34, and Ahearn, *Zukofsky's "A"*, 85.

12. *"A"* 94–95.

13. *"A"* 96–97.

14. *"A"* 98–99.

15. *"A"* 49.

16. The second stanza varies this as "Labor light lights in air, in earth, on earth" (*"A"* 104).

17. *"A"* 105.

18. These notes are no longer extant; see Ahearn, *Zukofsky's "A"*, 231–32.

19. From an undated note on the prosody of "A"-8 (HRC).

20. On mathematical poetics in "A"-8 and "A"-9, see Ahearn, *Zukofsky's "A"*, 231–41, and Peter Quartermain, *Disjunctive Poetics: From Gertrude Stein and Louis Zukofsky to Susan Howe* (Cambridge: Cambridge University Press, 1992), 70–89.

21. *"A"* 50.

22. Ahearn, *Zukofsky's "A"*, 235, 239.

23. "Of Notes and Horses," *Louis Zukofsky: Man and Poet*, ed. Carroll F. Terrell (Orono, ME: National Poetry Foundation, 1979), 189.

24. T. S. Eliot, *Selected Prose*, ed. Frank Kermode (London: Faber & Faber, 1975), 32.

25. LZ to Peter Quartermain, 18 October 1968.

26. See Kevin J. H. Dettmar, *The Illicit Joyce of Postmodernism: Reading Against the Grain* (Madison: University of Wisconsin Press, 1996), 137–73.

27. John Cage, *X: Writings '79–'82* (Middletown, CT: Wesleyan University Press, 1983), 149.

28. The MS of the first half of "A"-9 is dated 9 August 1938–1 April 1940 (HRC). On "A"-9, see Quartermain, "'Not at All Surprised by Science'"; Jeffrey Twitchell-Waas, "Tuning the Senses: Cavalcanti, Marx, Spinoza and Zukofsky's 'A'-9," *Sagetrieb* 11 (Winter 1992): 57–91; and Hugh Kenner, "Loove in Brooklyn," in *Historical Fictions: Essays* (San Francisco: North Point, 1990), 122–31.

29. In his *Sonnets and Ballate of Guido Cavalcanti* (1912), in the long essay "Cavalcanti" (1928), and in Canto 36 (1934); LZ probably knew all of these versions.

30. *First Half of "A"-9* (New York: privately printed, 1940), 2; LZ follows the text of EP's *Guido Cavalcanti: Rime* (Genoa: Edizioni Marsano, 1932). The English translation is from Maria Luisa Ardizzone, *Guido Cavalcanti: The Other Middle Ages* (Toronto: University of Toronto Press, 2002), 167.

31. Ezra Pound, *Literary Essays*, ed. T. S. Eliot (New York: New Directions, 1968), 170, 168.

32. *"A"* 106.

33. *First Half*, 4, 6, quoting Karl Marx, *Capital,* trans. Eden and Cedar Paul (New York: Dutton, 1932), 8, 58.

34. *"A"* 107; "Restatement," *First Half,* 40.

35. *"A"* 108; "Restatement," *First Half,* 41.

36. *Literary Essays*, 168.

37. London: Macmillan, 1932.

38. "The 'Form,'" *First Half,* 37.

39. *"A"*-9 (Stuttgart: Futura 5, edition hansjörg mayer, 1966).

40. "Foreword," *First Half,* 1.

41. *"A"* 107, 105.

42. *First Half,* 34.

43. LZ to EP, 23 February 1940 (Beinecke).

44. *First Half,* 35, LZ's ellipses. "A loin laoo boddere" is collected in LZ, *Selected Poems*, ed. Charles Bernstein (New York: Library of America, 2006), 152–54.

45. In a letter to EP of 7 December 1940 (Beinecke), LZ said he had the pamphlets on hand, but was holding on to EP's copy because of the uncertainty and high rates of air mail.

46. EP to James Laughlin, late November 1940, *Ezra Pound and James Laughlin: Selected Letters*, ed. David M. Gordon (New York: New Directions, 1994), 123.

47. WCW to LZ, December 1940 (*Williams/Zukofsky* 278).

48. WCW to LZ, 31 March 1941 and LZ to WCW, 1 April 1941 (*Williams/Zukofsky* 279); *"A"*-9 (first half) appeared in *Poetry* 58, no. 3 (June 1941).

Interchapter *Numbers and Horses*

1. CZ, "1927–1972," *Paideuma* 7, no. 3 (Winter 1978): 371; the "birthday," that is, which he celebrated; see Chapter 1.

2. EP to Hubert Creekmore, February 1939, *Selected Letters, 1907–1941*, ed. D. D. Paige (1950; New York: New Directions, 1971), 323.

3. *"A"* 563.

4. "A"-18, "A" 406; CZ discusses LZ's interest in Pythagorean number theory in Barry Ahearn, "Two Conversations with Celia Zukofsky," *Sagetrieb* 2, no. 1 (Spring 1983): 120–21. See also Michele J. Leggott, *Reading Zukofsky's 80 Flowers* (Baltimore: Johns Hopkins University Press, 1989), 76–78.

5. Walter Burket, *Love and Science in Ancient Pythagoreanism*, trans. Edwin L. Minar Jr. (Cambridge: Harvard University Press, 1972), 40.

6. See Christopher Butler, *Number Symbolism* (London: Routledge and Kegan Paul, 1970), 4–5. The most famous description of the "music of the spheres," the myth of Er in Plato's *Republic*, is revisited in LZ's "Pamphylian" (*CSP* 133).

7. *CSP* 215.

8. These numerological games are in the notes for *80 Flowers* at the HRC, and are quoted in Leggott, *Reading Zukofsky's 80, Flowers* 13–14.

9. See Leggott, *Reading Zukofsky's 80 Flowers*, 17; "number-tumbling" is Leggott's phrase (14).

10. "A" 138.

11. *Prepositions+* 6, quoting *Philebus*, 55e.

12. Wisdom of Solomon 11:21; see S. K. Heninger Jr., *The Subtext of Form in the English Renaissance: Proportion Poetical* (University Park: Pennsylvania State University Press, 1994), 41.

13. *CSP* 213; MS dated 27 March 1959 (HRC).

14. "A" 351.

15. *CSP* 16–17.

16. Guy Davenport, *Every Force Evolves a Form: Twenty Essays* (San Francisco: North Point, 1987), 102–3.

17. "A" 376, 359, 388.

18. LZ to Babette Deutsch, 27 March 1961 (Berg).

19. *CSP* 28, draft dated 22 February 1924, "Student Days" (HRC).

20. Guy Davenport, *The Geography of the Imagination: Forty Essays* (San Francisco: North Point, 1981), 51.

21. *Bottom* 1.39.

22. "A" 7.

23. "A" 20.

24. "A" 175.

25. *Prepositions+* 63.

26. "A" 560, 535.

27. *Romeo and Juliet*, II.ii.107–8.

28. *CSP* 325.

Chapter Eleven *The Home Front: 1940–1945*

1. The MS of "Paris" (HRC) is dated 10 June–31 July 1940. On "Paris" ("A"-10), see Bruce Comens, *Apocalypse and After: Modern Strategy and Postmodern Tactics in Pound, Williams, and Zukofsky* (Tuscaloosa: University of Alabama Press, 1995), 152–58.

2. *"A"* 113.

3. *"A"* 115, 118.

4. *"A"* 116, 117.

5. *"A"* 120; see Barry Ahearn, *Zukofsky's "A": An Introduction* (Berkeley: University of California Press, 1983), 209–10.

6. *"A"* 114.

7. *"A"* 112, 116, 121, 122.

8. WCW to LZ, 3 April 1941; LZ to WCW, 5 April 1941 (*Williams/Zukofsky* 280–81).

9. TS description of *La France en Liberté* sent to LN on 7 August 1940 (HRC); the HRC holds an undated prospectus for the magazine.

10. WCW to LZ, 2 October 1940 (*Williams/Zukofsky* 272); LZ to Carl Rakosi, 6 August 1940 (HRC); LZ to WCW, 27 November 1940 (*Williams/Zukofsky* 276).

11. LZ to LN, 30 October 1940 (HRC); see CZ's list of LZ's jobs in Carroll F. Terrell, "Louis Zukofsky: An Eccentric Profile," in Terrell, ed., *Louis Zukofsky: Man and Poet* (Orono, ME: National Poetry Foundation, 1979), 63.

12. A TS of "Abe Fink, Begorrah" is in the HRC.

13. MS dated 19 January 1941 (HRC).

14. *CF* 188, 186.

15. The MS of *Ferdinand* (HRC) is dated February 1941–19 June 1942.

16. LZ to WCW, 25 August 1942 (*Williams/Zukofsky* 283).

17. LZ sent a copy of the synopsis, along with the first two chapters of the novella, to LN in 1942 (HRC).

18. *CF* 183, 220.

19. *CF* 240.

20. *CF* 264.

21. LZ to WCW, 28 August 1941 (*Williams/Zukofsky* 287–88).

22. WCW to LZ, 21 June 1942 (*Williams/Zukofsky* 304).

23. LZ to WCW, 9 April 1942 (*Williams/Zukofsky* 299).

24. The MS of *"It was"* (HRC) is dated as being begun 4 August 1941; LZ seems to have finished the composition in August 1941 and returned to revise the piece in 1954.

25. *CF* 181–84.

26. Keith Alldritt, *The Poet as Spy: The Life and Wild Times of Basil Bunting* (London: Aurum, 1998), 97–100.

27. FBI dossier on LZ, report dated 22 October 1951; LZ to WCW, 10 November 1942 (*Williams/Zukofsky* 309).

28. LZ to LN, 25 January 1941 (HRC).

29. LZ's TS and MS notes for the reading, dated 23 January 1941 (HRC).

30. LZ to WCW, 9 April 1942 (*Williams/Zukofsky* 300). The symposium took place on 23 March 1941.

31. Peter Quartermain, *Disjunctive Poetics: From Gertrude Stein and Louis Zukofsky to Susan Howe* (Cambridge: Cambridge University Press, 1992), 70; Barry Ahearn reports that the pamphlet "was still to be had for the asking in the 1960s" (*Zukofsky's "A"*, 100).

32. LZ to WCW, 4 October 1940 (*Williams/Zukofsky* 275); LZ to Carl Rakosi, 7 November 1940 (HRC); New Directions published Rakosi's *Selected Poems* in December 1941.

33. The history of the Decker Press is told in James Ballowe, "Little Press on the Prairie," *Chicago Reader* (May 3, 1996): 16, 33–35, and on Marcus Williamson's "Decker Press" website (http://www.connectotel.com/patchen/decker.html). The details of the Decker Press's finances are unclear, since the publisher's records were largely destroyed after the press's demise in 1950.

34. For a description of this TS, see Marcella Booth, *A Catalogue of the Louis Zukofsky Manuscript Collection* (Austin: Humanities Research Center, University of Texas, 1975), 34–35.

35. *CSP* 73.

36. At this point, Zukofsky still believed that his birthday was January 29 rather than January 23.

37. *CSP* 64–65.

38. TS dated 17 March 1934 (HRC).

39. LZ to LN, fragment dated by LN 1945?, but probably 1941. LZ would echo these lines in the last sentence of *Ferdinand*.

40. *CSP* 34, MS dated 27 November 1923.

41. *CSP* 43.

42. *CSP* 46, 47.

43. LZ to WCW, 22 October 1941 (*Williams/Zukofsky* 293–94); "An Extraordinary Sensitivity: Louis Zukofsky's *55 Poems*," *Poetry* 60, no. 6 (September 1942): 338–40; reprinted in *Something to Say: William Carlos Williams on Younger Poets*, ed. James E. B. Breslin (New York: New Directions, 1985), 129–31.

44. LZ to LN, 21 January 1942 (HRC), noting that CZ was meeting with "the president of her school" "to discuss raises."

45. LZ to WCW, 18 June 1942 (*Williams/Zukofsky* 302).

46. LZ to WCW, 8 September 1942 (*Williams/Zukofsky* 305); notations on an HRC TS of "A"-1 through -7 indicate that LZ revised the first seven movements ("A"-7 was untouched) between 19 July and 6 August 1942.

47. LZ to Mary Barnard, 17 January 1940 (Buffalo).

48. *AOA* 113; *"A"* 2.

49. *AOA* 118; *"A"* 6.

50. LZ to WCW, 8 September 1942 (*Williams/Zukofsky* 305).

51. *Prepositions+* 152–54.

52. WCW to LZ, 7 November 1942 (*Williams/Zukofsky* 308); "Dometer Guczul," *View* 3, no. 3 (Fall 1943).

53. LZ to WCW, 8 September 1942 (*Williams/Zukofsky* 305).

54. LZ to Carl Rakosi, 10 December 1942 (HRC).

55. Quartermain, *Disjunctive Poetics,* 44; see also LZ to Hugh Kenner, 4 July 1973 (HRC).

56. John Paul Russo, *I. A. Richards: His Life and Work* (Baltimore: Johns Hopkins University Press, 1989), 297–98.

57. *Prepositions+* 155, 160–61, LZ's emphases.

58. *Prepositions+* 163; LZ here anticipates postwar attacks on Basic as an instrument of "linguistic imperialism" (see Russo, *I. A. Richards,* 403–4).

59. *Prepositions+* 163.

60. *CSP* 102. The MS (HRC) notes the time of PZ's birth; "Dinty" is PZ; "her" originally read "Sophie," presumably CZ's younger sister.

61. LZ to LN, undated fragment (HRC).

62. LZ to Hugh Kenner, 4 July 1973; WCW to LZ, 22 December 1944 (*Williams/Zukofsky* 351).

63. LZ to WCW, 7 September and 25 December 1945 (*Williams/Zukofsky* 357, 360–61).

64. James Laughlin to EP, 17 September 1945, *Ezra Pound and James Laughlin: Selected Letters*, ed. David M. Gordon (New York: New Directions, 1994), 138.

65. LZ to WCW, 25 December 1945 (*Williams/Zukofsky* 360).

Chapter Twelve *A New Life: 1946–1951*

1. Published as section 2 of "A Song for the Year's End" (*CSP* 111–12); MS dated 16 April 1946 (HRC).

2. LZ to LN, 7 January 1945 (HRC).

3. Humphrey Carpenter, *A Serious Character: The Life of Ezra Pound* (Boston: Little, Brown, 1988), 583–91, 603–6; many of the broadcasts are

collected in Leonard Doob, ed., *"Ezra Pound Speaking": Radio Speeches of World War II* (New York: Greenwood Press, 1978).

4. Carpenter, *A Serious Character* 621, 632–33.

5. Quoted in Omar Pound and Robert Spoo, eds., *Ezra and Dorothy Pound: Letters in Captivity, 1945–1946* (New York: Oxford University Press, 1999), 12–13.

6. LZ to LN, undated but probably May 1935 (HRC).

7. LZ to WCW, 25 December 1945 (*Williams/Zukofsky* 361).

8. *Prepositions+* 165–66; originally published in Charles Norman, *The Case of Ezra Pound*, with opinions by Conrad Aiken, E. E. Cummings, F. O. Matthiessen, William Carlos Williams, Louis Zukofsky (New York: Bodley, 1948).

9. Published simultaneously with *Anew*, and also in the Pocket Poetry series, was *New Goose*, Lorine Niedecker's first collection. Jacket copy, *Anew* (Prairie City, IL: The Press of James A. Decker, 1946).

10. *CSP* 89.

11. *CSP* 103; one might compare this account to Samuel Taylor Coleridge's explanation of the unfinished state of "Kubla Khan."

12. *CSP* 77.

13. *CSP* 103.

14. *CSP* 88.

15. *CSP* 93.

16. *CSP* 103–4.

17. *CSP* 91; LZ dates the visit 1 June 1941, the poem 6 June 1941.

18. *The Oxford Book of English Verse*, ed. Christopher Ricks (Oxford: Oxford University Press, 1999), 216.

19. *CSP* 99; "After Charles Sedley" was originally subtitled "(a valentine)," and is dated 14 February 1943.

20. WCW to LZ, 26 March 1946 (*Williams/Zukofsky* 366).

21. *Something to Say: William Carlos Williams on Younger Poets*, ed. James E. B. Breslin (New York: New Directions, 1985), 161, 166, 165, 167. "A New Line Is a New Measure: Louis Zukofsky's *Anew*" was published in the *New Quarterly of Poetry* 2, no. 2 (Winter 1947–48): 8–16.

22. On the editing of *The Wedge*, see *Williams/Zukofsky* 549–54, and Neil Baldwin, "Zukofsky, Williams, and *The Wedge*: Toward a Dynamic Convergence," in *Louis Zukofsky: Man and Poet*, ed. Carroll F. Terrell, (Orono, ME: National Poetry Foundation, 1979), 129–42.

23. "The Pink Church," *Briarcliff Quarterly* 11 (October 1946); details of CZ's compositional projects from CZ Dossier.

24. LZ to LN, 1947 (HRC); another letter to LN (undated) describes a second session of performing *Pericles* for Van Doren and his wife.

25. LZ to LN, probably October or November 1945; details of LZ's employment from CZ Dossier.
26. LZ to LN, undated (1946) letter (HRC).
27. LZ to LN, 7 February 1947 (HRC).
28. *Prepositions+* 3.
29. MS (HRC), dated "(started ca. May 1945)"–22 December 1946.
30. *Prepositions+* 3–4.
31. *Prepositions+* 5, 7.
32. *Prepositions+* 8.
33. *Prepositions+* 10.
34. *Prepositions+* 218.
35. LZ to LN, dated 1947 by LN (HRC).
36. LZ to WCW, postmarked 9 June 1947 (*Williams/Zukofsky* 389).
37. MS dated 22 August 1947 (HRC); revised version *CSP* 121–22.
38. LZ to LN, undated (HRC).
39. LZ to LN, summer 1947 (HRC).
40. LZ to LN, undated (LN dates it 1948?), (HRC).
41. "'Recencies' in Poetry," *Prepositions+* 204.
42. WCW to LZ, 26 June 1948; LZ to WCW, 28 June 1948 (*Williams/Zukofsky* 197–98).
43. LZ to EP, 18 June 1948; LZ to WCW, 28 June 1948 (*Williams/Zukofsky* 398).
44. *Test* 4, 5; compare "*A*" 215, 218, 221.
45. *William Carlos Williams and James Laughlin: Selected Letters*, ed. Hugh Witemeyer (New York: New Directions, 1989), 87; CZ Dossier notes the print run.
46. Wallace Stevens to LZ, 13 October 1948 (HRC).
47. LZ to LN, 14 April 1948; LZ to LN, 19 May 1949 (HRC).
48. Dahlberg told Robert M. Hutchins in 1958 that he had been "a humble academic charwoman at Brooklyn Polytechnic College for over three years, where I gave courses in composition and in the *inhumanities*"; *Epitaphs of Our Times: The Letters of Edward Dahlberg* (New York: George Braziller, 1967), 23.
49. LZ to LN, undated (HRC).
50. *CF* 298.
51. *CSP* 124–25; the MS for Section I of the poem is dated 13–16 August–4 September 1949. The background to the poem is elucidated in a note by LN on the back of an undated (1950?) letter from LZ (HRC).
52. *CSP* 125; "*A*" 223.
53. The letters are in the HRC; they appear in "*A*" 216–23.
54. LZ to LN, 20 May (?) 1951, LZ to LN, 14 June 1951 (HRC).

55. See the draft of the first eight chapters of *Little* (HRC).

56. Arnold Wand (Al Wand's son) to author, 18 November 2000; PZ explains many of *Little*'s pseudonyms in "The Baron Speaks," his afterword to *Collected Fiction* (294–303).

57. Sam Tanenhaus, *Whittaker Chambers: A Biography* (New York: Random House, 1997), 203.

58. Tanenhaus, *Whittaker Chambers*, 324.

59. FBI dossier on Louis Zukofsky, reports dated 22 October 1951 and 11 May 1953.

60. Tanenhaus, *Whittaker Chambers*, 340.

61. CZ, quoted in Carroll F. Terrell, "Louis Zukofsky: An Eccentric Profile," in Terrell, *Louis Zukofsky: Man and Poet*, 51.

62. Author interview with Guy Davenport, 6 July 1998, in which Davenport recounted a September 1965 conversation with CZ.

63. CZ, quoted in Terrell, *Louis Zukofsky: Man and Poet*, 51–52.

64. FBI dossier on LZ, report dated 1 November 1951, summarizing a 30 October 1951 interview with Whittaker Chambers.

65. FBI dossier on LZ, report dated 11 May 1953.

66. While the contents page of *"A"* dates the second half of *"A"*-9 "1948–1950," the only dated drafts of that section are from July and August 1950. That contents page dates *"A"*-11 "1950," but only the rhyme scheme clearly dates from that year; the poem's first draft is dated 11 April 1951, its final draft 12 May 1951.

67. The first draft of *"A"*-12, in nine blue exam books, is dated 22 June–19 October 1951.

68. LZ to LN, 12 April 1950 (HRC).

69. *"A"* 155.

70. *"A"* 143; PZ's Hebrew name was Chenaniah, "for song / (Grace), instructed in song" (*"A"* 145).

71. *"A"* 156.

72. LZ to LN, undated (HRC).

Chapter Thirteen *"A"- 9 (second half) through "A"-12*

1. It is unclear when LZ decided to make the second half of *"A"*-9 a Spinozan reworking of the first half.

2. *"A"* 109.

3. Baruch Spinoza, *The Ethics and On the Correction of the Understanding*, trans. Andrew Boyle (New York: Dutton, 1967), 74 (Part I, Note to Proposition XLVII).

4. *CSP* 99.

5. Barry Ahearn, *Zukofsky's "A": An Introduction* (Berkeley: University of California P), 104.

6. Spinoza, *Ethics*, 209 (Part V, Propositions XI and XIII).

7. *Bottom* 1.29 quotes Part V, Proposition XIII, of the *Ethics*, and LZ will return to its phrasing again and again, as when he claims that he has presented the huge range of quotations in the "Definitions" chapter "so the definition of love in Shakespeare may flourish" (1.267).

8. *Bottom* 1.39.

9. Spinoza, *Ethics*, 219 (Part V, Note to Proposition XXXVI).

10. On "A"-11, see Ahearn, *Zukofsky's "A"*, 115–24, and Hugh Kenner, "Too Full for Talk: 'A'-11," in *Louis Zukofsky: Man and Poet*, ed. Carroll F. Terrell (Orono, ME: National Poetry Foundation, 1979), 195–202.

11. *"A"* 124.

12. See Ezra Pound, *Translations*, enlarged ed. (New York: New Directions, 1963), 120–23.

13. *"A"* 125.

14. *"A"* 23, 14.

15. Kenner, "Too Full for Talk," 201.

16. *American Poetry: The Nineteenth Century, Volume One*, ed. John Hollander (New York: Library of America, 1993), 217.

17. LZ to EP, 23 February 1940 (Beinecke); see also *"It was."*

18. *Paracelsus: Selected Writings*, ed. Jolande Jacobi, trans. Norbert Guterman (New York: Pantheon, 1951); I quote from the paperback edition (Princeton: Princeton University Press, 1988), which is identical in text but different in pagination from LZ's copy. According to the inscription in the HRC copy, the Dahlbergs gave the book to LZ on 13 March 1951.

19. *"A"* 124 25, Jacobi, ed., Paracelsus, *Selected Writings*, 40, xxxv, lxiii.

20. Spinoza, *Ethics*, 177.

21. Spinoza, *Ethics*, 180.

22. Spinoza, *Ethics*, 114.

23. *"A"* 258.

24. On "A"-12, see Ahearn, *Zukofsky's "A"*, 124–28, and Burton Hatlen, "From Modernism to Postmodernism: Zukofsky's 'A'-12," in *Upper Limit Music: The Writing of Louis Zukofsky*, ed. Mark Scroggins (Tuscaloosa: University of Alabama Press, 1997), 214–29.

25. *"A"* 126; Hatlen, "From Modernism to Postmodernism," 225.

26. *"A"* 130.

27. *"A"* 127.

28. *"A"* 128.

29. Ahearn, *Zukofsky's "A"*, 126; Hatlen, "From Modernism to Postmodernism," 219, 227.
30. *"A"* 126.
31. *"A"* 129.
32. *"A"* 132; Sessions, "How a Difficult Composer Gets That Way," *New York Times*, 8 January 1950, reproduced in *Roger Sessions on Music: Collected Essays*, ed. Edward T. Cone (Princeton: Princeton University Press, 1979), 169–71.
33. *"A"* 130; see Spinoza, *Ethics*, 214 (Part V, Note to Proposition XXIII).
34. *"A"* 138, 143, 146, 159–61; on Buber, see John Taggart, *Songs of Degrees: Essays on Contemporary Poetry and Poetics* (Tuscaloosa: University of Alabama Press, 1994), 200–201.
35. *"A"* 169.
36. *"A"* 175.
37. *"A"* 175–76.
38. *"A"* 214.
39. *"A"* 239.
40. *"A"* 128, 18.
41. *"A"* 155.
42. *"A"* 221.
43. *"A"* 205.
44. *"A"* 261, with misprint corrected.
45. *"A"* 261.
46. *"A"* 244, 257.
47. *"A"* 252–57.
48. *Prepositions+* 212, *"A"* 195, 257.

Interchapter *Spinoza: Geometry and Freedom*
1. LZ to LN, undated (HRC).
2. Biographical details from Steven Nadler, *Spinoza: A Life* (Cambridge: Cambridge University Press, 1999). On the *marrano* experience, see Yirmiyahu Yovel, *Spinoza and Other Heretics: Volume 1, The Marrano of Reason* (Princeton, NJ: Princeton University Press, 1989).
3. See Stuart Hampshire, *Spinoza* (1951; rev. ed. Harmondsworth: Penguin, 1962), 58–62.
4. Baruch Spinoza, *The Ethics and On the Correction of the Understanding*, trans. Andrew Boyle (New York: Dutton, 1967), 15 (Part I, Proposition XVI); *Ethics*, 11 (Part I, Proposition XV); *Ethics*, 38–39 (Part II, Propositions I and II).
5. Roger Scruton, *Spinoza (Past Masters)* (Oxford: Oxford University Press,

1986), 49–50, glossing *Ethics*, 24 (Part I, Note to Proposition 29). For other explications of *natura naturans* and *natura naturata*, see Hampshire, *Spinoza*, 46, 54; Nadler, *Spinoza*, 231.

6. Spinoza, *Ethics*, 84–85 (Part III, Definitions I–III).

7. Spinoza, *Ethics*, 211 (Part V, Proof to Proposition XX); *Ethics*, 219 (Part V, Note to Proposition XXXVI), 223–24 (Part V, Proposition XLII); *Ethics*, 224 (Note to Proposition XLII).

8. *Criterion* 8, no. 32 (April 1929): 420, MS dated 26 January 1927 (HRC); Chana Zukofsky died 29 January 1927.

9. Spinoza, *Ethics*, 15 (Part I, Proposition XVI).

10. *CSP* 11.

11. LZ to Carl Rakosi, 6 January 1931 (HRC).

12. *"A"* 23; The most thorough examination of Spinoza in *"A"* is Stephen Rex Whited's "Louis Zukofsky and Baruch Spinoza: An annotated reading of *"A"*-1 through *"A"* 12," unpublished PhD dissertation, University of Kentucky, 1992.

13. See *"A"*-6, *"A"* 46, as well as an undated typescript, "Matter that Thinks: Or Notations towards Action" (HRC), and an undated (1936?) letter to [Kenneth] Burke, [Isidore] Schneider, and [Edwin] Burgum (HRC); Scruton, *Spinoza*, 113.

14. *Bottom* 1.16.

15. *Bottom* 1.16, first ellipsis mine; Spinoza, *Ethics*, 212–13.

16. *Bottom* 1.79; *Prepositions+* 170.

17. Spinoza, *Ethics*, 213–14 (Part V, Note to Proposition XXIII).

18. *"A"* 130.

19. *"A"* 199.

20. See, for instance, "Influence," *Prepositions+* 187.

21. *"A"* 187.

22. Spinoza, *Ethics*, 209 (Part V, Proposition XI).

23. See Hampshire, *Spinoza*, 16–21; the phrase "clear and distinct" is Descartes'.

24. *Prepositions+* 170; LZ exaggerates: there are eight definitions and seven axioms at the start of *Part I* of the *Ethics*; successive parts introduce further definitions and axioms.

25. *Bottom* 1.45.

26. *"A"* 127.

27. *Prepositions+* 171.

28. *"A"* 128.

29. Frederick J. E. Woodbridge, *Nature and Mind: Selected Essays* (New York: Columbia University Press, 1937), 19, my emphases.

30. *Prepositions+* 194, 196n.1.
31. *Prepositions+* 8.

Chapter Fourteen *The Great World: 1952–1957*

1. James E. B. Breslin, "Poetry," *The Columbia Literary History of the United States*, ed. Emory Elliott et al. (New York: Columbia University Press, 1988), 1079.

2. Tom Clark, *Charles Olson: The Allegory of a Poet's Life* (New York: Norton, 1991).

3. Charles Olson, *Charles Olson and Ezra Pound: An Encounter at St. Elizabeths*, ed. Catherine Seelye (1975; New York: Paragon House, 1991), 37; by 1945 it seems Olson was familiar at least with LZ's name.

4. Charles Olson, *Collected Prose*, ed. Donald Allen and Benjamin Friedlander (Berkeley: University of California Press, 1997), 239, 240.

5. *Prepositions+* 211.

6. Olson, *Collected Prose*, 247.

7. "'Recencies' in Poetry," *Prepositions+* 207.

8. Olson, *Collected Prose*, 247; LZ, *Prepositions+* 203.

9. LZ to Thomas Merton, 8 May 1967 (TMSC).

10. In Carroll F. Terrell, "Louis Zukofsky: An Eccentric Profile," in *Louis Zukofsky: Man and Poet*, ed. Carroll F. Terrell (Orono, ME: National Poetry Foundation, 1979), 73.

11. CZ in Terrell, "Eccentric Profile," 73.

12. See LZ to CC, 26 November 1960 (HRC).

13. Robert Duncan, "As Testimony: Reading Zukofsky These Forty Years," *Sagetrieb* 7, no. 3 (Winter 1978): 424–25.

14. Robert Duncan, "For a Muse Meant," *Selected Poems*, ed. Robert J. Bertholf (New York: New Directions, 1993), 37.

15. RD to LZ, June 1947 (HRC); LZ to RD, 20 July 1947 and 7 August 1947 (Buffalo); Duncan, "As Testimony," 421.

16. See the "Chronology" in *Robert Creeley's Life and Work: A Sense of Increment*, ed. John Wilson (Ann Arbor: University of Michigan Press, 1987), 21–26.

17. Robert Creeley, *Collected Essays* (Berkeley: University of California Press, 1989), 69.

18. Author interview with Robert Creeley, 15 March 2000.

19. Creeley, *Collected Essays*, 69–70.

20. Hugh Seidman, Allen Ginsberg, Robert Creeley, and CZ, "A Commemorative Evening for Louis Zukofsky," *American Poetry Review* 9, no. 1 (January/February 1980): 26, 24.

21. Author interview with Creeley, 15 March 2000; CZ, "A Commemorative Evening," 26; LZ to Robert Creeley, 11 October 1955 (Washington University).

22. "What I Come to Do Is Partial," in Wilson, *Robert Creeley's Life and Work*, 75–77, reprinted from *Poetry* 92, no. 2 (May 1958): 110–12.

23. *CSP* 134, MS dated 28 January 1952.

24. *CSP* 145–46, 148, MSS dated 12 February 1953 and 13 February 1954.

25. *CSP* 157, MS dated 6 February 1956.

26. LZ to LN, 27 December 1953 (HRC); *CSP* 144–45, MS dated 27 December 1953.

27. LZ to LN, 21 January 1952 (HRC).

28. *CSP* 135–38, MS dated 6–15 July 1952.

29. EP to LZ, 24 June 1954 (HRC).

30. David Gordon, "Zuk and Ez at St. Liz," *Paideuma* 7, no. 3 (Winter 1978): 582–84.

31. EP to LZ, 11–12 July 1954, *Pound/Zukofsky* 218.

32. *CSP* 147 (with second MS line omitted), MS dated 28 July 1953.

33. *The Cantos* (New York: New Directions, 1995), 449.

34. According to notes on the 28 July 1953 MS (HRC).

35. *CSP* 146–47, revisions dated 21 January 1955.

36. See my "'There Are Less Jews Left in the World': Louis Zukofsky's Holocaust Poetry," in *Shofar: An Interdisciplinary Journal of Jewish Studies* 21, no. 1 (Fall 2002): 63–73.

37. Jenny Penberthy, *Niedecker and the Correspondence with Zukofsky, 1931–1970* (Cambridge: Cambridge University Press, 1993), 221; LZ recalled Vancouver and Victoria in a 23 January 1956 letter to Edward Dahlberg (HRC); he gave LN a Los Angeles hotel address on 19 July 1954 (HRC).

38. *"A"* 298–99.

39. *CSP* 107, MS dated 25 February 1945.

40. Jonathan Williams recounts the press's history in "The Jargon Society," in *Blackbird Dust: Essays, Poems, and Photographs* (Turtle Point Press, 2000), 114–22; see also Steven Clay and Rodney Phillips, *A Secret Location on the Lower East Side: Adventures in Writing, 1960–1980* (New York: New York Public Library/Granary Books, 1998), 114–15.

41. Jonathan Williams, *A Palpable Elysium: Portraits of Genius and Solitude* (Boston: Godine, 2002), 64.

42. Jonathan Williams, a manuscript entitled "Zoo-cough's Key's Nest of Poultry" and dated 1964 (HRC); this is a draft of a publication announcement for the Jargon Society's 1964 reprint of *A Test of Poetry*.

43. LZ to JW, 11 May 1955 (Buffalo).
44. Williams, *Blackbird Dust*, 116–17; JW, *A Palpable Elysium*, 64.
45. JW to LZ, 18 February 1956 (HRC); JW, postcard announcement of edition, 24 March 1956 (HRC).
46. Williams, "Zoo-cough's Key's Nest of Poultry."
47. LZ to JW, 15 January 1956 (Buffalo).
48. LZ to JW, 1 March 1957 (Buffalo).
49. BB to LZ, 3 November 1948 (HRC).
50. *CSP* 122, MS dated 14 November 1948 (HRC); "Romantic Portrait" dated 20 May 1948.
51. *CSP* 135; the whole of "Spook's Sabbath" dated 6–15 July 1952 (HRC).
52. *CSP* 114, MS dated 11 January 1948 (HRC).
53. LZ to EP, 1 October 1956 (*Pound/Zukofsky* 214).
54. LZ to EP, 19 October 1956 (Beinecke); LZ to LN, 27 October 1956 and 29 June 1956 (HRC).
55. *CF* 199; while I have been very reluctant to draw biographical details from Zukofsky's roman à clef *Little*, this one proved irresistible.
56. LZ to WCW, 1 December 1956 (*Williams/Zukofsky* 476); LZ to WCW, 28 December 1956 (*Williams/Zukofsky* 477).
57. LZ to D. G. Bridson, 25 April 1957 (Lilly).
58. LZ included an (unfortunately undated) itinerary of their European trip in a 27 September 1957 letter to JW (Buffalo).
59. LZ to Gael Turnbull, 16 March 1957; Gael Turnbull to author, 21 June 2000.
60. Keith Alldritt, *The Poet as Spy: The Life and Wild Times of Basil Bunting* (London: Aurum, 1998), 111–46.
61. BB to LZ, 11 April 1957 (HRC).
62. Alldritt, *Poet as Spy*, 148; LZ to LN, 14 July 1957 (HRC).
63. LZ to LN, 16 July 1957 (HRC).
64. T. S. Eliot to LZ, 18 July 1951 and 10 October 1951 (HRC).
65. LZ to LN, 16 July 1957 (HRC).
66. *CSP* 90, MS dated 7 May 1944; see Cristina Giorcelli, "A Stony Language: Zukofsky's Zadkine," in *The Idea and the Thing in Modernist American Poetry*, ed. Giorcelli (Palermo: Ila Palma, 2001), 109–39. In addition to the 27 September 1957 letter to JW (Buffalo), I have relied on a long letter to LN of 20 September 1957 (HRC) for details of the Zukofskys' European trip; most of the incidental Zukofsky quotations in what follows are from this letter.
67. Guy Davenport, "Zukofsky," in *The Geography of the Imagination: Forty Essays* (San Francisco: North Point, 1981), 110.

68. Canto XI, *Cantos* 51.

69. See William Walsh, "Cid Corman," in *Dictionary of Literary Biography, Volume 193: American Poets Since World War II, Sixth Series*, ed. Joseph Conte (Detroit: Gale Research, 1998), 65–75; CC himself provides a detailed autobiography and an account of *Origin* magazine in the Introduction to *The Gist of Origin* (New York: Grossman, 1975), xv–xxxvii.

70. See Charles Olson, *Letters for Origin: 1950–1956*, ed. Albert Glover (1969; New York: Paragon House, 1989).

71. CC recounts his meeting with the Zukofskys in "Meeting in Fierenze," *Sagetrieb* 1, no. 1 (Spring 1982): 120–24.

Chapter Fifteen *Going Westward: 1958–1960*

1. LZ to LN, 20 September 1957 (HRC).

2. *CSP* 168; MS dated 1 July, 4 July, 4 August, and 30 August 1957 (HRC).

3. *CSP* 171–99; MSS dated Summer 1957–1 September 1958 (HRC).

4. *CSP* 171.

5. *CSP* 179–80, 175, 186, 188, 194–95.

6. See Robert Von Hallberg, *American Poetry and Culture, 1945–1980* (Cambridge: Harvard University Press, 1985), 62–92.

7. *CSP* 190–91.

8. *CSP* 198–99.

9. LZ to WCW, 30 September 1951 (*Williams/Zukofsky* 446); see also *Williams/Zukofsky* xviii.

10. Paul Mariani, *William Carlos Williams: A New World Naked* (New York: Norton, 1981).

11. WCW to LZ, 23 October 1958 (*Williams/Zukofsky* 502).

12. Marianne Moore to LZ, 6 October 1948 and 12 October 1948 (HRC).

13. LZ to Jonathan Williams, 23 September 1957 (Buffalo); LZ quotes Moore in a 23 September 1957 letter to JW (Buffalo); LZ, undated fragment to LN (HRC).

14. LZ summarizes the history of the project in a 23 September 1958 letter to Navaretta (Buffalo).

15. LZ to JW, 28 September 1957 (Buffalo).

16. Jonathan Williams, "Zoo-cough's Key's Nest of Poultry," 1964 TS in HRC.

17. Emanuel Navaretta to WCW, 22 October 1957 (Yale); see *Williams/Zukofsky* 481.

18. LZ wrote WCW to this effect on Thanksgiving Day, 1957, but decided not to send the letter: "Bill was too sick and I decided to let the poem speak for itself" (*Williams/Zukofsky* 543–44).

19. LZ to WCW, 12 December 1957 (*Williams/Zukofsky* 481–84); the piece was finally published in *"A" 1–12* (Kyoto: Origin Press, 1959), and is reprinted in *Something to Say: William Carlos Williams on Younger Poets*, ed. James E. B. Breslin (New York: New Directions, 1985), 264–67.

20. LZ to JW, 6 January 1958 (Buffalo).

21. LZ to Emanuel Navaretta, 23 September 1958 (Buffalo).

22. On the "For Paul" project, see Jenny Penberthy, *Niedecker and the Correspondence with Zukofsky 1931–1970* (Cambridge: Cambridge University Press, 1993), 57–74.

23. See *From This Condensary: The Complete Writing of Lorine Niedecker*, ed. Robert J. Bertholf (Highlands, NC: Jargon Society, 1985), 291–306.

24. LZ to JW, 26 December 1956 (Buffalo).

25. Penberthy, *Niedecker and the Correspondence*, 67.

26. Lew Ellingham and Kevin Killian, *Poet Be Like God: Jack Spicer and the San Francisco Renaissance* (Hanover: Wesleyan University Press, 1998), 52–53.

27. Ellingham and Killian, *Poet Be Like God*, 136.

28. LZ to RD, 14 May 1958 (Buffalo).

29. LZ to Ruth Witt-Diamant, 8 May 1958 (Berkeley).

30. For a more detailed description of *5 Statements for Poetry*, see my Introduction to "Additional Prose," *Prepositions+* 177–81.

31. *Prepositions+* 187; MS datelined "May 9, 1958."

32. A full list of variations between *5 Statements for Poetry* and its essays' earlier publications can be found in the notes to "Additional Prose," *Prepositions+*.

33. LZ to RD, 23 June 1958 (Buffalo); LZ to CC, 23 June 1958 (HRC).

34. LZ to RD, 8 July 1958 (Buffalo).

35. LZ to CC, 14 July 1958 (HRC).

36. Ellingham and Killian, *Poet Be Like God*, 136, 161.

37. LZ to CC, 24 January 1959, 7 March 1960 (HRC).

38. Ellingham and Killian, *Poet Be Like God*, 193.

39. LZ to RD, 13 August 1958 (Buffalo).

40. LZ to CC, 27 September 1958 (HRC).

41. CZ Dossier; the "publication" date of the collection was 26 September 1958.

42. *CSP* 161; this poem, which preceded the book's publication by eighteen months, is dated 30 March 1956 (HRC).

43. CZ, colophon to *Barely and widely* (New York: privately printed, 1958).

44. *CSP* 164, 168–69, MSS dated 2 February 1957 and 22 February 1958 (HRC).

45. *CSP* 170, MS dated 3 April 1958 (HRC).

46. *CSP* 165, MS dated 25–27 February 1957 (HRC).

47. *CSP* 189–90.

48. LZ to CC, 19, November 1958 and 25 November 1958 (HRC).

49. LZ to CC, 19 November 1958 (HRC).

50. George Oppen, *Selected Letters*, ed. Rachel Blau DuPlessis (Durham: Duke University Press, 1990), xv–xvi.

51. Mary Oppen, *Meaning a Life: An Autobiography* (Santa Barbara: Black Sparrow, 1978), 201–2.

52. Oppen to LZ, 7 (?) August 1958 (*Selected Letters*, 7–8).

53. LZ to CC, 22 June 1959 (HRC); see also LZ to LN, 19 June 1959 (HRC).

54. LZ to CC, 22 July 1959 (HRC).

55. *CSP* 211–12; LZ dates "Jaunt" to 20–25 July 1959.

56. LZ to CC, 22 July 1959; LZ to LN, undated fragment (HRC).

57. See Mary Oppen, *Meaning a Life*, 206–8.

58. LZ to CC, 20 December 1958 and 1 January 1959 (HRC).

59. LZ and CZ seem to have invested six hundred dollars for the printing of two hundred copies of *"A"* 1–12, of which they received one hundred fifty copies outright. See LZ to CC, 1 September 1959 and 9 September 1959 (HRC).

60. LZ to CC, 27 August 1959, 21 October 1959 (HRC).

61. LZ to CC, 23 December 1959 (HRC).

62. LZ includes a list of errata in a 27 December 1959 letter to CC (HRC).

63. LZ to CC, 15 November 1959 (HRC).

64. LZ to CC, 27 December 1959 (HRC).

Interchapter *Shakespeare: The Evidence of the Eyes*

1. William Carlos Williams, *Imaginations*, ed. Webster Schott (New York: New Directions, 1970), 258–59.

2. *Guide to Kulchur* (1938; New York: New Directions, 1970), 148.

3. *Prepositions+* 167.

4. On *Bottom*, see David Melnick, "The 'Ought' of Seeing: Zukofsky's *Bottom*," *MAPS* 5 (1973): 55–65; Mark Scroggins, *Louis Zukofsky and the Poetry of Knowledge* (Tuscaloosa: University of Alabama Press, 1998), 68–94; and Bob Perelman's Foreword to the Wesleyan University Press reprint of *Bottom* (vii–xiv).

5. *Bottom* 1.15, 1.39.

6. *Prepositions+* 171.

7. *Prepositions+* 170.

8. *Prepositions+* 194, 196n.1, 230.

9. *Prepositions+* 242, 170.

10. *Bottom* 1.19; *Hamlet*, II.ii.338–39.

11. *CSP* 213, MS dated 17 March 1959 (HRC).

12. See Stephen Orgel's Introduction to the play in *The Complete Pelican Shakespeare*, ed. Orgel and A. R. Braunmuller (New York: Penguin, 2002), 604–8.

13. *Bottom* 1.327.

14. CZ Dossier.

15. *Bottom* 2.6.

16. *Prepositions+* 9.

17. *Bottom* 1.37.

18. *Bottom* 1.13.

19. *Bottom* 1.13.

20. *"A" 1–12* (Garden City: Doubleday, 1967), dust jacket; *Prepositions+* 228.

21. *Prepositions+* 239.

22. *Bottom* 1.348, 1.341, 1.436.

23. *Bottom* 1.442–43. All editions of *Bottom* misprint the final word ἕνα for ἕνα, which makes no sense. My thanks to David Wray for confirming this for me, and for the translation that follows.

24. *Bottom* 1.436.

25. LZ to CC, 4 November 1959 (HRC); see Charles Norman, *Ezra Pound* (New York: Macmillan, 1960), esp. 305–20.

26. LZ to CC, 11 July 1960 (HRC).

27. LZ to WCW, 29 June 1960 (*Williams/Zukofsky* 526–27).

28. LZ mentions the compilation in several letters to LN in the spring and summer of 1953 (HRC).

29. LZ to WCW, 15 October 1960 (*Williams/Zukofsky* 532), "Preface" dated March 21, 1953–May 1, 1954; for a slightly different version, see LZ to CC, 27 September 1959 (HRC).

30. On Feldman and the HRC, see Nicholas A. Basbanes, *A Gentle Madness: Bibliophiles, Bibliomanes, and the Eternal Passion for Books* (New York: Henry Holt, 1995), 312–54.

31. Ransom quoted in Basbanes, *Gentle Madness*, 313.

32. LZ to LN, 10 February 1961 (HRC).

33. The "Collection Files" to the LZ collection at the HRC make it clear that initially the HRC had far more interest in the EP and WCW letters than in anything else LZ offered them.

34. F. W. Roberts (director of the HRC) to LZ, 17 October 1960 (HRC, LZ Collection Files).

35. LZ to LN, 10 February 1961 (HRC).

36. LZ to CC, 25 February 1960 (HRC).

37. Agreement between LZ/CZ and Lew David Feldman, 26 April 1961; agreement among LZ/CZ, Lew David Feldman, and the HRC, 28 September 1961 (HRC, LZ Collection Files). The HRC's Collection Files contain a record of the labyrinthine negotiations to print *Bottom*, though some details remain murky.

38. He was mistaken; he was still alive (though LZ, CZ, and Feldman had all died), when the University of California Press reprinted *Bottom* in 1987; it had been out of print for some years prior to that.

39. See LZ to CC, 25 April 1961 (HRC).

40. CZ Dossier; LZ to F. W. Roberts, 21 May 1961 (HRC, LZ Collection Files).

41. LZ to CC, 25 April 1961 (HRC); Kim Taylor to LZ and CZ, 5 August 1963 (HRC, LZ Collection Files).

42. LZ to Kim Taylor, 12 February 1964 (HRC, LZ Collection Files). The official publication date for the corrected *Bottom: on Shakespeare* was 17 February 1964 (CZ Dossier).

Chapter Sixteen *The Darker World: 1961–1963*

1. *CSP* 88–89; MS dated "Nov? 1939" (HRC).

2. *CSP* 245.

3. The dates at the beginning and end of the MS of *Catullus*–8 February 1958 to 19 October 1965–are misleading, since LZ finished the final fragments of the corpus (the "fragmenta") before tackling the long Carmen 64, which he completed on 1 February 1966; see LZ to CC, 2 February 1966 (SFU).

4. In a letter of 6 April 1962 to LN (HRC), LZ confesses that he never had a Latin class.

5. The MS of the Zukofskys' translation of Carmen 80, "Odi et amo," is reproduced on the cover of *Catullus (Gai Valeri Catulli Veronensis Liber)* (London: Cape Goliard Press, 1969). In LZ's hand are a comment by Walter Savage Landor, a quotation from *All's Well That Ends Well*, and earlier translations of the poem by Richard Lovelace, EP, Charles Lamb, and Thomas Moore.

6. CZ to Burton Hatlen, 12 September 1978, quoted in Hatlen, "Zukofsky as Translator," in Carroll F. Terrell, ed., *Louis Zukofsky: Man and Poet* (Orono, ME: National Poetry Foundation, 1979), 347n.7.

7. *CSP* 248–49; the Latin text from the Zukofskys' *Catullus*, n.p.

8. *Prepositions+* 234; the "Poet's Preface" was omitted from the 1969

Catullus and *CSP*. LZ had sent both documents to CC by November 1961; see LZ to CC, Thanksgiving 1961 (HRC).

9. LZ to CC, 20 November 1960 (HRC).

10. LZ to CC, 17 November 1961 (HRC).

11. LZ to CC, 16 February 1961 (HRC).

12. "From 'Bottom: on Shakespeare,'" *Poetry* 97, no. 3 (December 1960): 143–52; LZ to CC, 23 February 1961 (HRC).

13. Eliot Weinberger, *Written Reaction: Poetics Politics Polemics* (New York: Marsilio, 1996), 18.

14. LZ to CC, 23 March 1963 (HRC).

15. See Anne Day Dewey, "Denise Levertov," in *Dictionary of Literary Biography 165: American Poets Since World War II, Fourth Series*, ed. Joseph Conte (Detroit: Gale Research, 1996), 147–64.

16. Denise Levertov, "A Necessary Poetry," *Poetry* 97, no. 2 (November 1960): 102, 104.

17. Levertov, "A Necessary Poetry," 103–4.

18. Levertov, "A Necessary Poetry," 109.

19. LZ to CC, 27 May 1960 (HRC), in which LZ recounts the conversation and quotes much of Levertov's offending letter.

20. LZ to CC, 14 November 1960 (HRC).

21. "More Than Pretty Music," *National Review* 9, no. 20 (19 November 2003): 318–20.

22. LZ to CC, 14 November 1960; LZ to CC, 10 February 1960 (HRC).

23. LZ to CC, 25 April 1961, 2 May 1961, 8 May 1961 (HRC).

24. *The Gist of Origin, 1951–1971: An Anthology*, ed. Cid Corman (New York: Grossman, 1975), xxxi–xxxiii.

25. LZ to CC, 8 September 1959 (HRC).

26. LZ announced the completion of the first section of "A"-13 in a letter to CC, 21 June 1960 (HRC).

27. LZ to CC, 23 June 1960 (HRC).

28. LZ to CC, 24 September 1960 (HRC); the MS of "A"-13 is dated 23 September 1960.

29. Frank Samperi to LZ, 24 July 1957, 5 February 1958, 26 May 1958, 29 August 1961 (HRC).

30. Frank Samperi to LZ, 24 May 1964; Samperi's last extant letter to LZ is dated 9 September 1964 (HRC).

31. Hugh Seidman, "Louis Zukofsky at the Polytechnic Institute of Brooklyn (1958–1961)," in *Louis Zukofsky: Man and Poet*, ed. Carroll F. Terrell (Orono, ME: National Poetry Foundation, 1979), 100; LZ to CC, 9 May 1959 (HRC).

32. See *"Between Your House and Mine": The Letters of Lorine Niedecker to Cid*

Corman, 1960 to 1970, ed. Lisa Pater Faranda (Durham: Duke University Press, 1986).

33. *"A"* 300.

34. LZ to CC, 15 July 1961 (HRC).

35. LZ to LN, 7 January 1961; Ian Hamilton Finlay, *The Dancers Inherit the Party: Selected Poems* (Worcester: Migrant, 1960). On Finlay, see Yves Abrioux, *Ian Hamilton Finlay: A Visual Primer*, expanded ed. (Cambridge: MIT Press, 1992), 1–2.

36. On LN and Finlay, see Jenny Penberthy, "A Posse of Two: Lorine Niedecker and Ian Hamilton Finlay," *Chapman* 78–79 (1994): 17–22.

37. LN to LZ, [June?] 1961 (Jenny Penberthy, *Niedecker and the Correspondence with Zukofsky 1931–1970* [Cambridge: Cambridge University Press, 1993], 287); LZ to LN, 29 June 1961 (HRC).

38. LZ to Jessie McGuffie, 24 February 1962 (HRC).

39. "New Poetry Club Is Formed," *Polytechnic Reporter*, 18 February 1959; Seidman, "Louis Zukofsky at the Polytechnic Institute," 97–98.

40. Seidman, "Louis Zukofsky at the Polytechnic Institute," 97; LZ to CC, 23 December 1959 (HRC).

41. Hugh Seidman, "Poly's Poetic Professor," *Polytechnic Reporter*, 12 November 1959.

42. Seidman, "Louis Zukofsky at the Polytechnic Institute," 100.

43. Author interview with Hugh Seidman, 4 August 2003.

44. Michael Heller, unpublished autobiographical essay.

45. Ian Hamilton Finlay to LZ, 26 September 1963 and 14 October 1963 (HRC); Dick Sheeler to LZ, 14 October 1963; LZ to Ian Hamilton Finlay, 20 October 1963 (HRC).

46. Arnold Wand to author, 18 November 2000.

47. LZ to CC, 9 June 1962 (HRC).

48. *CSP* 231–32; draft dated 21 June 1962.

49. *"A"* 406.

50. New York: Grove, 1960.

51. LZ to CC, 9 October 1962, 27 September 1962, 26 April 1961 (HRC).

52. Patrick Meavor, "Robert Kelly," *Dictionary of Literary Biography 165: American Poets Since World War II, Fourth Series*, ed. Joseph Conte (Detroit: Gale Research, 1996), 125.

53. LZ to Robert Kelly, 18 May 1961 (Buffalo).

54. On Allen's soliciting work, see LZ to CC, 10 September 1959; on LZ's exclusion from the anthology, see LZ to CC, 22 May 1960 (HRC). While LZ admired many of the poets in *The New American Poetry*, he was dissatisfied with the anthology; see LZ to CC, 28 June 1960 (HRC).

55. See Steven Clay and Rodney Phillips, *A Secret Location on the Lower*

East Side: Adventures in Writing, 1960–1980 (New York: New York Public Library and Granary Books, 1998), 84–87.

56. Quoted in Clay and Phillips, *A Secret Location*, 86.

57. "Modern Times," *Kulchur* 4 (November 1961): 75–82.

58. *Arise, arise, Kulchur* 6 (Summer 1962): 66–100.

59. *5 Statements for Poetry* (Foreword; Program: "Objectivists" 1931; Sincerity and Objectification; "Recencies" in Poetry), *Kulchur* 7 (Autumn 1962): 63–84; *5 Statements for Poetry* (Poetry/*For My Son When He Can Read*), *Kulchur* 8 (Winter 1962): 75–86; *5 Statements for Poetry* (A Statement for Poetry [1950]), *Kulchur* 10 (Summer 1963): 49–53; "Ezra Pound: His Cantos (1–27)," *Kulchur* 11 (Autumn 1963): 39–56.

60. LZ to CC, 24 May 1961 (HRC).

61. JL to LZ, 1 June 1961; JL to LZ, 8 June 1961; LZ to CC, 9 June 1961; JL to LZ, 29 December 1960 and 9 January 1961; see also LZ to LN, 10 January 1961 (HRC).

62. LZ to CC, 9 June 1961 (HRC).

63. LZ first mentions the book project in a 21 June 1961 letter to CC (HRC).

64. Cid Corman, "Ryokan's Scroll," *Sagetrieb* 1, no. 2 (Fall 1982): 285–89.

65. *CSP* 203; MS dated 16 December 1960. The translation of Ryokan (reworked from CC's literal rendering) begins with "the / first / snow."

66. "*A*" 325.

67. LZ to CC, 12 June 1963 (HRC); LZ to Robert Kelly, 3 September 1963 (Buffalo).

68. "*A*" 326.

69. Paul Mariani, *William Carlos Williams: A New World Naked* (New York: Norton, 1981), 760.

70. WCW to LZ, 19 February 1960; Floss Williams to LZ, 9 March 1960 (*Williams/Zukofsky* 518); and WCW to LZ, 30 June 1960 (*Williams/ Zukofsky* 527). See Mariani, *William Carlos Williams*, 754.

71. LZ to WCW, 1 July 1960 (*Williams/Zukofsky* 527–28).

72. LZ to WCW, 12 November 1960, WCW to LZ, 14 November 1960 (*Williams/Zukofsky* 535–36).

73. Mariani, *William Carlos Williams*, 767–68; LZ's account of the funeral, from which quotations in this paragraph are taken, is in an 11 March 1963 letter to CC (HRC).

74. *CSP* 127, draft dated 29 October 1949; *CSP* 148, draft dated 3 August 1954 (HRC).

75. "*A*" 377–88.

76. LZ to Henry Rago, 21 May 1963 (Lilly).

77. Author interview with Michael Palmer, 27 December 1998; reading list from CZ Dossier.

78. *CSP* 233, draft dated 15 December 1963 (HRC). Michael Palmer and Clark Coolidge would print "After Reading" in the first issue of their magazine *Joglars* (Spring 1964), one of the crucial early forerunners of the "Language" movement.

Chapter Seventeen *Short Poems: Contingencies and Sequences*

1. George Oppen to LZ, 14 September 1962, in George Oppen, *Selected Letters*, ed. Rachel Blau DuPlessis (Durham: Duke University Press, 1990), 69–70.
2. LZ to CC, 27 September 1962 (HRC).
3. Charles Tomlinson, *Some Americans: A Personal Record* (Berkeley: University of California Press, 1981), 65–66.
4. George Oppen to Charles Tomlinson, 27 July 1963 (Oppen, *Selected Letters*, 383–84n.21).
5. LZ to CC, 7 February 1964 (HRC).
6. *Prepositions+* 168. *Found Objects* was published by Blue Grass, Georgetown, KY, in 1964, in an edition of six hundred copies.
7. George Oppen to LZ, 14 September 1962 (Oppen, *Selected Letters*, 69).
8. Johann Wolfgang von Goethe, *Conversations with Eckermann (1823–1832)*, trans. John Oxenford (San Francisco: North Point, 1984), 7.
9. *Prepositions+* 194, 189, 207, 208.
10. *CSP* 214.
11. *CSP* 228–29.
12. *Prepositions+* 194.
13. *CSP* 215.
14. See Marcella Booth, *A Catalogue of the Louis Zukofsky Manuscript Collection* (Austin: Humanities Research Center, University of Texas, 1975), 119–20.
15. *CSP* 115, MS dated 1943?–1944 (HRC).
16. *CSP* 115, MS dated 25 February 1940 (HRC).
17. *CSP* 116, MS dated 31 March–3 April 1943 (HRC).
18. *CSP* 116–17, MS dated 3 April 1948; 121, MS dated 4–5 August 1940 (HRC).
19. *CSP* 120, MS dated 1 April 1943 (HRC).
20. *CSP* 119, draft dated 3–4 December 1941 (HRC).
21. Ludwig Wittgenstein, *Philosophical Investigations*, trans. G. E. M. Anscombe, 2nd ed. (New York: Macmillan, 1958), 32e.
22. *The Interpreter's Bible, Volume IV: Psalms and Proverbs* (New York: Abingdon Press, 1955), 638–39.
23. Ezra Pound, *Personae*, rev. ed., ed. Lea Baechler and A. Walton Litz (New York: New Directions, 1990), 95–96.

24. *CSP* 145; MS dated 12 February 1953 (HRC).

25. *"A"* 124.

26. *CSP* 145–46; MS dated 14 February 1953 (HRC).

27. *CSP* 148; MS dated 13 February 1954 (HRC).

28. *CSP* 149; draft dated 3 August 1954 (HRC).

29. *CSP* 151–52; MS dated 17 January 1955 (HRC).

30. *CSP* 152; MS dated 2–5 March 1955 (HRC).

31. See LZ to CC, 30 August 1961 (HRC).

32. *Prepositions+* 242.

33. For a more detailed reading, see my *Louis Zukofsky and the Poetry of Knowledge* (Tuscaloosa: University of Alabama Press, 1998), 95–114.

34. *CSP* 214; draft dated 15 January 1959 (HRC).

35. *Prepositions+* 243.

36. *CSP* 215, 217; MSS dated 13 June 1959 and 23 March 1960 (HRC).

37. LZ to LN, 10 February 1962; see also LZ to CC, 10 February 1962 (HRC).

38. *CSP* 222; the HRC MS dates "The Old Poet" as "(notes from 11/25/60 on / Feb. 22–26/62)."

39. *CSP* 223.

40. LZ mentions Cage explicitly in his 1968 discussion of "The Old Poet" with L. S. Dembo; see *Prepositions+* 234.

41. *CSP* 223–24.

42. *Prepositions+* 235.

43. *CSP* 224–27.

44. *CSP* 227–29, 231.

45. *CSP* 230; LZ identifies the "sweet fat friend" in a 9 March 1962 letter to CC (HRC).

46. LZ to CC, 27 September 1959 (HRC).

47. *CSP* 234; MS dated 1 February 1964 (HRC).

48. *Poesia Americana del '900*, ed. Carlo Izzo (Parma, 1963), 977.

49. *CSP* 239.

Chapter Eighteen   *Becoming a Classic: 1964–1966*

1. LZ to JW, 28 November 1960 (Buffalo).

2. Steven Clay and Rodney Phillips, *A Secret Location on the Lower East Side: Adventures in Writing, 1960–1980* (New York: New York Public Library/ Granary Books, 1998), 92–93, 115.

3. Front matter, *A Test of Poetry* (Highlands, NC: Jargon Society/Corinth Books, 1964).

4. Denise Levertov to LZ, 6 May 1964 (HRC).

5. Denise Levertov to LZ, 16 May 1964 (HRC).

6. LZ discusses these dealings in a 16 July 1964 letter to JW (Buffalo); clearly Norton was fudging its figures: the two volumes of *ALL* combined amount to only 246 printed pages.

7. Denise Levertov to LZ, 17 June 1964 (HRC).

8. LZ to JW, 16 July 1964 (Buffalo); why LZ opted to present his books out of chronological order—*Barely and widely* appearing before *Some Time*—is unclear, but probably involved the relative size of the two volumes of *ALL*: a collection that included *Barely and widely*, *I's (pronounced eyes)*, and *After I's* would be dwarfed by one including LZ's first three collections.

9. LZ to RC, 16 July 1964 (Stanford), LZ to CC, 16 July 1964 (SFU).

10. Nathaniel Tarn to LZ, 22 June 1964; Tom Maschler (editorial director at Jonathan Cape Ltd.) to LZ, 2 June 1965 (HRC).

11. Drafts of the note are dated 17 August 1958 and 4 September 1962 (HRC).

12. The texts of "An Objective" and the 5 *Statements* versions of the "Objectivist" essays can be compared by consulting the "Additional Prose" section of *Prepositions+*; see my introduction for a discussion of Zukofsky's cuts and revisions (*Prepositions+* 177–81).

13. LZ to CC, 25 September 1966 (SFU); on Adams and the Russians, see *Prepositions+* 124.

14. *Prepositions+* xv.

15. Donald Carroll to LZ, 5 October 1967 (HRC).

16. George Rapp to LZ, 18 October 1967 (HRC).

17. LZ to CC, 9 January 1964, 21 January 1964 (HRC).

18. LZ to CC, 21 January 1960 (HRC).

19. TS of Kelly's introduction, CZ Dossier.

20. LZ to CC, 1 February 1964 (HRC).

21. LZ to CC, 27 April 1964 (SFU).

22. LZ quoted in Charles Tomlinson, *Some Americans: A Personal Record* (Berkeley: University of California Press, 1981), 70.

23. LZ to CC, 14 July 1964, 8 August 1964 (SFU).

24. "*A*" 435–35; draft dated 30 October 1964 (HRC).

25. *Test* 125.

26. "*A*" 376; draft dated 23 May 1963 (HRC).

27. See the MS materials dated 8 May 1963, which are immediately followed by the first draft of "A"-16; inserted in the margin is a reference to the September 1963 Birmingham church bombing (HRC).

28. LZ to CC, 25 July 1966 (SFU).

29. LZ to CC, 17 August 1964 (SFU).

30. The draft of "A"-14 is dated 13 August–14 September 1964; that of "A"-15, 3 October–1 December 1964; and the first passage of "A"-18, 26 December 1964 (HRC).

31. LZ to CC, 18 December 1964 (SFU). CZ, in Carroll F. Terrell's "Louis Zukofsky: An Eccentric Profile" (*Louis Zukofsky: Man and Poet*, ed. Terrell [Orono, ME: National Poetry Foundation, 1979], 63), dates LZ's retirement to August 1966, but his correspondence with CC and LN, his extended trip to Lexington in fall 1965, and the couple's stay at Yaddo into the first months of 1966 make it clear that LZ retired at the end of the 1964–65 academic year.

32. So LZ described his students to Tomlinson; see *Some Americans*, 66.

33. LZ to CC, 13 November 1964 (SFU).

34. LZ to Guy Davenport, 16 February 1965.

35. LZ quoted in Tomlinson, *Some Americans*, 69.

36. *Agenda* 3, no. 6 (December 1964).

37. "Past the Wit of Man," the *Nation*, 1 March 1965, 232, 235.

38. "Paperbacks," *New York Sunday Herald Tribune*, 3 January 1965, 2.

39. LZ to Hugh Kenner, 6 January 1965 (HRC).

40. *The Poetry of Ezra Pound* was published in 1951 by New Directions and Faber & Faber; Kenner recounts its composition and his own early career in "Retrospect: 1985," a preface to the 1985 University of Nebraska Press reprint (1–9).

41. LZ to Hugh Kenner, 13 February 1963, 18 April 1963 (HRC).

42. Author interview with Guy Davenport, 6 July 1998, correlated with the agenda of the visit in the CZ Dossier; the visit took place 27–30 September 1965.

43. George Evans and August Kleinzahler, "An Interview with Carl Rakosi," in *Carl Rakosi: Man and Poet*, ed. Michael Heller (Orono, ME: National Poetry Foundation, 1993), 80–81.

44. LZ to Carl Rakosi, 27 December 1965 (HRC).

45. LN to CC, postmarked 8 June 1965, Lorine Niedecker, *"Between Your House and Mine": The Letters of Lorine Niedecker to Cid Corman, 1960 to 1970*, ed. Lisa Pater Faranda (Durham: Duke University Press, 1986), 59.

46. See LN to CC, 18 September 1965, Niedecker, *"Between Your House and Mine,"* 71–72.

47. LZ to CC, 4 October 1965 (SFU).

48. LN to CC, 7 and 14 October 1965, Niedecker, *"Between Your House and Mine,"* 73–74; there is no trace of LN's TS or carbon copy at the HRC.

49. LZ to CC, 30 July 1965 (SFU); LZ to Guy Davenport, 17 July 1965.

50. LZ to CC, 13 August 1965 (SFU); the play's performance dates were 7, 12, 13, 14, 19, 20, 21, and 27, August 1965.
51. LZ to CC, 28 July 1965 (SFU).
52. LZ to CC, 19 October 1965 (SFU).
53. *Poetry* 107, no. 1 (October 1965); the reviewers were Robert Creeley and Thomas Clark.
54. "After Sedley, After Pound," the *Nation*, 1 November 1965, 311–13.
55. *Finally a Valentine*, January 1965, Stroud, Gloucestershire, England: The Piccolo Press (500 copies); *An Unearthing*, June 1965, Harvard Yard, Cambridge, MA: Adams House and Lowell House Printers (77 copies); *I Sent Thee Late*, June 1965, Harvard Yard, Cambridge, MA: LHS (20 copies) (see *"A"* 391).
56. *Iyyob* (London: Turret Books, 1965), in an edition of one hundred copies.
57. In August 1965.
58. LZ to PZ, 29 October 1964.
59. LZ to Guy Davenport, 11 December 1965.
60. LZ to CC, 16 February 1961 (HRC).
61. LZ to Guy Davenport, 4 January 1965.
62. LZ to Guy Davenport, 11 December 1965; LZ to CC, 14 February 1966 (SFU).
63. LZ to CC, 2 February 1966 (HRC); composition dates for "A"-19 and "A"-18 from the MSS in the HRC.

Interchapter *Translation: The "Literal" Meaning*

1. James Laughlin, *Pound as Wuz: Essays and Lectures on Ezra Pound* (St. Paul: Graywolf Press, 1987), 130.
2. *CSP* 285.
3. *Catullus, Tibullus, Pervigilium Veneris* (Cambridge: Harvard University Press, 1962), translation by F. W. Cornish.
4. Alan Brownjohn, "Caesar 'ad Some," *New Statesman* 78 (1 August 1969); Burton Raffel, "No Tidbit Love You Outdoors Far as a Bier," *Arion* 8 (1969); Robert Conquest, *Encounter* 34 (May 1970); these three reviews quoted from Burton Hatlen, "Zukofsky as Translator," in *Louis Zukofsky: Man and Poet*, ed. Carroll F. Terrell (Orono, ME: National Poetry Foundation, 1979), 349.
5. "Pegasus Impounded," *Poetry* 14 (1919): 55.
6. Ezra Pound, "Notes on Elizabethan Classicists," in *Literary Essays*, ed. T. S. Eliot (New York: New Directions, 1968), 232, 227.
7. See Ming Xie, "Pound as Translator," in *The Cambridge Companion to Ezra*

Pound, ed. Ira B. Nadel (Cambridge: Cambridge University Press, 1999), 204–23, and Steven G. Yao, *Translation and the Languages of Modernism: Gender, Politics, Language* (New York: Palgrave Macmillan, 2002).

8. Xie, "Pound as Translator," 204.

9. Ben Jonson, *Timber*, quoted in J. P. Sullivan, *Ezra Pound and Sextus Propertius: A Study in Creative Translation* (Austin: University of Texas Press, 1964), 18; see 17–23 on Pound's translation as "imitation."

10. Hugh Kenner, "Louis Zukofsky: All the Words," in *Mazes: Essays* (San Francisco: North Point Press, 1989), 315.

11. *"A"* 13.

12. The Bosquet translations are reprinted in Terrell, ed., *Louis Zukofsky: Man and Poet*, 161–62.

13. On *Catullus*, see Hatlen, "Zukofsky as Translator," 365–70, Guy Davenport, "Zukofsky's English Catullus," in Terrell, ed., *Louis Zukofsky: Man and Poet*, 365–70; David Gordon, "Three Notes on Zukofsky's *Catullus*," in Terrell, ed., *Louis Zukofsky: Man and Poet*, 371–81; Yao, *Translation and the Languages of Modernism*, 209–33; and Daniel Hooley, *The Classics in Paraphrase: Ezra Pound and Modern Translators of Latin Poetry* (Selinsgrove, PA: Susquehanna University Press, 1988), 55–69; the definitive discussion is David Wray's "'cool rare air': Zukofsky's Breathing with Catullus and Plautus," *Chicago Review* 50, nos. 2/3/4 (Winter 2004/5): 52–99.

14. "Zukofsky's English Catullus," 369.

15. See David Wray, *Catullus and the Poetics of Roman Manhood* (Cambridge: Cambridge University Press, 2001); I am especially indebted to the provocative parallels Wray draws between Catullus and Zukofsky (36–52). For the "Manhattan Mauler," see LZ to EP, 15 March 1935 (*Pound/Zukofsky* 166).

16. *Prepositions+* 225.

17. *Prepositions+* 231.

18. *Prepositions+* 20.

19. *"A"* 359; the MS of *"A"*-15 (HRC) includes marginal indications of the relevant Hebrew Bible passages.

20. *CSP* 345; see Michele J. Leggott, *Reading Zukofsky's 80 Flowers* (Baltimore: Johns Hopkins University Press, 1989), 27–28 on the misprint of "gook" for "geek."

21. *"A"* 539.

22. This note and the Welsh poems, along with Price's lengthy description of Welsh poetic traditions and brief explanation of the pronunciation of Welsh, are among the manuscript materials for *Little* (HRC).

23. *CF* 48.

24. *CF* 119.
25. Wray's point, in his "'cool rare air.'"
26. *CF* 40, 45.
27. *"A"* 175, *Prepositions+* 244.

Chapter Nineteen *"A"-13 through "A"-20*

1. See Barry Ahearn, *Zukofsky's "A": An Introduction* (Berkeley: University of California Press, 1983), 129–67, which also considers "A"-13 through -20 in a single chapter.
2. LZ to Robert Creeley, Summer 1964 (Stanford).
3. "Supplement: On Rhythm from America," *Agenda* 11, nos. 2–3 (Spring–Summer 1973): 39, 66.
4. Henry James, *Literary Criticism: French Writers, Other European Writers, The Prefaces to the New York Edition*, ed. Leon Edel (New York: Library of America, 1984), 1323.
5. LZ to CC, 21 June and 23 June 1960 (HRC).
6. See LZ to CC, 25 August 1960 (HRC); LZ gave CC permission to print this letter in *Origin* 1 (April 1964), thereby alerting his readers to the musical parallels.
7. *"A"* 263, 264.
8. *"A"* 274.
9. *"A"* 280.
10. *"A"* 284; LZ to CC, 22 September 1959 (HRC). LZ followed the Khrushchev visit on television.
11. *"A"* 289.
12. *"A"* 296.
13. *"A"* 306–7.
14. See Ahearn, *Zukofsky's "A"*, 38.
15. *"A"* 309, 311.
16. *"A"* 311–12.
17. *"A"* 312.
18. *"A"* 15.
19. *"A"* 315.
20. *"A"* 319–25; the lines sample *Paradise Lost* (in order) from IV.73 to XII.577.
21. *Test* 71–72.
22. LZ to CC, 12 April 1963 (HRC). LZ's markings in *The Poems of John Milton*, ed. James Holly Hanford, 2nd ed. (New York: Ronald Press Co., 1953) indicate that for "A"-14 he used both *Paradise Lost* and passages quoted from Milton in Hanford's "The Life of John Milton" (3–23). It

is clearly a teaching text, for LZ has marked various passages to be read aloud in class; LZ's marginalia is heavy and often combative.

23. See Harry Gilonis, "Dark Heart: Conrad in Louis Zukofsky's '*A*'," the *Conradian* 14, nos. 1–2 (December 1999): 92–101, and Mark McMorris, "Postcolonial '*A*': Empire and Nation in Louis Zukofsky's American Movements, '*A*'-14–'*A*'-17," *Xcp: cross-cultural poetics* 8 (2001): 11–22.

24. "*A*" 318–19.

25. "*A*" 354, 353.

26. MS dated 3 October–1 December 1964 (HRC).

27. "*A*" 361.

28. "*A*" 359.

29. "*A*" 361, 364.

30. "*A*" 368.

31. "*A*" 371–2; see *The History of the Decline and Fall of the Roman Empire*, ed. David Womersley (London: Penguin, 1994), 2.509–16.

32. "*A*" 372.

33. LZ to CC, 11 September 1960 (HRC).

34. In the book list he prepared in the last years of his life, LZ dated his copy of Gibbon 1954; on Gibbon and Marx, see Guy Davenport, *The Geography of the Imagination: Forty Essays* (San Francisco: North Point, 1981), 194.

35. "*A*" 375.

36. Quoted in Michele J. Leggott, *Reading Zukofsky's 80 Flowers* (Baltimore: Johns Hopkins University Press, 1989), 118–19.

37. "*A*" 356.

38. Ahearn, *Zukofsky's "A"*, 139.

39. "*A*" 389.

40. "*A*" 390.

41. "*A*" 393.

42. "*A*" 393.

43. "*A*" 393, 392.

44. "*A*" 399.

45. "*A*" 420.

46. On Mallarmé in "*A*"-19, see Kenneth Cox, *Collected Studies in the Use of English* (London: Agenda Editions, 2001), 256–70, and Serge Gavronsky, *Mallarmé spectral ou Zukofsky au travail* (La Souterraine, France: La main courante, 1998) and "Borrowing Mallarmé," *L'Esprit Créateur* 40, no. 3 (Fall 2000): 72–85.

47. Gavronsky, "Borrowing Mallarmé," 74; Jacques Scherer, *Le "Livre" de Mallarmé* (Paris: Gallimard/NRF, 1957); Mallarmé to Verlaine, 16

November 1885, quoted in Gordon Millan, *A Throw of the Dice: The Life of Stéphane Mallarmé* (New York: Farrar Straus & Giroux, 1994), 252.

48. *"A"* 423.

49. *"A"* 431; LZ alludes here to Mallarmé's sonnet "Le tombeau d'Edgar Poe," which describes Poe attempting "donner un sens plus pur aux mots de la tribu"; Mallarmé, *Œuvres complètes*, ed. Henri Mondor and G. Jean-Aubry (Paris: Bibliothèque de la Pléiade/Gallimard, 1945), 70.

50. LZ to Guy Davenport, 23 September 1967; *"A"* 422, 427.

51. *"A"* 420.

52. So LZ identifies it in a marginal note in the MS of "A"-19 (HRC).

53. *"A"* 434.

Chapter Twenty *Retiring: 1966–1969*

1. Mina Loy, *Lunar Baedeker and Time-Tables* (Highlands, NC: Jargon Society, 1958), dust jacket blurb.

2. LZ to CC, 2 July 1966 (SFU).

3. Keith Alldritt, *The Poet as Spy: The Life and Wild Times of Basil Bunting* (London: Aurum, 1998), 148–52.

4. BB to Tom Pickard, 30 March 1967, quoted in Peter Makin, *Bunting: The Shaping of His Verse* (Oxford: Clarendon, 1992), 324.

5. The draft of the poem is dated 15 August 1966 to 14 May 1967 (HRC).

6. LZ to Guy Davenport, 3 December 1969.

7. *"A"* 438.

8. Biographical information on Morris Zukowsky is drawn from an 11 November 2000 letter from Daniel Zukowsky (his son) to the author, as well as a 15 February 2001 interview with Florence Feigenblum (his daughter).

9. Sam Tanenhaus, *Whittaker Chambers: A Biography* (New York: Random House, 1997), 56–57; Tanenhaus locates the bookstore in Greenwich Village, while Florence Feigenblum puts it "around 14th and Union Square."

10. On Morris Zukowsky and the book trade, see LZ to CC, 29 July 1960 (SFU).

11. In a 14 April 1952 letter to LN, LZ records an urgent request for twenty-five dollars from his brother.

12. *Autobiography* 33; on *Hiawatha*, see LZ to CC, 28 June 1960 (HRC).

13. *"A"* 507.

14. *"A"* 437.

15. LZ to Mollie Gassner, 6 April 1967 (HRC); the letter includes a copy of a letter to Robert Brustein of Yale, offering the same lines (*"A"* 476–81)

for "any commemorative publication that Yale may have in mind" for Gassner.

16. *"A"* 477.

17. *"A"* 143.

18. A point made by David Wray in his "'cool rare air': Zukofsky's Breathing with Catullus and Plautus" (*Chicago Review* 50, nos. 2/3/4 [Winter 2004/5]: 52–99), an essay from which I have borrowed a number of observations on "A"-21.

19. *"A"* 442; see *"A"* 5.

20. *"A"* 456–57.

21. *New York Times*, 3 August 1967; see *"A"* 499–500.

22. Harvey Shapiro, "Thinking of the Zukofskys," *Paideuma* 7, no. 3 (Winter 1978): 391.

23. *"A"* 500.

24. On Nathaniel Tarn and Jonathan Cape, see Shamoon Zamir, "Bringing the World to Little England: Cape Editions, Cape Goliard and Poetry in the Sixties. An Interview with Nathaniel Tarn with an Afterword by Tom Raworth," *Comparative Criticism* 19 (1997): 263–86; Tarn further clarified his relationship to LZ's publications in an e-mail to the author, 27 November 2003.

25. LZ to Guy Davenport, 15 September 1966.

26. LZ to RC, 20 November 1966 (Stanford); see also LZ to CC, 12 July 1967 (SFU).

27. *Prepositions+* 228.

28. The MS of *Little* is dated as follows: "Chapter 1–8 completed Nov. 12, 1950 / Revised 8/8/67. 1959: Outline drawn up from various notes 1950–9. / Other notes 1960 on. Resumed writing Oct 4/67" (HRC).

29. According to LZ's note in the margins of an 11 August 1967 letter from John Martin, Martin had requested a book on 29 July, LZ replied 2 August, and Martin sent out a contract on 6 August 1967; the revisions of the first eight chapters of *Little* are dated 8 August 1967 (HRC).

30. See PZ, "The Baron Speaks," unpaginated afterword to *Collected Fiction*.

31. *CF* 174–75.

32. Thomas Merton, "Louis Zukofsky: The Paradise Ear," in *The Literary Essays of Thomas Merton*, ed. Brother Patrick Hart (New York: New Directions, 1981), 128.

33. LZ to Thomas Merton, 21 February 1967 (TMSC).

34. Thomas Merton to LZ, 11 March 1967 (TMSC).

35. LZ to Guy Davenport, 21 March 1967.

36. Thomas Merton to LZ, 15 April 1967; LZ to Thomas Merton, 20 April 1967 (TMSC).

37. Thomas Merton to LZ, 23 June 1967 (TMSC).

38. LZ to Thomas Merton, 5 July 1967 (TMSC).

39. LZ to Thomas Merton, 2 January 1968 (TMSC).

40. LZ to CC, 30 December 1968 (SFU).

41. CZ Dossier.

42. LZ to GD, 31 January 1968.

43. L. D. Dembo to LZ, 16 January 1968 (HRC).

44. *Prepositions+* 229–30.

45. *Prepositions+* 232.

46. L. S. Dembo and Cyrena M. Pondrom, eds., *The Contemporary Writer: Interviews with Sixteen Novelists and Poets* (Madison: University of Wisconsin Press, 1972), 173.

47. LN to CC, 21 May 1968, Lorine Niedecker, *"Between Your House and Mine": The Letters of Lorine Niedecker to Cid Corman, 1960 to 1970*, ed. Lisa Pater Faranda (Durham: Duke University Press, 1986), 164.

48. Zamir, "Bringing the World to Little England," 267–69.

49. Tom Maschler to LZ, 3 January 1968 (HRC).

50. Tom Maschler to LZ, 21 July 1967 (HRC).

51. Tom Maschler to LZ, 6 September 1968 (HRC).

52. John Martin to LZ, 6 September 1968 (HRC).

53. John Martin to LZ, 16 April 1969 (HRC).

54. LZ's introduction to the *Autobiography* is dated 17 February 1962.

55. I have been unable to determine whether *Midcentury Authors*, announced for 1967 by the H. W. Wilson Co., New York, ever actually published LZ's biographical statement (it does not appear in the CZ Dossier list of publications), but in a 29 July 1967 letter to Hugh Kenner (HRC), LZ makes it clear by extensive quotation that that statement was substantially the same as the prose passages of the *Autobiography*.

56. *Autobiography* [7].

57. *"A"* 564, CZ's explanatory directions for the entire score; specific sources are found at the end of *"A"*-24, *"A"* 804–6.

58. The first version was begun on 24 December 1966 and completed 24 May 1967.

59. CZ lists this as a preface in her Year-by-Year chronicle of LZ's works, and it is printed as such, *before* the work as a whole, in the 1972 Grossman Publishers' *"A"*-24; in the one-volume *"A"* it follows *"A"*-24 (*"A"* 806).

60. *Prepositions+* 167.

61. LZ to CC, 8 September 1959 and 10 October 1959 (HRC); see the

interview with Eshleman in Lee Bartlett, *Talking Poetry: Conversations in the Workshop with Contemporary Poets* (Albuquerque: University of New Mexico Press, 1987), 52.

62. *Caterpillar* 3/4 (April/July 1968): 270.

63. LZ to CC, 9 June 1969 (SFU).

64. LZ to Hugh Kenner, 2 June 1969 (HRC); Guy Davenport, "Zukofsky," in *The Geography of the Imagination: Forty Essays* (San Francisco: North Point, 1981), 107.

65. LZ to CC, 31 May 1969 (SFU).

66. LZ to LN, quoted in LN to CC, 10 June 1969 (Niedecker, "*Between Your House and Mine*," 195); LZ to Hugh Kenner, 2 June 1969 (HRC).

67. Edward Lucie-Smith, "Hushed Symbols," the *Sunday Times*, 18 May 1969, 60.

68. Raymond Gardner, "Poet in Pressed Pants," the *Guardian*, 14 May 1969, 6.

69. See Donald Davie, "Kenneth Cox's Criticism," in *Under Briggflatts: A History of Poetry in Great Britain, 1960–1988* (Chicago: University of Chicago Press, 1989), 234–44.

70. Kenneth Cox to LN, quoted in LN to CC, 10 June 1969 (Niedecker, "*Between Your House and Mine*," 195).

71. *Prepositions+* 169.

72. *Prepositions+* 171.

73. *The Gas Age: Louis Zukofsky at the American Embassy, London, May 21, 1969* (Newcastle-upon-Tyne: Ultima Thule Books, 1969); LZ, note dated 3 December 1970 on a 28 September 1970 letter from Michael Shayer (HRC); *Prepositions+* 169.

74. Michael Shayer to LZ, 28 September 1970 (HRC).

Interchapter *Quotation*

1. T. S. Eliot, *On Poetry and Poets* (1957; New York: Noonday, 1961), 131.

2. T. S. Eliot, *Selected Prose*, ed. Frank Kermode (London: Faber, 1975), 38.

3. This "taxonomy" is borrowed from Leonard Diepeveen, *Changing Voices: The Modern Quoting Poem* (Ann Arbor: University of Michigan Press, 1993).

4. "*A*" 561; see Alison Rieke, "'Quotation and Originality': Notes and Manuscripts to Louis Zukofsky's '*A*'," in *Lawrence, Jarry, Zukofsky: A Triptych—Manuscript Collections in the Harry Ransom Humanities Research Center*, ed. Dave Oliphant and Gena Dagel (Austin: Harry Ransom Humanities Research Center, 1987), 101.

5. "*A*" 313.

6. LZ to Henry Rago, 18 January 1967 (Lilly).

7. LZ to CC, 13 August 1960 (HRC).

8. Barry Ahearn, *Zukofsky's "A": An Introduction* (Berkeley: University of California Press, 1984), 191.

9. Patricia Hutchins, *Ezra Pound's Kensington: An Exploration 1885–1913* (London: Faber, 1965), 150–51.

10. Here I disagree with the premises of Michele J. Leggott's extraordinary *Reading Zukofsky's 80 Flowers* (Baltimore: Johns Hopkins University Press, 1989). Leggott argues that LZ consciously "legitimize[d] use of the draft material" when he bequeathed his papers to the HRC: "Texas was in effect written into the history of the work; Texas was an ultimate insurance policy against the black holes of neglect into which the very difficult too readily falls" (32). Leggott stops somewhat short of Rieke, who argues that "anyone looking for a complete *A* must also seek its notes.... They are as much a part of the complete *A* as its cover and its index" ("'Quotation and Originality,'"104).

11. "Of Notes and Horses," in *Louis Zukofsky: Man and Poet*, ed. Carroll F. Terrell (Orono, ME: National Poetry Foundation, 1979), 189.

12. *"A"* 175–76.

13. *"A"* 185.

Chapter Twenty-one *At Port: 1970–1978*

1. LZ to Mary Ellen Solt, 19 April 1966 (Lilly).

2. *"A"* 407.

3. LZ to Henry Rago, 18 January 1967 (Lilly).

4. LZ to CC, 9 June 1969 (SFU).

5. For a caustic account of the Hine editorship, see Eliot Weinberger, "Pegasus at the Glue Factory," in *Written Reaction: Poetics Politics Polemics* (New York: Marsilio, 1996), 18–22.

6. Daryl Hine to LZ, 11 July 1969; LZ to Daryl Hine, 14 July 1969 (HRC). LZ took this paragraph seriously enough for CZ to include "To Daryl Hine for Nov. 1969 *Poetry* for Henry Rago" in her "Year by Year Bibliography" of LZ's writings.

7. Carroll F. Terrell, "Louis Zukofsky: An Eccentric Profile," in *Louis Zukofsky: Man and Poet*, ed. Terrell (Orono, ME: National Poetry Foundation, 1979), 74.

8. *Poetry's* recent editor Joseph Parisi made something of a cottage industry of trying to erase all marks of Zukofsky's association with the magazine.

9. *Prepositions+* 131.

10. *Little* MS materials (HRC).

11. *CF* [xiii].

12. "End of the Sixties," *Hudson Review* 23, no. 1 (Spring 1970): 181; *Chicago Panorama*, 13 September 1970.

13. "'A'-9 (première partie)," *Siècle à Mains* 12 (Spring 1970): 25–30.

14. LZ to Anne-Marie Albiach (draft letter), 9 March 1969 (HRC).

15. *Les Lettres Nouvelles* (special bilingual issue), 1970–71, 30–36.

16. *Da A*, trans. Giovanni Galtieri (Parma: Guanda Editore, 1970).

17. *Ferdinand*, trans. Aurora Campos and Juan Antonio Matesanz (Barcelona: Barral Editores, 1970).

18. *Svetova Literatura* 1 (1970), 64–86; the translator was Hana Zantovska.

19. Paul G. Hayes, "'At the Close—Someone': Lorine's Marriage to Al Millen," in *Lorine Niedecker, Woman and Poet*, ed. Jenny Penberthy (Orono, ME: National Poetry Foundation, 1996), 74.

20. LN to Gail and Bonnie Roub, November 1970, Lorine Niedecker, *"Between Your House and Mine": The Letters of Lorine Niedecker to Cid Corman 1960–1970*, ed. Lisa Pater Faranda (Durham: Duke University Press, 1986), 241.

21. *Prepositions+* 24.

22. *Prepositions+* 138.

23. See Alan Golding, "The 'Community of Elements' in Wallace Stevens and Louis Zukofsky," in *Wallace Stevens: The Poetics of Modernism* (Cambridge: Cambridge University Press, 1985), 121–40, and Mark Scroggins, *Louis Zukofsky and the Poetry of Knowledge* (Tuscaloosa: University of Alabama Press, 1998), 259–71.

24. *Prepositions+* 31–32.

25. *Prepositions+* 34.

26. *Prepositions+* 27, 30.

27. *Prepositions+* 27.

28. *Prepositions+* 37.

29. On the tape, see Joseph Cary to LZ, 9 June 1971 (HRC); on the notion of *Prepositions* with an "addendum," see LZ to Guy Davenport, 29 December 1971; the transcription and revised version of the talk are in the HRC.

30. George F. Butterick, "With Louis Zukofsky in Connecticut," *Credences* (new series) 1, nos. 2 & 3 (Fall/Winter 1981/1982): 158.

31. William T. Moynihan (head of the University of Connecticut English Department) to LZ, 20 May 1971 (HRC).

32. LZ to William T. Moynihan, 20 May 1971 (HRC); the syllabus is in the HRC.

33. Butterick, "With Louis Zukofsky in Connecticut," 158–60, 162.

34. Butterick, "With Louis Zukofsky in Connecticut," 160, 162; LZ to CC, 20 December 1971 (SFU).

35. Butterick, "With Louis Zukofsky in Connecticut," 162.

36. John Paul Taggart, "Intending a Solid Object: A Study of Objectivist Poetics," unpublished dissertation, Syracuse University, 1974.

37. LZ to Guy Davenport, 31 January 1968.

38. 15 January 1972.

39. LZ to CC, 4 July 1972 (SFU).

40. Norman Taylor, ed., *Taylor's Encyclopedia of Gardening, Horticulture, and Landscape Design*, 4th ed. (Boston: Houghton Mifflin, 1961); *Gray's Manual of Botany*, ed. Merritt Lyndon Fernald, 8th ed. (New York: American Book Co., 1950); *The Century Dictionary: An Encyclopedic Lexicon of the English Language*, ed. William Dwight Whitney, 10 vols. (New York: Century, 1895); I have derived the dates of LZ's acquisitions of these books from the book list CZ compiled after LZ's death.

41. Santa Barbara: Unicorn Press, 1970; the publication date was 4 May.

42. New York: The Phoenix Bookshop, 1970.

43. For a painstaking account of the compositional chronology of "A"-22 and -23, see Michele J. Leggott, *Reading Zukofsky's 80 Flowers* (Baltimore: Johns Hopkins University Press, 1989), 5–11.

44. LZ and CZ were at Bellagio from 9 November to 14 December 1972; see LZ to Jane Allen (of the Rockefeller Foundation), 16 December 1972 (HRC).

45. The performances, in association with the Theatre for Ideas, took place on 14, 15, 16, 21, 22, and 23, June 1973.

46. LZ to Guy Davenport, 23 June 1973, LZ to Hugh Kenner, 7 June 1973 (HRC); Davenport, *The Geography of the Imagination: Forty Essays* (San Francisco: North Point, 1981), 105.

47. Eric Mottram, "1924–1951: Politics and Form in Zukofsky," *MAPS* 5 (1973): 76–103.

48. Fielding Dawson, "A Memoir of Louis Zukofsky," in *Louis Zukofsky: Man and Poet*, ed. Carroll F. Terrell (Orono, ME: National Poetry Foundation, 1979), 107, 108.

49. LZ to Hugh Kenner, 16 March 1975 (HRC).

50. This description of the Port Jefferson house relies on Barry Ahearn's unpublished memoir of his December 1977 visit; Nathaniel Tarn mentioned LZ's aim of reducing his library in a 27 November 2003 e-mail to the author.

51. See Leggott, *Reading Zukofsky's 80 Flowers*, 17–19.

52. *"A"* 562.

53. Leggott, *Reading Zukofsky's 80 Flowers*, 11.

54. *"A"* 562.

55. Leggott, *Reading Zukofsky's 80 Flowers*, 11.

56. LZ to Hugh Kenner, 30 January 1974 (HRC); LZ to Guy Davenport, 11 November 1973.

57. The reading was originally scheduled for 18 December 1973 (CZ Dossier); see Robert Grenier to LZ, 28 November 1973 (HRC).

58. Details of the 9 May 1973 Franconia reading from an author interview with Bob Perelman, 27 February 1999.

59. WCW to LZ, 7 April 1928 (*Williams/Zukofsky* 5).

60. Robert Grenier, "On Speech," in *In the American Tree: Language, Realism, Poetry*, ed. Ron Silliman (Orono, ME: National Poetry Foundation, 1986), 496.

61. LZ to Hugh Kenner, 1 May 1973 (HRC).

62. Hugh Kenner, *The Pound Era* (Berkeley: University of California Press, 1973), 323–25, 405–6, and *A Homemade World: The American Modernist Writers* (New York: Knopf, 1975), 164–68, 187–93.

63. CZ to Mary Anne Kenner, 8 August 1975 (HRC).

64. LZ to Hugh Kenner, 13 March 1976 (HRC).

65. Barry Ahearn, "The Aesthetics of 'A'," doctoral dissertation, Johns Hopkins University 1977, revised and published as *Zukofsky's "A": An Introduction* (Berkeley: University of California Press, 1983).

66. CZ Dossier.

67. As recalled by Carroll F. Terrell, "Conversations with Celia," *Paideuma* 7, no. 3 (Winter 1978): 587; Terrell's recollection might well be influenced by LZ's 1948 statement "Work/Sundown" (*Prepositions+* 165).

68. See the table of composition dates in Leggott, *Reading Zukofsky's 80 Flowers*, 364–68.

Chapter Twenty-two *"A"-21 through "A"-24*

1. *"A"* 214. On "A"-24, see Marnie Parsons, "A More Capacious Shoulder: 'A'-24, Nonsense, and the Burden of Meaning," in *Upper Limit Music: The Writing of Louis Zukofsky*, ed. Mark Scroggins (Tuscaloosa: University of Alabama Press, 1997), 230–56, and Guy Davenport, "Zukofsky's 'A'-24," *Parnassus* 2 (Spring–Summer 1974): 15–24.

2. William Harmon, "Louis Zukofsky: Eiron Eyes," in *American Poetry 1946 to 1965*, ed. Harold Bloom (New York: Chelsea House, 1987), 76.

3. *"A"* 564.

4. *"A"* 564.

5. *"A"* 803.

6. *"A"* 557.

7. *Twelfth Night*, V.iv.48. These identifications are from Alison Rieke, *The Senses of Nonsense* (Iowa City: University of Iowa Press, 1992), 223–24.

8. *"A"* 525.

9. Michele J. Leggott's *Reading Zukofsky's 80 Flowers* (Baltimore: Johns Hopkins University Press, 1989), 4–11, provides a painstaking description of the MS materials for "A"-22 and -23.

10. *"A"* 511.

11. *"A"* 525.

12. *"A"* 535.

13. *"A"* 539.

14. *"A"* 539, 563.

15. *"A"* 539; the song is identified as Aranda in the MS materials.

16. *"A"* 540–43.

17. *"A"* 535, 537.

18. *"A"* 552.

19. This is only approximately true of "A"-22; with the opening lyric, "AN ERA / ANY TIME / OF YEAR," its first section has 103 lines, its last section 97. "A"-23 is more perfectly symmetrical.

20. *"A"* 536.

21. *"A"* 538.

22. *"A"* 562.

23. *"A"* 562–63; for detailed readings of the "living calendar," see Leggott, *Reading Zukofsky's 80 Flowers*, 66–67, and my *Louis Zukofsky and the Poetry of Knowledge* (Tuscaloosa: University of Alabama Press, 1998), 245–51.

24. CZ to Hugh Kenner, 16 February 1979 (HRC); LZ to Hugh Kenner, 13 March 1976 (HRC).

25. *"A"* 517, *"A"* 496; see CZ to Hugh Kenner, 16 February 1979 (HRC).

26. LZ to Hugh Kenner, 13 March 1976 (HRC).

27. CZ to Hugh Kenner, 15 January 1979 (HRC).

Chapter Twenty-three 80 Flowers *and "Gamut: 90 Trees"*

1. Essays on *80 Flowers* include David Levi Strauss, "Approaching *80 Flowers*," in *Code of Signals: Recent Writings in Poetics*, ed. Michael Palmer (Berkeley: North Atlantic, 1983), 79–102, and Kent Johnson, "A Fractal Music: Some Notes on Zukofsky's Flowers," in *Upper Limit Music: The Writing of Louis Zukofsky*, ed. Mark Scroggins (Tuscaloosa: University of Alabama Press, 1997), 257–75. I am deeply indebted to Michele J. Leggott, *Reading Zukofsky's 80 Flowers* (Baltimore: Johns Hopkins University

Press, 1989), a monumental and painstaking study that is unlikely ever to be superseded.

2. The preliminary notes for *80 Flowers* (HRC) are quoted in Leggott, *Reading Zukofsky's 80 Flowers*, 12.

3. Carroll F. Terrell, "Louis Zukofsky: An Eccentric Profile," in *Louis Zukofsky: Man and Poet*, ed. Carroll F. Terrell (Orono, ME: National Poetry Foundation, 1979), 66–67.

4. *CSP* 325; MS dated 25–27 December 1974 (HRC).

5. "*A*" 92, "*A*" 393; see Leggott, *Reading Zukofsky's 80 Flowers*, 16.

6. Leggott, *Reading Zukofsky's 80 Flowers*, 14.

7. As punctuated in LZ's notes (HRC); see Leggott, *Reading Zukofsky's 80 Flowers*, 74–89.

8. *CSP* 346; see Leggott, *Reading Zukofsky's 80 Flowers*, 255.

9. *CSP* 350, and Davenport, *Every Force Evolves a From: Twenty Essays* (San Francisco: North Point Press, 1987), 110; see Leggott, *Reading Zukofsky's 80 Flowers*, 218–22.

10. *CSP* 325.

11. Leggott, *Reading Zukofsky's 80 Flowers*, 22; Leggott presents a transcript of LZ's discussion of "Bayberry" on 369–72.

12. Leggott, *Reading Zukofsky's 80 Flowers*, 28, quoting C. Freeman Keith to LZ, 4 January 1978.

13. This according to the full-page publication announcement in *Paideuma* 7, no. 3 (Winter 1978); I have been unable to determine whether *80 Flowers* was announced in other venues as well.

14. *CSP* 351.

15. Leggott, *Reading Zukofsky's 80 Flowers*, 28.

16. Note quoted in Leggott, *Reading Zukofsky's 80 Flowers*, 17; I have silently omitted LZ's strike-throughs, which Leggott reproduces.

17. I have followed Leggott in referring to the latter work as "Gamut: 90 Trees."

18. Leggott, *Reading Zukofsky's 80 Flowers*, 30; Leggott examines the "90 Trees" project on 29–31 and 359–61.

19. *CSP* 355.

20. The single misprint in *80 Flowers*, "gook" for "geek" in the first line of "Bearded Iris" (*CSP* 345), is explained in Leggott, *Reading Zukofsky's 80 Flowers*, 27–28.

21. *Six sets of typesetters*: the Origin Press "*A*" *1–12* (1), corrected for the Cape "*A*" *1–12* (2); the Cape "*A*" *13–21* (3); the Grossman "*A*" *22 & 23* (4); the Grossman "*A*"-*24* (5); and the University of California Press itself (6). While California used photoreproductions of the Cape "*A*" *13–21* and

the Grossman *"A"-24* and *"A" 22 & 23*, it attempted to remedy the many
faults in the Origin/Cape *"A" 1–12* when resetting that text, introducing
new ones in the process.

22. CZ, in Terrell, "Louis Zukofsky: An Eccentric Profile," 69.

23. On LZ's last days, see CZ in Terrell, "Louis Zukofsky: An Eccentric
Profile," 70, and Fielding Dawson, "A Memoir of Louis Zukofsky," in
Terrell, *Louis Zukofsky: Man and Poet*, 111.

Afterword *1978–1980*

1. *Mazes: Essays* (San Francisco: North Point, 1989), 311; first published in
the *New York Times Book Review*, 18 June 1978.

2. The contract for "Zukofsky's Eye" is in the Kenner papers at the HRC,
as is the essay on "The Translation," which is mentioned in CZ to Hugh
Kenner, 27 February 1979 (HRC); James Laughlin, in a 13 March 1981
letter to PZ (HRC), expresses great interest in a Kenner-edited volume of
Williams–Zukofsky letters.

3. *Paideuma* 7, no. 3 (Winter 1978): 375.

4. *Paideuma* 7, no. 3 (Winter 1978): 374.

5. "Conversations with Celia," *Paideuma* 7, no. 3 (Winter 1978): 585–600.

6. Carroll F. Terrell, *Louis Zukofsky: Man and Poet* (Orono, ME: National
Poetry Foundation, 1979).

7. The CZ Dossier dates the first performance, at the Grand Piano Coffee
Shop, to 29 June 1978; Bob Perelman, who played the piano ("should
have been harpsichord," he notes), remembers it as taking place in April;
see Perelman, "'A'-24," in *The L=A=N=G=U=A=G=E Book*, ed. Bruce
Andrews and Charles Bernstein (Carbondale: Southern Illinois University
Press, 1984), 292.

8. Hugh Seidman, Allen Ginsberg, Robert Creeley, and Celia Zukofsky, "A
Commemorative Evening for Louis Zukofsky," *American Poetry Review*
9, no. 1 (January/February 1980): 22; the event took place on 18 April
1979.

9. "A Commemorative Evening," 23.

10. "A Commemorative Evening," 24.

11. "A Commemorative Evening," 26.

12. Mandel, who had taken on the directorship earlier that year, had hoped
to invite LZ to read at the Poetry Center as the first event of his tenure
in that position (author interview with Tom Mandel, 19 July 2004).

13. Robert Duncan, "Reading Zukofsky These Forty Years," *Paideuma* 7,
no. 3 (Winter 1978): 421.

14. Lyn Hejinian recalled some of these groups in her contribution to a

panel of tributes to LZ at the "Poetries of the 1940s: American and International" conference at the University of Maine, Orono, 23 June 2004; see Watten's own contribution to the 2004 Orono panel, "Tribute to Zukofsky," <http://www.english.wayne.edu/fac_pages/ewatten/zukofsky.html>.

15. I have sifted this version of the event from the account of David Levi Strauss, a student and follower of RD's, as published six years later in *Poetry Flash* and quoted in De Villo Sloan, "'Crude Mechanical Access' or 'Crude Personism': A Chronicle of One San Francisco Bay Area Poetry War," *Sagetrieb* 4, nos. 2 & 3 (Fall & Winter 1985): 243–45; Barrett Watten's "Three Tests of Zukofsky" (<www.english.wayne.edu-fac_pages-ewatten-post03.html>); e-mails from Barrett Watten and Ron Silliman; a telephone interview with Tom Mandel; and reflections on the event by Silliman ("Wild Form," <http://wings.buffalo.edu/epc/authors/silliman/wildform>) and Eleana Kim ("Language Poetry: Dissident Practices and the Making of a Movement," Part 6, "The New Americans vs. the Treed Americans," <http://home.jps.net/~nada/language6.htm>).

16. David Levi Strauss, quoted in Sloan, "'Crude Mechanical Access,'" 244.

17. Watten, in "Three Tests of Zukofsky," is particularly good on what was at stake in this clash between "textualist" and "authorial" readings of LZ.

18. Poet Tom Clark titled his two pieces on Language writing "Stalin as Linguist"; see *The Poetry Beat: Reviewing the Eighties* (Ann Arbor: University of Michigan Press, 1990), 65–83.

19. Silliman, in "Wild Form," perceptively notes the "fundamentalism" implicit in both Duncan's and Levi Strauss's readings of LZ.

20. CZ to Hugh Kenner, 7 June 1978 (HRC).

21. So indicated on the TS, which is dated 22 October 1978.

22. CZ, *American Friends* (New York: C. Z. Publications, 1979), [5].

23. "A"-12, "A" 214.

24. "1939–1978" was reproduced in facsimile in the French magazine *fin* 17 (juillet 2003): 50–72, with a brief introduction by Mark Scroggins.

25. Author interview with Sophie Rubin, 9 November 2000.

Appendix *Zukofsky, Reisman, Niedecker*

1. Carroll F. Terrell, ed., *Louis Zukofsky: Man and Poet* (Orono, ME: National Poetry Foundation, 1979), 31–74.

2. Barry Ahearn, "Two Conversations with Celia Zukofsky," *Sagetrieb* 2, no. 1 (Spring 1983): 113–31.

3. *Sagetrieb* 10, no. 3 (Winter 1991): 139–50. The actual publication date of the issue was somewhat later, since it includes as a postscript a letter from Reisman to Hatlen dated 6 March 1992.

4. Reisman's "On Some Conversations" fixes the date as "St. Patrick's Day 1986" (139).

5. Breslin's article "Lorine Niedecker: Composing a Life," in Susan Groag Bell and Marilyn Yalom, eds., *Revealing Lives: Autobiography, Biography, and Gender* (Albany: SUNY Press, 1990), 141–53, repeats the story in her text, but offers as evidence only the following endnote: "My information about Niedecker's stay with Zukofsky comes from interviews with two people who have requested anonymity" (234n.12). Those "two people" are clearly Mary Oppen and Jerry Reisman.

6. Jenny Penberthy, ed., *Lorine Niedecker: Woman and Poet* (Orono, ME: National Poetry Foundation, 1996), 35–38.

7. *The Selected Letters of George Oppen*, ed. Rachel Blau DuPlessis (Durham, NC: Duke University Press, 1990), 93.

8. Mary Oppen, *Meaning a Life: An Autobiography* (Santa Barbara, CA: Black Sparrow, 1978), 145.

9. Reisman, "On Some Conversations," 149.

10. The letters, as yet uncatalogued, are in the LZ Collection at the HRC.

Index